1900 **INGREDIENTS**

1900 INGREDIENTS

A CLASSIC REFERENCE ENCYCLOPEDIA OF WORLD FOODS

CHRISTINE INGRAM

southwater

This edition is published by Southwater, an imprint of Anness Publishing Ltd,
Hermes House, 88–89 Blackfriars Road, London SE1 8HA; tel. 020 7401 2077; fax 020 7633 9499
www.southwaterbooks.com; www.annesspublishing.com

If you like the images in this book and would like to investigate using them for publishing, promotions or
advertising, please visit our website www.practicalpictures.com for more information.

UK agent: The Manning Partnership Ltd;
tel. 01225 478444; fax 01225 478440; sales@manning-partnership.co.uk

UK distributor: Grantham Book Services Ltd;
tel. 01476 541080; fax 01476 541061; orders@gbs.tbs-ltd.co.uk

North American agent/distributor: National Book Network;
tel. 301 459 3366; fax 301 429 5746; www.nbnbooks.com

Australian agent/distributor: Pan Macmillan Australia;
tel. 1300 135 113; fax 1300 135 103; customer.service@macmillan.com.au

New Zealand agent/distributor: David Bateman Ltd;
tel. (09) 415 7664; fax (09) 415 8892

Publisher: Joanna Lorenz
Managing Editor: Linda Fraser
Senior Editor: Susannah Blake
Copy-editor: Rosie Hankin
Proofreaders: Linda Doeser, Hayley Kerr, Molly Perham and Madeline Weston
Design: Nigel Partridge
Photography: Steve Baxter, Nicki Dowey, Amanda Heywood, Janine Hosegood,
Don Last, William Lingwood and Steve Moss
Picture Research: Nansong Lue, Gary Murphy, Joanne Pickering and Joanna Skordis
Production Controller: Ben Worley

NOTES
Bracketed terms are intended for American readers.
For all recipes, quantities are given in both metric and imperial measures and, where appropriate, in standard cups
and spoons. Follow one set of measures, but not a mixture, because they are not interchangeable.
Standard spoon and cup measures are level. 1 tsp = 5ml, 1 tbsp = 15ml, 1 cup = 250ml/8fl oz.
Australian standard tablespoons are 20ml. Australian readers should use 3 tsp in place of
1 tbsp for measuring small quantities.
American pints are 16fl oz/2 cups. American readers should use 20fl oz/2.5 cups in place of 1 pint when measuring liquids.
Electric oven temperatures in this book are for conventional ovens. When using a fan oven, the temperature will probably
need to be reduced by about 10–20°C/20–40°F. Since ovens vary, you should check with your manufacturer's
instruction book for guidance.
Medium (US large) eggs are used unless otherwise stated.

CONTENTS

FOOD TODAY

In recent years, improvements in refrigeration and freezing methods, modern packaging and inexpensive air freight have provided the means of transporting fresh produce across continents quickly and cost effectively. Commercial growing, harvesting and processing yields high quality foods at a low cost and has made exporting in large quantities feasible. From fresh fish, meat, fruit and vegetables to seasonings, herbs and spices a wide variety of products are now available all over the world. After centuries of enjoying food and cooking based on seasonal local produce, eating habits have started to change, becoming more eclectic and infinitely more flexible.

While chefs have always been quick to experiment with new foods, the wide availability and ever-increasing range of international ingredients means cooks at home can enjoy trying out new foods as well. Browsing through cookbooks or magazines and watching television cookery programmes can provide an endless source of inspiration, making it easy to appreciate the range of recipes and the cross-culture combination of ingredients that are now commonly used in cooking.

Below: A woman in South-east Asia sells spices for local consumption.

There is such a variety of produce available that the consumer is often spoilt for choice. With the help of this comprehensive guide you can discover new products and how to use them and rediscover old favourites. Each ingredient is described in detail, with tips on selecting the best and useful storage hints. Basic preparation and cooking methods are supported by step-by-step techniques. There is also advice on using ingredients – from simple serving options to sophisticated dishes.

Above: Vietnamese rice growers plant their crop in the fertile paddy fields of the Mekong Delta.

VARIETY AND CHOICE

With the advent of food preservation and packaging the international availability of even the most perishable products has increased. Dairy creams are widely available including thick, pouring and whipping as well as cultured for a fresh tang or sour edge. Yogurt too is available in many varieties including live, Greek (US strained plain) or set. French fromage frais, the lightest of all fresh cheeses, is often classed with creams and yogurts because of its versatility in cooking.

There is even a choice of different types of butter from creamy unsalted (sweet) types to regional salted butters. Knowing a little about the similarities and differences between these dairy foods, and their cooking properties, makes is easier to put them to optimum use, or to substitute one for another if necessary in cooking or when serving.

Cheeses of all types are produced worldwide and even the smallest food shops stock a wonderful range for cooking or eating. The extensive choice ranges from locally and nationally produced cheeses to popular or more obscure international varieties. Fresh;

matured; semi-hard or hard; white or blue, or with the addition of extra flavouring ingredients, identifying the main groups is the best way to find your way around the world of cheese.

Selecting the finest fish can become a real pleasure with a little basic knowledge. On any large fresh fish counter you will find fish from around the world, from bright-skinned parrot fish from tropical waters to species from cold oceans such as cod. Fresh shellfish such as lobsters and clams are commonly available while cooked or prepared seafood will also usually be offered. The fish chapter explains what you should look out for when buying fish, how best to prepare it (or to get the fishmonger to prepare it for you) and how to cook it. A good fishmonger will be able to advise you on what to buy and can make life easier by boning, filleting and skinning the fish.

Supermarkets and butchers alike offer a fantastic selection of meat and you can find a wide choice of breeds, various rearing methods and different feeds as well as displays of international and conveniently prepared ready-to-cook cuts. Meats once considered too expensive, rare or unobtainable such as venison, ostrich or kangaroo are now displayed alongside the more familiar cuts of beef, pork and lamb. The section on meat, game and poultry highlights how to buy for best results, with cuts matched to different cooking methods to help ensure succulent and full-flavoured dishes.

The array of fruit and vegetables in most supermarkets, markets and ethnic stores is a colourful indicator of the global food culture we can enjoy today. Root and leafy vegetables are likely to be flanked by pungent fresh herbs, set against a backdrop of tropical fruit. Knowing how to pick out produce at its seasonal best and identifying treats for which it is worth adapting what you were planning to cook is all part of the fun of knowing ingredients.

Right: Fish and shellfish from around the world are now widely available in supermarkets and markets.

commonly used to add an individual flavour to both sweet and savoury dishes. Many are available fresh as well as dried, contributing quite different flavour twists to a wider variety of dishes. In addition to individual herbs, spices and aromatics, spice blends and pastes are well-established as seasoning ingredients in their own right.

Store-cupboard (pantry) ingredients can be made into quick, simple meals or combined with fresh produce to make easy dishes. The store cupboard can be a source of inspiration and gourmet treats, including anything from high-quality bottled and canned

Left: French onion and garlic growers collect their harvest ready for local and international distribution.

Dried fruit is used freely and to great effect in contemporary cooking, bridging the gap between the glorious fruit-rich, sweet and spicy meat casseroles of North African cooking and classic compotes and cakes produced in many Western kitchens. As well as the more commonly found dried grapes – raisins, currants and sultanas – there is an excellent choice of dates, prunes, figs, apricots, pears and peaches. Tropical mango, papaya, pineapple and banana are also readily available. With a little guidance on their textures, sweetness and flavour, and some imaginative ideas, these ingredients can be used, cooked or raw, to great effect in savoury or sweet dishes.

Only a few generations ago nuts were reserved for festive occasions, now they are available all year and the choice is extensive. Pistachios, macadamias, pecans and cashews are as common as walnuts and almonds, and infinitely versatile in savoury dishes, salads, sauces, baking and desserts.

The wonderful fusion of flavours used in contemporary cooking often results from the careful use of the right herb, spice or aromatic. Herbs, spices and aromatics from all over the world are

Right: Farmers in South-east Asia sell fresh, seasonal vegetables at a market.

ingredients to pickles and conserves. Classic storecupboard ingredients include staples such as grains, beans, pastas and noodles, and oils, vinegars, sauces and condiments, as well as other sweet flavourings. Oils, derived from olives, nuts and seeds, all have their own characteristics and react differently to heating. Some may be best suited to cooking, while others are better suited to flavouring. Vinegars and other fermented condiments such as soy sauce and *nam pla* (fish sauce) are versatile in all sorts of cooking.

Sugar and sweeteners are available in many forms and are an essential ingredient in baking and desserts as well as in a variety of savoury dishes. From the common white grains and highly refined icing (confectioners') sugar to varieties of full-flavoured and moist brown sugars that evolve in earlier processing stages, the choice is diverse. Syrups and treacle (molasses) originate from sugar cane or beet or from other plant sources such as maple syrup. Sugar and its products may be the most popular sweeteners nowadays but honey has been used as a sweetener for far longer. Depending on the country and region of origin, honey is subtly scented and flavoured by the plants surrounding the hives.

Chocolate, in its various forms, is one of the most popular sweet foods throughout the world and may be eaten as it is or used as an ingredient or flavouring. Coffee and tea are grouped with chocolate. While tea is primarily served as a drink, coffee is a popular flavouring in sweet cookery as well as a popular drink.

CHOOSING THE VERY BEST

While food fashions come and go, essential good-quality ingredients will always form the basis on which cuisines and culinary cultures are established. As chefs, professional and home cooks alike seek out and experiment with new flavours and cooking styles, the guidelines on how to select the finest foods remain the same. Choosing fresh, good-quality ingredients is the first stage in any great culinary adventure.

If you have a basic understanding of the processing and presentation of essential ingredients you will be well prepared to select the best from the rest and this book will help you do just that.

When you seek inspiration or ideas, just dip into the pages of this book until you find the food that takes your fancy. When faced with a new ingredient, the detailed description and preparation guidelines will help you to identify and make the most of the food, from its

Above: Coffee grown in tropical climes is exported all over the world to be enjoyed for everyday consumption.

essential preparation to suggestions for serving it to best advantage. Whether you are an experienced cook or a beginner, this book has something for everyone – from fascinating insights into how food is used and enjoyed all over the world to tips and hints on using the best international ingredients.

EGGS, DAIRY PRODUCTS AND FATS

*These foods are staples in almost every kitchen in the world and have
been used in cooking for thousands of years. Eggs, milk and dairy
products such as yogurt can be enjoyed on their own, as a food in
their own right, but they can also be combined with other ingredients
to create a multitude of sweet and savoury dishes. Butter and other
hard fats are an essential ingredient in many dishes, adding a
wonderful depth of flavour and richness, and can help to enhance the
taste and texture of other ingredients.*

EGGS

Almost all eggs are edible and, around the world, the eggs of all types of birds – farmed and wild – as well as reptile and turtle eggs are eaten. Eggs are incredibly versatile and can be cooked on their own, either boiled, poached, fried or scrambled, or combined with other ingredients to make any number of dishes from omelettes and soufflés to sauces, pancakes, pasta and cakes.

HEN'S EGGS

These are the most commonly found eggs in the West. Domesticated hens lay billions of eggs each year. Certain breeds are selected for commercial production, chosen to suit the environment in which they are reared and also for the type of

Above: (Left to right) Hen's egg, bantam egg and quail's egg

Right: Bantam eggs have a similar flavour to hen's eggs but are only about half the size.

Below: Hen's eggs range in colour from white to light brown, dark brown or speckled dark tan.

eggs they produce. The most popular hen's eggs come from cross-bred birds such as Isabrown and Hy-Line, but some smaller breeders rear hens such as Black Maran, Brahma, Indian Game and Silkies who produce very small, dainty white eggs that are good for baking and young children's meals. Rhode Island Reds are excellent layers and produce the classic light brown egg. Other breeds such as Marans lay speckled, deep tan to darkish brown eggs, while Araucanas lay eggs that have a very pretty pale blue shell.

BANTAM EGGS

Because bantams are about half the size of ordinary hens, their eggs are also much smaller. Bantams may be natural dwarf animals or specially bred miniatures of the larger breeds. Bantam eggs taste similar to hen's eggs and can be used in the same way as full-size eggs, but you will need to use more eggs than required in a standard recipe. Bantams tend to be kept by small-scale or specialist farmers, so their eggs are not widely available. However, they can sometimes be found in farm shops or farmers' markets.

QUAIL'S EGGS

These tiny eggs are the smallest of all commercial eggs. They are only about a third of the size of hen's eggs and are available in delicatessens and specialist shops, and may also be found in some supermarkets. Quail's eggs have dark-speckled, pale shells and make an attractive garnish to a dish when hard-boiled (hard-cooked) and served in the half shell. The shelled eggs are also excellent in starters and canapés. As long as they have not been overcooked by boiling too hard, quail's eggs have a delicate, light, almost creamy texture and flavour. They can be cooked in much the same way as hen's eggs.

Below: Quail's eggs, with their attractive colouring and delicate flavour, were once expensive and difficult to find, but are much more common nowadays.

Above and right: Duck eggs are very pretty and can vary in colour from pale blue and green to white.

DUCK EGGS

These are bigger than hen's eggs, weighing about 90g/3½oz, and their shell colour can vary from very pale green-blue to white. Duck eggs have a slightly higher fat content and oilier texture than hen's eggs. Their rich flavour and golden yolks make them ideal for baking and produce beautiful sponges. The whites are not suitable for making meringues and become slightly rubbery when set, so are not to everyone's taste when plainly cooked. Duck eggs are often laid in muddy places, so they should be washed and well cooked. Boiling for a minimum of 10 minutes is advisable.

Domesticated ducks originated from wild waterfowl. Their eggs are available from speciality food shops, butchers and delicatessens. Store in the refrigerator and eat as soon as possible. Allow them to return to room temperature before cooking.

GOOSE EGGS

These are at least twice the size of hen's eggs, weighing about 200g/7oz, and they are a pure chalky white. The shells of goose eggs are usually very hard. Like ducks, geese are fairly messy birds, so wash the eggs in their shells, then cook thoroughly to kill any harmful bacteria that may be lurking.

Stronger in flavour than hen's eggs, goose eggs are slightly milder and less rich than duck eggs. They can be cooked simply and eaten on their own and are excellent in mildly flavoured baked dishes such as vegetable gratins and quiches. They are available in season from specialist butchers, delicatessens and farm shops.

Left: Goose eggs have a very hard, chalky white shell and can be twice the size of hen's eggs.

Above: Guinea fowl eggs are similar in size to bantam eggs.

GUINEA FOWL EGGS

Related to pheasants, guinea fowl lay eggs that are about half the size of hen's eggs and weigh about 25g/1oz. The eggs are light brown and very regular in colour and have a delicate flavour. They are ideal for garnishing dishes or adding to salads and are also good for baking. They are available from specialist breeders.

TURKEY EGGS

These eggs weigh about 75g/3oz. They have creamy white shells with light brown speckles. The smaller eggs of young birds tend to be paler than those of older birds. There is little difference in taste between turkey and hen's eggs. Turkeys are farmed in most parts of the world but their eggs are rarely available to buy because the birds are usually bred for their meat. The eggs are therefore reserved for hatching. However, outside the main breeding season you may find a local farmer who has some to spare. They are particularly good for baking.

Above: Large, pointed turkey eggs have attractive pale speckled shells and a delicate flavour.

PHEASANT EGGS

Similar in size to guinea fowl eggs, pheasant eggs vary in colour from buff to green-blue or olive, and they may be speckled. They have quite a strong flavour and can be boiled and added to salads, baked, or cooked in most other ways. They are available from game dealers and some farm shops. Crack each egg into a cup before adding it to other ingredients in case it is bad.

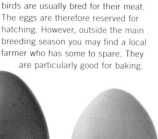

Left: (Left to right) Turkey egg, pheasant egg and guinea fowl egg

Left: A large ostrich egg can weigh a hefty 450g/1lb or more.

Above: Emu eggs have a very distinctive dark blue-green shell.

OSTRICH EGGS

Since ostrich meat has grown in popularity, ostrich eggs have become increasingly available. An ostrich egg weighs 450g/1lb or more. It has a comparatively strong flavour and is best used in baking. The pale shells are very thick and hard to crack. Laying is seasonal, during the summer, and the eggs are usually sold by breeders, delicatessens and specialist shops.

EMU EGGS

The Australian emu is slightly smaller than the ostrich. These birds are protected in their natural habitat and a special licence is needed for collecting their eggs. However, the birds are occasionally farmed for their meat and eggs. They have a winter laying season, during which time one bird will lay about 20 dark blue-green eggs, which have very hard shells. They are best used in baking, but they can be scrambled or cooked in savoury dishes.

WILD BIRD EGGS

In most Western countries the eggs of wild birds are protected by legislation, as a blanket measure to safeguard any species whose populations are in decline. Special licences need to be obtained for collecting

the eggs from gulls, such as the great black-backed gull, the lesser black-backed gull and the herring gull. Because they nest in inaccessible places, collecting can be difficult. Gull eggs are now eaten instead of plover eggs, which used to be thought of as a great delicacy. Gull eggs are dark spotted green and brown and have a mild fishy flavour. On some islands in the north of Scotland, it is possible to obtain a licence to collect gannet and fulmar eggs. Wild bird's eggs are available in season from specialist food shops and game dealers.

PRESERVED EGGS

In China, and among the Chinese communities throughout South-east Asia, preserved eggs are very popular. There are two main types and both use duck eggs. This is partly because duck eggs are bigger and have a stronger flavour than hen's eggs, but it is also because the yolk of a duck egg contains more fat. The more common type is the salted duck egg. The other is the so-called thousand-year-old egg.

Salted eggs are made by coating raw duck eggs in a salt and mud paste and then packing them into earthenware urns for 30–40 days. These eggs should be boiled or steamed and can then be eaten on their own or used as part of the filling in cakes for festivals.

Thousand-year-old eggs are preserved with a coating of wood ash and slaked lime and are then left for up to 100 days. By the time they are used, the egg whites have turned to pale brown jelly and the yolks have become creamy and tinged with green. Thousand-year-old eggs are eaten uncooked and have a milder flavour than the salted egg.

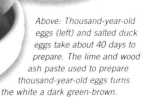

Above: Thousand-year-old eggs (left) and salted duck eggs take about 40 days to prepare. The lime and wood ash paste used to prepare thousand-year-old eggs turns the white a dark green-brown.

EGG KNOW-HOW

When buying, storing and cooking eggs, there are a few useful tips that will ensure you enjoy eggs at their best.

Egg Sizing

Eggs are sized by minimum weight. Size does not make any difference when you are cooking eggs to serve in individual portions such as when poaching or frying but, when baking, the size of an egg can be important. Use the chart below to check that you are using the right weight of egg, even if you cannot buy the correct size.

Below: Avoid cracked eggs, which may become infected with harmful bacteria.

Above: Fresh eggs can be stored safely for 3–4 weeks in the refrigerator. They should be stored pointed end down.

Right: Fresh eggs can be stored in a basket in a cool, well-ventilated place for up to a week.

Below: Eggs are sold according to size. Medium is the most frequently used size in most recipes.

Storing Fresh Eggs

While eggs look as if they are sealed, the shells are, in fact, porous, making eggs vulnerable to bacteria and odours. To protect them from any smells, they should be stored in their box or in a special egg compartment in the refrigerator, at or below 4°C/39°F. In these conditions eggs can be stored safely for 3–4 weeks. Bring them to room temperature before using them, especially when making meringues.

If you regularly use eggs quickly and have a suitable cool area, away from sunlight, then the eggs can be stored in a wire or wicker basket or in their box. They will keep safely for about a week as long as the temperature does not exceed 20°C/68°F.

Minimum Weight	EU Classification	USA Classification
73g/2½oz	XL (very large)	Jumbo
63g/2¼oz	L (large)	X Large
53g/2oz	M (medium)	Large
45g/1¾oz	S (small)	Medium
40g/1½oz		Small
35g/1¼oz		Peewee

Above: Store beaten egg in a bowl covered with clear film (plastic wrap) in the refrigerator.

Above: Store egg yolks in a small bowl, covered with cold water to prevent their outer membrane from hardening.

Below: Egg whites can be frozen in an airtight container. Defrost overnight in the refrigerator and use immediately.

Storing Cooked Eggs

Cooked eggs should be stored only if they are cooked right through. If hard-boiled eggs are left in their shells, they will develop a dark, bluish ring around the yolks, which can look unappetizing.

Shelled eggs can be stored in the refrigerator, loosely wrapped in clear film (plastic wrap), for 1–2 days. Do not store them for any longer as they will soon acquire a sulphurous smell.

Testing for Freshness

When it comes to eggs, how old is too old? The recommendation for shops is that they should sell only eggs that are less than 21 days old. This is a very safe recommendation. If eggs are stored under the correct conditions, they can be safe for up to 28 days.

If you have an egg that may be older than this, err on the side of caution and just throw it away. If you are in any doubt as to the age of your eggs, break each egg individually into a cup before mixing it with any other ingredients. The smell will be your final test, as bad eggs have an unmistakably unpleasant odour.

A simple way to check for freshness is to drop an unbroken egg into a glass of water. A fresh egg will sink straight to the bottom and sit on the base of the glass. An egg that is slightly older, but still safe to eat, will stay in the middle and an old egg that should be thrown away will float at the surface.

Below: Whole eggs, out of their shell, can be stored in an airtight plastic container in the refrigerator.

Checking the Age of an Egg

As an egg ages, its structure and appearance change, allowing you to judge its age.

A 3-day-old egg will have a plump yolk and two layers of white.

By the time an egg is 12 days old, the yolk will become much flatter and the two layers of white will not be as distinct.

A 21-day-old egg will have a very flat yolk and will have completely lost the definition between the two layers of white.

MILK

Often referred to as a complete food, milk is one of our most widely used ingredients. Cow's milk remains the most popular type: it is slightly sweet, mild and subtle in flavour. Most of it comes from Friesian cows, but milk from Jersey and Guernsey cattle is also available. The milk used for making various types of cheese comes from some 50 different breeds of cow.

Most of the milk that we buy has been pasteurized. This means that it has been heated to a temperature that eradicates any potentially dangerous bacteria, but does not affect the flavour of the milk. Unpasteurized milk, also known as raw or untreated milk, is becoming increasingly available as people acquire a taste for untreated products. Herds used to provide untreated milk must always be certified. This involves the farms being stringently tested to ensure no dangerous bacteria are present. It is recommended that babies, young children, the elderly, pregnant women and anyone with an impaired immune system should avoid drinking unpasteurized milk.

Below: (From left to right) Goat's milk, cow's milk, ewe's milk and vegetarian soya milk all have their own subtly distinct appearance and flavour.

WHOLE MILK

This milk, as the name suggests, is simply the fresh milk from the cow, with nothing added or taken away, although it is usually pasteurized. During the summer, when pastures are lush, the cream rises to the top, but come winter, the creamy top of the milk becomes less apparent. With the growing concern about the effects of saturated fat and cholesterol, full-cream whole milk has become less popular.

SEMI-SKIMMED AND SKIMMED MILK

This is milk from which part or almost all the fat has been removed. Semi-skimmed (low-fat) milk has a fat content of 1.5–1.8 per cent, and skimmed milk has a maximum fat content of 0.3 per cent, although 0.1 per cent is more usual. Skimmed milk contains half the calories of full-cream milk and only a fraction of the fat, but nutritionally it is virtually on a par, retaining most of its vitamins, calcium and other minerals. However, removing almost all the fat also removes the fat-soluble vitamins A and D. As a result, skimmed milk is not suitable for young children. Fortified skimmed milk with added vitamins and calcium is available.

CHANNEL ISLAND OR BREAKFAST MILK

Milk from Guernsey or Jersey cows is the creamiest milk of all. It is pale yellow in colour and has a superb rich flavour, owing to its high fat content.

HOMOGENIZED MILK

When milk is homogenized, the fat particles are broken up and dispersed evenly throughout it. The cream is blended into all of the milk, instead of floating to the surface, which it does when it is left to its own devices. Homogenized milk has a richer flavour that is not to everyone's taste.

LONG-LIFE AND UHT MILK

Milk labelled as long-life has been pasteurized, homogenized and then kept at a high temperature for long enough to destroy bacteria. The process gives the milk a rather odd, burnt caramel flavour, but it is nevertheless a useful stand-by as it will keep unopened for at least a week. However, once it has been opened, keep it in the refrigerator and treat as you would normal milk.

UHT (ultra-heat treatment) milk will keep, unopened, for even longer than long-life milk. This milk has been heated briefly to a high temperature (132°C/270°F). Although the taste is affected, it does not have quite the same caramelized flavour as long-life or sterilized milk. Unopened UHT milk can be stored, without refrigeration, for up to three months. Once opened, store in the refrigerator and treat it as fresh milk.

BUTTERMILK

Traditionally, buttermilk was made from the thin, milky, rather unstable liquid left over after butter-making. Nowadays, it is more likely to be made from skimmed milk, mixed with milk solids and then cultured with lactic acid, which ferments under controlled conditions. It has a creamy, mild, sour taste and makes a distinctive addition to desserts. It is widely used in baking because it gives cakes and soda bread a moist texture and helps aerate them. Buttermilk is low in fat, containing only 0.1 per cent.

GOAT'S MILK

This makes a useful alternative to cow's milk for people who are intolerant to lactose. The lactose in cow's milk can cause severe indigestion, and intolerance to dairy products often manifests itself in eczema or sinus congestion. Goat's milk is nutritionally similar to cow's milk, but is easier to digest, and it can be used in just the same way as cow's milk. It has a distinctive, musky and aromatic flavour that is stronger than that of cow's milk.

Soya Milk

This is a non-animal derived milk often used as a substitute for other milks by vegans and by those allergic to any form of dairy milk. It is made from pulverized soya beans, is suitable for both cooking and drinking, and is used to make yogurt, cream and cheese. Soya milk is interchangeable with cow's milk, although it has a slightly thicker consistency and a nutty flavour that is quite different. It also tends to curdle in very hot tea or coffee.

Some soya milk has added sugar, so it is advisable to check the label before buying. Chocolate- and fruit-flavoured soya milk, and versions fortified with extra vitamins and calcium, are widely available in health food shops and larger supermarkets.

Above: (Left to right) Evaporated and condensed milk are two and a half times as concentrated as ordinary whole milk.

WATER BUFFALO MILK

This type of milk is most famously used in Italy and some other countries for making mozzarella cheese, but it is also sometimes sold in cartons for drinking or for cooking. It is a pure ivory-white colour, with an earthy, slightly nutty flavour.

EWE'S MILK

Like goat's milk, ewe's or sheep's milk can be used by those who have an intolerance to cow's milk. It is creamier than goat's milk, with a milder, less assuming flavour. Ewe's milk cheeses are said to be recognizable by their subtle taste of roast lamb and lanolin, and these flavours, though less marked, can be detected in the milk, too. Ewe's milk can be used in the same way as cow's milk and its sweetness is said to make it especially suitable for desserts and puddings.

EVAPORATED AND CONDENSED MILK

Sold in cans and available whole or skimmed, evaporated milk is simply a homogenized milk with a considerably reduced water content so that it is almost twice as concentrated as ordinary milk. It is most useful for making desserts and sweets, either diluted with water or straight from the can. The high heat applied during processing gives it a very distinctive flavour. As the milk is sterilized in the can, it can be stored, unopened, almost indefinitely. Condensed milk is simply evaporated milk to which sugar has been added to thicken and sweeten it. It is mainly used for making desserts and sweets (candies).

Buying and Storing

Always check the label when buying fresh milk. Manufacturers and retailers are obliged to give a "best before" or "sell-by" date on the carton. Unpasteurized raw milk has a green foil top. Always store milk in the refrigerator, where it will last for 3–4 days. Stored outside the refrigerator, especially if the room is warm, it will sour very quickly.

Below: Buttermilk has a distinctive creamy, yet acidic flavour and is often favoured as an ingredient in baking.

CREAM

The fat content of cream varies quite considerably depending on the amount of butterfat it contains: half-cream contains about 12 per cent fat, single cream 18 per cent, double cream 48 per cent and clotted cream, which is the highest, contains about 55 per cent. The fat content affects both the texture and the keeping qualities of the cream.

DOUBLE/HEAVY CREAM

This is the thickest cream, used for serving with fruit or for whipping and decorating desserts or filling profiteroles and éclairs. It is very versatile and can also be used to enrich savoury dishes. It does not curdle when boiled on its own and can be added to most hot dishes. However, double cream may curdle if combined with very acidic ingredients. Thick, spoonable cream and pourable double cream are also now available. Extra-thick double cream has been homogenized and is not suitable for whipping.

WHIPPING CREAM

This cream contains sufficient butterfat to trap the air bubbles and therefore to increase in volume. It is also often used as a slightly less rich alternative to double cream in sauces. It will not separate when heated. When whipped the cream should double in volume and be light and airy. Be careful not to over-whip cream as it will turn to butter. This may also happen when whipping cream on a very hot day; add a spoonful of cold milk to each 150ml/¼ pint/⅔ cup of cream as it thickens to prevent this happening. Always chill cream before whipping it and, if possible, chill the bowl and the whisk, too. Beat the cream firmly, but not too vigorously. There is no remedy for overwhipped cream, but the resulting butter can still be used.

SINGLE/LIGHT CREAM

This thinner, lower-fat cream cannot be whipped as it does not contain enough butterfat. Nevertheless, it is excellent for enriching sauces and soups. Unlike double or whipping cream, single cream will separate if heated too fiercely. If heating cream for a custard or for making a hot sauce, scald it as you would milk. Whisking in flour or sugar will also help prevent cream

from separating. Extra-thick single cream has been homogenized. If you are planning to freeze a dish that is enriched with cream towards the end of the cooking time, such as a goulash or soup, it is advisable to freeze it without adding the cream. Reheat the dish fully, then lower the heat and add the cream.

SOURED CREAM

This thick-textured cream is treated with lactic acid, which gives it its typical tang. It is not the same as cream that has turned sour through age. Full-fat soured cream contains about 20 per cent fat, although low- and non-fat versions are also available. It can be used in the same way as cream and is ideal for making dips and cheesecakes, for enriching soups and sauces, and as topping for baked potatoes. Care should be taken when cooking, as it can curdle if heated to too high a temperature or too rapidly. Soured cream does not contain enough butterfat to be whipped.

You can make your own soured cream by adding 5–10ml/1–2 tsp lemon juice to 150ml/¼ pint/⅔ cup double or single cream, depending how thick you want it to be. Mix thoroughly and set aside for about 30 minutes, or until it has thickened. It will not taste exactly the same as commercially soured cream, but makes a good substitute for cooking.

SMETANA

Originally made in Russia and Eastern Europe, this rich version of buttermilk is made from a mixture of skimmed milk and single cream with an added culture. It has a similar fat content to strained yogurt (about 10 per cent) and should be treated in the same way. Smetana can curdle if it is heated too rapidly and should not be allowed to boil. Add smetana towards the end of the cooking time.

Above: (Clockwise from top left)
Single cream, whipping cream and
double cream

Above: Smetana, also called smatana and smitane, is a good low-fat substitute for cream.

CRÈME FRAÎCHE

This rich, cultured French cream is similar to soured cream, but is milder tasting. Its high fat content, at around 35 per cent, means that it does not curdle when cooked. Crème fraîche is delicious served with fresh fruit and may be used to enrich soups and casseroles and as a basis for dips. Crème fraîche should not be whipped.

PANNA DA CUCINA

This Italian cream is used for cooking, often as the basis of creamy pasta sauces. It is sold in little tubs, often joined together in pairs. Panna da cucina is a long-life product and makes a good storecupboard (pantry) standby. It is widely available in Italian delicatessens.

CLOTTED CREAM

This thick cream is made by heating milk, then, as it cools, skimming it of its thick creamy crust. The rich, golden coloured cream is a speciality of Devon and Cornwall, where it plays the central role in a cream tea, served with scones, butter and strawberry jam (jelly). It is also often served with desserts.

HALF CREAM

This is a thin, light cream with a fat content of about 13 per cent. It is suitable for adding to coffee, using to enrich sauces and dressings, and for serving with breakfast cereals. Its low butterfat content means that it is not suitable for whipping.

READY-WHIPPED CREAM

This cream is sold in aerosols and is a heat-treated product. It contains added sugar, stabilizers and a propellant and is not really whipped cream at all but an unstable foam that will collapse if left to stand for any length of time.

LOW-FAT CREAMS

Single, double and whipping cream are all available in low-fat versions, each type containing about half the fat of its full-fat equivalent. These creams are made from a blend of buttermilk, vegetable oils and butter and can be used in place of ordinary cream.

LONG-LIFE CREAM

UHT (ultra-heat treatment) versions of many types of cream, including whipping, single and half cream, are widely available. Although the flavour is not the same as ordinary cream, these long-life varieties make useful store-cupboard (pantry) items. However, they must be kept in the refrigerator and treated in the same way as fresh cream once they have been opened.

Storing Cream

Fresh cream should always be kept in the refrigerator and used within one or two days of purchase. Crème fraîche, however, will keep in the refrigerator for 10–14 days. UHT cream should be kept in a cool place and, once opened, treated in the same way as fresh cream and used within one or two days.

Cream with a butterfat content of over 35 per cent can be frozen. Lower fat creams such as single cream will separate on thawing, but can be frozen if incorporated into a dish. Half-whip double and whipping cream before freezing, pack in a suitable container and freeze for up to three months. To use frozen cream, thaw overnight in the refrigerator, or in a cool room for several hours. Whipped cream can also be frozen in rosettes. Pipe rosettes on to greaseproof paper (baking parchment) and freeze, then pack into a rigid container. Frozen rosettes should be placed on the dish to be decorated before thawing.

*Above:
Soured
cream and
crème fraîche can
be used to enrich casseroles
and soups and to top baked potatoes.*

YOGURT

Praised for its health-giving qualities, yogurt has earned a reputation as one of the most valuable health foods. Yogurt is rich in calcium, phosphorus and B vitamins, but the different types vary considerably in nutritional value. It is also a good dairy alternative for people who cannot tolerate the lactose in cow's milk, as they find they can eat cow's milk yogurt.

The bacteria present in live yogurt ensure that it is easily digestible: it may stimulate the friendly bacteria in the gut and suppress harmful bacteria, so aiding digestion and relieving gastro-intestinal problems.

The fat content of yogurt ranges from 0.5g per 100g for very low-fat or virtually fat-free yogurts, to 4g per 100g for whole-milk yogurt. The consistency may be thin or thick. Greek (US strained plain) and Greek-style yogurts, which are made from cow's or ewe's milk, contain about 10g of fat per 100g – just enough to prevent them from curdling during cooking. However, although these yogurts are higher in fat than other types of yogurt, they still

Below: (Clockwise from top left) Thick cow's milk yogurt, thin cow's milk yogurt, Greek-style yogurt, soya yogurt, goat's milk yogurt and sheep's milk yogurt.

contain less fat than cream and they are a healthier alternative. Lower fat yogurts can also be used instead of cream, but are best used in uncooked dishes. Strained yogurt has its watery whey removed to make it thicker and richer, and it has a similar fat content to Greek-style yogurt.

NATURAL/PLAIN YOGURT

Cultures are added to milk to produce natural yogurt. It has a smooth, creamy texture and a fresh, tangy, slightly acidic flavour. Natural yogurt can be used in both sweet and savoury dishes (though it should not be overheated), dressings and marinades, and to make refreshing drinks such as fruit smoothies and the classic Indian drink, lassi.

SET YOGURT

In the past, this type of yogurt was mainly found in France, but is now widely available in most supermarkets. The yogurt is made from low-fat milk and is allowed to incubate and set in the pot, rather than being packaged after "maturing". Set yogurt has a more solid appearance and texture but is still smooth and creamy on eating. Set yogurt can be used for cooking but is best enjoyed on its own.

GREEK/STRAINED YOGURT

This thick, creamy, strained yogurt may be made from cow's or ewe's milk. It has a mild flavour because of its high fat content, which counteracts the natural acidity found in other yogurts. It may be used in sweet or savoury dishes and makes a delicious dessert served simply with honey or fruit.

GOAT'S MILK YOGURT

Rich-tasting, goat's milk yogurt is ideal for people allergic to dairy products. It has a slightly acidic flavour and is useful in cooking because it does not curdle when added directly to hot food.

LONG-LIFE YOGURT

To increase its keeping qualities, yogurt may be pasteurized. This also kills off any beneficial bacteria and the cultures, so long-life yogurt cannot be used as a starter for making your own yogurt.

FROZEN YOGURT

This iced dessert makes a delicious alternative to ice cream. It has a slightly sharp flavour and is usually lower in fat than regular ice cream.

SOYA YOGURT

This dairy-free yogurt is made from soya milk and is widely available from most wholefood stores and supermarkets.

Buying and Storing

Live yogurt has a limited shelf life so it is best to check the "best before" or "sell-by" dates on the label before buying. Also look for the word "live" on the label because this signifies that the yogurt has been fermented with a live starter culture bacteria that is beneficial to health. Bio yogurts that contain extra bacteria (frequently *Lactobacillus acidophilus* or *Bifido-bacterium bifidum*) have a milder, creamier flavour than other yogurts.

Always check the label for added ingredients. Many commercially-made yogurts contain unnecessary amounts of sugar, flavourings and additives, including starch to thicken them. Some yogurts, especially low-fat varieties, may contain gelatine, an animal by-product, making them unsuitable for vegetarians.

Always store yogurt in the refrigerator, where it will keep for about 4 days. If you make your own yogurt at home, store in the refrigerator and eat within a few days of making.

Cooking with Yogurt

Yogurt is a useful culinary ingredient, but it does not respond well to heating. It is best added at the end of the cooking time, just before serving, to prevent it from curdling. High-fat yogurts are more stable, but it is also possible to stabilize and thicken low-fat yogurt by stirring in a little cornflour (cornstarch) blended to a paste with water before cooking. It is an excellent marinade and can form the base for sauces and dips.

Making Yogurt

It is easy to make yogurt at home – simply use live yogurt as a starter and ensure that it is as fresh as possible. Once you have made the first batch, you can reserve some of it as the starter to be a culture for the next batch. Do not use too much starter or the yogurt may become sour and grainy. When the yogurt has been made, it can be stored in the refrigerator for 4–5 days.

Dissolving a little dried milk in the milk, before adding the starter, will produce a thicker yogurt.

1 Pour 600ml/1 pint/2½ cups whole, semi-skimmed or skimmed milk into a pan and bring to the boil. Remove the pan from the heat and leave the milk to cool to 45°C/113°F.

2 If you do not have a thermometer, you can use your finger – the milk should feel slightly hotter than is comfortable on your skin. Pour the warm milk into a medium-size, sterilized bowl.

3 Whisk 15–30ml/1–2 tbsp live yogurt into the milk. Cover the bowl with clear film (plastic wrap) and insulate with several layers of dishtowel. Leave to stand in a warm place for 10 hours, or until set. Transfer to a clean container.

Making Fruit Yogurt

Fruit purée can be stirred into natural (plain) yogurt to make a simple dessert.

1 Purée 250g/9oz soft fresh fruit by pressing through a fine sieve.

2 Stir the fruit purée into 600ml/1 pint/ 2½ cups natural (plain) yogurt and serve immediately.

Making Drained Yogurt

Draining yogurt produces a soft cheese similar in taste and texture to ricotta, quark or curd (farmer's) cheese.

1 Lay a 30cm/12in square of muslin (cheesecloth) on a plate. Tip 600ml/ 1 pint/2½ cups natural (plain) yogurt on to the muslin, then lift into a strainer. Leave to drain for 1 hour.

2 Gather up the edges of the muslin and tie with string. Hang the cloth over the bowl and leave to drain for at least three hours. Unwrap the cloth and tip the curds into a bowl. Stir in salt and flavourings to taste.

BUTTER AND FATS

There is a wide choice of hard fats for both cooking and spreading and, in these health-conscious days, many people opt for the low-cholesterol, polyunsaturated varieties. Nevertheless, notwithstanding health warnings, butter is still the preferred spread for bread and toast, and almost all professional cooks choose butter in cooking, whether it's for sauces, pastries or cakes.

The very best butters mostly come from France. They are unsalted (sweet) and have a slightly sweet flavour and smooth texture. There are also a huge number of blended butters, which are produced in any number of countries, although among the favourites are Australia and New Zealand, Denmark, Ireland and England.

There are two basic types of butter – sweet cream and lactic, which may be salted or unsalted. In Britain and the United States, sweet cream butters tend to be favoured, while in Europe, butters tend to be lactic.

Butter can be made from any kind of milk. For example, in India, butter is made from water buffalo milk and in the Middle East it is made from ewe's milk.

UNSALTED/SWEET BUTTER

This butter has a mild aroma and a slightly sweet flavour and is particularly suited for making sweet pastries and cakes. It also makes an excellent table butter, although some people, who are accustomed to the more distinctive flavour of salted butter, may find it rather bland and insipid.

SALTED BUTTER

Butter was originally salted to preserve it for the winter months when fresh butter was not made. Today, salt is still added to butter and is normally the only added ingredient. The salt not only adds flavour but still has a preserving effect and salted butter will keep fresher for longer than the unsalted variety.

Right: There is a huge range of butters, margarines and spreads available, with fat contents that vary from about 40 per cent in low-fat spreads to 80 per cent in butters and margarines.

Different brands often have varying amounts of salt added, and it is a matter of taste which you prefer. Some very salty butters are not ideal for baking and should be avoided if you are making desserts or cakes. Butter with less than 3 per cent salt does not have to be labelled salted, but is sometimes labelled slightly salted.

CLARIFIED BUTTER

This type of butter is used for cooking. It is made by slowly melting butter and then skimming off the milk solids that rise to the top and pouring or spooning the melted fat off the sediment that is left in the pan. The result is a rich golden liquid. Because it contains no milk solids, clarified butter can be heated to a higher temperature than ordinary butter and is excellent for butter sauces and certain fried dishes.

Making Clarified Butter
Clarified butter should always be made with unsalted (sweet) butter.

Melt the butter over a low heat. Skim off the froth, then carefully pour the layer of clear fat into a bowl and chill. Discard the milky residue, or add it to soups.

Above: Ghee is widely used in Indian cooking, particularly for frying spices at the beginning of recipes.

GHEE

This type of clarified butter originated in India but is now produced in many other countries. It has a stronger, more caramelized flavour than clarified butter because it is heated for a little longer in the clarifying process. It is also made from a stronger flavoured cream. Ghee is usually sold in cans and, as it no longer contains milk solids that will rapidly go off, it is not necessary to keep it in the refrigerator.

SWEET CREAM BUTTER

This is also known as fresh cream butter and is made from unripened cream. It can be salted or unsalted and is particularly popular in the United States. It has a soft, creamy texture and a creamy buttery taste.

Below: Butter is widely used in cooking and can add a wonderful depth of flavour to many dishes. It is ideal for making cakes and desserts.

LACTIC BUTTER

This is the type of butter traditionally made in Denmark, Holland and France. The cream is mostly pasteurized, inoculated with a culture that ripens the butter, then pasteurized once more to arrest the ripening process.

WHEY BUTTER

This is a by-product of cheesemaking. Whey butter is made by separating the residue of cream from the whey drained from cheese curds, then churning it into butter. It has a strong, salty, cheese flavour and is available from farm stores and cheesemakers.

CONCENTRATED BUTTER

Specially developed for use in cooking, concentrated butter is produced by removing milk solids, salt and other impurities, leaving about 96 per cent butterfat. It can be heated to higher temperatures than ordinary butter and less of it is required – about 75g/3oz/ 6 tbsp concentrated butter for every 90g/3½oz/7 tbsp ordinary butter. To use it for baking, extra liquid must be added. Concentrated butter will keep for three months in the refrigerator.

BUTTER SUBSTITUTES

There are many butter-type products on the market. They are designed to taste and look like butter but are actually made from combinations of animal and vegetable fats, colouring, stabilizers and preservatives. Some have the same fat content as butter, although others contain a large proportion of water, less fat and have fewer calories.

Making Flavoured Butters

Flavoured butters can make good accompaniments for both sweet and savoury dishes. Herb and garlic butters are delicious with fish or grilled (broiled) meat, while sweet-flavoured butters can go well with steamed puddings.

1 Put 115g/4oz/½ cup unsalted (sweet) butter in a bowl and beat with a wooden spoon or an electric beater until soft. Add 30–60ml/ 2–4 tbsp chopped fresh herbs and season with salt, pepper and a dash of lemon juice. Beat to mix.

2 Transfer the butter to a piece of greaseproof (waxed) paper and shape into a roll. Wrap and chill. Serve cut into slices.

VARIATIONS
• To make mustard butter, beat 15ml/ 1 tbsp Dijon mustard into the butter in place of the herbs and omit the lemon juice. Flavour with 5ml/1 tsp citrus juice and the juice of 1 lemon.
• To make anchovy butter, crush about 8 canned anchovy fillets to a smooth paste, then beat into the butter. Add ground black pepper and a little lemon juice to taste.
• To make garlic butter, peel and crush 3 garlic cloves, then beat into the butter. Season with salt and pepper.
• To make brandy butter, add twice the weight of the butter in icing (confectioners') sugar. Cream the sugar with the butter, then add 10ml/ 2 tsp brandy and gradually work it into the sweet butter mixture.

MARGARINE

Along with butter, margarine is widely used for cooking and baking. Some brands are now as popular as butter for spreading, and much effort has been spent in the last 30 years to make margarine indistinguishable from butter in taste. Unfortunately for margarine manufacturers, margarine can't quite copy butter's unique melting point. Butter melts almost exactly at blood temperature, so that it literally melts in the mouth.

Most margarines are made from vegetable fat. Many brands also include milk, whey or animal fats so, if you need to avoid dairy products, always check the label. Hard margarine is made from hydrogenated fats. The process of hydrogenating solidifies fats, but it also turns healthy polyunsaturated fats into unhealthy saturated fats.

Margarine is not the best choice for cooking because it tends to burn easily. Soft margarines and low-fat margarines, which tend to have high water contents are even more unsuitable and should only be used for spreading.

Hard margarine was once favoured for pastry-making, and many people still prefer this. Soft margarine is usually not recommended for pastry although it can be used if combined with a harder fat such as lard or butter.

Below: Margarine is often favoured as a healthy alternative to butter, even though many margarines contain just as much saturated fat.

Below: Lard is excellent for pastry and produces wonderfully light, crumbly results.

LARD

This hard, white fat comes from pork, and is made by rendering pork fat and then allowing it to cool. It was once strong tasting, and was the popular fat for frying and deep-frying. Convenience and greater health awareness mean that lard is no longer very popular for frying, although it is still used by some pastry cooks; if used half-and-half with butter, it produces an excellent light, crumbly pastry. Some traditional cuisines, such as Cajun cooking, still favour lard.

SUET

This is the hard white fat that surrounds the kidneys of lambs or oxen. It was once popularly used for dumplings and steamed puddings such as jam roly-poly and steak and kidney pudding, but is now thought of as a rather old-fashioned ingredient and is not as widely used. If bought fresh, suet needs to be grated or shredded. This can be a slightly tricky business as the shredded fat can be rather sticky. To make the job easier, sprinkle a little flour over the suet before and during grating to prevent it sticking. Ready-shredded suet is also available in packets and is much more convenient to use.

SHORTENING

The name shortening could be applied to all fats as it simply means that, in pastry-making, the fat is capable of producing a short (crumbly) crust. The greater the proportion of fat used in pastry, the shorter (and crumblier) the result. Conversely, the more flour that is used in proportion to fat, the tougher the pastry will be.

The shortening available in shops is normally a blend of vegetable and animal fats – mainly lard and dripping and vegetable oils. However, some of the cheaper products contain fish oils.

Below: Suet is one of the key ingredients for dumplings, and for all kinds of steamed puddings.

Shortening is always pure white in colour and has no discernible flavour. It is only popular for frying if underlying subtleties of flavour are not required. For pastry, however, it is far more popular. Its soft fluffy texture makes it very easy to rub in and for many people it is the preferred fat for savoury short-crust pastries, producing a light and crumbly result.

VEGETABLE FATS

There are a number of vegetarian forms of suet, lard and shortening. Like hard margarine, the oils are hydrogenated to make them solid. They have a mild flavour and creamy texture and are useful for frying and baking. Vegetable ghee is a clarified vegetable fat and is very similar to clarified butter and ordinary ghee. It is however, much cheaper than clarified butter or ghee.

Buying and Storing Butters and Fats

Ideally, butters and fats should be bought in small quantities, enough for a week at a time. They should be well-wrapped in greaseproof (waxed) paper or foil to prevent them absorbing the smells of other foods and stored in the refrigerator. Soft margarines should be stored in their plastic tubs.

Hard fats such as butter and lard should be removed from the refrigerator an hour or so before using and allowed to return to room temperature. They should be returned to the refrigerator as soon as possible, especially if the weather is warm, as they will inevitably turn rancid, becoming unusable for cooking or spreading.

Cooking with Butter and Fats

Butter adds a superb richness to both sweet and savoury foods. It can be blended with herbs and/or garlic for spreading on to bread or melted to make a delicious dip for vegetables such as asparagus or globe artichokes. Butter mixed with chopped parsley makes a wonderful accompaniment to simply-cooked fish, or blended with Roquefort cheese, it makes a perfect accompaniment to steak. Butter sauces such as Hollandaise, Béarnaise, beurre

Making Rich Shortcrust Pastry

This basic pastry can be made with butter, margarine or white fat.

1 In a large mixing bowl, rub 115g/4oz/½ cup fat into 225g/8oz/2 cups plain (all-purpose) flour.

2 Blend 1 lightly beaten egg yolk and a little cold water into the mixture to form a smooth dough. Chill for 10 minutes before using.

Making Flaky Pastry

This quick version of flaky pastry has a wonderful buttery flavour and crisp texture. It can be made with butter or a mixture of butter and lard or shortening.

1 Put 175g/6oz/¾ cup butter and/or fat in the freezer for 40 minutes until it is very hard. Sift 225g/8oz/2 cups plain (all-purpose) flour and a pinch of salt into a bowl and chill.

2 Holding the butter in a piece of foil, coarsely grate it into the flour.

3 Stir the butter into the flour and sprinkle 90ml/6 tbsp chilled water over the mixture. Stir to form a dough.

4 Bring the dough together, wrap in clear film (plastic wrap) and chill for at least 40 minutes before using.

Making Rough Puff Pastry

This quick version of puff pastry uses a mixture of butter, for flavour, and lard or shortening, for a crisp texture.

1 Cut 175g/6oz/¾ cup chilled butter into dice and combine with 250g/9oz/2¼ cups sifted plain (all-purpose) flour and a pinch of salt.

2 Stir 5ml/1 tsp lemon juice into 120ml/4 fl oz/½ cup water and add to the dry ingredients. Mix with a knife, then knead on a floured surface.

3 Roll the pastry to a thin rectangle. Fold the lower third over the centre and the top third over that. Wrap in clear film (plastic wrap) and chill for 15 minutes. Repeat four times.

blanc and beurre noir are the corner-stones of much French cookery and butter is invariably used for patisserie by French pastry chefs. Butter also imparts a wonderful flavour when used for frying but you should add a little oil to prevent the butter burning, or use clarified butter.

Hard margarines can be used in almost all the same ways as butter although they will not give the same depth of flavour. Margarines with a high water content are not suitable for frying.

Soft margarines are good for making cakes but are not suitable for pastry. Margarine is not suitable for greasing baking tins (pans) as it will break down and become sticky when heated. Lard, on the other hand, does not break down at high temperatures and so is perfect for greasing or for roasting vegetables such as potatoes. Shortening, lard or a mixture of fats can be used for savoury shortcrust pastry, but for flaky or sweet pastries, butter has a superior flavour and gives a much better result.

CHEESE

Thousands of years ago, it was found that surplus milk, left to curdle, then drained and salted, was good to eat. Since then, cheesemaking has evolved into a sophisticated process. Today there is a huge range of cheeses to enjoy, and new ones are being developed all the time. Most are made from cow's milk but there are also cheeses made from goat's milk, sheep's milk and some from water buffalo milk. The type of milk, its fat content and the method used to make the cheese all help to define its individual character.

HARD CHEESES

To make hard cheese, the curds are put under pressure to remove more of the whey. In the first instance, this is done by cutting the curds more finely, then heating and draining them. Salt is then added and the curds may be cut again (the process varies among different types of hard cheeses). The cheese is then either placed in a perforated mould, wrapped in cloth or pressed into shape and wrapped. Most traditional hard British cheeses are wrapped in cloth, sealed with lard and left for weeks or even years to mature. European cheeses are often left in brine overnight, or sometimes, longer to seal the rind, and then left to ripen for several months, if not years, as in the case of Emmental and Cantal.

This elaborate system for making cheese has been developed and refined over centuries and there is huge scope for variation. The type of milk used, the way in which the curd is cut, how quickly and for how long it is reheated and whether the curd is cut again, all contribute to the character of the cheese. The maturing process is also significant. The longer a cheese matures, the harder it will become. Block hard cheeses that are wrapped in a special plastic wrap mature faster and retain much more moisture than those wrapped in cloth, and consequently the cheese has a softer texture than traditionally matured types. The fat content of a hard cheese will depend on a number of factors, including the type of milk used, but is commonly around 45–50 per cent.

ENGLAND

The past couple of decades have seen a revolution in English cheesemaking and many old recipes have been revived.

BASING

This mild Caerphilly-type cheese made from goat's milk is lightly pressed, moist and crumbly. It has a pleasant acidity and a hint of herbaceous goat's milk. It ripens within two months and becomes smooth and more creamy as it matures.

Above: Berkswell is one of the truly great modern English cheeses.

BERKSWELL

This sheep's milk cheese is sold at four months when the hard, crusty, ridged rind has an aroma of lanolin. Berkswell is hard and chewy and has an almost granular texture. Each bite reveals more of its complex flavours, which include roasted nuts, caramelized onions and meadow flowers with a prickly tang. It is suitable for vegetarians.

BUFFALO

Available since 1996, this is an unusual English cheese, not least because it is made from the milk of water buffalo which, rather incongruously, roam the Cotswold Hills. It is firm yet supple, with a creamy feel and an interesting flavour that hints of almonds with a citrus tang. It may be served as a table cheese or grilled (broiled). It is suitable for vegetarians.

CHEDDAR

Since the sixteenth century, the hard cow's milk cheese made in the Mendip Hills near the Cheddar Gorge has been referred to as Cheddar. The cheese undoubtedly goes back to earlier centuries, perhaps even to Roman times, when the process of

Right: Buffalo is the only hard buffalo's milk cheese made in England. It is produced in Hereford and Worcester in 2kg/4½lb wheels.

making hard cheese was introduced to Britain. A good Cheddar has a unique, wonderful flavour with a bite that is both firm and yielding. It should have a fresh aroma and a nutty, savoury yet sweet taste. It is a favourite table cheese and is widely used for cooking.

Over the centuries, emigrants to Canada, the United States, Australia, South Africa and New Zealand have taken with them the recipe for this cheese, and Cheddar has been copied more than any other British cheese. For the connoisseur, these copies are not really Cheddars at all. Indeed, for them the best and only real Cheddars are those produced by the handful of farmhouse Cheddar makers whose dairy herds graze on the hills of Somerset, Devon and Dorset. All are made using unpasteurized milk, which is considered the better choice for the characteristic tangy, nutty taste.

Chewton This Cheddar from Chewton in Somerset is firm, with a full flavour. The rind is nutty, and the interior suggests cheese and onion, with a hint of butter.

Above: (Left to right) Only a limited number of cheesemakers produce traditional cloth-bound Cheddars: Green's, Keen's, Quicke's and Montgomery's. Cheddar accounts for about 70 per cent of all cheese eaten in Britain, but much of it is factory-made and imported from other countries.

Denhay Hand-made and matured on the farm in Bridport, Devon, Denhay is nutty and rich with a strong savoury tang. The Denhay Dorset Drum is a smaller version of the traditional Denhay Cheddar. The Dorset Drum matures more quickly and has a dense, chewy texture and mellow nuttiness. The small size of cylinder, known as a truckle, makes this cheese an excellent gift. It is suitable for vegetarians.

Green's This cheese, made by three generations on the same farm in Glastonbury in Somerset, has a savoury flavour with a tangy bite. It is matured for 12 months or more. Each cheese is hand turned until it reaches its peak.

Keen's Made in Wincanton, Somerset, this nutty, smooth, creamy cheese has a full-bodied flavour and a fresh green tang. It has been made on the farm since the beginning of the twentieth century using milk from its own herd.

Montgomery's This wonderfully rich cheese made in Yeovil in Somerset has a spicy acidity and a fruity finish.

Quicke's This Cheddar is made by the Quicke family in Exeter, Devon. It is firm and chewy and has a buttery texture and nutty aroma.

CHESHIRE

Cheshire is one of England's oldest and finest cheeses; it was even mentioned in the Domesday Book in the eleventh century. By the 1930s, more than 400 farms were producing Cheshire, but today there are less than a handful of cheesemakers who still make the traditional cheese. As a result of the dominance of large supermarket chains, most of the cheeses produced today are factory-made and lack any real depth of character. However, there is a growing demand for traditionally-made Cheshire.

Cheshire derives its distinct character from the salt marshes on which the cattle graze. The hallmark of a good Cheshire is its fine, moist, somewhat

Below: Crumbly, white Cheshire has a wonderfully mild flavour.

Above: Coquetdale is ripened in caves where it can come into contact with the natural flora and moulds that live on the walls and roofs.

crumbly texture. A few local cheese-makers are now producing traditional cloth-bound Cheshire using raw milk.

Cheshire makes an excellent table cheese and is good for snacks. It is also good for grilling (broiling) and grating.

COQUETDALE

This fine farmhouse cheese is made in Northumberland, through which the River Coquet runs. Its maker based the cheese on the French Saint-Nectaire, but found that the natural flora and moulds that live in the old caves where the cheese was matured affected it differently and the recipe began to change. The final result is a soft, supple cheese with a wonderful balance of sweet-savoury flavours, and a nutty, slightly salty finish. It is very good served as a table cheese and is suitable for vegetarians.

CORNISH YARG

This hand-made table cheese is produced from a traditional seventeenth century recipe. The cheese is covered in fresh nettle leaves, which contrast with the white interior and impart a slight flavour to the fresh-tasting cheese that is not unlike Caerphilly. As Cornish Yarg matures, a greyish hue covers the nettles and the interior softens. It is suitable for vegetarians.

Below: Cornish Yarg has a distinctive crusty, grey rind.

COVERDALE

Made in North Yorkshire, near its namesake village, this cheese has been revived after an absence of about 50 years. Coverdale is mild and buttery and has a sharp, clean taste and firm, open texture. It is suitable for vegetarians.

Below: Coverdale is a cloth-bound, cow's milk cheese that is matured in four to five weeks.

Left: Curworthy develops a rounded taste with age and is a good table cheese, as well as being suitable for cooking.

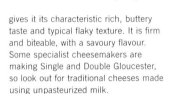

flavour of the herb was incorporated. Ideally the cheese should be aged for at least nine months, and mottled with natural-looking herbs. Much of the Sage Derby produced today is reconstituted cheese, coloured with streaks of vegetable dye and artificially flavoured. The result is a waxy cheese with an overpowering flavour, which bears little resemblance to the traditional farmhouse cheese.

Above: Double Gloucester is a firm, mellow, nutty-tasting cheese with a delicious zesty tang.

CURWORTHY

This cheese is made by a local Devon cheesemaker using milk from the farm's own Friesian cows. Although relatively new, it is based on an old seventeenth century recipe. Curworthy has a creamy texture and a smooth, melted butter taste. It is suitable for vegetarians and may be served as a table cheese. Curworthy is good for grilling (broiling) and grating.

DERBY AND SAGE DERBY

Once a traditional farmhouse cheese, Derby was the first cheese in Britain to be made in a factory. The unfortunate result of this is that today there are very few farmhouse cheeses produced and Derby is consequently rather bland. It is similar in texture to Cheddar, but is softer and more open, with a melted-butter taste. Derby can be served as a table cheese or grilled (broiled).

Sage Derby is a speciality cheese that was created in the seventeenth century for eating at harvest suppers. Sage (a herb valued at the time for its health-giving properties) was added to Derby cheese and as the cheese matured, so the

Right: Sage Derby may be mottled green throughout or, as here, have a central layer of sage-speckled cheese.

DOUBLE AND SINGLE GLOUCESTER

Both Double and Single Gloucester cheese have been made since the sixteenth century. They were originally cloth-bound, round cheeses made from the milk of the native Old Gloucester cows. Single Gloucester is smaller, made from skimmed milk, and is meant to be eaten while it is still young. The full-cream (whole) milk in Double Gloucester

gives it its characteristic rich, buttery taste and typical flaky texture. It is firm and biteable, with a savoury flavour. Some specialist cheesemakers are making Single and Double Gloucester, so look out for traditional cheeses made using unpasteurized milk.

DOUBLE WORCESTER

A smaller version of Double Gloucester, this cheese is made in the neighbouring county of Worcestershire. Like Double Gloucester, it has a firm, breakable, flaky texture and is a distinct deep tangerine-orange in colour. It is made with unpasteurized milk from Friesian cows, and hand milking contributes to its unique flavour, which is mellow and rounded and reminiscent of citrus zest.

DUDDLESWELL

This cheerful-looking truckle has a firm, somewhat flaky texture that melts in the mouth, releasing a sweet, almost caramel flavour with a hint of brazil nuts and fresh hay. It can be served as a table cheese and is good grated.

FRIESLA

This sheep's milk cheese from Devon has a sweet and fragrant flavour. It is based on Dutch Gouda and takes its name from the Friesland Islands, where both the world's finest milking sheep and this cheese

HERRIOT FARMHOUSE

This hard farmhouse cheese from North Yorkshire is made using sheep's milk and is based on a nineteenth-century recipe. It is an unpressed hard cheese, being firm, moist and crumbly, with a zesty taste and a soft sweetness. It is suitable for vegetarians.

LANCASHIRE

Throughout the Industrial Revolution, Lancashire cheese was the staple food of the local mill workers. The first factory-made Lancashire appeared in 1913 and today most of this cheese comes from creameries. When it is young, the traditional cheese is known as Creamy Lancashire, when the texture is mouthwateringly moist and crumbly. As the cheese matures, the flavour intensifies and the cheese becomes known as Tasty Lancashire.

The best Lancashire cheeses are the genuine farmhouse cheeses, such as Mrs Kirkham's Tasty Lancashire, which is made with a combination of three days' curd to give a slightly mottled texture and a great depth of flavour.

Left: Hereford Hop is a traditional English cheese that was revived in 1988.

originate. It is a pleasant table cheese, appealing to a wide range of palates, and its creamy, melting texture makes it an excellent introduction to the distinctive flavour of sheep's milk cheese for those who have never tried it before. It is suitable for vegetarians.

GOSPEL GREEN

This small Cheddar-style table cheese is slightly softer and less dense than classic Cheddar but with a good flavour. The unpasteurized cheese, named after the hamlet in Surrey where it is made, is matured for four to eight weeks in truckles of various sizes. It is good for grilling (broiling), grating and sauces and is suitable for vegetarians.

HEREFORD HOP

This supple, Caerphilly-like cheese has an unusual rind of toasted hops. The hops are crunchy, with the slightly yeasty flavour associated with beer, while the cheese is mellow, sweet and buttery. It always makes an attractive addition to any cheese board.

Above: Mrs Kirkham's Tasty Lancashire is a superb farmhouse cheese with a sharp, peppery flavour and a mouth-puckering finish.

LEAFIELD

This sheep's milk table cheese from Oxfordshire has been revived from a sixteenth-century recipe created by the monks of Abingdon Abbey who, it is recorded, made three "ponders" (tons) of sheep's milk cheese a year. The cheese is hard, dense and chewy with a certain fruitiness and a nutty flavour. It is suitable for vegetarians.

LINCOLNSHIRE POACHER

This unpasteurized cheese is made from milk from Holstein cow's milk. It is a tasty table cheese and can be grilled (broiled) and grated.

*Above:
Malvern is
delicious served as
a table cheese with a
firm texture and creamy taste.*

MALVERN

Made in Hereford and Worcester, this sheep's milk cheese is a modified version of Wensleydale. Firm and dry, yet dense and creamy in the mouth, Malvern is ideal for people allergic to cow's milk. It has a sweet, butterscotch flavour, with a surprising salty aftertaste. It is suitable for vegetarians and can be grilled (broiled) and grated.

MENALLACK FARMHOUSE

This attractive unpasteurized Cornish truckle cheese is a deep golden yellow in colour. When young it is smooth and creamy, but as it ripens it takes on a wonderful rich, savoury tang to balance the acidity. It is suitable for vegetarians.

NORTHUMBERLAND

Produced by the same makers as Coquetdale, this is a moist, firm cow's milk cheese with a sweet, fruity nose. The flavour is robust, with a tart bite that lingers on the palate. It is matured slowly in the old stone cellars of a farm where cheesemaking is reputed to have been going on since 1296. It is a good table cheese and is suitable for vegetarians.

RED LEICESTER

Leicester cheese was being produced in volume by the late eighteenth century. The cheese obtained its bright orange-red colour from the natural dye annatto. However, during World War II, all cheese producers had to make National Cheese, a moist cheese similar to Cheddar, and the practice of adding annatto to Leicester was banned. When the colour was eventually returned to the pale, wartime version, it became known as Red Leicester to distinguish it from the tasteless wartime version. A good Red Leicester has a firm body and a close, flaky

*Above:
(Top to bottom)
Lincolnshire Poacher and
Leafield are both farmhouse cheeses.*

texture. Ideally, Red Leicester should be matured for six to nine months. The flavour is delicately sweet. There is a suggestion of green-grass bitterness behind the more distinct butterscotch and nut flavours. Red Leicester is an excellent table cheese and is good for grilling (broiling) and grating.

*Above: Red
Leicester can be
eaten young but it
improves with age.*

RIBBLESDALE GOAT

Created in 1982, this delicious modern farmhouse cheese from North Yorkshire is made from unpasteurized goat's milk. It is sought after for its fresh delicate flavour. The firm texture is similar to that of a young Gouda and the taste is reminiscent of chicory and almonds, with just the faintest trace of misty hills and wild herbs.

Above: Spenwood is a modern farmhouse cheese.

Below: Ribblesdale Goat is produced in a 2kg/4½lb wheel with a smooth rind, covered with wax.

The sharp whiteness of the cheese is further enhanced by its distinctive, white wax coating. There is also a version made with cow's milk.

Ribblesdale Goat can be served as a table cheese and is very good for grilling (broiling) and grating. It is suitable for vegetarians.

SPENWOOD

Made in Berkshire, Spenwood is an unpasteurized sheep's milk cheese with a pale yellowish-grey interior and a firm, crusty natural rind. It is produced in 2kg/4½lb rounds. Hard and seemingly dry, the cheese is surprisingly creamy in the mouth, melting to release a distinct sweet caramel flavour, which is superbly balanced with acidity. With age, the taste of flowers and ground nuts becomes more pronounced. It is a good table cheese and is suitable for grilling (broiling). It is suitable for vegetarians.

STAFFORDSHIRE ORGANIC

This smooth and creamy, yet firm, cow's milk cheese is one of the few pressed, hard, organic cheeses made in Britain. Herb and chive varieties are available, but the most interesting version contains wild garlic. Staffordshire Organic makes a tasty table cheese and is good for grilling (broiling) and grating. It is suitable for vegetarians.

SWALEDALE

This cheese, named after one of the most beautiful of the dales is a classic Yorkshire cheese, made in the valley of the River Swale. It is soaked in brine before being left to mature in humid cellars, where the yellow rind acquires the attractive mould that prevents the light cream-coloured interior from drying out. Softer than Wensleydale and a little moister, it has the freshness of the misty Yorkshire dales and

Above: Staffordshire Organic is a modern farmhouse cheese with a firm, Cheddar-like rind.

the typical acidity and bite associated with dale cheeses. Swaledale can be made with either cow's or sheep's milk. Of the cow's milk version, there are two additional varieties – one flavoured with chives, garlic and apple mint and the other that is soaked in Old Peculiar, a rich, dark ale from North Yorkshire. Swaledale is a fine table cheese and is suitable for vegetarians.

Below: Swaledale cow's milk cheese has a very attractive appearance, a refreshing flavour and a soft, moist texture that make it a welcome addition to any cheese board.

Above: Tyning is a modern, sheep's milk farmhouse cheese from Avon.

TALA

This Cornish sheep's milk cheese comes in small drums – 400g/14oz and 1.8kg/4lb. It is creamy and full-bodied and has a sweet, aromatic flavour and the slight suggestion of lanolin and aromatic rosemary that is typical of sheep's milk cheeses. Gentle smoking seems to underscore the sweet caramel nature of the cheese. The smooth, hard, brushed rind is yellowish-grey and may have beautiful pinkish moulds. Tala is an excellent table cheese, and is suitable for vegetarians.

TYNING

This modern farmhouse cheese is hard, almost brittle and slightly oily. It is popular both as a table cheese and for grating into cooked dishes. It is made from unpasteurized sheep's milk and has the characteristic burnt-caramel flavour of such cheeses. Young Tyning has a very refreshing fruity tang and, when mature, acquires an intensity of wonderful contrasting flavours. The cheeses are shaped rather like a flying saucer. They have a natural rind and weigh between 2.25kg/5lb and 3.25kg/7lb.

WELLINGTON

This superb modern British cheese is made in a similar way to Cheddar but is much smaller – 2kg/4½lb rounds, as opposed to 26kg/57lb cylinders. Wellington is made in Berkshire but owes its beautiful yellow colour to Guernsey milk. It has a smooth and creamy texture, but with a sharp Cheddar bite. As it ripens, its flavour becomes more intense and sharp with a finish of parsley, celery and chives. It is an excellent table cheese and is suitable for vegetarians.

WENSLEYDALE

This is one of the most famous cheeses of the Yorkshire Dales and it is now produced by a number of small creameries and cheesemakers. Based on a recipe that can be traced back to the Cistercian

monks who came to England from Normandy with William the Conqueror in the eleventh century, the cheese is wrapped in muslin (cheesecloth) and matured in cellars. Originally it was made using sheep's milk, a tradition that is being revived by some local cheesemakers and which is doing much to restore its reputation as a great cheese.

Good Wensleydale has a supple, crumbly moist texture, resembling a young Caerphilly, and a fresh, acid flavour. It is a good table cheese.

WHITE STILTON

This is a younger version of regular Stilton but without its growth of blue mould. White Stilton is a pale cheese with a mild and crumbly texture and a pleasant lemon-fresh flavour. It has none of the punch of its more mature blue cousin. It is a good table cheese and is delicious served in salads. It is suitable for vegetarians.

Above: Wensleydale, made in 4.5kg/10lb or 21kg/46lb cylinders, is traditionally eaten with apple pie – its refreshing flavour balancing the sweetness of the fruit.

Left: White Stilton has a much milder flavour than its maturer blue-veined counterpart.

Above: Doolin is turned by hand and matured slowly to bring out the best in the high-quality local milk.

Left: Coolea is a modern, farmhouse cheese made in West Cork.

Mature Doolin has a much more distinctive fruity character; and Vintage Doolin is a deep golden colour, has a fine grainy texture and a rich, lingering buttery flavour with a tang. Doolin is a very versatile cheese and is good for grating, grilling (broiling) and making sauces, as well as serving as a table cheese. It is suitable for vegetarians.

IRELAND

There is no early record of cheese-making in Ireland, but a new generation of cheesemakers are rediscovering old recipes and creating new ones.

COOLEA

This cheese is made by a Dutch family who have settled in Ireland. The Gouda-style cheese, made from unpasteurized cow's milk, is considered to be as good as any made in Holland, while having its own unique character. The rich grazing produces a rich, nutty cheese with a fruity tang. Coolea is a tasty table cheese and is good for making sauces.

DOOLIN

This Gouda-style cheese, matured in a similar yellow waxed rind is produced in the county of Waterford. There are three versions: Young Doolin, which is sold after only two months, is rather bland;

GABRIEL

This unpasteurized cow's milk Gruyère-type cheese from West Cork is full of flavour and has a fruity zing. Lightly salted in brine, it is cured for many months with neither wax nor plastic to hinder ripening. It is a fine table cheese, produced in wheels weighing 6.75–27kg/15–60lb.

LAVISTOWN

Crumbling and fine, Lavistown resembles a Cheddar cheese but is rather less compact. Produced in Kilkenny in South-east Eire, it is made to a Swaledale recipe and has a sharp, refreshing acidity and a green, leafy taste. It is very good served as a table cheese and is suitable for vegetarians.

SCOTLAND

Although several hard cheeses are produced in Scotland, Dunlop is the only indigenous hard cheese.

CAIRNSMORE

This sheep's milk cheese from Galloway sometimes has a slightly lopsided shape and the rind develops a series of furry moulds as it reaches maturity. The cheese has a musty aroma and the texture is firm, rather like Cheddar but moister. It is made from April to October and has an aromatic, nutty flavour with the typical sweetness of sheep's milk.

DUNLOP

First made in the time of James II by Barbara Gilmour, Dunlop is a sweet, cow's milk cheese. Making Dunlop went on to become a flourishing industry in the eighteenth and nineteenth centuries, then all but died out until the end of the 1980s when it was produced again still using traditional methods. A good table cheese, it is firm yet springy, very mild and buttery, with the sweetness of fresh milk. It is suitable for vegetarians.

GOWRIE

Wrapped in locally made linen to produce a natural rind, Gowrie is a large and impressive cheese. It is made using traditional Cheddar techniques but is softer and less dense, more closely resembling Dunlop.

Below: Pale, round Dunlop is an unpasteurized hard cheese from Ayrshire.

ISLE OF MULL

The milk from the Isle of Mull produces a pale cheese, but this lack of colour is not reflected in its flavour, which is surprisingly powerful. Isle of Mull has the classic tang of Cheddar and is laced with savoury overtones of garlic and onions with just a hint of herbs. The cheese is made using traditional methods, and the dairy herd is fed hops during the winter which perhaps explains its powerful punch. It is a fine table cheese and is also good for grating and grilling (broiling). As well as the hefty cylinders in which it is traditionally made, Isle of Mull is available in a smaller gift size with flavourings such as herbs, caraway seeds and (bell) peppers.

LOCH ARTHUR FARMHOUSE

An organic unpasteurized cheese made using traditional Cheddar techniques, Loch Arthur Farmhouse is firm and dry and almost melts in the mouth revealing a wonderful, nutty character. Its tangy flavour is much less aggressive than mature Cheddars, so the fragrance and subtleties of the organic milk are allowed to come through. It is great served as a table cheese and is suitable for vegetarians.

ORKNEY EXTRA MATURE

Produced on the island of Orkney, which is renowned for the richness and flavour of its milk, this is a delicious strong-bodied Cheddar. The cheese is matured for at least 12 months and, like other well-aged hard cheeses such as Parmesan, tiny crystals of calcium lactate can sometimes be found in the cheese,

Right: Isle of Mull Cheddar clearly shows the marks of the cloth in which it was bound on its pale rind.

Above: Orkney Extra Mature Cheddar has a creamy, nutty flavour, with a hint of burnt onion.

Above: Loch Arthur Farmhouse is a traditionally made, cloth-bound Cheddar made using organic milk.

adding another dimension of bite to the final product. A versatile cheese, Orkney Extra Mature Cheddar is perfect for salads, snacks, grating and making sauces, as well as being an excellent table cheese.

SERIOUSLY STRONG CHEDDAR

This blockbuster of a Cheddar is aged for 18–24 months, and the flavour is strong and savoury with a mouthwatering tang to balance the creamy richness. The texture is sometimes slightly crunchy, owing to the calcium lactate crystals that form in old, hard cheeses. For the Scottish market the cheese is coloured with the red dye annatto, while a natural version, described as white, is available for those on the English side of the border. It is a good table cheese and can be used for grating, grilling (broiling) and sauces.

WALES

Caerphilly is probably the best-known of all the Welsh cheeses but there are a number of other modern, hard cheeses.

ACORN

This firm yet crumbly table cheese with a golden, crusty rind is loosely based on an old-style Wensleydale. Made from sheep's milk, it melts in the mouth, releasing the flavours of cream caramel and crushed nuts, with a citrus finish. It can also be used for grating.

Below: A good Caerphilly has a moist texture and wonderfully tangy flavour.

Below: Llangloffan has a pitted rind that bears the imprint of the cloth in which the cheese is bound.

CAERPHILLY

Made in 900g/2lb and 3.25kg/7lb wheels, Caerphilly is named after the village where it was first produced in 1831. Caerphilly is only lightly pressed and has a higher moisture content than other traditional British cheeses, which allows it to ripen more quickly. The brine baths, in which Caerphilly was traditionally soaked overnight, also helped to seal in the moisture and the saltiness that resulted proved very popular with Welsh miners who had lost salt from their perspiring bodies during their labours.

Caerphilly is the only traditional Welsh cheese still made today, and there are several cheese-makers who continue to produce it by the traditional methods. While a good factory-made Cheddar can still retain something of the character of a traditionally made cheese, the same thing is not true of Caerphilly. This ivory-white cheese needs the love and attention of a cheesemaker and it is always worth seeking out a traditionally-made cheese. When still young, a good Caerphilly has a fresh citrus taste and a moist, friable yet supple texture. As the cheese matures, the edges become wonderfully creamy and the flavour becomes more rounded. Caerphilly is an excellent table cheese and is the perfect choice for a ploughman's lunch. It is also the essential ingredient in a really good Welsh rarebit. Caerphilly is suitable for vegetarians.

CWMTAWE PECORINO

An Italian cheesemaker living in Wales makes this Pecorino-style cheese using the milk from his flock of 140 sheep that roam the wild grasses of the Brecon Beacons. In keeping with tradition, the sheep are milked only from April until November.

When young, Cwmtawe Pecorino is creamy, not grainy like its world-famous Italian cousin, and has a ridged, brownish rind. It can be served as a table cheese but is also good for grating and can be used as Italian Pecorino. A smoked version is also available. Unlike Italian Pecorino, Cwmtawe Pecorino is suitable for vegetarians.

LLANBOIDY

This unpasteurized Cheddar-like cheese is made in Pembrokeshire from Red Poll cow's milk. Llanboidy takes two to four months to ripen and is made in 4.5kg/10lb wheels. It has a crusty, wrinkled, yellow rind. The interior has a firm yet crumbly texture with a dense and creamy consistency. The aroma is of fresh-cut hay and meadows and the cheese has a mouthwatering, sharp, green and grassy tang. Llanboidy is delicious served as a table cheese and is also very good for grilling (broiling).

Caerphilly in England

The economic advantages of this quick-ripening Welsh cheese were soon recognised by the major makers of Cheddar in Somerset. Their large cheeses were made in cylinders, took months to mature, occupying valuable space and creating cash flow problems in the interim. Caerphilly on the other hand, weighed less and it ripened in a week, but would keep for two to three months. The Somerset cheesemakers were able to make the small, Welsh cheeses during the summer months when milk was abundant, and still produce their Cheddars. Today, one of the best-known makers of Caerphilly is in Somerset, rather than Wales.

LLANGLOFFAN FARMHOUSE

This hand-made, modern, farmhouse cheese comes from Pembrokeshire. It is made to a new recipe but follows traditional methods using unpasteurized milk from Brown Swiss and Jersey cows. The cheese has a rich, crumbly texture that melts in the mouth, and a fresh fruity flavour that has a hint of fire on the finish. A chive and garlic version of the cheese is also available. It is an excellent table cheese and is suitable for vegetarians.

PENBRYN

This organic, cow's milk cheese from Carmarthenshire is based on Dutch Gouda. Penbryn is firm, yet creamy, with a host of flavours that have been described as nutty, fruity, grassy, sweet and buttery. The natural rind of the 2.25kg/5lb rounds of cheese has a dusting of blue and white moulds and wild yeasts. Penbryn is good served as a table cheese.

TEIFI

This organic, unpasteurized farmhouse cheese is made from cow's milk. It is similar to a Gouda in both shape and texture. It is made in 450g/1lb, 900g/2lb and 3.5–4.5kg/8–10lb millstones with a smooth, polished rind. The deep sunshine-yellow interior has a firm, dense texture and a fairly fruity flavour when young. At it matures, the cheese becomes hard and almost flaky. A smoked version of the cheese is also produced, as are versions flavoured with fresh nettle leaves and aromatic cumin. Teifi is good served as a table cheese and is suitable for vegetarians.

Making Welsh Rarebit

This classic dish of toasted bread topped with a deliciously rich, creamy cheese sauce can be made with either beer or milk. Beer gives the sauce a mellow, hoppy taste and a wonderful country flavour. For an authentic feel, use Caerphilly, but any hard cheese will do.

1 Coarsely grate about 130g/4½oz Caerphilly or other hard cheese.

2 Put the grated cheese in a heavy pan and mix in 10ml/2 tsp plain (all-purpose) flour and 10ml/2 tsp mild mustard. Pour in 60ml/4 tbsp beer or milk and stir well to combine.

3 Heat gently, stirring until creamy. Do not allow to boil. Meanwhile, lightly toast 4 thick slices of country-style bread under the grill (broiler).

4 Pour the melted cheese on to the toast and spread to the edges. Grill (broil) until the cheese mixture is golden brown. Sprinkle with paprika or cayenne pepper and serve.

VARIATIONS
• To make Buck Rarebit, top Welsh Rarebit with a poached egg and a rasher or two of grilled bacon.
• Alternatively, top Welsh Rarebit with grilled tomatoes or caramelized onions.

TYN GRUG

Made in Cardiganshire, Tyn Grug is an organic unpasteurized cheese. Made in large cylinders (7.5kg/16½lb and 15kg/33lb), this cow's milk cheese is loosely based on Cheddar, with a Swiss influence. The result is a cross between a Cheddar and a Swiss Gruyère. Tyn Grug has a rough, deep yellow rind and a dense and firm interior with a slightly grainy texture. It has a complexity of flavours that are gradually released on to the palate. At first there is a hint of young celery leaves, then a rich Gruyère nuttiness and finally a peppery acidity on the finish. It is a good table cheese and is suitable for vegetarians.

Left: (Left to right) Tyn Grug and Teifi are wonderful modern hard cheeses. They are both unpasteurized and organic and have a delightful flavour.

FRANCE

Although France is more commonly associated with soft white cheese such as Brie and Camembert, the French also produce wonderful hard cheeses.

ABBAYE DE BELLOC (AOC)

From the Pays Basque, this traditional farmhouse cheese was originally made by Benedictine monks from locally-produced milk. The sheep's milk cheese has a firm, dense and creamy texture. The taste resembles burnt caramel and there is a distinctive lanolin aroma. Serve as a table cheese or grill (broil).

AOC

To preserve and protect the traditions and experience of centuries of French cheesemaking, the Appellation d'Origine Contrôlée (AOC) system was established, as it had been for wine. Each cheese protected by the system must comply with strictly enforced rules that govern the following:

• The area where cattle may graze
• The origin and type of feed provided for them
• The breed of cattle that furnish the milk
• When the cheese is made
• How the cheese is made
• The shape and size of the cheese
• How the cheese is stored

The regulations often mean that cattle may only graze on permanent pastures that are organically managed, rather than ploughed and re-sown every year. The use of silage or other fermented or man-made feed is prohibited.

The AOC rules guarantee the quality of France's famous cheeses, protecting them against imitations and giving the consumer the confidence to buy raw milk cheeses. Some AOC cheeses are made in huge factories, others on tiny farms, but all proudly respect and uphold the traditions of their own particular area.

Right: Abbaye de Belloc is good for grilling, grating and making sauces, as well as serving as a table cheese.

ARDI-GASNA

In Basque, *ardi-gasna* means sheep's cheese. Ardi-Gasna has remained virtually unchanged for centuries and there are still a few shepherds who make the long journey with their flocks up to the high mountain pastures of the Pyrénées. Here they make their cheese in stone huts in late spring and early summer. Seldom found outside the region, Ardi-Gasna cheeses are highly prized. The cheese has a hard texture but feels rich in the mouth. The flavour is clean and fresh with a slightly sweet nuttiness.

BEAUFORT (AOC)

This cheese is also known as Gruyère de Beaufort. Gruyère gets its name from the time when kings sent their tax collectors, known as *agents gruyers*, to collect taxes from the cheesemakers. Beaufort is made in mountain chalets in the Savoie region, and it dates back to the time of the Roman Empire. It has an irresistible smoothness, despite its rather hard appearance. Beaufort can be served as a table cheese, or used for snacks, fondues or pies.

Below: Beaufort is a traditional cow's milk cheese that owes its superb flavour to the flowers, sweet grasses and herbs of the high pastures where the cows graze.

Above: Every Cantal cheese is stamped with the AOC logo.

CANTAL (AOC)

One of the oldest French cheeses, this was originally produced by putting the curd into a wooden cylinder called *le formage*, from which it is believed the word *fromage* (cheese) is derived.

Cantal Fermier is produced during the summer months, while Cantal Laitier is a pasteurized cheese made all year round. When young, Cantal is moist, open-textured and springy with a tangy flavour. As it matures, it becomes more like a strong Cheddar. Cantal is good as a table cheese or for grating.

COMTÉ (AOC)

The French make two Gruyères – Beaufort and Comté. Comté is sweeter than Beaufort with a piquant fruity flavour. Like Beaufort, Comté can be used for fondues as well as gratins, snacks and canapés.

LAGUIOLE (AOC)

Made in the Auvergne, this is a cheese with an ancient pedigree. Laguiole has a supple to firm texture and, although not so compact as English Cheddar, has certain similarities such as a pleasant nutty sweetness. Connoisseurs consider it to be one of the truly great French cheeses. It is especially delicious when made from *transhumance* milk – which is produced between late May and mid-October, when the cows are taken to the flowering pastures in the mountains. Use as a table cheese, and for snacks, grating and grilling (broiling).

LARUNS

From the Pyrénées, this sheep's milk cheese has been made by shepherds in mountain huts for generations. When young, it has a supple texture and is mild and nutty, making it excellent as a table cheese and for snacks. As it ages, it becomes hard and brittle with a sharper flavour and is best used for grating and cooking.

MIMOLETTE FRANÇAISE

This cheese originated in Holland and was probably introduced to France when Flanders was part of that country. Basically, it is a matured Edam that has been allowed to ripen for six to nine months. By this time, the pieces have to be chiselled off in granite-like chunks. When young, it has a subtle aroma and

Right: Laruns is a sheep's milk cheese from the Pyrénées.

a mellow, nutty taste. The mature cheese is intensely fruity with a powerful tang. The bright tangerine colour is due to the natural dye annatto. It is popular as a cooking cheese or as a snack to wash down with a glass of beer.

TOMME D'ABONDANCE (AOC)

For centuries, this deep golden-yellow cheese has been made in mountain chalets in Savoie, near the border between France and Switzerland. The cheese has a distinct, fruity tang with a hint of yeast. Firm, yet supple and grainy in texture, it is made from unpasteurized, skimmed cow's milk.

Above right: Tomme d'Abondance is a delicious table cheese and is also good for melting.

Above: Laguiole has been made in the Auvergne region since at least the fourth century BC (and was earlier described by Pliny the Elder), although the quantities produced have been dramatically reduced in recent years.

Left: Mimolette Française, also known as Boule de Lille, is at its best when aged, but it can also be enjoyed while still quite young.

ITALY

Since Roman times, cheese has played a major role in the Italian diet and records of cheesemaking date back to before the fourth century BC.

ASIAGO (DOC)

This traditional farmhouse cheese is made in the Vicenza and Trento regions of Italy. There are two distinct types of Asiago. The first, a young, lightly pressed cheese made from whole milk in small dairies, ripens in 20–30 days. It is pale yellow and springy with a delicate, sweet, undemanding flavour and fragrance and is very popular in Italy and elsewhere. Asiago d'Allevo is the mature cheese, taking 12–24 months to ripen. Although it is made with skimmed milk, long maturation gives it a fruity, slightly sharp flavour with a compact granular interior full of small holes. In the same way as Parmesan, Asiago can be grated and then used as a condiment.

DOC

Italy operates a system to protect certain indigenous cheeses. The Ministry of Agriculture and Forestry in Italy, in conjunction with a consortium of cheesemakers, have identified suitable candidates for Denominazione di Origine Controllata (DOC) regulation. They also agree standards of production and determine areas where the cheeses in question could be made. To date, 26 cheeses have been given DOC classification, and more will likely follow. Inspectors regularly visit cheesemakers checking that cheeses sold under the DOC label comply with regulations.

Identifying and promoting indigenous cheeses in this way helps to protect them from being copied, while guaranteeing the consumer a specified level of quality. It also brings to the attention of the public artisan cheeses that might otherwise have become extinct.

Above:
Young Asiago
is pale yellow and springy, becoming deep orange and granular as it ripens.

BRA (DOC)

This cheese is named not after the place where it is made but where it was originally sold. The people of Bra, in Piedmont, used to buy young cheeses from the herdsmen of the Alpine valleys and mature them in their own cellars. There are two different types of Bra sold today. The traditional hard version is matured for three to six months, when the colour darkens and the flavour intensifies. The second, less popular version, is sold young at 45 days when it is still soft. This is made in small dairies mostly from pasteurized milk.

CANESTRATO PUGLIESE (DOC)

Named after the simple, hand-woven reed basket in which it is pressed and drained, Canestrato Pugliese is a flavoursome pecorino. Like most sheep's milk cheeses, it has a burnt-caramel taste, while the texture is a typical grana, being hard and grainy, and therefore well suited to grating. It may also be served as a table cheese.

Right: Pale yellow Grana Padano is made from unpasteurized cow's milk and has a grainy texture.

FIORE SARDO (DOC)

This is the sweetest of the pecorinos, with a caramel sweetness and a mouthwatering, salty tang. It can be used as a table cheese, for grating, cooking and for snacks.

GRANA PADANO (DOC)

Grana is the generic name for the hard, grainy cheeses that are used in Italy as grating cheese. The most famous examples of grana are Grana Padano and Parmigiano Reggiano, often known simply as Parmesan. The cheese should taste fresh, fruity and sweet; never sour or dull. The pale yellow interior should be hard, grainy and crumbly. Use as a table cheese, for grating, in sauces or as a condiment.

MONTASIO (DOC)

This cheese has been produced as long ago as the thirteenth century, when it was made wholly from sheep's milk. Today unpasteurized cow's milk is mostly used, but the cheese is still made following the traditional method: the evening milk is partially skimmed (the cream being used to make mascarpone) and then mixed with the whole morning milk. The cheese is pale yellow, and the body is firm with small holes. A good Montasio is creamy, rich and fruity with a hint of pineapple. It should be quite tangy, not unlike a medium Cheddar. As well as a table cheese, Montasio can be used for grating and in sauces.

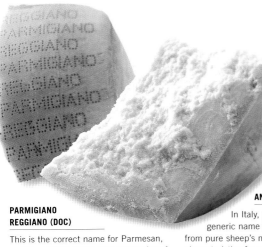

PARMIGIANO REGGIANO (DOC)

This is the correct name for Parmesan, and the cheese is the most expensive of all the grana. In Italy, it is sold in large rough grainy (never waxy) chunks, chiselled from the shiny drum. The name of the cheese is emblazoned on the rind so that even the smallest piece may be authenticated. The aroma is sweet and fruity, the colour a fresh straw-yellow (never greyish), and the taste exquisite: fruity, strong and rich. It will keep for months in the refrigerator, but the rough surface may grow some mould that needs scraping away. One feature of Parmigiano Reggiano is that it is made from partially skimmed milk. The evening milk is left in vats overnight. Next morning, the slightly soured cream is skimmed off to make mascarpone and the skimmed milk is combined with fresh morning milk. The process of cheesemaking then begins, and this takes between 18 and 48 months.

Parmigiano Reggiano is widely used in numerous traditional recipes. It is also served as a table cheese or grated to be used as a condiment.

Right: (Clockwise from top left) There are several different types of Pecorino, including Sardo, Toscano and Romano.

Left: The classic Italian cheese Parmigiano Reggiano has many culinary uses and is used widely in Italian cooking.

PECORINO ROMANO, SARDO AND TOSCANO (DOC)

In Italy, pecorino is the generic name for cheeses made from pure sheep's milk. Each cheese is characteristic of a specific area and of a particular breed of sheep. Pecorino is a hard, grainy cheese that can be used in the same way as Parmesan.

Pecorino Romano (DOC) This has been made in the countryside around Rome for centuries. It takes 8–12 months to mature, during which time it develops its characteristic flavour – salty with a fruity tang that becomes steadily more robust. The compact interior is white to pale yellow with irregular small eyes. It should feel moist yet granular, and it is a superb grating cheese.

Pecorino Sardo (DOC) There are two styles of this pecorino from Sardinia. Pecorino Sardo Dolce is matured for 20–60 days and is delicate and sweet; Pecorino Sardo Maturo, ripened for up to 12 months, is dry, hard and more granular, developing a sharpness and salty tang as it matures. Use as table cheeses or for grating as a condiment.

Pecorino Toscano (DOC), from Tuscany, is supple, fruity and aromatic. Generally smaller than other types of pecorino, Toscano ripens more quickly.

TOMA (DOC)

This mountain cheese of the Piedmont region has been made in various shapes and sizes for generations. Although it now comes under the DOC umbrella, there are as many variations as there are small dairy farms in the Vale d'Aosta. The young cheese, which is made from cow's milk, is sweet and milky. It can be served as a table cheese or can be used for cooking.

SPAIN

Wherever you go in Spain, from the barren plains of Extremadura to the majestic beauty of the Sierra Nevada, you will find delicious cheeses.

CASTELLANO

This is made in the Castile-León region of Spain, the largest cheesemaking region in Spain, accounting for 85 per cent of pure sheep's milk cheeses. Many cheeses in this area that were once made by shepherds or cheese-makers, are now made in factories or in co-operatives, and Castellano, like many traditional cheeses, has become more uniform. Nevertheless, it is still possible to find a good Castellano made by artisan cheesemakers whose cheeses carry motifs of flowers, geometric patterns or initials. These cheeses have a delicate, crème-caramel flavour, offset by a fresh acidity and a hint of salt.

GARROTXA

This modern goat's milk cheese is made north of Barcelona in Catalonia. It is based on an old recipe and is created using farmhouse methods. The cheese is a creamy pale yellow and has a firm yet springy texture. The flavour is fresh, but with underlying subtleties of walnuts and fresh young grass.

Below: Garrotxa is produced in 1kg/2¼lb rounds and has a natural rind covered in thick, furry, grey mould.

IDIAZABAL

This Basque sheep's milk cheese has been made by shepherds for centuries. It was traditionally sold at the end of September when the shepherds and their flocks were forced down from the mountains by the first snows of winter. It has a compact texture with a few pin-prick holes. It is dry but not crumbly. The rind carries the marks of the wooden moulds in which it is drained. The characteristic smoked flavour was originally the result of the cheese's having been stored in the smoky atmosphere of the shepherds' huts. Cheesemakers continue to make the cheese in the way their fathers and grandfathers did, and a good Idiazabal carries the Spanish Denominación de Origen (DO) stamp of approval.

Above: (From left to right) Manchego aged 4, 6 and 10 months: its flavour and texture vary depending on how long it has been matured.

Below: Mahon was originally a sheep's milk cheese, but has been made from Friesian cow's milk since they were first imported to Minorca during the eighteenth century.

MAHON

This unpasteurized cheese comes from Minorca and is well worth looking out for when visiting the island. It is sold as a fresh cheese, a few days after being made, but is best loved as a hard cheese, when it has a slightly granular texture, like that of Parmesan. The cheese is a distinctive cushion shape with a dent in the centre. The ivory interior, with its small irregular holes, contrasts with the bright orange rind whose colour comes not from bacteria but from being rubbed with butter, paprika and oil. The taste is sharp with a salty tang because the sea surrounds the hills where the cattle graze.

MANCHEGO

This sheep's milk cheese comes from the La Mancha region. The cheese has been made in this area since Roman times although much has changed since then; the plains are irrigated and there are vineyards where there were once only hardy La Mancha sheep.

To qualify for the famous Manchego label, the cheese must be firm and dry, yet rich and creamy. Only sheep's milk

Below: Zamorano was once made by itinerant cheesemakers, travelling from farm to farm. The cheeses were then often matured in the underground "caves" of neighbouring vineyards.

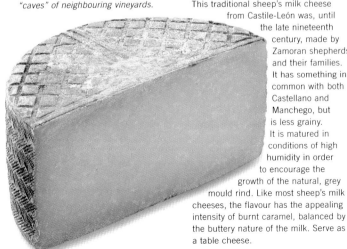

Right: Idiazabal has been made in the high pastures of the Urbia and Aralar mountains for centuries.

from La Mancha may be used, and the very distinctive markings found on the waxed rind must be visible. The cheese itself should be ivory in colour with small irregular eyes, and the flavour should be rich and nutty with a full burnt caramel flavour. Serve as a table cheese or use for grilling (broiling).

QUESO IBERICO

This cheese is unique in Spain for being made using cow's, goat's and sheep's milk. Regulations require that it contain not less than 25 per cent and not more than 40 per cent of any one type of milk. The flavour of the cheese has elements of all three types of milk used. The creamy texture melts in the mouth, gradually releasing a rich, full-bodied nuttiness before delivering a fruity tang on the finish.

ZAMORANO

This traditional sheep's milk cheese from Castile-León was, until the late nineteenth century, made by Zamoran shepherds and their families. It has something in common with both Castellano and Manchego, but is less grainy. It is matured in conditions of high humidity in order to encourage the growth of the natural, grey mould rind. Like most sheep's milk cheeses, the flavour has the appealing intensity of burnt caramel, balanced by the buttery nature of the milk. Serve as a table cheese.

PORTUGAL

The climate on mainland Portugal does not lend itself to cheesemaking, but those cheeses that are made there are absolutely outstanding. A few cheeses with ancient pedigrees are produced on small farms or dairies in isolated valleys and mountainsides. The milk of the agile, tenacious goats is luscious, thick and aromatic, making superb cheese.

SÃO JORGE/ILHA DE SÃO JORGE

This cheese comes from São Jorge, a small island in the Azores. The high plateaux and craters, reminders of the island's volcanic past, give way to lush pastures. A Flemish settlement was established on the nearby island of Faial in the fifteenth century. Isolated from the mainland, the islanders were self-sufficient, and cheesemaking was established here and on neighbouring islands. The Azores were the last stop for explorers *en route* to the New World, so the cheeses were much sought after. Like Gouda, São Jorge improves with age and keeps well, so it continues to prove popular with seafarers such as the transatlantic yachtsmen, who call at the Azores for provisions. Over the centuries the recipe has been adapted to the local conditions: the result is a unique cheese with the appearance of Dutch Gouda but the sharp, savoury tang of Cheddar.

SWITZERLAND

Early in history, cheese was used as a currency in Switzerland. Much of what was made was taken over the Alps to be exchanged with the Romans for rice, spices and wine.

APPENZELLER

This cheese dates back to the time of Charlemagne. Its quality and character are protected by strict rules and it is at its best when made in mountain chalets, from the milk of the summer pastures. The dry, flat, pale yellow to orange rind gains its colour from being washed in spices, white wine and salt. The yellow interior is firm and dense with a few peanut-sized holes scattered throughout. A young Appenzeller has a buttery, fruity flavour, but when it is more mature it has a fuller flavour. Use as a table cheese or for melting and grilling (broiling).

EMMENTAL

The history of Emmental can be traced back to 1293. It takes its name from the valley of the upper Emme River and is now made throughout Switzerland, wherever there are high pastures. Although it resembles Gruyère, the aroma is sweeter and the flavour unmistakably fruity, with the underlying flavour of fresh-cut-hay. It is also smoother and more elastic than Gruyère, with holes about the size of hazelnuts. It is a wonderful melting cheese and is the traditional cheese, along with Gruyère, for fondue. It can also be served as a table cheese or in a ploughman's lunch.

FRIBOURGEOIS

This cheese can be traced back through the centuries and it is documented that it was served to the wife of Duke Sigismund of Austria in 1448. The cheese has a full-bodied flavour and a meaty quality. It resembles a small Gruyère, with a spicy, rather than nutty, taste that intensifies when the cheese is grilled (broiled) or melted.

Left: Emmental, like all Swiss hard cheeses, is subject to very strict quality control.

Right: Gruyère is similar to Emmental, but is a much deeper yellow.

Above:
Appenzeller
almost certainly originated in Appenzell, but is now also produced in St Gallen.

GRUYÈRE

Like Emmental, Gruyère has been made in the Alps for centuries. Each of the enormous cheeses (20–45kg/44–99lb) is made by a group of farmers, since it takes 400 litres/88 gallons of milk to produce a single 35kg/77lb wheel. The texture is dense and compact, yet flexible, and it has a rich, creamy flavour – at first fruity, then revealing earthy and nutty characteristics that linger on the palate. It is excellent in fondues but is less stringy than Emmental when heated, so is better used for gratins, grilling (broiling) and in soups.

Left: Royalp-Tilsiter, made in the St Gallen region is a popular breakfast cheese in Switzerland.

ROYALP-TILSITER

Compared with Switzerland's ancient cheeses, this is a relative newcomer, having been introduced in the latter half of the nineteenth century by a Swiss cheese-maker who had learned to make Tilsiter while in eastern Prussia after the Franco-Prussian war. The rich, creamy milk of the alpine pastures produced a cheese with a robust smooth texture and small distinct holes, unlike the original Tilsiter, which had irregular cracks running through it.

Royalp-Tilsiter is smaller than other Swiss cheeses. The unpasteurized cheese is lightly pressed and ripened for at least two months, but is better after six months. To distinguish it from other Tilsiter cheese, it is known as Royalp abroad. Royalp-Tilsiter makes a good table cheese or it can be used for melting and grilling (broiling).

SAANEN

This is a very hard, brittle cow's milk cheese, with a deep yellow interior that is intensely fruity. It is quite similar to Parmesan or Sbrinz and is a good grating and cooking cheese that will keep almost indefinitely. Saanen was traditionally reserved for special occasions, when pieces of the cheese would be shaved off and served with a glass of fruity, local wine.

SAPSAGO

The unusual, pale lime green colour of this cone-shaped cheese results from the addition of fenugreek. Sapsago is very

hard and gritty and melts like Parmesan when heated. It has an astringent, salty, sour and mouth-watering flavour and is not a cheese to be taken lightly.

SBRINZ

This is thought to be the cheese Pliny the Elder referred to as *Caseus Helveticus* in his writings in the first century AD. The method of production is similar to that for Parmesan and the cheeses have similar characteristics. Sbrinz has the same fresh, pineapple taste and aroma against a background of ground nuts, and a deliciously spicy finish. It is not so potent as Parmesan, but, nevertheless, it makes a good and usually significantly cheaper alternative as a table cheese or for grating.

TÊTE-DE-MOINE

It is often said that the name of this cheese, which means head of the monk, derives from its shape. However, the cheese was originally actually called Bellelay, after a monastery in the Jura Mountains. But following the French Revolution, it was renamed Tête-de-Moine after the monks who made it.

Tête-de-Moine has a strong, earthy flavour. It is usually served in thick strips or ruffles, made by passing it through a machine called a girolle. The ruffles are used to garnish salads, platters of cooked meats and other dishes. It is also delicious served as a table cheese.

Left: Fresh-tasting Sbrinz has been made in central Switzerland for more than 2,000 years.

Above: Tête-de-Moine is commonly served shaved into decorative ruffles.

HOLLAND

More than half the land in Holland is below sea level, and the sea is held back only by the intricate system of dykes and canals that was begun by the Romans. The superb grazing on this reclaimed land, known as Polders, is the foundation on which the cheeses of Holland were built. Surprisingly, unlike other major cheese-producing countries of Europe, which produce a vast range of cheeses, Holland concentrates on only two – Gouda and Edam, which is a semi-soft cheese – upon which all other Dutch cheeses are based.

With nearly a third of Dutch land dedicated to dairy farming, cheese plays a significant role in the economy and over 75 per cent of the annual production is exported. Most cheese is made in highly-mechanized factories, which has, sadly, led to the decline in artisan cheesemakers. The few that remain largely make farmhouse Goudas.

BOERENKAAS

The name of this semi-hard cow's milk cheese is derived from the Dutch word *boer*, meaning farmer, and the word *kaas*, meaning cheese. Boerenkaas is made in the traditional way, with the only modern touch being the porous plastic coating that is painted on to the newly-formed cheese to protect it during the months of slow ageing. When young, this semi-hard, cow's milk cheese is nutty and rich, with a dense, creamy texture and a fragrance reminiscent of meadow pastures and fresh hay. With age, the flavour intensifies, becoming stronger and fruity. Very small calcium crystals, like those found in Parmesan, develop in a well-aged cheese. It may be served as a table cheese and is often enjoyed sliced for breakfast. It is also delicious melted and served in sandwiches.

DUTCH MIMOLETTE

Known as Commissiekaas in Holland and Dutch Mimolette everywhere else, this cheese is actually a matured Edam coloured with carrot juice. It is seldom found outside northern Europe but is a truly magnificent, fruity cheese and looks like a giant orange with rough, pitted skin. At around five months it has a firm, compact and slightly oily texture, with a fruity aroma and nutty flavour. When aged, the colour darkens to a deep orange, the texture becomes rock-hard, granular and brittle and the flavour becomes more pronounced. It is fruity with a hint of orange zest and the nutty flavour intensifies to reach a mouthwatering crescendo.

FRIESEKAAS

This large, round semi-hard cheese is spiced with a combination of cumin and cloves and is quite similar to Leyden. The 10kg/22lb cheeses are made with cow's milk and ripened for three to 12 months. Friesekaas is served as a table cheese, often for snacks or breakfast, and is very good for grilling (broiling).

Left: Due to the decline in artisan cheese-making in Holland, Boerenkaas is becoming increasingly hard to find.

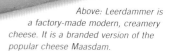

Above: Leerdammer is a factory-made modern, creamery cheese. It is a branded version of the popular cheese Maasdam.

GOUDA

Gouda accounts for more than 60 per cent of the cheese produced in Holland. It is made in huge rounds, within a smooth, yellow, waxed rind. Mature Gouda (18 months plus) is coated in black wax, which contrasts starkly with its deep yellow interior.

Gouda has many imitations. Other European countries, notably Sweden, have adopted the Dutch style of cheesemaking and produce cheeses similar to Gouda and since the nineteenth century, the United States and Australia have been making farmhouse versions, meticulously adhering to the traditional methods.

When only a few months old, Gouda is firm, smooth and supple with a scattering of small holes. The flavour is sweet and fruity and the cheese is wonderful in snacks or as a table cheese. Mature Gouda has a more granular texture and, at this stage, is suitable for grating and using for cooking and grilling (broiling).

LEERDAMMER

This boulder-shaped, semi-hard cheese is made from cow's milk. It has a smooth, natural rind, which may be waxed, and is one of the better-known factory brands of Maasdam. Other factory brands include Ronduer, Goyweter and Fricotal. Serve as a table cheese or use for grilling (broiling).

GERMANY

It was not until the arrival of the Franks and the rule of Charlemagne in the ninth century AD that the cheeses of Germany really began to emerge.

ALLGÄUER EMMENTALER

The mountain pastures and the cattle of southern Bavaria are similar to their Swiss counterparts and since the German makers of Allgäuer Emmentaler adopted the same stringent standards of quality maintained by the Swiss, it is almost impossible to tell Allgäuer Emmentaler and Swiss Emmental apart. It has a delicious fruity flavour. Use for grilling (broiling), melting or snacks.

BAVARIAN BERGKÄSE

Bergkäse simply means mountain cheese and is a smaller version of Allgäuer Emmentaler. Firm but supple, and almost chewy, Bergkäse is a superb melting cheese. It is only made in the summer months from the milk of cows grazing the mountain pastures.

TILSIT

This smooth, supple cheese is filled with tiny irregular holes and is encased in a crusty rind. The aroma is mildly pungent, while the flavour is buttery and fruity with a spicy tinge. The original Tilsit was apparently discovered by Dutch cheesemakers living in Tilsit (then in East Prussia). They were trying to make Gouda but various factors combined to create a cheese that was markedly different, especially in relation to the rind.

Above: Leyden has the city's emblem of crossed keys imprinted on the rind.

LEYDEN

Also known as Leidsekaas, this cheese is made on farms around the university city of Leiden. It has a similar texture to Gouda but, because it is made with semi-skimmed (low-fat) milk it feels slightly drier. The curd is coloured with annatto and mixed with cumin seeds before being pressed and washed in brine. (The traditional custom of treading the seeds into the curds has now been replaced by machine.) The aromatic cumin contrasts well with the creamy nutty character of the cheese.

MAASDAM

This large, boulder-shaped cheese was created in the early 1990s as an alternative to the more expensive Swiss Emmental. Although there are some similarities with Emmental, Maasdam is higher in moisture and therefore more supple. The flavour is sweet and buttery, with a fruity background.

Right: Maasdam is delicious served as a snack or breakfast cheese.

Left: Belgian Beauvoorde was created in the early 1900s by Arthur Djes.

OTHER EUROPEAN HARD CHEESES

Throughout the rest of Europe, there are a number of delicious hard cheeses that are worthy of note, all with their own unique appearance, texture and flavour.

BERGKÄSE (AUSTRIA)

This cheese closely resembles Bavarian Bergkäse, with the same creamy, fudge-like flavour. The holes in the cheese are smaller than those in the German cheese.

BEAUVOORDE (BELGIUM)

This semi-hard hexagonal, cow's milk cheese has an open texture that is firm, yet supple, with a mild flavour and a spicy aroma.

GJETOST (NORWAY)

This semi-hard cheese is noticeably less compact that most hard cheeses. The unusual fudge-coloured cheese is made from the whey and was originally made entirely from goat's milk, although now it is more often made with a blend of goat's and cow's milk or pure cow's milk. The pure cow's milk version is called

Right: Gjetost is Norway's most popular cheese.

Mysost and the pure goat's milk version, Ekta Gjetost. Gjetost has a distinctly sweet flavour and a rather unusual aromatic quality that is not to everyone's taste. It is traditionally eaten for breakfast, but may also be served as a dessert, with coffee and is also used in cooking, melted into savoury dishes.

Above: Jarlsberg has a springy texture and sweet, slightly nutty flavour.

JARLSBERG (NORWAY)

This old Norwegian cheese, based on Emmental, was all but forgotten before its rediscovery in the mid-1900s. Today it is extremely popular and a great deal of Jarlsberg is exported, particularly to the United States.

Made from the rich milk of the high summer pastures, Jarlsberg is sweeter and less nutty than Emmental. Although it lacks the depth of that great cheese, Jarlsberg has a pleasant flavour. The paste is golden yellow, with holes of various sizes. It is good served as a table cheese and can also be used for melting, grilling (broiling) and for snacks.

NÖKKELOST (NORWAY)

This is the Norwegian version of the Dutch cheese Leyden and has been made in Norway since the seventeenth century. It comes in 5–12kg/11–26lb wheels or blocks flecked with cumin seeds and is marked with the imprint of crossed keys (*nökkel* in Norwegian), the emblem of the city of Leiden.

GREVÉOST/GREVÉ (SWEDEN)

Often known simply as Grevé, this cow's milk cheese is a slightly milder, more commercial copy of Swiss Emmental. It is supple and dense in texture, with some large holes. It is pale yellow, has a creamy texture and a sweet, slightly nutty flavour, which becomes more pronounced as the cheese matures, but it lacks the depth and character of Emmental. Serve as a table cheese or use for grating and melting.

MESOST (SWEDEN)

Like a number of Swedish cheeses, Mesost is made by caramelizing the whey, a practice that is peculiar to Scandinavia. The whey is heated so that the residual proteins and fats separate. The liquid slowly evaporates to leave a sticky, toffee-like mass of caramelized milk sugars. The cheese is then left to set before being cut into blocks and wrapped for sale. The cheese can be anything from a pale tan to dark coffee in colour and looks rather like fudge. Mesost has a creamy caramel flavour with a strangely bitter aftertaste.

HERRGÅRDSOST (SWEDEN)

Meaning manor house in Swedish, Herrgårdsost is an all-round family cheese, created at the beginning of the twentieth century as an alternative to Gruyère. Although there are similarities between the two – it melts easily and keeps well – it is a much softer and more supple cheese, with smaller round holes. Herrgårdsost has a mild nuttiness and fresh tang.

Above: Grevé is a modern semi-hard cheese made from cow's milk.

Making Fondue

A fondue is a mixture of melted cheeses and wine. The addition of cornflour (cornstarch) prevents the cheeses and wine from separating, while garlic and Kirsch add extra flavour. Any combination of cheeses may be used. A classic Swiss fondue is made with a mixture of Emmental, Gruyère and Appenzeller or Raclette, while in Norway, the cheese mixture might include Gjetost and Jarlsberg, and in Sweden, Herrgårdsost and Grevé might be used.

1 Cut a clove of garlic in half and rub it over the inside of a cquelon (fondue pan) or deep pan.

2 Mix 5ml/1tsp cornflour (cornstarch) with a little dry white wine. Set aside. Pour 300ml/½ pint/1¼ cups dry white wine into the pan and heat gently.

3 Grate 3 x 350g/12oz portions of different hard melting cheeses.

4 Place about one third of the grated cheeses in the pan. Stirring continuously, cook over a low heat until the cheese starts to melt and the liquid begins to bubble.

5 Stir the cornflour mixture into the pan, then add the rest of the cheese, a little at a time. Stir in a little Kirsch and ground black pepper to taste.

6 Serve the hot fondue at once with cubes of bread, crudités and cherry tomatoes for dipping.

PRÄSTOST (SWEDEN)

The word *prästost* means priest's cheese and dates back to the sixteenth century, when farmers regularly paid a tithe in milk to the local pastor. It was then the job of the pastor's wife to make the milk into cheese to be sold at the local market. The pastor's personal popularity was as important a factor in success at the marketplace as his wife's skills in cheesemaking. Today, Prästost is made only in factories.

It is a supple, semi-hard cheese with a pale yellow rind covered in fine cloth and with a yellow wax coat. The interior has a slightly mushy texture and many irregular, rice-sized holes. It has a mellow to robust, sweet-sour flavour with a sharp, fruity aftertaste. A version washed in whisky and known as Saaland Pfarr is also produced. It has the robust character of a French washed rind cheese. Prästost may be served as a table cheese.

SVENCIAOST (SWEDEN)

Svencia is the Latin name for Sweden and is here used to describe a range of cheeses made in the traditional Swedish style that were introduced to compete with the cheeses of the Netherlands such as Edam and Gouda. Available in different sizes, these semi-hard, cow's milk cheeses are frequently waxed and sold in a variety of flavours, including cloves, cumin and caraway. The texture is moist and supple and the cheese has a number of small holes. It has a pleasant, fresh acidity that matures to a more assertive piquancy.

VÄSTERBOTTENOST (SWEDEN)

This firm and very crumbly semi-hard cheese has small irregular eyes and some trapped moisture. Västerbottenost, which was invented in the middle of the nineteenth century in West Bothnia, is still exclusive to the area. It has a granular texture and a definite, fruity bite, and is excellent for grating and melting in sauces.

Above:
Maribo is a
traditional cow's milk cheese
made either in a round or a block.

TUTUNMAA (FINLAND)

This semi-hard breakfast cheese was probably introduced to Finland in the sixteenth century. The cheese is smooth and creamy, with a richness and depth of flavour that owes much to Finland's excellent grazing pastures. The texture is firm and open and the flavour is aromatic, with a slightly sharp tang.

MARIBO (DENMARK)

Similar to the more famous Danish semi-soft Danbo, Maribo is widely available in Denmark (though seldom exported). It is firm and somewhat dry, scattered with irregular holes. It is usually coated with wax and may be flavoured with caraway seeds. Use as a table cheese or for grilling (broiling).

SAMSØ (DENMARK)

In the early nineteenth century, the Danish king saw the potential for diversifying cheesemaking in his country. Consequently, he invited a Swiss cheesemaker to advise the Danish farmers. The result was Samsø, named after the island of Samsø.

Looking rather like a pale Emmental, Samsø has a supple, elastic texture with a few irregular-sized holes. When young, it tastes mild and buttery. However, the Danes prefer it aged, when it develops a definite sweet-sour pungency and a distinct hazelnut flavour. It is a good table cheese and can be used for grilling (broiling), grating and fondues.

ABERTAM (CZECH REPUBLIC)

The unusual ball-shaped cheese, with its thin yellow to orange rind, comes from the Czech spa town of Karlovy-Vary (formerly Carlsbad). The natural pastures of this mountainous part of Bohemia provide the native sheep with a rich diet that is revealed in the robust flavour of the hard, pressed cheese. Serve Abertam as a table cheese or use for melting and grilling (broiling).

BALATON (HUNGARY)

Named after the beautiful Laka Balaton, this Hungarian cheese has a firm, compact texture with a scattering of small holes. The flavour is quite mild with a pleasant acidity. Serve as a table cheese or use for grilling (broiling).

OSCHTJEPKA (SLOVAKIA)

Made for centuries in the magnificent Carpathian mountains, this supple, elastic cheese is made from cow's and sheep's milk. Most of it is still made in the traditional way by the shepherds themselves. Soured milk is pressed into balls, each about the size of a melon, and then hung from the ceilings of mountain chalets to drain. The aromatic smoke from the shepherds' fires gradually dries the cheese and helps to create its unique flavour. Oschtjepka is good for grilling (broiling) and melting.

MANUR (YUGOSLAVIA)

Also known as Mandur, this unusual traditional farmhouse cheese is unique to Serbia. The fresh milk (either cow's or sheep's, depending on the season) is gradually heated until it boils. It is then cooled until hand-hot and a mixture of buttermilk, fresh whey and rennet is added. Once set, the curd is placed in a cloth and allowed to drain before being salted, shaped and dried. It ripens in a few days. It is used mainly for grating as a condiment or in soup.

OSZCZPEK (POLAND)

One of the few remaining traditional cheeses to be found in Poland, this semi-hard cheese is made in the Tatra Mountains and is similar to the Slovakian cheese, Oschtjepka. It is made from cow's and sheep's milk. The kneaded curd is pressed into hand-carved wooden moulds. Once drained, the young cheeses are traditionally stored in the eaves of the house where they gradually absorb the smoke from the fire. Oszczpek comes in various shapes and sizes, although it is usually oval and the smooth rind which may be pale yellow, or dark brown if the cheese has been heavily smoked. It may be served as a table cheese and also used for grilling (broiling) and melting.

Right:
Samsø
has a
firm, buttery
texture and a sweet,
slightly nutty flavour.

GRAVIERA (GREECE)

Made in the Dodoni region and on the islands of Naxos and Crete, Graviera is a Gruyère-type cheese. After feta, it is the most popular of the Greek cheeses and is ideal for all occasions. As with many Greek cheeses, it can be made from cow's, goat's or sheep's milk according to the season, although most of today's Graviera is made from cow's milk. It has a firm yet supple texture, tiny holes and a rich, creamy feel. The hard, cooked rind has a criss-cross pattern created by the cloth in which the cheese was drained. Graviera from Crete is made from sheep's milk and is much sought after for its delicate fragrance and burnt-caramel taste, which becomes richer and nuttier when the cheese is baked. The island of Naxos produces a wonderfully nutty cow's milk Graviera in a small, local co-operative. Graviera may be served as a table cheese and as a snack and is traditionally used in savoury pastries.

Below: Graviera is one of the most popular cheeses in Greece. It may be made from cow's, goat's or sheep's milk.

KEFALOTIRI (GREECE)

This cheese, usually made from sheep's milk, although sometimes goat's milk, was already well known by the time of the Byzantine era. It is said to take its name from the *kefalo*, a Greek hat. Historically, it was the first cheese to be made at the start of a new season. As soon as the young lambs were weaned, the sheep's milk was used to make this pale cheese. The colour varies a little from white to yellow and the firm, dry cheese has numerous irregular holes. The flavour is pleasantly fresh with a distinct taste of sheep's milk and a slightly sharp finish. It is a popular breakfast cheese and is good for grating, baking and snacks.

Most of the Kefalotiri sold outside Greece comes from Cyprus.

Left: Kefalotiri is an unpasteurized sheep's milk cheese made with full-cream (whole) milk. In Greece, it is known as a male or first cheese to indicate this.

MIHALIC PEYNIR (TURKEY)

There are numerous cheeses made in Turkey, most of them by traditional methods in small local farmhouses and dairies. Most are fresh or soft, creamy cheeses, but some hard cheeses, such as Taze Kaser, which misleadingly translates as fresh cheese, and Eski Kaser (old cheese), which is quite similar to Pecorino, are produced. Peynir is the Turkish word for cheese and the majority of cheeses go by the name of the village where they are made. However, Mihalic Peynir is made in Bursa, on the Sea of Marmara, south of Istanbul. Like the majority of locally produced Turkish cheeses, it is made from unpasteurized sheep's milk. The curds are divided into small portions, stirred in hot water and left in water to harden. Next, they are twisted in a cloth to force out the whey. After shaping, the cheese is salted and dried and then stored in brine to preserve and protect it until it is needed. Mihalic Peynir comes in various shapes and sizes, often as balls or slices, and is smooth and white with no rind. It has a rich texture and flavour and is used fresh in salads or in baked dishes. It is suitable for vegetarians.

Cheeses from India and the Middle East

Very few hard cheeses are made in the Middle East. Fresh cheeses, like feta or soft curds rolled in chopped herbs, are still the preferred types of cheeses in Arab countries – a tradition that dates back centuries. Karut, made in Afghanistan and north-west India, is one of the few hard cheeses. More commonly seen is Paneer, an Indian curd cheese that is often made in the home and cooked in curries.

THE UNITED STATES

Mass production in the early 1900s did a great deal to destroy traditional farmhouse cheeses in the United States. During the previous century a huge number of different cheeses were produced on local farmsteads by European-born emigrants. But with a need to feed a soaring population, there was a move to produce cheese on a massive scale. Small-volume producers were inevitably eased out of the market and the country was left with factory-made processed cheeses, which were easy to use but sanitized, sterilized and standardized. The first all-American cheese was Brick, which was first made by John Jossi, a cheesemaker of Swiss extraction, in 1877. He discovered the process of squeezing fresh curd between two bricks. The result was a brick-shaped cheese similar to the popular German Limburger, but firmer and more rubbery. It was ideal for cutting and had a mild aroma and taste. Today Brick is vacuum-packed in slices, strings or blocks and is sold right across the United States.

CHEDDARS

There are numerous Cheddars in America, but the best are those produced using unpasteurized milk and made by the traditional farmhouse method.

Grafton Cheddar This is an example of an excellent white Cheddar. It is made in Vermont where the local dairy herds graze the rich mountain grasslands. The result is milk high in butterfat that makes a cheese which is rich and creamy with plenty of character.

Shelburne Cheddar This cheese from Vermont is made using the traditional cheddar-making process. It has a firm, biteable texture, and the milk yielded by Brown Swiss cows give the flavour a wonderfully rich complexity. It may be used as a table cheese or for cooking.

Tillamook Cheddar This Cheddar from Oregon is made using milk that has been heat-treated rather than pasteurized. The sharp, white, uncoloured Cheddar is made with animal rennet and has a mouthwatering, fruity tang. It must be more than 60 days old before being sold.

Above: Grafton Cheddar has a depth of flavour and character that can only be achieved with raw milk and long ageing. It is produced according to traditional methods.

Above: Shelburne Cheddar is matured for 18–24 months.

Above: Yerba Santa Shepherd's Cheese has a magnificent, rich taste with the characteristic flavour of goat's milk.

DRY JACK

This cheese was created in 1915 by a San Francisco wholesaler who found himself with an over-abundance of young Jack cheese. In order to make space, he stacked the Jack on the floor, hand-salting each one in the hope it would survive. Weeks later he found that the cheeses were fruity, rich and hard, not unlike Pecorino and Parmesan. He coated each cheese with oil, pepper and cocoa to imitate the lamp black being used on imported Italian cheeses at that time, and offered "Dry Jack" to his customers. A star was born and today, Dry Jack is among the finest cheeses in the world.

IDAHO GOATSTER

This hard goat's milk cheese from Idaho has a firm dry texture, similar to that of an Italian Pecorino. The flavour is nutty and pleasant. The cheese comes in large 2kg/4½lb rounds. The rind is rubbed with annatto, giving it an attractive orange-brown colour. It is a fine table cheese and is also good for grilling (broiling) and grating.

SALLY JACKSON

There is a range of goat's and sheep's cheeses from this Washington-based company. Made by farmhouse methods, they come wrapped in brandy-soaked chestnut leaves, giving a rustic look to the cheese and a subtlety to the flavour. This is delicious served as a table cheese and is also good for cooking.

TOSCANA

This magnificent American-style Pecorino made from sheep's milk has a hard and flaky texture with small eyes irregularly scattered throughout the cheese. At first, Toscana feels dry in the mouth, but it dissolves to reveal a symphony of flavours and aromas.

Below: Dry Jack has a rich, sweet, fruity and full-bodied taste that releases layer upon layer of flavour when cut.

VERMONT SHEPHERD

This modern, sheep's milk cheese was created in 1989. It has a firm, dense texture and a deliciously nutty flavour. It has a hard, rustic-looking natural rind. It is a tasty table cheese and is good for cooking.

YERBA SANTA SHEPHERD'S CHEESE

This modern farmhouse cheese from California is easily as good as any of the artisan goat's milk cheeses of Spain. It is very hard, dry and flaky with small holes. The intensity and diversity of flavour is magnificent and it has been a consistent award-winner. Serve as a table cheese or use for cooking.

Above: Sally Jackson's goat's cheese is rapidly becoming a star of the cheese world.

Canadian Cheeses

The early Canadian settlers from Britain and France were mainly trappers, traders and foresters with little interest in either farmsteading or cheesemaking. As a result, cheesemaking was slow to develop and it was the arrival of French Trappist monks that really began Canada's cheesemaking tradition. British immigrants gradually established dairy herds and set up co-operatives to process the milk into Cheddar. Today, Cheddar dominates the Canadian cheese market, although a growth of tourism and the skiing industry has brought about a dramatic increase in the sales of Canadian Raclette and Oka, a semi-soft, washed-rind cheese that was first produced by Trappist monks in their monastery in Quebec.

AUSTRALIA
AND NEW ZEALAND

Before the arrival of European settlers in the eighteenth century, who brought cows, sheep and goats with them, there was no cheesemaking by the indigenous peoples of Australia and New Zealand.

In Australia, cheese was made in kitchens on the isolated farms, but gradually, as herds grew, the dairy farms formed co-operatives. Until the late 1960s, Cheddars were the only cheeses being made, for it was largely the British and Irish who colonized Australia. However, the cheese revolution was fired by immigrants from Italy, Greece, Holland, Germany and Yugoslavia, who arrived in droves after World War II. Before long, European cheesemakers were setting up factories making cheeses such as Parmesan, Pecorino-style cow's milk cheeses, Edam and Gouda.

In New Zealand, the early settlers established co-operative dairies to process the milk from the many small and isolated farms. From the late 1840s, Cheddar became a major export to the home country. Today, very large volumes of cheese are exported to the United States, the Middle East, Russia and Japan. Over the past 30 years or so, the small co-operatives have merged, and New Zealand now has some of the largest and most efficient milk-processing factories in the world.

AIREDALE

This cow's milk cheese is compact, rather than elastic, in texture and is on the borderline between hard and semi-hard. Special red cheese "paint" conceals its deep sun-yellow centre and encourages the cheese to develop a real depth of flavour.

CHEDDARS

Despite the appearance of other cheeses in Australia, Cheddar still dominates the market. Much of the cheese is made on a large scale, but the best Cheddars are made in small dairies and farmhouses. Pyengana Cheddar is firm, but neither as hard or smooth as traditional Cheddar. It is, nevertheless, a rich and nutty cheese with a real depth of flavour.

New Zealand Cheddars are popular all over the world and there are numerous award-winning cheeses including Anchor Mild Cheddar, Tararua BONZ Cheddar and Marlborough Tasty Cheddar. Unlike farmhouse Cheddars, the cheeses are pressed into shape and then matured in special clear film. They are never so hard as cheeses matured in cloth, but if aged for 18 months or more, they develop a firm, biteable

Below: Pyengana Cheddar is not as hard as some Cheddars.

texture and the flavour intensifies. Degrees of strength are categorized Mild, Medium, Mature, Tasty, Extra Mature and Vintage.

Barry's Bay Cheddar (New Zealand) This is the only traditional clothbound Cheddar still being made in New Zealand. It is made in large cylinders, which are first waxed and then left to mature for six to 36 months. The result is a firmer texture than that of Cheddars made in blocks and matured in plastic.

Pyengana Cheddar (Tasmania) This is a firm clothbound cheese, which is neither as hard nor as smooth as traditional Cheddar. However, it still has a rich, nutty taste with a strong, sharp flavour.

Left: Australian Surprise Bay Cheddar has a distinctive red wax covering.

GOUDA (NEW ZEALAND)

Several resourceful Dutch cheesemakers emigrated to New Zealand in the 1980s. Combining traditional cheesemaking methods with modern practices, they recreated the cheeses of their homeland. Among these are gouda. (Other hard cheeses produced include Edam, Leiden and Maasdam.)

Four Herb Gouda This organic vegetarian Gouda from Christchurch is made by cheesemakers from Holland. When Rients Rympa and his wife decided to emigrate to New Zealand, they spent a year studying and learning about cheese and now have a thriving business. Their cheese, under the Karikaas name, is familiar throughout South Island. The cheese is creamy, rich and nutty, and marries well with the flavour of the fresh, finely cut herbs that are distributed through it. Fresh Herb Gouda is suitable for vegetarians.

Mahoe Aged Gouda This very firm, smooth cheese from Kerikeri has a slightly pliable texture that is almost chewy. It has a fruity, fresh tang and a rich, buttery flavour. It is a consistent medal-winner at the New Zealand Cheese Awards.

Mercer Gouda This boulder-shaped Gouda from Hamilton is sold at varying stages of maturity. Some Mercer Goudas are with cumin, cracked pepper, garlic or herbs. It is excellent as a table cheese or for grilling (broiling).

Meyer Vintage Gouda This cheese is another popular Gouda from Hamilton. The makers, Ben and Fieke Meyer, are also Dutch émigrés who brought with them a passion for cheese and a belief in the traditional methods of their native Holland. Meyer Vintage is firm, smooth, dense and creamy and the peach-coloured interior is fruity. Some Meyer Goudas are plain, while others are flavoured with cumin, cloves or pepper.

HEIDI GRUYÈRE (AUSTRALIA)

Swiss cheesemaker Frank Marchand is responsible for producing this Tasmanian version of the famous Swiss cheese, which is made according to traditional methods. Heidi Gruyère is made from Friesian cow's milk in 20–35kg/44–77lb wheels. The cheese has a firm supple texture, similar to that of the French

Above: Heidi Gruyère is a sweet and fruity farmhouse cheese with a wonderful texture and a classic, crusty rind that looks almost polished.

cheese, Beaufort, with tiny crunchy crystals and a profusion of flavours. The more mature the cheese, the better its flavour. Like Gruyère, it can be used as a table cheese, for grilling (broiling) and for fondues. Made with non-animal rennet, it is suitable for vegetarians.

ST CLAIRE (AUSTRALIA)

This cow's milk cheese from Tasmania is made in the style of traditional Gruyère. It is deep yellow in colour and has a smooth, firm and slightly rubbery texture. It is sweeter and milder than traditional Gruyère and has a fairly mellow, fruity finish. It is good for grating, grilling (broiling) and serving as a table cheese.

St Claire is made by one of Australia's oldest manufacturers of Continental-style cheeses, Lactos, which was founded in 1955. Lactos makes a number of other cheeses, including Edam and Gouda. St Claire is its only Gruyère-style cheese.

South African Cheese

Most cheeses sold in South Africa today are factory-made copies of Gouda and Cheddar, which is not surprising, given that the majority of European immigrants who first settled in this country came from Holland and Great Britain. Small amounts of feta, Edam and Brie are produced locally, and it is possible to obtain industrial imports of European cheeses, but cheeses that are uniquely South African are fairly difficult to come by.

Cheesemakers such as Christine Briscoe are doing their best to change the situation, however. Christine farms Ayrshires in Kwa-Zulu Natal, some 3,000 miles from her main market, Cape Town. This does not prevent her from ensuring her cheeses are delivered in peak condition to the wine farms where they sell extremely well. She simply air-freights them in from Durban. Her range, sold under the name Galtee Mare, consists

mainly of English-style territorials like Sage Derby, Leicester and Cheddar, and she also makes two blues. All her cheeses are hand-made.

The Harris family also farm in Natal, but their herd consists of Jerseys, not Ayrshires. They make small volumes of several cheeses under the name Bellavigne. These include Saint-Paulin, Tilsit and a soft, creamy, sweet cheese that looks similar to Edam.

Fairview Estate, a wine farm near Paarl, in the Western Cape, has been producing a soft, Brie-style blue since the early 1980s. It can be found in supermarkets and speciality shops.

The booming tourist industry will undoubtedly lead to a demand for more locally produced cheeses, as has happened elsewhere in the world. When it does, South African cheesemakers – as determined and dedicated as any of their international colleagues – will come into their own.

SEMI-SOFT CHEESES

Softer than traditional hard cheeses, these cheeses – such as Raclette, Edam and Monterey Jack – characteristically have a supple elastic feel. As with hard cheese, the curd is cut or chopped to release some of the whey, then placed in moulds and lightly pressed to speed up draining. After washing in brine to seal the rind, the cheese is placed in ripening rooms, either sealed in plastic to prevent a rind from forming or left to its own devices, so that gradually a leathery rind forms.

UNITED KINGDOM

There are relatively few semi-soft cheeses from the United Kingdom. Most of the harder cheeses are allowed to ripen to a firm, rich maturity but the revival of some of the traditional methods by modern cheesemakers has produced some fine examples of this type of cheese.

LODDISWELL AVONDALE (ENGLAND)

A semi-soft cheese from Devon, Loddiswell has a firm, almost dry texture and a fragrant aroma. Behind the creamy flavour lies an unusual hint of aniseed and a sweet, sherbet-like zing. It is suitable for vegetarians.

ORANGE GROVE (ENGLAND)

This is a cross between a cream cheese and a cheese dessert, and would be best described as a speciality cheese. The cheese comes in large 2kg/4½lb rounds, with a layer of finely chopped orange peel through the middle. More candied oranges are used to decorate the top, so that the whole looks not unlike an orange cheesecake. The cheese itself is slightly tart, but rich. It is suitable for vegetarians.

WATERLOO (ENGLAND)

This washed curd cheese from Berkshire is made from Guernsey cow's milk. It has a thick, pinkish rind dusted with white moulds and a smooth, supple interior. The cheese is a rich yellow colour with a sweet, full-bodied flavour. It starts life mellow and fruity, but as the interior reaches the point where it starts to run, the cheese acquires a vegetal taste.

Above: Orange Grove is almost a cross between a dessert and a cheese.

WIGMORE (ENGLAND)

This unassuming sheep's milk cheese retains the sweetness of the milk and develops a truly voluptuous consistency. It has a burnt-caramel flavour, blended with hints of macadamia nuts and roast lamb. It is suitable for vegetarians.

CROGHAN (IRELAND)

This organic goat's milk cheese from Wexford is loosely based on Gouda. It is round, with a smooth, brown-pink, leathery rind and a pale, smooth interior. It has an intense flavour with an aromatic finish.

DURRUS (IRELAND)

This modern farmhouse cheese from West Cork is made from cow's milk. It is round in shape and has a fawn, zipper-patterned rind with blotches of blue, grey and white mould. When young, the interior is buttery and mild with a slightly acidic flavour that mellows out to a silky-smooth compact cheese resembling a French Tomme.

GUBBEEN (IRELAND)

This small, attractive cheese from Cork in the south of Ireland is a modern farmhouse cheese. It has a distinctive terracotta-coloured rind that is flecked with fine white and pale blue moulds. The cheese has an earthy sweetness, both rich and savoury. Use as a table cheese. It is suitable for vegetarians.

MILLEENS (IRELAND)

Also from the Republic of Ireland, this time West Cork on the Beara Peninsula, Milleens is an attractive small cheese, with a wrinkled pinkish-orange rind. It has the sweet-sour taste associated with genuine Trappist cheeses, with a firm, supple texture. It has a powerful aroma. At its peak, the paste becomes almost fluid and the flavour is yeasty and savoury with a herbaceous tang. It matures in four to 10 weeks. Serve as a table cheese.

Left: Gubbeen is a full-flavoured, rich and savoury cheese from Ireland.

ORLA (IRELAND)

This attractive sheep's milk cheese is made in Cork. It sits between being a semi-soft and hard cheese, depending on the degree of maturity. When young, it is semi-soft, with a supple texture. At this stage the typical flavour of burnt-caramel is present, but is less pungent than the hard, mature cheese, which is sharp and salty.

BISHOP KENNEDY (SCOTLAND)

This semi-soft cheese from Perthshire is known not least because it is smeared with whisky during maturation. The cheese is named after a fifteenth-century bishop of St Andrews. It is smooth and velvety with a spicy finish. When the cheese is mature, it almost runs and virtually hums with flavour. It is suitable for vegetarians.

ST ANDREWS (SCOTLAND)

This sticky cheese from Perthshire is one of only two Trappist-style cheeses made in Scotland. Produced in 2.2kg/5lb discs or squares, the deep-orange rind contrasts with the pale yellow interior. St Andrews has a supple holey texture and a sweet-sour, slightly yeasty flavour. Serve as a table cheese.

Left: Bishop Kennedy, an unusual modern Scottish cheese, includes a dash of whisky in its wash.

CELTIC PROMISE (WALES)

This dumpling-shaped cheese is made in Carmarthenshire from unpasteurized cow's milk. It has a smooth, brine-washed rind, ranging in colour from orange to terracotta with a dusting of moulds. It has a supple, smooth texture and a spicy and aromatic flavour. Use as a table cheese. It is suitable for vegetarians.

ST DAVID'S (WALES)

Made in Monmouthshire, St David's is a washed-rind cheese with a wonderful pliable semi-soft texture. It has a pungent, yeasty taste, with an under-current of smoked bacon and the texture is supple and squidgy. Like most washed-rind cheeses, it has an orange rind; the interior is pale yellow. Serve as a table cheese. It is suitable for vegetarians.

Above: St Andrews is a modern unpasteurized Scottish cheese.

Right: Celtic Promise has a pungent flavour.

Right: St David's is one of the only two Welsh washed-rind cheeses.

Right: Dauphin is often shaped like a dolphin or a fish but may also be brick-shaped.

Below: Le Brin is a modern cheese with a mild, sweet, almost perfumed aroma and taste.

Left: Fromage Corse is a traditionally-made cheese. It is covered in dried wild herbs and has the robust flavour typical of goat's milk cheeses.

FRANCE

Most of the semi-soft cheeses made in France today are traditional varieties such as Morbier and Mariolles, but there are also some new creations such as Le Brin.

AISY CENDRÉ

This speciality cow's milk cheese from Burgundy is made by immersing a local cheese (usually Epoisses) in a bed of ashes for at least one month. Slow to ripen, Aisy Cendré has a white, salty, chalky centre surrounded by a softer, earthy-tasting outer layer. Brush off the layer of ash before serving as a table cheese. Olivet Cendré is a similar type of cheese.

DAUPHIN

The brick-red rind of this goat's milk cheese gives way to a firm, yet supple interior. The fresh curds are flavoured with tarragon and peppers and, when matured, the cheese takes on a spicy flavour with a yeasty aroma. It is delicious served as a table cheese.

FROMAGE CORSE

This fresh goat's milk cheese from Corsica is mainly available only on the island. For centuries it has been made by the local people for the local people and is still made by traditional methods. The supple interior is sometimes runny, with small holes. It has a robust flavour.

LE BRIN

This small, hexagonal, cow's milk cheese has a thin reddish rind dusted with white penicillium mould. It was created in the 1980s as a milder version of the traditional washed-rind cheeses. It is made by the ultra-filtration method rather than by using rennet to separate the curd from the whey. The cheese is velvety smooth, like English custard, and has a mild, sweet aroma and flavour. It resembles its soft-white rinded cousin, Pavé d'Affinois. Le Terroir is a similar cheese.

LE FIUM'ORBO

This round, sheep's and goat's milk cheese from Corsica is a farmhouse version of Fromage Corse. It has a pungent nose but with a more delicate flavour suggesting herbs and flowers. It is an ancient cheese that has been made by shepherds for centuries.

LIVAROT (AOC)

This small round French cheese has a smooth, glossy, brown washed rind with white and occasional bluish moulds. Originally made by monks in the Livarot area of Normandy, the cheese is now made on a more commercial scale, although the AOC regulations should help to maintain its ancestry. It is a smooth, supple-textured cheese with a distinct, spicy flavour.

MORBIER

This cheese from the Jura mountains can be recognized by the dark, horizontal band that runs through its centre. Originally, this would have been a mixture of wood ash and salt but today it is more likely to be food colouring. Morbier is an elastic, springy cheese with a pungent, yeasty aroma. It can be used for snacks, grilling (broiling) and as a table cheese.

Above: The best Morbier cheeses are made by traditional methods.

Left: Mariolles was first made in the tenth century at the Abbaye de Mariolles in northern France, where St Hubert, the patron saint of cheese is buried.

MUROL

This ring-shaped, cow's milk cheese from the Auvergne has a thin, smooth, pinkish rind. It was invented by a local man in the 1930s, by stamping out the centre from several young Saint-Nectaire cheeses and ripening the rings. The interior is supple, creamy and very smooth and has a sweet, nutty flavour and aroma.

OSSAU-IRATY-BREBIS PYRÉNÉES

A number of farmhouse, artisan, co-operative and industrial sheep's milk cheeses made in the Béarn and Basque regions come under this umbrella. The regulations state that the affinage for the mountain sheep's milk cheeses must be at least 60 days for the small and 90 days for the larger ones. Coagulation can only be from rennet, and no milk may be used until 20 days after lambing. Cheeses that do not conform must be sold as simple Fromage de Brebis.

MARIOLLES

This square cheese is made in Flanders and is regarded as the forefather of all Trappist cheeses. Mariolles has a thickish, damp, brick-red rind with fine ridges. The interior is pale yellow, bouncy and porous, not supple and dense like many similar cheeses. The aroma is stronger and more pungent than the flavour, which is sweet-sour.

Right: Livarot was once known as the colonel because of the circles of sedge grass that encircled it.

Left: Pavé d'Auge is a traditional cow's milk cheese from Normandy, which is famous for its lush pastures. Pavé d'Auge has an aroma of cool cellars and a spicy taste.

Below: Raclette, from the Savoie region, is a very good melting cheese and is delicious served sliced and grilled on potatoes or vegetables.

Below: Pont L'Evêque has a pleasant springy and open texture and the cheese virtually glistens thanks to the richness of the milk.

PAVÉ D'AUGE

Pavé is the name given to the roughly square cobblestones you still see in old market-places in France. It is a charming name for this supple, creamy cheese with its reddish rind.

PONT L'EVÊQUE (AOC)

This is probably one of the oldest cheeses of Normandy. Pont L'Evêque is said to have originated in an abbey, although there appears to be no evidence to substantiate this. Despite being granted its AOC status to protect its history and good name, only around 2 or 3 per cent of the cheese is *fermier* (farmhouse) made; the majority comes from two large producers. To comply with AOC regulations and achieve the authentic taste and texture, the cheese must be regularly washed, brushed and turned to encourage bacteria to grow on the rind, and the milk must come from the local area. Pont L'Evêque is fairly pungent-smelling, but the taste is savoury and piquant.

RACLETTE

This ancient mountain cheese is common to the Savoie region. Although the cheese has a pleasant enough flavour, it comes into its own when heated in front of a fire or under a hot grill (broiler). Grilling intensifies its aroma and the melted cheese takes on a stringy, elastic texture.

REBLOCHON

Similar to Saint-Nectaire and Tamie, Reblochon, which comes from the Haute-Savoie region, has a supple, creamy texture. It has a warm, yeasty aroma with a sweet flavour reminiscent of crushed walnuts. It is good melted or served as a table cheese.

Below: Reblochon is a traditional cheese from the Haute-Savoie region. It is not unlike Saint-Nectaire and Tamie.

Above: Pungent-smelling Rollot from Picardy may be either round or heart-shaped.

ROLLOT

This cheese takes its name from the village of the same name. Under the tough, sticky rind, the pale yellow interior is firm yet supple, with a rather pungent, yeasty aroma and a fruity flavour. It can be quite salty and bitter if the rind has dried out.

SAINT-NECTAIRE

This soft, voluptuous cheese from the Auvergne region of France is cured on a bed of straw for eight weeks, and seems to absorb some of its earthy aroma. Like a large version of Reblochon, Saint-Nectaire is very creamy and rich, redolent of freshly-cut

grass. When selecting Saint-Nectaire, look for an oval, green label that declares it to be a *fermier* (farmhouse) cheese made from unpasteurized milk. A square, green label is used on the factory-made cheeses, which are usually made from pasteurized milk.

SAINT PAULIN

This mild, cow's milk cheese, which was first made in 1930, is based on the Trappist cheese, Port-du-Salut. It has a thin, washed rind that ranges in colour from pale yellow to bright mandarin orange.

TAMIE

From the Haute-Savoie, this traditional, farmhouse cheese, made by the monks of the Abbaye de Tamie, has an attractive rind with a sweet, earthy aroma. Under the rind, the interior is a creamy colour with a sweet, vaguely nutty flavour at first, followed by a more powerful tang. It is delicious served as a table cheese.

Left: Saint-Nectaire is a creamy, rich cheese from the Auvergne.

Above: Tamie de l'Abbaye has a soft, supple rind, ranging in colour from pinkish-brown to orange-pink.

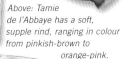

Left: Tomme de Savoie has a gentle, quite delicate flavour.

TOMME DE SAVOIE

This ancient mountain cheese from Savoie has a thick, furry, grey rind, which encases a firm, pale yellow cheese with a few small holes. It has a supple texture and a hint of gentle flavour. When searching out the best Tomme, look for *lait cru* on the label, the numbers 73 or 74 on an oval red, casein plaque and the logo of four red hearts and the word Savoie.

ITALY

Some of Italy's best-known cheeses such as Bel Paese, Stracchino and Taleggio are semi-soft.

BEL PAESE

Dante referred to Italy as *bel paese* (beautiful land). This later became the title of a book, which in turn proved the inspiration for Egidio Galbani when he sought a name for his soft, yielding cheese. Made in Lombardy, Bel Paese comes in large wheels in a shiny, golden, waxed rind. Underneath the rind, the ivory cheese has a delicate flavour.

Above: Bel Paese was invented in 1900 and has become one of Italy's most popular semi-soft cheeses.

Below: Casciotta di Urbino is an all-round cheese suitable for snacks and cooking.

CACIOCAVALLO

This is a large, gourd-shaped cheese and, like many Italian fresh cheeses, is made by the stretched curd method. The curd is pulled and stretched until stringy and is then divided into portions, kneaded into shape and matured. A cord is attached at the thin end for hanging up the cheese. Unlike mozzarella and Scamorza, which mature relatively quickly, Caciocavallo ripens very gradually. At three months, the cheese is sweet and supple and is best eaten as a table cheese. With further maturing – at least one and up to two years – it develops a full, mellow taste and intense, lingering aroma. As it matures, it becomes harder, when it can be used for grating and then used in grilled (broiled) and baked dishes. Smoked versions and a version containing a small lump of butter are also made.

CASCIOTTA DI URBINO

Casciotta describes the many small, artisan cheeses made in central Italy and some parts of the south. They can be made with cow's, goat's or sheep's milk and are popular with locals and tourists alike. Some have smooth oiled rinds; others have the basket imprint typical of Pecorinos. Casciotta di Urbino is said to be one of the best. The yellow rind gives way to a compact, straw-coloured interior. Sweet-tasting, with the aroma and flavour of warm milk, it is a delicate, subtle cheese. It is a good table cheese and can be used for cooking.

Above: Provolone may be made in a variety of shapes and in whatever size the cheesemaker feels like.

Below: Fontina is an excellent melting cheese and is delicious grilled.

FONTINA

There has been a cheese industry in the Valle d'Aosta since the eleventh century. Today the name Fontina is used proudly and exclusively to identify cheeses produced there. The best of these are made in mountain chalets between May and September, when the herds graze the alpine meadows. Fontina is dense, smooth and slightly elastic. The straw-coloured interior, with its small, round holes, has a delicate nuttiness with just a subtle hint of mild honey. When melted, as it frequently is (Fontina being the foundation of *fonduta*, a fondue-style dish), the flavour is earthy with a subtle suggestion of mushrooms and a fresh acidity. Fontina is delicious served as a table cheese and can be used for fondues or for melting and grilling (broiling).

PROVOLONE

This is one of the oldest of Italian cheeses. Made by the stretched curd method, Provolone comes in a variety of shapes and sizes but is best known as a small sausage with a thin, golden yellow rind, and is either waxed or wrapped in waxed paper. In Italy, Provolone can often be spherical, pear-shaped or even plaited (braided), and is found in most food stores, hanging from the ceiling on a waxed string. *Giganti* (monster) cheese, often made for special occasions or trade fairs, can be over 3m/10ft long. Mild *Dolce* is aged for two to three months, and is supple and smooth with a thin waxed rind. It is generally used as a table cheese. *Picante*, aged for 6–24 months, has a stronger, spicy flavour, and is darker with a hard rind.

QUARTIROLO LOMBARDO

This square, cow's milk cheese has a tender, pale pink rind that hardens with age. The interior is similar to a young Taleggio, and has a slightly crumbly, lumpy centre. Young cheeses have a fresh acidity and delicate fragrance, while more mature cheeses become dense and the fruity flavour stronger.

Below: Stracchino is a term that encompasses a range of cheeses, all of which are ideal for melting and grilling.

RASCHERA

This square cheese from the Cuneo region is made with the sweet milk from the Piedmontese cow. Raschera has a thin, reddish-yellow crust and a pale ivory interior scattered with tiny holes, which occasionally have a bluish tinge. When young, the cheese is supple and elastic, with a delicate sweet flavour that becomes richer, more aromatic and slightly tart as the cheese matures.

SCAMORZA

Similar in many ways to Provolone, Scamorza is another stretched curd cheese with a rubbery, stringy texture. It has a bland milky flavour when first made, and is more popular as the smoked version (Scamorza *affumicate*). It is often used in pasta dishes and is also served with ham, mushrooms or vegetables.

Left: Scamorza affumicate, like plain Scamorza, is traditionally made in the shape of money bags.

STRACCHINO

The name Stracchino is a generic term, used to describe a style of soft cheese that has been made in Lombardy since the twelfth century. The quality can vary considerably. A good Stracchino will have a supple, yielding texture and a fruity flavour.

TALEGGIO (DOC)

This soft square cheese of Lombardy is among the most famous of the Stracchina. Traditionally, Taleggio was matured in natural caves. The deep crevices provided a kind of natural air-conditioning that encouraged the spread of the moulds essential to create the cheese's unique aroma and taste. These caves are still used for maturing a sizeable proportion of the cheeses made. The squares of cheese have a rough, rosy crust, while the curd is very nearly at melting point and the centre elastic with some eyes. The aroma is sweet but insistent and the flavour deliciously fruity, rich and creamy. Serve as a table cheese or use for grilling (broiling) or for melting on polenta.

Left: Taleggio is a creamy cow's milk cheese with a unique aroma and taste.

Right: San Simon is rather unusually shaped as either a bullet or a pear.

Above: Edam is a good all-rounder and is excellent used for cooking.

OTHER EUROPEAN SEMI-SOFT CHEESES

These tend to be mild and supple with a wonderful texture and delicious taste.

SAN SIMON (SPAIN)

This cheese is from the Galicia region of Spain. It has been made for generations on the western tip of Spain, where the lush, green pastures nourish the Galicia cows. San Simon is lightly pressed, then smoked. It has a supple, open consistency and an attractive, polished rind which ranges in colour from honey to reddish-brown. The smoke gives the cheese a woody taste to add to the buttery quality and slight acidity from the milk.

EDAM (HOLLAND)

Named after the small port of Edam, just north of Amsterdam, this is probably the most famous of all Dutch cheeses. The red wax coat, first used in the fourteenth century, makes it a distinctive sight in delicatessens and supermarkets the world over. Most Edam is still produced from skimmed or semi-skimmed (low-fat) milk. Edam is mostly sold young, when the texture is still supple and elastic and the flavour is mild, sweet and nutty. A black wax coat indicates an Edam has been aged for at least 17 weeks. Some cheese is aged for 10 months. Both make good table cheeses, and the mature Edam is excellent for cooking.

Above: German Bruder Basil is a popular choice for snacks and is also a good grilling cheese.

BRUDER BASIL (GERMANY)

Made in Bavaria, Bruder Basil is the traditional version of the Bavarian smoked cheese, Rauchkäse, which is found almost everywhere. The smooth, firm, yellow cheese has small holes, and its taste is creamy and pleasantly smoky.

BUTTERKÄSE (GERMANY)

Made in both Germany and Austria, this cheese lives up to its name and has a buttery taste and colour. Very supple, but odourless and rather bland, it is best served with pickles and beer to give it life.

PASSENDALE (BELGIUM)

Produced in the Flanders region of Belgium, this cheese takes its name from the village of Passchendaele, where thousands of soldiers lost their lives in World War I. With its brown crust lightly dusted with white mould, it looks like a loaf of country bread. A modern cheese, based on an old monastic recipe, it is firm with small holes and has a mild and creamy taste.

RUBENS (BELGIUM)

A chubby cheese with a rich, smooth and subtle taste, Rubens is covered with a reddish-brown, protective coat. One of the many old Belgian cheeses revived in the 1960s, it carries a label bearing a portrait of the Flemish painter Rubens.

Above: Rubens is a smooth, subtle cheese.

GRÄDDOST (SWEDEN)

This rindless cow's milk cheese was created in 1961. It has a firm texture and small evenly distributed holes. The flavour is mild and creamy, with a fresh acidity. It is good for slicing, grilling (broiling) and serving as a table cheese.

HUSHÅLLSOST (SWEDEN)

This cow's milk cheese can be traced back over 700 years. *Hushållsost* simply means household cheese and it is very versatile. The pale, straw-coloured interior has a smooth, open texture and small, irregular holes. The flavour is mild and creamy and it is good for snacks and grilling (broiling).

DANBO (DENMARK)

This is one of the most popular of all the Danish cheeses. It is similar to Samsø and has a pale, elastic interior with a few peanut-sized holes. It has a mild, slightly aromatic flavour. Occasionally Danbo contains caraway seeds, which results in a much more pungent, spicy flavour.

ESROM (DENMARK)

Made from an old recipe that was rediscovered by the Danish Cheese Institute in 1951, Esrom is mild and buttery when young. As it ages, it develops a fuller, more robust flavour. The interior, which is scattered with small, irregular-shaped holes, is supple, elastic and generally quite sweet, although it can sometimes be pungent. It gains its name from the ancient monastery of Esrom.

Above: Havarti is good for snacks, slicing and grilling (broiling).

HAVARTI (DENMARK)

One of the better-known semi-soft cheeses of Denmark, Havarti contains numerous irregular holes throughout its pale interior. The flavour is creamy with an underlying but mild bite when young, which becomes more powerful and outspoken with age.

RIDDER (NORWAY)

Invented by Sven Fenelius, a Swedish cheesemaker, this cheese spread to Norway and is now made and copied the world over. It is open textured and elastic, not unlike the French Saint Paulin, with a buttery feel and a sweet-savoury taste. The aroma can be quite pungent if left wrapped in plastic for too long.

Above: Esrom, like most Danish cheeses, has to meet very high standards of quality imposed by the government.

Right: Danbo is also known as Christian IX or King Christian.

THE UNITED STATES

A handful of delicious, mild-tasting semi-soft cheeses are produced in the Unites States, one of the best known being Monterey Jack. They all have the typical elastic texture and gentle taste.

COUGAR GOLD

This cheese was established in 1948 by Washington State University. It was created to encourage the growth and quality of cheesemaking in the state. Cougar Gold remains popular today – partly, no doubt, due to the novelty of buying a cheese that is packed in a can. Cougar Gold is made from cow's milk in 1kg/2¼lb rounds. It is rindless and the cheese has a creamy, smooth, rich texture and a mellow cheese-and-onion-sauce aroma and taste. It is good served as a table cheese or for snacks.

Above: Sonoma Jack is now made in a wide variety of flavours – this version includes hot, spicy peppers.

Below: The rind of Sonoma Dry Jack is dusted with cocoa, giving it its distinctive colour.

FRESH JACK

This traditional farmhouse cheese is made in rounds of varying sizes. Fresh Jack has a natural, straw-coloured rind and the interior resembles Edam in texture, but is creamier and springier. It has a distinctive taste, which is aromatic with a hint of green-grass bitterness. Factory-made Fresh Jack tends to be bland, mild and milky, with a rather rubbery feel.

MONTEREY AND SONOMA JACK

The origin of Monterey Jack, although attributed to the Scot, David Jacks, can actually be traced back to the Spanish Franciscan monks who travelled north to California during the days of the missions. Finding themselves with surplus milk, they set about making *queso blanco*, a delicate creamy cheese that originated in Spain. David Jacks' contribution was to recognize the cheese's potential. He set up factories and by the mid-1880s was producing his own cheese. To distinguish his factory-made cheese from others on the market, it became known as Jack's cheese and eventually simply Jack cheese.

Monterey (Sonoma) Jack was so-called to differentiate it from the firmer, industrially produced Jack. Sonoma Jack has won the hearts of the American people. Its supple and moist texture and sweet, creamy taste is balanced by a citrus bite. It is thought to have been modelled on the traditional Scottish cheese, Dunlop. The cheese is now made in a wide range of flavours including hot pepper. Serve as a table cheese or use for grilling (broiling).

Above: Teleme develops a wonderful aroma when left to ripen.

MOSSHOLDER

This modern cow's milk cheese from Wisconsin is loosely based on the Trappist cheeses of Europe. Aromatic, pungent and meaty, the supple cheese is full of tiny holes that positively ooze flavour. It is regarded by cheese-lovers as one of the great American farmhouse cheeses. Serve as a table cheese or use for melting and grilling (broiling).

TELEME

The Peluso family have been making this traditional farmhouse cheese for three generations. Made from cow's milk in a 5kg/11lb square, Teleme is delicious when young and really comes into its own when ripened. The pale pinkish rind, dusted with rice flour and mottled with moulds and yeasts, literally bursts at the seams, and the aroma is utterly compelling.

Teleme was introduced to America by Greek immigrants over a century ago. It is based on Touloumotyri or Touloumi, a goat's milk cheese similar to feta but not as salty. The immigrants did not have access to goat's milk, so used cow's milk instead. Italian cheese-makers found the cheese to their liking, made a few adjustments, and Teleme was born. It is delicious served as a table cheese or used for baking and salads. It is suitable for vegetarians.

Peluso Cheese is one of only two companies currently making Teleme. They also produce Monterey Jack, Dry Jack, Halloumi and Raw Milk Cheddar.

AUSTRALIA AND NEW ZEALAND

The most popular of the antipodean semi-soft cheeses is New Zealand's rather unappetizingly-named Brick.

KINGRIVER GOLD (AUSTRALIA)

This round cow's milk table cheese from Victoria has a pinkish-orange rind with a dusting of mould. The interior is smooth, dense and voluptuous with random small holes. The flavour hints at warm cow's milk and has a slightly sharp finish.

ROMNEY (AUSTRALIA)

This sheep's milk cheese is made in Victoria. The cheese is named after the breed of sheep and it comes in two versions. The first, the young curd is shaped and drained in a mould, then waxed while still moist. The result is a fresh, moist and springy cheese with a mild sweet flavour. The second, Romney Mature, has a more intense flavour and a harder, flaky texture. To make this cheese the curd is bound in cloth and matured for up to six months.

Below: Romney Mature has a crusty rind with some pale grey mould.

Above: Brick is a very popular modern version of a traditional European cheese which came to New Zealand via the United States.

TOMME DE CHEVRE (AUSTRALIA)

This goat's milk cheese from New South Wales has a smooth, dense texture with a salty tang. It is slightly firmer than an unpasteurized French Tomme, and does not have the same depth of flavour.

WASHED RIND (AUSTRALIA)

This cow's milk cheese from Victoria is made in the Trappist style and has a sticky, orange rind, dusted with blue, grey and white moulds. The cheese has a meaty, pungent aroma with a soft, springy texture.

BRICK (NEW ZEALAND)

This cheese is based upon the traditional, monastery-style cheeses of Europe. The washed rind is typically burnt-orange in colour and the cheese has a pungent aroma with overtones of yeast and roast lamb. The pale yellow interior is smooth and dense, and the flavour is sweet and savoury with a spicy tang. It is suitable for vegetarians.

COLBY (NEW ZEALAND)

This block-shaped, rindless, cow's milk cheese has a soft, springy texture and a mild flavour. Colby has a higher moisture content than Cheddar and feels more elastic. It is also sweet, rather than savoury, and lacks the depth of flavour acquired by a good Cheddar so is seldom used in cooking.

PORT NICHOLSON (NEW ZEALAND)

This cheese has the characteristic sweet-sour, slightly smoked aroma and taste of the Trappist-style cheese Port-Salut, upon which it is based. It is, however, more supple and open-textured. The producers named the cheese after the magnificent harbour of New Zealand's capital city, Wellington.

Left: Port Nicholson may be served as a table cheese and is also excellent for both melting and grilling.

SOFT WHITE CHEESES

These are akin to fresh cheeses, except that the soft curds are left to mature for a few weeks. Their high moisture content, coupled with high humidity, encourages the growth of the classic white penicillium mould. The moulds help to break down the curd and contribute to the buttery, mushroomy flavour and texture of the cheese. The final result is a creamy, smooth, voluptuous interior. They are generally used as table cheeses, although they may be used in recipes.

UNITED KINGDOM

There is not a great tradition of soft white cheeses in Britain. The few that are produced are all modern cheeses.

BATH CHEESE (ENGLAND)

The producers of this cheese developed it after reading a description of a similar cheese made in Bath a century ago. When young, the cheese has a slightly grainy texture and a mild, slightly tart flavour. When aged, the soft, furry white rind yields to a soft interior which oozes on to the plate as it reaches perfection. The flavour has hints of mushroom balanced with a peppery bite.

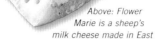

Above: Flower Marie is a sheep's milk cheese made in East Sussex. It comes in small 200g/7oz or much larger 1.6kg/3½lb squares.

BOSWORTH (ENGLAND)

This soft white cheese is produced in Staffordshire. The elegant cheese has an unexpectedly firm, breakable texture, rather than the usual Brie-like softness. It melts in the mouth rather like fudge, yielding up its sweet, nutty flavours with just a suggestion of goat's milk. It is suitable for vegetarians.

Below: Capricorn Goat is mild and creamy with a distinctive flavour and has a pure white rind of soft, furry mould.

CAPRICORN GOAT (ENGLAND)

Capricorn Goat is one of the best-known English goat's milk cheeses. It is a soft-white cheese with a mild yet distinct flavour. Slightly chalky, like unripe Camembert, when young, it becomes softer around the edges and is sometimes almost runny. The fresh, creamy flavour is very appealing. It is suitable for vegetarians.

EMLETT (ENGLAND)

This small cheese comes in discs and is made from unpasteurized sheep's milk. It has a delicious, yeasty aroma that penetrates the cheese and enhances the sweet acidity and characteristic nuttiness. The uneven Camembert-like rind encloses an unpasteurized, soft cheese that is a deep creamy yellow around the edge. If young, it may be slightly chalky and white in the centre. Like good Camembert, it melts in the mouth to reveal distinct yet subtle layers of flavour, including the sweetness of caramel and a slight hint of Brazil nuts.

FINN (ENGLAND)

This is the only triple cream cheese made in England. It is firm and amazingly rich, with a mild, fresh, creamy acidity. Suitable for vegetarians.

FLOWER MARIE (ENGLAND)

The thin, soft-white rind of sheep's milk cheese has a pink tint. The cheese has a wonderful texture, melting like ice cream in the mouth, and a lemony freshness. It is suitable for vegetarians.

GOLDEN CROSS (ENGLAND)

Made in East Sussex, this cheese is based on the traditional, French artisan cheese Sainte-Maure. Produced in small logs, it is easily recognizable by its dusting of salted ash. At first firm and slightly grainy, the cheese softens with age to a texture more like that of ice cream. The flavour is a blend of sweetness and acidity. It is suitable for vegetarians.

COOLEENEY (IRELAND)

This Camembert-style cheese comes from Tipperary and is made by hand. It has a full flavour with a distinct aroma of mushrooms when ripe. Its rich, semi-liquid interior is a result of the lush pastures for which Tipperary is famous.

ST KILLIAN (IRELAND)

Attractively boxed, this hexagonal Camembert-style cheese from Wexford has taken the market by storm. Although the rind can be a little smelly, the prevailing aroma is of mushrooms and cellars, while the soft, nearly melting interior has the rich, creamy flavour of warm butter. St Killian is suitable for vegetarians.

Above: Bonchester is a rich, buttery cheese from Scotland.

BONCHESTER (SCOTLAND)

The makers of this unique, Camembert-style cheese created it using the milk from their own herd. Theirs is one of the few farms to retain the old practice of resting the herd. The Jersey milk gives the cheese its rich butter-yellow colour and velvety texture.

PENCARREG (WALES)

Made in Cardiganshire, Pencarreg is a Brie-style cheese with a texture that feels like solid, whipped cream as it melts in the mouth. It has a buttery sweet flavour and mushroomy aroma.

Below: Cooleeney is a modern farmhouse cheese with a rich creamy texture. It is made in small and large rounds.

Left: Pencarreg is a Welsh organic cow's milk cheese.

Above: Somerset Brie is not as rich as classic French Brie, but it has a wonderful texture.

SHARPHAM (ENGLAND)

This unpasteurized, vegetarian cheese comes from Devon. It uses Jersey milk, which undoubtedly gives the cheese its unique taste. The Brie-type cheese has a wonderfully creamy texture with a hint of acidity and mushrooms in the flavour. Sharpham is produced in rounds and squares, weighing 250g/9oz, 500g/1/¼lb or 1kg/2¼lb. It is suitable for vegetarians.

SOMERSET BRIE (ENGLAND)

Probably the best-selling British soft-white cheese, Somerset Brie has a delicious set custard texture. The aroma and taste suggest mushrooms with a hint of green grass, with some acidity to give the cheese depth. It does not pretend to be like a French Brie, which is richer and more robust, owing to the differences in climate, soil, breed of cattle and production methods. It is suitable for vegetarians.

FRANCE

The vast majority of soft white cheeses come from France, with Brie and Camembert probably being the best-known and loved of their type. However, there are many other less well-known, but equally delicious examples of this type of cheese.

BOUGON

Although similar cheeses have been made in France for generations, Bougon, which is produced in the Poitou-Charentes region of France, was only recently made commercially. It is a smooth, voluptuous cheese with a taste that has been likened to a blend of tarragon, thyme and white wine. The Camembert shape is the most popular, but it also comes in pyramids, logs and very small rounds.

BOURSAULT

Also known as Lucullus, Boursault is similar to the fresh cheese, Boursin. Boursault has a high cream content, which means that the taste is smooth and almost buttery. The 200g/7oz white half-cylinders have a soft thin rind and the interior is solid rather than runny with a nutty finish and a refreshing citrus tang, balancing the creaminess. Délice de Saint-Cyr is a larger version of the classic Boursault.

Right: Boursault is a modern cheese made by a similar method to Brie, but it has a softer, thinner rind.

BRIE DE MEAUX (AOC)

This is the most famous of all the French soft white cheeses. It was first recorded in AD774 when the gourmet and soldier Charlemagne tasted it in Brie and ordered two batches to be sent to him annually in Aix. A perfect Brie de Meaux is smooth, voluptuous and not

Above: Brie de Meaux shows the marks of the straw mat on which it matures.

quite runny. It should have an aroma of mushrooms with the merest hint of ammonia. Like most French farmhouse cheeses, Brie de Meaux is made using unpasteurized milk. Traditionally the milk was supplied by the indigenous cows of the Ile-de-France region, but now they have been largely replaced by Friesian-Holstein cattle.

BRIE DE MELUN (AOC)

This Brie is produced in the same region as Brie de Meaux, but is sharper and has a slightly saltier flavour. The method of production relies on lactose-loving bacteria without the addition of rennet. A perfect Brie de Melun has a supple texture with a fresh, meadow scent.

BRILLAT-SAVARIN

This triple cream cheese from Normandy comes in 450g/1lb rounds. The cheese normally has a soft white rind which will eventually grow to a thick, velvety, white crust.

BUTTE

This is a commercially produced cheese that takes its name from its shape, which resembles a hillock. The cheese owes its rich, buttery texture to cream, which is added to the milk before it is coagulated. The fresh cheese melts in the mouth and has a mushroomy aroma and a salty, bitter tang.

CAMEMBERT DE NORMANDIE (AOC)

This classic soft white cheese is instantly recognizable by the little wooden boxes in which it is packed. Hundreds of producers in Normandy are permitted to make AOC Camembert. The finest have a fragrant aroma and taste of wild mushroom soup.

COEUR DE CAMEMBERT

This is a delicious variation of classic Camembert. The rind is removed from a semi-cured Camembert, and the cheese is then soaked in Calvados. Breadcrumbs are pressed into the cheese and a walnut garnish is added. The cheese has a rich, creamy texture and a faint apple aroma.

CAPRICE DES DIEUX

These pretty oval-shaped cheeses come in attractive boxes. The presentation possibly accounts for the popularity of the cheese, which is milky and pleasant, if rather bland. Its texture is also sometimes rather disappointing, tending to be elastic rather than supple.

CARRE DE L'EST

Made in the Champagne and Lorraine regions for generations, Carre de l'Est is ripened in cellars and encouraged to grow a soft white crust. The soft white cheeses have a Camembert-like rind and a flavour reminiscent of melted butter and warm mushrooms.

Right: Caprice des Dieux make a pretty addition to a cheese board, although their flavour can sometimes be bland.

Right: Coeur de Camembert au Calvados has a subtle flavour of apple brandy.

Right: Butte is a creamy cheese from the Ile-de-France. If allowed to ripen, the rind develops reddish pigmentation, and the inside softens.

Left: Brillat Savarin is named after the famous gastronome.

COULOMMIERS

This attractive unpasteurized cheese is similar to Brie both in looks and flavour. Known also as Petit Brie, it comes in small 400g/14oz rounds and has the same white penicillium mould. Some people prefer the cheese while still quite young, when the white mould is barely discernible; others prefer it when the cheese is ripe, at which point the aroma and flavour are more similar to a ripe Brie. Commercial versions are pleasant, but lack the depth of the traditional unpasteurized farmhouse cheese.

Above:
Chaource is a
soft, silky cheese
with a refreshing flavour.

CHAOURCE (AOC)

From the Champagne region of France, Chaource is another of the well-known soft white cheeses. Some people prefer it when young, when the rind has barely formed and the cheese is milky and slightly tart with a salty tang. Other cheese-lovers prefer to wait for the rind to thicken and develop ferments, which become slightly bitter. The interior is buttery, sharp and fruity.

Above:
Explorateur
was invented in
the 1950s in honour of
the US satellite, Explorer.

DREUX À LA FEUILLE

Made in the same region as Brie, this creamy cheese is recognizable by the chestnut-leaf wrapping which imparts a nutty, slightly aromatic taste.

EXPLORATEUR

This is a firm, creamy cheese with a grainy feel. It has a delicate aroma and the flavour has a salty, mushroomy tang.

FRINAULT

This cheese is similar to Camembert, but is matured in wood ash. It has a slightly firmer, less voluptuous texture, with a strong, spicy taste. It comes from the Orléanais region and is difficult to obtain outside that area.

LE FOUGERUS

This cheese, decorated with fern, is supple and almost runny when ripe. It resembles Dreux á la Feuille.

Above: Coulommiers is also
known as Petit Brie or
Brie de Coulommiers.

GAPERON

This attractive cheese comes from the Auvergne region of France. The small cheese, shaped like a tiny upturned basin, has a soft white rind and comes wrapped in raffia. Traditionally, this cheese and others like it were made in the home rather than by cheesemakers. Buttermilk was originally used, although skimmed milk is more often used today. The curds were kneaded with garlic and peppercorns before being pressed into the bowl-shaped moulds. Mild and milky, the cheese has a gentle acidity and spongy texture. The aromas of the garlic and peppercorns dominate the flavour.

GRATTE-PAILLE

A modern cheese from the Ile-de-France, Gratte-Paille takes its name from *gratte* (to scratch) and *paille* (straw), marking the fact that when bales of straw were carried through the narrow streets in summer, pieces of the straw would become wedged in the walls along the way. It is rich and creamy with an excellent flavour. The cheese comes in 300–350g/11–12oz bricks and is sometimes sold on small straw mats. It has a mushroomy flavour, developing a slight sharpness with age. It is one of the few soft white cheeses that is used in recipes.

NEUFCHÂTEL (AOC)

Unlike other soft white rinded cheese, Neufchâtel has a grainy texture. Although it has the aroma and taste of mushrooms, it is also quite sharp and salty. Some lovers of this cheese prefer it when it has been kept until the rind develops reddish pigmentation and a smell of ammonia. At this stage the taste is salty and acrid. Neufchâtel is available in various shapes such as squares, rounds, logs, hearts, loaves and cylinders. They weigh 100–200g/3¾–7oz. Some are unpasteurized. Gournay is a similar cheese.

Above: Gaperon is a popular choice for snacks and makes a decorative addition to a cheese board.

Below: Gratte-Paille is often served baked in pastries with chicken and vegetables. It is also a delicious table cheese.

Below: (Left to right) Olivet au Foin and Olivet Cendré are from Orléanais.

OLIVET AU FOIN AND OLIVET CENDRÉ

These unpasteurized cheeses are from the Orléanais region. Olivet au Foin is similar to Camembert, but is milder in flavour and not so soft when ripe. It is decorated with fine strands of hay (*foin*), the scent of which is absorbed into the cheese. Olivet Cendré is a similar cheese, but is cured for three months in wood ash from vines, giving the cheese a supple texture and a fairly pungent, spicy aroma. Similar cheeses include Vendôme Cendré and the Cendrés of Champagne and the Ardennes.

Above: Pavé d'Affinois does not require rennet for the cheesemaking process, only a culture to allow fermentation.

PAVÉ D'AFFINOIS

This square cheese from the Lyonnais region of France has a characteristic ridged rind. When young, Pavé d'Affinois is mildly scented and fairly bland. If allowed to ripen, the interior of the cheese literally melts but retains a firm, slightly chalky centre. The taste is similar to Brie. Suitable for vegetarians.

PITHIVIERS AU FOIN

Similar to Camembert, Pithiviers au Foin has a mild, milky, caramel flavour.

SAINT-ALBRAY

This distinctive disc-shaped cheese with a central hole has a reddish-brown rind, overlaid with white penicillium mould. It was invented in 1976 to appeal to those who found the flavour of Camembert too strong but who liked that type of cheese. Ripened in just two weeks, Saint-Albray develops a moist, rubbery texture and has a mild, creamy flavour. The shape makes it very practical for serving: it is marked into sections by indentations in the rind.

Above: Pithiviers au Foin, like Olivet au Foin is rolled in strands of hay or grass.

Above: Saint-Albray is a very stable cheese, so it survives the rigours of export successfully and is popular in many countries outside France.

VIGNOTTE/LES VIGNOTTES

From the Champagne and Lorraine regions of France, this is a very popular, triple-cream cheese. It is made from cow's milk in 150g/5oz cylinders or 2kg/4½lb discs that have a thick velvety-smooth penicillium rind. Vignotte has a light, airy, almost mousse-like texture, thanks to the careful ladling of the young curd into the moulds. The flavour is fresh and creamy, slightly lemony and salty. Unlike many soft white cheeses, it is used for grilling (broiling) as a well as serving as a table cheese.

OTHER SOFT WHITE CHEESES

Around the rest of the world, only a few other soft white cheeses are made. Most of these are based on the classic French soft white cheeses.

QUESO DEL MONTSEC (SPAIN)

This Spanish soft white cheese is made in the Catalonia region. It has a dense, grainy texture that feels creamy in the mouth, yet has a definite bite. It has a distinctive taste of goat's milk.

JINDI BRIE (AUSTRALIA)

In Australia, the milk for cheesemaking is pasteurized and this Brie is semi-stabilized, to give it a longer shelf life. The texture is rich and buttery with slightly sweet tones.

KANGAROO ISLAND BRIE (AUSTRALIA)

This brie is smooth and voluptuous with the sweet, creamy taste of mushroom soup. It melts like butter in the mouth. The cheese is made all year round and the curd is not stabilized, so it is subject to seasonal changes.

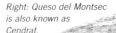

Right: Queso del Montsec is also known as Cendrat.

KING ISLAND CAPE WICKHAM BRIE (AUSTRALIA)

King Island guards the western entrance to Bass Strait, which separates Tasmania from the Australian mainland. Founded in 1902, King Island Dairy became a co-operative in 1939, but it was nearly 50 years later that the company started producing the cheeses that have made it famous. Cape Wickham is a stabilized cheese, which gives it a longer shelf life and prevents the interior from running. The flavour is sweeter and more buttery, and the consistency is elastic rather than runny.

TIMBOON BRIE (AUSTRALIA)

Timboon Brie, like other cheeses made by these cheesemakers from Victoria, uses only biodynamic milk (a type of organic milk). The cheese is not stabilized, and therefore has a more tempestuous nature and a greater depth of flavour than many cheeses of the same type from this part of the world. Because the milk is pasteurized the rind does not develop the wild yeasts and pigments that would give Timboon the authenticity of a traditional Brie, but it comes closer than most.

AORANGI (NEW ZEALAND)

This Brie-style cheese has been given a Maori name meaning white cloud, which perfectly describes the thick, white penicillium rind. The aim of the cheesemaker who created it – and many other cheeses – was not to produce an imitation of a European cheese, but rather, one that is uniquely of New Zealand. He wanted New Zealanders to buy local cheeses from choice and not because they were the only ones available. The cheeses are scrupulously turned to ensure an even coating of mould and the interior is creamy and of a consistent quality.

EVANSDALE FARMHOUSE (NEW ZEALAND)

Deeper in stature than traditional Brie, Evansdale Farmhouse from New Zealand has a soft white rind and a smooth, creamy texture that melts in the mouth. The flavour is reminiscent of mushrooms and melted butter. It is suitable for vegetarians.

Left: Jindi and Cape Wickham bries are Australian versions of the classic French soft white cheese.

WASHED-RIND CHEESES

These cheeses are characterized by an orangey-brown sticky rind. This is the result of dunking them, during the maturing process, in baths of salty water, wine or other alcoholic liquid. The process produces a robust cheese that encourages the development of orange, sticky bacteria, which help to break down the curd from the outside. The process was invented by Trappist monks to enhance their otherwise rather meagre diet on fast days. They are often referred to as Trappist or monastic-style cheeses. Washed-rind cheeses range from being rather spicy to outrageously piquant in taste and aroma. They are mostly served as table cheeses, but may be sliced for grilling (broiling).

FRANCE

Washed-rind cheeses are found right across Europe, and France has a particularly fine selection.

BAGUETTE LAONNAISE

This cheese is a favourite with lovers of strong cheese. The sticky, ridged, orange-brown rind hides a supple yet dense interior. As the cheese ages it develops a pungent, spicy nose and taste, and a finish reminiscent of the farmyard. It should not be kept in the refrigerator as the rind may dry out and the cheese will become quite bitter and unpleasant.

Right: Chaumes is a very popular, modern cheese produced by traditional methods. It may be served as table cheese and is also good for grilling.

CARRÉ DE L'EST

This cheese comes from Champagne and Lorraine. The washed-rind version of Carré de l'Est (it is also produced as a soft white cheese) is washed in brine and eau-de-vie to produce a pungent, ridged orange rind. Each cheese is turned and washed by hand to spread the colourful bacteria over it. The cheese has a runny interior with a smoked bacon flavour.

CHAUMES

Based upon traditional Trappist-style cheeses, Chaumes has proved to be one of the most popular of the modern, French washed-rind varieties. It could be seen as a stepping-stone between contemporary mass-production and specialist artisan cheesemaking

methods. The soft rind is a bright tangerine-orange in colour and the golden yellow interior is smooth, supple and quite rubbery. Although it looks as though it is about to run, the cheese is actually fairly dense and feels wonderfully rich and creamy on the tongue. The nutty, almost meaty taste and aroma are milder than you might expect. Port Salut is a similar cheese.

Left: Carré de l'Est is a small, square cheese. The washed-rind version has a stronger, more pungent flavour than the soft white form of the cheese.

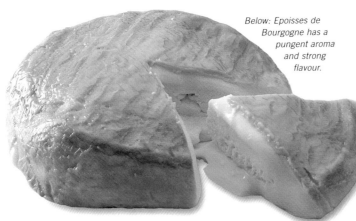

Below: Epoisses de Bourgogne has a pungent aroma and strong flavour.

GRIS DE LILLE

This cheese is sometimes known as Puant de Lille or Puant Macéré. The word *puant* means obnoxious or stinking – a term of endearment to those who love the rich flavour of this pungent cheese with its distinctive farmyard aroma. It is best used as a table cheese and for snacks.

LANGRES (AOC)

This is another cherished French cheese, made in the Champagne-Ardennes region. Monks who passed through the region during the Middle Ages probably introduced this cheese. The cheese is either cone-shaped or cylindrical with a hollow in the top. The brightly coloured rind is the result of continual washing; orange bacteria grow on the surface, as well as some white flora or yeasts. The cheese is notable for its pungent, smoked bacon aroma. When young, the texture is firm and grainy. With age, the rind starts to break down and becomes smooth-flowering and creamy, and the flavour intensifies. Sometimes *eau-de-vie* is poured into the top crater, adding a further dimension to an already powerful flavour. This is an excellent table cheese, and is also baked and used as a dip for vegetables.

CÎTEAUX

Like Epoisses de Bourgogne, this cheese comes from the Burgundy region, made still at the Abbaye de Cîteaux, which is set in the heart of the wine country. The monks at the abbey have a herd of around 200 red and white Montbéliard cows and prefer to keep production small, so it is difficult to find outside the area. It has a refreshing flavour and a melting texture. Serve as a table cheese.

Below: Langres has a distinctive hollow in the top because the curd is turned only twice during draining. The weight of the undrained whey, and its movement through the curd causes the centre to subside.

EPOISSES DE BOURGOGNE (AOC)

Right: Gris de Lille is a square cow's milk cheese with a sticky, pinkish-grey washed rind.

This is one of France's best-loved cheeses. Each cheese is washed by hand, using a small brush to spread the bacteria over and into the rind. The final wash is in alcohol, usually marc de Bourgogne. Like many French cheeses, Epoisses are enjoyed at different stages of their maturation by different people. Epoisse Frais (30 days) is a mere shadow of its aged counterpart, being firm, moist and grainy, yet still creamy with a fresh acidity and mild yeasty tang. At 40 days, the rind is orange-brown in colour. The pungent, spicy aroma is matched by the strong flavour. The cheese deserves to be served with a fine Burgundy or a spicy, aromatic white wine.

MAMIROLLE

This brick-shaped cheese has a bright orange rind and a sweet-sour, faintly smoked aroma and taste. The rind is finely ridged and the texture is supple and smooth. Serve as a table cheese or use for grilling (broiling).

MONT D'OR/VACHERIN HAUT-DOUBS (AOC)

In the days when the borders of France and Switzerland were less well defined, the local soft, washed cheese was called Vacherin Mont d'Or, regardless of which side of the mountain it came from. Later, the Swiss (who produce the pasteurized version) laid claim to the name and the unpasteurized French Vacherin became simply Vacherin Haut-Doubs or Mont d'Or. A good Mont d'Or has an aroma of chopped wood and mountain flowers, with a faint hint of fermentation and resin. The texture is full and creamy and the flavour suggests wild herbs. Production begins on 15 August, when the cows return from the mountain pastures. The cheese is available only from the end of September through to 31 March. Summer milk is taken to a local co-operative to create another great cheese, Gruyère de Comté.

Right: Munster Géromé has a pungent aroma and an intense flavour.

Right: Soumaintrain is often steeped in the local wine before it is eaten. This speciality is called fromage fort.

MUNSTER/MUNSTER GÉROMÉ (AOC)

The Vosges mountains are home to one of the smelliest and most delicious cheeses in the world. Those made in Alsace are called Munster, while the smaller versions from Lorraine are known as Géromé. The cheese owes its quite unique character to the unspoilt pastures of Alsace and the Vosgiennes. The cows who graze

here are renowned for giving high-protein milk. The cheese is constantly rubbed with brine over a period of two to three months. This causes the rind to develop its rich colour, which ranges from yellow-orange to russet, and the aroma to intensify. Don't let the smell put you off. The cheese is supple, with a flavour that is both sweet and savoury (almost yeasty), and an intense, spicy, aromatic finish. This is a wonderful table cheese and is good for making snacks and for grilling (broiling). It is traditional to enjoy the cheese with boiled potatoes, cumin seeds and local wine. Munster au Cumin is a popular variation. Langrés and Géromé are similar cheeses.

NANTAIS

Brittany has no native cheeses and had to wait until the early 1790s for a young priest who was on the run from the French Revolution to introduce cheese-making. This cheese, also known as Curé de Nantais or Fromage de Curé, celebrates that fact. It is a small, sticky cheese with a pungent, yeasty rind. The voluptuous, creamy interior has a rich, smoked bacon taste and spicy finish. Nantais is a square cheese, weighing 175–200g/6–7oz with a smooth, straw-coloured to ochre rind.

ROUY

This is a commercially made copy of the stronger, more pungent, traditional French washed-rind cheeses such as Langrés or Epoisses. Nevertheless, it is a good buy. Made in Burgundy, it is a square cheese with rounded corners. The terracotta-coloured rind is slightly sticky and may have some white mould.

SOUMAINTRAIN

Made in Burgundy, this traditional cheese is grainy and moist when young, with a mild lemony flavour. After six weeks in a humid cellar, where it is frequently washed in brine, it develops more character, the rind becoming more pungent and the interior developing a strong, spicy tang. Soumaintrain is sometimes immersed in ash to make Aisy Cendré, which is a local speciality.

TOURÉE DE L'AUBIER

The spruce bark belt gives this cheese a unique flavour. Creamy, sweet, yet pungent, it becomes almost runny when mature. The cheese is made in Normandy and comes in either small 200g/7oz rounds or much larger 2kg/4½lb rounds, with powdery white mould on its orange-red surface. It is made commercially and is widely available outside France.

Right: Tourée de L'Aubier was created as a pasteurized copy of the great French cheese, Mont d'Or.

PORTUGAL

One of the finest of cheeses produced in Portugal is a washed-rind cheese, which is often described as the king of Portuguese cheese.

SERRA DA ESTRELA

For centuries, shepherds have made this cheese in the mountains of the same name. Serra da Estrela has a characteristic orange-brown rind, which is leathery and slightly sticky. Made with sheep's milk, the cheese is coagulated using the flowers or leaves of a wild thistle. This gives the cheese a subtle but distinct character and affects the final texture. The curds are broken by hand, rather than cut, and matured in caves for one to four months.

Serra da Estrela is so soft that it is almost spreadable. It has a rich, perfumed intensity as a result of the superb grazing, and the sweet, slightly burnt-caramel character of the sheep's milk. When the cheese is allowed to age, the rind toughens and the interior becomes denser and more supple, when it can be sliced with ease. Serve as a table cheese.

Australian Washed-rind Cheeses

These cheeses are relatively new to Australia, having been created only in the late 1980s. Australian cheese-maker Fred Leppin developed English- and French-style cheese, but deliberately avoided simple copying in favour of creating new world versions. His semi-soft, washed-rind cheese, while made in the Trappist style, has different qualities from the original. The cheese has a meaty, pungent aroma with a soft, springy texture and the flavour seems to have absorbed the warm, minty aroma of the eucalyptus trees.

Fred Leppin's washed-rind cheeses – Whitelaw, Bass River Red, Wine Washed Rind, Cronwell, Ranceby, Loch and Kardella – have been greeted with great enthusiasm by cheese-lovers in Australia.

BELGIUM

This is one of the few countries outside France to produce a number of washed-rind or Trappist-style cheeses. Belgium's cheeses are virtually unknown outside her borders, but it is the washed-rind ones that are both the best-known and the best-loved.

BRUSSELSE KAAS

Made with skimmed milk, this cheese has a smooth, sharp, citric flavour and a strong and salty bite. It is shaped into rough rounds and packed in tubs. It is also known as Fromage de Bruxelles.

HERVE

This cheese comes in small 200g/ 7oz bricks and has a glossy, autumn-coloured crust that is pungent and yeasty. Beneath it, the supple, tender interior ranges from sweet to powerful and spicy, depending on how long the cheese has been ripened. Fairly small quantities of unpasteurized cheese are still made, and there is also a version made with double cream.

MAREDSOUS

This is another of Belgium's Trappist-style cheeses and is made by the monks at Maredsous Abbey. The large cheeses (1kg/2¼lb or 2.5kg/5½lb) are made from cow's milk, then lightly

Above: Maredsous is a large, loaf-shaped cheese with a firm orange rind, which sometimes has a very fine dusting of white mould.

pressed and washed in brine to create the firm orange crust and pungent aroma. The supple, smooth interior is pale yellow with a slightly smoky tinge. It is less pungent and has a somewhat milder flavour than Herve and is a little like the French washed-rind cheese, Saint-Paulin. Maredsous is usually served as a table cheese but is also very good used for grilling (broiling).

Right: Herve, from the Liège region of Belgium, is the country's most famous cheese.

PLATEAU DE HERVE

This lightly pressed cow's milk cheese has a pale yellow interior with a creamy consistency. Washed regularly in brine, it has the flavour without the pervasive aroma of Herve. Produced in a 1.5kg/3¼lb dome, the cheese is sold wrapped in foil.

POSTEL

The monks at the Abbey of Postel resumed making this classic Trappist cheese in the 1960s using the milk from their herd of 160 cows. Volume is small, but it is worth travelling to the abbey to buy it.

RAMEDOU

Also known as Piquant, this is a larger, more aggressive version of Herve. Ramedou often comes in 675g/1½lb rounds. Its larger size means that it takes longer to ripen, which gives the surface bacteria time to exude the powerful aroma for which it is known. It is known locally as stinking cheese and is best eaten in the open air with a glass of robust red wine or local beer. *Remoud* is an old Walloon word for rich milk.

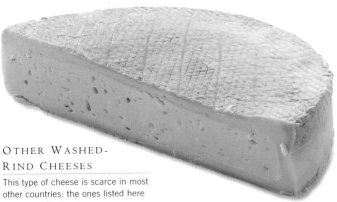

OTHER WASHED-RIND CHEESES

This type of cheese is scarce in most other countries: the ones listed here are among the best.

STINKING BISHOP (ENGLAND)

This is one of the few washed-rind cheeses in England. It is a large, half-cylinder shaped cheese with an almost glistening, orange-yellow rind. During the ripening process, the rind is washed and rubbed with perry, made with a local pear called Stinking Bishop. The cheese has a soft, almost spoonable interior and is a frequent prize-winner at the British Cheese Awards. It is suitable for vegetarians.

TORVILLE (ENGLAND)

This is an unusual cheese. The cheese-maker in Somerset, well-known for his traditional farmhouse Caerphilly, experimented some years ago by washing some of his fresh Caerphilly in the local scrumpy cider. The result was this salty sweet cheese.

ARDRAHAN (IRELAND)

Made by traditional farmhouse methods in West Cork, this cheese comes in small 400g/14oz rounds or large 1.6kg/ 3½lb wheels. It has a distinctive, earthy aroma. Beneath the brine-washed rind, which is encrusted with brown, ochre and grey moulds, the deep yellow interior is firm and slightly chalky. Its flavour is complex, with a zesty acidity underscoring the buttery, savoury character. It is suitable for vegetarians.

LIMBURGER (GERMANY)

Famous for its powerful aroma and distinctive taste, Limburger is one of Germany's most notable cheeses. The yellow interior hints at sweetness, but the overwhelming taste is spicy and aromatic, almost meaty. It is best when the texture is firm, yet yielding: it should not be allowed to become runny. Limburger originated with the cheese-loving Trappist monks in Belgium, and was hijacked by German cheese-makers in the nineteenth century. It may be served as a table cheese or melted over potatoes. It is suitable for vegetarians.

Left: Stinking Bishop may seem to have obtained its name as a result of its powerful, pungent aroma, but, in fact, it is named after the local variety of pears used to make the perry in which the rind is washed.

MÜNSTER (GERMANY)

This is a smooth, fairly soft, yellow cheese with a thin orange skin. Its mildly piquant flavour can become quite pungent as it ripens. In the Middle Ages the cheese was made by the monks at Munster Abbey in modern-day Alsace. When Alsace became part of Germany, the cheese became known as Münster, after the Westphalian town. Ownership of Alsace has switched from Germany to France several times, and the cheese is made on both sides of the border. It is also produced in the United States, where it is known as Muenster.

MONDSEER (AUSTRIA)

This round, cow's milk cheese from Salzburg is firm, yet moist, with an open texture and a few irregular eyes. The rind is deep orange, dusted with powdery white mould. The cheese has a slightly spicy aroma and a sweet-sour taste. It tends to be milder and less pungent than other washed-rind cheeses. Mondseer ripens in two to three months. It is delicious used for snacks and for grilling (broiling).

Above: Limburger has a distinctive ridged rind and an unmistakable aroma.

NATURAL-RIND CHEESES

These cheeses are simply fresh cheeses that have been left to drain for longer and in a drier atmosphere than a fresh cheese. These are the cheeses you see piled on wooden trestles in French markets. When young, they have a slightly wrinkled, cream-coloured rind. In time they dry out, the wrinkles become more pronounced and the character and flavour increases, along with the growth of bluish-grey moulds. There are few examples of this type of cheese in Britain, the United States and Australasia, as the majority of consumers are dubious about moulds. In France and elsewhere in Europe, however, there are a large number of these delightful cheeses, many of which are made using goat's milk.

Natural-rind cheeses are always small. They are excellent served as a table cheese and are also occasionally used in cooking. All the examples listed here come from France.

Left: Cabécou de Rocamadour is made in tiny discs weighing only 30–40g/ 1–1½oz.

ARÔMES AU GÈNE DE MARC

These small cheeses are made in various wine-making areas two to three months after the grapes have been pressed. Small immature cheeses such as Rigotte are macerated in vats of *marc* (fermenting grape skins and pips). The macerated cheeses are then rolled in the *marc* before being sold. The

Below: Banon is traditionally sold wrapped in crisp brown chestnut leaves and tied decoratively with raffia string.

cheese has a strong, bittersweet, yeasty taste and pungent aroma. When young, though, the cheese is moist with a smooth, creamy taste.

BANON

This cheese can be made of cow's, sheep's or goat's milk and is often a combination of all three. The small 90g/ 3½oz round cheese is traditionally sold wrapped in leaves. When young, the cheese is moist with a fresh vegetable flavour. As it ages, moulds and yeasts are produced on and under the leaves, which contribute to the flavour. Banon cheeses range from firm, mild and lactic to soft, creamy and tart, with a slightly nutty flavour.

Penamellera

This cheese from the Asturias region of Spain is named after the high peak that rises behind the village where the cheese has been made for centuries. Penamellera has a slightly greasy appearance and an oddly meaty smell. The interior is more elegant. Supple and dense, with a few small, irregular holes, it has a mellow, vaguely nutty taste. The finish is fresh and lemony. Penamellera may be made from cow's, goat's or sheep's milk. A number of similar cheeses are produced locally.

Above: Chabichou du Poitou is a traditional unpasteurized farmhouse cheese with a wonderful goaty flavour.

CABÉCOU DE ROCAMADOUR (AOC)

Often simply known as Rocamadour, these tiny discs with their creamy white rind have been made in the Midi-Pyrénées for centuries – ever since the locals domesticated the herds of goats and sheep that once roamed wild on the mountainside. Nowadays, they are sold in flat, wooden-slatted trays and are sometimes decorated with sprigs of wild herbs or wrapped in bacon strips, ready for grilling (broiling) and tossing into a salad. When the dense, creamy cheese is grilled, the nutty taste and distinctly goaty aroma intensify. The cheese is sometimes made with sheep's milk. Rocamadour may also be served as a table cheese or used for baking.

CHABICHOU DU POITOU (AOC)

This small, goat's milk natural-rind cheese comes in a 130g/4½oz cylinder. When mature, it has a distinctive dark bluish-grey mould that overlays the thin, white mould covering the cheese. The texture of this chèvre is firm and creamy rather than grainy, and the cheese has a fresh ground-nut flavour. Mothais is a similar cheese.

CROTTIN DE CHAVIGNOL (AOC)

This goat's milk cheese comes from the Loire region of France. The young cheese has an off-white, wrinkled rind with a mere suggestion of white and blue moulds. At eight days, Crottin de Chavignol has a gentle, aromatic, yeasty taste and a fine, moist texture. At 11 days, the interior softens, and the taste becomes nuttier and more full-bodied. At 20 days, the cheese is denser and creamier still. The flavour intensifies when the cheese is grilled (broiled).

Below: Mâconnais is often topped with chopped Muscat raisins.

Above: Grilled Crottin de Chavignol is the basis of the classic chèvre salad.

MÂCONNAIS

Small and elegant, this cheese can be made from cow's or goat's milk – or a mixture – depending on the season. When young, it has a dense, flaky interior. The subtle hint of tarragon in the flavour recalls the fruitiness of a young Chardonnay, and the cheese is the perfect partner for a Mâcon white wine. Serve as a table cheese, or use for grilling (broiling) or in salads.

PÉRAIL

This *fermier* (farmhouse) or artisan cheese has the softest, most delicate of rinds with a nutty aroma. Inside there is an even softer, caramel-like centre that has the freshness of meadow flowers. The cheese has the sweet taste of sheep's milk.

PICODON DE L'ARDÈCHE/PICODON DE LA DRÔME (AOC)

The thin rind of this goat's milk cheese has the scent of stone cellars and the hard, compact interior is aromatic. The cheeses are occasionally packed with herbs in jars of the local green olive oil. Serve as a table cheese or use for grilling (broiling) or baking.

POIVRE D'ANE

This dense, fine-grained cheese has an aromatic scent and flavour. Any variation in this is due to the milk from which it is made: sheep's milk in spring and early summer, goat's milk from the end of spring to the start of autumn, and cow's milk virtually all year round. The natural rind is white with a hint of blue or yellow, traditionally covered with a sprig of wild savory. Serve as a table cheese or use for cooking.

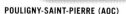

Above: Pérail is an attractive cheese made in 80–120g/3¼–4¼oz discs. Its pale, straw-coloured natural rind has a delicate pinkish tinge.

POULIGNY-SAINT-PIERRE (AOC)

This French chèvre, named after the eponymous village, is a distinctive truncated pyramid shape with a soft, wrinkled rind. It has earned itself various nicknames, the most common of which is the pyramid. To many people it epitomizes chèvre: it is wonderfully rustic, yet elegant. The rind is soft and ivory-coloured when the cheese is young. As it ages and dries, the rind becomes reddish-orange and acquires an array of beautiful moulds, which provide a contrast to the firm, pure white, slightly grainy interior. Tasting reveals a great complexity of flavours, including white wine and herbs, in particular tarragon, and a texture that is both creamy and nutty. A Pouligny-Saint-Pierre cheese with a red label was made in a dairy, while a green label indicates that the cheese is farmhouse-made.

Below: Pouligny-Saint-Pierre is a fine table cheese, goes well in salads and is good used for grilling.

Above: Picodon cheeses are similar to Pélardon cheese.

SAINT-MARCELLIN

This cheese is known to have been served to royalty as early as 1461. In those days it would probably have been made from goat's milk, but cow's milk is often used today. The texture of the young cheese varies from firm to very runny, and it has a mild, slightly salty flavour. When ripe, it is irresistible, with a slightly yeasty taste.

SAINTE-MAURE DE TOURAINE (AOC)

Sainte-Maure, a goat's milk cheese, is made both on small farms and in factories throughout Touraine. The freshly formed curd is scooped by hand into log-shaped moulds. Farmhouse cheeses have a piece of straw running through the centre. An ash coating provides a wonderful contrast to the stark white interior. Young cheeses are moist and grainy, but as the mould develops the cheese hardens and becomes more dense.

Below: (Left to right) Sancerre and Selles-sur-Cher are both classic, natural-rind goat's milk cheeses.

Above: Saint-Marcellin, a round cheese with a wrinkly rind, is dusted with a coating of white yeast. With age, a delicate blue mould and red and yellow pigments develop.

SANCERRE

This classic chèvre has a fine, wrinkled cream-coloured rind that hardens over time. It has a light, goaty smell and a slightly grainy texture that becomes dense and smooth. There is a fresh "white wine" fruitiness to the young Sancerre and a strong, nutty, goaty taste when aged. The white wine of the region is a perfect partner for this excellent table cheese.

SELLES-SUR-CHER (AOC)

The Loire is famous for its goat's milk cheeses. They come in a wide array of shapes – pyramids, rounds, truncated cones, hearts, logs and cylinders – but all have the same natural, blue-grey rind and many are lightly dusted with wood ash. Selles-sur-Cher is a classic example. The ash, mixed with coarse salt, is sprinkled over the cheese, adding visual appeal while facilitating the draining of the whey. The concept was probably introduced in the eighth century by Saracen invaders.

TOMME DE ROMANS

These attractive little cheeses are sold in wooden trays lined with straw. They have a slightly sour, grassy flavour with a delicate, nutty finish.

VALENÇAY

This well-known French chèvre, an elegant pyramid dusted with fine black charcoal, comes from the Cher Valley. When young, the white cheese can be seen through the ash, but the colours gradually merge and blue-grey moulds appear. The taste is at first fresh and citrus-like, but age gives the cheese a nuttier flavour and a distinctly goaty character. The commercially produced version is known as Pyramide.

BLUE CHEESES

These are neither pressed nor cooked. Most frequently, the curd is crumbled, eliminating much of the whey, then scooped into moulds. The blue mould is a strain of penicillium that is added to the milk before the rennet. Thin rods are threaded into the cheese, introducing air and causing the cheese to turn blue. The blue grows along the tunnels and into the nooks and crannies between the loose curd, producing the shattered porcelain look that typifies blue cheese.

UNITED KINGDOM

Stilton stands out as the jewel of British blue cheeses, but there are also some excellent modern cheeses based on traditional recipes from the past.

Below: Blue Vinny (back) and Blue Wensleydale (front) are both modern revivals based on old, traditional recipes.

Left: Beenleigh Blue is one of only three blue sheep's milk cheeses made in Great Britain.

BEENLEIGH BLUE (ENGLAND)

This moist and crumbly cheese has blue-green streaks through the white interior, and the typical burnt-caramel taste of fine sheep's milk cheese. Beenleigh blue melts on the palate, disclosing its strong, spicy flavour. It should be enjoyed as a table cheese and is good served with mead or sweet cider. It is suitable for vegetarians.

BLUE VINNY (ENGLAND)

This cheese is a revival of an old Dorset cheese. *Vinny* is the Old English word for veining, and the blue of the cheese comes from the family of penicillium moulds that occur naturally in the air. In the past, these spontaneously invaded the young, moist, open-textured curd, but today the blueing is not left to chance and the mould is added directly to the unpasteurized cow's milk. It is suitable for vegetarians.

BLUE WENSLEYDALE (ENGLAND)

This is a variation of the famous hard cheese from Yorkshire. Based on an original recipe that dates back to the eleventh century, it has recently been revived by several creameries in the Yorkshire Dales. Firmer than most blues and slightly crumbly, Blue Wensleydale has a spicy, blue tang with a slightly bitter, dark chocolate and chicory finish. It is suitable for vegetarians.

BUXTON BLUE (ENGLAND)

This firm pale orange cheese, interlaced with fine blue streaks, was created in 1994 to meet the growing demand from consumers and supermarkets for new cheeses. Buxton Blue is crumbly rather than hard. It has a milder flavour than most blue cheeses and has a hint of chocolate and burnt onions on the finish. It is suitable for vegetarians.

HARBOURNE BLUE (ENGLAND)

From Devon, Harbourne Blue is one of only three English hard, blue, goat's milk cheeses. The aroma suggests tropical fruit and it finishes with the hot, spicy tang associated with blues. It is produced in large, 5kg/11lb rounds and has a crusty, natural rind with some moulding. Suitable for vegetarians.

Above: Buxton Blue can be eaten as a table cheese or crumbled into soups.

SHROPSHIRE BLUE (ENGLAND)

Despite its name, this fairly new cow's milk cheese was invented in Scotland and then introduced to the Stilton makers in England. Shropshire Blue is made in large 8kg/18lb cylinders and has a crusty, deep orange-brown rind. The cheese is similar in style to Stilton but is distinguished by the wonderful, orange colour, created by the addition of the natural dye, annatto. The royal blue of the mould provides an attractive colour contrast. A good Shropshire Blue has a wonderful blue cheese taste, combined with an underlying hint of rich, buttery burnt caramel. It is suitable for vegetarians.

Above: Striking Shropshire Blue looks superb on a cheese board.

STILTON (ENGLAND)

In the early 1900s, Stilton makers formed an association to control how this cheese should be made. They also specified where Stilton could be made – only in Derbyshire, Nottinghamshire and Leicestershire. Stilton is punctuated with tiny holes where it has been pierced by stainless-steel needles to allow air to penetrate. The perfect Stilton should have the blue mould spreading out to the rind so that it looks like shattered porcelain. It should be rich and creamy with a clean, lasting, tangy finish. It is suitable for vegetarians.

BLUE RATHGORE (IRELAND)

Blue goat's milk cheeses are rare worldwide, but Britain boasts several, including Rathgore from County Antrim, which was created in 1989 to supply local and American markets. Problems with supply meant that production almost ceased until 1995, when the producer decided to start again. The cheese is moist and crumbly with a smattering of blue, giving it a spicy, slightly burnt taste. Through the blue you can still identify the almondy freshness of the goat's milk. It is good served as a table cheese or added to dressings. It is suitable for vegetarians.

CASHEL BLUE (IRELAND)

This cheese is made by Jane and Louis Grubb under the shadow of the Rock of Cashel, a bold outcrop overlooking the Tipperary plains. The milk comes from their own pedigree herd. When young, Cashel Blue is firm yet moist, with just a hint of fresh tarragon and white wine. With age, its true character emerges, mellowing to a rounder, more spicy style. The interior softens, then when the cheese is at the peak of perfection it collapses, providing a challenge for the retailer but a treat for the connoisseur. It is wonderful spread on warm walnut bread. It is available pasteurized, unpasteurized, vegetarian and non-vegetarian. It matures in 8–14 weeks.

DUNSYRE BLUE (SCOTLAND)

From Lanarkshire, this cheese is wrapped in foil to keep its rind moist. When aged, the smooth creamy-coloured interior is penetrated by chunky streaks of blue-green mould which imparts a spicy flavour to the cheese. The flavour is suggestive of the clover and grasses of the pastures where the cows graze. It is suitable for vegetarians.

LANARK BLUE (SCOTLAND)

This modern Roquefort-style cheese is made by Humphrey Errington, the same cheese-maker who produces Dunsyre Blue. He was the first person this century to milk sheep commercially in Scotland. Made using sheep's milk, the cheese has an aromatic, slightly sweet yet pungent flavour. The superb green-blue veins spreading through the cheese are the result of a Roquefort mould having been sprinkled into the vat before the cheese is curdled. It is then moulded by hand and left to mature for three months. This table cheese is suitable for vegetarians.

Below: Stilton is delicious eaten with Port at the end of a meal.

FRANCE

Some of the finest blue cheeses are made in France, of which Roquefort is probably one of the best-known.

BLEU D'AUVERGNE (AOC)

Named after the mountainous region where it is made, this moist, creamy cheese resembles Roquefort, although it is made with cow's milk. It has a piquant smell and a sharp, clean taste with a hint of herbs and butter. Bleu d'Auvergne is now made by large creameries, but the AOC regulations ensure that tradition is retained.

BLEU DU HAUT JURA (AOC)

Unlike most blue cheeses, this is made in the shape of a large, flat wheel which speeds the ripening process. The result is a cheese that is more supple and less creamy than other blues, with a mild taste. All blues made in the region are now officially named Bleu de Haut Jura.

BLEU DE LAQUEUILLE

This unpasteurized blue cheese comes in medium or large cylinders and is like a smaller version of Fourme d'Ambert. The blue is chunky rather than in streaks and the flavour is spicy, fresh and creamy, with a slightly salty tang.

BLEU DES CAUSSES (AOC)

This cheese is made in the Rouergue region and shares many similarities with its compatriot, Roquefort, except that it is made using cow's, rather than sheep's, milk. Like Roquefort, it is matured in limestone caves, where the natural fissures in the cave, called *fleurines*, allow fresh air currents to circulate and move the natural moulds through the ripening cheese. The result is a cheese that is firm-textured, but moister and spicier in flavour than other French blues. Fresh-tasting, with a sharp finish, it is a good, less salty alternative to Roquefort.

BRESSE BLEU

Developed during World War II, Bresse Bleu became popular as an alternative to stronger blue cheeses. The interior is rich and buttery. Like Brie, it melts in the mouth, and has a sweet, slightly spicy tang. Because of its dense, creamy nature, the blue mould must be injected into the cheese, rather than being added to the milk before coagulation. It forms pockets of blue-grey mould rather than fine streaks. Tiny mould spores from the rind may be carried into the cheese, forming patches of fluffy white mould within the cheese. Individual cheeses are small, so can be sold whole rather than in slices. Convenient packaging means that Bresse Bleu travels well and is widely available outside its country of origin.

Below: (Clockwise from bottom left) Bleu de Laqueuille, Bleu d'Auvergne, Bleu des Causses, Bleu du Haut Jura

Above: Fourme d'Ambert is easily recognized by its unusually tall, cylindrical shape.

Left: Roquefort is a superb table cheese and is widely used in dressings.

ROQUEFORT (AOC)

For over 2,000 years, shepherds have been maturing their cheeses in the deep limestone caves of Cambalou, which are famous for the blue moulds that exist naturally in the air. The traditional way of introducing the mould was to allow it to grow on loaves of rye bread placed beside the cheeses in the caves, and a version of this method is still practised by some cheese-makers today. Roquefort has a distinct bouquet and a flavour that combines the sweet, burnt-caramel taste of sheep's milk with the sharp, metallic tang of the blue mould. Crumbly, melt-in-the-mouth, refreshing, clean – all these words have been used to describe this great cheese.

SAINT-AGUR

Created in 1986, Saint-Agur is made from pasteurized milk and has a moist, creamy texture and spicy, blue-cheese taste. It is milder than most other French blue cheeses, with the mould evenly spread in patches.

Left: Saint-Agur is a modern cheese made in a distinctive hexagonal shape.

FOURME D'AMBERT

This cow's milk cheese is more supple and dense than most blues. The mould gathers in erratic patches rather than the more usual streaks and the flavour is savoury and slightly nutty.

OLIVET BLEU

This cow's milk cheese, made in 300g/11oz discs, is slightly grainy, with a distinct aroma and a taste of mushrooms, and a salty finish. Olivet Bleu resembles a mild Camembert. The word *bleu* refers to the rind, which is so white that it has an almost blue tinge.

ITALY

The most famous Italian blue cheeses are Dolcelatte and Gorgonzola. They are very good served as table cheeses and can be used in cooking.

DOLCELATTE

The word *dolcelatte* means sweet milk and the cheese has a luscious, sweet taste. Deliciously soft, it melts like ice cream in the mouth. The cheese appeals to those who find the more traditional blue cheeses such as Gorgonzola too strongly flavoured and robust.

Above: Deliciously mild Dolcelatte is also sometimes known as Gorgonzola Dolce (meaning sweet Gorgonzola).

DOLCELATTE TORTA

Created relatively recently, this cheese consists of thick layers of mascarpone cream alternating with the mild Italian blue cheese Dolcelatte. The cream mellows the blue cheese and Dolcelatte Torta has a texture more like ice cream than cheese. Dolcelatte Torta is really too rich to serve with

Above: Pungent Gorgonzola is also one of the world's oldest blue cheeses.

ordinary wine, but it is delicious accompanied by a smooth fortified wine, such as Madeira, or even a sweet Italian dessert wine to cut the richness. It is served as a table cheese, used in dips and spreads and over pasta.

GORGONZOLA (DOC)

Probably the most famous of Italy's blue cheeses, made by over 80 producers, Gorgonzola has become one of the world's finest blues. According to some, it was discovered inadvertently by an innkeeper in Gorgonzola, who found that his young Stracchino cheese had turned blue after a few weeks in his cool, damp cellars. The little village from which the cheese takes its name has long been subsumed by the city of Milan, although production is still concentrated in Lombardy. The greenish-blue penicillium mould imparts a sharp, spicy flavour and provides an excellent contrast to the rich, creamy cheese. It is usually sold wrapped in foil to keep it moist. A fine table cheese, Gorgonzola is also widely used in dressings and salads, and on freshly cooked pasta and gnocchi.

Left: Dolcelatte Torta is a deliciously rich and attractive-looking cheese.

OTHER BLUE CHEESES

Around the rest of the world, a number of other blue cheeses are made. Some of the best are listed here.

CAMBAZOLA (GERMANY)

This cheese is a modern success story. Since its creation in the 1970s, others have tried to copy it, but few have achieved the consistency of quality and texture. As the name implies, it is based on Camembert and Gorgonzola, and appeals to those who find other blue cheeses too ferocious, but still enjoy a little bite. The smooth, rich texture is achieved by adding cream to the milk, and the taste is slightly sweet-sour.

DANISH BLUE (DENMARK)

This cheese was developed as an alternative to Roquefort, although the cheeses are very different. The appeal of Danish Blue lies in its sharp, almost metallic taste, salty bite and creamy feel in the mouth. The interior is very white and makes an attractive contrast to the blue-black mould, which has a rather gritty texture and salty taste.

Right: Maytag Blue has a creamy texture and a fine depth of flavour. This is, in part, a result of the maturing process in cellars built into the side of a hill.

MYCELLA (DENMARK)

Often known as Danish Gorgonzola, this mild blue cheese takes its name from the mould that gives it its thin strands of greenish-blue: *Penicillium mycellium*. The veins in the cheese provide a pretty contrast to the very pale, creamy, almost buttery interior.

BERGÈRE BLEUE (UNITED STATES)

Made in New York State, Bergère Bleue is a Roquefort-style cheese with a rich aroma of lanolin and yeast. It melts in the mouth like butter, releasing the flavour of burnt caramel. The blue-green streaks give a spicy piquancy to the pale lemon-coloured cheese, which is moist and slightly crumbly.

MAYTAG BLUE (UNITED STATES)

Maytag Blue is made in the state of Iowa. It has a dense, crumbly texture, and, like Roquefort, it melts in the mouth, revealing a spicy flavour from the fine streaks of blue-grey mould that are scattered throughout the creamy, moist cheese. The finish is deliciously hot. It is suitable for vegetarians.

Above: Mild Cambazola is based on Camembert and Gorgonzola.

GIPPSLAND BLUE (AUSTRALIA)

This cheese is produced by the Tarago River Cheese Company in Victoria and is one of the country's finest and best-known blue cheeses. Using milk from their own herd, and occasionally making their own starter cultures, the Tarago River Cheese Company has adapted methods learnt in Europe to their own climate and grazing conditions. It was probably the first genuine farmhouse cheese to be made in Australia.

Gippsland Blue resembles Dolcelatte: it is sharp, yet sweet and buttery, with a spicy, lingering, blue-cheese tang. The chunky veins spread unevenly through the dense rich cheese. Shadows of Blue is milder than Gippsland Blue, with a Brie-like texture and taste, whereas Blue Orchid has a somewhat more vicious, intense nature.

MEREDITH BLUE

Although described as Roquefort-style, Meredith Blue is a mild and creamy blue cheese with a unique character. The sweetness of the sheep's milk comes through the distinct and spicy but not overly strong finish. This is a table cheese, available only seasonally.

FRESH CHEESES

These mild, soft cheeses are normally made from the warmed curds of milk. Lactic cheeses such as fromage frais are the simplest of all, requiring nothing but the addition of a souring culture to increase the acidity and give the cheese its characteristic sharp flavour. Most fresh cheeses, however, use rennet or a vegetarian alternative to set the cheese. The fresh cheese is placed in a sack or a small perforated container and is allowed to drain. Since no pressure is applied, the curd retains much of the whey and it is the moisture in the whey that determines how soft the cheese will be. Whey cheeses, the most famous of which is ricotta, are made solely from the thin liquid left over from making harder cheeses. These are relatively low in fat, but other fresh cheeses can be alarmingly high in fat, depending on whether full-fat (whole) or semi-skimmed (low-fat) milk has been used.

UNITED KINGDOM

The recipes for some fresh cheeses date back hundreds of years, while others are more recent creations.

BUTTON AND INNES (ENGLAND)

This modern, soft, mousse-like cheese comes from Staffordshire. It is one of Britain's finest goat's milk cheeses, with a texture that dissolves on the palate, and a flavour trailing a hint of almonds, honey and lemon. It is also available dusted with ash, pink peppercorns, nuts or herbs. It is suitable for vegetarians.

CERNEY

Named after the pretty Gloucestershire village of Cerney, this distinctive, fresh cheese is made from unpasteurized goat's milk. It has a mild, zingy, citrus taste, with a delicate goaty finish. The light, moist texture resembles fromage frais. Each of the small, truncated cones, weighing 240g/8½oz, is hand-made, and dusted with a fine layer of oak ash and salt. There are a number of variations, including Cerney Smoked, Cerney Pepper and Cerney Village.

Right: (Clockwise from top) Rosary Herb Log, Round and Dazel.

CORNISH PEPPER AND CORNISH HERB AND GARLIC (ENGLAND)

These large round cheeses are rich and moist, one sprinkled with peppercorns, the other mixed with herbs and garlic and rolled in chopped parsley. They are suitable for vegetarians.

OLDE YORK (ENGLAND)

This sheep's milk cheese resembles feta without the saltiness. It is creamy and soft and has a lemony zest and acidity offset by the subtle sweetness of sheep's milk. It is suitable for vegetarians.

PERROCHE (ENGLAND)

This fresh goat's-milk cheese has a subtle goaty taste that is clean and slightly almondy. The high moisture content gives it a light, fluffy texture but a short shelf-life. It is also made with herbs, such as tarragon, rosemary and thyme, and comes in small rounds or larger logs. Suitable for vegetarians.

ROSARY (ENGLAND)

Delicate, moist, soft and creamy, Rosary is subtly flavoured by the sprig of fresh herbs that is used as a decoration. Rosary Plain matures in one to two weeks, and has a fat content of 45 per cent. Flavoured versions include Rosary Herb Log, Rosary Round and Rosary Dazel. They are all suitable for vegetarians.

Above: Perroche may be plain (centre), or flavoured with herbs.

SUSSEX SLIPCOTE (ENGLAND)

The recipe for this unusual cheese is said to date back to the time of Shakespeare, the name deriving from the tendency of the young curd to mature too fast and slip out of its cheesecloth coat. The cheese is made from unpasteurized sheep's milk, the curd ladled into moulds with sufficient whey to give the finished cheese its light, mousse-like texture and refreshing, citrus acidity. It is sold in 115g/4oz rounds or in larger logs. Three varieties are available: plain, garlic and herb, and cracked peppercorn. They are all suitable for vegetarians.

VULSCOMBE (ENGLAND)

This fresh cheese from Devon is small and round. Vulscombe is unusual in that rennet is not used to separate the milk; coagulation occurs purely through the acidity of the milk. The cheese is moist but creamy and has a fresh, lemon-sorbet taste and just the merest hint of goat's milk. It is good served as a table cheese and may be used for grating. It is suitable for vegetarians.

CABOC (SCOTLAND)

This large chubby log-shaped cheese is rolled in oatmeal. Made with cream-enriched milk, it is buttery and wickedly rich, tempered by the toasted oats which give it a nutty, yeasty flavour. An indigenous Scottish cheese, still made to an ancient recipe, it was said to have been created by Mariota de Ile, daughter of a fifteenth-century MacDonald, Lord of the Isles. When she was 12 years old, she was in danger of being abducted by the Campbells, who planned to marry her to one of their own and seize her lands. She escaped to Ireland, learned how to make cheese

Left: Pant ys Gawn may be flavoured with herbs, garlic, chives or peppercorns.

and brought back the knowledge to her people. Caboc was popular for many years, then went into decline. It was revived by Susannah Stone, a descendant of Mariota, in 1962. It is mostly used as a table cheese, spread on oatcakes or bread. It is suitable for vegetarians.

CROWDIE (SCOTLAND)

Thought to have been introduced into Scotland by the Vikings in the eighth century, Crowdie, which comes either in logs or packed into tubs, has a slightly sour flavour, yet with a creamy, crumbly texture. A variation of Crowdie called *Gruth Dhu* (Black Crowdie), made with double cream, formed into oval shapes and covered with toasted pinhead oats and crushed peppercorns, is also available. It is suitable for vegetarians.

GALLOWAY'S GOAT (SCOTLAND)

This cheese, as the name suggests, comes from Scotland. The tiny, pure white balls of fresh goat's cheese are marinated with fresh herbs and garlic in jars of olive oil. Although the garlic is the overriding flavour, you can still identify the freshness of the herbs and the lemony character of the milk.

PANT YS GAWN (WALES)

This small, delightful goat's-milk cheese, shaped in discs or logs, has a very clean, fresh citrus flavour with a hint of tarragon. The texture resembles that of fromage frais. The soft moist curds are carefully drained in tiny moulds and are ready for sale in a few days, yet with clever packaging the cheeses have a remarkably long shelf-life. It is suitable for vegetarians.

Left: (Clockwise from top left) Vulscombe is available flavoured with herbs and garlic, topped with crushed peppercorns, or plain.

FRANCE

One of the simplest of all fresh cheeses is the French fromage frais, but France produces a number of other wonderful fresh cheeses as well.

BOULETTE D'AVESNES

This soft cheese comes from the north of France. It was traditionally made from buttermilk, but today is normally factory-made using milk, and has a fairly doughy texture. The small pyramid-shaped cheeses are red on the outside, achieved by the use of annatto or paprika, while the soft curd inside has been kneaded and mashed with parsley, tarragon, pepper and paprika to give the cheese a spicy flavour.

BOURSIN

This familiar foil-wrapped cheese is made using rich Normandy milk and cream, and so it is a high-fat cheese. It has a moist, creamy texture and sweet, rich flavour with a hint of acidity. It is among the few fresh cheeses made without rennet, using only a starter culture, which may account for its pleasant acidity. As well as the original cheese, there are several variations, including ones flavoured with garlic and herbs or cracked peppercorns. They are all suitable for vegetarians.

Below: Boulette d'Avesnes is an outrageously spicy cow's milk cheese.

Above: Boursin is a delicious, sweet, rich, creamy cheese that is equally suitable for spreading, baking and serving as a table cheese.

FIGUE

This very pretty fresh chèvre is made in the Aquitaine area of France. Mild and pure with a lemony acidity and the characteristic flavour of goat's milk, it is normally dusted with salt and ash, paprika or herbs.

FROMAGE FRAIS

This is one of the first cheeses made by man and is probably the simplest of fresh cheeses. Traditionally French, it is now made in many countries. Instead of rennet, the milk is coagulated using a bacterial culture, similar to that used for yogurt. The cheese is very soft and high in moisture, with a consistency not unlike whipped cream. It has a pleasant, slightly citrus flavour and can be used in cooking as well as for serving with fresh fruit or as a spread. Low-fat (*maigre*), double (*allégé*) and full-fat (*triple crème*) varieties are available. Fromage frais may be made with cow's, goat's and sheep's milk. It is suitable for vegetarians.

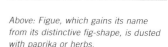

Above: Figue, which gains its name from its distinctive fig-shape, is dusted with paprika or herbs.

Left: Fromage frais varies in consistency from light and pourable to thick and quite firm, depending on the fat content.

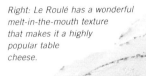

Right: Le Roulé has a wonderful melt-in-the-mouth texture that makes it a highly popular table cheese.

LE ROULÉ

The familiar logs of Le Roulé, with their green swirl of herbs and garlic, were introduced in the mid-1980s by the French company Fromagerie Triballat. The logs come in various sizes, and there are many exotic and eye-catching combinations: salmon and dill, chives, and even strawberries. Made with cow's milk, it is mostly eaten as a table cheese. It is suitable for vegetarians.

Below: Pélardon, a fresh cheese made from unpasteurized goat's milk, is made in several areas in the Languedoc.

PÉLARDON

Softer and more mousse-like than most goat's milk cheeses, the flavour of Pélardon suggests soured cream infused with walnut oil. When aged, the wrinkled, mould-covered rind has a distinct goaty aroma and an intense Brazil-nut sweetness.

PETIT-SUISSE

This cheese was invented by a Swiss cheese-maker called Charles Gervais in the nineteenth century. He decided to make a variation on the local cheese, Neufchâtel, by adding cream to the fresh curd and selling the result before the soft white rind could develop. The light, yet creamy texture and charming shape made Petit-Suisse an instant and major success.

RIGOTTE

These attractive cheeses come from the uplands of the Auvergne and Lyonnais area of France. They are made with unpasteurized cow's or goat's milk, according to the season; sometimes they are made with a mixture of both. They are at their best between mid-April and mid-November. Made in little cylinders, the rind is lightly coloured with annatto. Firm and grainy when a few weeks old, with a mild, lemony freshness, Rigotte becomes quite tart if allowed to dry. Some dry cheeses are marinated in aromatic oils flavoured with peppers and fresh herbs. The cheese absorbs the flavours while becoming creamier and the result is strangely reminiscent of saucisson or salami. Rigotte is also sometimes cured in wine. Known as *fromage fort*, these cured cheeses are best eaten with bread or toast. Rigottes that are matured in humid conditions develop the classic pale blue moulds. They acquire a nuttier flavour but still retain a slight bitterness of taste. Rigotte is good for grilling (broiling), goes well in salads and is a fine table cheese.

Below: Rigotte is produced in cylinders weighing 70–90g/2¾–3½oz and has a lightly coloured rind.

ITALY

Fresh cheeses are much used in Italian cooking. Mozzarella and ricotta are among the most famous, and the most versatile. They are used for pasta, pizzas, pastries and added to salads.

CRESCENZA

The texture of this square, or rectangular, cow's milk cheese from Lombardy varies considerably from one brand to another. The best examples are reputed to come from around Milan or Pavia. They are sold within a few days of making, wrapped in white waxed paper, and have a squidgy, moist texture and a fresh, clean acidity not unlike that of yogurt. Other cheeses can be more rubbery, jelly-like or even mushy, and low-fat varieties can be grainy. Crescenza should be ripened for no longer than 10 days, and eaten as soon as possible after that.

MASCARPONE

Technically speaking, mascarpone is not a cheese at all, but is rather a matured cream. Made from the cream skimmed off the milk used in making Parmesan, it is nevertheless described as a curd cheese and is similar to a cream cheese, although it is thicker and more buttery. Originally made in Tuscany and Lombardy, Mascarpone is

Left: Mascarpone is rich and luscious with a silky smooth texture that is particularly good for desserts.

now popular all over Italy and is the main ingredient of the most sensuous of Italian desserts, tiramisù. Rich and creamy, mascarpone is one of the richest fresh cheeses with a fat content of 75 per cent. It has an unassertive flavour, which means it is excellent in both sweet and savoury dishes and can also be served as a good alternative to double (heavy) cream. It is suitable for vegetarians.

MOZZARELLA

Mozzarella is probably the most famous of Italian fresh cheeses. It is a soft and springy white cheese with a mild flavour and is known as a stretched curd cheese, whereby the young curd is heated in the whey before it is stretched or kneaded until the strings do not break when they are stretched. Like most fresh cheeses, mozzarella is used to add texture rather than a specific taste to a dish. The juices, oils and flavours of the other ingredients are absorbed and intensified by the mild moist, open

layers of the spun curd. It is this, together with the fact that mozzarella melts to become wonderfully elastic, that has made it such a popular cheese.

A traditional mozzarella is made using water buffalo's milk, although increasingly cow's milk is used. Both have a mild flavour, but the cow's milk version is normally not as soft nor as delicately flavoured as that made from water buffalo's milk. The cheese is sold in whey, and should be floppy rather than rubbery and have moisture trapped between the layers of springy curd. If the cheese is lightly smoked it is called mozzarella affumicata. Blocks of mozzarella, which are sold in packets and are hard and rubbery, are adequate for only pizzas, but will never equal the fresh cheese in taste. Fresh mozzarella should be stored in water in the refrigerator and eaten within two days.

Right: Mozzarella is an excellent cooking cheese.

Making Tricolour Salad

For two people you need 150g/5oz of fresh mozzarella cheese, 4 large plum tomatoes, and an avocado.

1 Slice the cheese and tomatoes and arrange on two plates. Sprinkle with salt and leave for 30 minutes.

2 Slice the avocado and arrange on top. Sprinkle with chopped basil, olive oil and pepper and serve.

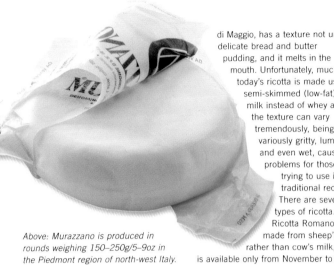

Above: Murazzano is produced in rounds weighing 150–250g/5–9oz in the Piedmont region of north-west Italy.

MURAZZANO (DOC)

This traditional farmhouse cheese is named for the village where it is made. It is pale and round, individually wrapped with a fine pale yellow rind. Although delicious as a table cheese, it is most often melted on pizzas or crostini or used in sauces and pastries. It is made of a mixture of cow's and sheep's milk. The texture is delicate and supple, and the taste fresh and milky with just a hint of the caramel that is characteristic of sheep's milk. Murazzano ripens in 4–5 days and has a fat content of 45 per cent.

RICOTTA

Ricotta is the most famous whey cheese, and is one of Italy's most delightful traditional cheeses. The whey is heated until milk solids come to the surface as small white lumps and these are skimmed off and drained in woven baskets. The result is a soft, moist, basin-shaped cheese that has a fat content of around 20 per cent.

Good ricotta should be firm, not solid, and consist of a mass of fine, moist, delicate grains, neither salted nor ripened. One of the finest, Fior di Maggio, has a texture not unlike delicate bread and butter pudding, and it melts in the mouth. Unfortunately, much of today's ricotta is made using semi-skimmed (low-fat) milk instead of whey and the texture can vary tremendously, being variously gritty, lumpy and even wet, causing problems for those trying to use it in a traditional recipe. There are several types of ricotta. Ricotta Romano is made from sheep's rather than cow's milk, and is available only from November to June. Ricotta Salata, which resembles feta, is salted and dried. Smoked ricotta is a speciality of northern Italy, while Sicily produces Ricotta Infornata, which is baked in the oven until it is lightly browned. Ricotta can be served as a dessert cheese with sugar and fruit, or used in a wide range of pasta and pastry recipes.

ROBIOLA DI ROCCAVERANO (DOC)

This traditional goat's milk cheese made in the village of Roccaverano in Lombardy, was once made exclusively of goat's milk, but is nowadays made of a mixture of cow's and goat's milk. Some Robiola di Roccaverano is still made on farms for family consumption, but the majority is made in small co-operatives, using pasteurized milk. The cheese can be eaten fresh, at just a few days old, when it is pure white, sweet and very moist, or once it has matured for up to 20 days. The mature cheese becomes pink to orange and takes on a sharper taste, but still retains the subtle taste characteristic of a goat's milk cheese. The pasteurized cheese is spreadable, with a smooth texture. It has a sweet-sour aroma and a taste that resembles melted butter, but can be quite salty. The unpasteurized cheese has a more complex flavour and a piquant aroma. Robiola di Roccaverano is eaten as a table cheese, and is also used in baking, for spreading, and for adding texture and flavour to sauces.

Left: (From left to right) Ricotta Salata and fresh ricotta

OTHER FRESH CHEESES

In other countries around the world, fresh cheeses are also made. Greek Feta is one of these, and has been made for centuries.

CUAJADA (SPAIN)

This Spanish fresh cheese originally came from northern Navarre, where the shepherds used the local thistle rather than animal rennet to coagulate the milk. This gave the cheese a unique floppier consistency in contrast to the modern equivalent, which is made by adding rennet to fresh milk and then heating it gently. The mixture is poured into small earthenware pots to set. In Spain, Cuajada is often served for breakfast with honey or fruit.

Above: Quark is soft and moist and is similar in flavour and texture to a very thick strained yogurt.

QUARK (GERMANY)

The word *quark* simply means curd. The cheese is said to date from the Iron Age, when nomadic tribes discovered the means of fermenting milk without the use of rennet. Quark can be made from whole, semi-skimmed (low-fat) or skimmed milk, or even buttermilk. It ripens within a few days. Soft and moist, like a cross between yogurt and fromage frais, it should taste lemon-fresh. Some versions have skimmed milk powder added and can be rather gritty. Quark is very versatile and can be used for spreading on bread, cooking, in cheesecakes, or served with fruit for breakfast. It is suitable for vegetarians.

PRINC'JEAN (BELGIUM)

This rindless, round, triple cream, cow's milk cheese has a rich texture. There is a crushed peppercorn version as well as a softer type, which has a white rind and creamy flavour. The small 150g/5oz round cheeses are packed into small, wooden crates for sale.

JUUSTOLEIPÄ (FINLAND)

This farmhouse cheese from Finland is quite distinctive, owing to its charred surface. It is made either from cow's or reindeer's milk. The curds are drained and pressed into rounds which are then held in front of a fire until the outer layer becomes toasted. The cheese has a mild flavour and creamy texture that contrasts with the charred crusty surface. It is served for breakfast or as a dessert.

Above: Juustoleipä is a speciality of Finland and Lappland.

BEYAZ PEYNIR (TURKEY)

Similar to feta, this traditional pure white, rindless cheese is the most popular of Turkey's cheeses. It is made throughout the country in factories, co-operatives and by shepherds. Vegetable rennet is used to clot the milk, then the curds are pressed for a few hours, chopped and strained, sometimes in attractive wooden or woven moulds. After draining, the cheese is cut into slices before being salted and covered with brine. It is usually stored in brine for more than six months, and is soaked in water or milk before use to remove excess salt. It is suitable for vegetarians.

Left: Cuajada is made using sheep's or goat's milk and is often served with fruit or honey.

FETA (GREECE)

This very simple cheese has an ancient pedigree, being first made by nomadic tribes needing to preserve the milk of their flocks of sheep and goats. In the *Odyssey*, Homer gives a detailed description of how the cheese is made, and virtually the same recipe and method is still used today. When the cheese is firm enough, it is cut into slices, liberally sprinkled with salt and then, after drying, packed into barrels and covered with brine. Feta will keep almost indefinitely stored in this way.

Feta can be made with cow's, goat's or sheep's milk or with any combination of the three. The creamy-white cheese is made in various shapes and sizes, though is often loaf-shaped, and has a smooth texture and no rind. Most feta that is sold commercially is made from pasteurized milk, but in rural parts of Greece, Turkey and Bulgaria, it is possible to find excellent feta that reflects the diversity and character of the milk from animals that graze the wild mountain pastures. Soak feta in cold fresh water or milk if you wish to remove some of its saltiness.

Below: Feta comes in various shapes and sizes but it is often loaf-shaped.

Right: Turkish Beyaz Peynir is popularly baked in many local dishes.

HALLOUMI (CYPRUS)

This stretched curd cheese is made in the eastern Mediterranean, Eastern Europe and the Middle East. It comes in small blocks, is shiny and white, and is often flavoured with chopped mint, adding flavour to an otherwise rather bland cheese. It has a fibrous, rubbery texture which is particularly suited to cooking. It can be sliced, then fried or grilled (broiled). In recent years it has become more popular, particularly among young chefs of Australia, New Zealand and the West Coast of the United States.

BRINZA/BURDUF BRINZA (ROMANIA)

This ancient sheep's milk, whose origins go back to Roman times, has been made for centuries. The white cheese is made in blocks and has a mild, moist, crumbly and slightly grainy texture. It is usually eaten within a few days of making, when it has a delicate, sweet character, but some is preserved in salt for use during winter, when it more closely resembles feta.

LIPTAUER (HUNGARY)

The Hungarians developed this cheese from a simple, white sheep's milk cheese called Liptoi, which was made by mountain shepherds. Liptauer may be made from cow's or sheep's milk and is spiced with paprika and sold in pots. Additional ingredients can include onions, caraway seeds, capers, or other ingredients, the proportions of which remain a closely guarded secret. Each family often has its own recipe.

LIPTOI (HUNGARY)

This white, mousse-like, sheep's milk cheese has been made by shepherds in the Tatra mountains for centuries. It has a subtle, sweet flavour and is mixed with various spices and herbs. There are as many recipes for this cheese as there are makers, as the recipes have been handed down from one generation to the next.

SIRENE (BULGARIA)

This traditional moist, crumbly cheese has a fresh lemony flavour and can be used in salads or as a table cheese, as well as in baking and spreads. It is normally made from unpasteurized sheep's or cow's milk.

CAPRIOLE BANON (UNITED STATES)

This delightful fresh goat's milk cheese comes from Indiana. The 185g/6½oz discs are wrapped in marinated chestnut leaves and look like exquisitely wrapped gifts. The aroma of the leaves permeates the soft creamy curd to really wonderful effect, creating a sensational blend of flavours. Capriole Banon is excellent served as a table cheese.

CHÈVRE DE PROVENCE (UNITED STATES)

This wonderful farmhouse cheese from Alabama has been described as an American treasure. The subtle flavour of the tiny discs of fresh, lemony goat's milk cheese is enhanced by its being packed in a mixture of olive oil and fresh herbs. Serve as a table cheese or use for spreading, baking, grilling (broiling), and in salads.

Right: Capriole Banon is wrapped in chestnut leaves marinated in brandy and wine.

*Above:
Cream cheese has a very long shelf life compared to most fresh cheeses. It will keep well, stored in the refrigerator for up to 60 days, depending on the precise method used to make and preserve the cheese.*

COTTAGE CHEESE (UNITED STATES)

With its healthy eating image, cottage cheese is one of the most popular varieties of cheese in the United States and is the choice for anyone following a low-fat diet. This soft, bland cheese, which originated in Europe, is made by allowing milk to curdle naturally and then cutting the curds into tiny cubes. This is heated with the whey until it reaches the desired texture and is then drained and rinsed. Salt and a little milk or cream are routinely added and many varieties are flavoured. Cottage cheese can be used in cooking but is mainly used for making snacks and in salads.

CREAM CHEESE (UNITED STATES)

This mild, velvety-smooth cheese has a refreshing lemony zing balanced by the buttery richness of cream. There are many different types of cream cheese, including low-fat, medium-fat and full-fat versions. Each of these versions may be further flavoured with a range of other ingredients, including pineapple, ham, smoked salmon, prawns (shrimp) and chives. Low-fat varieties may have a slightly grainy texture, which results from the addition of whey-powder. Cream cheese is widely used in both sweet and savoury recipes and for spreads, dips and uncooked cheesecakes.

ASADERO (MEXICO)

This is one of the most famous Mexican cheeses and is similar to the Italian cheese Provolone. *Asadero* means fit for roasting, and the cheese is mostly used in grilled (broiled) or baked dishes as it melts superbly. Originally from Oaxaca on the Pacific coast – and sometimes referred to as *queso Oaxaca* – the cheese is now widely produced throughout Mexico. It comes in a variety of shapes, including loaves and plaits, or it may be shaped into balls. The size also varies considerably, ranging from 225g/8oz to 5kg/11lb.

QUESO BLANCO (MEXICO)

Meaning nothing more precise than white cheese, queso blanco is made in most Latin American countries and is a cross between mozzarella and salty cottage cheese. Traditionally,

Above: Asadero is a supple white cheese with a flavour that ranges from quite bland to buttery and sweet.

queso blanco was always made from skimmed milk or whey coagulated with lemon juice, although recently some creameries have begun making it with full-cream milk and rennet. It can be sliced and fried, grilled (broiled), baked and used in salads.

QUESO FRESCO (MEXICO)

Based on the Spanish cheese Burgos, Mexican queso fresco (meaning fresh cheese) is soft and breakable, rather than crumbly. It has a grainy texture and a very mild, fresh flavour. It is made from cow's or goat's milk. It holds its shape well when heated and is used for grilling (broiling), baking and in salads. It is eaten within a few days of making.

Left: Yarra Valley feta is sold packed into small cans, immersed in olive oil flavoured with fresh herbs.

YARRA VALLEY PYRAMID (AUSTRALIA)

This small, pyramid-shaped goat's milk cheese may be plain or covered in ash. It is creamy, lemon-fresh and slightly salty and melts in the mouth like ice cream. If left to age, the Yarra Valley Pyramid becomes firmer and may develop some mould. There is also a Yarra Valley feta, which is sold packed into small cans. The little balls of salty, moist cheese are immersed in olive oil and fresh herbs to give extra flavour.

HIPI ITI (NEW ZEALAND)

This cylinder-shaped, sheep's milk cheese is packed with herbs in jars of oil. It is crumbly like feta, but only slightly salty, and has a fresh, lemony flavour. It gradually absorbs the flavours of the herbs and oil in which it is packed.

Central and South American Cheeses
Cheese was unknown in Central and Southern America until Spanish and Portuguese missionaries arrived in the sixteenth and seventeenth centuries. As cheesemaking became established, it was the mild, fresh *queso blanco* that proved most popular, partly because it suited the diet of the people and partly because the cool temperatures made it less important to mature the cheese. In Peru, the locals suspended sacks or skins of curds over slow-burning wood fires to speed up the draining process. More recently, in Chile, there has been a move to imitate the sheep's milk cheese of the Pyrenees. In Argentina, Italian immigrants started making a Parmesan-style cheese called Treboligiano, and a mozzarella-type cheese called Moliterno. In Brazil most of the cheese is imported, but some local cheese is made in the Minas Gerais region, north of Rio de Janeiro.

CREATING A CHEESE BOARD

The habit of serving cheese before dessert is practised by the French for the simple reason that it enables red wine from the main course to be finished with the cheese. Sweet, dessert wine can then be served with the blue cheeses (which, because they have the strongest flavour, should be eaten last) and follows through to accompany the sweet dessert course.

A cheese board can also be served as a main course for lunch. Serve a selection of cheeses with a lightly dressed, mixed leaf salad, pickles or chutney, fresh fruit and nuts, plus country-style bread. If you like, serve a selection of wines.

• The best cheese board is the one chosen with care and enthusiasm and served on a wooden board with chunks of bread and a robust wine.

• One superb cheese is better than three or four small, mediocre wedges, which can look mean.
• However, if you can, choosing several cheeses from different categories means you will have a variety of flavours and textures.
• Colour should come from the rinds of the cheeses. Decorate the board, using chestnut or oak leaves, fresh herbs or wild flowers.
• Serve fresh, crusty, country-style breads with cheese or choose plain, lightly salted biscuits (crackers).
• Serve fresh fruit separately.
• There are some wonderful alternatives to the basic round wooden or marble cheese board. Experiment with wicker trays, shallow baskets, a piece of driftwood or a tray covered with a linen napkin and grape leaves.

• Shapes will add interest to your cheese board. Where possible avoid having all the shapes of the cheeses the same. Instead, choose pyramids, logs, squares and cylinders.

A GOOD CHEESE BOARD SELECTION

Queso del Montsec This pretty soft white goat's cheese from Spain would look spectacular on any cheese board.
Le Brin This is a velvety smooth, modern semi-soft French cheese. It makes an excellent table cheese.
Sancerre and Selles-sur-Cher Goat's cheeses make a very useful addition to any cheese board. Both of these go well with a fruity white wine.

Below: A good cheese board should consist of a variety of cheeses with different flavours, colours and textures.

Beenleigh Blue From Devon, this is best enjoyed as a table cheese. Serve with English bread such as a crusty farmhouse or cottage loaf.

Cooleeney and Croghan Both from Ireland, these cheeses would make a superb choice to end a special meal. Cooleeney is a Camembert-style cheese, while Croghan is a semi-soft, brine-washed goat's cheese.

CHEESE BOARD ACCOMPANIMENTS

Bread There are almost as many breads as there are cheeses. The best are home-made or country-style breads. Walnut and raisin breads and olive breads are favoured by some, but plain, simple breads are often a better choice for serving with cheese as they do not take away from the natural flavours and textures of the cheeses.

Nuts Europeans often serve their cheese with fresh walnuts, hazelnuts or almonds in the shell. Pre-shelled nuts rarely have the same sweetness or freshness and can taste musty.

Pickles Serving pickles or chutney with cheese is a very English habit. These accompaniments are suitable for hard, mature cheeses such as Cheddar but their strong, piquant flavour can overpower more subtle cheeses. The best pickles and chutneys for serving with cheese are home-made and sweet, rather than hot and spicy.

Fresh Fruit Serve seasonal, preferably local fruit. Citrus fruit is usually too sharp, and tropical fruit generally too sweet – apples, pears, grapes and figs with their distinct yet subtle flavours are the perfect choice. Their texture goes well with the creaminess of the cheese.

Dried Fruit Dried figs, prunes and raisins are delicious with all styles of cheese. The Spanish make a number of delicious fruit pastes or *"cheeses"* from quinces, figs, almonds and raisins. These are delicious served with all types of cheese, particularly hard cheeses made from sheep's milk.

Savoury Touches Serve spring onions (scallions), olives, celery, fresh beans and crisp greens such as rocket or long leaf lettuces alongside the cheese board to help cleanse the palate.

SERVING CHEESE WITH WINE

As a very general rule, the whiter and fresher the cheese, the crisper and fruitier the wine should be. The heavier, richer soft cheeses can be partnered with a robust, rounded white such as a Chardonnay or a light red. The harder and darker the cheese, the heavier and richer the style of wine can be. On the other hand, most blue cheeses go superbly with sweet wines.

Perfumed or floral reds are too overpowering. So are heavy tannic wines – the tannin tends to steal the nutty richness of the cheese. If you wish to select one grape variety over any other for drinking with a cheese board, go for a Pinot Noir from the New World or a soft Burgundian Pinot Noir. However, white wines are often unexpectedly good partners, allowing the cheese and the wine a chance to show their characters in a way that a red wine may often fail to do.

Hard Cheeses As hard cheeses range from the mild to the outrageously tangy, almost any wine can be a potential match. However, a general rule is, the stronger the cheese, the bigger the character of the wine needs to be.

• *Mild*: Try something red and fruity, such as Fitou, Merlot or one of the Chilean reds.

• *Medium*: Côtes du Rhône or a New Zealand Cabernet Sauvignon would be good choices.

• *Strong*: A Californian Cabernet Sauvignon or even an Australian Shiraz would meet the challenge of a full-bodied cheese.

• *Extra Strong*: These cheeses can handle the rich sweetness of fortified wines such as Port or Madeira.

Semi-soft Cheeses Try a full-bodied gutsy white or a light fruity red. The firmer, more distinctly flavoured semi-soft cheeses are best suited to a Chianti, Rioja or Merlot.

Soft White Cheeses With a mild, slightly sharp, salty style, try a slightly sweet wine. Those with a richer, sweeter and creamier taste need a fruitier wine with a good balance of fruit and acidity. A New Zealand or Chilean Sauvignon Blanc would be an ideal choice. The

Above: Cheese and wine are natural partners, complementing and bringing out each other's flavours.

meatier Bries prefer a full-bodied, fruity red such as a Pinot Noir or even a rich, full-bodied white Chardonnay.

Washed-rind Cheeses These pungent cheeses go very well with beer. If you serve wine, try to choose a spicy Gewurztraminer or a robust red.

Blue Cheeses Milder blues need a light fruity white such as a Vouvray, Chenin Blanc or even a rosé, while the more piquant blues prefer robust, spicy reds such as the Rhônes or a Shiraz. Better still, serve a sweet wine such as Monbazillac or some of the sweeter wines from the New World. The absolute classic is the wonderful marriage of Roquefort with a Sauterne. The sharp, salty tang of the cheese is softened by the mellow bouquet of the wine, while the sweetness of the sheep's milk is underlined.

Fresh Cheeses Try fresh, light, crisp white wines such as a Sauvignon or Chenin Blanc; also try Frascati, Soave or Loire whites. Red wines are too heavy, unless the cheese is part of a stongly flavoured dish such as a pizza.

FISH AND SHELLFISH

The world's oceans and rivers are filled with fish and shellfish in a huge variety of shapes, sizes and colours, ranging from the small silver herring that roam in vast shoals in cold Atlantic waters to the rainbow-coloured parrotfish of tropical seas. With improved methods of transport, there is an increasingly wide range of fish and shellfish available. They may be eaten raw or cooked in any number of ways to delicious result, and have the added bonus of being incredibly nutritious, offering a good supply of protein, vitamins and minerals.

SEA FISH

There are two main categories of fish that are found in the sea: flat fish and round fish. Those that live on or near the seabed are known as demersal fish. These are "white" fish, whose nutritious oil is concentrated in the liver. Correspondingly, "oily" fish tend to swim in shoals near the surface of the sea; they are known as pelagic fish. In oily fish, the nutritious oil is dispersed throughout the flesh. Flat fish spend most of their time lying on the seabed and do very little swimming.

FLAT FISH

All flat fish start life with an eye on each side of their head like a round fish, and they swim upright like round fish, too. As they mature, however, they start to swim on one side only and one eye moves over the head on to the dark-skinned side of the body. Because they do not have to chase their food, their flesh is always delicate and white, without too much muscle fibre. They have a simple bone structure, so even people who are nervous of bones can cope with them. With the exception of flounder, flat fish are seldom found outside European waters. Dover sole, turbot and halibut rank among the finest fish.

Left: Brill was once, rather unfairly, known as the poor man's turbot.

Left: Dabs are at their best when really fresh, either grilled or pan-fried.

BRILL

These fish live on the bottom of the Atlantic, Baltic Sea and Mediterranean. Similar to turbot in appearance and taste, brill has a fine, softish white flesh with a delicate flavour. Brill can grow to about 75cm/30in and can weigh up to 3kg/6½lb, but are often smaller. The fish have slender bodies and there are small, smooth scales on the dark grey skin on the top. The underside is creamy or pinkish-white.

Buying

Brill is considerably cheaper than turbot and available almost all year round as whole fish or fillets. There is a high percentage of wastage in flat fish, so you will need about 1.6kg/3½lb fish for four.

Cooking

Brill can hold its own with a robust red wine and is often cooked in a *matelote* (fish stew) or red wine sauce. Small fish are best cooked whole; they can be baked, braised, poached, steamed, pan-fried or grilled (broiled). Whole poached brill is excellent garnished with prawns (shrimp) or other shellfish. Fillets of brill *à l'anglaise* are coated in egg and breadcrumbs and pan-fried.

DAB/SAND DAB

These are found in shallow water on the sandy bottom of the Atlantic and off the coast of New Zealand. There are several related species of dab, none of which has much flavour. European and American dabs are small, lozenge-shaped fish that seldom grow to more than 35cm/14in. They have brownish, rough skin and a lateral line.

Buying

Dabs are only worth eating when they are very fresh. Near the seaside, you may find them still alive and flapping on the fishmonger's slab; if not, make sure they have glossy skins and a fresh smell. Dabs are usually sold whole, but larger fish may be filleted.

Cooking

Dabs have rather soft, insipid flesh. Pan-fry them in butter or grill (broil) them. Fillets can be coated in egg and breadcrumbs and fried. They benefit from strong flavourings.

HALIBUT

These fish live in the very cold, deep waters off the coasts of Scotland, Norway, Iceland and Newfoundland, migrating to shallower waters to spawn. They are voracious predators, eating almost any type of fish or crustacean, and will even devour birds' eggs that roll off cliffs.

Halibut are the largest of the flat fish, normally weighing between 3kg/6½lb and 15kg/33lb, but can weigh as much as 27kg/60lb. They have elegant, elongated greenish-brown bodies, with a rather pointed head and pearly white underside. The flesh is delicious with a fine, meaty texture.

Buying

Whole young halibut, called chicken halibut, weigh about 1.6–2kg/3½–4½lb and will amply serve four. Large fish are almost always cut into steaks or fillets. Go for steaks taken from the middle rather than from the thin tail, where the proportion of bone to flesh is very high. As bone is a good heat conductor, steaks from the tail end are liable to dry out more rapidly during cooking than middle-cut steaks. Allow 175–200g/ 6–7oz per serving. Fresh raw halibut can be used for ceviche, sashimi and sushi. Beware of Greenland halibut, which is a different species and a vastly inferior fish.

Cooking

Chicken halibut can be baked, braised, poached or cooked *à la bonne femme*, with shallots, mushrooms and white wine. The flesh of large halibut can be rather dry, so steaks and fillets should be braised or baked with wine or stock.

FLOUNDER

These fish are found in many parts of the world, from Europe to New Zealand. In the United States there are summer, winter and sand flounders. The mottled greyish-brown skin has orange spots and the fish is round. They can grow to 50cm/20in, but usually measure only 25–30cm/10–12in.

Above: Halibut is one of the largest fish eaten and can grow to 4m/13ft long.

Buying

Like dabs, flounders must be bought and eaten when extremely fresh. Look for fish with glossy skins and a fresh smell.

Cooking

Flounder can be baked, braised, poached, steamed or grilled (broiled). Fillets are good dipped in egg and breadcrumbs and pan-fried in butter.

Left: Flounders usually live close to the shore and are sometimes found in estuaries.

PLAICE

These are found in the Atlantic and other northerly waters, and also in the Mediterranean. They have a distinctive-looking greyish-brown skin with orange spots on their backs. These spots are very bright when the fish is fresh. The underside is pearly white. They can grow up to 90cm/3ft long and weigh up to 7kg/15½lb, but the average weight is 400g–1kg/14oz–2¼lb. They have soft, rather bland white flesh, which can sometimes lack flavour and texture.

Buying

Plaice must be very fresh or the flesh tends to take on the texture of cotton wool. These fish are available all year round, whole or as fillets, but are best avoided in the summer months, when the flesh is flaccid and tasteless. When fresh, the orange spots on the dark skin will be bright and distinctive. Fillets with dark skins are cheaper than white-skinned ones, but there is no difference in flavour. There is a lot of wastage on plaice, so you should allow a whole 350–450g/12–16oz fish per serving or a 175g/6oz fillet.

Cooking

Any sole or brill recipe is suitable for plaice. Deep-fried in batter, plaice is a classic fish-and-chip shop dish. Whole fish or fillets can be coated in egg and breadcrumbs and pan-fried. Alternatively it can be steamed or poached. Plaice benefits from strongly flavoured sauces and accompaniments, such as anchovies or fennel. It is easy to digest so makes good invalid food.

For plaice *à la florentine,* bake a whole fish or white-skinned fillets in stock and white wine, lay it on a bed of cooked spinach, cover with a cheese sauce and grill (broil) until bubbling and browned.

Above: Megrim, also known as meg, is a very small fish.

MEGRIM

This yellowish-grey translucent fish is mainly found south of the English Channel and seldom grows to more than 50cm/20in in length. Megrim have dryish, rather bland flesh and are not considered by some to be worth eating. It is rarely eaten in France and Italy. In Spain, Megrim are called *gallo.*

Buying

Megrim are either sold whole or as fillets. They need to be extremely fresh, so always make sure you smell them before you buy. Allow 350g/12oz or at least two fillets per serving.

Cooking

Whole fish can be coated in batter or breadcrumbs and deep-fried, or poached or baked. Fillets are best crumbed and deep-fried. Megrim can sometimes be rather dry, so use plenty of liquid. The skin tends to be quite tough and coarse, so it is best to remove it before or after cooking. Megrim are probably best used for making fish cakes.

Above: Plaice is a somewhat bland fish but, despite this, is still very popular.

DOVER SOLE

Arguably the finest fish of all, Dover sole have firm, delicate flesh with a superb flavour. They live mainly in the English Channel and the Atlantic, but can be found in the Baltic, Mediterranean and North Sea. Their weight ranges from 200g/7oz to 1kg/2¼lb and they may grow as long as 45cm/18in.

Left: Dover sole (top) and lemon sole (bottom) are similar in name and appearance but are not related.

Buying

Sole are at their best three days after being caught, so if you are sure that you are buying fish straight from the sea, keep them for a couple of days before cooking. The skin should be sticky and the underside very white. A 225g/8oz fish will serve one person. If you want to serve two, buy a fish weighing at least 675–800g/1½–1¾lb (which will yield four decent-sized fillets, but could prove costly). If you ask the fishmonger to fillet it for you, keep the bones and trimmings so that you can make fish stock.

Cooking

There are numerous recipes for sole, but a plain lightly grilled (broiled) fish served with a drizzle of melted butter and lemon juice is hard to beat. Skin both sides before cooking. Small sole can be coated in egg and breadcrumbs and pan-fried or deep-fried; larger specimens can be poached, steamed or cooked in butter *à la meunière*. Fillets can be fried, poached in wine, rolled into paupiettes or served with an elaborate sauce. Famous recipes include *à l'anglaise*, *à la dieppoise*, *à la bordelaise*, Walewska and Yvette, with ingredients ranging from crayfish tails to truffles and mussels to white wine.

LEMON SOLE

Known as the yellowtail flounder in the United States, lemon sole is related to dab, plaice and flounder rather than to Dover sole. It is also known as lemon dab and lemon fish. They are found in the North Sea and Atlantic Ocean and around the coast of New Zealand. They lead largely stationary lives on the stony or rocky seabed and vary enormously in size depending on local conditions. Generally, weights range between 350g/12oz and 1.75kg/4lb.

Lemon sole has a soft white flesh, similar to that of plaice but slightly superior and sweeter in flavour. It is a good alternative to the more expensive Dover sole. Because of the similarity of their names, lemon sole suffers in comparison with Dover sole, although it is a fine fish in its own right.

Buying

Lemon sole are available all year round and are sold whole or as fillets. They must be very fresh and should have a tang of the sea.

Cooking

Lemon sole are best cooked simply – grilled (broiled) or fried in butter or deep-fried in a light batter. You can use any dab, plaice or Dover sole recipe. Lemon sole is also a good choice for *fritto misto* – Italian mixed fried fish – goujons and goes well in fish terrines. It is especially suited to steaming Cantonese-style with root ginger, sesame seed oil and soy sauce. It is usually easier to remove the skin after cooking, but it can be done at the same time as filleting.

OTHER TYPES OF SOLE

There are a number of other flat fish related to sole. Sétau is a small brown sole, about 7.5–10cm/3–4in long. It is fished off the south-west coast of France. Sand sole or partridge sole, found in the Atlantic Ocean, is a small, dark, striped fish very similar in appearance to Dover sole. Dakar or Moroccan sole is a long fish with large scales. It has a fairly bland flavour but is extensively fished.

TURBOT

These fish live on the seabed in the Mediterranean, Atlantic and Black Sea. Recently they have been introduced to New Zealand coastal waters. They can also be farmed successfully, and this has improved both the quality and the size of the fish.

Weighing as much as 11.25kg/25lb, and growing up to 1m/39in in length, turbot have tiny heads and large, almost circular bodies with tough, warty brown skin. What turbot lacks in appearance, however, it makes up for in texture and taste. Prized since ancient times, it was called king of Lent in the Middle Ages.

Buying

Turbot is extremely expensive to buy, especially the large wild specimens. Farmed fish are cheaper, but can be fatty. Turbot should have creamy-white flesh; do not buy fish with a blue tinge. It is available all year round, sold whole or as steaks and fillets. A small young turbot weighing 1.6kg/3½lb will feed four people. There is a lot of wastage, so if your fishmonger fillets a whole turbot for you, ask for the bones and trimmings, so that you can make fish stock.

Above: A small young turbot is known as a chicken turbot.

Cooking

To cook chicken turbot, grill (broil) it or poach in white wine and fish stock. Traditionally, turbot was poached in milk to keep the flesh pure white, then served with hollandaise sauce. Almost any cooking method is suitable for turbot, except perhaps deep-frying, which would be a waste; it is essential not to overcook this exquisitely delicate fish. Creamy sauces made with lobster, mushroom, parsley or chives go well with plainly cooked turbot. Chunks of poached turbot, dressed with a piquant vinaigrette, make a superb salad and, in the unlikely event of there being leftover turbot, it is delicious served cold with a little home-made mayonnaise.

A wide range of sumptuous and elaborate turbot recipes has been created by almost all the great chefs of history. In bygone days, diamond-shaped *turbotières*, or turbot-kettles, were important kitchen utensils. They were cooked with crayfish tails and truffle sauce, scallops, vermouth and champagne, and even grapes and tea.

Above: Turbot is a delicious but expensive fish.

WITCH

Also known as Torbay sole, witch are mostly caught off the south-west coast of England. A member of the plaice family, it has an elongated body like a Dover sole, with a straight lateral line on the rough, greyish-brown skin. The flesh is rather insipid.

Buying and Cooking

Witch are available all year round, but are only worth eating if very fresh. They are best grilled (broiled), and need plenty of seasoning.

Left: Witch are best cooked on the bone.

Cleaning and Preparing Flat Fish

Flat fish are generally sold already cleaned, but it is easy to gut them yourself if necessary. Four fillets can be obtained from a single fish, two from each side. However, they won't be equal in size.

1 To gut the fish, trim off the fins with sharp kitchen scissors. Using a sharp knife, make an incision just below the gills, then insert your fingers and pull out the innards, including the roe. (The roe can be retained if you like to eat it.) Wrap the innards in several layers of newspaper before disposing of them.

2 To fillet the fish, lay it on a board with the dark skin facing upwards and the head pointing away from you. Using a large sharp knife, carefully cut around the head and right down the centre line of the fish, taking the blade of the knife all the way through to the backbone.

3 Working from the head to the tail of the fish, insert the point of the knife under the flesh at the head end. Starting with the left-hand fillet, hold the knife almost parallel to the bones and carefully free the fillet with long stroking movements.

4 Turn the fish around so that the head is towards you and remove the second fillet in the same way.

5 Turn the fish over and repeat the process on the other side, starting with the left-hand fillet and then the right.

Skinning Whole Flat Fish

Traditionally, Dover sole are skinned only on the dark side, but other flat fish such as flounder and plaice are skinned on both sides.

1 Lay the fish on a board with the dark skin facing up and the tail pointing towards you. Using a sharp knife, slit through the skin just below the tail and loosen it on both sides.

2 Using a cloth, hold the tail down firmly with one hand. Use the other hand to pull away the skin.

Round White Fish

There are many different families of fish within this large group, including sea bass, sea bream and cod.

SEA BASS

Called *loup de mer*, meaning sea wolf in French, the sea bass belongs to a huge family that includes the grouper, in itself an enormous fish family. Sea bass live in small shoals close to rocky coasts in Britain and the Mediterranean. They can also be found in saltwater lakes and some large river estuaries. They can weigh up to 7kg/15¹/₂lb, but the average weight is 1–3kg/2¹/₄–6¹/₂lb. Sea bass are one of the finest fish, with a firm flesh and a delicate flavour.

Buying

Sea bass are available all year round, as whole fish or as fillets. They are best in spring and early summer, before they spawn. Line-caught wild sea bass have the finest texture and flavour, but farmed fish are an acceptable and much cheaper alternative. Look for bright, silvery skin and clear eyes. Allow about 200g/7oz per serving.

Cooking

Sea bass is a versatile fish; it has very few bones and the firm flesh holds its shape well during cooking. It can be grilled (broiled), baked, braised, poached, shallow fried, stir-fried or steamed. A whole poached sea bass, skinned and served cold with home-made mayonnaise, makes an impressive and delicious party dish.

SEA BREAM

There are approximately 200 species of sea bream. They are found in all warm and temperate coastal waters including the Atlantic, up to the Bay of Biscay. The gilt-head bream, which is also known as royal bream, is considered to be the finest of all sea bream. Its dense, juicy white flesh has been prized for thousands of years.

Above: Sea bass is as good to eat as it is to look at.

Buying

Sea bream are sold whole or as fillets. There is a high percentage of wastage. Gilt-heads are farmed successfully in the Mediterranean. Fresh gilt-head bream should have bright, shiny scales.

Cooking

All bream have numerous wide scales that must be removed before cooking – otherwise the diner will experience a very unpleasant mouthful. Whole gilt-head bream can be treated like sea bass or sole – baked, grilled (broiled), poached, steamed in seaweed or braised. The flesh should be scored in several places on both sides before the fish is grilled (broiled) or baked whole to ensure even cooking. The dense flesh is robust enough to withstand spicy or aromatic flavours. Gilt-head fillets can be baked, pan-fried or grilled (broiled). Raw fresh fish can be used to make sashimi.

RED BREAM

This tall, rosy-red fish has a pronounced black spot above the pectoral fin on each shoulder. Red Bream is usually sold filleted. It is found in northern European waters, but swims south in winter to spawn.

Cooking

Extremely fresh red bream can be eaten raw as sashimi. Whole fish and fillets should be cooked in the same way as snapper, bass or red mullet.

Other Breams

Black bream This is a brownish-grey fish with firm flesh and a good flavour. Cook in the same way as other bream.

Dentex Popular in Mediterranean countries, dentex is best eaten when young and no more than 30cm/12in long. The fish can be grilled (broiled) or baked in a dish with plenty of herbs.

Porgy Also known as pagre, this is a North American relative of the bream. Bake, grill (broil), poach, steam or braise, whole or as steaks.

Above: (From front) Gilt-head bream, red bream and black bream

GURNARD

Also known as sea robin, piper and gurnet, gurnard are prehistoric-looking fish, found in the Atlantic and the Mediterranean, and living on or near the seabed, using their "fingers" to seek out the crabs, prawns (shrimp) and small fish that live in the sediment. There are several types of gurnard; all have lean white flesh with a firm texture but generally rather insipid taste.

Buying

Gurnard are bony fish with a rather unexceptional flavour, so they tend to be cheap. They are usually sold whole; ask the fishmonger to remove the spiny fins and the skin. As they have such large heads, there is a lot of wastage.

Right: Scorpion fish is an essential ingredient for making an authentic bouillabaisse.

Above: Gurnard, although not particularly flavoursome, makes an attractive and colourful addition to fish stews and soups.

Tub gurnard This larger variety is orangey-brown with bright orange pectoral fins. They are excellent swimmers and sometimes leap right out of the water, giving them their alternative name of flying gurnard.

SCORPION FISH

These members of the gurnard family are found in the Mediterranean, off the coast of North Africa and in the warmer Atlantic waters. The brown scorpion fish, which is actually grey, is rarer and has a finer flavour than the red variety.

Buying and Cooking

Scorpion fish are usually sold whole. A 2kg/4½lb fish will serve only four. Scorpion fish is best known as an essential ingredient in traditional bouillabaisse. Whole fish can also be baked or braised with fennel.

Cooking

Small gurnard are best used in soups and stocks. (The heads make very good stock.) Larger fish can be braised or baked and are good with an onion or mushroom and herb stuffing. Take care when eating gurnard, because of the bones. Fillets can be coated in breadcrumbs and fried, or steamed and served with a Mediterranean-style sauce. Any recipe for red mullet is suitable for cooking gurnard, although the flavour will not be so fine.

Varieties

Grey gurnard These fish are brownish-grey in colour with silvery bellies. The lateral line should be removed before the fish is cooked.
Red gurnard The most attractive member of this family, the red gurnard also has the finest flavour and is sometimes substituted for red mullet.
Trigle lyre gurnard This also has a pink or red body with a lighter underbelly.

COD

There are actually several fish that belong to the cod family, including haddock, hake, ling, whiting and many other related species of white-fleshed fish. Most of them come from the Atlantic and other cold northerly waters, although hake is found in the warmer waters of the Mediterranean and is particularly popular in Spain and Portugal.

Cod itself can grow to a length of 6m/19½ft, weighing up to 50kg/110lb, but most commercially fished cod weighs between 3kg/6½lb and 8kg/18lb. They prefer to live in cold water with a high salt content. For years, cod were so plentiful that they were regarded as an inferior fish, fit only to be fried then served with chips, or masked with an unpleasant floury white sauce. All too often, the succulent, flaky white flesh was overcooked, making it watery or dry. Today, overfishing has depleted stocks and cod has become relatively scarce and more highly acclaimed.

Buying

Cod is most commonly trawled or netted, which can damage the delicate flesh, so try to buy line-caught fish. When buying a whole small cod or codling, the skin should be shiny and clear. There is a lot of wastage in whole cod and fillets or steaks are more economical and, indeed, more widely available. Shoulder steaks have the finest flavour. Try to buy thick cuts from the shoulder or middle of the fish and check that the flesh is very white.

Above: Haddock is one of the most popular members of the cod family but has suffered from overfishing.

Cooking

Cod holds its texture well and can be cooked in many different ways, but it is essential not to overcook it. The flavour is robust enough to take quite strong and spicy accompaniments such as capers, garlic and cheese. Whole fish can be poached in a court-bouillon and served cold with mayonnaise, green sauce or tartare sauce. Cod can also be baked or roasted in the oven or braised in white wine.

Most cooking methods are suitable for cod fillets and steaks, except grilling (broiling), which can destroy the delicate, flaky texture of the flesh. Cod are very good poached, steamed, braised in tomato sauce or topped with a crust of breadcrumbs and herbs and baked. They are also delicious floured and sautéed, or coated with batter and deep-fried. Fresh and smoked cod fillets can be used to make delicious fish cakes, croquettes, fish pies, salads and mousses.

HADDOCK

Called scrod in the United States, haddock are shoaling fish that live on the seabed of cold northern seas in Europe and North America. They are often considered to be interchangeable with cod. However, haddock is smaller and has a whiter, more delicate flesh, which is both softer and less flaky than cod.

Buying

Fresh haddock is at its best in winter and early spring, when the cold has firmed up the flesh. You may find whole small haddock (weighing 450g–2kg/ 1–4½lb) at the fishmonger's, but the fish is usually sold in fillets. The flesh should be firm.

Cooking

Fresh haddock is a versatile fish, which can be cooked in the same way as cod. If cooking whole haddock, leave the skin on to hold the flesh together.

Haddock is the perfect fish for deep-frying, making it ideal for serving with chips. It also makes excellent fish lasagne and pie, especially when the fresh fish is mixed with an equal quantity of smoked haddock.

Below: Cod is an immensely versatile fish that can be cooked in any number of ways and served with a vast range of sauces.

*Right: Hake has fragile
flesh and requires
quite careful
handling.*

HAKE

In the United States, hake is
known as ling or whiting, which can
cause confusion. It is found in most
temperate and cold waters, and is the
most elegant member of the cod family.
The fish can be trawled or caught on
long lines, but due to overfishing, it is
becoming quite scarce and expensive.

Buying

Try to buy line-caught fish, which has a
better texture. The fish should be very
fresh or it becomes flabby. The flesh
has a pinkish tinge and should feel soft
to the touch; it should never feel limp.

When calculating how much to buy,
allow for about 40 per cent wastage for
whole fish. Keep the head, as it makes
particularly delicious soup and
excellent fish stock.

Hake is usually sold as
cutlets or steaks. Those cut
from near the head have the
best flavour. The fish has few
bones and these are easy to
remove. Avoid buying fillets,
as they tend to disintegrate
during cooking.

Cooking

Whole hake can be
poached, baked or
braised in wine, lemon
juice and fresh herbs or
in a tomato sauce. Like all
fish, it should never be overcooked.
Steaks can be grilled (broiled), coated
in egg and breadcrumbs and deep-
fried, or sautéed in olive oil and garlic.
They can also be layered with potatoes
and onions, or with tomatoes and
cheeses and baked *au gratin*. Cooking
en papillote or wrapped in leaves is
especially good, as it helps to prevent
the fragile flesh from breaking up.

LING

This slender-bodied,
mottled bronze fish is the largest
relative of the cod and can grow to a
length of 1.8m/6ft and a weight of
14kg/31lb. It lives in the Atlantic, often
in proximity to rocks, where it feeds on
round and flat fish.

A smaller relative of the ling is found
in the Mediterranean. Rock ling are also
very popular in Scandinavian countries,
where they are frequently salted and
dried and sold under the names of
lutfisk or *klipfisk*.

Buying

As with all fish, the best
ling are line-caught. You
may be able to find small whole
ling, but the fish is more commonly
sold as fillets or middle-cut cutlets.
It is not a widely available fish,
perhaps because its rather
unattractive, eel-like appearance
puts people off.

Cooking

Ling has firm flesh with
a fairly good flavour and
is sometimes substituted for monkfish.
Whole fish can be baked or braised, or
made into casseroles, soups, pies and
curries. Fillets and cutlets can be grilled
(broiled) or pan-fried and served with
a flavoursome sauce. It also goes well
with robust flavours, such as garlic,
prawns (shrimp) and spinach.

COLEY

Also known as
saithe, coalfish and
pollock, coley live in shoals
in cold and salty, deep and
shallow waters. They were
traditionally regarded as cod's
poor relation, owing to their unappealing
greyish-coloured flesh.

Buying

Coley are sometimes sold whole,
weighing 1–4kg/2¼–8½lb, but are more
usually sold as steaks, cutlets and
fillets. The unattractive grey flesh looks
off-putting, but whitens during cooking.
It should feel firm to the touch. Coley
must be extremely fresh, or the flesh
will become woolly and unpleasant.

Coley is less fine than cod in texture
and flavour. Rubbing the flesh with
lemon juice helps to whiten it, but the
colour can also be masked by coating
the fish in batter or using it in a fish
pie, casserole or fish cakes. It will
withstand robust flavours and can be
baked, grilled (broiled) or fried,
and is good in fish soups.

*Left: Ling is not widely
available, as most
goes to the food
processing
industry for
smoking or
drying.*

POLLACK

Although smaller than cod, pollack can still grow to a length of 1m/39in and weigh up to 9kg/20lb. It is also known as greenfish and lythe. It has a greeny brown body with pale orange blotches. Pollack is usually sold as fillets, cutlets or steaks, and is at its best in autumn and winter. If you need a whole fish, look out for a superior line-caught specimen. Although the flavour is not so fine as cod, haddock or hake, it is an economical buy.

Cooking

Pollack has a drier texture and less pronounced flavour than cod, so it benefits from a creamy, highly-flavoured sauce. It is good for fish pies and soups and can be baked, braised, deep-fried or sautéed. It is suitable for any recipe for cod, haddock, hake or ling, and works particularly well with many Indian recipes for baked fish.

TORSK

Also known as tusk, this smaller member of the cod family lives in the northern part of the North Atlantic. It is popular in Scandinavia, but not so well known elsewhere. Confusingly, *torsk* is the name for cod in Scandinavia, and actual torsk is known as *brosme*. It is 45–60cm/18–24in long on average, but can grow bigger, and it is reddish-brown in colour. It may be cooked in the same ways as haddock and cod.

WHITING

Previously known as merling and similar in appearance to haddock, whiting are small fish with greenish-grey skin and a silvery belly. They grow to 30–40cm/12–16in long and can weigh as much as 2kg/4½lb, although 350–500g/12oz–1¼lb is more usual. They are found all over the Atlantic, from Iceland to northern Spain. They have tender flesh and an unassuming flavour and are a popular alternative to haddock, although they are a good buy in their own right for certain recipes.

Buying

Whiting is available all year round. It is thought of as being rather dull and is thus relatively cheap. Although not a spectacular fish, whiting does not deserve this reputation; for certain dishes it is well worth buying. It should be bought as fresh as possible, as the flesh breaks down very rapidly and it quickly becomes impossible to fillet or skin. Fillets should be pearly white and feel soft, but definitely not flabby. Whiting are small, so allow two fillets per serving.

Cooking

The whiting's tender flesh makes it an ideal basis for a soup as it contributes a velvety texture. Whiting is a versatile fish that can be coated in breadcrumbs or batter and fried. It is also good pan-fried, grilled (broiled) or poached in wine or a court-bouillon and served with a lemony sauce or flavoured butter. It is best cooked by indirect

Above: Whiting has a delicate flavour and extremely tender, highly digestible flesh, making it the ideal fish for soups, quenelles and mousselines.

heat. Whatever cooking method you use, make sure the whiting is well seasoned. As it is delicately flavoured and easily digested, whiting is a good choice for invalids and the elderly.

POUTING

Also known as pout, this is a poor (and cheap) relation of the whiting. It needs to be eaten very fresh, as the fish goes off extremely quickly. As pouting are relatively small (about 25cm/10in long) buy a whole fish if possible, and ask the fishmonger to fillet it. Cook as soon as possible, as you would for whiting.

Above: Pouting is good for soups, fish cakes and fish balls.

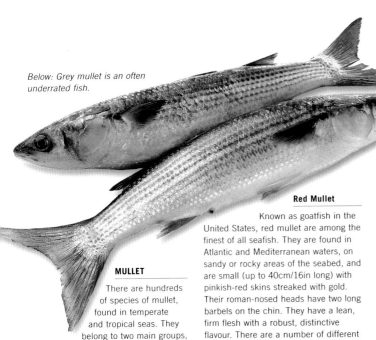

Below: Grey mullet is an often underrated fish.

MULLET

There are hundreds of species of mullet, found in temperate and tropical seas. They belong to two main groups, grey and red, which are unrelated in both appearance and flavour.

Grey Mullet

These are found in coastal waters and estuaries all over the world. There are several different varieties.
Golden mullet This is the finest of the grey mullet. It is one of the smallest, growing only to about 45cm/18cm.
Thin-lipped mullet This has a golden sheen and a pointed snout. There is also a thick-lipped mullet.
Common or striped grey mullet This is the largest of all the mullets.

Buying

Except in France, you are unlikely to find any differentiation between the varieties. Choose fish that come from the high seas rather than estuaries, as the latter can taste muddy and flabby. Grey mullet are usually sold whole – ask the fishmonger to scale and skin them.

Cooking

Grey mullet must be scaled before being cooked. Any muddiness can be eliminated by soaking the fish in several changes of acidulated water. Whole fish are very good stuffed with fennel and grilled (broiled) or with a buttery sauce.

Red Mullet

Known as goatfish in the United States, red mullet are among the finest of all seafish. They are found in Atlantic and Mediterranean waters, on sandy or rocky areas of the seabed, and are small (up to 40cm/16in long) with pinkish-red skins streaked with gold. Their roman-nosed heads have two long barbels on the chin. They have a lean, firm flesh with a robust, distinctive flavour. There are a number of different varieties, including *Mullus surmeletus* and *Mullus barbatus*. Mullet are known by different names including woodcock of the sea, *rouget* in France, *triglia* in Italy, and *salmonete de roca* or *salmonete de fango* in Spain.

Buying

Red mullet is very perishable, so it is essential to buy extremely fresh fish. They should have very bright skins and eyes and feel very firm. Because they are small, they are usually sold whole, but large fish are sometimes filleted. The flesh is quite rich, so a 200g/7oz fish will be ample for one person. Ask the fishmonger to scale and gut it for you but keep the liver, which is a great delicacy.

Cooking

The best way to cook red mullet is by grilling (broiling) and pan-frying. Score the sides before grilling (broiling) a whole fish to ensure even cooking. Red mullet goes well with the Mediterranean flavours of olive oil, saffron, tomatoes, olives, anchovies and orange. They can be cooked *en papillote* with flavourings such as fennel or basil. Baking or grilling (broiling) the fish with the liver inside is a traditional cooking method.

Below: Red mullet has a rich, sweet flavour and a wonderful texture.

WRASSE

This large family of fish is notable for
its varied and dazzling colours. Wrasse
range from steely blue to green, orange
and golden; in some species the sexes
have different colours. All wrasse have
thick lips and an array of sharp teeth.
They are small fish, seldom growing
to more than 40cm/16in in length.
Wrasse are found in both Atlantic and
Mediterranean waters, living near rocky
coasts and feeding on barnacles and
small crustaceans.

The most common variety of wrasse
is the ballan wrasse, which has
greenish-brown skin, with large scales
tipped with gold. Male and female
cuckoo wrasse have strikingly different
coloration; the males are steely blue
with almost black stripes, while the
females are orangey-pink with three
black spots under the dorsal fin. The
name of the five-spotted wrasse is

*Above: When buying common wrasse,
look for bright skin and eyes.*

*Below: The skin of the brown-spotted
wrasse is very decorative.*

self-explanatory, while the brown
spotted wrasse is completely covered
in spots. Rainbow wrasse have spiny
dorsal fins and a red or orange band
along their body. Some of the mottled
blue-green wrasse have a slight
resemblance to the parrotfish, to which
they are distantly related.

Buying

Wrasse are available in spring and
summer. Look for scintillating skin and
bright eyes. Ask the fishmonger to scale
and clean the fish for you. Allow at least
400g/14oz per serving.

Cooking

Most wrasse are fit only for making
soup or stew, but some larger varieties,
such as ballan wrasse, can be baked
whole. Make a bed of sliced onions,
garlic, smoked bacon and potatoes,
bake at 200°C/400°F/Gas 6 until soft,
then add the wrasse, moisten with white
wine and bake for 10–15 minutes.

Scaling Round Fish

Smooth-skinned round fish, such as trout and mackerel, do not need scaling. However, for others such as sea bass and mullet, it is essential to remove the scales. Always scale fish before filleting if you are going to cook it with the skin on.

Ideally, you should use a proper fish scaler to do the job, but the back of a round-bladed knife will do almost as well. Work in the sink, preferably under running water, or the scales will fly all over your kitchen.

1 Wash the fish under cold running water. Cut off the three fins that run along the stomach, and the dorsal fins, using strong, sharp scissors. Take care with the dorsal fins, as they can have sharp spines.

2 Hold the fish firmly by the tail (a clean cloth will give a better grip). Using a fish scaler or the back of a knife, and working from tail to head under running water, scrape against the lie of the scales to remove them.

3 Wash the fish again under cold water to detach any clinging scales.

Cleaning Round Fish

Round fish can be cleaned in two different ways – either through the belly or through the gills.

1 To clean through the belly, starting at the site of the anal fin, slit open the fish from tail to head.

2 Pull out the innards. Keep any roes and the livers of red mullet, but discard everything else. Use a tablespoon to make sure the cavity is empty, removing any blood vessels. Wash under cold water and pat dry with kitchen paper.

3 To clean through the gills, lay the fish on its back. Make an incision in the bottom of the belly, near the tail and snip the end of the innards.

4 Cut through the bone under the lower jaw. Open the gill flaps and gently pull out the innards. Wash the fish under cold running water.

Filleting Round Fish

It is very quick and simple to remove the fillets from a fish.

1 Lay the fish on a board, lift the gill fin and make a diagonal cut behind the fin to the top of the head.

2 Insert the knife halfway down the fish close to the backbone. Cut towards the tail, keeping the knife flat to the bone. Lift up the fillet, turn the knife towards the tail and slide along the bone to free the fillet. Turn the fish over and repeat on the other side.

OILY FISH

These fish, which include herring, mackerel and sardines, have always been popular because they are cheap and nutritious. In recent years they have received an excellent press, owing to their health-giving properties. They contain protein, vitamins A, B and D, and Omega-3 fatty acids, which are thought to reduce the risk of clogged arteries, blood clots, strokes and even

Above: Herring fillets may be pan-fried, marinated, soused or pickled.

Below: Herring has been an important part of the north European diet for centuries, but stocks are now depleted.

cancer. People who eat fish regularly tend to live longer – the Japanese, who are among the world's greatest fish eaters, have one of the lowest death rates from heart disease.

Oily fish live near the surface of the sea, congregated in shoals. The largest family of oil-rich fish are the herring.

HERRING

These are mostly known by the name of the region where they are located, including the North Sea, Norwegian and Baltic. There are countless different varieties of herring, each confined to its own sea area. They seldom grow to more than 35cm/14in and their oily flesh can be cured in many ways, including smoking, salting, drying and marinating in vinegar and spices.

Buying

Like all oily fish, herring must be absolutely fresh or they will taste rancid. As herrings contain numerous soft bones, you might ask the fishmonger to bone or fillet them for you. They can be gutted either through the belly or through the gills, leaving the roe inside.

Boning a Herring

Herrings contain a large number of small bones, which are best removed before cooking.

1 Having removed the fins and gutted the fish, open it out and lay it on a board, with the skin side up. Press down along the backbone.

2 Turn the fish over and gently pull the backbone away from the flesh. Cut off at the tail and pick out any small loose bones. Rinse the fish under cold running water and pat dry with kitchen paper.

Cooking

Their oiliness makes herrings ideal for grilling (broiling) and barbecueing. Score whole fish on both sides to ensure even cooking. Herrings are good served with an acidic sauce such as gooseberry or mustard to counteract the richness. Whole herrings and fillets are delicious rolled in oatmeal and pan-fried in bacon fat, and served sprinkled with lemon juice. They can also be baked with a stuffing of chopped onions, breadcrumbs and apples, or wrapped in bacon and grilled (broiled).

ANCHOVIES

These small, slender fish live in tightly packed shoals and can be found throughout the Mediterranean and the Black Sea, and the Atlantic and Pacific. They seldom grow to more than 16cm/ 6¼in in length; the average is 8–10cm/ 3½–4in. They have steely blue backs and shimmering silver sides.

Buying

Ideally, fresh anchovies should be cooked and eaten straight from the sea. The best anchovies come from the Mediterranean and are at their peak in early summer. By the time they have been exported they will have lost much of their delicate flavour.

Preparing and Cooking

You are unlikely to find a fishmonger willing to clean anchovies for you, but they are easy to prepare at home. To gut them, cut off the head and press gently along the body with your thumb to squeeze out the innards. To fillet, run your thumbnail or a stubby blunt knife along the length of the spine from head to tail on both sides and lift off the fillets.

Whole anchovies can be grilled (broiled) or fried, or lightly coated in egg and flour and deep-fried. Fillets can be fried with garlic and parsley, or marinated for 24 hours in a mixture of olive oil, onion, garlic, bay leaves and crushed peppercorns.

Above: Pilchards mostly go to the canning industry.

Above: Sardines, which are actually just young pilchards, are perfect for grilling (broiling) or for cooking over a barbecue.

Left: Fresh anchovies are rarely found outside the Mediterranean but they are widely available in supermarkets, either preserved in salt or oil. In Spain, marinated fresh anchovies are often served as a tapas dish.

SARDINES AND PILCHARDS

Sardines take their name from the island of Sardinia, where they were once abundant. Like anchovies, they are a shoaling fish and are found throughout the Mediterranean and Atlantic. Pilchards are actually the same fish, just larger and more mature.

Buying

Sardines are at their best in spring and early summer. They do not travel well, so try to buy fish from local waters. Small sardines have the best flavour, but larger fish are better for stuffing. Allow 3–5 sardines per serving.

Preparing and Cooking

Sardines should be scaled and gutted before being cooked. This is easy to do; just cut off the head almost through from the backbone and twist, pulling it towards you. The innards will come away with the head. Whole sardines are superb grilled (broiled) or barbecued, which crisps the skin. They can be coated in breadcrumbs, fried and served with tomato sauce, made into fritters or stuffed with capers.

SPRAT

These small silvery fish look very similar to sardines or immature herrings, but are squatter. Today they are often smoked or cured, or sold as fishmeal.

Cooking

Sprats can be cooked in the same way as anchovies and sardines. They have very oily flesh and are delicious when fried in oatmeal or deep-fried in batter.

MACKEREL

These shoaling fish are found in huge numbers in the North Atlantic, North Sea and the Mediterranean. The streamlined fish are easily identified by their beautiful greenish-blue skin. The flesh is smooth, pale and beige-pink.

Above: Sprats are best cooked simply – by grilling (broiling) or frying.

Below: Whitebait are tiny fish that are usually eaten whole, heads and all.

Buying

The flesh of mackerel is meaty, with a distinctive full flavour. The fish is delicious when extremely fresh, but not really worth eating when past its best. It is in its prime in late spring and early summer, just before spawning. Look for firm fish with iridescent skin and clear, bright eyes. Small mackerel are better than large fish. Larger specimens are sometimes sold filleted, either fresh or smoked. Mackerel is a popular canned fish, and may be canned in either oil or tomato sauce.

Cooking

Whole mackerel can be grilled (broiled), barbecued, braised or poached in a court-bouillon, white wine or cider. Make several slashes on both sides of each fish before cooking over direct heat. Like herrings, they need a sharp sauce to counteract their richness; classic accompaniments are gooseberry, sorrel, horseradish or mustard sauce. Fillets can be cooked in the same way as herring – either coated in oatmeal and fried, or braised with onions and white wine. Raw fillets can be marinated in sweet-and-sour vinaigrette to make a delightful appetizer or snack.

Above: Mackerel is a handsome, nutritious fish with a rich flavour.

WHITEBAIT

This name is given to tiny silver fish – only about 5cm/2in in length – that are caught in summer as they swim up estuaries. They may be immature sprats or herrings, or a mixture of both fish.

Buying and Cooking

Whitebait are available fresh in spring and summer, and frozen all year round. Allow about 115g/4oz per person when serving as a starter.

Whitebait are cooked and eaten whole, complete with heads. They are delicious deep-fried and served with brown bread and butter. Prepare them for cooking by dunking in a bowl of milk and then shaking them in a plastic bag containing flour seasoned with salt and cayenne pepper. Deep-fry until crisp.

BLUEFISH

Found in the Mediterranean and American Atlantic waters, bluefish are hugely popular in Turkey. The flesh is softer and more delicate than that of mackerel, but they can be cooked in the same way.

TUNA

Also called tunny, tuna has been a popular food for centuries. The fish were highly prized by the Ancient Greeks, who mapped their migratory patterns in order to fish for them. They are a member of the mackerel family and are found in warmer seas throughout the world, as far north as the Bay of Biscay.

A shoal of immense tuna fish travelling through the high seas is a magnificent sight. These beautiful, torpedo-shaped fish can grow to an enormous size – up to 700kg/1,540lb – although they may be as small as 1–1.5kg/2¼–3lb. They have immensely powerful muscles and firm, dark, meaty flesh. There are many varieties of tuna, although as a result of centuries of overfishing, only about half-a-dozen varieties are sold commercially.

Buying

Tuna is usually sold as steaks or larger pieces, often already skinned. This makes it an extremely economical purchase, as there is no waste. It is a very substantial and filling fish, so allow about 175g/6oz per person. Depending on the individual variety, the flesh may range from pale beige-pink to deep dark red. Do not buy steaks with heavy discoloration around the bone, or which are dull-looking and brownish all over. The flesh should be very firm, dense and compact.

Cooking

Tuna becomes greyish and dry when overcooked, so it is essential to cook it only briefly over a high heat, or to simmer it extremely gently with moist ingredients, such as tomatoes and (bell) peppers. It has become fashionable to sear it fleetingly, leaving it almost raw in the middle; if this is not to your taste, cook it for about 2 minutes on each

Above: Bluefin tuna is generally considered to have the finest flavour of all tuna.

side – but no longer. It is especially good marinated in herbs, spices and wine or sherry before grilling (broiling). A ridged pan is a particularly good way of cooking tuna and it is also an excellent fish for the barbecue. Very thinly sliced raw tuna, dressed with olive oil, balsamic vinegar and capers is a popular Italian antipasto. Raw fish should always be extremely fresh.

Varieties

Albacore Also known as white tuna, and longfin owing to its unusually long pectoral fins, this tuna is found in temperate and tropical seas. Albacore has pale, rosy flesh with a colour and texture resembling veal. Because its rosy-white flesh is so akin to veal, albacore is often cooked in similar ways – as escalopes or larded with anchovy fillets and pork back fat, and braised. It is frequently used for canning.

False albacore, a comparatively small tuna weighing about 15kg/33lb, is found only in warmer waters, generally off the coast of Africa. It is sought-after in Japan, where it is used for sashimi.

Bonito and skipjack These fish fall into a category somewhere between tuna and mackerel. There are two main types of bonito: Atlantic *(Sarda sarda)* and skipjack or oceanic *(Katsuwonus pelamis)*. Bonito are inferior to true tuna in quality and taste, with pale, meaty flesh which can sometimes be rather dry. It is best braised or used for casseroles and chowders. It goes well with strongly-flavoured ingredients such as fennel. Skipjack are usually used for canning. They are popular in Japan where they are known as *katsuo* and are often made into dried flakes, which is a main ingredient of *dashi* (stock).

Frigate mackerel Despite its name, this small fish is actually a tuna which is found in the Pacific and Indian Oceans. Some are small enough to cook whole.

Yellowfin These large tuna are fished in tropical and equatorial waters. They have pale pinkish flesh and a good flavour. Confusingly, they are called *albacore* in France, whereas albacore are called *thon blanc* (white tuna).

Blackfin These smaller tuna are fished in the same waters as yellowfins. They are called bigeye in the United States.

Bluefin Considered by many to be the finest of all tuna, bluefin are also the largest. They are found in the Bay of Biscay, the Mediterranean and tropical seas. In Italy and Spain, bluefin goes by the same name as tuna – *tonno* and *atún*, respectively; in France it is called *thon rouge*, on account of its red flesh.

MIGRATORY FISH

Certain species of fish undertake an astonishing annual mass migration from one area to another to spawn or feed. They follow a specific route, although how they know which route to take remains a mystery. Each year, salmon and sea trout migrate from the sea to spawn in the fresh water of the river; having spawned, they return to the sea and so the pattern continues. Eels, on the other hand, travel from rivers and lakes to spawn in salt sea water, entailing a journey of thousands of miles. The whole process is truly one of nature's miracles.

Above: Atlantic salmon is a majestic-looking and wonderfully flavoured fish.

SALMON

Known as the king of fish, salmon is probably the most important of all fish, prized by sportsmen and gastronomes alike. Although salmon spends most of its life in the sea, it is spawned in fresh water and returns to the very same river to spawn itself. Salmon are found in all the cold northern waters of Europe and America. When young salmon first migrate to the sea, they are called smolts. After a year or two of voracious feeding, they reach a weight of 1.2–2kg/2½lb–4½lb and then they make their first spawning run; these young fish are called grilse. Some fish may spawn only once or twice in their lifetime; others spawn up to four times.

Thanks to farming, salmon is easily available and affordable. Unfortunately, the quality is variable and wild salmon is universally considered superior, with those from Scottish or Irish rivers taking the crown. However, salmon from Norwegian waters, and those from Greenland, Canada and the West Coast of the United States are all excellent.

Buying

Salmon are sold whole, as steaks, cutlets, fillets and large middle and tail cuts. The best (and most expensive salmon) are wild fish. Wild salmon are sleeker, with firmer, lustrous skin and deep pink flesh. Farmed salmon is far more commonly available. It is also available all year round, unlike wild salmon, which is available only from spring to late summer. When buying, check that the flesh is firm. It should be dark pink – not pale or greyish – with creamy marbling and not too much fat. The flesh should be firm, not flabby. Salmon heads are heavy, so if you buy whole salmon allow 350g–400g/12–14oz per serving. If buying cutlets or steaks, you will need only 200g/7oz per person.

Cooking

There is almost no limit to the ways in which you can prepare and cook salmon. It can be eaten raw as salmon tartare, sashimi or sushi. It can be marinated in oil, lemon juice and herbs, or salted and marinated with sugar and dill to make *gravadlax*. It can be poached, pan-fried, seared, grilled (broiled), baked or braised, *en papillote* or enveloped in pastry as *saumon en croûte* or *coulibiac*. Poached salmon is delicious hot or cold; a whole fish poached in a court-bouillon makes a superb festive dish served with plain or green mayonnaise and cucumber. It is also excellent with a spicy salsa.

Hot poached salmon can be served with a hollandaise or rich seafood sauce. If you do not have a fish kettle large enough for a whole salmon, wrap the fish in foil, moisten with white wine, then bake. Salmon fillets can be thinly sliced into escalopes and flash-fried, or sandwiched together with fish or shellfish mousse and baked or braised.

Below: Salmon steaks and fillets are one of the simplest ways to enjoy salmon. They need little preparation and are delicious simply cooked.

SALMON TROUT OR SEA TROUT

Although they are closely related to the brown trout, salmon trout differ from other trout species in that they migrate to the sea like salmon, returning to the rivers in autumn. There are also some subtle differences in appearance. They seldom grow to more than 3kg/6¹/₂lb in weight. They have fine dark pink flesh, as a result of feeding on crustaceans. The fish is beautifully succulent and has a delicate, mellow flavour.

Buying

Salmon trout are always wild, but are not so expensive as wild salmon. They are sold whole – a 2kg/4½lb fish will serve four to six people. They should be very bright and silvery with an almost golden sheen to the scales.

Cooking

Salmon trout are versatile fish. Cook them as you would salmon. They are best prepared simply to avoid detracting from their fine, delicate flavour. Like salmon, the fish can also be marinated in lemon juice, oil and herbs and eaten raw.

EELS AND ELVERS

There are more than 20 members of the eel family. Some, like morays and conger eels, are permanent residents of the ocean; the *Anguillidae* family are freshwater fish. They are born in the Sargasso Sea and are carried on the ocean currents to the coasts of Europe and North America. When they enter the estuaries, they are tiny transparent creatures. As they mature their skin colour

Above: Adult eels are at their best in the autumn, when they have turned silver with almost black heads.

changes first to yellow, then to green, then silver. At this stage, the eels begin the long journey back to the Sargasso Sea, where they spawn and then die.

Buying

You may find tiny elvers for sale in spring; they are a great delicacy. Adult eels are available in the autumn, and farmed eels all year round. Eels should be bought alive, as they go off quickly. Ask the fishmonger to skin and chop them into 5cm/2in lengths.

Cooking

Toss tiny elvers in seasoned flour and deep-fry. Soak in acidulated water first to remove the mud. Eel can be fried and served with a simple sauce, or poached. If grilling (broiling), marinate it first, then wrap in streaky bacon. There are many traditional recipes for eel pie.

Above: Salmon trout closely resemble salmon, but are smaller and have a less streamlined shape.

EXOTIC FISH

These fish live in the tropical and subtropical waters of the world – the South Pacific, Caribbean and Indian Ocean – and in warm Atlantic seas. Many have beautiful markings and are strikingly coloured, although they never have quite as good a flavour as those from colder climes. Do not be alarmed at the prospect of cooking unfamiliar fish; they can be cooked in the same way as other species.

PARROTFISH

These fish are found in tropical and subtropical seas throughout the world. They live in large numbers around coral reefs. They have hard, parrot-like beaks with which they nibble the coral, and brightly coloured bodies in a variety of vibrant hues – green, blue, red and multi-coloured. The largest is the rainbow parrotfish, which can grow up to 1m/39in. They look better than they taste, having firm but insipid flesh.

Buying

Many supermarkets now stock pretty parrotfish. Make sure that the colours are clear and bright. The average fish will feed one person; a larger 800g–1kg/1¾–2¼lb fish will serve two. Larger fish are sometimes sold filleted, or can be filleted on request.

Cooking

Parrotfish can be rather bland, so spice them up with tropical flavours, such as coconut milk, garlic, chilli and lemon grass. Whole fish can be braised or baked; they go well with spicy salsa.

MAHI MAHI

Also known as dorade, dorado, lampuka and dolphinfish, although it is no relation to the dolphin, this is a large fish, weighing on average 2.5kg/5½lb, but some have been known to grow to ten times that weight. The name mahi

mahi is Hawaiian and they are very common fish around this island as well as neighbouring ones. In fact, mahi mahi live in almost all the warm seas of the world, including the Mediterranean. They are among the fastest swimmers of the fish kingdom, travelling at a top speed of 80 km/50 miles per hour.

Buying

Available from spring to autumn, mahi mahi is sold as steaks or fillets. Do not buy frozen fish, as it is completely lacking in flavour.

Cooking

The Hawaiians eat this fish raw and it can be prepared like *gravadlax*. It is good grilled (broiled) or barbecued, and it goes well with spicy flavours such as garlic and chilli, and is delicious served with a piquant salsa. In Malta, it is traditional to bake mahi mahi in a pie with vegetables.

Below: Mahi mahi is a very versatile fish that can be cooked in any number of ways.

Above: Vibrant parrotfish lose a little of their colour during cooking.

FLYING FISH

There are various species of flying fish, which can be found in the Caribbean, the Pacific and warm Atlantic waters. They fly through the air, using their large wing-like spineless pectoral fin, starting below the water at high speed and bursting through the surface into the air. They then expand their pectoral fins and glide for about 30 seconds, before dropping back into the water.

Buying

Flying fish are usually displayed whole so that customers can admire their exotic shape. Large fish are sometimes filleted. They do not travel well, so are best eaten soon after being caught.

Cooking

Whole fish or fillets can be dusted in seasoned flour and then deep-fried, baked *au gratin* or braised.

POMFRET

Also known as butterfish in the United States, ray's bream dollar fish and pumpkinseed fish, these small silvery fish look rather like coins as seen through the eyes of Salvador Dali. A variety of pomfret is found in the Mediterranean, but the best-flavoured fish comes from the Indian and Pacific Oceans and they are highly prized in India and Thailand. Pomfret are found off the north-west coast of the United States.

Buying

Pomfret are available most of the year, either fresh or frozen. Small fish weighing about 400g/14oz are sold whole and will feed one person. Fillets from small fish are rather thin, so it is best to choose a larger fish if possible and ask the fishmonger to fillet it.

Cooking

Whole pomfret can be grilled (broiled), fried, baked, poached or steamed. It goes with spices and Oriental flavours.

POMPANO AND JACK

This large family of fish comprises more than 200 species. All are oily fish, similar to mackerel, but with a stronger flavour. Jacks vary enormously in size and shape, but all have forked tails and virtually scaleless, iridescent skin. Pompano and Jack are found in warm seas all over the world, including the Louisiana and Florida coasts. In Australia and New Zealand, yellowtail jack are known as kingfish.

Buying

Pompano and Jack are available all year round. They are generally sold whole, but may be filleted. Outside Florida, you are likely to find only farmed pompano, but this is of excellent quality.

Cooking

Jack can be cooked in the same way as mackerel. The robust flesh lends itself to spicy Oriental flavours. Pompano and Jack can be stuffed with seasoned breadcrumbs or crab meat and baked, grilled (broiled) or barbecued. Pompano is a feature of New Orleans cooking.

Left: Tilapia is also known as St Peter's fish.

Above: Red Emperor snappers have a fine, delicate flavour.

SNAPPER

There are more than 250 species of snapper. The best known, red snapper, come from deep waters around the coasts of Florida and Central and South America. Other varieties are found in warm waters from the Atlantic to the Caribbean and Indo-Pacific.

Buying

Snapper are available all year round, sold whole or as fillets or steaks. Many of the fish sold as red snapper are a different, inferior species; true American red snapper have red eyes. A whole fish weighing about 800g–1kg/1¾–2¼lb will feed two people.

Cooking

Snapper can be baked, grilled (broiled), poached, steamed and pan-fried. It lends itself to exotic and Caribbean flavours such as chilli and coconut.

TILAPIA

Technically, tilapia are freshwater fish. They are found in the Nile and other warm rivers, but can also live in saltwater and are found in tropical seas. There are many varieties of tilapia, with colours ranging from grey to bright red.

Buying and Cooking

Tilapia are available all year round. Much is now farmed. Small fish are sold whole, but larger fish are filleted. A 675g/1½lb fish will serve two. Whole tilapia can be stuffed and baked, grilled (broiled) or barbecued. Fillets can be lightly coated in egg and breadcrumbs or batter and then deep-fried.

DEEP-SEA AND GAME FISH

Deep in the world's oceans live several varieties of fish that rarely come close to the shore. Many have odd shapes and vibrant colours. Most edible deep-sea fish are found around the coasts of New Zealand, South Africa and South America. The Caribbean is home to huge game fish and keen fishermen will pay vast sums for a day's sport.

SWORDFISH

The elongated upper jaw of the swordfish represents up to one-third of its total length. These fish live in deep waters around the world and are known as both culinary and game fish. They occasionally migrate into northern European seas, but are more commonly found in the Mediterranean. They can grow to an enormous size, sometimes weighing up to 600kg/1,320lb. Their excellent white, meaty flesh is low in fat.

Buying

Fresh swordfish is available all year round, usually as steaks. Frozen fish is also available, but is best avoided. A 150g–165g/5–5½oz portion will provide an ample serving. Try to buy fairly thick steaks, as thinner ones have a tendency to dry out during cooking.

Cooking

Swordfish tends to dryness, so needs careful cooking. Baste it frequently with oil when grilling (broiling) or barbecueing and serve with olive oil or a herb butter. Swordfish makes excellent kebabs and can withstand a robust or spicy sauce. It is delicious marinated in olive oil, lemon

Left: Shark loin is firm and well flavoured.

juice, garlic and herbs, then seared in a very hot ridged pan or char-grilled. Swordfish can also be braised or stewed with a selection of Mediterranean vegetables such as (bell) peppers, tomatoes and aubergines (eggplant).

SHARK

The shark, and other members of this large family, are curious in that they have no bones. Their skeletons are made entirely of cartilage. The shark family varies in size from the small dogfish to the huge basking shark, which can weigh up to 4,000kg/8,800lb. Edible sharks include porbeagle, blue shark, mako, tope and several different types of dogfish.

Buying

Shark is sold as steaks, loin or fillets. The flesh has a faint smell of ammonia, which disappears during cooking if the shark is fresh. However, after a week or so, it becomes very pungent and nothing will get rid of it.

Cooking

Shark meat is a match for robust and aromatic flavours and is excellent in curries. Steaks can be grilled (broiled), pan-fried or barbecued. They can be dry, so marinate in olive oil and lemon juice, or lard them with pork back fat.

Varieties

Blue shark The white flesh of this shark is not considered particularly palatable, but the fins are used to garnish the famous and expensive Chinese delicacy shark's fin soup.

Dogfish Known also as huss, flake, rigg or rock salmon, dogfish are small members of the shark family. Only certain types are commonly eaten, namely the lesser spotted dogfish, the spur-dog and the nursehound. The flesh is white or pinkish with a firm texture and a good flavour. Like shark, dogfish is boneless. Dogfish is sold skinned, often in fillets. It is cheap and there is very little waste, so it makes an economical buy, but the fish must be very fresh. It can be cooked in the same way as monkfish and skate.

Mako shark Belonging to the family of mackerel sharks, mako are swift surface swimmers. They live in subtropical and temperate warm seas. Prized by game fishermen, they have a habit of raiding and damaging fishing nets and lines. Mako shark is usually sold as loin or fillets. The flesh is firm but flavourless and benefits from a long, robustly flavoured marinade before it is cooked.

Above: Swordfish may grow to 5m/16½ft.

BARRACUDA

These are fearsome-looking game fish with long slender bodies. Their sharp teeth are capable of delivering a vicious bite and they strike fear into the hearts of divers, who often encounter these alarming fish on coral reefs.

Barracuda are found in warm waters, mainly in the Pacific and Caribbean, but sometimes in warmer Atlantic seas. Young fish travel in schools, but older ones are solitary. They are full of curiosity and will follow divers around reefs and even walkers along the shore. There are about twenty species. The largest is the great barracuda, which has dark bars and scattered black blotches on its greenish skin. This fish can grow to over 1m/39in in length. Other species include the yellowtail and small Pacific and Mexican barracudas. All have meaty, rich, rather oily flesh, which has the reputation of being toxic, possibly owing to an accumulation of toxins from the fish they eat. Play safe by not eating raw barracuda; properly cooked, it is perfectly safe.

Above: Barracuda is also known as becune and sea pike.

Buying

Small barracuda, up to 3kg/6½lb, make the best eating. Ask the fishmonger to scale and fillet them. Larger fish are often sold already filleted. Barracuda is available all year round.

Cooking

The firm, rich flesh of barracuda lends itself to Asian and exotic spices and flavours such as ginger, lemon grass and chillies. It is oily, so avoid cooking it with butter, cream or too much oil.

Small whole barracuda can be grilled (broiled), barbecued, baked or poached; fillets or steaks can be marinated in spices. In Portugal, steaks are grilled (broiled) first, then marinated afterwards and eaten either hot or cold.

Below left: Marlin, which can be found in the Caribbean, is seasonally available as loin and steaks.

MARLIN

The marlin is a magnificent-looking billfish, renowned for its speed and endurance. Its name comes from the greatly elongated upper jaw, which forms a bill or spear. It lives in warm seas throughout the world and can attain enormous weights of 300kg/660lb, though the average size is 160–200kg/352–440lb. The striped marlin is slightly smaller than the blue marlin. The deep pink flesh is high in fat and has a firm texture, but the flavour is rather bland.

Buying and Cooking

Marlin is available in summer as loin and steaks. Try to buy cuts from smaller fish if possible. Cook as for swordfish, or cut into cubes and marinate with lime or lemon juice to make ceviche.

SAILFISH

With similar elongated jaws, the sailfish resembles marlin but looks even more spectacular. It has a streamlined body and a blue dorsal fin which it unfurls like a sail to travel through the water at speeds of 96 km/60 miles per hour.

Buying and Cooking

Treat sailfish in the same way in which you would marlin. The flesh is best marinated in oil, garlic and herbs, then char-grilled or cooked on a ridged grill (broiling) pan or on a barbecue.

MISCELLANEOUS FISH

There are a number of fish that do not fit neatly into any obvious category.

RAY AND SKATE

It is virtually impossible to distinguish between ray and skate on the fishmonger's slab, since only the "wings" are sold. They are both flat, cartilaginous fish, related to the shark. They are found in both cold and temperate waters, living a sedentary life on the seabed. The best-flavoured variety is the thornback. Other

Below: Skate wing has a good texture and the flesh is delicate and sweet-tasting, turning white on cooking.

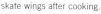

edible varieties include the butterfly or mirror skate and the spotted skate. Normally only the wings are eaten, but the cheeks and small medallions from the tail are regarded as a delicacy. The liver is also highly prized by gourmets.

Buying

Skate is available most of the year but is best in autumn and winter. Smaller wings are sold whole; if you want a larger piece, ask for a middle cut. Even fresh skate smells faintly of ammonia; the smell will disappear during cooking.

Cooking

Before cooking skate, wash it well in cold water to eliminate the ammoniac smell. If the skin is still on, leave it and scrape it off during cooking. The classic skate dish is *raie au beurre noir* (with black butter). Poach the wings in water acidulated with a little vinegar or court-bouillon for about 10 minutes, then drain and sprinkle with capers. Brown some butter (do not let it burn and blacken) and pour it over the fish. Skate can also be grilled (broiled).

HOKI

Related to the hake, hoki has the same white flesh and flaky texture. They can be found around the coasts of Southern Australia and New Zealand. In Australia hoki are called blue grenadier; in New Zealand they are whiptail or blue hake. A similar species to hoki is found around South America.

Buying

Hoki is available all year round, as fillets, loin and other cuts. It is used to make fish fingers or ocean sticks.

Cooking

The delicate white flesh is suitable for most cooking methods, particularly frying. It can sometimes taste insipid so is best served with a robust tomato-based sauce or a creamy sauce. It can also be used for kebabs.

Below: Hoki fillets can be cooked in a variety of ways but are very good fried.

Skinning Cooked Skate

It is easiest to remove the skin from skate wings after cooking.

1 With a blunt knife, scrape off the skin from the thicker part of the skate wing towards the edge.

2 Discard the skin. Scrape the flesh off the cartilage in the same way.

ORANGE ROUGHY

Known as sea perch in Australia, orange roughy were once believed to inhabit only Icelandic waters. In the 1970s, however, large numbers were found in the deep waters around New Zealand. They belong, like John Dory and monkfish, to the "looks ugly, tastes delicious" category of fish, with massive heads and conspicuous bony ridges. The pearly-white flesh is similar in texture to that of cod, but has a sweet, shellfish flavour.

Buying

Orange roughy is available all year round, usually as fillets. You may be lucky enough to find fresh fish, but most is frozen at sea.

Cooking

Orange roughy holds together well when cooked, which makes it suitable for most cooking methods. Its almost crab-like flavour marries well with other seafood. It can be used for soups and stews, and is good poached, pan-fried, roasted or steamed. It can also be dipped in batter or coated with egg and breadcrumbs and deep-fried.

GARFISH

Also known as needlefish, there are more than fifty species of garfish. Most inhabit tropical seas, but some, like the garfish, are found in cooler waters, and one species is found only in freshwater. Many people find the needle-like appearance of the garfish off-putting, despite (or perhaps because of) their vibrant silver and blue-green colouring and their long spear-like beaks.

Garfish can grow to 2m/6½ft, but are more common up to 80cm/32in. Their bones are a phosphorescent green even when cooked (this coloration is completely harmless), and even their flesh has a greenish tinge, although this whitens on cooking. Despite these physical disadvantages, garfish are good to eat, with firm flesh from which the backbone can easily be removed, since you can hardly miss it.

Buying

Garfish are sold whole. If you do not want to serve it that way, ask the fishmonger to clean the fish and cut it into 5cm/2in chunks.

Cooking

To cook a whole garfish, wash it inside and out, rub the cavity with lemon juice, then curl the fish round and stick the pointed beak into the tail end so that it forms a ring. Brush with a marinade of olive oil, lemon juice, garlic and chopped parsley and grill (broil) or barbecue for about 15 minutes, basting frequently. Chunks of garfish or saury can be coated in seasoned flour and pan-fried in butter and oil, or stewed with onions and tomatoes. They are gelatinous fish, so make excellent soups and stews, or fish couscous.

Above: Orange roughy has a delicate, almost sweet flavour that is reminiscent of crab.

OPAH

Variously called moonfish, sunfish or mariposa, this beautiful, slim, oval fish is found in warm waters throughout the world, but so far only solitary specimens have been caught. It has a steel-blue back shading into a rose-pink belly, with silver spots all over its body. It has red fins, jaws and tail, and, unusually, is the only member of its family. The opah is toothless and scaleless, and can grow to an enormous size. Some specimens weigh over 200kg/440lb and measure more than 2m/6½ft, though the average weight is 20kg/44lb. The flesh is salmon-pink, with a flavour similar to tuna.

Buying

Should you be lucky enough to find opah on the fishmonger's slab, ask for it to be cut into steaks or escalopes.

Cooking

Treat opah in the same way as salmon or tuna, taking great care not to overcook, and serve with a creamy sauce or mayonnaise.

Below: Garfish tends to be unpopular because of its green bones.

JOHN DORY

These fish were sacred to Zeus, hence the Latin name of *Zeus faber*. The olive-brown bodies of these fish are so slim that they look almost like upright flat fish. Dories have extremely ugly faces and spiny dorsal fins from which long filaments trail. Their most distinguishing feature is a large black spot ringed with yellow right in the middle of their bodies; this is said to be the thumbprint of St Peter. The story goes that the saint lifted a John Dory in the Sea of Galilee, leaving his thumb and finger prints on either side, and found in its mouth a gold coin, which he used to pay the

Below: Despite its unattractive appearance, John Dory is one of the most delicious of all fish, with firm, succulent white flesh, similar to turbot and Dover sole.

unpopular tax collectors. This fable is highly unlikely, since John Dory are not found in the Sea of Galilee, but in the Atlantic. Those from American coastal waters are known as American dories, while fish from the eastern Atlantic, from Britain and Norway to Africa, and from the Mediterranean, are European dories. Another species, from the southern hemisphere, lives in the Indo-Pacific Ocean.

Buying

Thanks to its large head, almost two-thirds of a dory's weight is wastage, which makes it a very expensive fish. Small dories weighing 1–2kg/2¼–4½lb are sold whole; a 1kg/2¼lb fish will feed two people. For fillets, buy the largest fish you can afford, and allow 150–200g/5–7oz per serving.

Cooking

Whole fish can be grilled (broiled), braised, baked, steamed or poached; boiled and served with mayonnaise makes a popular Venetian and Catalan dish. Its succulent flesh goes well with Mediterranean flavours such as tomatoes, fennel, red (bell) peppers, olives and saffron. Fillets can be cooked in the same way as sole, brill and turbot. They are superb served with a red wine, white wine or creamy sauce.

Right: The ugly monkfish is very fashionable and therefore rather expensive to buy. It is really only the flesh on the tail section that is valued.

> **Bouillabaisse**
> This Provençal fish soup is really more of a stew than a soup, and was originally cooked on the beach by fishermen, using those fish that had little market value. It can contain John Dory, monkfish and other Mediterranean fish, plus small crabs and other shellfish, all cooked together with tomatoes, potatoes and onions, and flavoured with garlic, olive oil and saffron.

MONKFISH

This extraordinarily ugly fish has an enormous, gruesome-looking head equipped with a "rod and lure" to catch its food; hence its alternative name of anglerfish. Monkfish have a huge mouth fringed with lethally sharp teeth and a dangling rod, which is actually the first spine of the dorsal fin, on its nose. Its comparatively small body has brown, scaleless skin.

On the fishmonger's slab, the only part of a monkfish you are likely to see is the tail, since the head is almost always removed because of its extreme ugliness, disproportionate weight and the fact that only the cheeks are worth eating. The flesh found on the tail is quite another matter; it is quite delicious, and is the reason why monkfish is considered to be one of the finest of all fish, with a superb firm texture and a delicious sweetness, rather like lobster meat. In fact, some unscrupulous caterers have been known to pass off monkfish as lobster or scampi. The only bone the tail contains is the backbone, which makes it especially easy to prepare and pleasant to eat. Monkfish liver is not widely available but, if you can get it, it is a great delicacy.

Buying

Monkfish is available all year round, but is best in spring and summer before spawning. It is sold as whole tails, fillets or medallions. A whole tail can weigh as much as 3.5kg/8lb, but on average weighs 750g–1.5kg/1^1/$_2$–3lb. Generally speaking, the larger the tail, the better the quality; avoid thin, scraggy tails. For tails with the bone in, allow about 200g/7oz per person.

Cooking

One of the best ways to cook a whole monkfish tail is to treat it like a leg of lamb; tie it up with string, stud with slivers of garlic and thyme or rosemary leaves, anoint with olive oil and roast. Monkfish can also be grilled (broiled), made into kebabs, pan-fried, poached and served cold with garlicky mayonnaise, or braised in white wine, with saffron and cream. It goes well with other seafood such as salmon, red mullet and shellfish, and is used in hearty fish soups. Thin escalopes are delicious marinated in olive oil and lemon juice, then coated with flour and sautéed in butter.

Below: Monkfish tail has a superb firm texture and a delicious sweetness.

Preparing Monkfish Tails

The tails are the best part of the monkfish. Because of their high water content, fillets should be cooked with very little liquid. They are easy to prepare.

1 Grasp the thick end of the tail firmly with one hand and peel off the skin with the other, working from the thick to the thin end.

2 Carefully pull off the thin, dark or pinkish membrane.

3 Fillet the tail by cutting through the flesh on either side of the backbone with a sharp knife (there are no small bones). The bone can be used to make stock.

FRESHWATER FISH

There is a wide variety of freshwater fish, but not in large quantities, and so, commercially, it has never been worth netting these fish. The exception, of course, are fish like salmon and trout, which are generally farmed. Carp and char are now increasingly being farmed, too, and may sometimes be found at a fishmonger's. The majority of other freshwater fish, such as pike, grayling and roach, are caught only by anglers.

Freshwater fish, as a rule, have a delicate and less robust flavour than seawater fish. To be enjoyed at their best, they should be cooked as soon as possible after being caught.

TROUT

The pretty, iridescent, green and brown spotted rainbow trout is the fish you commonly find in supermarkets and on the fishmonger's slab. This is the farmed variety of trout. It is widely available, relatively inexpensive and the delicate, succulent and sweet flesh is universally appreciated.

Brown trout, sometimes called lake trout, are the wild trout of British rivers. They look significantly more robust than their rainbow cousins, having a brown skin with red and dark grey spots. Their flesh is more succulent than that of rainbow trout and is quite delicious. It is creamy white when cooked, whereas the flesh of rainbow trout is pink. Unfortunately, brown trout are hardly ever seen for sale and are usually available only to the friends and families of fly-fishers.

Right: Golden trout are farmed hybrid trout, which taste similar to rainbow trout.

Buying and Cooking

Trout are available all year round. The fishmonger will clean the fish but it is commonly cooked, unfilleted, as a whole fish. Unless the trout are very large, allow one fish per person.

Trout are wonderfully versatile fish. They can be grilled (broiled), pan-fried, baked or barbecued. They can also be poached in a court-bouillon, cooked in beer, or steamed. The traditional way of cooking brown trout is *au bleu*, when very fresh fish are poached in stock acidulated with vinegar, which turns them a delicate shade of blue.

Above: Rainbow trout (top), unlike brown trout (bottom), are easy to find.

Rainbow trout can be cooked with more robust flavourings, such as anchovies or bacon. Both rainbow and brown trout are good served cold with mayonnaise or other creamy dressings.

GRAYLING

You'll be lucky to find this for sale at the supermarket or fishmonger's, but if you do – or a fisher friend drops one by – then you are in for a treat. It is similar in many ways to the brown trout, with a fine flavour and texture. Grayling tend to be relatively small fish, rarely heavier than 900g/2lb and often as small as only 225g/8oz. They need to be eaten as soon as possible after catching, and do not travel or keep well. Before cooking, pour boiling water over the fish and scrape off the scales with a blunt knife. Pan-fry or grill (broil), brushing it first with melted butter. You can also use trout or salmon recipes for cooking grayling.

BARBEL

These fish live in fast-flowing rivers. They have brown backs, yellowish sides and white bellies. Barbel have rather tasteless flesh and are extremely bony, so they are not regarded as prime river fish. They are popular in the Loire and Burgundy regions of France, where they are typically poached or braised with a red wine sauce.

Below: Bream has a rather bland taste and is best used in braised dishes and fish stews.

Cooking

Barbel need strong flavours to enhance their intrinsic blandness. Small young fish can be grilled (broiled) and served with a well-seasoned butter; larger fish (weighing up to 1.75kg/4lb) are best used in a hearty, robust stew such as *matelote*.

BREAM

These fish, with their flat oval greenish-brown bodies covered with gold scales, are more attractive in their looks than in their taste. The bony flesh is soft and bland, and can sometimes taste muddy, since bream live in the silt near the bottom of pools and slow-flowing rivers.

Cooking

Bream is best used in braised dishes and stews with other fish, but it can also be grilled (broiled) or baked, stuffed or seasoned with strong flavours such as garlic and pungent herbs, and brushed with olive oil or butter to baste its rather dry flesh. Before cooking, the fish should be thoroughly cleaned with salt and lemon or vinegar, and then soaked in acidulated water for several hours. This process will eliminate any muddy flavour.

Below: Catfish are traditionally coated in oatmeal and deep-fried, and served with tartare sauce.

CATFISH

These fish take their name from the long whiskery barbels, resembling a cat's whiskers, that help them to locate their prey in the muddy river waters where they live. The catfish has a broad flat head and belly, and smooth, scaleless, somewhat slimy skin. There are dozens of different species, ranging from tiny fish to gigantic ones weighing several hundredweight. Catfish are extremely hardy and can live out of water for a considerable time. These fish are found all over the world, but the best fish for eating are the American species known as bullheads, which have firm, meaty, rather fatty white flesh and very few bones. In Louisiana and other southern parts of the United States these are being farmed in increasing quantities to produce an important food source.

Cooking

The classic southern American cooking method for catfish is to coat it in cornmeal, deep-fry it and serve with tartare sauce. It can also be grilled (broiled) or pan-fried in butter, stuffed and baked, or cooked like eel, whose flesh it resembles. The tough skin must be removed before cooking. Catfish also makes a good addition to fish soups and stews, cooked with garlic and tomatoes. However it is cooked, it needs plenty of flavouring with salty powerful tastes such as anchovies, bacon or olives, herbs and olive oil.

GUDGEON

Small white fish with large heads and thick lips, gudgeon have delicious, delicate flesh. They live at the bottom of lakes and rivers all over Europe and freshly caught and crisply fried gudgeon were once a common sight in cafés on riverbanks in France, where they are known as *goujon*.

Cooking

Gudgeon must be gutted and wiped clean before cooking. Coat them in flour or very light batter and deep-fry until very crisp and golden. Sprinkle with salt and serve with lemon wedges.

CHAR

The char is a member of the salmon family. There are several varieties: the common char is found in the deep lakes of the French and Swiss Alps; the Arctic char comes from northern Europe and Canada. The wild fish is now a rarity in Britain, but since the fish is farmed today, it can occasionally be found in fishmongers.

Buying and Cooking

Char is sold whole or in convenient fillets. It can be cooked as you would trout – steamed, baked or pan-fried. It goes well with a rich sauce.

CARP

This is one of the few freshwater fish that is extensively farmed, and it is popular in Chinese and Jewish cooking. It is traditionally eaten on Christmas Eve in Poland and other Catholic countries.

Buying and Cooking

Carp is usually sold whole and will give a generous serving for four people. Before cooking, pour some boiling water over the fish and remove the scales with a knife or your fingernails. Fillets are sometimes available.

   Carp can be poached and served with a robust sauce, or stuffed and gently baked to keep the flesh moist.

Above: Carp rouge, with its pinkish-red irridescent scales, is one of the prettiest fish on the fishmonger's slab.

Below: Carp is a member of the minnow family.

Below: The pike is a long-bodied fish with a pointed head and jaw, and a mouthful of vicious-looking teeth.

PIKE

Pike are a native freshwater fish, renowned for their predatory nature. They can grow to a massive 18kg/40lb and the muskellunge of north-eastern North America can be even bigger. They have a firm white flesh, which can be dry. The pike is much admired in France, where it is used for *quenelles de brochet*, and it is highly regarded in the United States.

Buying and Cooking

Pike is available from certain specialist fishmongers, normally in autumn and early winter. Larger specimens are cut into steaks, but smaller fish can be found whole. Whole fish can be stuffed and baked, or poached. Serve with a simple sauce. Alternatively, use the flesh to make *quenelles*, a fish mousse made with beaten egg and cream, shaped into small ovals and poached in a little water or fish stock.

PERCH

This fish has a greenish-gold skin and coral fins, and a spiky dorsal fin on the humped back. It can reach a weight of 3kg/6½lb, but the average weight is only about 500g/1¼lb. Perch are highly prized for their firm, delicate flesh, but are only rarely available.

Pike perch, also known as zander, has firm, wonderfully flavoured flesh and tastes even better than perch. It can grow quite large, sometimes weighing up to 5kg/11lb, and fillets are delicious and meaty.

Buying and Cooking

Perch should be absolutely fresh, and since it doesn't freeze well you'll need to eat it on the day it's caught. Prepare the fish carefully to remove the stubborn scales and sharp spines. The whole fish can be pan-fried, grilled (broiled), baked or poached. Pike perch can be cooked in the same way.

STURGEON

A weird and wonderful creature, sturgeon is best known for its roe, caviar. This large fish spends most of its life in the sea, but comes into the rivers to spawn. It is only at this point that the fish is intentionally caught, after which the roes are removed and the fish is cut into steaks or fillets.

Cooking

The white flesh is firm and closely textured. It is likened to veal and is often treated in a similar way, being larded with anchovy fillets and garlic before being roasted.

ROACH

Although roach has a good flavour, it has an irritating number of bones.

Cooking

Small roach can be fried with other tiny fish to make a *friture*. If you don't mind the bones, larger fish can be grilled (broiled), fried, or baked in white wine.

Right: Roach has firm white flesh with a good flavour. Their greenish roe, which turns red when cooked, is good to eat.

Above: Sturgeon steaks may be poached in white wine, or baked in a sauce.

SHAD

This member of the herring family is categorized as a freshwater fish as, like salmon and trout, it spawns in freshwater. The fish has a good flavour but is unpopular on account of its huge number of tiny bones. Try to remove as many bones as possible before cooking, and then check for bones again once the fish is cooked. It can be stuffed and baked or cooked *à la meunière*.

TENCH

This fat-bodied relative of the minnow has a coppery-green body covered with small scales and a thick coating of slime. Tench are hardy, fighting fish, which make great sport for anglers. They live in sluggish streams and have a tendency to taste muddy, but they make a good addition to a fish stew. They can also be baked or fried, and should be served with a robustly flavoured sauce to enliven the rather bland flesh. They must be scaled and thoroughly cleaned before cooking; scalding them with boiling water helps remove the scales.

WHITEFISH

These members of the salmon family are silvery-white in colour. They resemble trout, but have larger scales and smaller mouths. Whitefish live in cold, clear lochs and lakes in northern Europe and America. In Britain, they are sometimes called vendace or powan. They have a pleasant texture and flavour, somewhere between trout and grayling, but not as fine as either.

SMOKED AND PRESERVED FISH

Once one of the most ancient ways of preserving fish, smoking is used today less for preserving and more for imparting a unique flavour. There are two methods – cold- and hot-smoking – which give very different results. For both methods, the fish must first be dry-salted or soaked in brine. The fish are then smoked over different types of wood, all of which impart their own unique, distinctive taste. Other flavourings such as jasmine tea may also be used.

COLD-SMOKED FISH

To produce good quality cold-smoked fish requires a high degree of skill because it is difficult to get the flavour and texture just right. The cold-smoking process is done at a temperature of about 30–35°C/86–95°F, which cures but does not cook the fish. Some cold-smoked fish such as salmon, halibut and trout, are eaten raw; others such as kippers and haddock, are usually cooked although they can be marinated and eaten just as they are.

SMOKED SALMON

This is one of the best loved of all smoked fish. Smoked salmon is made by brining the fish, then dry curing it in sugar with flavourings such as molasses or whisky, and smoking it over wood chips (usually oak). Different woods give a different flavour to the salmon; some Scottish and Irish salmon is smoked over a fire made from old whisky barrels, which imparts a subtle flavour of the spirit. The colour varies from pale pink to deep brownish-red.

Buying and Serving

Smoked salmon is usually sold ready-sliced with the paper-thin slices separated by sheets of transparent paper. Whole sides are sliced and the slices are re-assembled to restore the shape of the fillet. Avoid buying sliced fish that is not layered with paper as the delicate slices stick together. The thinner the salmon is sliced, the better. Top-quality smoked salmon should be eaten just as it is, served with thinly sliced brown bread and butter. Cheaper salmon or trimmings can be stirred into scrambled eggs, omelettes, quiches or flans, mixed into pasta or puréed to make mousses.

Left: Smoked halibut has been coated in honey and smoked over beech and juniper, giving it a pale golden exterior.

SMOKED HALIBUT

Sold thinly sliced and interleaved with paper like smoked salmon, smoked halibut has translucent white flesh and a delicate flavour. It can be eaten as it is or used like smoked haddock. The flavour can be enhanced with a mild, creamy horseradish sauce.

COLD-SMOKED TROUT

A cheaper alternative to smoked salmon, this looks like salmon but has a more delicate flavour. It can be eaten in the same way as smoked salmon.

SMOKED STURGEON

Smoked sturgeon has a pale pinkish flesh with a rich flavour and a succulent texture. It should be thinly sliced across the grain. As it is a great luxury, it should be treated like the very best quality smoked salmon.

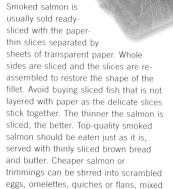

Left: Smoked salmon is one of the most popular of all smoked fish.

Below: Smoked sturgeon is rare and expensive, and tastes superb.

Left: Finnan haddock should be boned and skinned after cooking.

Finnan Haddock

These are distinctively pale, whole split haddock (with the bone left in), named after the Scottish village of Findon, where the special smoking process originated. It gives the fish a pale corn colour and a subtle smoked flavour. Cook as you would haddock. It is excellent simply grilled (broiled).

KIPPERS

Herrings are briefly brined, then hung up in pairs and smoked over oak fires for 4–18 hours to produce kippers. Dye is often added to the brine, resulting in deep reddish-brown kippers, but the best are undyed.

Buying and Cooking

Look for plump kippers; lean ones can be dry. As a rule, the darker the fish, the poorer the quality. Frozen boil-in-the-bag kipper fillets are convenient but have a flabby texture and insipid taste.

To avoid cooking smells, put kippers in a heatproof jug, head down, and pour over boiling water. Leave for about 10 minutes, by which time the kippers will be cooked. Kippers are also good grilled (broiled) skin-side up or fried in butter. They make a delicious breakfast dish, topped with a poached or fried egg.

Boning Cooked Kippers

Removing the bones from cooked kippers is very simple.

1 Run the point of a sharp knife around the edge of the kipper to lift up the skin.

2 Run the knife point down the backbone and lift off the flesh. Discard the skin and bones.

SMOKED HADDOCK

Smoked haddock comes in various forms, from bright yellow dyed fillets to pale, naturally cured fillets.

Buying and Cooking

Avoid buying dyed smoked haddock. It is now known that the dyes used can be carcinogenic; dyed fillets are also often flavoured with artificial chemicals to simulate the effect of smoking.

Smoked haddock is succulent and delicious. It is usually eaten hot, but thinly sliced fillets can be marinated and eaten raw as a starter. Smoked haddock can be grilled like kippers, or poached in milk or water. Serve with butter or topped with a poached egg.

BLOATERS

These are ungutted herrings that are briefly salted, then smoked for about 12 hours. The guts impart a gamy flavour and the enzymes they contain cause the herrings to become bloated during smoking.

Cooking

Bloaters do not keep well and should be eaten within a few days. Always gut them before serving. They can be eaten as they are in salads and sandwiches, or mashed into a paste with lemon juice and cayenne pepper, or grilled (broiled) and served with butter.

Left: Bloaters, although still available, are not as common as they once were.

HOT-SMOKED FISH

Fish that are cured or hot-smoked at a temperature of 80–85°C/176–185°F, which both cooks and cures them, need no further cooking. Trout, mackerel, eel and herrings can all be hot-smoked. Recently it has become fashionable to hot-smoke salmon, producing a very different flavour and texture from that of salmon that has been cold-smoked.

ARBROATH SMOKIES

These hot-smoked haddock have been beheaded and gutted but left whole. They have deep golden skin and soft pale gold flesh with a more delicate flavour than cold-smoked haddock. In their native Scotland, they are a favourite breakfast or supper dish. As smokies are sold whole, ask the fishmonger to split them open for you. Grill (broil) gently and serve with plenty of butter. When mashed with butter and lemon juice, Arbroath smokies make a delicious and easy-to-prepare pâté.

SMOKED EEL

This fish has a rich, dense texture and can be eaten only in small quantities. The skin, which is easily removed, is black and shiny and the flesh has a pinkish tinge. The eel can be served on its own as an hors d'oeuvre, with horseradish or mustard sauce to cut the richness, or made into a salad or pâté.

Above: Smoked sprats make a delicious snack or starter served with toast.

It is delicious served on a bed of celeriac rémoulade (grated celeriac in a mustard-flavoured mayonnaise). Smoked eel also makes a good addition to a platter of mixed smoked fish.

When buying smoked eel, check that the skin is shiny and has not dried out. You will need 90g/3½oz per person.

Below: Arbroath smokies are always sold in pairs, tied with string.

BRISLING, SILD AND SPRATS

These small, hot-smoked herrings with rich oily flesh are usually skinned and filleted and served cold as a starter with brown bread and butter. They are also very good brushed with melted unsalted (sweet) butter and lightly grilled (broiled), then served with toast.

Left: Smoked fillets of freshwater eels are very rich and should be served with a tart sauce to cut through the richness.

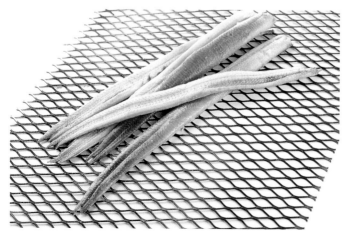

Left: Rich-tasting buckling is best served simply for a starter or snack, with a wedge of lemon for squeezing.

Below: Smoked sea trout is just as expensive as smoked salmon and makes a wonderful alternative.

Bottom: Smoked mackerel is widely available and very versatile. It is delicious served in both hot and cold dishes.

BUCKLING

These are large, fat, ungutted herrings with a rich flavour. They are best eaten cold with bread and butter, but can be mashed into a paste or grilled (broiled) and served with scrambled eggs.

SMOKED MACKEREL

This has a rich flavour and a succulent velvety-smooth texture. The fillets are sold loose or pre-packed. They are sometimes coated in a thick layer of crushed peppercorns. Smoked mackerel can be eaten cold in a salad, or with horseradish sauce and lemon. It makes an excellent pâté and can be flaked and added to an omelette or quiche. Try it instead of smoked haddock in a kedgeree. Allow one fillet of fish per person.

To skin smoked mackerel, lay the fish on a board, skin-side up. Starting at the tail end, peel back the skin towards the head. Pull away any fins together with their bones.

SMOKED TROUT

Among the finest of all hot-smoked fish, trout should be plump and moist, with a beautiful golden-pink colour. The flesh has a delicate flavour and is less rich than smoked herring or mackerel. The best smoked trout is first brined, then gutted and smoked over birch with the addition of a little peat for a smokier flavour. Smoked trout is usually sold as skinned fillets, but you may occasionally find them whole, with the head on. Skin them like smoked mackerel.

Smoked trout is delicious served on its own with dill or horseradish sauce. It can be made into mousses or pâtés and is also served in salads, omelettes and flans. Allow one fillet per person as a starter; two as a main course.

PICKLED, DRIED AND SALTED FISH

There are many other ways of preserving fish – techniques that were perfected by our ancestors, to ensure that food was always available, even during lean months. Pickling has always been a good way of preserving oily fish, although it is not suitable for more delicate fish. Drying is a particularly useful way of preserving fish and has been used throughout the world since prehistoric times. Even today, in remote communities, traditional methods of drying fish, with long ropes strung with split and salted fish hung out to dry like washing, are a common sight.

PICKLED HERRING

Curing in vinegar or brine is an effective way of preserving fish. It is particularly well suited to oily fish such as herrings. Herring fillets are normally marinated in vinegar and spices, then coated in a soured cream sauce.

Left: Pickled herrings, in all shapes and forms, are a particular speciality of most countries in northern Europe.

Below: Bismarck herring are delicious served with soured cream and crisp, freshly baked bread rolls.

Above: Maajtes herring take on a brownish-pink colour as a result of the curing process.

MAAJTES HERRING

Fat young female herrings (*maajtes* means maiden or virgin in Dutch) are skinned and filleted before they are lightly cured in salt, sugar, spices and saltpetre. In Holland and Belgium they are eaten with chopped raw onion. The Scandinavian equivalent is *matjes*. These have a stronger flavour and are generally eaten with some sour cream and chopped hard-boiled (hard-cooked) egg.

BISMARCK HERRING

Also called Baltic herring, the herrings are split in the same way as kippers and marinated in white wine vinegar and spices, ranging from red (bell) peppers to juniper berries. The fillets are layered with onion rings and carrot rounds.

ROLLMOPS

These consist of herring fillets rolled up, with the skin side out, around whole peppercorns and pickling spice, and secured with wooden cocktail sticks (tooth picks). The rolls are then marinated in sweetened white wine vinegar with gherkins and onion slices. Thinly sliced onion rings are sometimes incorporated in the herring rolls. They are good served with rye bread, and a cucumber salad dressed with a sour cream and dill sauce.

Above. Swedish gravadlax is made from really fresh salmon fillet.

Above: Pretty silver-skinned rollmops have a wonderfully tart flavour.

Below: Jellied eels, once a favourite dish in London's East End, fell out of favour for many years and seemed almost to have disappeared from sight. Now, however, they are enjoying a revival in popularity.

GRAVADLAX

A wonderfully succulent and tasty Swedish speciality, gravadlax (or gravlax) has achieved a great popularity in recent years. It is fresh, raw salmon fillet that has been cured with dill, sugar, salt and coarse peppercorns. Gravadlax is widely available, often packed with a sachet of dill-flavoured mustard sauce which makes the perfect – and authentic – accompaniment. Gravadlax may be served as an hors d'oeuvre; it makes a tasty filling for baguettes and rolls; or it may be eaten with a salad.

JELLIED EELS

In Britain, market stalls selling this traditional Cockney dish are now becoming increasingly rare, but jellied eels are widely available frozen and in cans. Jellied eels are made by boiling pieces of eel in a marinade of white wine vinegar and herbs, then leaving them in the liquid with masses of chopped fresh parsley until the mixture sets to a light jelly. Serve jellied eels with thick slices of bread and butter.

Home-cured Gravadlax

To make gravadlax for eight people, you will need 1–1.2kg/2¼–2½lb fresh middle-cut salmon, boned and cut lengthways into two fillets.

1 In a bowl, combine 30ml/2 tbsp coarse sea salt, 30ml/2 tbsp sugar, 15–30ml/1–2 tbsp coarsely crushed peppercorns and a good handful of chopped fresh dill.

2 Lay one salmon fillet skin-side down in a non-metallic dish. Cover with a generous layer of the curing mix. Lay the second fillet on top, skin-side up, and sprinkle on the remaining curing mix.

3 Cover with clear film (plastic wrap). Place a wooden board on top of the salmon and weight down with heavy cans or weights.

4 Place the fish in the refrigerator and leave for at least 72 hours, turning the salmon every 12 hours and basting it with the juices that have oozed out.

5 To serve, using a sharp knife, slice the gravadlax on the diagonal, a little thicker than you would for smoked salmon. Serve with a sweet mustard and dill sauce.

SALT COD AND STOCKFISH

The most common commercial dried fish is cod, and its relatives haddock, ling and pollack. When dried, these look – and feel – like old shoe leather, but once reconstituted in water, the flesh softens and tastes delicious when cooked. Stockfish is not salted before being dried. Whatever the type, dried cod must be soaked for many hours in cold water.

BOMBAY DUCK

Why this dried small transparent fish from the Indian sub-continent should be called Bombay duck, no one knows for sure. As soon as the fish is caught, it is filleted and hung on cane frames to dry. Bombay duck looks and tastes vaguely like very strongly flavoured pork scratchings. It is served as an appetizer or used as a garnish for curries and rice dishes.

SHARK'S FIN

Dried shark's fin is highly prized in China. The fins from the many species of sharks which inhabit the Indo-Pacific Oceans are sun-dried and preserved in lime. In its dried state, shark's fin looks like a bushy beard, but after soaking it reconstitutes into a gelatinous, viscous mass with a texture resembling calf's foot jelly. It is highly nutritious and is eaten as a tonic.

SALTED FISH ROE

Caviar is made from lightly cured sturgeon roe, and is the most expensive luxury food in the world. It has a unique texture and an elusive and incomparable flavour. The three main types of caviar take their names from the species of sturgeon from which the eggs come.

The rarest and most expensive is Beluga. The dark grey eggs are quite large and well separated. Oscietra is golden or yellowish-brown with smaller grains and an oily texture. Sevruga is the least expensive caviar, coming from the smallest and most prolific fish. It has small, pale, greenish-grey grains and a markedly salty flavour.

Grey mullet roe, which is dried, is regarded as a great delicacy and is very nutritious. The orange roe is salted, then dried and pressed.

Salmon caviar is made from vibrant orange-pink salmon roe. The eggs are much larger than sturgeon caviar and have a pleasant, mild flavour and an excellent texture.

Lumpfish roe is sometimes known as mock or Danish caviar, this is the roe of the Arctic lumpfish. The tiny eggs are dyed black or orange-red and look pretty as a garnish for canapés.

Above: Salt cod needs to be soaked for at least 48 hours before cooking.

Below: Bombay duck looks like chunks of wood and has a very strong smell.

Below: Shark's fin has very little flavour of its own but, when cooked, has a very interesting gelatinous texture, which is highly-prized in Chinese cooking.

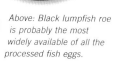

Left: Caviar

Above: Black lumpfish roe is probably the most widely available of all the processed fish eggs.

Left: Red lumpfish roe makes a good garnish, but use only at the last minute as the dye can leak out and spoil the dish.

CANNED FISH

This is a useful store-cupboard (pantry) ingredient. While it never has the subtle texture and flavour of fresh fish, canned fish can be excellent in its own right.

ANCHOVIES

Fillets are preserved in oil (olive oil is best) in small oblong cans or bottled in jars. The salty fillets are a staple ingredient of salade niçoise and tapenade (olive and anchovy paste), and are used as a topping for pizzas and crostini. They can be mashed into butter as a topping for grilled (broiled) fish, or chopped and mixed into tomato sauces. Anchovies enhance the flavour of many non-fish dishes (roast lamb, for example) without making them taste fishy. Once opened, anchovies perish quickly, so try to use the whole can or jar at once. Any leftovers should be submerged in oil and kept for only a day or two.

PILCHARDS

These fish are older sardines. They lack the subtle flavour of their younger siblings, so are usually canned in tomato sauce.

SALMON

Canned salmon is quite different in flavour and texture from fresh fish, but is useful to have in the store cupboard (pantry). It is richer in calcium than fresh salmon, because the bones are softened during the canning process and can easily be eaten. Canned salmon was once the mainstay of sandwiches, salads, fish cakes and fish pies, but it has been overshadowed by

Right: Canned tuna is a useful store-cupboard standby and is perfect for salads, snacks, sandwiches and other quick meals.

inexpensive farmed fresh salmon. Canned salmon is available in several grades, the most expensive having the best flavour and texture. Canned salmon is good for making mousses, soufflés and fish cakes.

SARDINES

These were the first fish to be canned; in 1834, a canning factory opened in Brittany to process the sardines that abounded on the Breton coast. For years, tiny Breton sardines were the best, but they have all but disappeared and most sardines canned in France now come from North Africa. Large numbers of sardines are also canned in Spain and Portugal. The finest sardines are fried in olive oil before canning. Most sardines are be-headed and gutted before being packed raw, complete with backbones, in groundnut or olive oil. Inferior or damaged fish are packed in tomato or

Left: The best canned sardines are packed in olive oil.

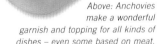

Above: Anchovies make a wonderful garnish and topping for all kinds of dishes – even some based on meat.

mustard sauce. Sardines in olive oil are the best; the more expensive varieties are left to mature for at least a year to soften the bones and mature the flavour. The best way to enjoy canned sardines is to serve them whole on hot toast. They can also be mashed with lemon juice and cayenne pepper to make a simple pâté.

TUNA

In recent years, canned tuna has received a bad press because dolphins were often caught in the tuna nets and slaughtered unnecessarily. Canners have now become more ecologically aware and most tuna is line-caught. The best canned tuna is the pale albacore, which is usually canned in one solid piece. Cheaper varieties, such as skipjack and yellowfin, are often sold as chunks or flaky broken pieces. Tuna comes packed in olive oil (the best), vegetable oil or brine, which is healthier and lighter. Canned tuna is a versatile ingredient that can be served with pasta, used in sandwiches and salads and made into a pâté or fish loaf. It is used in the classic Italian dish *vitello tonnato*.

CRUSTACEANS

This family of shellfish is truly enormous and includes crabs, lobsters, crayfish, and prawns and shrimps. They can be virtually any shape or size, their distinguishing feature being that their skeleton (carapace) is on the outside, concealing a soft and delicious flesh. Crustaceans may require considerable effort to prepare, cook and eat, but they are well worth it.

CRABS

There are dozens of varieties of crab, ranging from the hefty common crabs that will make a meal for several people, to the tiny shore crabs that are the size of a fingernail, and are good only for making soups. Crabs travel many hundreds of kilometres (miles) in a year from feeding to spawning grounds, and are often caught in baited pots sited on the seabed far from shore. As crabs outgrow their shells, they shed them. They then grow a new carapace, which, at first, is soft. These soft-shell crabs are a delicacy and can be eaten whole.

Above: Soft-shell crabs are highly prized and often eaten deep-fried.

Below: Blue crabs can grow to about 20cm/8in, but are usually sold smaller than this.

Above: Common brown crabs are available all year round.

Female crabs, which are known as hens, have sweeter flesh than the males but they are smaller and their claws contain less flesh.

BLUE CRAB

These have steel-grey bodies and bright, electric blue legs and claws. They are found in American waters along the Gulf of Mexico and Atlantic coasts, and are highly prized for their white meat.

SOFT-SHELL CRABS

These blue crabs have shed their hard carapaces, leaving them deliciously tender, with sweet creamy flesh. They are extremely delicate and do not keep or travel well, so they are generally sold frozen, although you may find fresh soft-shell crabs in the United States in the summer months.

COMMON EDIBLE OR BROWN CRAB

These are the best-known edible crabs, found on Atlantic coasts and parts of the Mediterranean. They are the perfect crabs for boiling to serve cold with mayonnaise. Their claws contain plenty of firm meat. As well as serving cold with a dressing, they are also delicious deep-fried.

Preparing a Live Crab

Many people are put off cooking crabs because of the preparation, but it is relatively simple.

To kill a crab humanely, chill it by submerging it in ice, or leave it in the freezer for a couple of hours until it is comatose. When the crab is no longer moving, lay it on its back, lift up the tail flap and look for a small hole at the base of a distinct groove. Drive an awl or sturdy skewer into this hole, then carefully push the skewer between the mouth plates between the eyes. The crab is now ready for cooking.

Alternatively, the live crab can be killed and cooked simultaneously. Either plunge it into a pan of boiling salted water, bring it back to the boil and cook for 10–12 minutes; or place it in a pan of cold salted water and bring it slowly to the boil.

The latter method is reckoned to be more humane. Either way, calculate the cooking time from when the water boils, and do not boil the crab for more than 12 minutes, whatever its size.

DUNGENESS OR CALIFORNIA CRAB

These trapezium-shaped crabs are found all along the Pacific coast. Similar to common edible crabs, they can be cooked and eaten in the same way.

KING CRAB

Looking like gigantic spiny spiders, king crabs are hideous to look at, but very good to eat. A mature male king crab can weigh up to 12kg/26lb and measure 1m/39in across. Their triangular bodies are bright red with a pale creamy underside. Only male king crabs are sold. The flesh is delicious and is one of the few crabmeats that can be successfully canned.

Below: Every part of the king crab is good to eat, including the claws.

SPIDER CRAB

These pink crabs have spiny shells and long slender legs, which make them look like spiders. Those found along Atlantic coasts measure about 20cm/8in across, but those found in Japanese waters measure up to 40cm/16in.

Below: Spider crabs do not have a pair of large claws, but there is plenty of meat in the legs.

Above: Swimming crabs have an extra pair of legs, shaped like paddles.

SNOW CRAB

Also known as queen crabs, these crabs from the North Pacific have roundish, pinkish-brown bodies and very long legs. The delicious, sweet flesh is difficult to remove from the body, but the claw meat is more accessible. Snow crab meat is usually sold frozen or canned.

STONE CRAB

Similar in appearance to king crabs, stone crabs live at great depths. They have a superb flavour, but are usually sold frozen or canned rather than fresh.

SWIMMING CRAB

The main distinguishing feature of swimming crabs is their extra pair of legs, shaped rather like paddles. Among the many species of swimming crabs are mud or mangrove, shore and velvet crabs. Shore crabs are eaten in Italy in their soft-shelled state; they also make delicious soup. Mud crabs, with their excellent claw meat, are popular in Australia and South-east Asia.

Buying and Cooking

Always buy live crab whenever possible, so that you can be absolutely sure of freshness. A crab is normally cooked by dropping it into boiling water. An alternative, and possibly more humane way, is to put the live crab in cold water and slowly bring the water to boiling point. Once the crab is cooked the crabmeat can be used in numerous ways. The sweet, succulent meat is rich and filling, so it needs a light touch when cooking it.

Recipes include devilled crab, where the meat is removed from the shell and cooked with mustard, horseradish, spices and breadcrumbs; crab mornay, in which the meat is combined with a Gruyère cheese sauce enriched with sherry and mushrooms; and potted crab. The flesh marries well with clean Asian flavours such as lime juice, coriander (cilantro) and chilli; combined with these, it makes the perfect summer salad. Crabmeat is excellent in fish cakes such as Thai crab cakes. It also

makes excellent soup: a classic Scottish dish is partan bree, a creamy crab soup made with fish stock, milk and rice.

In the shell, crab can be boiled and served with mayonnaise, steamed with aromatics or baked with ginger and spring onions. Soft-shell crabs may be lightly coated in flour and deep-fried. *Molecchie fritte* is a Venetian speciality in which the crabs are soaked in beaten egg before being fried. In China, soft-shell crabs are served with a spicy garnish of chilli or fresh root ginger.

Removing Meat from a Cooked Crab

1 Lay the cooked crab on its back on a large chopping board. Hold the crab firmly with one hand and break off the tail flap. Twist off both the claws and all the legs.

2 Stand the crab on its head and insert a heavy knife between the body and shell. Twist the knife firmly to separate them so that you can lift the honeycomb body out.

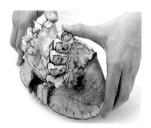

3 Alternatively, hold the crab firmly and use your thumbs to ease the body out of the shell.

4 Remove and discard the feathery, grey gills (they are unattractively but colourfully known as dead men's fingers), which are attached to either side of the crab's body.

5 Press down on the top shell to detach the spongy stomach sac – this is found directly behind the mouth. Cut the honeycomb body into quarters with a large heavy knife.

6 Using a skewer or a lobster pick, carefully prise out all the white meat and put it into a bowl.

7 Use a teaspoon to scoop out all the creamy brown meat from the back shell, then scoop out the thin solid brown meat from inside the flaps. The brown meat can be used to make a delicious sauce.

8 Crack open the claws and legs with a mallet (or use the back of a heavy knife), then remove the claw meat in the largest possible pieces. Pick or scrape out the leg meat with a lobster pick or a skewer. The smallest legs can be kept whole and used to make a delicious shellfish stock.

LOBSTER

This is the ultimate luxury seafood. The uniquely firm, sweet flesh of lobster has a delicious flavour and many people regard them as the finest crustaceans of all. The best lobsters live in cold waters, scavenging for food on the rocky seabed. Like crabs, they moult every couple of years, casting off their outgrown shells. Their colour varies according to their habitat, from steely blue to greenish-brown to reddish-purple; all turn brick-red when cooked.

Lobsters must be bought live or freshly boiled. The powerful pincers that they use for catching and crushing prey can be dangerous. If you buy a live lobster, make sure that the pincers are secured with a stout rubber band.

CANADIAN OR AMERICAN LOBSTER

The hardiest species of lobster, these are found in large numbers in the waters around Canada and the North American Atlantic; the Maine lobster is probably the best-known. They resemble the European lobster but are greener in colour and the claws are slightly rounder and fleshier. Although these lobsters make excellent eating, their flavour does not quite match that of the European lobster.

Below: Maine lobsters are air-freighted live to European supermarkets.

Right: Canadian lobsters are abundant in North Atlantic waters.

EUROPEAN LOBSTER

Coming from England, Scotland, Ireland, Norway and the Brittany coast in France, these lobsters are regarded as having the finest flavour of all. They have distinctive blue-black colouring and are sometimes speckled with bright blue. European lobsters are becoming increasingly rare and expensive. During the more fruitful summer months, they are often held as live stock in massive holding tanks built into the sea.

Right: European lobsters can grow to a formidable 4.5kg/10lb, but the most convenient size is 1.2–1.3kg/2½–3lb, which will comfortably feed two people.

SLIPPER/SQUAT LOBSTER

There are over fifty species of these warm-water lobsters. They have wide, flattened bodies and spindly clawed legs. The best-known squat lobsters are the Australian "bugs", which include the Balmain and Moreton Bay bugs. The comparatively small tails contain deliciously sweet flesh. Squat lobsters are seldom sold in Europe, but can occasionally be found in France, where they are called *cigales* (grasshoppers). Italians call them *cicala di mare* and in Spain they are called *cigarra*.

Buying

Live lobsters should smell very fresh and still be lively and aggressive when picked up. The tails should spring back sharply when they are opened out. Check that the lobster has both its claws – if one is missing, make sure the price is reduced. Live lobsters should be cooked on the day you buy them. If you cannot pop them straight into the cooking pot, wrap them in slightly wet newspaper or cover with a very damp dishtowel and keep in the coldest part of the refrigerator.

Lobsters are often sold cooked, but it is preferable to buy them live and cook them yourself. Always buy cooked lobsters from a reputable supplier. The colour of the lobster should be vibrant, and it should feel heavy for its size. The tail should be tightly curled under the body. Allow 450g/1lb lobster per person.

Cooking

There is very little in the lobster that is inedible – only the stomach sac, a small transparent bag that will probably have grit or sand in it, and the thin dark

---

Preparing and Cooking Live Lobster

1 The most humane way to kill a live lobster is to render it unconscious by placing it in a freezerproof dish or tray and covering it with crushed ice. Alternatively, put the lobster in the freezer for 2 hours.

2 When the lobster is very cold and no longer moving, place it on a chopping board and drive the tip of a large, sharp heavy knife or a very strong skewer through the centre of the cross on its head. According to the experts, death is instantaneous.

3 If you can't face stabbing the lobster, put it in a large pan of cold, salted water and bring slowly to the boil. The lobster will expire before the water boils.

4 Alternatively, you can add the comatose lobster to a large pan of boiling water. Plunge it in head first and immediately clamp on the lid. Bring the water back to the boil. If cooking two lobsters in the same pan, wait until the water comes back to the boil before adding the second one. More than two should be cooked separately.

5 Lower the heat and simmer the lobster gently for about 15 minutes for the first 450g/1lb. Allow a further 10 minutes for each extra 450g/1lb, up to a maximum simmering time of about 40 minutes.

6 When cooked, the lobster will turn a deep brick-red. Drain off the water and leave to cool, if not eating hot.

7 Remove the meat from the lobster, and keep the shells to use in a shellfish stock or soup.

intestinal system that runs the length of the body and can be removed with the point of a knife. Do not discard the tomalley, the creamy grey-green liver, which has an exquisite flavour.

All types of lobster are best cooked simply to really enjoy their delicate flavour. They can be boiled in salted water or in a court bouillon and served hot with melted butter or cold with mayonnaise. A boiled lobster can be the crowning glory of a seafood platter. They can also be grilled (broiled) or fried in the shell with oil and butter.

Classic French cookery has many rich lobster recipes that reflect the luxurious quality of these crustaceans. These dishes, which are usually served with rice to offset the richness, include

lobster newburg, with a cognac and sherry-flavoured cream sauce; *lobster bretonne*, with prawns (shrimp) and mushrooms in a white wine sauce; and *lobster thermidor*, with its luxury béchamel sauce flavoured with shallots, tarragon, chervil and white wine.

Lobster is superb with fresh pasta. It can be used as a filling for ravioli, or tossed into tagliolini with plenty of lemon juice and butter. Cold boiled lobster can be diced and made into a lobster cocktail, or added to a salad. More modern recipes combine lobster with Asian flavours, such as ginger, lemon grass and star anise, but these spices should be used in moderation to avoid overpowering the delicate flavour of the lobster.

Grilling Lobster

One of the simplest ways to cook a lobster is to grill (broil) it.

1 Boil the lobster for 3 minutes, drain, split lengthways and clean.

2 Meanwhile, preheat the grill (broiler) to high. Lay the lobster halves cut-side up in a grill pan, brush with melted buttter and grill for 10 minutes, spooning on more melted butter halfway through.

If the lobster has already been killed, do not parboil. Simply split in half and grill for 12 minutes.

Preparing Cooked Lobster

1 Hold the body of the lobster firmly in one hand and twist off the claws.

2 Hold the lobster the right way up on a chopping board. Insert a large sharp knife at right angles to the seam between the body and the head and press down firmly to split the body and tail lengthways.

3 Turn the lobster round to face the other way and cut firmly through the head. Separate the lobster into two halves and discard the stomach sac.

4 Twist off the legs and then flatten them lightly with the back of the knife. Use a lobster pick or a skewer to remove the flesh.

5 Break the claws into sections. Hold the larger section of the claw, curved side down, in one hand and pull off the smaller pincer. Twist off the lower section of the claw at the joint.

6 Gently crack the claw shell with a mallet or the end of a rolling pin and remove the flesh.

1 Hold the crayfish between your finger and thumb and gently twist off the tail.

2 Hold the tail shell between your thumb and index finger, twist and pull off the flat end; the thread-like intestinal tract will come away. Peel the tail.

3 Hold the head and thorax in one hand. Use the other index finger to prise off the whole underside, including the gills and innards, and discard these.

4 Finally, gently twist off the claws and discard the head.

CRAWFISH

These crustaceans are very similar to lobsters except that they have spiny shells, chunkier bodies and no claws. They are known variously as spiny lobsters, rock lobsters, langoustes and crayfish (not be confused with freshwater crayfish, however). Crawfish are found on the rocky seabed in many parts of the world. The colour of their shells varies according to where they come from and may be dark reddish-brown, brown with pale spots, pink or bluish green. All turn pink or red when cooked. Crawfish have dense, very white flesh, very similar to that of lobster, but with a milder flavour. Crawfish from the Atlantic are the finest and sweetest of all. Crawfish from warmer waters can be a little coarse.

Buying and Cooking

Crawfish are generally sold cooked. Females have the better flavour, so look for the egg sac underneath the thorax. Because there is no claw meat, allow one 450g/1lb crawfish per person.

Crawfish can be cooked in much the same way as lobster; they benefit from spicy seasonings and are excellent in Asia-inspired recipes.

Above: Crayfish, also known as écrevisse, may take as long as seven years to reach adulthood.

CRAYFISH

These miniature freshwater lobsters grow to a maximum length of 10cm/4in. Confusingly, they are usually called crawfish in the United States, where they are a feature of New Orleans cooking. They have a superb flavour and whatever their colour when alive, turn a glorious deep scarlet when cooked. Over 300 species of crayfish are found in streams throughout Europe, the United States, Africa and Australia, although, sadly, most of the European species have been wiped out.

Buying and Cooking

Fresh crayfish should be bought alive. There is a lot of wastage, so you will need 8–12 crayfish per serving. Keep the shells to make stock or soup.

Crayfish feature in many luxurious dishes, including *bisque*, sauces and mousses. They are superb poached in a court bouillon for about 5 minutes and served hot with lemony melted butter or cold with mayonnaise. Only the tail and claw meat is eaten.

*Left:
Langoustines are
a rare and
expensive
treat.*

LANGOUSTINES, DUBLIN BAY PRAWNS AND SCAMPI

Closely related to each other and somewhat smaller relatives of lobsters, langoustines, Dublin Bay prawns and scampi are virtually indistinguishable. Langoustines have pink, smooth-shelled narrow bodies with long, thin, knobbly claws. Originally found off the coast of Norway, they are still sometimes known as Norway lobsters, but today they are caught all along the Atlantic coast, in the Adriatic and western Mediterranean. As a general rule, the colder the water in which langoustines live, the better their flavour will be.

Buying

Langoustines deteriorate very rapidly once caught, so they are often cooked and frozen at sea. Live langoustines are, therefore, something of a rarity in Britain, although you will often find them in continental Europe. This tends to make them expensive, which, combined with the fact that there is little meat on them, turns them into a luxury dish. Nevertheless, if you are lucky enough to find live langoustines and can be certain of cooking them very soon after purchase, they will be an excellent buy. It is important to check that they are still moving. They are at their best from late spring to late autumn. Unlike other crustaceans, langoustines do not change colour when cooked, so make sure you know what you are buying. Whole langoustines are graded by size; larger specimens are better value, as they contain more meat. They are also available frozen, often as scampi tails. If they have already been shelled, allow 115g/4oz per person, and you will need twice this quantity if the langoustines are shell-on.

Cooking

These shellfish should be cooked very briefly. Roast them in olive oil and garlic in a hot oven for 3–5 minutes; split them and grill (broil) or barbecue for about 2 minutes on each side, or poach in a court bouillon and serve hot with melted butter. Whole langoustines are delicious served cold with mayonnaise or marie-rose sauce. Many recipes require the shelled tails only. They can be baked *au gratin* in a creamy sauce with mushrooms and Gruyère cheese, or served Scottish-style in a whisky-flavoured sauce. They are often included in paella and can be substituted for tiger prawns in many Chinese and South-east Asian recipes. They may be cooked in the same ways as lobster, but for a much shorter time.

Classic langoustine recipes include *beignets de langoustines*, where the tails are coated in a light batter, deep-fried and served with tartare sauce, and brochettes, when the tails are marinated in olive oil, lemon juice, parsley, garlic, *herbes de Provence* and a pinch of cayenne pepper before threading on to skewers and grilling (broiling).

PRAWNS AND SHRIMP

Known collectively as shrimp in the United States, prawns and shrimp are the world's most popular crustaceans. Thousands of species are found in all the world's oceans, as well as in fresh water. Technically, there is no difference between shrimp and prawns; the names are merely an indication of size. In the fish trade, any prawns measuring less than about 5cm/2in are known as shrimp. Most prawns have narrow tapering bodies, curled under at the tail, and long antennae. As is the case with other crustaceans, prawns that come from colder waters have a better flavour than those from warm waters.

COMMON PRAWN

Also called the pink shrimp, these translucent, brownish, cold-water prawns can grow up to 10cm/4in in length. They are found in deep waters in the Mediterranean and Atlantic, but related species are found all around the world. The French and Italians consider these prawns the best of all; they have an excellent flavour and turn a glorious red when cooked.

DEEP SEA PRAWN

Sometimes sold as large shrimp, these cold-water prawns live at great depths in the North Sea. They have translucent pink bodies which turn a pale salmon colour when cooked. They are almost always sold ready cooked, and have a delicate, juicy flavour.

MEDITERRANEAN PRAWN

These large cold-water prawns can measure up to 20cm/8in in size. They are also known as blue or red shrimp, and the colour can vary considerably – the heads can be anything from blood-red to deep coral – but,

once cooked, they turn a brilliant red. The flesh is delicious and extremely succulent. Mediterranean prawns are sold cooked and should be served just as they are, with mayonnaise and French bread. In Spain they are popular in tapas bars, and they are often partnered with garlic mayonnaise. Allow about 3 prawns for each person as an appetizer.

Right: Common prawns are much prized for their fine flavour and texture.

Left: Common shrimp are intensively fished in the English Channel and the North Sea.

COMMON SHRIMP

Sometimes called the brown shrimp, these small cold-water shrimp have translucent grey bodies and measure only about 5cm/2in. They live in soft sand in shallow waters, emerging at night in darker camouflage to hunt for their prey. When cooked, they turn brownish-grey. Their small size makes them difficult to peel, but they can be eaten whole and their flavour is incomparable, with a wonderful tang of the sea. They are the traditional choice for potted shrimp: shrimp are briefly fried in unsalted butter, flavoured with cayenne, nutmeg and mace, and then packed in ramekins to set.

Left: Mediterranean prawns are best served with mayonnaise.

Peeling and Deveining Prawns

It often looks pretty to leave the tail section on the prawn for serving.

1 Hold the prawn and pull off the head and legs. Peel off the shell.

2 Make a shallow incision down the centre of the back of the prawn. Pick out the black vein and discard.

GULF SHRIMP

These warm-water prawns come from the Gulf of Mexico. They are usually bright red, but may sometimes be a greyish-pink. They can grow up to 40g/1½oz in weight, and have succulent flesh.

JAPANESE PRAWN

These large warm-water prawns can grow to a length of 23cm/9in. They have yellowish tails, flecked with black. They are found throughout the Indo-Pacific region and in the Red Sea.

TIGER PRAWN

Also known as king prawns and, in the United States, as jumbo shrimp, tiger prawns are a huge warm-water variety, found throughout the Indo-Pacific region. They can grow up to 33cm/13in in length and are ideal for barbecueing and grilling (broiling). In their raw state, they are a translucent greenish-grey in colour. Although their flavour is not so good as that of cold-water prawns, tiger prawns have succulent flesh with plenty of bite. In Europe, they are seldom sold fresh, but they freeze well and are available both peeled and in the shell. Peeled tiger prawns usually have the end of the tail left on so that they can be eaten with the fingers.

Cooking

The cardinal rule with any prawn or shrimp is not to overcook them, as this makes them tough and chewy. Ready-cooked prawns are best eaten without any further cooking. Serve them simply with mayonnaise or wedges of lemon and brown bread and butter, or use them in a salad or prawn cocktail. If you do cook them, use them in a dish such as a pasta sauce where they need only be heated through. They add extra flavour and texture to other fish dishes, such as fish pies, terrines and flans, and combine well with other shellfish. Small prawns and shrimp make an excellent filling for omelettes, bouchées and tartlets.

Raw prawns can be boiled briefly in salt water or a court bouillon and are delicious grilled (broiled), barbecued or deep-fried in batter. Combined with squid and other fish, deep-fried prawns are an essential ingredient of an Italian *fritto misto*. Briefly fried in butter and olive oil they make a superb warm salad combined with scallops. Warm-water prawns are also very good for using in stir-fries, curries and kebabs. Chopped and mixed with garlic, fresh ginger and fresh coriander (cilantro), warm-water prawns make a delicious filling for steamed wontons.

Both prawns and shrimp may be used for making sauces to serve with fish. The classic *sauce crevette à l'anglaise* is based on a rich butter sauce to which anchovy essence, cooked, peeled prawns or shrimp and cayenne pepper are added, while adding shrimp butter to a creamy, cider-flavoured sauce will turn any plainly-cooked fish into a feast.

Above:
Tiger prawns
are succulent
and they look impressive.

MOLLUSCS

This family of shellfish is normally divided into two main groups: gastropods, which include whelks and winkles, and bivalves, which include clams and mussels.

GASTROPODS

These molluscs are distinguishable by their single external shell.

ABALONE

Owing to their decreasing food source, which is a particular type of seaweed that is susceptible to pollution, abalone are becoming increasingly rare. They are found in certain countries, including France, the Channel Islands, where they are known as ormers, and off the coast of California, where the fishermen compete with the endearing sea otters, for whom the abalone is their main source of food.

Buying and Cooking

In Europe there is a long closed season for abalone, and they are available for only a few days in early spring. You are more likely to find fresh abalone in the United States, Australia and the Far East, where they are increasingly

*Below: Abalone are also known as ear shells or sea ears (*oreilles de mer*) because of the rimmed, curved shape of their shells.*

farmed. Abalone is often sold sliced and tenderized ready for cooking. It is also available canned, frozen and dried.

If buying fresh, remove the intestinal sac and dark membrane and skirt before cooking. Abalone flesh must be beaten vigorously with a wooden mallet to tenderize it. In Japan, it is then sliced thinly and eaten raw as sashimi. If it is to be cooked, the approach is the same as for squid – either very brief or long, slow cooking. Thin slices can be sautéed quickly in hot butter, or cut into strips and deep-fried in batter or egg and breadcrumbs. It is also good stir-fried and flavoured with oyster sauce and soy sauce.

CONCH

Pronounced "konk" rather than "konch", this mollusc is a very large relative of the humble whelk. It has a distinctive spiral shell with a series of knobs and a pointed end. The shells are greatly sought-after as ornaments and musical instruments. The pinkish flesh is flavoursome, but can be very chewy, and must be well beaten to tenderize it before eating.

Above: Canned abalone tends to have a slightly rubbery texture.

Buying and Cooking

In their native countries, conches are available all year round. The best are young specimens and they are generally sold out of their shell. After tenderizing, conch meat can be marinated and eaten raw or cooked in a chowder. Some conches can cause stomach upset; the risk of this is reduced if the conch is boiled in two changes of water.

LIMPETS

These molluscs have grey-coloured conical shells, 3–7cm/1¼–2¾in in diameter. They are found throughout the world, clinging tightly to rocks. The inner shells of Atlantic limpets are orangey-yellow, while those of Mediterranean limpets are iridescent blue. When the tide goes out, they nestle into holes in the sand, emerging at night to crawl in circles around their holes in search of food. Limpets have quite a good flavour, but the small amount of flesh they contain can be very tough. They are not available commercially, so you will have to harvest them yourself – but it is vital to check that the shore is not polluted.

Cooking

Wash the limpets and then boil them in sea water or heavily-salted water for 5–7 minutes, or cook the flesh in seafood dishes or soups. Alternatively, grill (broil) with butter in each shell.

Above: Whelks look like large, pointed snails, but are most often sold already shelled.

WHELKS

Smaller relatives of the conch, whelks have attractive spiral shells measuring up to 10cm/4in. They have rather chewy, pinkish flesh with a good flavour. They are often sold cooked and shelled.

Buying and Cooking

Whelks should be bought alive; check that the operculum – the horny flap covering the opening of the shell – is tightly closed. They are sometimes sold ready-boiled and removed from the shell, but these can be rather dry. You will also find whelks pickled in vinegar, or ready-cooked and bottled in brine. It is unwise to gather whelks from the shore yourself.

The best way to cook whelks is to boil them in sea water or heavily-salted water for about 5 minutes. Use a toothpick to prise the flesh out of the shell. The flesh of large whelks can be sautéed after boiling, or deep-fried in batter. Whelks can be used instead of clams in a chowder, can be added to cooked shellfish dishes or salads or sautéed in garlic butter.

WINKLES

These tiny marine snails have thick greenish-brown or black shells, each with a pointed end. Most grow no larger than 4cm/1½in long, 1cm/½in wide and contain a mere morsel of rather chewy flesh.

Above: Winkles are tiny and dark brown or black.

Buying and Cooking

Fresh winkles should be bought alive; check that the operculum is tightly closed. They are also available cooked and bottled in vinegar.

Winkles should be well rinsed in several changes of water and then left in a bowl of lightly salted water for several hours to disgorge any impurities. Like whelks, winkles need only brief cooking. Serve as a French-style appetizer with vinegar or mayonnaise, or as part of a shellfish platter. The flesh can be taken out of the shell and tossed in garlic butter. Winkles may be used to make a sauce to serve with fish.

Cooking and Picking Whelks

Winkles can be cooked and picked in the same way but should be cooked for only 5 minutes.

1 Bring a large pan of salted water to the boil. Drop in the whelks and simmer for 10 minutes. Drain.

2 Using a sharp pin or a cocktail stick (toothpick), remove the operculum if it is still covering the opening of the shell, then pull out the flesh and eat.

BIVALVES

This group of molluscs have attractive
hinged external shells that house soft,
delicate flesh inside and includes
clams, mussels and oysters.

CLAMS

There are hundreds of species of clam,
ranging from the aptly-named giant
clam which can grow to a length of
1.3m/4¼ft, to tiny pebble-like Venus
and littleneck clams. Americans are
passionate about clams and eat them in
all sizes and forms. Their enthusiasm
has spread to Europe, where clams are
now extensively farmed. Large species
have very thick warty shells; small
varieties have smooth shells marked
with fine circular striations. Clams have
a fine, sweet flavour and lovely, firm
texture. They can be enjoyed eaten both
cooked and raw.

Cherrystone/Littleneck clam These small
clams have an attractive brown and
white patterned shell. They are actually
quahogs, the popular name deriving
from their size. The smallest are the
baby littlenecks, with 4–5cm/1½–2in
shells. The slightly larger cherrystones
(about 7.5cm/3in in diameter) are about
five years old. Both are often served
raw on the half shell; cooked, they
make wonderful pasta sauces. Larger
quahogs, which are unsuitable for
eating raw, are known as steamer
clams. They have quite a strong flavour
and are often used for making clam
chowder or pasta sauces.

*Above: Palourde or
carpetshell clams are very tender
and can be eaten raw.*

*Below: Praire, or
Warty Venus
clams*

*Above: Cherrystone clams are among
the smallest varieties of clam.*

Geoduck clam
These enormous
clams are the largest of all American
Pacific shellfish and can weigh up to
4kg/8½lb. Half the weight consists of
two siphons, which are extended
to more than 1.3m/4¼ft to take
in and expel water. Unlike the
soft-shell clam, the geoduck
cannot retract these
siphons into the shell,
and they are often
sold separately.
Geoducks can
bury themselves
up to 1.2m/4ft
deep in sand and it
takes two
people to prise
them out. The siphons
and flesh are sliced before cooking.

Palourde/Carpetshell clam These small
(4–7.5cm/1½–3in) clams have attractive
grooved brown shells with a yellow
lattice pattern. The flesh is exceptionally
tender, so they can be eaten raw, but
are also good grilled (broiled).

Praire/Warty Venus clam This smallish
clam measures 2.5–7.5cm/1–3in. The
thick shell has concentric stripes, some
of which end in warty protuberances.
These clams are widely distributed on
sandy coasts, from Africa to Europe.
They are often eaten raw on the half
shell, but are also excellent cooked.

Razorshell/Razor clam Resembling a cut-throat razor, these clams have striped gold and brown tubular shells and delicious flesh. They are often served raw, but can be cooked. They can be found on sandy beaches at low tide, but they can burrow into the sand at great speed.

Opening Clams

The easiest way to open clams or razor-shells is by steaming them. However, this method is not suitable if the clams are to be eaten raw like oysters.

1 Protect your hand with a clean dishtowel, then cup the clam in your palm, holding it firmly. Work over the bowl to catch the juices.

2 Very carefully, insert the blade of a sharp, pointed knife between the two shells. Run the knife away from you to open the clam, twisting it to force the shells apart.

3 Cut through the hinge muscle attaching the shells, then use a spoon to scoop out the muscle on the bottom shell and discard.

Soft-shell/Long-neck clam The shells of these wide oval clams gape slightly at the posterior end, inspiring the nickname "gapers". They burrow deep into sand and silt, and have a long tube that acts as a siphon for taking in and expelling water. This siphon can be eaten raw, or made into chowder or creamed dishes.

Cooking

Small clams and razorshells can be eaten raw, steamed or cooked in soups and sauces. Larger clams can be stuffed and baked or grilled (broiled) like mussels, cut into strips and deep-fried in batter or breadcrumbs, or stewed with white wine or onions and tomatoes. Steamed clams can be added to salads or sauces or used as a garnish. Never throw away the juices they contain; these are extremely nutritious and delicious, and can be used for drinks, stock or soup.

COCKLES

Although traditionally thought of as a typically British food, cockles are in fact found all around the world. Their two equal heart-shaped shells are 2.5–4cm/1–1½in long and have 26 defined ribs. Inside each cockle lies a morsel of delicate flesh and its coral.

Buying

Fresh cockles are sold by volume; 1 pint weighs about 450g/1lb. Those with paler flesh are said to taste better than those with dark flesh. The colour of the shell is an indication of the colour of the flesh, so choose cockles with pale shells. Shelled cockles are available frozen and bottled in brine or vinegar.

Cooking

Cockles are full of sand, so must be soaked in salted cold water for several hours before eating. They can be eaten raw or boiled and served with vinegar and brown bread and butter. They are good steamed, stewed with tomatoes and onions, or made into soup. Cockles can be added to risotto, pasta and other seafood dishes or served cold as an hors d'oeuvre or salad.

Above: The flesh of razorshell clams looks slightly gelatinous but tastes delicious served raw or cooked.

DOG COCKLE

With their large, flat striated shells, dog cockles resemble scallops. There are four known species of these tropical and warm-water bivalves – the true dog cockle, the bittersweet cockle, the violet bittersweet and the giant bittersweet. All are perfectly good to eat, but have a coarser texture and flavour than true cockles. They should be soaked in cold salted water and can be cooked in the same way as cockles and mussels.

Below: Cockles are found in sandy coastal areas throughout the world.

MUSSELS

Once regarded as the poor relation of the shellfish family, mussels are now very popular, but still fairly cheap. Unlike other bivalves, they do not use a muscly foot to anchor themselves to rocks and poles, but attach themselves with a "beard" or byssus. Clumps of mussels are found growing wild on sea shores throughout the world. They are easy to harvest but it is essential that the waters they come from are unpolluted. Their sweet tender flesh is nutritious and versatile. Nowadays, most commercial mussels are farmed.

Varieties

Blue or European mussel These are from cold British waters and are considered the best and most succulent. They are large with sweet flesh, which in the female is a beautiful orange; males have a paler, cream-coloured flesh.
Green-lipped mussel Green-lipped mussels come from New Zealand. They can grow to over 23cm/9in and are very substantial. They earn their name from the green lip around the internal border of the shell. They are ideal for stuffing, but their flavour is not so good as that of blue mussels.

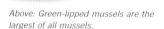

Above: Green-lipped mussels are the largest of all mussels.

Buying

Most mussels are farmed and are usually cleaned. They are available all year round and are cheap, so buy more than you think you will need to allow for wastage: 1kg/2¼lb will provide a generous meal for two people. Shelled mussels are available frozen, smoked and bottled in brine or vinegar.

Cooking

Mussels are enormously versatile. They can be eaten raw or steamed simply as in *moules marinières*. They are also good steamed with Mediterranean or Asian flavours. Large mussels can be stuffed and baked or grilled (broiled) with flavoured butter, bacon or pesto. They can be wrapped in bacon, then threaded on to skewers and grilled (broiled); cooked in cream, wine or cider; deep-fried, or used in omelettes, soufflés, soups, curries, pasta sauces, or seafood salads. The national dish of Belgium is *moules frites*, fried mussels with chips, served with a glass of beer. For an hors d'oeuvre, serve cold steamed mussels *à la ravigote*, with a vinaigrette flavoured with chopped hard-boiled egg, fresh herbs and gherkins.

Left: Blue mussels are said to have the finest flavour.

Preparing and Steaming Mussels

Never cook mussels that do not close when tapped, and discard any that do not open once cooked.

1 Wash the mussels in plenty of cold water, scrubbing them well to remove any sand or mud.

2 Give any open mussels a sharp tap with the back of a knife and discard any that fail to close.

3 Pull out and discard the fibrous "beard" that sprouts between the two halves of the shell.

4 Put the mussels into a large pan, cover with a lid and steam them until they open. Discard any that remain closed once cooked.

OYSTERS

One of life's luxuries, oysters evoke passionate feelings – people tend to either love or loathe them. Their unique, salty, iodized flavour and slippery texture may not appeal to everyone, but their reputation as an aphrodisiac has contributed to their popularity and they are highly prized all over the world. It was not always so; for centuries oysters were regarded as food for the poor. It was their growing scarcity, resulting from overfishing, that led to their popularity increasing.

Varieties

Eastern/Atlantic oyster This has a rounded shell, like those of the native oyster. It has a mild flavour.

Native oyster Natives are slow-growers, taking three years to reach their full size of 5–12cm/2–4½in. Their round shells

Below: Native oysters are the finest of all oysters, and the most expensive.

Bottom: Gigas are the most widely farmed variety of oyster in the world, as they are resistant to disease.

vary in colour from greyish-green to beige, depending on their habitat, and they have a wonderful, delicate flavour. Natives are named after their place of origin. Among the best known are the French Belon, the English Whitstable, Colchester and Helford, the Irish Galway and the Belgian Ostendes.

Pacific/Gigas oyster A large oyster with a craggy, elongated shell, these are the most widely farmed oyster. Their texture is not so fine as that of natives, but their large size makes them more suitable for cooking than other oysters.

Oyster Cultivation

Centuries of overfishing and disease have decimated the world's natural stocks of oysters, a sad state of affairs that has been somewhat alleviated by oyster farming. Oysters have been farmed since Roman times, but cultivation has now become a highly lucrative business, despite being very labour-intensive and very slow.

Oysters need constant cosseting from the moment of hatching. A single oyster produces up to a hundred million eggs each breeding season, of which only ten oysters will survive long enough to end up on your plate. It takes at least three years to produce an oyster of marketable size; natives take up to seven years and the giant "royals" take ten years to mature. The minuscule spats must first be caught and encouraged to settle on lime-soaked tiles or slates.

After about nine months, they are transferred to oyster parks, where they are enclosed in wire grills and carefully nurtured while they feed on plankton. After being left to grow for two or three years, they are placed in nets and fattened for about a year in shallow beds or claires. The final stage of the lengthy process involves placing them in clean beds for several days under stringent hygiene conditions to expel any impurities.

Portuguese cupped oyster These oysters come from Portugal (and Spain and Morocco). They have scaly greyish-brown shells, one of which is slightly concave. They are considered finer than gigas, although their flesh is rather coarse, but not as good as natives.

Opening Oysters

Ideally, you need a special oyster knife to open oysters. If you haven't got one, use a strong knife with a short, blunt blade.

1 Scrub the shells under cold running water. Wrap one hand in a clean dishtowel and hold the oyster with the cupped shell down and the narrow hinged end towards you.

2 Push the point of the knife into the small gap in the hinge and twist it between the shells until the hinge breaks. Lever open the top shell.

3 Slide the knife carefully along the inner edges of the top shell and sever the muscle that joins the oyster to the shell. Lift off the top shell, leaving the oyster in its juices in the bottom shell.

Below: Portuguese oysters have coarse flesh.

Sydney rock oyster

Farmed extensively in New South Wales, this oyster is famed for its sex-changing abilities, which make it extremely fertile. It grows quickly, has a good flavour, but is difficult to open.

Buying

The age-old rule that oysters should only be bought when there is an "r" in the month still holds good in the northern hemisphere, mainly because their flesh becomes unpleasantly soft and milky during the summer breeding season from May to August.

Cooking

Oysters are best eaten raw with just a squeeze of lemon or a dash of Tabasco sauce. If you prefer to cook them, do so very briefly. They are delicious lightly poached or steamed and served with a *beurre blanc* or champagne sauce; stuffed and grilled (broiled) as in oysters Rockefeller; or as an addition to steak and kidney pie.

SCALLOPS

These bivalves have two fan-shaped shells, one flat and the other curved, with grooves radiating out from the hinge to the edge. They are found on sandy seabeds in many parts of the world from Iceland to Japan. Unlike many bivalves, they do not burrow into the sand, but "swim" above the seabed by opening and closing their shells. There are about three hundred species of scallop throughout the world, ranging in colour from beige to brown, salmon-pink, yellow and orange. The most common species is the common or great scallop, whose reddish-brown shell grows up to 5–6cm/2–2$\frac{1}{2}$in. Scallops have long been associated with beauty. Botticelli painted the goddess Venus as she was born from a scallop shell.

Buying

Scallops are available almost all year round, but are best in winter when the roes, called corals, are full and firm. The finest are individually hand-caught by divers; needless to say, they are also the most expensive. If you buy scallops in the shell, keep the shells to use as serving dishes for all sorts of fish recipes. Allow 4–5 large scallops per person as a main course, three times

Below: King scallops have firm white flesh and, at the right time of year, orange or pale red corals.

Below: Queen scallops are quite small, but are just as delicious as larger scallops.

Queen scallops These miniature scallops, sometimes known as "queenies", measure only about 3cm/1¼in across. Their cream-coloured shells are marked with attractive brown ridges and they contain a small nugget of white flesh and a tiny pointed coral. Queen scallops are cheaper than large ones, but they have the same sweet flavour. They are often sold out of the shell; you should allow at least a dozen per person.

Baking Scallops in their Shells
For four people, you will need twelve scallops and four shells.

1 Butter the shells and sprinkle with fresh breadcrumbs. Put three scallops in each shell and season with a pinch of cayenne, a little chopped parsley and lemon juice.

2 Cover the scallops with white sauce. Mix a little pepper with a cupful of fresh breadcrumbs and sprinkle over the top. Top with small knobs of butter.

3 Bake in a fairly hot oven for about 20 minutes and serve immediately.

this number if they are small. Scallops are also available shelled. Always try to buy scallops with their delicious coral. Avoid frozen scallops, which tend to have little or no taste.

Cooking

The beard and all dark-coloured parts of the scallop must be removed before they are cooked and eaten. If the scallops are large, slice the white flesh in half horizontally. Scallops need only the briefest of cooking to preserve their firm yet tender texture. Alternatively, they can be thinly sliced and eaten raw, with a little lemon juice and olive oil.

Whole scallops in the shell can be baked in the oven; seal the shells with a flour and water paste to trap the juices. They are equally delicious wrapped in bacon and grilled (broiled); coated in egg and breadcrumbs and deep-fried; pan-fried for about 30 seconds on each side; stir-fried with colourful vegetables; or steamed with ginger and soy sauce. They are well suited to cooking on skewers, and make wonderful pâtés and mousses. A classic dish is Coquilles St Jacques, in which poached scallops and corals are sliced, returned to the half shell and coated with Mornay sauce, then grilled (broiled) or baked until brown. A border of mashed potato is sometimes piped around the edge.

Opening Scallops in the Oven
The easiest way to open scallops is to place them, rounded side down, on a baking sheet and put them in an oven preheated to 160°C/325°F/Gas 3 for a few moments until they gape sufficiently for you to complete the job by hand.

1 Spread the scallops in a single layer on a baking sheet. Heat them until they gape open, then remove them from the oven.

2 Grasp a scallop in a clean dishtowel, flat side up. Using a long, flexible knife, run the blade along the inner surface of the flat shell to cut through the muscle that holds the shells together. This done, carefully ease the shells apart.

3 Lift off the top shell. Pull out and discard the black intestinal sac and the yellowish frilly membrane.

4 Cut the white scallop and the orange coral from the bottom shell. Wash them both briefly under cold running water. Remove and discard the white ligament that is attached to the scallop flesh.

CEPHALOPODS

Squid, octopus and cuttlefish come under the heading of cephalopods and are more closely related to snails than to fish. They are highly developed creatures with three-dimensional vision. They can also change colour according to the environment. Their name derives from the Greek meaning head with feet. The bulbous head contains the mouth, which has two jaws, rather like a parrot's beak. This is surrounded by tentacles covered with suckers, which are used for crawling and seizing prey.

Most cephalopods also contain an ink sac that emits a blackish fluid designed to repel predators and provide a "smokescreen" when under attack. This fluid – always referred to as ink – can be used for cooking.

SQUID

These cephalopods have elongated heads and slender, torpedo-shaped bodies that end in a kite-shaped fin. Their internal shell is a transparent "quill" that looks like a piece of clear acetate. They have ten tentacles, two of which are very long. The most common squid is the long-finned squid or calamary, which is found throughout Europe. It has smooth, sandy-red skin and weighs up to 2kg/4½lb.

Below: Squid is available all year round and does not suffer from freezing.

Cleaning and Preparing Squid

1 Rinse the squid thoroughly under cold running water. Holding the body firmly in one hand, grasp the tentacles at the base with the other hand and gently but firmly pull the head away from the body. As you do this, the soft yellowish entrails will come away with it.

2 Use a sharp knife to cut off the tentacles from the head of the squid. Reserve the tentacles, but discard the hard beak in the middle. Discard the head and entrails.

3 Carefully remove the ink sac and reserve. Store it in the refrigerator, in a small bowl of cold water to prevent it from breaking.

4 Peel the purplish-grey membrane away from the body and discard it.

5 Pull out the "quill", then wash the body under cold running water.

6 Cut the body, flaps and tentacles to the required size for your recipe.

Buying

Whole squid are sold fresh or frozen and are available all year round. Make sure they contain their ink sac. Some fishmongers and supermarkets also sell squid ink separately. Squid is also available ready-cleaned, which saves a great deal of labour. Whole tentacles and rings are available frozen, sometimes as part of a mixed platter of *fruits de mer*. You can also buy ready-battered squid rings for deep-frying, but these are best avoided. Allow about 200g/7oz of squid per person.

Cooking

The cardinal rule with squid is to cook it either very briefly or for a long time; anything in between and it becomes tough and rubbery. The bodies can be

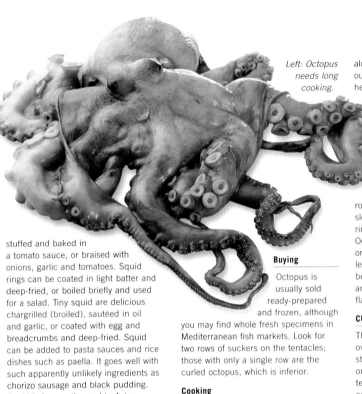

Left: Octopus needs long cooking.

stuffed and baked in a tomato sauce, or braised with onions, garlic and tomatoes. Squid rings can be coated in light batter and deep-fried, or boiled briefly and used for a salad. Tiny squid are delicious chargrilled (broiled), sautéed in oil and garlic, or coated with egg and breadcrumbs and deep-fried. Squid can be added to pasta sauces and rice dishes such as paella. It goes well with such apparently unlikely ingredients as chorizo sausage and black pudding. Squid is frequently used in Asian recipes and lends itself to flavourings such as ginger, chilli, garlic and lime. The ink can be used to colour and flavour home-made pasta and risotto.

OCTOPUS

Unlike cuttlefish and squid, the octopus has no internal shell, nor does it possess catching tentacles or fins. The creatures spend their lives lurking in clefts in the rocks on the seabed, blocking the entrance to their hidey-holes with shellfish and stones. Their eight equal-size tentacles have two rows of suckers. It is the largest of the cephalopods and can grow to a length of 5m/16½ft. The larger an octopus grows, the tougher it becomes, so smaller specimens make better eating. The flesh is firm and sweet. Octopus ink has a much stronger flavour than cuttlefish or squid ink.

Buying

Octopus is usually sold ready-prepared and frozen, although you may find whole fresh specimens in Mediterranean fish markets. Look for two rows of suckers on the tentacles; those with only a single row are the curled octopus, which is inferior.

Cooking

Octopus needs long slow cooking. Before including it in a recipe, it is a good idea to blanch or marinate it. If the octopus has not been prepared

Below: Cuttlefish is much underrated, yet is quite delicious.

already, cut off the tentacles and press out the beak from the head. Discard the head, turn the body inside out and discard the entrails. Rinse it thoroughly, then pound the body and tentacles with a mallet to tenderize them before cutting them into strips. Simmer the octopus in stock or salted water for at least 1 hour, until tender. Octopus can be stewed with Mediterranean vegetables and/or robust red wine, or stuffed and baked slowly. Small specimens can be cut into rings and sautéed gently in olive oil. Octopus is best served warm in a salad or dressed with a simple olive oil and lemon vinaigrette. Whole octopus can be casseroled slowly in its own juices and ink, although the ink has a strong flavour that is not to everyone's taste.

CUTTLEFISH

The common cuttlefish has a flattened oval head with brownish camouflage stripes on the back and light coloration on the underside. It has eight stubby tentacles and two long tentacles for catching its prey. These are kept rolled up and hidden in openings near its mouth. Cuttlefish are comparatively small, with bodies measuring 25–30cm/10–12in. When unfurled, the catching tentacles double its length. As is the case with all cephalopods, the smaller the cuttlefish, the more tender the flesh. The smallest species is the Mediterranean little or dwarf cuttlefish (*Sepiola*), which grows to only 2–6cm/ ¾–2½in. They are delicious, but time-consuming to prepare as the tiny cuttlebones must be removed before cooking.

Cooking

Tiny cuttlefish are delicious left whole and sautéed quickly in olive oil and garlic or deep-fried. They make a good addition to rice dishes. Larger specimens can be cooked like squid. A classic Spanish dish is cuttlefish cooked in its own ink.

OTHER EDIBLE SEA CREATURES

The sea is full of weird and wonderful creatures whose strange appearance belies their delicious taste. They may be soft and gelatinous, like jellyfish, warty like sea cucumbers, or menacingly spiny like sea urchins, but somewhere in the world they will be regarded as a great delicacy and are well worth trying.

Above: Dried jellyfish is a very popular ingredient in Asian cooking, in which it is valued both for its texture and flavour.

JELLYFISH

These strange-looking, transparent creatures with their dangling tentacles, look rather like open parachutes. They inhabit every ocean of the world, but are eaten almost exclusively in Asia, where they are dried and used in a number of seafood dishes.

Buying and Cooking

You will find dried jellyfish in any Asian food store, together with jellyfish preserved in brine. Both types must be soaked in several changes of water before use, changing the water often and squeezing the jellyfish each time to get rid of as much of the fishy smell as possible. In China, slices of dried jellyfish are scalded in boiling water until they curl up, then drained and served in a dressing of soy sauce, sesame oil and rice vinegar. They are also added to shellfish or chicken stir-fries. In Japan, crisply fried strips of jellyfish are served with vinegar and are sometimes combined with sea urchins.

SEA CUCUMBER

It is not difficult to understand why these odd creatures are not a popular addition to Western menus. Warty and cucumber-shaped, they rejoice in the alternative name of sea slug. The prickles along their backs are actually feet, which enable them to crawl along the seabed. However, they are considered a great delicacy in Japan and China, where they are reputed to be a great aphrodisiac.

Buying and Cooking

In Japan, the sea cucumber is sliced and eaten raw as sashimi. It is also available dried, but requires many hours of soaking to make it palatable. During soaking, the sea cucumber doubles in bulk and becomes gelatinous in texture.

SEA SQUIRT

There are over 1,000 species of sea squirts, small invertebrates whose bodies are enclosed in thick leathery "tunics". They have two orifices or spouts through which they siphon water, and attach themselves to the seabed or rocks and crevices. They can be found in the Mediterranean, where they are a popular, if esoteric, food, particularly in Spain and the south of France, where the local name, *violet,* refers to their resemblance to a purple fig.

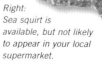

*Right:
Sea squirt is available, but not likely to appear in your local supermarket.*

Above: Sea cucumber features in a number of extremely complicated Asian recipes, which take an enormous amount of time and effort to prepare. They have an unusual taste and texture that are often not to everyone's liking.

Buying and Cooking

Sea squirts are not widely available. They can accumulate toxins, so should never be eaten if they come from polluted waters. Enthusiasts eat these unusual creatures by splitting them in half, then scooping out the soft yellow part inside and eating it raw, despite the strong aroma of iodine.

Opening Sea Urchins

The best implement for opening sea urchins is a knife known as a *coupe oursin*. Failing this, use very sharp scissors and wear rubber (latex) gloves to protect against the spines.

1 Hold the sea urchin on a board and cut around the soft tissue on the underside using a *coupe oursin* or a pair of sharp scissors.

2 Lift off the top of the sea urchin and remove the mouth and innards, which are inedible. Keep the juices to flavour shellfish sauces, egg dishes or soup.

3 Use a teaspoon to scoop out the bright orange coral.

SEA URCHIN

One of the most unpleasant experiences a holidaymaker can have is to tread on the long, poisonous spines of a sea urchin. To lovers of seafood, however, eating these marine creatures is one of life's great gastronomic pleasures. There are over eight hundred species of sea urchin, found all over the world, but only a few are edible. The most common European variety is the *Paracentrotus lividus*, a greenish or purplish-black hemispherical creature which measures about 7.5cm/3in across, and whose shell is covered with long spines, rather like those of a hedgehog. The females are slightly larger than the males and are said to taste better. Only the orange or yellow ovaries or gonads (known as the coral) are eaten; these have a pungent taste reminiscent of iodine. In France, sea urchins are variously known as *oursin*, *châtaigne de mer* (sea chestnut) and *hérisson de mer* (sea hedgehog); in Italy, they are *riccio di mare*, and in Spain *erizo de mar*.

Buying and Cooking

Overfishing has made sea urchins rare and expensive. The best are the purple or green urchins with long spines; short-spined, whitish species have an extremely strong flavour and are best used in cooked dishes. Look for sea

Above: Sea urchins are considered a delicacy in Japan and in many Mediterranean countries. Only a few of the over eight hundred varieties are edible.

urchins with firm spines and a tightly closed mouth (on the underside). If you find a source of fresh sea urchins, they can be kept in the refrigerator for up to three days.

Sea urchins are eaten raw. The top is sliced off, rather like a boiled egg, and the insides are scooped out with a teaspoon. The best implement for opening sea urchins is a purpose-made *coupe oursin* but, failing this, very sharp scissors will do just as well. They may also be used to flavour sauces, pasta, omelettes and scrambled eggs. They make wonderful soup, which can be served in small portions in the shell and eaten with a teaspoon. The shells can also be used as containers for other seafood such as langoustines cooked in a sea urchin sauce.

SEA VEGETABLES

As well as fish and other seafood, the sea and the seashore provide a wealth of edible seaweeds and vegetables. Some grow entirely in the sea, either completely submerged or washed by tides. Others, such as samphire, grow only in the marshes near the sea, nourished by the salty waters and sea breezes. The West has only relatively recently re-discovered the extraordinary variety and value of these foods, but in the East they have been used for centuries, valued for their versatility, flavour and nutritional benefits. Sea vegetables are reputed to have a number of health-giving benefits.

Above: Arame, also known as sea oak, has a mild flavour and a wonderful texture. It is delicious added to salads, or hot in stir-fries and Asian-style soups.

Above: Wakame is quite a soft-textured type of seaweed.

LAVER

A relation of nori, laver is found around the shores of Britain, but it is not cultivated. Laver is used in regional cooking, particularly in Wales, Scotland and Ireland. It is cooked into a thick dark purée, which can be spread on toast or mixed with oatmeal to make the Welsh delicacy, laverbread. It can be added to sauces and stuffings. Available ready-cooked in cans from health food shops, laver has a strong flavour and should be used sparingly at first.

WAKAME

This sea vegetable is often confused with its relative, kombu, because it looks very similar until it is soaked, when it changes colour from brown to a delicate green. Wakame has a mild flavour and is one of the most versatile of all sea vegetables. It is an excellent source of vitamin C and B vitamins. To use wakame, soak briefly in cold water and use in salads and soups; or toast in the same way as nori, crumble and use as a condiment.

ARAME

Sold in delicate black strips, arame has a mild, slightly sweet flavour and, if you haven't tried sea vegetables before, it is a good one to start with. It needs to be soaked before using in stir-fries or salads, but if using in moist or slow-cooked dishes, such as noodles and soups, it can be added straight from the packet. Arame is rich in iodine, calcium and iron and is reputed to help with high blood pressure.

Preparing Arame

Soaking and cooking times will vary slightly depending on how the arame is to be used.

1 Rinse the arame in a sieve under cold running water, then place in a bowl and cover with cold water. Leave to soak for about 5 minutes – it should double in volume. Drain and place in a large pan.

2 Pour fresh cold water into the pan and bring to the boil. For use in salads and stir-fries simmer for about 20 minutes until the arame is tender.

KELP

Also known as kombu, kelp is now farmed in Britain. A brown sea vegetable, it is usually sold in dried strips, although in Japan it is available in many forms. It has a strong flavour and is used in slow-cooked dishes, soups and stocks – it is essential in the Japanese stock dashi. A small strip of kelp added to dried beans while they are cooking will soften them and increase their digestibility.

DULSE

Purple-red dulse has flat fronds that have a chewy texture. It needs to be soaked until soft before adding to salads, noodle dishes, soups and vegetable dishes. For hundreds of years dulse was popular in North America and northern Europe, particularly Ireland and parts of Scotland. Because of its salty, tangy flavour, it needs a bland foil such as potatoes, as in the Irish dish "dulse champ", a mixture of mashed potatoes, dulse and plenty of butter.

SAMPHIRE

There are two types of samphire. Marsh samphire grows in estuaries and salt marshes, while rock samphire grows on rocky shores and cliffs. The type sold by a fishmonger is marsh samphire; rock samphire has an unpleasant flavour and should be avoided. Marsh samphire is also known as glasswort or sea asparagus, as its shoots are similar to sprue, small asparagus shoots.

Below: Kelp or kombu has a number of delightful local names, such as fingerware and grockle.

Right: Nori sheets and flakes have a delicate texture and mild flavour.

Although samphire grows easily, it is not cultivated and is available only for a short season, normally in late summer and early autumn. Samphire has a salty, iodine flavour and a pleasant, crisp texture. It goes well with fish and seafood. However, it can be enjoyed simply steamed and dipped in melted butter.

Buying and Cooking

When in season, good fishmongers get regular stocks of marsh samphire, and it should look bright and fresh. Buy it as you need it, as it will not keep for long.

Wash samphire under cold running water, then steam over a pan of boiling water for no more than 3 minutes. Alternatively, blanch it in boiling water for 3–5 minutes and drain. It can be eaten raw, but blanching removes some of the saltiness. To eat samphire, draw the shoots through the teeth to peel away the succulent part from the thin central core.

NORI

Nori is sold in thin purple-black sheets, which turn translucent green when cooked. It is one of the few sea vegetables that does not require soaking. Nori is processed by being chopped, flattened and dried on frames, like paper. In Japanese cooking, the sheets are used to wrap delicate small parcels of vinegar-flavoured rice, fish and vegetables. Toasted nori can be crumbled and used as a garnish.

Toasting Nori

Nori can be toasted, either over an electric hob plate or over a gas burner, until it is very crisp, then crumbled and used as a garnish for salads, soups and stir-fries.

1 Hold a sheet of nori with a pair of tongs about 5cm/2in above an electric hot plate or gas hob for about 1 minute, moving it around so it toasts evenly. It will turn bright green and become crisp.

2 Leave the nori sheet to cool for a few moments, then crumble.

MEAT, POULTRY AND GAME

From the commonly eaten meat and poultry such as beef,

chicken and turkey, to more unusual meats such as buffalo

and alligator, meat, poultry and game play a major role in

cuisines throughout the world. New breeding and butchery

pratices have resulted in leaner, healthier and more affordable

cuts, and few foods are as versatile, as widely enjoyed,

or as satisfying and nourishing.

BEEF AND VEAL

Probably on of the most varied of meats, beef provides a full-flavoured ingredient for stewing, succulent cuts for roasting and tender steaks for speedy grilling (broiling). In broths, soups and stews or extravagant dishes fit for banquets, there are all types of cuts to suit every occasion.

Since more humane rearing methods have been adopted, veal is becoming increasingly popular in Britain and the United States, although it has always been a favourite in many parts of Europe, including France, Italy, Spain, Germany and Austria. It has a mild flavour and a melt-in-the mouth texture. It is now available in most supermarkets as well as from specialist butchers.

Beef and veal are excellent sources of high-quality protein, providing all the essential amino acids required for growth and body maintenance. Beef, particularly, is an excellent source of iron, in a form that is easily absorbed by the body. It also provides zinc and a variety of other minerals. Along with other meat, beef is an important source of many of the B vitamins.

Buying Beef

Good beef is hung for weeks – up to five or six with planned variations in temperature – rather than days, which allows time for the muscle to mature and the fat to develop. However, in practice, most beef tends to be hung at a consistent temperature – 2°C/36°F – for five to six days. Beef has a full flavour, becoming succulent and tender when cooked. Well-matured meat is a deep rich burgundy brown in colour, not bright red, and the fat is creamy rather than white. The best roasting cuts are those that have an even marbling of fat, which provides flavour and keeps the meat moist and juicy as it cooks.

Look for meat that has been properly butchered. The key signs are cleanly cut meat, which has been neatly and evenly trimmed, with meat that follows the line of the muscle and bone. The bones should be smooth, without any sign of splinters. Smaller cuts such as steaks should be of uniform thickness so that they cook evenly.

Buying Veal

Veal is best judged by its colour: the whiter the meat is, the greater the proportion of milk in the diet of the calf. Pale meat is tender with a delicate flavour. Older veal is pink or rosy pink, rather than white, often with a layer of creamy white fat. If it is brown, it is either very old or very stale and should be avoided. Veal has very little fat and cuts are often larded – threaded with strips of fat – before being roasted to keep them moist.

Storing

Beef and veal should always be kept on a low shelf in the refrigerator, below and away from cooked foods and ingredients that are to be eaten raw.

As a general rule, when buying pre-packed meat, always check and observe the use-by date on the packet. Pre-packed meat, which is securely sealed, should be stored in its packaging. If the packaging is damaged and there is any danger of meat juices escaping, or if the meat is bought loose and wrapped in a bag, remove it from its packaging and place in the refrigerator unwrapped, in a large dish covered with a lid or clear film (plastic wrap).

As a guide to buying meat that is not pre-packed, minced (ground) meat and small cuts of veal are best eaten on the day of purchase, but small roasts, chops and steaks will keep for two to three days and larger roasts may be stored for up to five days.

Both beef and veal freeze well, particularly smaller pieces. Wrap tightly and freeze: veal can be frozen for up to six months and beef for up to a year. Thaw the meat thoroughly before cooking, ideally overnight in the refrigerator because slow thawing helps to preserve its texture. Never re-freeze raw meat that has been thawed.

Below: Sirloin is considered by many to be the most tender cut of beef.

BASIC CUTS OF BEEF

Butchering techniques for beef differ according to country or regional traditions. Many large supermarkets and good butchers offer a wide selection of classic international cuts. With the increasing popularity of easy-to-prepare, boneless meat, many non-traditional cuts are also available.

Cuts from the top of the animal, along the middle of the back, are tender because they are taken from muscles that perform comparatively light work. These include the most expensive cuts that can be cooked quickly by grilling (broiling) and frying as well as roasting. Cuts from the neck, shoulders and lower legs – the parts of the animal that work hardest – are tougher and coarser in texture, and are less expensive. They require longer cooking by moist and gentle methods such as braising and stewing. However, when properly cooked, these cuts have an excellent flavour and they are usually very lean.

FORERIB/RIB

Also known as best rib, this is a high quality cut that is available either on the bone or boned and rolled for roasting (the bigger the better). Forerib is very lean and tender. It is also sold cut into thick slices (steaks) for grilling (broiling) or frying.

SIRLOIN

Traditionally said to have acquired its name after the epicurean English king Henry VIII knighted a rib of beef with the words, "Arise, Sir Loin". More prosaically, its name probably derives from the French *sur loin*, meaning on top of the loin. Also known as best end loin, the sirloin is frequently cut into steaks, including entrecôte, porterhouse or T-bone. This is a lean, tender cut from the back of the animal for roasting – on the bone or boned and rolled – or grilling (broiling) and frying when cut into steaks.

Entrecôte steak A prime quality steak cut from the thin end of the boneless sirloin. The word *entrecôte* literally means between the ribs.

Porterhouse steak Traditionally a large steak – about 5cm/2in thick – cut from the wing end of the sirloin, but it is also sometimes used for steaks cut from the rib of beef.

T-bone steak Cut across the sirloin, this steak takes its name from the T-shaped bone it contains. It also includes the lean fillet or "eye".

New York steak Also known as New York strip or shell steak, this is taken from the prime eye of meat from the sirloin or porterhouse area.

Sirloin steak A classic American cut, this name also appears on packaged steak in British supermarkets. The steaks may be boneless or pinbone, wedgebone or flatbone, depending on which part of the sirloin they were cut from.

Above: Entrecôte and porterhouse are both thick and juicy cuts.

Above: T-bone steak is usually large and can serve two modest diners.

Right: New York steak is a boneless strip of loin.

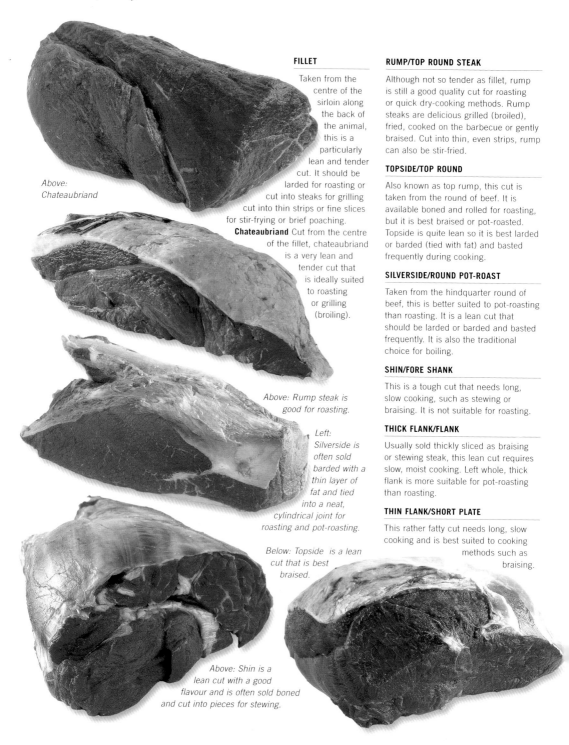

FILLET

Taken from the centre of the sirloin along the back of the animal, this is a particularly lean and tender cut. It should be larded for roasting or cut into steaks for grilling cut into thin strips or fine slices for stir-frying or brief poaching.

Chateaubriand Cut from the centre of the fillet, chateaubriand is a very lean and tender cut that is ideally suited to roasting or grilling (broiling).

RUMP/TOP ROUND STEAK

Although not so tender as fillet, rump is still a good quality cut for roasting or quick dry-cooking methods. Rump steaks are delicious grilled (broiled), fried, cooked on the barbecue or gently braised. Cut into thin, even strips, rump can also be stir-fried.

TOPSIDE/TOP ROUND

Also known as top rump, this cut is taken from the round of beef. It is available boned and rolled for roasting, but it is best braised or pot-roasted. Topside is quite lean so it is best larded or barded (tied with fat) and basted frequently during cooking.

SILVERSIDE/ROUND POT-ROAST

Taken from the hindquarter round of beef, this is better suited to pot-roasting than roasting. It is a lean cut that should be larded or barded and basted frequently. It is also the traditional choice for boiling.

SHIN/FORE SHANK

This is a tough cut that needs long, slow cooking, such as stewing or braising. It is not suitable for roasting.

THICK FLANK/FLANK

Usually sold thickly sliced as braising or stewing steak, this lean cut requires slow, moist cooking. Left whole, thick flank is more suitable for pot-roasting than roasting.

THIN FLANK/SHORT PLATE

This rather fatty cut needs long, slow cooking and is best suited to cooking methods such as braising.

Above: Chateaubriand

Above: Rump steak is good for roasting.

Left: Silverside is often sold barded with a thin layer of fat and tied into a neat, cylindrical joint for roasting and pot-roasting.

Below: Topside is a lean cut that is best braised.

Above: Shin is a lean cut with a good flavour and is often sold boned and cut into pieces for stewing.

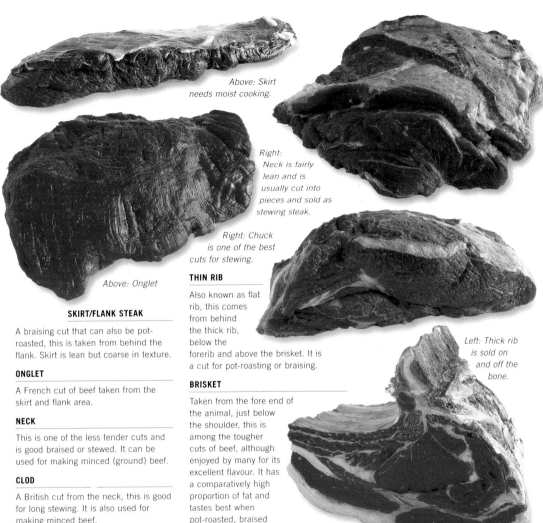

Above: Skirt needs moist cooking.

Above: Onglet

Right: Neck is fairly lean and is usually cut into pieces and sold as stewing steak.

Right: Chuck is one of the best cuts for stewing.

Left: Thick rib is sold on and off the bone.

Below: Brisket

SKIRT/FLANK STEAK

A braising cut that can also be pot-roasted, this is taken from behind the flank. Skirt is lean but coarse in texture.

ONGLET

A French cut of beef taken from the skirt and flank area.

NECK

This is one of the less tender cuts and is good braised or stewed. It can be used for making minced (ground) beef.

CLOD

A British cut from the neck, this is good for long stewing. It is also used for making minced beef.

CHUCK AND BLADE/CHUCK, BLADE POT-ROAST, ARM POT-ROAST AND SHOULDER

Often sold as braising steak, these are braising or stewing cuts, benefiting from long slow cooking to give tender results.

THICK RIB/FLANK-STYLE RIB

Also known as top rib, this is taken from the forequarter beneath the chuck and blade and above the brisket. It is often boned and rolled, but is best roasted with the bone in, as it helps conduct heat. It can also be cut into steaks and either pot-roasted or braised.

THIN RIB

Also known as flat rib, this comes from behind the thick rib, below the forerib and above the brisket. It is a cut for pot-roasting or braising.

BRISKET

Taken from the fore end of the animal, just below the shoulder, this is among the tougher cuts of beef, although enjoyed by many for its excellent flavour. It has a comparatively high proportion of fat and tastes best when pot-roasted, braised or stewed. It is also used to make classic salt beef.

MINCED/GROUND BEEF

The paler the mince, the higher the fat content, so look for dark mince, which will have a higher proportion of lean meat. The percentage of fat must be displayed on the label of pre-packed mince. Use for burgers, meatballs, meat loaves and meat sauces.

BASIC CUTS OF VEAL

There is an increasingly wide range of veal cuts available from specialist butchers and larger supermarkets. There are large cuts suitable for roasting and braising and smaller cuts for the quicker cooking methods of frying, griddling and grilling (broiling). The following is a guide to the various basic cuts of veal.

FILLET/ROUND

A boneless cut taken from the hindquarters. This is usually sliced into escalopes (scallops) of veal, but it can be roasted whole (known as boneless rump roast in the United States).

LOIN/LOIN AND SIRLOIN

Taken from the back of the animal and available on the bone or boned and rolled, this cut is ideal for roasting.

CHOPS

Taken from the loin, these are on the bone and are usually grilled (broiled), griddled or pan-fried.

BREAST

This can be roasted on the bone, or boned, stuffed and rolled before roasting. Alternatively, it can be cut up into separate riblets for grilling (broiling).

LEG

This is a good quality cut for roasting. This large, tender cut is often boned and stuffed before cooking.

Right: Veal chops, which resemble T-bone steaks are good for both grilling and frying.

Above: Fillet is usually cut into escalopes and is great for quick pan-frying.

Above: Leg is a large, lean cut of veal that is great served stuffed and roasted.

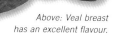

Above: Veal breast has an excellent flavour.

Left: This large, prime veal joint is a combination of loin and fillet and is available from specialist butchers.

KNUCKLE

The end of the leg, this is bony and used mainly for boiling or stewing, but it can also be braised. It is usually sold cut crossways into thick slices.

CUTLETS

These are taken from the neck end of the loin, and are usually griddled, grilled (broiled) or pan-fried.

SHOULDER

Also called the oyster, this can be boned, stuffed and rolled and makes an excellent, relatively economical cut for roasting. However, it is quite an awkward shape. Shoulder can also be cut into chunks for stewing or used as a pie filling.

BEST END/RIB

This is usually sold on the bone for roasting and is juicy and tender. Ask the butcher to remove the chine bone (part of the back bone), so that it can be carved more easily. Best end is also sold in cutlets (small chops) for frying.

MINCED/GROUND VEAL

This pale pink mince is available ready made in some stores, but it is more usual to select the meat and then ask the butcher to mince it for you. It may be used for meat loaf, pasta sauces and in stuffings.

Right: Knuckle is the bonier end of the hind leg and is often cut into thick slices and is best loved for its use in the rich Italian stew, osso bucco, which is traditionally served with risotto alla Milanese.

Above: Cutlets are cut from the neck end of the loin and are good cooked quickly by grilling (broiling), griddling and frying.

Right: Shoulder of veal is often sold boned and rolled and makes a very good roast.

Above: Best end of neck is one of the tougher cuts of veal so is better pot-roasted, braised or stewed.

PREPARING BEEF AND VEAL

Depending on the cut, beef and veal can be prepared in a number of ways.

Boning

Beef and veal can be cooked on or off the bone. Boneless joints are easier to carve and serve. They can be stuffed or cut up, for example into cubes or dice.

1 To bone a rib of beef, select a sharp knife with a fine, flexible blade as it will follow the shape of the bones.

2 Using a gently cutting motion, rather than slicing into the meat, follow the rib bones with the blade of the knife, gradually working down from the tops of the bones. Follow the shape and curve of the bone, easing the meat away from the bone as it becomes free.

3 Carefully cut through the cartilage around the base of the bone, keeping the eye of the meat whole and as neat as possible. When it is free, remove the bone and set aside or reserve for making beef stock.

4 Trim off any excess fat from the boned joint of meat.

Barding and Larding

These are both methods of introducing fat to very lean joints, to keep them moist and succulent during cooking and to add flavour to the meat.

Barding is simply wrapping fat around or over lean meat – thin slices of either pork or beef fat can be used. Barding is often obvious on lean, rolled roasts bought from the supermarket where the meat is wrapped in a separate coating of fat. Streaky (fatty) bacon can also be used for barding. The outer covering of fat bastes the meat, preventing it from drying out before it is cooked through.

Larding involves more preparation than barding. It is the technique of threading strips of fat (usually chilled pork fat) through lean meat, with the use of a larding needle, to keep it moist from the inside as the fat melts during roasting. The strips of fat, known as lardons, can be rolled in herbs or spices before being threaded through the meat. With some slightly less tender cuts, or if the larding needle is blunt, it may be necessary to pierce holes through the meat with a fine metal skewer before threading the fat through. A specially-designed larding needle has a small gripping device to hold the strip of fat when it is inside a hole.

1 To lard meats that will be cooked by slow, moist methods, insert the needle following the grain of the meat, then attach a strip of fat and gently push the needle through. Lard the meat at regular intervals to keep it evenly moist.

2 To lard meats that are to be roasted, thread the strips of fat into the outside of the meat in long stitches.

Tying a Roast

Tying a boneless roast helps to keep it in shape and promotes even cooking. The roast may be stuffed first, if required, making sure that the cavity is large enough to contain the stuffing so that it is not squeezed out when the roast is tied. Fine string is used for tying a roast and is available from all good cook's shops – however, fine parcel string is also adequate. It is a good idea to use cooking string or trussing thread and store it in a plastic bag so that it is kept clean, ready for use.

1 Roll, fold or arrange the meat into a neat shape. Then tie a piece of fine string lengthways around the roast and secure it with a double knot.

2 Tie the string around the roast at regular intervals, about 2.5cm/1in apart. Knot and trim the ends as you go. Apply even pressure when tying each length of string to avoid squeezing the meat more in some places than others.

3 Once cooked, leave the roast to stand, still tied, for about 10 minutes before carving. Using a pair of kitchen scissors, snip the tightly tied string in several places and remove before slicing and serving the meat.

Tenderizing Steak

Pounding meat breaks down the tissue fibres and helps to give a tender result. This is particularly important with thicker pieces of tender cuts that will be cooked rapidly by grilling (broiling) or pan-frying. It is not necessary for meat that will be cooked by a slow process such as braising. Marinating with wine, vinegar or a papain-rich fruit juice such as papaya or pineapple also helps to tenderize steaks and chops. For perfect results, pound the meat before setting aside to marinate.

1 Place the steak on a board and cover it with greaseproof (waxed) paper. Alternatively, lay the meat between two sheets of greaseproof paper.

2 Pound the meat evenly with a rolling pin or meat mallet.

Meat Mallets

Also known as a meat tenderizer, steak hammer or steak/meat batt, the meat mallet is a useful kitchen tool. It was originally made of wood, but nowadays it is more commonly made from steel or cast aluminium. It is shaped like a hammer and has one plain and one ridged, notched or toothed side. Wooden meat mallets often have a ridged steel surface on one side. The textured surface is for tenderizing meat such as steaks cutlets and escalopes (scallops), and the smooth surface is for flattening it. The meat mallet is heavy in proportion to its size, and you do not need to use a lot of force when pounding the meat.

Cutting Meat for Braising or Stewing

Tougher cuts of meat cook much more evenly and quickly when they are cut into small, neat similar-size pieces for stewing or braising.

1 Trim the meat of excess fat and any gristle, membranes or sinew.

2 Cut the meat across the grain into 2.5cm/1in thick slices, using a large, sharp knife. These slices can be braised or casseroled, especially when preparing braising steak, rather than stewing steak.

3 To cut stewing steak into cubes for making casseroles and stews, first cut the slices lengthways into thick strips or fingers. Then cut the strips of meat crossways into cubes measuring 2.5–5cm/1–2in.

Mincing Beef

Making your own minced (ground) meat allows you to select the cut and trim off any excess fat. Stewing or braising cuts are ideal, especially for making long-cooked meat sauces, but rump (round) steak can be minced for making burgers and similar minced beef dishes.

A food processor can be used for mincing meat, and this will give a finer texture. Trim the meat well and cut it into small, even cubes, then process it in small batches for even results, pulsing the power on and off. Take care not to over-process.

1 To use a traditional mincer (grinder), trim the meat and cut it into pieces, then feed it into the top of the mincer, while turning the handle. Use a coarse blade if you are going to use the meat in a long-simmered sauce. For meat loaves or meatballs use a medium blade. For fine mince, pass the meat through a coarse blade first, then through a fine blade.

2 To finely chop steak, use a pair of very sharp knives, one in each hand, and a rhythmic chopping action. Use the flat blades to scrape meat from the sides of the board, turning it over and inwards in batches for even chopping.

COOKING BEEF AND VEAL

Tender cuts such as beef fillet or veal escalope (scallops) can be quickly fried or grilled (broiled), whereas tougher meat needs a longer cooking time.

Pan-fried Beef

This is the traditional cooking method for steaks. Use a good quality heavy pan, preferably non-stick. Butter burns unless it is clarified, so heating a little oil in the pan first and adding the butter just before the steak helps to avoid this.

1 Use kitchen paper to grease the pan with a little sunflower oil.

2 Heat the pan until it is very hot before adding a knob (pat) of butter.

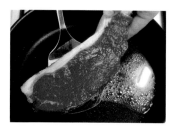

3 Add the steak and cook for the required time.

Pan-fried Veal

There are many tender cuts of veal, suitable for pan-frying. Escalopes (scallops) are the classic cut for this method of cooking.

1 Place a veal escalope between two sheets of clear film (plastic wrap) or greaseproof (waxed) paper, or place on a board and cover with clear film. Use the wooden side of a meat mallet to beat the veal out thinly and evenly, being firm but gentle. Repeat with the remaining escalopes.

2 Use a heavy frying pan, preferably non-stick, and heat until very hot. Smear with enough butter and oil to prevent the meat from sticking. Add the veal escalopes when the fat is sizzling and cook for 1–2 minutes. Turn and cook for 1–2 minutes on the second side. Serve immediately, with the pan juices poured over. Or make a simple sauce by adding a splash of sherry and some cream to the pan juices.

Cooking Times for Pan-fried Beef
The cooking time for steak depends both on the cut and on how well cooked you like your beef. For very rare fillet steak, cut about 2.5cm/1in thick and allow 1 minute on each side; for rump (round) steak allow 2 minutes on each side. For rare steak, allow 2 minutes each side for fillet; 3 minutes for rump. For medium steak, allow 2–3 minutes for fillet, 2–4 minutes for rump. For well-done steak, allow 3 minutes, then reduce the heat and allow a further 5–10 minutes.

Stewing, Braising and Casseroling

These are long, slow and moist methods of cooking either in the oven or on the hob (stovetop). The meat is simmered slowly at a low temperature in liquid – wine, water, beer or stock. This is ideal for tough, inexpensive cuts such as shin (fore shank) and brisket. Stewing steak is tougher and needs longer cooking than braising steak.

1 Trim off any excess fat and cut the meat into 2.5cm/1in cubes.

2 Toss the meat in seasoned flour, shaking off any excess. This coating browns to give the casserole a good flavour and thickens the cooking liquid.

3 Heat 30ml/2 tbsp sunflower oil in a flameproof casserole. Add the meat in batches and cook over a high heat, turning the cubes to brown on all sides.

4 When the meat is well browned, use a slotted spoon to remove it before adding the next batch. If necessary, heat extra oil before adding more meat.

5 Add sliced or chopped onions and other vegetables to the remaining fat and juices in the casserole and cook, stirring occasionally, for 5 minutes.

6 Return the meat to the casserole with any juices that have accumulated, then pour in the cooking liquid. Stir to loosen the residue from the pan and heat until simmering. Simmer gently on the hob or in the oven until the meat is tender. The casserole may be covered for the entire length of the cooking or uncovered towards the end to allow excess liquid to evaporate and the sauce to thicken.

Roasting Beef

Large roasts give best results, allowing time for the outside to brown and the fat to melt and become crisp before the centre of the meat is overcooked. Forerib or sirloin are good cuts for roasting. The fillet can be roasted, but it is very lean and should be larded, then basted well during cooking.

Roasting times for beef

Weigh the roast and calculate the cooking time as follows:

On the bone
- For rare beef: 20 minutes per 450g/1lb at 180°C/350°F/Gas 4, plus 20 minutes
- For medium beef: 25 minutes per 450g/1lb, plus 25 minutes
- For well-done beef: 30 minutes per 450g/1lb, plus 30 minutes

Off the bone
- For rare beef:15 minutes per 450g/1lb at 180°C/350°F/Gas 4, plus 15 minutes
- For medium beef: 20 minutes per 450g/1lb, plus 20 minutes
- For well-done beef: 25 minutes per 450g/1lb, plus 25 minutes

---

Roasting Veal

Allow 25 minutes per 450g/1lb at 180°C/350°F/Gas 4, plus an extra 25 minutes, for veal on or off the bone.

Roasting Techniques

There are two different methods: either place the cold roast in the oven or briefly sear it first. When cooking a very large roast, it is easier to place it in a roasting pan fat side up and roast for the calculated time. The comparatively long cooking allows plenty of time for the fat to melt and brown.

Alternatively, with a medium-size roast, browning the fat first on the hob (stovetop) gives a better result, as the cooking time is not long enough to cook the fat thoroughly in the oven. The traditional theory was that this sealed in flavour, but that is not scientifically correct; however, it does help to prevent the joint shrinking unevenly.

1 Preheat the oven to 180°C/350°F/Gas 4. Heat a little oil in a frying pan and sear the roast on all sides, particularly the fat. Season well and place on a rack in a roasting pan, fat side up. Place in the oven.

2 Roast the meat for the calculated time. A meat thermometer is useful for checking progress and to determine when the meat is cooked. Heat the spike of the thermometer in very hot water and insert it into the thickest part of the roast: 60°C/140°F indicates that the meat is rare, 70°C/158°F gives a medium result and 75°C/167°F means the meat is well done.

3 Cover the roast with foil and leave to stand for 10 minutes before carving. This allows the temperature to even out and the fibres to relax.

Carving a Rolled Roast

Allow the cooked roast to stand and relax for 10 minutes, then remove the string before carving.

1 Place the roast on a board and use a carving fork to hold firmly in position. Cut the meat into even, thin slices using a gentle sawing action.

Carving Rib of Beef

Allow the roast to stand for 10 minutes before carving it.

1 Place the roast on a board and hold firmly with a carving fork. Cut along the bone between the meat and the ribs to remove the meat from the bones.

2 Set the bones aside. Turn the roast on its side and carve even slices across the grain of the meat.

LAMB

Delicious in roasts, superb in chargrilled kebabs and inimitable in full-flavoured stews or casseroles, lamb is one of our best-loved and most popular meats. Unlike beef and pork, which are often forbidden for religious reasons, lamb features in all meat-eating cuisines, from the tagines of Morocco to spicy curries from India.

Although lamb is a fatty meat, particularly that produced from some of the mountain breeds, the fat content largely depends on the breed and the rearing methods. Much of the meat available now is no longer fatty and, today, farmers are rearing leaner animals that still have excellent flavour.

Lamb is a high quality protein food. It is an excellent source of iron in a form readily absorbed by the body and it is a good source of zinc. It is also an important source of valuable B vitamins and useful minerals, including copper, manganese and selenium.

Buying

Meat from milk-fed baby lamb is very pale and looks rather like veal; meat from sheep less than a year old has slightly darker pink flesh, while meat from sheep more than a year old is known as mutton and has a darker flesh with a stronger flavour. Prime lamb is taken from five- to seven-month-old animals and is often known as spring lamb (sometimes called summer lamb or early lamb).

When choosing lamb, look for firm, slightly pink meat with a fine-grained velvety texture. The fat should be creamy white, firm and waxy. Avoid meat that looks dark and grainy in texture, surrounded by yellow fat. Meat that shows signs of drying out should also be rejected.

Storing

Lamb should be stored on a low shelf in the refrigerator, well away from cooked food and ingredients that will be eaten raw. Place the meat in a covered dish large enough to contain any drips. Pre-packed meat should be left in its packaging and used by the date given

Above: Chump chops are good for pan-frying and grilling (broiling).

on the packet. Meat, chops and steaks that are bought loose should keep for two to four days, larger roasts for up to five days. Minced (ground) lamb should be eaten within a day of purchase.

Lamb freezes well. Place in freezer bags and seal them tightly. Store small cuts for up to three months, larger cuts for up to six months. Thaw meat overnight in a dish in the refrigerator.

BASIC CUTS

Prime cuts are taken from the top of the carcass, along the middle of the back. They comprise the muscle least used during the life of the animal and therefore provide the most tender meat. These are the cuts to cook quickly, by grilling (broiling) and frying, as well as roasting; they can also be cooked slowly by moist methods such as stewing.

Cuts from the neck and lower legs or shanks – parts that had to work hardest when the animal was alive, are cheaper, but they need slower, gentle cooking in a casserole, stew or pot-roast until they are tender. They may be sold as stewing lamb.

Right: Saddle is a huge roasting joint taken from both sides of the carcass.

LOIN

Usually sold as a roast, sometimes boned, stuffed and rolled, this prime cut is good for roasting. Loin chops have a small T-bone (part of the backbone from which they are cut) and can be griddled, grilled (broiled) or pan-fried.

NOISETTES

Boned and rolled loin, tied with string, then sliced into neat rounds, these are good to pan-fry, sauté, griddle, grill (broil) or cook on the barbecue.

CHUMP CHOPS

These are cut from between the leg and the loin, and they have a small round bone in the middle.

SADDLE/LOIN ROAST

Sometimes called a double loin of lamb, this is a large roast, ideal for special occasions. It consists of the whole loin taken from both sides of the carcass.

DOUBLE LOIN CHOPS

Sometimes called Barnsley chops or butterfly chops, these are cut from a saddle of lamb. They are suitable for grilling (broiling), frying or braising.

LEG

A tender cut, often divided into fillet and shank, which is sold on the bone or boned. Leg is ideal for roasting, or the cubed meat can be used in a wide variety of braised or casseroled dishes. It can also be grilled (broiled) or cooked on the barbecue. It is also known by its French name of *gigot*.

Below: Leg and leg steaks are tender.

GUARD OF HONOUR

This consists of a pair of racks tied together with the fat on the outside.

SHOULDER

A succulent and tender cut, which can be roasted on or off the bone, braised or stewed. Boneless shoulder can be cubed for casseroles, kebabs and pies, or minced (ground).

BREAST

A long thin cut, which tends to be fairly tough and fatty. When boned, stuffed and rolled it can be roasted slowly or braised.

LAMB STEAKS

Cut across the leg, with a small round of bone in the middle, these can be pan fried, grilled (broiled) or braised.

Below: Guard of Honour, made from two racks of lamb, makes an attractive and impressive roast.

RACK/RIB

The French *carré d'agneau* is taken from the best end of neck. This can be roasted on the bone or boned, stuffed and rolled. It is a good cut for a small number, particularly suitable for two people. It is also sold as chops, each with one rib bone, for grilling (broiling) or frying.

CROWN ROAST

In French this is known as the *couronne*. It is made by tying two racks ends together in a circle to resemble a crown.

SCRAG END AND MIDDLE NECK/NECK SLICE AND NECK FILLET

Ideal for stewing, braising and casseroling, these are the traditional cuts for Irish stew and Lancashire hot pot. The main eye of lean meat from the middle neck is sold as fillet of lamb, which is good for grilling (broiling).

SHANK OR KNUCKLE

An economical, yet flavourful cut, this is best cooked slowly and gently – stewed, casseroled, pot-roasted or braised.

MINCED/GROUND OR CUBED LAMB

Quick and convenient, this can be used for pies, baked dishes such as moussaka and kebabs.

Above: Racks of lamb can be sold trimmed and chined or with the chine bone left intact.

Right: Minced and diced lamb are popularly used in many classic dishes from around the world.

PREPARING LAMB

The large tender cuts of lamb from the shoulder and leg may be boned before roasting, which makes the meat much easier to carve.

Boning a Shoulder

Removing the blade and shoulder bones means the roast can be stuffed, if you like, rolled and tied.

1 Scrape back the flesh back to reveal the wide end of the blade bone.

2 When the edge of the bone is free, follow the shape of the blade to cut the meat off the bone. Do this on both sides of the large flat bone.

3 Carefully cut through the ball and socket joint to separate the blade and shoulder bones.

4 Hold the shoulder open and pull the blade bone away from the meat, scraping off any meat from the narrow end of the bone.

5 Cut and scrape the meat away from the shoulder bone, then pull the bone free. If stuffing the meat, open out the boned shoulder and spread the stuffing evenly over it. Roll up and tie with string to secure the stuffing.

Boning a Leg

Removing the bone before roasting makes space for stuffing the leg, if required, and the roast joint is easier to carve than a joint with the bone in.

1 Using a sharp knife, carefully trim off the layer of fat from the outside of the leg and cut through the tendons at the bottom of the shank.

2 Cut around the pelvic bone and through the tendons, then remove the pelvic bone.

3 Scrape the flesh away from the shank bone, cut the tendons on the leg joint and remove the shank bone.

4 Cut around the leg bone, then twist and remove it.

Butterflying Leg of Lamb

This is a good way to prepare lamb if you are planning to cook it on a barbecue. It can also be stuffed and rolled for roasting.

Bone the leg of lamb, then cut it lengthways and open it out. To keep the meat opened out flat, insert metal skewers widthways.

Preparing Rack of Lamb

The best end of neck, or rack (rib) of lamb, is taken from one side of the rib cage. There are usually six to nine cutlets (chops) in a rack.

1 Using a sharp knife, carefully cut off the skin and most of the fat.

2 Place the rack on its side and cut off the chine bone (part of the back bone) with a meat cleaver. (Some racks of lamb are sold ready chined.)

3 Cut the fat off the ribs down the top 5cm/2in from the bone ends. Turn the meat over and then score between each of the bones.

4 Cut and carefully scrape away the meat and connective tissue from between the bones.

Preparing Crown Roast

This is an attractive way to prepare racks of lamb for roasting. If you like, the central cavity can be filled with stuffing before roasting.

1 Prepare two racks of lamb, then, using a sharp knife, carefully cut the tissue between each rib so that both the racks can be bent.

2 Stand one rack and bend it into a semicircle, with the meat outside, to form the shape of one side of the crown. Push the ribs outwards at the top so the crown will sit up straight.

3 Bend the second lamb rack into a semicircle shape and put the two racks together to form a crown. Tie string around the crown at 2.5cm/1in intervals to keep the racks in place.

Preparing Guard of Honour

This popular traditional dish consists of a pair of racks of lamb interlocked like soldiers' swords. It makes a very impressive dish for a special dinner.

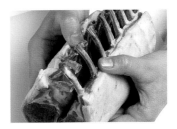

1 Prepare two racks of lamb, then hold one rack of lamb in each hand with the meat facing inwards. Push the racks firmly together, so that the two sets of bones interlock.

Cutting Noisettes

These are thick slices cut off the boned and rolled loin. They can be pan-fried, chargrilled or griddled. They cook evenly and quickly, and many people prefer them to meat on the bone. The cooking time depends on the thickness of the noisettes.

1 Trim off the thin fatty edge of the flap along the side of the boned loin, then tie the meat neatly into a cylinder shape at 6cm/2½in intervals with string. The first length of string should be 1.5cm/¾in from the end of the meat. Trim the string as you go.

2 Cut the loin into 3cm/1¼in thick slices between the pieces of string. Flatten each noisette slightly with the blade of the knife.

COOKING LAMB

However it is cooked, lamb tastes wonderful flavoured with garlic and with fresh herbs such as rosemary, thyme, oregano and basil.

Pan-Frying

This is the traditional method for cooking lamb steaks or chops and is also a useful method for medallions.

1 Preheat the pan thoroughly, then grease it lightly with a little oil before adding the meat. As soon as the medallions are browned (about 2–3 minutes), turn and cook the second sides. Transfer the cooked medallions to warmed plates and keep warm.

2 Stir double (heavy) cream into the cooking juices with a sprinkling of fresh thyme leaves, salt and pepper. Heat until boiling to make a rich sauce.

Griddling Noisettes

Cook noisettes of the same thickness so they cook in the same length of time.

Heat a ridged griddle until hot, then add a little oil or butter. When the oil is hot or the butter foaming, add the noisettes and cook for 4–5 minutes. Turn and cook for 4–5 minutes on the other side.

Grilling

Cooking lamb cutlets or chops under the grill (broiler) is quick and healthy, allowing the fat to drip away during cooking. The high heat seals the meat quickly to lock in the juices and give a succulent result. Sprigs of rosemary can be inserted into the meat before cooking to add a delicious flavour.

1 Trim off any excess fat around the cutlets with a sharp cook's knife. Season well with salt and black pepper.

2 Make a slit through the fat into the flesh and insert a sprig of rosemary. Preheat the broiler to high.

3 Place the cutlets on a lightly oiled rack over a broiler pan and cook under the hot broiler. Allow 4–6 minutes on each side, turning halfway through.

Braising

Leg steaks are an excellent choice for braising on a bed of root vegetables. Prepare the vegetables such as carrots, swede (rutabaga), parsnips and onions cutting them into chunks, then place them in a flameproof casserole.

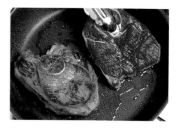

1 Heat a little oil in a frying pan; brown the lamb steaks quickly on both sides.

2 Lay the lamb steaks on top of the vegetables. Add stock to the frying pan used for browning the meat and bring to a boil, stirring to mix. Pour on to the steaks – it should cover the vegetables and part-cover the meat. Cover and simmer gently for 45–60 minutes.

Pot-roasting Lamb Shanks

Lamb shanks are tender and delicious when pot-roasted in the oven or on the stove, on a bed of chopped vegetables moistened with a little red wine or well-flavoured stock, in a covered casserole.

1 Heat a large, heavy frying pan and add a little sunflower or olive oil. When the oil is hot, add the lamb shanks, in batches if necessary, and fry them over high heat, turning them occasionally using tongs, until they are well browned on all sides.

2 Meanwhile, prepare a bed of thickly sliced or roughly diced vegetables such as carrots, leeks and onions layered with sprigs of fresh thyme, bay leaves, rosemary, or other aromatic herbs in a large, deep, flameproof casserole.

3 Add the lamb shanks and pour in enough robust red wine or stock to just partially cover the vegetables.

4 Cover the casserole with a tight-fitting lid or aluminum foil and cook in a preheated oven at 180°C/350°F/Gas 4 for 1–1½ hours, until the lamb is very tender. Check halfway through cooking and add more liquid if necessary.

Roasting Lamb

Lamb is often served rare or medium rare. A meat thermometer is useful for checking the internal temperature of the meat. Insert it into the thickest part.

1 Weigh the roast. Cut small, deep slits all over the meat, using the point of a small knife. Press thin slivers of peeled garlic and small fresh rosemary or thyme sprigs into the slits.

2 Lay the leg of lamb in a roasting pan, fat side up, and sprinkle the layer of fat generously with salt.

3 Cover the cooked meat with foil and leave to stand for about 10 minutes to relax before carving.

Flavouring Roast Rack of Lamb

Rack of lamb can be flavoured with herbs and spices before roasting. First, heat a little oil in a frying pan and brown the meat, fat side down, in the hot oil. Remove from the pan and leave to cool. Spread the fat with 15ml/1 tbsp Dijon mustard, then press a mixture of chopped fresh herbs, spices and dried breadcrumbs into the mustard.

Roasting Times for Lamb

Weigh the roast and calculate the cooking time accordingly.

For rare lamb Roast the meat in a preheated oven at 230°C/450°F/Gas 8 for 10 minutes, then reduce the oven temperature to 180°C/350°F/Gas 4, and cook the lamb for the remaining time, allowing 18 minutes per 450g/1lb plus an extra 18 minutes. The internal temperature of the roast should be 60°C/140°F.

For medium lamb Roast at 230°C/450°F/Gas 8 for 10 minutes, then at 180°C/350°F/Gas 4 for a further 25 minutes per 450g/1lb, plus an extra 25 minutes. The internal temperature of the meat should be 70°C/158°F.

For well cooked lamb Roast at 230°C/450°F/Gas 8 for 10 minutes, then at 180°C/350°F/Gas 4 for a further 30 minutes per 450g/1lb plus an extra 30 minutes. The internal temperature of the meat should be 80°C/176°F.

Carving Leg of Lamb

The secret to carving a leg of lamb is to allow it to rest sufficiently after roasting before trying to carve it.

1 Place the roast on a board and hold firmly in place with a carving fork.

2 Using a sharp carving knife, start by cutting a V-shaped wedge of meat from the top of the leg, near to but not right at the thin end. Gently cut down through the thick part of the meat as far as the bone.

3 Holding the meat firmly at the leg end, carve slices following the first cut made for the wedge. These are the prime slices of meat. Turn the roast over and cut small slices down across the grain to remove the remaining meat.

Carving Rack of Lamb

This method is also used for crown roast and guard of honour: scoop out any stuffing with a spoon before cutting between the cutlets. Remember to remove the pieces of string from a crown roast before carving.

Cut between the individual rib bones and serve the roast rack as individual cutlets (chops).

PORK

This comparatively inexpensive meat and it is also the most versatile, generally tender and with an excellent flavour. Although forbidden among Jewish and Muslim people, the pig has long been an important source of food in communities throughout Europe, Asia and South and Central America. Pigs are inexpensive and easy to look after. They will eat virtually anything and, unlike sheep and cattle, do not need a large area of land on which to graze. Until less than 50 years ago, pigs were reared in suburban backyards, fattened on kitchen leftovers and killed by the local butcher.

Although it was once thought of as a fatty meat, modern breeding, rearing and butchering has resulted in pork becoming one of the lowest fat meats. In addition, the fat it does contain is less saturated than that found in other meats. Pork is a high quality protein food, a good source of iron, zinc and B vitamins. It also provides many other trace elements, including copper, manganese and selenium.

Buying

Look for firm, pale pink flesh, which is moist but not damp or oily. The fat should be white, not yellow, and the bones should be tinged with red. The skin should be dry and silky, not slimy or damp. Most pigs are slaughtered at around 6 months, when they yield meat with a fine texture. Coarse flesh and hard white bones indicate the animal is older and the meat less tender.

Storing

Keep pork on a low shelf in the refrigerator, well away from and below cooked food and food that is to be eaten raw. This is important to avoid cross contamination by meat juices that may drip on to food that is to be eaten uncooked. Ideally, the meat should be placed on a rack in a dish and covered with an upturned bowl or lid so that moisture can be retained while air can circulate freely. Pre-packed meat is best kept in its packaging as long as this is sealed. Always check the use-by dates on packaged meats. As a guide when

buying loose meat, minced (ground) pork will keep for one to two days; pork cuts and roasts for three to four days. Pork can be frozen for four to six months.

BASIC CUTS

From ears to trotters (feet), almost every part of the pig can be eaten. As for other meats, there are prime roasts and cuts that grill (broil) well; unlike other meats, the carcass does not yield very tough cuts. With careful trimming to remove sinews and excess fat, the majority of the meat is tender.

LOIN

On the bone or boned, when the meat can be rolled, this is a lean cut and one of the best for roasting.

LOIN CHOPS

A prime choice for grilling (broiling), griddling, cooking on the barbecue or frying, these large tender chops can also be braised in delicious casseroles.

TENDERLOIN/FILLET

A boneless eye of lean meat from the hindquarters, this equivalent of fillet of beef is taken from under the ribs and backbone. It is a lean, fine-textured cut of pork and good for grilling (broiling) or pan-frying. If roasted, it cooks quickly and should be basted frequently or cooked in a roasting bag.

Left: Loin on the bone

Above : Loin chops

CHUMP/HIND LOIN

This is a lean cut from the hindquarters. Whole cuts are ideal for roasting, but make sure that the backbone has been sawn to make carving easier.

Below: Chump or hind loin is delicious served roasted.

Below: Tenderloin or fillet is good for quick-roasting.

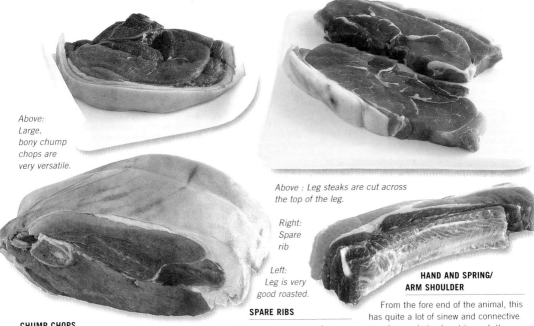

*Above:
Large,
bony chump
chops are
very versatile.*

*Above : Leg steaks are cut across
the top of the leg.*

*Right:
Spare
rib*

*Left:
Leg is very
good roasted.*

CHUMP CHOPS

Cut from between the loin and the leg, chump chops can be grilled (broiled), griddled, roasted, fried or stewed.

LEG/HAM

The hind leg is sold whole or split into two. A whole leg makes a marvellous roast for a large number of people. Leg steaks can be grilled (broiled), griddled, fried, stewed or braised. Thin slices off the leg are prepared as escalopes (scallops).

LEG FILLET

Also known as fillet of the leg, this cut is taken from across the top of the leg, including the bone in the middle. It is very tender and good for roasting.

KNUCKLE/SHANK

This is cut from the lower part of the leg and provides delicious, succulent meat when roasted slowly.

SPARE RIB AND SPARE RIB CHOPS

These cuts are taken from the fore end of the animal and sold either whole or cut up into spare rib chops. Suitable for slow roasting, braising and casseroling, grilling (broiling) or griddling.

SPARE RIBS

Chinese-style spare ribs are cut from the belly rather than from the neck end of the carcass. They are best either grilled (broiled) or cooked on the barbecue and should be marinated first.

BLADE/BLADE SHOULDER

Taken from the fore end and sold on or off the bone, this cut can be roasted or pot-roasted (if whole) but is mostly boned, trimmed, then cut into cubes for casseroles, kebabs or similar dishes.

SHOULDER STEAKS

Marbled with fat, with or without the bone, these can be grilled (broiled), griddled, pan-fried, stewed or braised.

HAND AND SPRING/ARM SHOULDER

From the fore end of the animal, this has quite a lot of sinew and connective membranes but, when trimmed, the meat is tender and has an excellent flavour. It is suitable for slow roasting or braising whole, or it can be cubed.

BELLY/SIDE

Today, this traditionally fatty cut tends to be leaner. It can be rolled to make a roast, used for mincing (grinding) or making sausages. It can be roasted, pot-roasted, grilled (broiled), griddled, cooked on a barbecue or stewed.

Below: Knuckle of pork and boneless leg fillet are good for roasting.

PREPARING PORK

Pork can be quite fatty so trim any excess fat from the meat as you prepare it for cooking.

Preparing Fillet of Pork

1 Lift the edge of the fatty membrane and peel it away from the fillet. You can do this with your fingers, but it helps to run the blade of a sharp knife down the underside of the membrane.

2 To cut strips of fillet, lay the trimmed fillet on a chopping board, with one of the narrow ends facing you. Using a long sharp knife, cut the meat length-ways into 8mm/⅓in wide strips.

3 To cube the fillet, cut across the strips to make even-size cubes, measuring about 2.5cm/1in. These are ideal for cooking as kebabs.

Flattening Fillet

One flattened fillet of pork is the right size to serve two people.

1 Trim off all fat and remove the fatty membrane from the fillet. Hold the top of the fillet and use a long sharp knife to cut a slash, about 4cm/1½in deep into the meat.

2 Pull the cut edges apart and cut to within 1cm/½in of the opposite edge.

3 Lay the fillet out on a sheet of clear film (plastic wrap) on the work surface. Fold back the top slice to open the meat to double its original width. Cover the fillet with a second sheet of clear film. Use the flat, wide side of a meat mallet or a rolling pin and carefully and evenly beat out the fillet to the required thickness.

Cutting Medallions

1 Trim off any fat and the thin membrane from the pork fillet then, working from the thick end, cut off slices at a slight angle to make neat round medallions of equal thickness.

2 Place the slices on a work surface between two sheets of clear film (plastic wrap) and then beat to the required thickness using the flat side of a wooden mallet or a rolling pin.

Stuffing Pork Chops

Loin chops can be boned and stuffed before they are cooked to add extra flavour. The chops can simply be slashed horizontally from the round, meat side, but they are especially good when trimmed and boned.

1 First trim off the fat from the chops. Use a sharp knife and work from the narrow end of the chop, carefully removing the rind with the band of fat.

2 To remove the bone, cut the flesh along the line of the bone, keeping the knife as near as possible to the bone. Pull the bone away as you cut and twist the point of the knife to free the meat from the corner of the bone.

3 Cut a shallow slit about 4cm/1½in long into the rounded side of the chop, halfway up its depth. Press the blade deeper into the chop, but not right through to the other side, and cut with a backwards and forwards action, using the point of the knife blade to hollow out a deep, wide pocket almost to the edges of the meat.

4 Open up the pocket in the chop and push in the stuffing, using your fingers. Press firmly to distribute the stuffing evenly throughout the cavity.

Stuffings for Pork Chops

If you prefer a light stuffing, mix the suggested ingredients below just as they are. For a firmer mixture, you can bind them with some fresh white breadcrumbs.

• Shredded rocket (arugula) mixed with cored and diced eating apple. Peel the apple first if you like.

• Chopped ready-to-eat dried apricots, finely shredded spinach, chopped (cured) ham and chopped fresh parsley.

• Peeled and chopped roasted (bell) peppers with crushed garlic and finely chopped eating apples.

Boning Loin

You can either buy loin ready-boned, or bone it yourself. Boning has two advantages: you can flavour the loin of pork with a tasty stuffing and the cooked meat is also far easier to carve.

1 Using a sharp knife, remove the skin and fat by cutting them off close to the meat. Fold back the fat and skin as you remove them.

2 Holding the loin firmly in position on the board with one hand, carefully cut between the ribs. Do not to cut any further down into the meat than the thickness of the ribs.

3 Using a meat cleaver or large chef's knife, carefully cut down behind the ribs, keeping the blade as near to the bones as possible.

4 Work the blade down and around the chine bone, lifting the bones away from the meat as they are cut free.

5 Open out the loin and lay it flat, then cut two slits lengthways into the meat, taking care not to cut right through. Arrange the stuffing in the slits, using your fingers to push it in firmly.

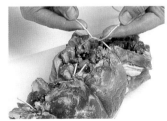

6 Carefully roll up the loin from one long side and tie securely with fine string in several places along its length to secure the stuffing.

Stuffing for Loin of Pork

Mix together 1 diced dessert apple, a finely chopped onion, some white breadcrumbs and a little white wine vinegar. Season with black pepper.

COOKING PORK

Pork is a tender meat, and most cuts can be roasted or baked, or cooked using other dry cooking methods. Hocks and trotters (feet) are the exceptions: they should be boiled to soften the connective tissue and release the small amount of well-flavored meat they yield. Once boiled, hocks can be trimmed, stuffed and roasted. Some cuts such as hand and spring have more sinews and benefit from slow roasting but, unlike beef, pork has no areas of tough muscle that need long, slow cooking to become tender.

Pan-frying

This is a traditional method for cooking pork chops and steaks. Use a heavy frying pan, preferably non-stick.

1 Dab a little sunflower oil on kitchen paper and use to grease the pan. Heat the pan until it is very hot (almost smoking). Add the meat and cook for about 3 minutes on each side.

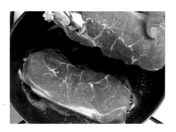

2 Alternatively, pan-fry lean cuts in a mixture of butter and oil. Heat the oil in the pan before adding the butter. (Unless it is clarified, butter heated on its own is liable to burn.) When the oil and butter are sizzling add the meat.

Stir-frying

This is a quick cooking method for thin, even strips or fine slices of pork. The majority of pork is suitable for stir-frying as long as all the sinew, membrane and fat are trimmed; prime cuts such as fillet are ideal. Most supermarkets sell pork ready cut into fine strips for stir-frying. Use a wok or a large, heavy frying pan over a high heat.

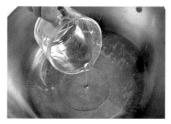

1 Heat a little oil in the wok or pan until it is smoking hot.

2 Add the pork in batches and stir-fry over high heat. Remove the cooked meat before adding a fresh batch. If you add too many strips at once, the temperature will drop and the meat will not cook quickly enough.

Stewing, Braising and Casseroling

These are all long, slow, moist methods of cooking, which can be done in the oven or on the stove. The meat is simmered gently in a flavourful liquid such as wine, water, beer or stock. This is a good cooking method for hand and spring or blade pork.

1 Trim off any excess fat and cut the meat into even-size cubes, measuring about 2.5cm/1in.

2 The meat may be tossed in seasoned flour before cooking if a flour-thickened sauce is required. This gives a dark, rich result. Shake off any excess flour before browning the meat.

3 Heat 30ml/2 tbsp sunflower oil in a flameproof casserole. Add the meat in batches, a handful at a time, and cook over high heat, turning frequently, until the meat is browned on all sides.

4 Use a draining spoon to remove each batch of meat from the casserole, and let the casserole reheat before adding the next batch. Add a little more oil if necessary before adding the meat.

5 Add any flavouring vegetables such as leeks, onions and carrots, to the casserole and cook in the remaining fat and juices, stirring occasionally, until softened and beginning to brown.

6 Return the meat to the casserole and pour in the liquid. Bring to a boil on the stove. Simmer gently or transfer to a preheated oven and cook until the meat is tender. The casserole may be covered for the entire length of the cooking time or it may be uncovered toward the end of the time to let some of the cooking liquid evaporate to thicken the sauce.

Griddling Pork

This method of frying is particularly suitable for pork. A griddle is a ridged pan, and the best types are those with a non-stick coating. The fat drains away from the meat into the deep ridges and the meat is seared with a lined pattern.

1 Preheat the griddle until it is almost smoking. Brush the meat very lightly with a little oil. (Sunflower or safflower oil, which are very mild and will not flavour the meat, are ideal.)

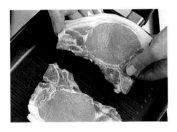

2 Add the meat to the hot griddle. Don't crowd the pan – cook in the meat in batches if necessary.

3 Cook for 3 minutes, then turn the meat and cook for a further 3 minutes on the other side, or until well browned and cooked through.

COOK'S TIP
A pair of tongs is useful for turning the chops during cooking. At the end of cooking, if the fat attached to the meat is not well browned, use the tongs to hold the chops with the rim of fat on the griddle. Turn the fat to brown it along its length.

Grilling

Cooking pork chops under the grill (broiler) is quick and healthy as it allows the fat to drip away into the grill pan during cooking. The intense heat of the grill seals the meat quickly, helping to keep the juices in and producing really succulent results.

1 Preheat the grill (broiler) until very hot. Trim off any excess fat from around the chops using a sharp cook's knife.

2 Brush the chops with a little sunflower or safflower oil, then place on an oiled rack under the grill (broiler).

3 Cook the chops for about 3 minutes, then turn the meat using a pair of tongs and cook for 3 minutes on the other side, or until they are well browned and cooked right through.

Roasting Pork

Most people prefer pork well-cooked. If you like a slightly rarer result – although the meat should not be served very pink – reduce the roasting time slightly.

1 Use a meat thermometer to check the internal temperature of the meat. Insert it into the centre of the thickest part, making sure that it does not touch any bone. Pork is usually done when the temperature reaches 80°C/176°F.

2 Cover the roast with foil and set aside for 10 minutes to rest before carving.

Roasting Times for Pork
Weigh the roast and calculate the cooking time accordingly.
For well-cooked pork
Allow 10 minutes at 230°C/450°F/Gas 8, then 30 minutes per 450g/1lb, plus an extra 30 minutes, at 180°C/350°F/Gas 4 for roasts still on the bone.
For boned and rolled roasts
Allow 35 minutes per 450g/1lb, plus an extra 35 minutes at 180°C/350°F/Gas 4. Remember to weigh stuffed roasts after they have been stuffed.

OFFAL

Known as variety meats in the United States, offal is the term for the offcuts from the carcass, including the edible internal organs, tail, feet and head. In everyday use, it usually means liver, kidneys, sweetbreads, tripe and heart.

The nutritive value depends on the type of offal, but it is generally a good source of animal protein, while being lean and lower in fat than meat. Liver and kidney are especially rich sources of iron, vitamin A and B complex vitamins, including folic acid.

Buying

Offal should always be fresh. Check sell-by dates on pre-packed offal and buy from a supermarket where the offal is neatly displayed in uncluttered refrigerators that are not overfilled. When buying offal loose from a butcher, it should always look fresh, moist and clean, with an even bright colour and texture, and it should smell fresh.

Storing

Always leave sealed pre-packed offal in its container and use it by the date given on the packet. Transfer offal bought loose to a deep dish and cover it tightly with clear film (plastic wrap) or a close-fitting lid. Use loose offal within 24 hours of purchase. Store in the refrigerator, in the coldest part, and where any drips that may escape will not be able to contaminate other foods.

Foie Gras

In France, where *foie gras* is a speciality, varieties of goose are bred especially for this purpose. Fattened goose liver, produced by force-feeding the geese, is pale and creamy in texture. It tastes wonderful and is considered a great delicacy by gourmets. However, the way it is produced makes it a controversial ingredient in some parts of the world and many people prefer not to eat it.

LIVER

This has a fine, close texture and a pronounced flavour. Calf's (veal) liver has the finest texture and lightest flavour. It is quite expensive and is regarded as a prime cut in Western cooking. Lamb's liver also has a mild flavour. It is inexpensive, readily available and widely used as a main ingredient in its own right, as well as for pâtés. Pig's liver and ox liver are strong in flavour and they have a coarser texture. Pig's liver is a particularly good ingredient for rich pâtés. Chicken, turkey and duck

Below: (Clockwise from top left) Chicken, goose, turkey and duck livers.

Above: (Top to bottom) Pig's and lamb's kidneys

Below: (Top to bottom) Ox and veal kidneys

livers are similar to each other in size, flavour and texture. They are significantly lighter in flavour, fine textured and rich. They are more versatile than the other types of liver. Goose liver is larger and paler in colour.

KIDNEY

All kidney has a distinctive taste, although this varies depending on its origin. Lamb's kidneys are small, tender and comparatively delicate in flavour. They are either cooked halved or whole. Veal kidneys are also very tender. Ox kidney is strongly flavoured and firm in texture. It is the classic ingredient for British steak and kidney pie (although lamb's kidney is often used instead for a lighter flavour). Pig's kidney is also strongly flavoured and used in terrines.

Above: Lamb's liver has a delicate flavour and is good used in pâtés.

Right: Calf's liver is also known as veal liver in the United States.

Above: (From top to bottom) Ox, veal and lamb's tongues

TONGUE

Ox tongue is sold fresh or cured in brine; veal tongue is popular in France. Lamb's tongues are sold fresh and, being smaller, they are put to a quite different use. A large tongue (usually of ox) is part-boiled so that the thick layer of skin can be removed, then the remaining, trimmed meat requires lengthy cooking to make it tender. The cooked meat can be used in hot dishes or pressed and served as a cold meat (a particular British speciality). Small lamb's tongues can be casseroled.

Below: Shin bones from cattle are the source of bone marrow.

Right: (Top to bottom) Calf's and lamb's sweetbreads

TAIL

Oxtail is usually chopped across into chunks. It has a large amount of creamy white fat covering a modest proportion of dark red meat. It requires long, slow and moist cooking, until the meat leaves the bone. Oxtail has a rich flavour and is good in soups, stews and terrines.

BONE MARROW

Found in hollow bones, this is a pale, fatty substance that has a full flavour. When poached, the marrow can be scooped out and used to enrich soups, stews, sauces and risottos. It is also served hot as a spread for bread or toast, or as a topping for canapés.

TROTTERS AND FEET

Pig's trotters (feet) and calf's feet can be bought whole or split in half. They are boiled to make stocks that set firmly when cold. They can also be used to enrich stews.

TRIPE

This comes from the stomach of a cow. Tripe from the first stomach (the rumen) is plain in texture, but that from the second stomach (the reticulum) has the typical honeycomb texture. Tripe is sold cleaned, washed and blanched (or often fully cooked), when it is creamy white in colour. It is easily digestible and very nutritious. Tripe has a distinctive flavour – not strong, but pronounced and able to dominate even spicy sauces. It is usually stewed with onions in milk to make a pale blanquette, for example, or in a spicy tomato sauce with onions and dried mushrooms in Polish style.

CHITTERLINGS

These are pig's intestines used as sausage casings or chopped up as part of the filling. They can also be cleaned, blanched and grilled (broiled) or pan-fried. Chitterlings are popular in France and the United States.

SWEETBREADS

Sweetbreads are the thymus glands taken from the neck and heart of young animals such as calves and lambs. They are pale and delicate with a tender meaty texture when braised or boiled. They are often pressed and fried or sautéed after blanching.

HEART

Lamb's heart is the most tender and lightest in flavour. Pig's heart is larger and slightly coarser; beef or ox heart is big, but not very tender. All need long, slow cooking and careful preparation.

BRAINS

Lamb's and veal brains are pale pink and delicate. Once rinsed, soaked and blanched they can be pan-fried, sautéed or braised.

Below: Chicken hearts are very small.

PREPARING AND COOKING OFFAL

Offal does not keep well and must be prepared and cooked quickly.

Trimming Liver

Most liver is sold trimmed and ready to cook, but still check it for any stray tubes or areas of membrane.

1 Trim off any patches of pale gristle or small pieces of tube that may remain. Use a small, sharp pointed knife to cut out the trimmings.

2 A fine skin or membrane sometimes remains on the surface of the liver, often in patches where it has not been thoroughly trimmed. Rub your fingertips over the liver to feel the membrane, then gently pull it away. For pan-frying, cut the liver into neat, even slices about 1cm/½in thick. Cut slightly thicker slices for grilling (broiling).

Cooking Liver

Liver should be cooked through, but remain slightly pink (not rare) in the middle, when it will be tender and succulent. If the liver is cooked over a medium heat for too long, it will become tough, hard and dry before it browns.

1 Melt a little butter in a heavy frying pan and add the slices of liver when it is foaming hot.

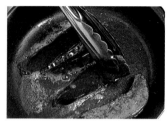

2 Cook briefly over fairly high heat until browned underneath, then turn and cook the slices on the second side.

3 If you prefer to grill (broil) liver, brush it with a little melted butter or vegetable oil and cook under a hot grill (broiler) for 3–4 minutes per side.

4 Liver may also be cut into pieces, threaded on to kebab skewers with cherry tomatoes, onion wedges and bacon, and then grilled (broiled) or cooked on the barbecue.

Trimming Kidneys

Kidneys are surrounded by a pad of firm fat which is usually removed before they are sold. (The fat surrounding ox kidneys is used for suet.) The white "core" that lies in the middle of the kidney should also be removed, together with any blood vessels.

1 If the fat is still in place, snip or cut it, then slide and pull it away from the kidney. Peel off the thin, transparent membrane covering the kidney to prevent it from shrinking when cooked.

2 Using a sharp knife, carefully cut the kidney in half horizontally.

3 Use sharp kitchen scissors to snip out the central white core together with any tubes and pale core.

Cooking Kidneys

Lamb's kidneys are tender and they cook quickly. Griddling is a good alternative to pan-frying or grilling (broiling) them.

1 Heat the griddle until very hot, then add a little butter or oil and heat it again for a few seconds.

2 Lay the halved kidneys on the griddle, cut-side down, and cook until browned and firm underneath. Turn and cook the second side until browned.

Cooking Tongue

Ox tongue is usually sold cleaned and ready to cook.

1 Place the prepared tongue in a large pan with cold water to cover. Add flavouring ingredients and aromatics such as carrot, celery, onion and a bouquet garni. The vegetables should be cut into large chunks.

2 Bring slowly to the boil, skim off any scum that rises to the surface, then reduce the heat to a steady simmer. At this stage spices, such as peppercorns, cloves, coriander seeds and juniper berries can be added. Cover and simmer for 3–4 hours, or until the meat is tender. Remove from the heat and leave the tongue to cool in its cooking liquid until it is cool enough to handle.

3 Drain the tongue and discard the cooking liquid. Cut away any tough, white gristle at the wide end of the tongue if necessary (this root may already have been completely removed), then peel off the thick skin.

4 Cut the tongue up and reheat in a sauce. Alternatively, it can be curled into a small round dish and weighted, then allowed to cool completely.

5 Pressed tongue should be unmoulded and sliced thinly. It can then be served in the same way as cooked ham. It is excellent with mustard or pickles.

Extracting Marrow from Bones

Ask the butcher to saw the marrow bones into 7.5cm/3in long pieces. To serve the bone marrow as an appetizer or as a spread for toast, brush the bones with a little oil or melted dripping and roast at 200°C/400°F/Gas 6 for 45 minutes, or until well browned. Alternatively, roast them at the same time as a cut of meat.

Alternatively, poach the bones in salted boiling water for 2–3 minutes to soften the marrow, then drain well and use the handle end of a teaspoon to scoop out the marrow. Poached bone marrow can be used to enrich stock and sauces or in a risotto, or it can be seasoned and served as a spread.

Preparing Sweetbreads

1 Soak the sweetbreads in a bowl of cold water for at least 2 hours, changing the water several times. Rinse them well: they are ready for cooking when all signs of blood have been soaked or rinsed away.

2 Drain the sweetbreads, place in a pan and cover with plenty of cold water. Bring to the boil, then immediately lower the heat and simmer gently for 5 minutes, until the sweetbreads have become firm and white.

3 Drain the sweetbreads and peel off the membrane. Remove any pieces of gristle or fat and ducts. Cool and chill until firm. When firm, the sweetbreads can be sliced or cut into pieces, coated in flour and pan-fried, then simmered in a sauce. Sweetbreads are also good coated in egg and breadcrumbs, fried and served with lemon wedges.

Preparing Brains

Brains are prepared in the same way as sweetbreads, by thorough rinsing, soaking and blanching, then trimming. They are then poached in a sauce or lightly pressed under weights until cold, when they can be sliced and coated with breadcrumbs and pan-fried. Brains have a creamy texture when cooked.

Pot-roasting Trotters

Trotters (pig's feet) are sold cleaned and ready for cooking. Rinse and dry them, then singe off any hairs with a lighted match or candle. Heat a little oil in a heavy pan or flameproof casserole and brown the trotters on all sides. Remove from the pan or casserole. Add thickly sliced onions and carrots, peeled garlic cloves and herbs, then replace the trotters on the bed of vegetables and aromatics. Pour in enough water, stock or wine to cover the vegetables. Cover and cook in the oven at 180°C/350°F/Gas 4 for about 2 hours, turning the trotters occasionally, or until they are golden brown and tender.

SAUSAGES AND SALAMI

Sausages are meat mixtures, usually enclosed in casings. Originally they were produced from all the offcuts from the carcass – offal (variety meats), fatty or tough scraps or irregular pieces of meat. Mixed with herbs, spices, flavouring ingredients, salt and saltpetre for preservation, the meat was packed into lengths of intestine or other suitable organs, tied firmly and hung to dry and cure. These were not neat little uniformly cylindrical products, even though they were, in effect, one of the earliest forms of convenience food. The casings often created sausages of different lengths, widths and shapes: haggis, the classic Scottish sausage of lamb offal packed in a sheep's stomach, is a good example.

Although casings were used for hanging and curing sausages intended for long-term storage, they were not essential. The mixture was sometimes pressed into shape, then coated with fat, flour or breadcrumbs. British faggots and the French *crepinette* are both types of sausage, shaped into small balls, then wrapped in caul, the thin lacy membrane of fat that surrounds the pig's stomach.

Sausages were once simply the way of using up and preserving all of the pig after it was killed. Salt and pepper, spices, herbs and garlic were often added to provide additional flavour and piquancy, but basically sausages were the food of the poor. In areas where pigs were forbidden, or didn't or couldn't live, fish and even vegetable sausages were made, but again, these were simple foods. Today, however, sausages have become quite fashionable among discerning food-lovers and people will travel some distance for certain, special French sausages or Italian salamis.

The nutritional value varies widely, because each type of sausage contains different ingredients, or varying proportions of the same ingredients. As a rule, sausages tend to have a high fat content compared to lean meat, poultry or offal, but low-fat and lean versions are also produced.

Below: Scottish haggis

FRESH SAUSAGES

These are raw and ready to cook – the British pork sausage is a typical example. The range of fresh sausages available varies according to food fashions and their popularity. There is an incredible choice, from coarse or fine meat sausages made according to traditional recipes, to quite bizarre combinations of seasonings, vegetables, fruit, nuts and even cheese added to basic meat mixtures. The selection changes according to the whim of the producer, whether it be a small local butcher or a large food manufacturer.

Britain is known for fresh sausages: pork and beef are the main types, but chicken, turkey, venison and game are all available. Italy, France and Germany each have their own specialities, but these countries are famed for cured sausages. The following is an overview of the international variety of fresh sausages.

Andouillettes and andouilles Andouillettes, and larger andouilles, are made with pork, chitterlings, pepper, wine and onions and may be smoked. Despite their appearance, they taste delicious.

Bordeaux sausage This is a small highly seasoned French sausage.

Bratwurst A pale, fine-textured, German smoked sausage for frying, the bratwurst is made with pork or veal, milk and chopped onions seasoned with salt, pepper and mace.

Cambridge sausage This traditional English pork sausage is made with twice as much lean meat as fat and is flavoured with herbs and spices. It may be either grilled (broiled) or gently fried.

Chipolatas Slim, fine-textured pork sausages, these are a British breakfast favourite. Chipolatas were once known for their high quality, but today's skinless versions do not compare with the traditional chipolata. A long length of chipolatas is known as a string of sausages.

Cotechino This is a readily available, popular Italian coarse pork sausage flavoured with white wine and spices.

Cumberland sausage A coarse-textured British pork sausage seasoned with black pepper, this is traditionally very long, not twisted into links, but usually curled and cooked in a round.

Below: (Clockwise from the top left) Beef and Guinness, pork, apple and pork chipolatas, venison, pork and beef, Cumberland are just a few of the fresh sausages produced in Britain.

Above: (Clockwise from top right) German sausages include frankfurters, bratwurst, bockwurst, knoblauchwurst.

Lincolnshire sausage This traditional British pork sausage is flavoured with sage and thyme.

Luganeghe A long, thin pork sausage, this variety is popular in northern Italy.

Merguez This is a deep red and very spicy Algerian sausage made of beef and mutton, or sometimes goat. It is flavoured with red pepper and is usually served with couscous.

Oxford sausage This famous British sausage is made from a mixture of pork and veal.

Salchicha A small and fragrant fresh pork sausage, this is Spanish in origin.

Salsiccie This Italian fresh sausage is ready for cooking and can be poached, fried or grilled (broiled). Salsiccie sausages are made according to local recipes, of which there are many types. *Salsiccia* is simply the Italian word for sausage.

Salsiccie casalinga Meaning home-made sausage, salsiccie casalinga is a short, fat rustic Italian sausage usually made with pure pork.

Saveloy This British smoked sausage is made from pork and beef. It also contains lights (lungs) and a little saltpetre, which gives it a reddish hue.

Thick link sausage
This is the standard British sausage, sometimes referred to as "links". Fine or coarse pork, pork and beef or beef are the most common versions. There are traditional regional recipes and a huge range of contemporary flavours.

Toulouse sausage/ Saucisson de Toulouse
A coarse pork sausage, this is herbed, highly seasoned and flavoured with garlic. It is an essential ingredient of cassoulet and can also be grilled (broiled) or fried and eaten with mashed potatoes and fried apple rings.

Classic Ingredients

Fat in modest amounts is an important ingredient in the traditional sausage, adding flavour and keeping the mixture moist. Fatty cuts of pork such as belly (side) are ideal for making sausages. Beef and veal are used alone or combined with pork. Fresh bread is a traditional ingredient for binding the mixture; dried breadcrumbs and other cereals are inferior mainly because they are often added in large quantities when they absorb too much excess fat instead of allowing it to baste and flavour the meat before draining away. Cheaper sausages are made using inexpensive and bulky filling ingredients, with excessive quantities of dried herbs, or even artificial flavours, and colouring agents, added to compensate for the lack of taste and colour. Better quality sausages use moderate amounts of fresh or dried herbs such as thyme, sage, parsley or marjoram often combined with spices, such as mace, nutmeg, coriander and pepper.

Above: Salchicas are long, thin, rustic sausages from Spain.

Below: (Clockwise from the top) Classic Italian sausages include cotechino, luganeghe, salmelle, salsiccie casalinga.

Above: Large and meaty, Toulouse sausages, which are flavoured with garlic and herbs, may be sold in links or in continuous lengths that need to be cut into pieces.

Casings and Coatings

Intestines or chitterlings are the traditional casings for fresh sausages, but synthetic alternatives are widely used. Skinless sausages are also available and some mixtures can be coated in flour or dipped in egg and fresh or dried breadcrumbs.

Buying Fresh Sausages

When purchasing pre-packed products, check the packet for information on the ingredients and choose only sausages that contain a high percentage of meat. The fat content of sausages will come under nutritional information; low-fat sausages are normally labelled as such in large lettering on the packet. Whether packed or loose, look for sausages made with a large proportion of high quality meat and natural seasonings or flavouring ingredients. Look at the texture, colour and plumpness of the sausage. Avoid products that are a strange, artificial colour compared to the ingredients they contain. Fresh sausages should look plump and well filled, without sagging skins, but not so full that they look fit to burst. They should look moist and fresh. Reject any with dried patches or ends, discoloured areas, or those that are wet, slimy or weeping. Smell is, of course, a good indicator of freshness and it is unwise to buy from a store or counter which smells unpleasant.

Storing Sausages

Leave pre-packed sausages in their sealed wrapper and store them in the coldest area of the refrigerator. Use before the date given on the

Below: Chorizo sausages are quite spicy.

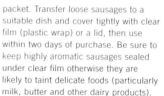

packet. Transfer loose sausages to a suitable dish and cover tightly with clear film (plastic wrap) or a lid, then use within two days of purchase. Be sure to keep highly aromatic sausages sealed under clear film otherwise they are likely to taint delicate foods (particularly milk, butter and other dairy products).

Many types of fresh sausage freeze well, but this depends entirely on the ingredients they contain. Sausages highly flavoured with garlic should be at least double wrapped, otherwise they will taint the other foods in the freezer.

CURED AND SMOKED SAUSAGES

These are preserved sausages, and salami is probably the best known of this type. There are literally thousands of salamis and smoked sausages. With almost every supermarket and delicatessen in town selling an extensive range of their own favourites, the choice is becoming quite bewildering. Some cured sausages are served thinly sliced, raw, in the same way as Italian salami; others are cooked before serving. Some are served either raw or cooked according to taste. These are examples of preserved or part-preserved sausages; in culinary terms, the curing and ageing produces a mature flavour, which is the main characteristic now that modern refrigeration and freezing are the more practical and safer methods for the long-term preservation of meat products.

Birnenformige This is a pear-shaped German salami.

Chorizo A coarsely textured spicy red sausage, this is made of air-cured pork or a mixture of pork and beef and pimentos. This cured sausage from Andalucia can be eaten raw or cooked and is an essential ingredient in the Spanish bean stew *fabada asturiana*. All chorizo sausages are spicy and some varieties are especially hot. They are widely used in both

Above: Coppa is an unusual northern Italian sausage with an irregular shape.

Spanish and Mexican cooking and may be fried or grilled (broiled), as well being added to stews. (*Longaniza* is a Portuguese version of chorizo.)

Coppa di Palma/Coppa Also known as *coppa crudo*, this is a salted and dried sausage that is something between a raw, cured ham and a sausage in both flavour and texture. It comes from the neck or shoulder of pork and the casing is made of natural skin. *Coppa* has a roughly rectangular shape and a rich deep red colour. It comes from Lombardy and Emilia Romagna in the north of Italy.

Danish salami Danish salamis are made from pork and veal and have quite a high fat content. The popular varieties are fine and fairly soft in texture, light rather than well matured, but well seasoned with spices and with a salty, smoky flavour. The characteristic bright red or pink colour results from artificial colouring.

Felinetti From Parma, these are delicate small salami made with white wine, whole peppercorns and garlic.

Finocchiona This large pure pork salami is mottled with quite large pieces of fat and flavoured with fennel.

Right: Felinetti is claimed by many to be the finest Italian salami.

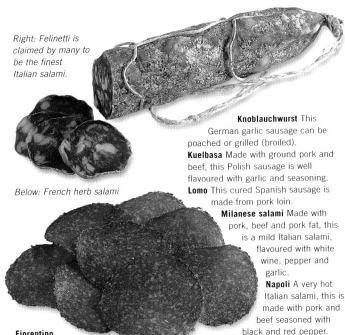

Below: French herb salami

Fiorentino
One of the many types of salami from Tuscany, this is made with pork and lean meats combined with fat. It is quite large, measuring about 10cm/4in in diameter.

French herb salami This cured meat is highly flavoured with garlic, dried and smoked, then finished with a thick coating of herbs. Like most French salamis, it keeps very well.

French pepper salami Made from a mixture of pork and beef, this French salami is mixed with coarse chunks of fat and seasoned liberally with whole black peppercorns.

Fuet This Spanish cured sausage is long and thin in shape, and firm in texture.

Italian salami There are dozens of different regional specialities throughout Italy, and almost every town has its favourite preparation.

Kabanos There are various types of this Polish sausage, some that are suitable for cooking and others for serving cold. They are highly spiced and smoked.

Katenrauchwurst A firm, dark German sausage, this is made with coarsely cut smoked pork.

Knoblauchwurst This German garlic sausage can be poached or grilled (broiled).
Kuelbasa Made with ground pork and beef, this Polish sausage is well flavoured with garlic and seasoning.
Lomo This cured Spanish sausage is made from pork loin.
Milanese salami Made with pork, beef and pork fat, this is a mild Italian salami, flavoured with white wine, pepper and garlic.
Napoli A very hot Italian salami, this is made with pork and beef seasoned with black and red pepper.
Pepperoni Made from coarsely chopped pork and beef, this Italian cured sausage is highly seasoned with red pepper.
Spanish salchichon This is a cured sausage or salami.
Toscana A fairly coarse Italian salami, this variety is seasoned with peppercorns.

Preserving Methods

There are many different methods of curing or smoking, the majority still based largely on traditional principles of preservation. Salt and saltpetre (potassium nitrate) are used to preserve the meat, while spices and herbs are used for flavouring. Other ingredients can be added for flavour, including vegetables, wine and spirits. Sugar or other sweetening agents may be added, particularly when the salt is used in the form of a brine rather than dry.

For cured or dried sausages, the mixture is packed into the casing and hung in an airy environment (usually cool, but sometimes hot) until dried. The middle of the mixture dries more slowly than the outside and it ferments slightly, which is all part of the curing process, giving many salamis and cured sausages their tangy flavour. Smoking is another way of drying and imparting flavour to the cured sausages or meat. The wood used imparts its own flavour.

Above: Kuelbasa

Above: Fuet is usually bought whole for slicing at home.

Above: Spanish lomo is made from cured pork loin.

Buying

There is such a huge range of sausages now available that it is difficult to make general comments about buying them. Cured sausages, cured and cooked meats must be fresh. Avoid dull or dried-out and off-colour products. The meats or sausages should be freshly sliced for you; many supermarkets and delicatessens slice popular products in advance to save time, but check that the slices are recently cut. Meats that have been sliced for many hours will look dry, especially around the edges, and these should be rejected. Pre-packed products vary greatly in quality but it is usually easy to assess them by appearance and price.

Storing

The old-fashioned larder (pantry) is the ideal place for hanging whole cured meats, salamis or sausages. The refrigerator is the practical option for modest amounts and today's household. Store all cooked and cured meats in the refrigerator, away from uncooked foods that may contaminate them. Leave pre-packed products in their sealed wrapping. Transfer loose sliced meats to a plate and cover with clear film (plastic wrap) or wrap closely in greaseproof (waxed) paper, folding the edges together firmly to seal them, then place this in a greaseproof paper bag. Again, in practice, clear film (plastic wrap) is the most readily available and practical of coverings. Cooked meats and sausages should be used within four to five days of purchase; salamis and cured sausages can be stored for longer, depending on whether they are whole or sliced. Sliced products should be used within a week; whole sausages will keep for about two weeks.

Chinese Sausages

Wind-dried Chinese sausages are shrunken, hard and wrinkled. They are made with pork and/or offal, flavoured with spices and are slightly sweet. Most large Chinese supermarkets offer a selection, some strung and hanging loose, others in shrink-wrapped packs. The sausages vary in colour from pink-red to dark brown-red and the latter tend to be made with a high percentage of offal. Check the ingredients list or go by colour, selecting the paler sausages for a light, meaty flavour or the dark colour for a distinct offal taste. The sausages should be steamed for 30–45 minutes, until plump and tender, then sliced on the diagonal and served as part of a selection of cooked wind-dried foods or used in a variety of dishes. Chinese sausages may be stir-fried or added to braised dishes.

Other well-known cured and dried Chinese meats are pork and the rather spectacular-looking ducks, which are opened out and then flattened.

Below: Milanese salami

Below: Napoli salami

Right: Try to buy cured sausages, such as this Toscana, freshly sliced.

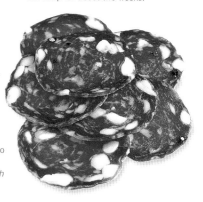

COOKED SAUSAGES

These include products for slicing such as garlic sausage; or for spreading such as liver sausage. There are also other sausages that may be reheated or cooked again, for example frankfurters.

Bierschinken This pork and ham sausage has added pistachio nuts.

Bierwurst This is a pork and beef sausage, usually quite spicy and flavoured with garlic.

Black pudding This British blood sausage is usually highly spiced and dotted with fat. It is poached ready for further cooking.

Bockwurst This delicate white sausage is made with pork and veal, chopped chives, parsley, milk and eggs.

Boudin blanc A French white pudding, this is made from chicken, veal, rabbit and/or pork, enriched with cream and white wine.

Boudin noir This French blood sausage is poached ready for further cooking.

Butifarra bianca This is a traditional Spanish poached white sausage, which is made from pork.

Butifarra negra A Spanish blood sausage, this is similar to morcilla.

Crepinette This French offal (variety meats) mixture is shaped into a sausage or ball and coated in caul fat. It is sold cooked ready for reheating.

Extrawurst This large, pale pink, smooth sausage is made from pork and beef. It slices easily.

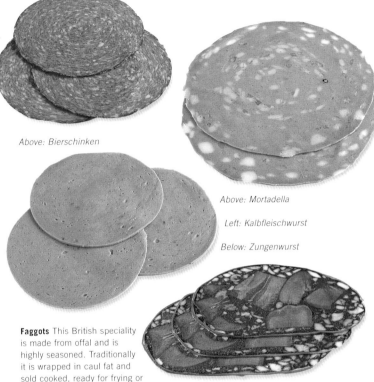

Above: Bierschinken

Above: Mortadella

Left: Kalbfleischwurst

Below: Zungenwurst

Below: Black and white puddings

Faggots This British speciality is made from offal and is highly seasoned. Traditionally it is wrapped in caul fat and sold cooked, ready for frying or poaching.

Frankfurter Originally a cold smoked sausage made with pork and salted bacon fat, the name frankfurter has been adopted for any cooked sausage with a smoky flavour that is suitable for making hot dogs.

Haggis This large Scottish sausage is made of diced sheep's liver, lungs, heart, onion and suet, seasoned with spice and bound together with oatmeal. Traditionally, it is packed into a sheep's stomach ready for lengthy boiling. Nowadays, it is sold cooked, ready for reheating.

Kalbfleischwurst This is a pale pink, very fine, large veal sausage.

Mettwurst This pork and beef sausage varies in texture and can be sliced or spread.

Morcilla Morcilla blood sausage is usually highly seasoned and very spicy.

Mortadella This large cooked pork sausage, flavoured with garlic, is smooth and studded with pistachio nuts and pieces of fat.

Pfeffer plockwurst This unusual square sausage is coated with very coarsely ground black pepper.

Presskopf Presskopf is a flavourful sausage made with pork, veal and beef.

Schinken Jagdwurst Made from finely minced (ground) pork with diced pork fat, this sausage is flavoured with small pieces of ham.

Schinken kalbfleischwurst Made from pork, beef and veal, this sausage contains ham and a little garlic.

White pudding This is a British white sausage containing either pearl barley or groats, suet, leeks, rusk, milk, herbs and sometimes cloves, salt and pepper. It is sold ready for grilling (broiling), poaching or baking.

Ham, Bacon and Cured Meats

In the past, curing was a traditional way of preserving meat. It has remained popular today because of the delicious flavour it imparts to the meat.

Ham

The word ham originally referred only to fresh meat from the upper part of an animal's hind leg. It was not until the seventeenth century that it was applied specifically to meat from a hog or pig. The word still retains this meaning in the United States, but in Britain, it began to be associated with only salted, dried or smoked meat and it now refers exclusively to cured pig meat. For convenience and to avoid confusion, all references to ham in this section apply to cured pig meat. The term ham is most widely used for the cooked or ready-to-eat product or for the dry cured hams that are eaten raw as well as cooked. Gammon steaks, taken from the cured leg, are also sometimes referred to as ham.

The hind legs and the loin make the best cured pork and ham. For the very finest ham, farmers are particularly careful about the diet on which the pigs are fed. In Parma, for example, pigs are fattened on parsnips.

Every region has its own traditional method and recipe for curing ham, first in dry salt or brine and then sometimes smoked over a hardwood fire. The brine can be varied by the addition of sugar or molasses, herbs, spices or berries. Finally, the ham is left to dry and mature. The temperature and humidity during the drying or smoking and drying can be varied to produce different results. The geographical differences are still evident in the names of the hams available today: Prosciutto di Parma from Emilia-Romagna in Italy; Virginia ham from the American South; Westphalian ham in western Germany; and York ham, Bradenham ham, Cumberland ham, Wiltshire ham and Suffolk ham from England.

Some dry-cured, smoked hams are eaten raw. Italian prosciutto is probably the most famous, in particular the much-loved Parma ham. Bayonne ham is the French equivalent to Parma,

Serrano ham comes from Spain and in Germany, Westphalian ham is also eaten uncooked. All are sliced to tissue-paper fineness before serving. They can also be cooked for use in some dishes.

Buying

Cooked ham should be evenly coloured and have a slightly crumbly surface. Whenever possible, ask for the ham to be carved from the bone, rather than buying the pre-cut product. When buying uncooked ham such as prosciutto look for deep pink flesh and creamy white fat. The ham should be moist, but not damp, and should lay flat; it should not be dry and curled at the edges. As with cooked ham, buy uncooked ham freshly sliced. Look for a supplier who is able to cut large, paper-thin slices. The rind and some of the fat should be trimmed off before the ham is sliced. Reject broken slices or slices that are too thick to be served raw.

Storing

Ham should be kept in the refrigerator. Leave pre-packed meat in its wrapping and use by the recommended date. Wrap loose ham in greaseproof (waxed) paper and clear film (plastic wrap) and store away from raw, fresh meat.

Above : Prosciutto is a highly-prized Italian ham that is partially cured under weights to flatten it.

HAMS FOR EATING RAW

There are numerous hams the world over that are intended to be eaten raw. All have been cured, although in different ways, and then are normally air-dried. Raw hams can be lightly cooked, or added to hot dishes, such as risotto and pasta. However, to enjoy them at their best, they should be eaten in their raw state.

Prosciutto di Parma and Prosciutto crudo
Italy is famous for its *prosciutto crudo*, salted and air-dried ham that requires no cooking. The most famous of these hams, prosciutto di Parma, comes from the area around the city of Parma, where Parmesan cheese is also made. Although they are said to be fattened on parsnips, the pigs in this region are fed partly on the whey left over from the cheese-making process, which makes their flesh very mild and sweet. Because they are always reared and kept in sheds and never allowed to roam outdoors, they tend to be rather fatty. Parma hams are made from the pig's hindquarters, which are lightly salted and air-dried for at least one year

(and sometimes up to two). The zone of production of Parma ham is restricted by law to the area between the Taro and Baganza rivers, where the air and humidity levels are ideal for drying and curing the hams. In fact, every year thousands of ready-salted hams are sent here from neighbouring regions to be dried and cured in the unique air around Parma.

San Daniele This is another Italian prosciutto, regarded by some as superior even to Parma ham. The ham comes from the Friuli region of northern Italy, from pigs that are raised on a diet of acorns. It is this diet that gives the ham its distinctive flavour, while the flesh is leaner since the pigs are kept outside. It is also a richer colour. San Daniele is produced in much smaller quantities than Parma ham, which makes it even more expensive and desirable.

Other prosciutto crudo A number of raw, cured hams is produced in several other regions of Italy, notably a light and delicate prosciutto from the Veneto in the north-east of the country. They are also made in Tuscany and elsewhere in Friuli and Emilia-Romagna.

Bayonne ham This is the best known of all the French raw hams, coming from the Basses-Pyrénées region, although it is now produced all over France. Traditionally, it is cured using a locally produced wine, which gives the ham its distinctive flavour. It is best eaten raw

Below: Serrano ham may be left to mature in the snow of the Spanish mountains after which it is named.

Above: San Daniele ham is leaner and, some would claim, superior to Italy's more famous prosciutto di Parma.

like prosciutto, but can be used in cooking, added to casseroles or quickly fried and served with eggs.

Jambon d'Ardennes Produced in both northern France and neighbouring Belgium, this ham is popular thinly sliced and served raw and may also be heated gently in butter.

Jambon de campagne The name simply means country ham and includes numerous raw hams from all over France. The Dordogne region produces some of the best and other hams of varying quality come from Alsace, Auvergne, Brittany, Burgundy, Limousin, Morvan, Toulouse, Touraine and the Vosges. The best ones are produced by local farmers, rather than commercial manufacturers. Serve with

crusty, country-style bread and unsalted (sweet) butter. French country hams also feature in a number of regional specialities.

Serrano ham This is the most famous and delicious of all Spanish hams. The variety called *jamón de Jabugo* comes from the region of Huelva in the Sierra Morena mountains (*serrano* means from the mountains), west of Seville near the Portuguese border. The small, Iberian free-range pigs feed on acorns from the acorn cork, giving the meat a fine flavour. The ham, which is cured and air-dried, is chewy and distinctly sweet, and is excellent simply served on plain bread. It is rose-coloured and usually displayed in stores with the marking of a black hoof as a guarantee of its authenticity. Other types of mountain ham are produced in Caceres, Granada and Salamanca.

Presunto This is a lightly cured, smoked ham from Portugal. It has a pleasant flavour and is usually served thinly sliced as an appetizer.

Schwarzwalder The strong flavour of this Black Forest ham from Germany is something of an acquired taste. It is smoked after curing in a strong brine.

Mainz ham The lengthy process involved in producing this popular German ham results in an excellent flavour. It is first cured in brine, then desalinated and soaked in brandy before being smoked for a prolonged period.

Westphalian ham This is the most famous of all German hams and is traditionally smoked over ash or beech wood, after having been cured with juniper berries, which give the ham its distinctive flavour. It is an attractive, reddish-brown colour. It is excellent served on German dark rye bread such as pumpernickel. Westphalian ham is protected by a trademark.

Lachsschinken This German ham is recognized by its white, pork-fat wrapping. Inside the ham is pink and moist. It can be bought cut into wafer-thin slices; if you buy it whole, chop it into small dice.

COOKED HAM

These hams need to be cooked before being eaten, and whole hams are sold uncooked, for cooking at home. If you buy an uncooked ham, it benefits from a lengthy soaking, and is then normally simmered before being skinned, glazed and baked. The curing process differs from one type of ham to another: some are cured in brine, sometimes with sugar, honey or molasses added; others are smoked after curing. There are some exotic hams such as the fine Chinese ham, Unnan, and the Japanese ham, Jinhua, which are only available from specialist outlets.

Bradenham ham This ham from Wiltshire is one of the most famous of English hams. The skin is black, while the flesh is deep red. Cured with molasses, it has a noticeably sweet, but robust flavour. If you buy it uncooked, soak it for several days to remove the excess salt.

York ham This is another very popular English ham. Cured by the dry-salt method, it is then smoked over oak, which helps to develop its delicious mild flavour. It is available both uncooked, to cook at home, or cooked on the bone from delicatessen counters. It may be served hot or cold.

Suffolk ham Also known as Seager, Suffolk ham is basted, after curing with salt, with honey or treacle, old ale and spices. It is then hung until mature, giving it a well-rounded flavour.

Irish ham Also known as Belfast ham or Ulster Roll, this dry-salt cured ham comes from Northern Ireland. The ham is smoked over peat which gives it a very distinctive flavour.

Prosciutto cotto Italy also produces a wide range of cooked hams, usually boiled. They can be flavoured with all sorts of herbs and spices. Cooked ham is sometimes served

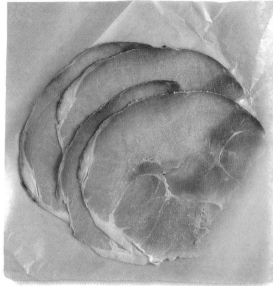

Above : Prosciutto cotto is less famous than the crudo, or raw version.

as an *antipasto* together with raw ham, but it is more often eaten in sandwiches and as part of a snack.

Kentucky ham This fine ham comes from Hampshire hogs that are fattened first on acorns and beans and then on grain. After dry-salting, the meat is smoked slowly over hickory and applewood or sassafras wood and then matured for up to 12 months.

Smithfield ham This is a popular ham from Virginia in the United States, but is not the same as Virginia ham.

Free-range pigs are fed first on hickory nuts and acorns, then on peanuts and then finally, on corn. After dry-curing, the meat is heavily smoked over hickory and applewood. It is usually sold cooked and may be eaten hot or cold.

Virginia ham This sweet-flavoured, moist ham comes exclusively from razorbacks fed on peaches and peanuts. After dry-curing, the ham is flavoured with molasses and pepper. It may be smoked over hickory and applewood or simply matured for a year.

Country-cured ham This group consists of other high-quality American hams. Hams that are mass-produced are usually known as city hams and are inferior. The best country-cured hams come from Georgia, Kentucky, Tennessee and Virginia, where the pigs are often allowed to roam and forage freely and are fattened on peaches and nuts.

Jambon de Paris In France, ham sold for boiling is known as *jambon de Paris* or *jambon blanc*, while boiled ham is called *jambon glacé*. It may be unsmoked or lightly smoked.

Prague ham First salted and brined for several months, this ham from the Czech Republic is then smoked over beech wood. It has a sweet flavour and is usually sold cooked.

Above: York ham is now made in countries all over the world.

COOKING HAM

If the ham is cured by a traditional method, it may be very salty and should be covered in cold water and left to soak for 12 hours or even longer if it is large. Meat today is often cured by modern methods and soaking is not always necessary and may result in insipid meat. However, ask the butcher for advice (or check the label). As a guide, meats cured by traditional methods are generally available from specialist stores, high-quality butchers or by mail order. Leaving the rind on for most of the cooking period helps to keep the meat in shape.

1 Weigh the ham and calculate the cooking time at 20 minutes per 450g/1lb, plus 20 minutes extra.

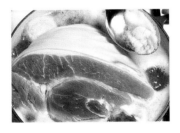

2 Put the ham in a large pan with enough fresh cold water to cover. Bring to the boil and skim off the scum that rises to the surface. Lower the heat and simmer for 30 minutes.

3 Drain the ham and discard the water. Then return the ham to the pan and pour over fresh cold water to cover. Add flavouring ingredients such as a coarsely chopped apple or onion, wine or a few cloves and bring to the boil.

4 Cover the pan and simmer gently for the calculated cooking time (beginning timing at this stage).

5 While the ham is still hot the rind will come off easily, leaving a smooth surface on the fat. Leave the ham to cool slightly in its cooking stock, then lift out of the pan on to a dish and drain while still hot. Use a sharp knife to loosen the rind, then fold it back as you peel it off, cutting between it and the fat. This will leave an even layer of fat on the surface.

6 The fat can be finished off by rolling it in fresh breadcrumbs. Or it can be scored and studded with cloves if it is to be baked. Hold the bone end firmly and with a sharp knife score lines across the fat, then score in the opposite direction to mark diamond shapes.

7 Stud the ham with cloves, placing one in each diamond of fat.

8 Place the ham on a rack inside a baking tray. Sprinkle generously with demerara (raw) sugar, pressing it lightly on to the fat.

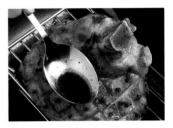

9 Bake the ham until the sugar melts and browns, giving the fat an attractive glaze. When preparing a freshly cooked, hot ham, simply place it in a preheated oven at 200°C/400°F/Gas 6 and re-heat for about 20 minutes.

10 If the ham has cooled, it should be glazed in a preheated oven at 180°C/350°F/Gas 4 until thoroughly reheated and browned.

Glazing Mixtures

Instead of using demerara (raw) sugar, try one of the following glazing mixtures:
- apple juice mixed with honey or maple syrup
- soy sauce combined with brown sugar and medium or dry sherry
- brush the the ham with English (hot) mustard, before sprinkling it with demerara sugar.

BACON AND GAMMON

Normally (although not exclusively), bacon is the cured meat taken from the back and sides of the pig. Gammon (cured ham) comes from the hind leg and hind quarters. Both are available as larger cuts as well as rashers (strips). There are three curing methods for bacon, using dry coarse salt, brine, or a mixture of salt, sugar, seasonings and preservatives. After salting, the meat is sometimes smoked.

Bacon slices and larger cuts are cut from the fore quarter and gammon from the hind quarter. Collar (blade shoulder) from the front of the carcass is sold as large cuts, for boiling, or as wide, fairly lean rashers. These are economical, but not so tender as the rashers from the middle of the carcass. Cuts from the fore quarter are ideal for boiling, giving an excellent flavour, or for dicing and stewing or adding to soups. Offcuts, either in chunks or small dice, are the trimmings from both bacon and gammon. Offcuts tend to be inexpensive and ideal for flavouring.

Buying

All bacon can be bought either smoked or unsmoked. Unsmoked bacon is sometimes known as green bacon (though it is not green in colour). If you are not sure whether bacon is smoked or unsmoked, check the colour. Smoked bacon has a richer fat and a golden-orange rind. Unsmoked flesh is paler, and the fat and rind are white and cream respectively.

Good quality bacon has clear, pink, moist, but not wet, meat with an even layer of creamy white fat. The rind, if it has one, should be thin and elastic, but its colour will depend on the method of curing and/or smoking. Bacon should never smell unpleasant.

Storing

Check and observe the use-by date on pre-packed bacon. Leave the bacon in its pack, then when it is opened, store any leftovers in clear film (plastic wrap) or a plastic container with a lid. Follow the storage instructions on the packet. If you buy good quality loose bacon, wrap it in greaseproof (waxed) paper

Above : Gammon steaks are thick slices taken from the boned hind quarter.

and place in a plastic bag. Bacon will keep for up to three weeks in the refrigerator. Keep it in the coolest part of the refrigerator, away from ingredients that will be eaten raw.

Bacon and gammon – and ham, for that matter – do not freeze well as the salt used in curing promotes rancidity once they are frozen. Commercially vacuum-packed bacon, gammon and ham have a slightly improved freezer life. The storage time depends on the curing process. As a general rule, it is not worth freezing high quality bacon and ham cured by traditional

methods, as they keep for only two to three weeks and tend to be inferior when thawed. However, meat cured by modern methods will keep for a month. In some cases, manufacturers suggest a freezer life of up to three months. This short time also applies to cooked dishes containing bacon – they will keep for up to only four weeks, as the bacon becomes rancid on longer storage and taints the dish.

Below: Middle bacon or through cut comprises long rashers with a mix of lean bacon from the back of the carcass and streaky bacon.

Below: Back bacon rashers are very lean, with a layer of fat on the edge.

Above : Streaky bacon is the belly end of through-cut bacon.

MIDDLE GAMMON

The gammon is the cured leg. This may be cooked on the bone or boned and rolled. The middle gammon is a prime cut taken from the wide part of the leg. This can be boiled or baked, or cooked by a combination of both methods, first par-boiling, then finishing in the oven.

Below: Pancetta is a fatty Italian bacon – unsmoked round, rolled slices of cured pork belly.

Below: Smoked pancetta is usually sold in flat slices or thin strips, rather than being rolled, like unsmoked pancetta.

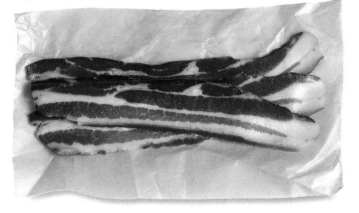

GAMMON STEAKS

Gammon steaks are made from thick slices cut from the middle gammon after it has been boned.

GAMMON KNUCKLE

This is the end of the gammon and usually includes the bone although it can be boned and rolled. Knuckle is good for boiling or baking ir can be trimmed, cubed and added to stews.

MIDDLE OR THROUGH-CUT BACON

This comprises the back and streaky bacon in a long, continuous piece. It is good for grilling (broiling).

BACK BACON

From the back, this is a leanest cut of bacon. The widths of the rashers (strips) vary according to their position along the carcass and the size of the carcass. Bacon chops are thick slices of cured back. They can be grilled (broiled), baked, pan-fried or prepared by the same methods as pork chops.

STREAKY/FATTY BACON

Traditionally, streaky bacon was always very fatty, but it is less so now as modern breeding programmes and rearing methods have produced pigs with a smaller amount of fat. This is the belly end of the middle or through-cut. It is best grilled (broiled), but can also be used for barding the breasts of poultry and game birds before roasting.

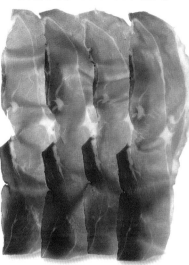

Above: Speck is a thinly-sliced, smoke-cured bacon that has been air-dried.

PANCETTA

This fatty bacon is the Italian equivalent of streaky bacon and can be bought in strips or round slices cut from a roll. It is cured by traditional methods and may be unsmoked or smoked.

SPECK

This fatty bacon is made from pork belly (side), which is smoke-cured over beechwood with herbs and spices, then air-dried. Sometimes it is covered with peppercorns or dried herbs, which add a distinctive flavour. It comes from the Tyrol, near the Swiss border with Germany, which explains its German-sounding name. Use it for adding flavour to soups, stews and sauces. Schinkenspeck is a leaner version.

*Above: Fatty lardo
is mainly used with other ingredients.*

LARDO

This is another Italian-style bacon. It is extrmely fatty and is always used as a basis for pan-frying and flavouring other ingredients, usually in the form of a *soffrito* – a mixture of diced bacon and chopped onions.

LARD DE POITRINE

This is the French equivalent of streaky bacon and can be extremely fatty. It can be unsmoked or smoked (*poitrine fumé* or *lard fumé*). Use to enrich stews or for coq au vin. It may also be sprinkled on warm salads or baked potatoes.

TOCINO

This is the Spanish version of speck, made by storing the bacon in salt crystals, which gives it a strong flavour.

COOK'S TIP
Classic warm salads are made with strongly flavoured salad leaves, such as baby spinach, escarole, rocket (arugula) or frisée, dressed with fried, still warm lardons and the bacon fat, which wilts the leaves.

COOKING BACON

Bacon rashers (strips) can be grilled (broiled), griddled or fried. They are used in a wide variety of ways in cooking, wrapped around ingredients to flavour them and prevent them from drying out during cooking, or cut up and cooked with other foods as a flavouring ingredient. When cooking whole bacon rashers, trim off the rind first, if the rind is still intact, then snip the fat at regular intervals to prevent the rashers from curling up and cooking unevenly.

Frying

This is the traditional way of cooking bacon for breakfast.

1 Grease the frying pan with a little mild-flavoured oil on a pad of kitchen paper – there is no need to add any more, as the bacon will yield plenty of fat during cooking.

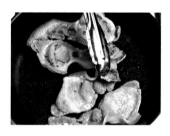

2 Lay the bacon rashers in the frying pan and fry over a medium-high heat for 4–8 minutes, turning once.

Cooking in the Microwave

This is a convenient way of cooking bacon, although it is not a great time-saver, as other methods are almost as quick. However, you do avoid having to wash a frying pan or grill (broiler) afterwards. If you like your bacon crisp, this method is not suitable.

Place 4 rashers of bacon in a single layer on a microwaveproof plate and cover loosely with a sheet of kitchen paper. Microwave the bacon on High for 3–4 minutes.

Grilling

Cooking bacon under the grill (broiler) allows the fat to drip away from the meat. This makes it a healthier cooking method and is perfect when the minimum of fat is required.

1 Preheat the grill (broiler) and arrange the bacon rashers (strips) on a rack in the grill pan.

2 Grill (broil) the rashers for about 4 minutes. Turn the rashers and grill for 4–5 minutes on the other side. Remove with tongs and serve.

Making Lardons

Small strips of bacon may be used to enrich and flavour stews and casseroles, fill omelettes, sprinkle over baked potatoes or garnish warm salads. Ready-made lardons are available from supermarkets, but it is easy and much less expensive to make your own. You can use either smoked or unsmoked bacon. Buy it in a single piece.

1 Bring a pan of water to the boil. Add the bacon and blanch for 5–10 minutes, depending on the size. Drain well.

2 Using a sharp knife, cut off and discard the skin. Trim off any excess fat, but do not remove all of it, as it is required for adding flavour.

3 Carefully cut the bacon into slices about 5mm/¼in thick, then cut the slices across into small batons. The lardons are then ready to use according to the recipe.

CURED MEATS

Preserving meat and meat products by salting and/or drying to prevent decay has long been used to cure buffalo meat and beef, as well as European sausages and hams. For example, pemmican is a dried meat mixture prepared by Native Americans as a trail food. Dried buffalo, bison or venison is pounded with fat, seasonings and dried cranberries or other fruit, then packed into intestines or skins made from buffalo hide. In Mexico sun-dried strips of buffalo meat were known as *charqui*, which later became jerk beef or jerky.

Pork is a main ingredient for cured meat products and French butchers, in particular, have a proud tradition of pork butchery, known as *charcuterie*, including the preparation of a wide variety of cured hams and sausages. Italy is famed for its fabulous hams and inimitable regional salami. However, there are other cured meats made using pork and other meats such as beef. The following is a small selection of the types available.

BILTONG

This African cured meat consists of air-dried and smoked strips of beef, buffalo, antelope, venison or ostrich.

BRESAOLA

An Italian dried beef fillet (tenderloin), this meat is salt-cured and air-dried for a couple of months until it is a deep rich red colour. It is excellent served thinly sliced, with olive oil, lemon juice and chopped fresh parsley.

Below: Biltong is chewy, but sustaining dried beef from Africa.

Above: Bresaola is similar to prosciutto but made from beef.

Right: British corned beef is compressed and canned.

BÜNDNERFLEISCH

The Swiss equivalent to bresaola, this cured meat is flavoured with white wine before being salted and dried.

CORNED BEEF

Originally derived from the name corns, the grains of salt used in brine prepared for salting beef, this is the American term for salt beef or pickled beef. In Britain, the name is used exclusively for compressed canned pieces of salt beef. It is used for sandwiches and salads.

OX TONGUE

This is usually sold cooked and pressed as a cold meat. It is available smoked, corned or pickled and all types have a strong flavour.

PASTRAMI

A spiced smoked beef which is sometimes eaten hot, but is more usually served cold. Although the name originates from the Romanian *pastrama* (from the verb *pastra* meaning to preserve), the word is actually Yiddish. The classic way to serve pastrami is in a sandwich made with rye bread – particularly in Jewish delis of New York city. Romanian *pastrama* is similar but may include other meats besides beef such as pork, goat and goose.

SALT BEEF

Known as corned beef in the United States, this beef, usually brisket, is soaked in brine with seasonings and spices. It is available uncooked for boiling and serving hot, or sold cooked with other cold meats on deli counters. Salt beef sandwiches made with rye bread or bagels, served with sweet dill pickles, are a staple part of Jewish-American deli cuisine.

SMOKED PORK LOIN

This is a compact round nugget of lean pork, which resembles a neat sausage. *Lomo ahumado* is a Spanish speciality of cured and smoked pork loin that it is thinly sliced and served raw, rather like prosciutto, as a tapas.

CHICKEN

Being small and easy to keep, hens have been domesticated for thousands of years. In the days when small traditional farms were dotted all over the countryside, chickens were kept for their eggs and killed only when they were past their laying best. Eventually, old roosters were also sent to the pot – for a thorough boiling or stewing. As intensive rearing became more commonplace, chickens gradually became an everyday food. Today, public pressure has meant that some farmers are returning to more old-fashioned rearing methods, but battery-reared chickens are still widely available.

The higher the standard of welfare under which chickens are reared, the better. Whether the end concern is the welfare of the poultry or the quality of the meat, the means to both are the same. If you want good quality chicken, buy those that have been well reared.

Chicken is rich in high quality protein, providing all the essential amino acids required by the body. It provides B group vitamins and iron, as well as copper and selenium. The white meat is low in fat (the fat is found in and under the skin) and contains less saturated fat than other meat.

Below: (From left to right) Corn-fed, free-range and organic chickens are a few of the different varieties of chicken available.

ROASTING CHICKEN

Sometimes called a roaster, this is a young cockerel (rooster) or hen, about 12 weeks old. They usually weigh up to 3kg/6½lb. Older, larger birds (up to 20 weeks old) and weighing up to 4.5kg/10lb are often available as well.

STEWING OR BOILING CHICKEN

Also known as a boiling hen or fowl, this is an older bird. It requires long, slow simmering, as the flesh is tough, but its flavour is excellent. Boiling fowl are not readily available today as demand tends to be low, but they can normally be ordered from any good butcher. Stewing chickens are used in fricassées, pies, casseroles, stews and for galantines and soups.

CAPON

This is a young cockerel (rooster) that has been castrated and then fattened on a special diet to make it plump and flavourful. The practice is now prohibited in many countries. A capon weighs 2.7–4.5kg/6–10lb, with a large proportion of white meat to dark.

POUSSIN

The French name for a young chicken, these small birds are 4–6 weeks old and weigh 350–675g/12oz–1½lb. Each provides an individual portion. Poussins, also sometimes called spring chickens, are tender and delicate in flavour – some would say lacking in flavour. They can be roasted, when they benefit from a moist well-flavoured stuffing, and can also be spatchcocked (butterflied) and grilled (broiled), pan-fried or cooked on the barbecue.

DOUBLE POUSSIN

This poussin weighs about 900g/2lb and is about six weeks old. Double poussins are big enough to serve two people. They are tender, but lack flavour. Include a rich-flavoured stuffing when roasting, and marinate before frying or grilling (broiling).

CHICKEN PORTIONS

There is a wide range, both on and off the bone, with or without skin. Quarters include either the leg or the wing joint, the latter having a larger portion of breast meat. The leg joint includes the thigh, with just a small area of breast meat. Other portions include thighs, drumsticks and wings, which have little meat. Breast portions are sold on or off the bone, skinned or unskinned; these prime

portions include only the white meat. Boneless breast portions are often sold as fillets. Supremes include the wing bone, while part-boned breasts still have the short piece of bone leading into the wing and the fine strip of breastbone.

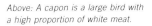

Above: A capon is a large bird with a high proportion of white meat.

Below: A young roasting chicken can weigh up to 3kg/6½lb.

Below: A poussin is a young bird.

ROCK CORNISH HEN

This small North American cross-breed was developed from White Rock and Cornish chickens and is sometimes called a Rock Cornish game hen. These small birds are 4–6 weeks old and can weigh up to 1.2kg/ 2½lb. The flesh is white and flavourful, but the ratio of bone to meat is high, so each hen will usually serve one person.

GUINEA FOWL

These domesticated fowl have been raised in Europe for many centuries but they originally came from West Africa. They are tender with slightly dry flesh. Cook as for chicken or pheasant, but at a high temperature – for example roast at 230°C/450°F/Gas 8 for 25–30 minutes. Alternatively, guinea fowl can be braised or casseroled.

Buying

Chicken can be bought fresh, chilled or frozen. Look for birds with a clear soft skin, without blemishes or bruises. A soft thin skin shows that the bird is young. The bigger the bird, the better its value because the proportion of meat to bone is higher. As well as whole birds, chicken is available in portions such as legs, wings, thighs, breast portions and drumsticks. The portions may be on the bone or boneless, with or without skin. Sliced, diced and minced (ground) chicken is available. Breast meat strips, marinated cuts and stuffed portions are all sold fresh or frozen.

Apart from the standard intensively reared chicken, there is quite a wide choice of birds raised by different farming methods. These are available either as whole birds or cut into handy portions.

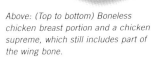

Above: (Top to bottom) Boneless chicken breast portion and a chicken supreme, which still includes part of the wing bone.

Free-range birds These are not reared in battery conditions. Laws about the ways in which free-range chickens are reared vary according to country of origin.

Corn-fed chicken Corn-fed chickens are easily recognized by their bright yellow skin. The colour fades during cooking and the meat yields golden fat that also diminishes in colour during cooking.

Organic birds These chickens are raised in humane conditions, fed on a natural and (usually) traditional-style diet. Standards relating to the particular scheme or terms by which the birds are classed as organic are usually outlined on the packaging.

Storing

Whole chicken should be placed in a deep dish, covered with a plate or clear film (plastic wrap) and kept in the refrigerator. Giblets are usually wrapped separately and placed within the cavity. These should be removed from the chicken and stored in a separate dish. Wrapped chicken or chicken pieces can be kept in the wrapper, but check that the packs are sealed before storing. Use packed chicken by the date suggested or loose chicken within two days of purchase. Cook giblets for gravy or stuffing within 24 hours.

Raw fresh chicken can be frozen successfully. Remove the giblets, if necessary. Wrap portions individually in freezer film. Pack the chicken or portions in a freezer bag and seal tightly. Thaw the chicken overnight in the refrigerator, if possible.

PREPARING SMALL POULTRY

These techniques are suitable for chicken, as well as other poultry, and game birds such as pheasant.

Jointing a Bird

Although it is possible to buy ready-prepared portions, it is easy to cut up a bird at home.

A bird can be cut into various pieces, depending on what is called for in the recipe. For example, it can be cut into four or eight pieces. Use a sharp knife and poultry shears for cutting through meat and bone. Poultry shears have very sharp, curved and pointed blades for intricate cutting and a notch to hold bones securely when cracking them.

The following instructions give four small pieces from each side of the bird, eight pieces in total – two wings, two breasts, two thighs and two drumsticks.

1 Put the bird breast-side up on a chopping board. Use a sharp knife to remove the leg by cutting through the thigh joint. Repeat on the other side.

2 Following the line of the breastbone and using poultry shears, cut the breast in half as cleanly as possible.

3 Turn the bird over and cut out the backbone. Leave the wings attached.

4 Cut each breast, leaving a portion of the breast meat attached to the wing.

5 Cut each leg through the knee joint to separate the thigh from the drumstick.

6 Using poultry shears, cut off the wing tip at the first joint.

Preparing a Chicken for Roasting

Very little preparation is needed to roast a chicken, but the following techniques help to keep the bird in shape so that it looks attractive when cooked, and make carving easier.

Removing the Wishbone

The wishbone is the arched bone at the neck end of the bird. It does not have to be removed before cooking, but the breast meat can be carved more easily without it.

1 Using a small, sharp knife pull back the skin from the neck cavity and cut around the wishbone.

2 Scrape away the meat from the wishbone, then cut it away at the base and pull it out.

Making a Lucky Wish

When the roast bird is served, it is traditional for two people to pull the wishbone. Each person is allowed to use only the little finger to hold the end of one side. Once pulled and snapped, the person with the larger arched top of the bone is entitled to make a wish.

Trussing with Skewers

The aim of trussing a bird is to ensure that when cooked it looks attractive. This is a quick and useful method for preparing a larger bird that is more rigid and firmer in shape.

1 Push a metal skewer through both sections of the wing, into the skin of the neck and out through the other wing.

2 Push the second skewer through the thighs and the tail cavity.

Trussing with String

With a smaller bird, trussing with string helps to keep it in a neat compact shape during roasting.

1 Lay the bird down with the breast uppermost and away from you. Tuck the wing tips and neck flap underneath.

2 Tie a piece of string around the legs and under the flap of skin.

3 Bring the string back towards the neck end, passing it between the legs.

4 Turn the bird over and wrap the string around the wings to keep them flat. Finally, pull the string tight to bring the wings together and tie neatly.

COOK'S TIP
Although it is most usual to truss a chicken before roasting, it is also a good idea to do so before pot-roasting or preparing a dish such as the classic French poule au pot, where the bird is cooked whole. Always snip and remove the string before carving and serving.

Spatchcocking a Bird

Also called butterflying, this is a method of splitting and flattening a whole bird so that it can be cooked quickly.

1 Tuck under the wings and remove the wishbone from the neck end. Turn the bird over and, holding it firmly with one hand, split it along each side of the backbone with poultry shears. Remove and discard the backbone.

2 Place the bird on a chopping board with the breast side uppermost. Press down firmly with the heel of one hand on the middle of the breast to flatten out the bird.

3 Push a metal skewer through the wings and breast. Push a second metal skewer parallel to the first, through the thighs and the tip of the breast.

Preparing Boneless Breast Fillets

Boneless chicken breast fillets are readily available in the supermarket, but the advantage of preparing fillets yourself is that the rest of the carcass can be cut up and used to make a well-flavoured stock or soup.

1 Cut the bird into portions, but keep the breasts whole.

2 Carefully pull the skin and membrane away from the breast. Use a small, sharp knife to cut the meat off the rib bone and any remaining breastbone.

3 Cut away the thin white central tendons from the chicken breast.

4 Trim away any pieces of fat and untidy edges from the breast to make a neat fillet.

Preparing Escalopes

A chicken breast yields two escalopes (scallops). A similar technique can also be used with other poultry. A duck breast will yield about three escalopes, and a turkey breast can be sliced into several escalopes depending on the size of the breast portions.

1 Place the skinless boneless breast fillet flat on a chopping board and, using a large sharp knife, carefully slice it in half horizontally. To cut an even slice, hold your hand flat on top of the chicken breast as you cut to prevent it from moving.

2 Lay each slice of chicken between sheets of greaseproof (waxed) paper or baking parchment in turn and beat out gently until thin and flat using a meat mallet or rolling pin.

Safety First

When preparing and cooking poultry, wash all utensils, surfaces and hands afterwards to avoid contamination. Remember to wash any spoons used to lift or stir part-cooked poultry before using them with the cooked poultry.

Cutting Strips for Stir-Frying

Tender poultry is ideal for stir-frying. It can be cut into really small pieces and cooks very quickly.

Lay a flattened escalope (see left) on a board and using a sharp kitchen knife, cut it across into fine strips.

Boning Chicken Thighs

When boned, the thighs yield a neat nugget of well-flavoured meat.

1 Use a sharp knife to loosen the skin, then pull it away from the meat.

2 Carefully cut the flesh lengthways along the main thigh bone, then cut the bone out, trimming the meat close to the bone, and then lift it away. Continue cutting out the bones, leaving the meat open and flat.

COOKING POULTRY

Whole chicken, poussin and guinea fowl are easy to roast, requiring the minimum of attention. Chicken portions may be griddled or pan-fried.

Roasting Chicken

When cooking a slightly larger bird, requiring longer cooking, you may need to cover the top of the breast loosely with foil when it is light golden brown. Remove the foil for the final 15 minutes of cooking time.

To test if chicken is cooked, pierce the thickest area of meat with the point of a knife. First check the juices – if there is any sign of pink (blood) the meat is not cooked. Check the meat at the base of the cut. It should be firm and look white – if it is pink and soft, the bird is not cooked. On a whole bird, the area just behind the thigh is thickest and takes longest to cook.

1 Rub the breast and the top of the bird generously with butter. If you are stuffing the bird, stuff it at the neck end only before trussing, and then tuck the neck skin under.

2 Place the bird breast down in the roasting pan for the first 30 minutes of the cooking time.

3 Turn and baste the bird, then continue cooking for the calculated time, basting it every 15 minutes.

4 When completely cooked, remove the roasting pan from the oven and cover tightly with foil. Leave it to rest in a warm place for 10–15 minutes: this will make the flesh easier to carve.

Pan-Frying

Escalopes (scallops) and boneless breast portions cook very quickly, so they are ideal for speedy pan-frying over a high heat. Breast meat on the bone takes longer. Uneven, thicker portions require careful cooking and turning. Boneless thighs take about 15 minutes; drumsticks take 30 minutes or longer.

1 Heat a small amount of olive oil in a non-stick frying pan.

2 Add the chicken pieces to the hot oil and cook until they are lightly browned on one side.

3 Turn the pieces and cook until lightly browned on the second side. Reduce the heat to prevent the pieces from becoming too brown before they are cooked through and continue cooking gently until the meat is cooked.

Griddling Boneless Breast Fillets

This is a healthy way of cooking, allowing fat to drain away between the ridges of the pan.

1 Brush the breast fillets with a little vegetable or sunflower oil.

2 Preheat the griddle until it is almost smoking, then lay the boneless breast fillets on it.

3 Cook for 3–4 minutes, until the meat is well browned underneath, firm and white inside. Turn the fillets over using tongs and cook until the second side is browned and the meat is firm and white throughout but still tender.

> **Roasting times for chicken, poussin and guinea fowl**
> Preheat the oven to 200°C/400°F/ Gas 6. Weigh the bird when it has been trimmed and with any stuffing added.
> **Chicken**: allow 20 minutes per 450g/1lb, plus 20 minutes extra.
> **Poussin**: allow 25–40 minutes total roasting time.
> **Guinea fowl**: allow 15 minutes per 450g/1lb, plus 15 minutes extra.

TURKEY

The turkey came originally from America and was first domesticated by the Aztecs in Mexico. Turkeys were introduced into Europe by the Spanish and they soon became a popular choice in France, Italy and Britain, too.

When early settlers from Britain, France and Holland crossed the Atlantic to North America, the vast flocks of turkey that roamed wild provided them with sustenance. They were plentiful and so easy to trap or shoot that the older children of the family were given the responsibility of catching them. The Native Americans meanwhile taught the new settlers the rudiments of farming, and in November 1621, on the first anniversary of their arrival, the Pilgrims entertained the locals to a feast. at the centre of which was the turkey. Ever since, this has been the traditional bird served at Thanksgiving.

Turkey is a lean source of protein and provides B vitamins, phosphorous, potassium, magnesium, zinc and iron.

Above: The majority of turkeys are white-feathered, like this Norfolk turkey.

BRONZE BIRDS

These are dark-feathered birds and the skin may be spotted with slightly dark stubble remaining after plucking. Norfolk Bronze is popular and Norfolk Black is a very plump-breasted bird with a good flavour. American Bronze is another traditional turkey. Cambridge turkeys are also a traditional British bird; when they are crossed with the American Bronze, the Cambridge Bronze is the result. Bronze birds were the traditional turkeys before white birds became so popular and they have been enjoying a revival during the past 15 years. They are reared non-intensively on traditional lines and allowed to mature naturally. This has helped their revival as consumers are becoming more concerned about rearing methods.

Above: Bronze turkey has very juicy and flavoursome flesh.

WHITE BIRDS

In the United States, the White Holland is a popular breed. The majority of British turkeys are white-feathered, including Norfolk turkey. However, they do not have the superior flavour of bronze or dark-feathered birds, which are becoming increasingly popular.

FREE-RANGE AND ORGANIC BIRDS

Both free-range and organic turkeys are available, and information on the rearing conditions is normally provided by the supermarket, butcher or farm store where you buy them. Birds that are labelled free-range should be checked carefully before buying, as this is not necessarily an indication of the quality of the bird. For the best turkey, seek out a source of organic birds, preferably ones from a recommended or known farm.

WILD TURKEY

These birds are smaller than the domestic fowl and have a strong, gamier, but truly delicious flavour. Wild turkey can still be found in the United States, although not in the large flocks that once existed when European settlers first arrived.

CUTS OF TURKEY

As well as whole birds, there is a variety of prepared cuts available. This is as a result of a marketing drive to persuade people to buy turkey all year round, rather than just for festive occasions.

PART-BONED BREAST

This is a large roast consisting of the unskinned breast meat and bone which has been removed from the rest of the carcass. Usually taken from large birds, these can weigh as much as a whole small turkey and will serve a reasonably large party of people. The roast can be stuffed under the skin. Half breasts are also available. Smaller whole breast roasts, taken from more modest size turkeys and suitable for two or three people, are becoming increasingly popular. They are available on the bone, as well as boned.

BONELESS BREAST

This is usually taken from one side of the breast, and neatly rolled or shaped with the skin around the outside. The quality is very variable. Take care to distinguish between a boneless breast and a roast of "re-formed" turkey meat, made up of scraps and offcuts moulded into a roast under skin or a layer of fat (enclosed in netting). It also often contains a high proportion of water.

BREAST FILLETS

These are skinless, boneless slices taken from the turkey breast portion.

TURKEY DRUMSTICK

With the right preparation, a turkey leg can usually serve four people. Turkey drumsticks have a lot of sinew running through the brown meat, as well as fine bones, which makes them tough and awkward to eat. They can be roasted, but are better quickly browned, then stewed or braised until the meat is falling off the bone and is succulent.

DICED TURKEY

Used mainly for pies and casseroles, this is often the darker meat from around the thigh and leg area.

Below: A Norfolk Black has a plump breast and a wonderful full flavour.

STIR-FRY TURKEY

These are long, thin strips of white breast meat. Cheaper packs may include some dark meat and small pieces rather than thin strips.

MINCED/GROUND TURKEY

Minced turkey meat is good for pies, sausages and burgers or other recipes in which minced pork or beef would be used. It is not so strongly flavoured as minced beef, but has more taste than minced chicken and is usually less expensive than both.

Buying turkey

Turkeys are available fresh, chilled or frozen all year round. When buying a whole bird, look for a plump well-rounded breast and legs and clear, soft and evenly coloured skin. Avoid birds that are bruised, with blemishes or torn skin or any that have been badly or unevenly plucked. Turkeys vary enormously in weight.

The average bird weighs from about 2.75kg/6lb to 11.5kg/25½lb, but 18kg/40lb specimens have been known. The average weights are 4.5–6.3 kg/10–14lb. Very large turkeys are less common these days, although they are still available on festive occasions such as Christmas and Thanksgiving, and modern breeders tend to concentrate on medium and smaller birds to suit today's smaller families.

Storing Turkey

Place the bird in a large, deep dish and cover it completely with clear film (plastic wrap). Store it in the coolest part of the refrigerator, making sure that it does not come in contact with other foods. Turkey cuts or diced meat can be kept in the wrapper, but check that the packs are sealed before storing.

Thaw a frozen bird in the refrigerator for 2–4 days or a small bird at room temperature for 48 hours. It is unlikely that you will be able to fit a whole turkey into the microwave for thawing, but frozen portions can be thawed in this way; follow the manufacturer's advice for thawing chicken.

What's in a Name?

The name turkey has an odd derivation. Guinea fowl, imported by Britain from Africa via Portugal and turkey was known as turkeycock or turkeyhen. When Europeans first encountered the American turkey, they thought that it was related to the guinea fowl and called it by the same name.

PREPARING TURKEY

These days, birds are sold cleaned and ready for stuffing or cooking. However, some cooks like to rinse out the cavity under cold running water and then pat it thoroughly dry with kitchen paper before starting preparation.

Thawing Frozen Turkey

A frozen turkey must be thawed completely before cooking. Unwrap it and place it on a rack in a deep dish so that liquid that drips from the bird as it thaws runs below the rack. Cover with clear film (plastic wrap) and place in the refrigerator. Allow two to three days for a 4.5kg/10lb bird. Allow three to four days for a 6.8kg/15lb bird.

Stuffing Turkey

Never stuff turkey in advance of cooking. The stuffing can be made in advance, but the turkey should not be stuffed until just before it is placed in the oven. Weigh the stuffing and add this to the weight of the bird before calculating the cooking time. Truss the bird, then cook for the calculated time. Never shorten the cooking time because although the meat may appear cooked, extra time must be allowed for cooking the stuffing thoroughly.

Adding Aromatics

It is generally recommended to place aromatics in the body cavity of the bird and pack the stuffing under the skin covering the breast. Cut a large onion in half and stud each half with 4–6 cloves. Place this in the body cavity of the bird. Cut an orange and a lemon into quarters and add these, together with 3–4 bay leaves, 4–6 fresh sage sprigs and 2–3 fresh thyme sprigs. Add 1 cinnamon stick or 1 blade of mace for a festive hint of warm spice.

Stuffing the Breast

This is the most popular method. Loosen the skin over the breast meat and insert stuffing underneath it. It is a good idea to introduce some stuffing here, even when stuffing the cavity, as this protects the delicate breast meat during long cooking.

Making Stuffing

Minced (ground) meat, particularly pork or sausagemeat, are traditional stuffings for turkey, as are mixtures based on breadcrumbs. Rice is also a popular base for stuffings. For modern recipes, loose combinations of fruit or vegetables are easy to make and taste delicious. These are normally spooned out, but stiffer mixtures that are sliced along with the meat are still popular.

Flavourings

One of the purposes of a stuffing – as well as to make the meat go further – is to add a complexity of tastes to a bird. Stuffings therefore need to be well flavoured, with herbs, spices, citrus fruit or strongly flavoured vegetables. The flavourings must complement, not compete with, the meat. The binding ingredients such as breadcrumbs or rice give the necessary bulk to a stuffing, but it is the other ingredients that give the flavour.

Making Stuffing Balls

Any stuffing that is not used for the bird can be rolled into small balls about the size of walnuts. Add these to the roasting pan, arranging them around the bird, for the final 15 minutes.

Stuffing the Neck End

It is traditional to use two stuffings for turkey. Here sage and onion stuffing is used to fill the neck end of the bird.

1 Fold back the flap of skin at the neck end, then use a small sharp knife to cut out the wishbone, working right around the bone and cutting the meat as close to the bone as possible. Cut the bone free at the base on both sides.

2 Press the stuffing inside the shallow neck cavity. Turn the bird over and pull the neck skin over the stuffing. Truss the bird to secure the flap of skin in place. If necessary, use a metal skewer to keep the skin in place while trussing with string.

Stuffing the Body Cavity

The stuffing can be prepared in advance and chilled separately from the bird. It can then be placed in the bird just before roasting. Weigh both bird and stuffing, then add the weights together to calculate the cooking time.

1 Thoroughly rinse the body cavity of the bird under cold running water, then drain it well. Wipe the turkey, inside and out, with kitchen paper.

2 Insert the stuffing, but do not pack it in too tightly.

> **Flavouring Sausagemeat Stuffing**
> Good herb combinations to add to a basic sausagemeat stuffing include 30ml/2 tbsp each chopped fresh tarragon and parsley or 15ml/1 tbsp chopped fresh thyme and 45ml/3 tbsp chopped fresh parsley.

Roasting Turkey

Turkeys are easy to roast, but require a little more attention than smaller birds. Check that the oven shelves are in the correct position before heating the oven.

1 Place the prepared stuffed bird on a rack in a large roasting pan.

2 Smear the breast generously with butter (this helps to keep the meat moist), season with salt and ground black pepper and place in the oven.

Making Sage and Onion Stuffing

This is a classic stuffing, which is suitable for all types of poultry.

1 Melt 25g/1oz/2 tbsp butter in a frying pan. Add 4 finely chopped onions and cook for 10–15 minutes until soft but not browned. Set aside to cool.

2 Add the onions to 115g/4oz fresh white breadcrumbs and 60ml/4 tbsp chopped fresh sage. Season well with salt and ground black pepper, then add 1 beaten egg and about 120ml/4fl oz/½ cup chicken stock to bind the stuffing.

3 Baste the turkey from time to time during cooking. When the breast has browned, cover with foil to protect it and continue cooking.

4 Remove the covering foil for the final 20 minutes of cooking. To check if the meat is cooked, insert a skewer into the thickest part of the thigh. If the juices run clear and the meat is white, it is cooked. If the juices are pink and the meat is soft and pink, the turkey is not ready; return it to the oven and check again after 20 minutes.

5 Remove the turkey from the oven and cover it closely with foil. Leave to rest for 15 minutes before carving. This will even out the temperature and make it easier to carve. If you wish to make gravy in the roasting pan, transfer the bird to a carving plate.

Carving Turkey

1 Remove the trussing string. Hold the bird steady in position with a carving fork. Cut off the legs, then cut these in half or carve the meat from the bones.

2 Make a horizontal cut across the breast above the wing.

3 Carve neat and even vertical slices off the breast. Repeat on the other side of the bird. Arrange the slices on a warmed platter. Add the turkey legs or sliced meat to the platter or set them aside for serving separately. Scoop out the stuffing and serve with the meat.

Roasting times for Turkey

Preheat the oven to 180°C/350°F/ Gas 4. Calculate the cooking time, according to the weight of the bird (remember to weigh the bird and stuffing separately and add the two together for total weight). Use the following as a guide to time, checking and basting regularly during cooking. It is difficult to estimate the exact time when cooking large birds, as the shape and proportion of breast meat and exact quantity and position of stuffing all influence the result.

• For birds up to 4.5kg/10lb, allow 20 minutes per 450g/1lb, plus an extra 20 minutes.

• For birds over 4.5kg/10lb, allow 18 minutes per 450g/1lb, plus an extra 20 minutes.

• For birds over 6.8kg/15lb, allow 15 minutes per 450g/1lb, plus an extra 20 minutes.

DUCK AND GOOSE

Ducks were probably first domesticated in China, where they have long been appreciated for their eggs. The European birds were domesticated from the wild mallard, as indeed were North American varieties. Athough geese have been domesticated, they have defied the intensive rearing methods. They are not prolific layers and they are one of the few remaining sources of seasonal food.

Duck and goose are high protein foods. They contain B vitamins and some minerals. Both are good sources of zinc and also provide phosphorous, potassium, magnesium and iron. Being high in fat, they should not feature frequently in a healthy diet, but they are excellent foods for special occasions. Lean duck breasts are a good choice for those who appreciate the flavour of the rich meat but would prefer to avoid the high fat content of birds with skin on.

Below: Aylesbury duck has pale, tender meat and is a traditional favourite.

Left: Canada goose is a popular variety.

DOMESTICATED DUCK

Modern breeding methods have produced leaner ducks, with a good amount of breast meat and only a fine layer of fat under the skin. They are available as whole birds and portions.
American Long Island and British Aylesbury These fairly fatty ducks have a deep, rich flavour.
Barbary or Muscovy and Nantes The Barbary is a big bird providing a good portion of firm breast meat. The Nantes, popular in France, is smaller, more tender and with a delicate flavour. Both varieties have less fat and thin skins.
Rouen The meat of this duck is more like game in both taste and texture.

GOOSE

This large, fatty bird traditionally survived by pecking about and foraging for any available food. Found on poor farms because it was economical to keep and a good source of meat and fat, a special bird would always be fattened for Christmas. It is also the traditional celebration bird and has always been a gourmet treat for both the rich and poor. In Britain, a young goose (known as green goose because it had been fed on grass) was served at Michaelmas in September, while an older goose was served at Christmas.
Canada goose This is the most popular variety of bird which, at around 2.7kg/6lb, easily serves six.
Greylag and Pinkfoot The greylag is smaller than the Canada goose, and the pinkfoot smaller still. Both are well-flavoured birds.
Whitefront This is the smallest goose, averaging about 2.5kg/5½lb in feather.

Buying

Look for light skinned, plump birds. They should smell fresh and be soft and moist, with no bruises, blemishes or feathers. Goose is seasonal, but is also available frozen.

Storing

Cover loosely with greaseproof (waxed) paper and keep on a plate in the bottom of a refrigerator so the juices don't spill on to and contaminate other foods. Be especially careful to keep the uncooked bird away from any cooked meats you have in the refrigerator.

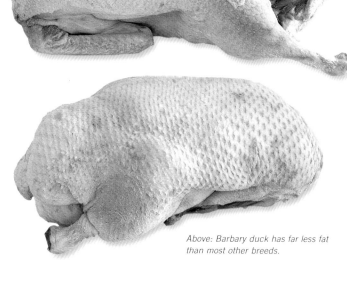

Above: Barbary duck has far less fat than most other breeds.

Right: Mallard is the most commonly available wild duck.

Above: Duck breast and leg portions

WILD DUCK

This is far less fatty than domesticated duck, which is important when you come to cook it. Generally, most recipes for duck can be adapted to either bird, but it may be necessary to add a little fat when cooking the game bird. Duck taken from inland water is preferable to that from salty water (the latter tend to have a fishy flavour and their flesh is fairly oily). Wild duck are at their best between October and December.

Plump mallard is the largest and most common of all the wild ducks. It has a more intense flavour than domesticated duck and is excellent for roasting. One bird serves two to three people. Teal is one of the smallest wild ducks and highly prized by gourmets, and canvasback, widgeon, gadwall, pintail and pochard are also available. Young birds are tender, but older ones can be quite tough and need long, slow cooking in a casserole.

WILD GOOSE

The Canada goose (which averages about 4.75kg/10½lb in feather or 2.7kg/6lb dressed) is one of the plumpest and tastiest of geese and one bird is usually sufficient to serve six people. As with wild duck, try to avoid wild geese from salty water; those which have been feeding on grass or stubble taste much better than those which have been living and feeding on marshland.

Above: (Top to bottom) Oven-ready cock and hen pheasants

OTHER WILD FEATHERED GAME

It is important to check the extent of damage to wild game that has been shot, as removing lead shot from a carcass can be a tedious and time-consuming operation.

PHEASANT

By far the most plentiful and popular of game birds, pheasant was introduced to Europe from China. They are often sold in pairs, a male and female, known as a brace. The hen is more tender and smaller than the cock; it will serve three, while the cock will serve four. A young bird can be roasted; an older fowl should be stewed or casseroled.

Above: Pheasants are relatively cheap game birds because they are easy to rear, so stocks of wild birds can be supplemented before the season opens.

GROUSE

Native to Scotland, where it is regarded as the king of feathered game, but also found elsewhere in the British Isles, grouse has a wonderful rich, gamey flavour. One bird provides a good single portion. Young birds are usually roasted or grilled (broiled); older birds are cooked in a casserole.

PARTRIDGE

There are two main types: the French or red-legged partridge, which was introduced into England in 1673, and the indigenous English or grey-legged partridge. The red-legged bird is bigger, but the flavour of the grey bird is often preferred. Partridge can be roasted, stewed or braised. Partridge are not very big – serve one per person.

QUAIL

The quail is native to the Middle East. They are available all year round. One provides an appetizer, but you will need two per person as a main course.

Above:
Red-legged and
grey partridges

Below: Quail

PIGEON

Cheap, plentiful and available all year round, the pigeon is found wild the world over. Although it has never been held in particularly high esteem, it is surprisingly tasty, as it feeds extensively on cereals. Wood pigeons are the best buy, being meaty birds and usually about 450g/1lb in weight. Serve one of these richly flavoured birds per person. Pigeons can be braised on a bed of vegetables and herbs; cooked in a salmis, where the birds are first roasted, then finished in a sauce; or they can be turned into pigeon pie.

The squab is a young pigeon and these small birds are now reared commercially for eating, although they are usually only available in the spring. Squabs weigh about 375g/13oz. They have meaty breasts and are more tender than older wild pigeons, so can be simply barded with pork fat or bacon and then roasted at a fairly low temperature for about an hour and served with the flesh still pink and juicy. They can also be braised or split in half and grilled (broiled).

WOODCOCK

This long-beaked bird has a wonderful rich flavour. Woodcock can be roasted, braised, grilled (broiled) or cooked on a barbecue. It is a small bird, so allow one per person.

SNIPE

This is a tiny long-legged marsh bird with a very long beak. Like the woodcock, it is seldom seen for sale in the butchers' or game dealer's; you are more likely to come across snipe if you, or someone you know, shoots (hunts). It is best roasted, although small ones can be grilled. Split the birds in half and flatten them out first. Serve one or two birds per person.

Above: Pigeon is a meaty bird.

Above:
Squab, young
pigeon, is now
reared for the
table.

Left: Snipe is
highly prized.

Below: Woodcock
is full of flavour.

PTARMIGAN

This is a member of the grouse family, but it is rarely seen because its preferred habitat is a high stony mountainside. The flavour of the meat varies according to the wild mountain food that the bird has been eating.

CAPERCAILLIE

This magnificent bird, which weighs about 4kg/9lb, resembles a very large grouse. It was hunted to extinction in Britain by the end of the eighteenth century. Today, it is found in the mountainous regions of northern Europe and has been reintroduced to Scotland. Although splendid looking, it is a forest forager so has a disappointing flavour.

FURRED GAME

From the mighty moose to the humble rabbit, furred game provides flavourful meat that can be roasted or cooked slowly in stews or casseroles.

DEER

The word venison was originally used to describe the meat of any furred game animal. Today, in Britain and Australia, venison means the meat from deer, although in America it is used more broadly, to include meat from elk, moose, reindeer, caribou and antelope.

Venison is a dark, close-textured meat with very little fat; what there is should be firm and white. If it is in good condition and a prime cut such as saddle (back) or loin it will be juicy and tender and is best served rare. Other cuts such as shoulder are often marinated and benefit from long and gentle cooking to bring out the flavour of the meat. A naturally lean meat, the little fat it contains helps to enhance the taste of the meat and will keep it moist and juicy as it cooks.

RABBIT

Originally from Africa, wild rabbits are now found all around the world. Rabbit and hare belong to the same family and are often confused with each other. Nevertheless, they are different, even to the eye in the field and especially to the cook in the kitchen. Rabbit is smaller and its flesh is pale and mild in flavour.

Below: (Clockwise from left) Venison prime cuts include loin, haunch, best end and fillet.

Above: Farmed rabbit is readily available in supermarkets.

Below: Cultivated hare has dark, lean meat.

Wild rabbit is usually bought whole and fresh, while farmed rabbit can be bought cut into pieces. The meat of the the female is more tender than that of the male.

HARE/JACK RABBIT

Originally from Europe, hares, are now found the world over. They are larger than rabbits with longer ears and powerful hind legs. The meat is dark, lean and healthy, and (in a young animal) very tender. Its flavour is stronger than that of rabbit. Hare can be roasted whole or in pieces and used in casseroles, stews or terrines. Older hares are usually jugged (cooked in a casserole, set in a pan of water). The water bath tempers the heat, so the meat is cooked very gently and slowly. Many traditional French dishes call for the back or saddle, or the saddle and hind legs only. The classic Tuscan pasta dish *pappardelle al lepre* includes rabbit.

Above: (Clockwise from top right) Wild boar saddle, chops and fillet can be treated in the same way as pork.

When buying rabbit or hare make sure that the meat is lean with very little visible fat. Avoid carcasses that show signs of injury, disease or having been clumsily shot.

WILD BOAR

Found across Europe, Central Asia and North Africa, wild boar has been hunted for many years. It was hunted to extinction in Britain in the seventeenth century, but is still found in numbers in Europe. The meat of wild boar is dark and has a strong taste. Because there is little fat present, it can be dry and tough, although its flavour is excellent. When buying wild boar look for firm pink flesh that is moist but not damp or oily. The fat should be white, not yellow.

NEW MEATS

Beef, lamb, pork, chicken, turkey, duck and goose are long established as international meats, but there is also a wide selection of other types that have, until comparatively recently, rarely been sampled away from their countries of origin. Modern farming, rearing, butchering, food transportation, communications and marketing have fuelled interest in different culinary cultures and traditions.

Unlike exotic fruit and vegetables, many of the animal food sources have less visual appeal and they rarely sound exciting. These meats may not have the same immediate impact as aromatic fruit or bright vegetables, but they are

Below: Alligator is a light-coloured, delicately flavoured meat

Above: Minced ostrich meat is wonderfully tender and succulent.

steadily gaining acceptance and arousing the interest of enthusiastic cooks and experimental diners, as they are often extremely lean and tender.

ALLIGATOR

There is a long tradition of cooking alligator in the southern states of America, particularly in Louisiana. Fears of extinction meant that alligators in the wild were protected and so farming was introduced. This was so successful that wild alligators are on the increase.

Alligators are farmed (and found in the wild) right across the southern states, from Texas to the Carolinas, but the Mississippi delta is the heartland. The meat from young alligators is eaten. It is white, flaky and tender, almost a cross between fish and chicken, with a hint of the texture of pork, and it can be cooked by the same methods as chicken or tender meat. A Cajun favourite is to cook it in sauce piquante, a spicy tomato and chilli sauce.

CROCODILE

Crocodiles are larger than alligators, although part of the same family, and are found in the northern part of the Nile delta, the swamps of Florida and Asia, from Australia and the Philippines right across to southern India. The meat is popular in the Northern

Above: Crocodile meat can be cut into fillets and steaks.

Territory of Australia, where both fresh-water and marine species are farmed. Like alligator meat, it is tender with a delicate flavour, similar to chicken or pork, but slightly flaky. It is available as steaks or fillets. Cook crocodile in the same way as chicken portions, by pan-frying, grilling (broiling) or braising.

OSTRICH

This bird is native to Africa, where it has been eaten since prehistoric times. It is now farmed in North America and Western Europe. Ostrich meat is dark in colour and finer in texture than beef. It is a lean meat with a full flavour that is stronger than beef but not quite so pronounced as game. It is sold as prepared cuts, including slices, steaks and fillets. Minced (ground) ostrich meat is also available. Prepare and cook ostrich as for tender beef steaks, by grilling (broiling), pan-frying, stir-frying, roasting, braising or on the barbecue. Minced ostrich can be used for burgers, meatloaves and sauces.

KANGAROO

This is a generic name applied to different Australian species, including large red and small grey kangaroos, wallaroos and wallabies. Kangaroo has long been a traditional part of the Aborigine diet and is now internationally available. It is a dark, fine-textured meat with a strong flavour, more pronounced than beef; it has been compared to hare (jack rabbit), but depending on the cooking method, it is not necessarily that rich. Sold as prepared cuts, including steaks and

*Above: Kangaroo meat is lean and
tender with a delicate flavour and
should be cooked carefully as it can
easily dry out.*

*Above: Emu
is a prime example
of how the new meats appeal
to the health-conscious, as it is high
in iron and low in cholesterol.*

slices, kangaroo is also available as
a smoked meat. In terms of cooking
methods, it is best treated as beef.
Forerib, sirloin or fillet (tenderloin)
cuts are sold for roasting, while rump
(round), sirloin or fillet steak are
suitable for grilling (broiling) or pan-
frying. Low in fat, it is best served rare
or medium-rare. Kangaroo is a good
ingredient for casseroles and stews.

EMU

The emu is indigenous to Australia,
where it is farmed as well as being
found in the wild. In fact, it was the first
game meat to be farmed in Australia
It is now also successfully farmed in
Europe, notably in France. Emu meat
is dark and extremely lean, darker
than beef but softer in texture. It has a
flavour that is similar to venison, but not
quite so gamey. Emu should be cooked

in the same way as tender beef.
It is also smoked and sold as
a cured meat, and used for
making sausages. Available
as prepared cuts, including
fillet, steaks, cubed and
minced meat, emu can be
grilled (broiled), roasted, pan-
fried, braised or cooked
on the barbecue.

BUFFALO

The Cape buffalo
is hunted and eaten in Africa,
where it is air-dried and smoked to
make biltong. In Asia, two main types
of water buffalo, the river buffalo and
the swamp buffalo, are found in huge
numbers. In North America, the
equivalent is the bison. Buffalo meat is
similar to beef, with corresponding cuts
that can be roasted, grilled (broiled),
pan fried, stewed or braised.
However, buffalo is not
usually so tender as
beef and benefits
from being well
marinated.
The exception
is the meat from
young water buffalo,
especially the females, which is tender.

LLAMA

In South America, the llama has long
provided transport, clothing and a
source of milk and meat, particularly
among the Peruvian Incas. To modern
tastes, younger llamas are more tender
and appetizing than older beasts, which
tend to be dried and turned into jerky or
charqui. Roast a cut or leg of llama;
pan-fry in a little oil or griddle cutlets
(small chops) or loin chops or cook
them on the barbecue.

Buying and Storing New Meats

When they are available from the
supermarket, the majority of these
meats are neatly prepared ready for
cooking and displayed in sealed packs.
Labelling information always includes a
use-by date and, often, instructions or
suggestions for basic cooking methods
and recipes. Always treat them as you

would other fresh meat, by storing the
sealed pack in the coldest area of the
refrigerator. Specialist butchers offer a
wider selection of cuts and they will also
be able to give expert advice on which
cuts to buy and on appropriate cooking
methods, too. Place loose meat on a
deep plate or dish and cover with clear
film (plastic wrap) or a lid. Do not
refreeze previously frozen meats.

Making Crocodile Parcels

This method keeps the delicate
flesh moist and is suitable for both
crocodile and alligator fillets.

1 Season the fillet well and rub it all
over with your chosen flavouring
ingredients. Here, finely chopped
garlic and chillies are used. Cut the
fillet into neat, even-size portions.

2 Wrap each portion of meat in a
piece of baking parchment or
greased greaseproof (waxed) paper.
Fold the edges of the paper
together and tuck the ends under
to seal. Place in a roasting pan and
cook in a preheated oven at
200°C/400°F/Gas 6 for 20 minutes.
Serve immediately.

VEGETABLES

Around the world there are hundreds of different types of vegetables, which come in a huge variety of shapes, sizes and colours. Each one has its own unique flavour and texture and can be used in numerous ways. Vegetables offer a rich supply of valuable nutrients and including them in your everyday diet is essential for good health.

THE ONION FAMILY

Known as alliums, there are more than 300 distinct species in this family. For culinary purposes, the best-known species are the onion, shallot, leek, bunching onions, garlic and chives. Although there are some wild forms, most varieties are known only in their cultivated form. The one thing all members of the onion family have in common is their characteristic pungent smell and flavour.

ONIONS

Throughout the world, onions are one of the most widely eaten vegetables. They are used as the basis of numerous savoury dishes – either gently fried until soft, or fried more fiercely until golden brown, then added to give a wonderful depth and flavour. There are several different varieties of onions, of different strengths, and most are distinguishable by their size and colour.

YELLOW ONIONS

These are the most common type of onion. They are characterized by a light brown skin and greenish-white to pale yellow flesh. There are many different varieties but, despite this, yellow onions

Below: Spanish onions are usually fairly large with a mild flavour and are ideal for most culinary purposes.

Below: Red onions are often used raw in salads and relishes.

are often known simply as Spanish onions, regardless of their place of origin; in the United States, Bermuda is the similar generic name. For culinary purposes, Spanish onions are usually large, round and mild.

Other types of yellow onions include brown onions, which have thick brown skins, and French onions, which have a stronger, slightly more pungent flavour.

Generally, the younger and greener the onion, the more pungent the flesh will taste. Several varieties of yellow onion have been favoured for the mild sweetness of their flesh, such as the Vidalia from the North-western states of America. Yellow onions are suitable for most kitchen purposes. Large round onions are very good for baking, stuffing or cutting into rings; longer or squatter onions are better for slicing and are good for roasting whole.

RED ONIONS

As with yellow onions, there is a great variety in the shape and size of red onions, but they are all characterized by their shiny, papery purple-red skins. The flesh is white, but stained red at the edges of each layer. Red onions usually have a much milder, sweeter flavour than yellow onions and are often used raw in salads, salsas, relishes, antipasti and marinated dishes. When slices of red onion are tossed with acidic vinegar or citrus juice their colour is released and the slices will turn a deep, uniform pink. Red onions are also good roasted, though they are less well-suited to basic frying, when they have less flavour than other varieties.

WHITE ONIONS

These are usually medium to large onions with a papery, white outer skin and white flesh. They tend not to vary as much in size, shape and flavour as yellow and red onions. They are usually fairly strong in flavour. White onions may be used for general cooking, but many people consider them too strong to eat raw. Their even size and shape make them good for stuffing or baking.

Below: White onions usually have a strong, pungent flavour and are best used for cooking, rather than using raw.

GRELOTS

This is the French term for small, flattish onions with a green skin and very white flesh. They are generally mild-flavoured with a crisp bite. Various types of this onion are often labelled salad onions in supermarkets and food stores. They are very like a bulbous spring onion (scallion). They are used extensively sliced raw in salads, but are good in many quick-cooked dishes such as omelettes and frittatas or sliced into stir-fries. They are less useful for general frying or long-cooked recipes because they tend to disintegrate.

CIPOLLA OR BORETTANE ONIONS

These are quite small, flattish or squat onions with a pale golden skin and pale yellow flesh, while some varieties are tinged with pink. Cipolla or borettane onions are popular in Italy and some varieties are grown in France, too. They have an excellent, sweet flavour with an agreeable strength of taste. Because they are small and have such a characteristic shape, they are usually peeled and cooked whole. They are excellent caramelized or cooked *à la grecque* in a mixture of olive oil, wine and spices. They are also excellent for roasting whole, bottling and pickling.

Below: Cipolla onions are often found in Italian markets are excellent for braising, pickling and in salads.

Above: Silverskins are strong-flavoured onions that are used for pickling.

Right: Yellow pickling onions have a milder flavour than silverskins and may be used for casseroles and stews.

PICKLING ONIONS

This is a general term for many different varieties of small onion. Some varieties may simply be immature yellow or red onions; others have been specially bred to produce small onions. White silver-skin pickling onions are very strongly flavoured and are nearly always used for pickling. They are also sometimes added to martinis. Yellow and red pickling onions are usually larger and milder than the silverskin varieties. They also keep much better than silverskins. These small onions are usually used whole and can be pickled in spiced vinegar, roasted or caramelized, or added to casseroles and stews.

Buying and Storing

Onions will keep well if stored in a cool, dry place. Do not store them in the refrigerator, as they will go soft. Onions do not keep well once cut, so it is worth buying onions in assorted sizes to avoid having bits left over.

Cooking

The volatile compounds in onions that cause the eyes to water are driven off during cooking, which is why the flavour of cooked onion is never as strong as raw onion. The flavour of onion also depends on the method of cooking. Boiled onion or chopped onion added to soups or casseroles has a strong, more "raw" flavour. Frying or sautéing briefly, or sweating over a very low heat until soft and translucent, gives a mild flavour. When fried until golden brown, onions develop a distinct flavour, both sweet and savoury that is superb in curries and with grilled (broiled) meats.

SHALLOTS

These are a distinct sub-species of onions, distinguished by clusters of several bulbs at the leaf base. Most are smaller than onions, composed of finer layers, and they contain less water.

BANANA SHALLOTS

These are the largest variety and get their name from their elongated shape. They have a smooth tan skin and a slightly milder flavour than other shallots.

PINK SHALLOTS AND ÉCHALOTE GRISE

These very strongly flavoured shallots are popular in France. Pink shallots have a reddish skin and pink-tinged flesh; échalote grise are paler but still have a pinkish cast to the flesh. They have a crisp texture and pungent, but not harsh, flavour, which is good raw and cooked.

BROWN/ENGLISH/DUTCH SHALLOTS

These are probably the most commonly-found shallots in food stores. They are small and tan-skinned, and often separate into subsidiary bulbs when peeled. They are an excellent general-purpose shallot and have a reasonably mild flesh with a good flavour.

Below: Banana shallots have a milder flavour than other shallots.

Above: French shallots have a very strong flavour and are good in sauces.

ASIAN/THAI RED SHALLOTS

These small, round red bulbs are used extensively in the cookery of many South-east Asian countries. They vary from strong to exceptionally strong in taste and are used most commonly in spice pastes, when they are pounded with other ingredients. Because of their low water content they are also good for slicing and frying to make crisp-fried shallots, which are common as a garnish on Thai salads and curries.

CHINESE "SHALLOTS"

These are actually a different species (Allium chinense) and not a shallot at all. It is a wild species that is cultivated in China (*jiao tou* in Cantonese or *rakkyo* in Japanese). They are grown mainly for pickling, and that is the form in which they are found in the West.

POTATO ONIONS

These alliums are related to shallots and belong to the Aggregatum group of the onion family. The species is peculiar among the onions in that it develops entirely underground, in the same way as garlic. Because of this, it is a little hardier than other onions and shallots and, in the past, it was often planted in

autumn. Potato shallots form clumps of small, yellow-skinned onions that store well. As many as eight small onions may form per clump. These onions were once more popular than they are now, especially in the mild west of England and Ireland, from where they were taken to the United States. They filled a gap between the end of the stored autumn-cropping onions and the new crop of shallots in late summer. Today, the potato onion is regarded as a bit of an oddity, and is mainly restricted to the herb patch, but the bulbs are of good flavour and are as useful as ordinary onions.

Buying and Storing

Shallots should be firm without any green shoots. They will keep well for several months in a cool dry place.

Cooking

Shallots are excellent roasted whole, caramelized or pickled. Raw, they are an essential ingredient in salad dressings and a wide range of French dishes. Cooked, shallots are used in many sauces that need the flavour of onion but not its bulk. Shallots have a low water content, so they can burn and toughen easily and care should be taken when frying.

Below: Pink shallots have a strong flavour and crisp texture.

Above: Garlic is often sold in strings that keep well hung in a cool, dry place.

GARLIC

Garlic is an ingredient few cooks would be without. As a general rule, the smaller the garlic bulb, the stronger the flavour. Most garlic sold in shops, however, is not classified in either shape or form and in practice you will simply pick up whatever you need, either loose, in bunches or on strings. Garlic grown in a hot climate is likely to be the most pungent, and fresh new season's garlic has a subtle, mild flavour that is particularly good if it is to be used raw, for example in salads and for dressings.

Garlic is reputed to have therapeutic properties, the most significant of which is that it lowers blood cholesterol, thus helping prevent heart disease. Raw garlic contains a powerful antibiotic and there is evidence that it has a beneficial effect against cancer and strokes, and increases the absorption of vitamins.

ELEPHANT GARLIC

There is some confusion in food stores between this variety and large-growing varieties of true garlic. Elephant garlic is actually more closely related to the leek than to garlic proper. It has a mild, creamy, garlic flavour and the cloves are very large in comparison with those of ordinary garlic.

Above: Garlic sold loose allows the shopper to buy just one bulb.

SOLO GARLIC

This is a variety of garlic that has been specially bred to develop just one, large clove, making it easy to peel and prepare. It is useful for dishes using a lot of garlic, but expensive to use in any quantity. The flavour is fairly mild.

WET/NEW SEASON GARLIC

This may simply be labelled "fresh" or "green" garlic. Typically, in the northern hemisphere, this is ready in late spring to early summer, when the papery skin has not fully developed and dried out. Usually the head is used whole: it is creamy white, streaked and flushed with green and pink, and has a delicious mild flavour that is ideal for European garlic soups and to roast whole.

Smoked garlic usually consists of large, whole heads of garlic that have been hot-smoked so that they are partly cooked and infused with wood smoke. They have a light, tan-brown exterior skin that should be peeled before the cloves are used for crushing into mayonnaise, for making garlic butter, or for tossing with pasta.

Garlic shoots are considered a great delicacy in many areas of southern Europe (Italy, France and Spain) and are used in much the same way as chives or spring onions (scallions).

They are also much used in Chinese stir-fries. Soup made from garlic shoots is a great favourite and is considered a splendid health tonic – a cleanser for the blood and circulation. Shoots are also pickled for use later in the season in relishes, salads and sauces.

Buying and Storing

Garlic bulbs should be firm and round with clear, papery skins. Avoid any that are beginning to sprout. Garlic bulbs keep well stored in a cool, dry place; if the air is damp they tend to sprout and if it is too warm the cloves eventually turn to grey powder.

Cooking

Garlic is an almost universal favourite for flavouring in cuisines all around the world. It is used raw in dressings, salsas, butters and salads. It is an ubiquitous ingredient in most spice pastes, Spanish salsas, Italian pestos and Mexican moles. It is also used in all types of cuisine in dressings, marinades, soups and stews.

Garlic alters in flavour according to how it is prepared and for how long it is cooked. Crushed garlic, either raw or briefly cooked, is the most pungent and strongly flavoured; a whole head of garlic, slowly roasted, will have a mellow, nutty, toasty flavour.

Below: Young wet, or new season, garlic has a particularly sweet, mild flavour.

Left: Large leeks have a mild, sweet flavour when cooked and make an excellent addition to soups and salads. They are also very good served on their own as an accompaniment.

LEEKS

These versatile alliums have their own distinct flavour. They are excellent cooked in pies and casseroles with other ingredients, braised in cream and served by themselves, or simmered in butter as an accompanying vegetable. Leeks are also wonderful in soups and broths, and have rightly earned the title "king of the soup onions". Cock-a-leekie from Scotland and *crème vichyssoise* invented by the chef of New York's Ritz Carlton, are two classic leek soups.

There are many different varieties of leeks, though there is little to choose between them in terms of flavour. Commercially grown leeks tend to be about 25cm/10in long and about 2cm/¾in in diameter. Leeks nurtured in home gardens can be left to grow to an enormous size, but these may develop a rather woody centre.

Below: Baby leeks are good steamed whole, then browned on a griddle.

Preparing and Cooking

It is important to wash leeks really thoroughly before cooking as earth and grit can get lodged between the white sections at the base. To prepare leeks, cut away the flags (leaves) and trim the base. Unless the leek is extremely fresh, or home grown, you will probably have to remove the first layer of white, then cut a slit from one end to the other through the centre of the leek. Wash under cold running water, pulling the sections apart so that the water rinses out any stubborn pieces of earth. Alternatively, slice the leeks and then rinse them thoroughly through a colander or strainer.

Leeks can be steamed or boiled, then added to a recipe, or sliced and fried gently in butter for a few minutes, then covered with a lid to sweat so they cook without browning. Unlike onions, leeks shouldn't be allowed to brown as they become tough and bitter.

Steamed or boiled leeks are good served with a Béchamel or cheese sauce. Leeks *à la Grecque* are cooked with wine, herbs and spices.

RAMP

Among the many wild onions and leeks, the Canadian ramp is perhaps the best known. Also known as the wild leek, ramp looks a little like a spring onion (scallion), but has a stronger and more assertive garlic-onion flavour. Choose unblemished, clear white specimens with bright, fresh leaves and store in a cool place, wrapped in a polythene bag.

Prepare and use ramp as you would spring onions (scallions). Trim the root end, then slice as required. Use in cooking or in salads, but remember the onion flavour is strong, so use sparingly.

Cleaning Leeks

Leeks need to be well washed to remove any earth and grit.

1 Cut off the base of the leek, then trim the green part. Remove any tough or damaged outer layers.

2 Cut the top green part of the leek lengthways and rinse well under cold running water, separating the layers to remove any hidden dirt. Slice or leave whole.

SPRING ONIONS/ SCALLIONS

Most of what are sold as spring or salad onions (scallions in the United States) are simply early-maturing varieties of onion. They should be grown quickly – in about eight weeks from sowing to harvesting – otherwise they become tough. In culinary terms, the distinction between different types of spring onion is purely one of size – they vary from the really tiny (thinner than a pencil) spring onions to those that are as large as a baby leek. Some varieties of spring onion have a markedly bulbous base, while others are more leek-like with no particular basal swelling.

Spring onions have a mild sweet flavour with a fresh, green snap, which makes them good in salads. Use thinner spring onions for salads and thicker ones for cooking. The leaves can be used as a substitute for chives. Red spring onions look pretty in salads but do not differ significantly in flavour from white spring onions. Unlike ordinary onions, spring onions do not store well. They can be kept for a few days in a cool place or in a refrigerator, but are best used really fresh.

Below: Small, thin spring onions can be enjoyed both whole or chopped finely.

Above: Bulb spring onions are the best type for dipping in batter and deep-frying.

Cooking

In Britain, spring onions are traditionally served whole (trimmed) in salads. They are good as crudités with a black olive tapenade and are excellent chopped or sliced into mixed or composite salads; they are widely used like this in the Middle East. They are a good addition to Mexican salsas. Spring onions are also excellent cooked, and are an essential ingredient in Asian stir-fries, because they cook quickly. They grill (broil) well, taking only a few minutes to cook. In Cataluña, in north-east Spain, they are widely used in this way: known as *calçots*, they are grilled over hot coals and served with all sorts of grilled meats and a nut/chilli sauce called *salsa romesco*. The tops of young spring onions may be used as a garnish in the same way as chives, and spring onion curls and brushes are popular garnishes in Chinese food.

BUNCHING OR WELSH ONIONS

These are very popular in China and Japan. They are called Welsh as a corruption of the Germanic *welsche*, meaning foreign. This name was probably given when they were first introduced into Europe from Asia. In Wales itself they used to be known as *holtzers* and they were once a popular

Above: Tree onions are hardy, clumping onions that grow well in herb patches.

flavouring because they grew in early spring when few other vegetables were available. They are also known as *chiboules* or *cibols*. In Chinese cooking, bunching onions are used in stir-fries in place of spring onions. The onion grows in clusters of bulbs, so individual onions may be removed, leaving the plant growing. The flavour is mild.

TREE ONIONS

These are true perennials for the herb patch. As with bunching onions, individual onions may be removed from the plant for use in the kitchen. Tree onions also form little bulblets at the tips of the stem, and as these swell, the weight of them bends the leaf over until it touches the ground, where the bulb will root. The bulblets may also be used in the kitchen. A particularly vigorous and tall form of the tree onion, known as the Catawissa onion, was a popular pot herb in America during the 19th and early 20th centuries.

Cooking

Both the basal stem and the green flags (leaves) may be used in sauces, stir-fries and salads. Tree onions are slightly tougher than spring onions, so do not grill (broil) well. The bulblets are good chopped in sauces and salad dressings.

SHOOTS AND STEMS

Vegetables in which the whole or part of the stalk is eaten (such as celery and fennel) are commonly classified as shoots. Some, like asparagus and the American fiddlehead fern, are early season vegetables. Others, such as the globe artichoke arrive later, while beansprouts, which grow all year round, are always available.

ASPARAGUS

Unless you grow your own, asparagus is definitely a luxury vegetable. Its price, even in season, sets it apart from other vegetables such as cabbages and cauliflowers, and it has a luxurious taste, too. The spears – particularly the thick, green ones that are at their best in early summer – have an intense savoury flavour that goes particularly well with simple but rich sauces such as Hollandaise sauce, or simply with hot melted butter.

Asparagus grows wild throughout Europe and has been eaten, and possibly cultivated, from at least the time of the ancient Greeks. There are many different varieties. Spanish and some Dutch asparagus is white with ivory tips; it is grown under mounds of soil and cut just as the tips begin to show. The purple variety is mostly grown in France, where the spears are cut once the tips are about 4cm/1½in above the ground. Consequently, the stalks are white and the tops tinged with green or purple. In contrast, the English and American asparagus, which is grown above the

ground, is entirely green. Arguments continue over which type of asparagus has the better flavour, with most growers expressing a preference for their own asparagus. Thin short asparagus are called sprue and are excellent when briefly steamed or stir-fried and added to salads. In Italy, they are served by themselves with shavings of Parmesan cheese.

Asparagus is reputed to have both nutritional and medicinal properties. It is rich in vitamins A and C, potassium, iron and calcium. It is a well-known diuretic and a mild laxative, and has been used as a tonic and a sedative, and to treat rheumatism.

Buying and Storing

Asparagus has a relatively short growing season from late spring to early summer. Today, it is available in the supermarkets almost all year round, but outside the season it will have been imported. It is still good, but it is expensive and will not have the flavour of home-produced asparagus.

When buying asparagus, the tips should be tightly furled and the stalks fresh and straight. It will keep for several days, if necessary. Untie the bundles and store in the salad drawer of the refrigerator. Or stand the asparagus in a jug (pitcher) of cold water in the refrigerator.

Cooking

Ideally, asparagus should be cooked in an asparagus kettle, so that the stalks are immersed in boiling water while the tips steam. Failing this, the bundle can be placed upright in a deep pan of boiling salted water, covered with a dome of foil and cooked for about 7 minutes until tender. Asparagus is also delicious roasted in a little olive oil, a method which intensifies the flavour.

Trimming Asparagus

Unless the asparagus comes straight from the garden, the ends will probably be tough and should be trimmed.

Trim away the tough ends of the stems and, if the bottom parts of the stem also feel hard, pare this away with a vegetable peeler.

Left: Asparagus is good served hot with melted butter and a sprinkling of coarsely ground sea salt.

Above: Crisp, raw fennel is delicious served thinly sliced in salads.

FENNEL

The vegetable fennel is closely related to the herb and spice of the same name. It is called variously Florence fennel, sweet fennel, *finocchio dulce* or Italian fennel. Like the herb, Florence fennel has the distinct flavour of anise, which goes particularly well with fish.

Buying and Storing

If possible, buy small tender bulbs. They should be clean and white with no bruises or blemishes, and the feathery leaves should be green and lively. Fennel will keep for a day or two in the salad drawer of the refrigerator.

Preparing and Cooking

Unless the bulbs are very young and tender, remove the first layer of skin, as it is likely to be tough (this can be used for making a stock). Fennel can then be sliced into slivers or rings. If thinly sliced, it can be served raw in salads. It contrasts well with apple, celery and other crunchy ingredients. Fennel is also excellent braised with onions, tomatoes and garlic.

FIDDLEHEAD FERN

Sometimes called ostrich fern, these shoots are a rich green colour and are normally about 5cm/2in long. They have a rather unusual flavour, somewhere between asparagus and okra, and have a slightly chewy texture.

To prepare and cook, trim the ends, then steam or simmer the fern in a little water or sauté in butter until tender.

CELERY

In Italy, celery has been eaten in salads for centuries. It has a distinct and individual flavour, sharp and savoury, which makes it an excellent flavouring for soups and stuffings, and is good on its own or in salads as well. The astringent flavour and crunchy texture of celery contrasts well with other ingredients in salads.

Basically, there are two types of celery available – green and white. These are not different varieties, but are the same plant reared in different ways. When allowed to grow naturally, the celery stalks are green. However, by banking up earth against the shoots, celery is blanched; the stalks are protected from sunlight and remain pale and white. Consequently, white celery is often "dirty" – covered loosely in soil – while green celery will always be clean. White celery, which is frost hardy, is only available in winter. It is more tender and tends to be less bitter than green celery, and is generally considered superior. Consequently, celery is usually thought of as a winter vegetable and is traditionally used at Christmas time, for stuffing or as a sauce to go with turkey.

Buying and Storing

If possible, buy unwashed white celery. It has a better flavour than the pristine but rather bland green variety. Look for celery with green fresh-looking leaves and straight stems. Celery will keep for several days in the salad drawer of the refrigerator. Limp celery can be revived by wrapping it in kitchen paper and standing in a jug (pitcher) of water.

Preparing and Cooking

If necessary, wash the celery and pull the stalks apart, trimming the base with a sharp knife. Cut into thick or thin slices according to the recipe.

When the stalks are served raw and whole, the coarse outer "strings" should be removed form each stalk by pulling them up from the base. Serve celery raw and finely sliced in salads. Braised celery is tasty, either whole or sliced.

Above: Celery has a subtle, yet distinctive, flavour of anise.

Above: Globe artichokes are good served with vinaigrette.

CARDOONS

These impressively large vegetables are closely related to the globe artichoke and have a superb flavour, a cross between artichokes and asparagus. Cultivated plants frequently grow to 1.8m/6ft in height. Once established, cardoons are kept pale as they grow. This process involves wrapping the stalks with newspaper and black bags for several weeks, so that when harvested in late autumn, the stalks are a pale green. The cardoon is a popular vegetable in southern Europe.

Preparing and Cooking

Cardoons should be thoroughly washed and the outside stalks discarded. As with celery, the coarse strings should be removed. They can be eaten raw in salads or cooked in various ways including frying, puréeing or boiling and serving with melted butter. In Spain, the vegetable is poached and served with chestnuts or walnuts. Only the inner ribs and heart are used.

Right: Cardoons are very popular in Italy but are not commonly available in either Britain or the United States.

GLOBE ARTICHOKES

These pretty vegetables are actually the buds of a large member of the thistle family. Served as a starter with melted garlic butter or vinaigrette, they make a lovely, and flavoursome beginning to a dinner party. The whole head is boiled or steamed and then the various parts are consumed. First, the globe-like bracts (leaves) are removed and the soft fleshy part at the base of each is eaten. As these are removed, the hairy tuft of the flower – known as the choke – is revealed. This is usually removed and discarded and then the base of the flower – known as the heart – is scooped out and eaten.

Buying and Storing

It is only worth buying artichokes when they are in season, although they are available most of the year. In winter, they tend to be small, dry specimens. At their best, artichokes should be fresh, crisp, with a bloom on their leaves and the inner leaves wrapped tightly round the choke. Artichokes will keep for 2–3 days in the salad drawer of the refrigerator but should be eaten as soon as possible.

Preparing and Cooking Artichokes

Globe artichokes look impressive but are actually very easy to prepare.

1 Hold the top of the artichoke and, using a sharp knife, remove the stalk and trim the base so that the artichoke sits flat. Trim off and discard the tips of the leaves and cut off the pointed top.

2 Cook the artichokes in a pan of boiling, salted water for 35–45 minutes until a leaf can be pulled out easily. Drain upside down.

3 If you intend to stuff the artichoke, pull out the central leaves, then scoop out the hairy choke with a teaspoon and discard.

Asian Shoots

These are now widely available in supermarkets in the West, and are excellent for adding to stir-fries and Chinese and Asian dishes.

Bamboo shoots In the Far East, edible bamboo shoots are sold fresh in the markets. The young shoots are stripped of their brown outer skins and the insides are then eaten. Fresh bamboo shoots can occasionally be found in Oriental stores. They have a mild but distinct taste, faintly reminiscent of globe artichokes, and they have a pleasant, fresh and crunchy bite.

Bean sprouts There are many varieties of sprouted beans available. The most commonly found are mung bean sprouts, which are widely used in Chinese and Asian cooking. They are fairly large, with a crunchy texture and delicate flavour. They can be eaten raw in salads or used in soups and stir-fries. Other sprouted beans include alfalfa, wheat berry, garbanzo, lentil and aduki bean.

Below: Water chestnuts make a wonderful, crunchy addition to stir-fries and braised dishes. The Chinese ones have a dark brown skin.

Palm hearts Fresh palm hearts are the buds of the cabbage palm tree and are considered a delicacy in many parts of the world. Blanch before cooking to eliminate any bitterness, then braise or sauté. Serve hot with a Hollandaise sauce or cold with a vinaigrette.

Below: Lotus root is a popular ingredient in Chinese and Japanese cooking.

Water chestnuts Water chestnuts are popular throughout Asia, cropping up in Chinese, Japanese, Korean and South-east Asian recipes. The name is slightly misleading because, while they do grow in water, they certainly aren't nuts. Instead they are corms, which are about the size of walnuts. There are several varieties, but the Chinese type, which are dark brown and look a bit like small daffodil bulbs, are the most widely available outside Asia. They have a soft skin that needs to be peeled away. Underneath the water chestnuts don't look very different from the canned variety.

Above: Sprouted mung beans have a delicate, fresh flavour and a refreshingly crunchy texture.

Water chestnuts have a sweet but unassuming taste. Their best feature is their texture, which is nice and crunchy, and they are also wonderfully juicy. Water chestnuts can be left whole, sliced or diced. They can be eaten raw in both savoury and sweet fruit salads, or added to stir-fries or braised dishes.

Lotus root Lotus root is used in cooking throughout Asia and is particularly popular in Chinese and Japanese cuisine. Raw lotus root looks like a string of fat sausages covered in black mud. But when cleaned, peeled and sliced, however, a beautiful pattern emerges in each cross section, the result of narrow channels that run through the root.

Lotus root has a mild and subtly sweet flavour and a wonderful crunchy texture. Clean carefully by scrubbing, then chop into sections, discarding the tough "necks". Peel off the outer skin. The flesh can then be cut into large chunks or the whole roots can be stuffed. Use as a vegetable by boiling briefly until tender.

ROOT VEGETABLES

These are the mainstays of our winter meals. Parsnips, turnips, swedes and potatoes combine to make wonderful warming stews. Jerusalem artichokes are another winter favourite and, as winter turns to spring, young carrots and Jersey potatoes appear. Exotic roots such as sweet potatoes and yams are available almost all year round, and root vegetables such as salsify can be enjoyed whatever the season.

POTATOES

This starchy root vegetable comes from South America and was introduced to England by early explorers of the New World. They were not an immediate success, being reviled as flavourless and suitable only for the poor. But by the 17th century they were popular throughout Europe, grown extensively in Ireland and many northern European countries and taking over from bread as a staple food. They are a good source of carbohydrate and vitamin C and other nutrients.

There are more than 400 varieties of potato. However, most of these are not widely available commercially and are generally only enjoyed by those who grow them themselves.

Below: Alex potatoes originated in Denmark and are good for home-growing.

Above: Anya potatoes have a waxy texture and a pleasant nutty flavour. They are good for salads.

Right: Maori Chief potatoes are best eaten within ten days of harvesting.

NEW POTATOES

These are not a particular variety, but are any potatoes that are harvested while small and young. Often labelled earlies, they appear in stores from May onwards and are smaller, sweeter and firmer than maincrop potatoes.

Alex With a creamy waxy texture and a good mild flavour, these potatoes are good for salads and are suitable for most cooking methods.

Anya These small finger potatoes have a knobbly oval shape with pale pink-beige skin, white flesh, a waxy texture and a pleasant nutty flavour.

Carlingford Available as both a new potato and as main crop, Carlingford has a close white flesh. They are suitable for most cooking methods.

Epicure These round, white-skinned potatoes have firm flesh, deep eyes and a very distinctive flavour.

Finger potatoes These thumb-sized, long baby potatoes are sometimes called finger potatoes or fingerlings. Among the many varieties are the German Lady's Finger. Since they are new crop potatoes, boil and then use in salads or serve with butter and parsley.

Jersey Royals Often the first new potato of the season, Jersey Royals have been shipped from Jersey for over a hundred years and have acquired an enviable reputation. Jersey Royals are kidney-shaped, with firm yellow flesh and a distinctive flavour. Boiled or steamed, then served with butter and a sprinkling of fresh chopped parsley, they cannot be beaten.

Linzer Delikatess These small, kidney-shaped potatoes look a little like Jersey Royals.

Maris Bard This is a regularly shaped, slightly waxy potato with white flesh.

Maris Peer This variety has dry firm flesh and a waxy texture. It doesn't disintegrate when cooked, so is especially good in salads.

Maori Chief These unusual potatoes from New Zealand have a dark purple-black skin and flesh, with a sweet potato flavour. The tender skin does not need peeling.

Above: Epicure have white skin and deep eyes.

MAINCROP POTATOES

These are available all year round and can be stored for many months.

Atlantic These oval to round potatoes have a light, scaly, buff skin and white flesh. They are mainly used for chips (US fries) and crisps (US chips).

Bel Rus These uniform, long, smooth potatoes have dark, thick, russeted skin and creamy coloured flesh. They are excellent in gratins and for steaming; the heavy russeting produces a thick, crunchy skin when baked.

Cara A large main crop potato, this variety is excellent baked or boiled.

Desirée This potato has a pink skin and yellow soft-textured flesh. It is good for all culinary purposes.

Estima This potato is widely available, though rather tasteless, with yellow flesh and pale skin.

Above: Desirée is a good all-round potato, for boiling, baking and roasting.

Francine This red-skinned, creamy-fleshed potato has an earthy taste and is excellent for gratins and steaming.

Frisia This oval potato has a creamy-yellow skin and white flesh with a moist, slightly waxy texture.

Goldrush This new, russet-type potato has light brown netted skin, white flesh and a good flavour.

Golden Wonder This russet-skinned potato was the original favourite for making crisps (US chips). It has a distinctive flavour and is excellent for baking. It is also good boiled and roasted.

International Kidney This variety of Jersey Royal are long and oval with very flaky white-yellow skin and creamy white flesh that has a lovely buttery flavour. They are slightly smaller than the Jersey Royal.

Kerr's Pink This cooking potato has a pink skin and pale, creamy flesh.

Above: Atlantic are mainly used for making into crisps and chips.

Above: Bel Rus are good for most cooking and are excellent baked.

King Edward Probably the best-known of British potatoes, King Edwards have a good flavour and a floury texture that makes them well suited for roasting and baking. Red King Edwards are virtually identical except for their skin colour. They, too, are good roasted or baked, but the flesh tends to disintegrate when they are boiled so they are really only suitable for mashing.

Maris Piper This widely grown variety of potato is popular with both gardeners and cooks because it is suitable for all kinds of cooking methods – baking, chipping, roasting and mashing. Maris Piper potatoes have a pale, smooth skin and creamy white flesh.

Above: King Edwards have a delicious flavour and wonderful texture.

Below: Maris Piper is a widely-grown and popular variety of potato.

Right: Nicola is an attractive potato that is excellent steamed or sautéed.

Nicola This oval-shaped potato has a smooth yellowish skin and deep yellow flesh. The texture is waxy with an excellent buttery taste. This potato is ideal for all-round use as well as being particularly good in salads. It is also good steamed and sautéed, and sliced for slow-cooked oven-baked dishes.

Penta These round white-skinned potatoes have quite deep pink-red eyes and a rich, creamy flesh. They tend to disintegrate when they are boiled and are better steamed.

Pentland Dell A long, oval-shaped potato, the Pentland Dell has a floury texture that tends to disintegrate when boiled. For this reason it is popular for roasting as the outside becomes soft when parboiled and then crisps up with the addition of fat during roasting.

Below: Knobbly Pink Fir Apples are an excellent salad potato.

Picasso These small oval potatoes have quite deep red eyes, pale skin and waxy flesh.

Pink Fir Apple This is an old English variety, with pink skin and yellow flesh.

Ratte This French potato has a smooth skin and waxy yellow flesh. It has a chestnut flavour and is particularly good in salads.

Red la Soda These round-oval potatoes have a smooth, deep-red skin, quite deep eyes and creamy white flesh.

Romano The Romano has a distinctive red skin with creamy flesh and is a good all-rounder, similar to Desirée.

Russet Burbank These potatoes are oval to long in shape, with russeted skin and pale yellow-white flesh, which is floury and full of flavour.

Sante These are oval or round potatoes with white or light yellow skin and flesh that has a firm, dry texture. They have become the most successful organic potatoes and are often sold young as new potatoes, too.

Wilja Introduced from Holland, this is a pale, yellow-fleshed potato with a good, sweet flavour and waxy texture.

Buying and Storing

Potatoes should be stored in a dark, cool, dry place. If exposed to the light, green patches develop which can be poisonous; if kept in the damp, they go mouldy. If buying in bulk, buy potatoes in paper sacks rather than polythene bags, as the humid conditions will cause them to rot. Similarly, if you buy potatoes in smaller quantities in polythene bags, remove and store in a dark place.

Maincrop potatoes will keep for several months in the right conditions but will gradually lose nutrients. New potatoes should be eaten as soon as possible, or at least within 2–3 days.

Preparation and Cooking

Most of the minerals and vitamins in potatoes are contained in or just below the skin. It is therefore better to eat potatoes in their skins, rather than peeling them. New potatoes should be washed under running water; older potatoes should be scrubbed.

If you peel potatoes, use a peeler that removes only the very top surface. Place them in a pan of water so they are just covered until ready to cook. Ideally, they should be cooked at once to avoid any loss of vitamin C.

Really new potatoes peel very easily, often just by being rubbed in your hands. You can tell a good new potato by how easily the skin rubs off. With a small sharp knife, scrape away the flaky skin and cook in just enough water to cover them completely.

Potatoes can be baked in their skins, boiled, steamed, sautéed, drizzled with oil and roasted or deep-fried to make chips (fries). Boiled potatoes are very good mashed with a little butter.

Left: Red la Soda potatoes have a pretty red skin and contrasting white flesh.

Below: Dutch Wilja potatoes have a good sweet flavour.

SWEET POTATOES

These have a distinctive sugary and spicy flavour which makes them an excellent addition to many savoury dishes.There are two types of this highly nutritious tuber: one has cream-coloured flesh, the other orange. The orange-fleshed variety has a higher nutritional content because it is richer in the anti-oxidant betacarotene. Both types are a good source of potassium, and contain plenty of nutritional fibre, vitamin C and carbohydrate.

Buying and Storing

When buying, choose small or medium-size specimens, as the larger ones tend to be rather fibrous. They should be firm and evenly shaped. Avoid any that seem withered, have damp patches or are sprouting. They will keep for about 8 days if stored in a cool place.

Left: Sweet potatoes contain useful nutrients.

Sweet Potato Crisps

Crisps (US chips) can be made with sweet potatoes instead of ordinary potatoes. Mix them with other West Indian vegetables such as plantains and yams and serve with pre-dinner drinks or as an accompaniment.

To prepare, peel the potato and slice very thinly with a sharp knife or a mandolin. Put the potato slices in a bowl of acidulated water until ready to fry. Drain, pat dry using kitchen paper and deep-fry in oil as they are, or dip into a mixture of flour blended with ground spices such as coriander, cumin and cayenne before frying.

Preparing and Cooking

Sweet potatoes can be cooked in any of the ways you would cook ordinary potatoes – roasted, boiled, mashed or baked. They also make delicious chips (US fries). If baking, scrub the potatoes well and cook exactly as you would ordinary potatoes. To boil, either cook in their skins and remove them after cooking, or peel and place in acidulated water. This prevents them from turning brown.

YAMS

These starchy root vegetables have been a staple food in many parts of the world for thousands of years. There are countless varieties, in different shapes, sizes and colours. The type you are most likely to find will be about the size of a small marrow. Sweet yams look like large potatoes and are normally covered with whiskery roots. All have a coarse brown skin and can be white- or red-fleshed.

Buying and Cooking

Buy firm specimens with unbroken skins. They can be stored for several weeks in a cool, dark place. To prepare and cook yams, peel away the skin and place in salted water. The skin and the layer underneath the skin contain the poison dioscorine. This is destroyed during cooking, but discard the peel carefully.

Yams can be used in the same way as potatoes and mashed, fried, sautéed or roasted. They have an affinity with spicy sauces and are delicious cut into discs, fried and sprinkled with salt and cayenne pepper.

TARO

Like yams, taro is a staple food in tropical regions. There are two basic varieties: a large barrel-shaped tuber and a smaller variety that is often called eddo or dasheen. They are all a dark mahogany brown with a rather shaggy skin. If possible, buy small specimens. Store in a cool dark place.

Below: Taro looks similar to a yam, but has a different and very unique flavour.

Below: Cassava is widely used in Caribbean cooking.

CELERIAC

This vegetable is actually the root of certain types of celery. Like cultivated celery, it is derived from the wild celery that is native to Europe and the Middle East. It came to the table much later than celery and is said to have been introduced to Britain from Alexandria in the early 18th century.

Celeriac is knobbly with a patchy brown-white skin and has a similar, though less pronounced, flavour than celery. Grated and eaten raw, it has a crunchy texture, but when cooked it is more akin to potatoes. It can be used in soups and broths, or can be cut into large dice and boiled and eaten in potato salads.

Thin slices of potato and celeriac cooked *au gratin* with cream is a popular way of serving this vegetable. If you can, buy smallish bulbs of celeriac. The flesh discolours when exposed to air, so as soon as it is peeled, plunge it into a bowl of acidulated water.

CASSAVA

This popular West Indian root is included in numerous Caribbean dishes. It is used to make tapioca and, in South America, a sauce and an intoxicating beverage are prepared from the juice. In Africa and the West Indies, cassava is eaten as a vegetable. It can be boiled, baked or fried, or cooked and pounded to a dough to make *fufu*, a traditional savoury African pudding.

Below: Knobbly celeriac comes from the same plant as celery and has a very similar flavour.

JICAMA

Also known as the Mexican potato or yam bean, this large root vegetable is a native of Central America. It was introduced to the Philippines by the Spanish and, from there, it spread to China where it is still popular today. It has a thin brown skin and white, crunchy flesh that has a sweet nutty taste. It can be cooked in the same ways as potatoes or sliced and added raw to salads.

Above: Jicama can be enjoyed raw or cooked.

Preparing Celeriac
The knobbly skin of celeriac needs to be removed before use.

Peel the celeriac carefully with a sharp knife and quickly immerse in a bowl of water with lemon juice added until ready to use.

SALSIFY AND SCORZONERA

These two closely related vegetables are members of the dandelion family. Both have long tapering roots, salsify having a white or pale brownish skin and scorzonera (also known as black salsify) having a black skin. Both salsify and scorzonera have a pale creamy flesh with a flavour that is reminiscent of artichokes and asparagus. Salsify is said to have the superior flavour, which has been likened by some to oysters.

Buying and Storing

Choose specimens that are firm and smooth and, if possible, still with their tops on, which should be fresh and lively looking. They will keep for several days stored in a cool dark place.

Preparing and Cooking

Scrub the root under cold running water, peel with a sharp knife and immediately place into acidulated water. Alternatively, the scrubbed root may be

Below: Scorzonera has a pale, creamy flesh underneath the dark skin.

Above: Scorzonera must be plunged into acidulated water if it is peeled raw to prevent the flesh discolouring.

peeled after cooking. To cook, cut into short lengths and simmer for 20–30 minutes until soft. Drain well, then sauté in a little butter and serve with lemon juice. Alternatively, the vegetables can be puréed for soup, or mashed.

JERUSALEM ARTICHOKES

These small knobbly tubers are thought to have come from the central United States and Canada, where they were cultivated by the Native Americans as long ago as the 15th century. They are related to the sunflower and have nothing to do with Jerusalem. One explanation for their name is that the Italian *girasole*, meaning turning to the sun, was corrupted to "Jerusalem" by English-speaking exporters.

Below: Jerusalem artichokes

Buying and Storing

Jerusalem artichokes are at their best during winter and early spring. They are invariably knobbly, but if possible buy neat ones with the minimum of knobs to save waste when peeling them. The skins should be pale brown without any dark or soft patches. If they are stored in a cool dark place they will keep well for up to about 10 days.

Preparing and Cooking

Jerusalem artichokes will discolour if exposed to the air, so place the peeled vegetable in a bowl of acidulated water until ready to cook. Because they are so knobbly, it is considered easier by many cooks to boil them in acidulated water in their skins and peel them afterwards. They can be cooked in many of the ways in which you would cook potatoes or parsnips. They are excellent roasted (although they tend to be rather soft), sautéed or dipped in batter and fried. For creamed artichokes, combine with potatoes in equal amounts.

PARSNIPS

These hearty, nutritious root vegetables have a long history. The Romans grew and cooked them to make broths and stews, and throughout the Middle Ages – before the potato had been introduced – they were the main starchy vegetable eaten by ordinary people. Nowadays, parsnips are available all year round, but they are still most popularly used to make warming winter soups and stews.

Parsnips are related to carrots and are similarly sweet, but with a distinct earthy flavour. They go well with other root vegetables and their flavour is greatly enhanced by the addition of spices and garlic.

Buying and Storing

It is often said that parsnips are best after the first frost, but many people like the very young tender parsnips available in the early summer. When buying parsnips, choose small or medium-size specimens. They should feel firm and be a pale ivory colour without any sprouting roots. Parsnips should be stored in a cool, dark place and will keep for 8–10 days.

Preparing and Cooking

Small parsnips need little or no peeling; just trim the ends and cook according to your preference or recipe. Larger parsnips will need to be peeled and may even need the woody core to be removed. To make roast parsnips, it is often easier to par-boil them for a few minutes before adding to the roasting dish. Young parsnips can be roasted whole but larger ones are best halved or quartered lengthways. To boil parsnips, cut them into pieces about 5cm/2in long and boil for 15–20 minutes until tender. They can then be served with butter and a sprinkling of parsley, or puréed. Adding a small pinch of grated nutmeg will greatly enhance the flavour of puréed parsnips.

Above: Parsnips are good added to soups and stews.

TURNIPS AND SWEDES/ RUTABAGA

Both members of the cabbage family, turnips and swedes are closely related to each other. Turnips have a distinctive peppery flavour, while swedes

Left: Small turnips with green tops have a wonderful flavour.

have a more earthy, full-bodied, sweeter taste. There are a number of different varieties, all of which are an excellent source of nutrients.

Navets From France, these small, round, squashed-shaped turnips are tinged with pink or purple.

Vertus Prized by the French, these turnips are long and carrot-shaped.

English turnips These are generally large and are mainly green and white.

Marian swede This is a yellow-fleshed variety with a strong, distinct flavour.

Merrick swede This has a watery flavour that is more like turnip than swede.

Buying and Storing

Select the smallest, youngest specimens available. They should be firm, smooth and unblemished, ideally with fresh green tops. Store in a cool dry place.

Preparing and Cooking

Trim young turnips, then simmer or steam until tender. They can also be served raw in a salad, thinly sliced or grated. Older turnips should be peeled and sliced or diced before cooking. Peel swedes to remove the skin, then cut into chunks. Be careful not to overcook or they will disintegrate.

Above: Swedes are very good served boiled and mashed.

Right: Young carrots are sweet and tender.

CARROTS

The orange carrot we know and love today came originally from Holland, but up until the Middle Ages, all carrots were purple. Gardeners often delight in such oddities, but you will be very lucky to find any purple specimens available in stores or supermarkets.

Carrots contain large amounts of carotene and vitamin A, along with useful amounts of vitamins B3, C and E. When eaten raw, they also provide potassium, calcium, iron and zinc but these are partly destroyed with cooking.

Buying and Storing

Almost all vegetables have a better flavour if they are grown organically, but this is particularly true of carrots. If possible, buy organic ones, or look for the young, pencil-thin carrots that still have their feathery tops attached. These young carrots can be eaten raw, or steamed for a few minutes. Older carrots should be unblemished and feel firm. Carrots should not be stored for too long, but they will keep for several days in a cool airy place or in the salad drawer of the refrigerator.

Preparing and Cooking

The age of carrots is a guide to how they should be prepared. The valuable nutrients lie either in or just beneath the skin, so if the carrots are young, simply scrub them. Medium-size carrots may need to be scraped with a knife before cooking them and large carrots will need to be scraped or peeled. Carrots can be cooked or eaten raw. To eat raw, they can be cut into julienne strips and tossed with a dressing, or grated into salads and coleslaw. They can be cooked in almost any way you choose. As an accompaniment, cut them into julienne strips and braise in butter and cider. Roasted carrots are delicious, with a melt-in-the-mouth sweetness. Par-boil large ones first, but younger carrots can be quickly blanched or added direct to the pan with a joint of meat.

BEETROOT/BEET

These purple roots have been eaten since Roman times. They have a dark purplish skin and a bright, vibrant pinkish-purple flesh. They contain valuable supplies of nutrients and are said to have excellent detoxifying properties. They may be eaten raw or cooked, and are also popular served as juice.

Buying and Storing

If possible, buy small beetroots which have their whiskers intact and have at least 5cm/2in of leaf stalk at the top; if they are too closely cropped they will bleed during cooking. Fresh beetroots will keep for several weeks if stored in a cool place.

Preparing and Cooking

To cook beetroot whole, rinse under running water. Cut the stalks to about 2.5cm/1in above the beetroot. Don't cut away the tapering root or the peel. The beetroot can then be baked in the oven, either in a little water in a casserole with a tight-fitting lid, or wrapped in foil and cooked like a baked potato. In a low oven, the beetroot will cook in 2–3 hours; it is cooked when the skin begins to wrinkle and can be easily rubbed away with your fingers. To boil beetroot, prepare as above and simmer for about 1 hour. Beetroot can also be served cold, grated or chopped in salads.

Beetroot tops are rich in vitamins A and C, iron and calcium. If you are lucky enough to get some, boil the greens for a few minutes, drain and serve with butter or olive oil.

Above: Beetroot can be served in a number of different ways: baked and served with sour cream, braised in a creamy sauce, grated in a salad, or used for the classic soup borscht.

GREEN VEGETABLES

Throughout the year greens of one sort or another are usually always available – whenever one green vegetable finishes another one comes into season. Cauliflowers, kale, broccoli and Brussels sprouts are all members of the cabbage family and, like the cabbage itself, are among the most nutritious of all vegetables. Spinach, too, is full of vitamins and minerals and is wonderfully versatile. Asian cabbages such as Chinese leaves or Pak-choi are now widely available and are quite delicious.

Right: Swiss chard comes in various colours.

SPINACH

This is arguably the most versatile of all the green vegetables. It is popular worldwide, with nearly every cuisine featuring spinach somewhere in its repertoire. It has a particular affinity with dairy products and in the Middle East, feta or helim cheese is used to make *boreks* and other spinach pies. The Italians are also particularly partial to spinach and often combine it with ricotta or Parmesan cheese in various dishes. In Italian *à la florentine* means that the dish contains spinach. Spinach also has an affinity with eggs and is delicious in soufflés and omelettes.

Spinach is an excellent source of vitamin C, if eaten raw, and beta-carotene. It also provides vitamin A, B vitamins, calcium, potassium and iron.

Above: Green, leafy spinach is highly nutritious.

Buying and Storing

Spinach grows all year round, so you should have no difficulty buying it fresh. The leaves should be green and fresh-looking; if they look tired and the stalks are floppy, shop around until you find something in better condition. Spinach reduces significantly when cooked; about 450g/1lb raw weight will serve two people when cooked. Store in the salad drawer of the refrigerator where it will keep for 1–2 days.

Preparing and Cooking

Always wash spinach thoroughly, being careful to rinse off any grit and removing any stones. Remove any tough stalks, then throw the leaves into a large pan with just the water that clings to them. Add a sprinkling of salt, cover the pan tightly and place over a low heat for about 4 minutes, shaking the pan now and then to prevent the spinach sticking to the bottom. The spinach will steam in its own liquid. As well as being delicious on its own, spinach can be chopped or puréed and mixed with a range of other ingredients with superb results.

SWISS CHARD

Although Swiss chard is often likened to spinach, the two plants are not related. The leaves have similarities, but chard is on an altogether different scale. Swiss chard leaves are large and fleshy with distinctive white ribs, and the flavour is stronger and more robust than spinach. Popular in France, it is baked with rice, eggs and milk in *tians*, and cooked in a pastry from Nice – *tourte de blettes* – a sweet tart filled with raisins, pine nuts, apples and Swiss chard bound together with eggs. It is combined with eggs in frittatas and tortillas.

Ruby or rhubarb chard has red ribs; other varieties have an almost golden-coloured stem. All have the same flavour. Swiss chard is rich in vitamins and minerals and contains oxalic acid.

Buying and Storing

Heads of chard should be fresh and bright green; avoid any with withered leaves or flabby stems. Store in a cool place and eat within 3–4 days.

Preparing and Cooking

The leaf needs to be separated from the ribs, which can be done roughly with a sharp knife or more precisely using scissors. The ribs can then be sliced. Either shred the leaves or blanch and use as food wrappers. Use Swiss chard in pies, frittatas and gratins. The leaves and ribs can be cooked together. Gently sauté the ribs in butter and oil, then add the leaves a few minutes later.

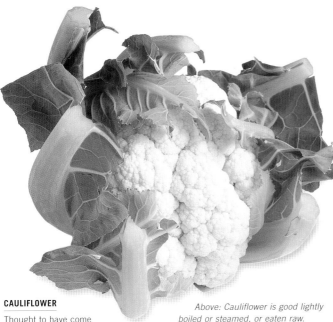

CAULIFLOWER

Thought to have come originally from China, and thence to the Middle East, the Moors introduced cauliflower to Spain in the 12th century. It is a member of the cabbage family and, like all members of the cabbage family, suffers terribly if overcooked. A properly cooked cauliflower should have a pleasant fresh flavour but, if overcooked, it will turn grey and become unpalatably soft, taking on a nasty rank flavour with an unpleasant aftertaste. All cauliflowers contain potassium, iron and zinc, but cooking reduces the amounts. They are also a good source of vitamins A and C.

Green and occasionally purple cauliflowers are available in the shops. They look pretty but are otherwise similar to white cauliflowers. Dwarf varieties of cauliflowers are now also commonly available.

Romanescoes These pretty green or white vegetables look like a cross between broccoli and cauliflower, but are more closely related to cauliflowers. They are quite small and need only the briefest cooking.

Broccoflower A cross between broccoli and cauliflower, this looks like a pale green cauliflower and should be cooked in the same way as other cauliflowers.

Above: Cauliflower is good lightly boiled or steamed, or eaten raw.

Buying and Storing

Cauliflower should be a creamy white colour with the outer leaves curled around the flower. The head should be unblemished without any discoloured areas. Keep cauliflowers in a cool place for no longer than 1–2 days.

Preparing and Cooking

Trim away the coarse base leaves. Large cauliflowers are best halved, quartered or broken into florets, or the outside will overcook before the inside is tender. Small cauliflowers can be cooked whole if wished. They are excellent steamed, or the florets can be stir-fried in oil to give a lightly browned finish. Cauliflower is also good served raw in salads or for crudités.

BROCCOLI AND SPROUTING BROCCOLI

The broccoli available in our shops today, with its neat green heads, is a relatively modern vegetable. Also known as calabrese, it was developed in Italy from the far less tidy purple sprouting broccoli that is widely grown in gardens, and can still be bought in some super-markets and farm stores. There is little to choose between them in taste; some people prefer the compactness of calabrese broccoli, others like the leafiness of the sprouting variety.

Buying and Storing

When buying, if possible choose loose broccoli rather than the pre-wrapped bundles because it is easier to check that it is fresh. Avoid broccoli that looks wilted or has damaged flowerheads or leaves. They can be stored in the refrigerator for 2–3 days.

Preparing and Cooking

Break broccoli into even-size florets (or lengths if using purple-sprouting) and cook in a little boiling water. Serve both varieties simply with butter and lemon juice or with a Hollandaise or béarnaise sauce as an accompaniment. They are also excellent stir-fried.

Above: Calabrese broccoli is the most commonly available variety.

Buying and Storing

Cabbages should be fresh-looking and unblemished. When buying, avoid any with wilted leaves or those that look or feel puffy. Savoys and spring greens will keep in a cool place for several days; firmer cabbages will keep happily for much longer.

Preparing and Cooking

Remove the outer leaves before cooking and cut the cabbage into quarters. Remove the stalk and then slice or shred according to your recipe or taste. For green or white cabbage, place the sliced or shredded leaves in a pan with a knob (pat) of butter and a couple of table-spoons of water to prevent burning. Cover and cook over a medium heat until the leaves are tender, shaking the pan or stirring. Red cabbage is commonly sautéed in oil or butter, then slowly braised with apples, currants, vinegar and spices.

CABBAGE

There are numerous varieties of cabbage but all share the same unfortunate characteristic of developing a rank smell and flavour if overcooked. This is due to a chemical, common to cabbage and other brassicas like cauliflower and turnips, which is activated during cooking. The answer is to avoid overcooking them.

Savoy cabbage This is a green cabbage with crimped or curly leaves. It has a mild flavour and is particularly tender.

Spring greens These have fresh loose heads with a pale yellow-green heart. They are available in spring and are delicious simply sliced, steamed and served with butter.

Green cabbage The early green, or spring, cabbages are dark green, loose, leafed and have a slightly pointed head. They have little or no heart as they are picked before this has had time to develop. Nevertheless they are a very good cabbage and all but the very outside leaves should be tender. As the season progresses, larger, firmer and paler green cabbages are available. These are a little tougher than the spring cabbages and need slightly longer cooking.

Above: (Clockwise from top) Savoy, green and white cabbages

Right: Red cabbage loses the wonderful vibrancy of its colour when cooked.

Red cabbage This pretty cabbage has smooth, firm leaves. When cooking, add a little vinegar to the water to prevent the colour fading. Red cabbage can be pickled or stewed with spices and flavourings.

White cabbage Sometimes called Dutch cabbage, this has smooth, firm pale green leaves. White cabbages are available throughout the winter. They are good cooked or raw. To cook, boil or steam and serve with butter.

Below: Spring greens have a delicate cabbage-like flavour.

KALE AND CURLY KALE

All kales are a variety of green-leafed vegetables of the brassica family. Most have thick stems and robust leaves that do not form a head, and curly leaves.

Collards Also known as collard greens, these are a popular green vegetable in the southern United States, grown during summer and autumn (fall) for harvesting in the spring. They are a good source of vitamin A.

Curly kale This is the most commonly available kale. It has wonderfully crimped and curly leaves.

Preparing and Cooking

To prepare, break the leaves from the stalk and discard any thick stalk. Keep the leaves whole or slice them before boiling in a little water for 3–5 minutes.

BRUSSELS SPROUTS

These have a pronounced and sweet nutty flavour, quite unlike cabbage although the two are closely related. They are traditionally served at Christmas with chestnuts and have an affinity with certain nuts, such as almonds and chestnuts.

Buying and Storing

Brussels sprouts should be small and hard with tightly wrapped leaves. Avoid any that are turning yellow or have loose leaves. They will keep in a cool place or in the salad drawer of a refrigerator for several days.

Preparing and Cooking

Trim away the base of the stalk and remove the outer leaves. If the sprouts are large, cut them in half or quarters, or slice thinly for stir-frying. Cook very briefly in small amounts of fast-boiling water. Alternatively, stir-fry with onions and ginger, in a little oil and butter.

KOHLRABI

Looking rather like a cross between a cabbage and a turnip, kohlrabi is a member of the brassica family, but unlike cabbages, it is the bulbous stalk

Above: Kohlrabi can be served as an alternative to carrots or turnips.

that is edible, rather than the flowering heads. There are two varieties: one purple, the other pale green. They both have the same mild and fresh tasting flavour, not unlike water chestnuts.

Buying and Storing

Kohlrabi is best when small and young, since larger specimens tend to be coarse and fibrous. It keeps well for 7–10 days if stored in a cool place.

Preparing and Cooking

If they are bigger than 5cm/2in in diameter, peel and slice the kohlrabi, then either boil them, or par-boil and bake in the oven. They can also be cooked long and slow in gratin dishes. Very small kohlrabi are tender and can be cooked whole.

Above: Kale with curly leaves is the most popular variety with cooks.

Right: Brussels sprouts taste good with onions and ginger, or with nuts.

CHINESE GREENS

Many Chinese and Asian greens are members of the brassica family and can be used in similar ways.

PAK-CHOI/BOK CHOY

Another member of the brassica family, pak-choi goes by many different names, including horse's ear and Chinese celery cabbage. The stalks are pale, and range from light green to ivory-white, and the glossy leaves, which are a distinctive feature of this vegetable, are dark green. Pak-choi is a perennial and several varieties are available throughout the year.

Although reminiscent of Chinese leaves, pak-choi is less delicate in flavour and has a distinctive taste of mild cabbage crossed with spinach. It can also have a slightly peppery finish.

Below: Chinese leaves are quick and easy to prepare and make a useful vegetable for winter salads.

Right: Pak-choi has a wonderful texture and flavour when stir-fried.

Buying and Cooking

Choose fresh specimens, with unblemished stalks and lively looking leaves, and use as soon as possible. To prepare, separate the leaves and stems, as the latter take slightly longer to cook. Baby pak-choi can be cooked whole or in halves or quarters. Pak-choi can be used inter-changeably with Chinese leaves for most dishes, although their flavour and colour differ. It is delicious when quickly braised, but should not be subjected to prolonged cooking. Only when very young and tender can it be eaten raw.

CHINESE LEAVES OR CABBAGE

Sometimes sold by its Chinese name, Pe-Tsai, Chinese leaves or cabbage has pale green, crinkly leaves with long, wide white ribs. Its shape is a little like a very fat head of celery, which gives rise to another of its alternative names, celery cabbage. It is pleasantly crunchy with a faint cabbage flavour. Chinese cabbage is an essential ingredient in many Asian recipes and is very good stir-fried with a tasty sauce.

Buying and Storing

Chinese leaves should look fresh and perky when on sale in the supermarket. Avoid any with discoloured or damaged stems. The leaves should be pale green and straight without blemishes or bruises. They will keep for up to six days in the salad drawer of the refrigerator.

Preparing and Cooking

Remove the outside leaves and slice as much as you need. If adding to salads, combine with something fairly forceful, like endive or rocket, and add a well-flavoured dressing. If adding to a stir-fry, cook with garlic, ginger and other fairly strong flavours.

Above: Chinese broccoli looks very similar to European sprouting broccoli.

CHINESE BROCCOLI

This is from the same family as mustard greens, but is more robust both in terms of texture and taste. It has long, slender stems, loose leaves and has tiny white or yellow flowers. Flowers, stalk and leaves can all be eaten and each has its own individual flavour. Once the thicker stalks are trimmed, the greens can be sliced and cooked in the same way as Chinese mustard greens.

CHINESE MUSTARD GREENS

Mustard greens are worth looking out for as they have an excellent flavour and are very good to eat. The plant is a member of the cabbage family, but is grown in Europe solely for its mustard seed. In India and Asia it has long been grown for its oil seed, but the Chinese developed the plant for its leaves as well. These are deep green and slightly puckered-looking, and have a definite mustard flavour, which can be quite fiery.

Young Chinese mustard greens can be used with lettuce to spice up salads. The older, tougher leaves are best stir-fried and then dressed with a light Chinese sauce. They are also good cooked with onion and garlic and served as a side dish to accompany pork or bacon.

Left: Choi sum has a light, mild flavour.

CHOI SUM

This is another type of cabbage, related to oilseed rape. The bright yellow flowers at the centre are responsible for its common name of Chinese flowering cabbage. It has bright green leaves and thin, pale green stalks that are slightly grooved. The flavour is mild and unassuming, and it is used in Chinese and Asian cooking, in stir-fries and in soups for its crisp texture.

Little preparation is required for choi sum. Wash and then shake off excess water. The stalks need only be trimmed, although if liked, they can be discarded, then blanched in stock for 10 minutes and served with oyster sauce. The leaves can be thickly or thinly sliced and used for soups and stir-fries, either solo or with other ingredients.

Garden and Wild Leaves

Several plants that are good to eat are available in the garden or grow wild, and can be picked for free. If picking your own dandelions or nettles, do so well away from roads.

Vine leaves All leaves from vines that produce grapes can be eaten when young. They make an ideal wrapping for various meats and vegetables.

Below: Dandelion leaves are generally only found in French markets.

They have a faintly lemon-cabbage flavour which can be detected at its best in good *dolmades*. The leaves need to be cooked briefly before using, so that they are pliable and don't crack when you wrap the food.

Dandelion leaves These can be added to salads or used in the French *pissenlits au lard*, where whole young dandelion plants are dressed in vinaigrette and then covered in finely chopped pieces of salt pork or bacon. They have a faintly spinach-like flavour. Dandelion leaves are popular in France but are not widely available elsewhere.

Sorrel This has a sharp, distinct, lemon flavour and the leaves are greatly prized in France, where they are used for soups and in various classic dishes. The young leaves are delicious in salads, or use the plant later

Left: Sorrel

in the year for sauces to accompany fish. It is commonly teamed with eggs and cream.

Nettles These have long been a popular green leafy vegetable: as well as being full of vitamins and minerals, they are both plentiful and free. They should only be picked when very young in the spring. Traditionally, they were gathered and eaten as a spring tonic. They may be served as a green vegetable, or used to make a tasty soup.

Orache Although not related to spinach, this beautiful red or golden-leaved plant is called mountain spinach, and its large leaves can be treated like spinach.

Fat hen This is a member of the goosefoot family and resembles spinach in taste, although it is milder. It grows wild as a weed.

PEAS, BEANS AND PODS

Probably the first vegetable to be cultivated by man, ancient peas and beans have been found in settlements from the late Stone Age onwards – that is, nearly 8,000 years ago. They are a highly nutritious vegetable, containing essential carbohydrates and proteins, as well as useful supplies of vitamins and minerals. They were particularly valuable to ancient man as they could be dried and stored, which meant that food was available throughout the year.

GARDEN PEAS

These are one of the delights of summer, although they are one of those vegetables that are best when absolutely fresh. Pick-your-own (if you don't grow them yourself) is the best way to enjoy peas at their best. There are many varieties of peas, some of which can be eaten whole, including the pod.

Peas are one of the few vegetables that taste almost as good when frozen. Because freezing takes place soon after picking, frozen peas often have a higher nutritional content than fresh, and are available all year round.

Right: Mangetouts (back) and peas in their pods (front)

Above: Snow peas (bottom) and sugar snaps (top) have a delicious flavour and should be eaten as fresh as possible.

Mangetouts These are eaten whole and are valued for their pods, rather than the peas, which never mature. Mangetouts have a delicate, sweet flavour. To prepare, young, freshly-picked mangetouts simply need to be topped, tailed and washed. They should be cooked only briefly to retain their delicate, mild flavour and crisp bite. They can be blanched or stir-fried and are also good served raw in salads.

Petits pois These are not, as you might expect, immature peas, but are a dwarf variety. They are wonderfully tender and have a sweet, delicate flavour. Gardeners grow their own, but petits pois are not available fresh in the shops as they are mainly grown commercially for canning or for freezing.

Above: Fresh green peas are now available ready-podded.

Snow peas/sugar peas/sugar snap peas These have the distinct fresh flavour of raw peas and are plumper and have more "snap" than mangetouts. They are delicious added raw to salads. They are also good steamed or boiled, but should only be cooked for about 1 minute or they will lose their wonderful flavour and texture.

Buying and Storing

Only buy really fresh peas; if they are old they are bound to be disappointing. In top condition, the pods are bright green and lively-looking; the more withered the pod, the longer ago they were picked. Use fresh peas as soon as possible.

Above: Corn on the cob is delicious boiled served with butter and a little salt and pepper.

Left: Baby sweetcorn can be eaten raw and are good in stir-fries.

SWEETCORN/CORN

To really savour its delightful sweetness, sweetcorn cobs should be eaten really fresh. This is why many gardeners make room in their vegetable patch for this impressive plant.

Baby sweetcorn is also now widely available. Baby sweetcorn cobs are picked when immature. They are cooked and eaten whole. They have a faintly sweet but rather bland flavour, and are mostly enjoyed for their pretty appearance and pleasantly crunchy texture. Sweetcorn is an excellent carbohydrate food and is rich in vitamins A, B and C. It contains protein, but less so than most other cereals. It is also a good source of potassium, magnesium, phosphorus and iron.

Buying and Storing

As soon as corn is picked, its sugar begins to turn to starch. The flavour fades and the kernels toughen, so the sooner it goes into the pot the better. Wherever possible, buy locally grown corn – buying it from a supermarket is inevitably a bit hit-and-miss.

Look for husks that are clean and green, and tassels which are golden, with no sign of matting. The corn itself should look plump and yellow.

OKRA

Originally from Africa, okra is a well-travelled vegetable that has insinuated itself into a surprising number of cuisines and is widely used in African, Caribbean, Creole and Indian cooking. The lantern-shaped pod contains rows of seeds that ooze a mucilaginous liquid when cooked. Although not liked by everyone, it is this stickiness that has made the vegetable so popular. It has a very subtle flavour and is particularly good combined with spicy flavourings.

Left: Okra adds a gluey thickness to stews and casseroles.

Buying and Storing

Choose young, small pods. They should be bright green, firm and slightly springy when squeezed. They will keep for a few days in the salad drawer of the refrigerator.

Preparing and Cooking Okra

If cooked whole, okra is pleasantly tender and not mucilaginous.

1 When cooking okra whole, trim the top but don't expose the seeds inside or the viscous liquid will ooze into the rest of the dish. If, however, this is what you want, slice thickly or thinly according to the recipe. If you want to eliminate some of the liquid, first soak the whole pods in acidulated water for about an hour before cooking.

2 The pods can be steamed, boiled or lightly fried, then added to other ingredients. Whether cooked whole or sliced, use garlic, ginger or chilli to perk up the flavour, or cook with Indian-inspired flavourings such as onions, tomatoes and spices.

Above: (Top to bottom) Broad beans, runner beans and Haricots verts are at their best when really fresh.

BROAD/FAVA BEANS

Beans are one of man's earliest foods and there is evidence that broad beans were being cultivated in Neolithic times. Broad beans grow in most climates and soils, and were a staple food throughout the Dark Ages and the Middle Ages, grown for feeding both people and livestock, until being replaced by the potato in the 17th and 18th centuries. Beans are high in protein and carbohydrates, and are a good source of vitamins A, B1 and B2. They also provide potassium and iron.

Buying and Storing

Buy beans as fresh as possible. The pods should preferably be small and tender. Use as soon as possible.

Right: Bobby beans (above) and French beans (below) are just two of the many varieties of green bean that are available in stores and supermarkets.

Preparing and Cooking

Very young broad beans, no more than 7.5cm/3in in length, have very tender pods and can be eaten whole; top and tail, then slice roughly. Usually, however, you will need to shell the beans. Older beans are often better skinned after they are cooked to rid them of the strong, bitter flavour. To cook the beans, plunge shelled beans into rapidly boiling water and cook until just tender. They can also be par-boiled and then finished off braised in butter. They are also good served puréed with a little fried garlic.

RUNNER BEANS

Native to South America where they have been cultivated for more than 2,000 years, runner beans are now widely grown by many home gardeners. Like all legumes, their roots contain bacteria that help renew nitrogen supplies in the soil.

Runner beans have a more robust flavour and texture than French beans and are distinct from green beans in several ways. They are generally much larger with long, flattened pods; their skin is rough in texture, although in young beans this softens during cooking; and they contain very attractive purple beans within the pods.

Buying and Storing

Always buy young beans as the pods of larger beans are likely to be tough. The pods should feel firm and fresh; if you can see the outline of the bean inside the pod it is likely to be fibrous, although you could leave the beans to dry out and use the dried beans later in the season. Ideally, the beans inside should be no larger than your small fingernail. Use runner beans as soon as possible after buying as they do not store well.

Preparing and Cooking

Runner beans need to be topped and tailed and may also need stringing. Carefully put your knife through the top of the bean without cutting right through, and then pull downwards; if a thick thread comes away, the beans need to be stringed, so do the same on the other side. The beans can then be sliced horizontally with a sharp knife or a slicer. Runner beans are best simply boiled and cooked until they are *al dente*.

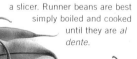

Right: Thai beans are very long.

GREEN BEANS

Whether you call them French beans, wax beans, haricots or green beans, they all belong to this large and varied family. One variety or another is always available in the supermarkets all year round and therefore they are one of the most convenient and versatile fresh green vegetables.

French beans These beans were introduced into Britain from France, hence their name. They include a range of green beans, including the snap bean and bobby bean. French beans are mostly fat and fleshy and when fresh should be firm so that they break in half with a satisfying snapping sound.

Haricots verts These are considered to be the best French beans and are delicate and slim in shape. They should be eaten when very young, no more than 6–7.5cm/2½–3in in length.

Thai beans These long beans are similar to French beans and can be prepared and cooked in the same way.

Yellow wax beans This is also a French bean and has a pleasantly mild and slighty buttery taste.

Buying and Storing

Whatever the variety, beans should be bright and crisp. Avoid wilted ones, or those with overly mature pods which feel spongy when lightly squeezed. Green beans do not keep well, so use as soon as possible after buying or picking them.

Preparing and Cooking

To top and tail green beans or French beans, gather them together in one hand then slice away the top 5mm/¼in, then do the same at the other end. If necessary, pull off any stringy bits. Plunge the beans into rapidly boiling water and cook until *al dente*. When overcooked, beans have a flabby texture and lose much of their flavour.

Drain and toss in butter or with fried shallots and bacon. For salads, cook green beans until just tender, then refresh under cold water. They are excellent with a garlicky vinaigrette.

LIMA BEANS

Known as butter beans when dried, the fresh lima beans are popular in the United States where they are sold mainly shelled. They are an essential ingredient in the native American dish *succotash*. Lima beans should be cooked in a little boiling water until tender. Elderly beans need skinning after they are cooked.

SOYA BEANS

Fresh young soya beans are very popular in Japan. They are delicious boiled and are often served whole as an hors d'oeuvre or as snacks. They are removed from the pods before eating.

Below: Fresh soya beans in their pods

Cooking Young Soya Beans

This method of cooking young soya beans in the pod is very popular in Japan. They are served as snacks with drinks, and make a healthy alternative to salted nuts and crisps (US chips). To eat them, it is acceptable to squeeze the pods with your teeth to push the beans out into your mouth.

1 Separate the pods from the stalks if they are still attached. Trim off the stem end and place in a bowl. Sprinkle the pods generously with salt and rub into the bean pods with your hands. Leave to stand for about 15 minutes.

2 Boil plenty of water in a large pan, then add the beans and boil over a high heat for 7–10 minutes, or until the bean inside the pods are tender but still crunchy. Drain immediately and refresh briefly under running water.

3 Serve hot or cold in a basket or a bowl with drinks. For extra saltiness, sprinkle the cooked beans with a little more salt.

SQUASHES

These are among the best-known autumn vegetables. Locally-grown courgettes are available from mid to late summer, as are the pretty pattypans. Marrows follow in late summer and then come the winter squashes – acorn squash, kabocha and pumpkins.

SUMMER SQUASHES

The delicately flavoured vegetables include marrows, courgettes (zucchini) and pattypan squashes.

COURGETTES/ZUCCHINI

These are the best loved of all the squashes as they are so versatile. They are quick and easy to cook and are succulent and tender with a delicate flavour. Unlike other squashes, they are available all year round.

Courgettes are basically immature marrows. The word is a diminutive of the French *courge*, meaning marrow; similarly zucchini means miniature *zucca*, Italian for gourd. Courgettes have a deep green skin, with firm pale flesh. The seeds and pith found in marrows have yet to form but are visible in mature courgettes. The prized baby courgettes have no suggestion of seeds or pith and the flesh is completely firm.
Yellow courgettes These have a yellow skin and are somewhat straighter than green courgettes. They have a slightly firmer flesh, but are otherwise similar.
Italian courgettes These very long, thin courgettes are grown in Italy. They are treated like ordinary courgettes but are strictly a bottle gourd.

Buying and Storing

Courgettes should be firm with a glossy skin. Avoid any that feel squashy or look limp or dull. Choose small specimens.

Preparing and Cooking

The tiny young courgettes need no preparation at all, and if they still have their flowers, so much the better. Larger courgettes should be topped and tailed, then prepared according to the recipe. Sliced courgettes can be steamed or boiled, but take care they do not overcook. Alternatively, they can be grilled (broiled), roasted or fried.

Above: (Left to right) Marrow, courgettes and pretty green and yellow pattypan squashes all have a delicate flavour and are delicious cooked simply or combined with other ingredients.

MARROW

The word marrow, as a general term, tends to refer to the summer squashes that are available at the end of summer and in the early autumn. There are a number of varieties of these large summer squashes.
Vegetable marrows This is the proper name for the large prize marrows beloved of harvest festivals. Buy small ones whenever possible.
Spaghetti squashes Long and pale yellow, these squashes can grow to an enormous size. They earned their name from the resemblance of the cooked flesh to spaghetti.
Custard marrows These are pretty, pale green squashes with scalloped edges, similar in flavour to courgettes.

Buying and Storing

Always select squashes that are firm with clear, unblemished flesh. Vegetable marrows and spaghetti squashes will keep for several months provided they are stored in a cool, dry place. Custard marrows will keep for up to a week.

Preparing and Cooking

First wash the skin, then, if it is tough, peel it away. For braised marrow, cut into chunks and discard the seeds and pith. To steam or sauté marrow, cut into thick slices or cut lengthways and discard the seeds and pith. Place chunks of marrow in a heavy pan with a little butter, cover and cook until tender. It can then be livened up with garlic, herbs or tomatoes. For stuffed marrow, blanch first, stuff, then cover or wrap in foil and bake in the oven.

PATTYPAN SQUASHES

These pretty, delicate little squashes look like tiny custard squashes. They can be pale green, yellow or white and have a slightly firmer texture than courgettes but a similar flavour. Make the most of their size and shape by steaming them whole until tender and serving as an accompaniment.

SUMMER CROOKNECKS

Pale yellow with curves at the neck and a bumpy skin, crooknecks can be prepared and cooked in the same way as courgettes.

WINTER SQUASHES

There are a huge number of varieties of winter squashes; many are known by several different names. When cooking, most are interchangeable, although it is best to taste dishes as you cook them, as they may require different seasoning.

PUMPKINS

The most famous of all the winter squashes, pumpkins are large, bright yellow or orange squashes with a deep orange flesh. They have a sweet, slightly honeyed flavour and are very popular in the United States.

English pumpkins These have a softer flesh than the American variety and are good for soups or, if puréed, combined with potatoes or other root vegetables.

BUTTERNUT SQUASHES

These perfectly pear-shaped squashes have a pale skin and orange flesh. Use in soups or in any pumpkin recipe.

ACORN SQUASHES

These are small and heart-shaped with a beautiful deep green or orange skin, or a lovely mixture of the two. Peel, then use as for pumpkins or bake whole, then split and serve with butter.

HUBBARD SQUASHES

These large squashes have a thick, hard shell that can range from bright orange to dark green. Large specimens are sold in halves or large wedges. They have a grainy texture and are best mashed with butter and seasoning.

Left: (Clockwise from top left) Butternut, orange acorn, little gem and green acorn squashes are all winter varieties.

Below: Kabocha squash are popular in Asian cooking.

DELICATA SQUASHES

These pretty squashes have a succulent yellow flesh, tasting like a mixture of sweet potato and butternut squash.

ONION SQUASHES

These round, yellow or pale orange squashes have a mild flavour, which is less sweet than pumpkin but still fruity or honeyed. They are very good in risottos and most pumpkin recipes.

KABOCHA SQUASHES

These bright green squashes have a pale orange flesh. They are similar in flavour and texture to acorn squashes and can be cooked in the same way.

Buying and Storing

All winter squashes may be stored for long periods. Buy firm, unblemished vegetables with clear smooth skins.

Preparing and Cooking

For larger squashes, or for those being used for soups or purées, peel and cut into pieces, removing the seeds.

To cook pumpkins and other winter squash, boil in a little water for about 20 minutes until tender, then mash and serve with butter and plenty of salt and pepper. Smaller squashes can be baked whole in their skins, then halved, seeded and served with butter and maple syrup. Pumpkin and other squashes can also be lightly sautéed in butter before adding stock, cream or chopped tomatoes.

EXOTIC GOURDS

While the squashes are native to the Americas, most gourds originated in the Old World – Africa, India and the Far East. However, over many centuries people and seeds have crossed continents, so that squashes and gourds are now common worldwide. Both belong to the family *Cucurbitacea* and both are characterized by their rapid-growing vines.

BOTTLE GOURDS

These are still a familiar sight in Africa, where they are principally grown for their dried shells rather than for their fruit. The gourds can grow to an enormous size and the shells are used as water bottles, and made into cups and musical instruments. The young fruit can be eaten, but it is extremely bitter and is normally only added to highly flavoured stews such as curries.

CHAYOTES

The chayote (pronounced chow-chow) is a popular gourd in many regions of the world and can be found in just about any ethnic supermarket. In each it is known by a different name: *christophine* is the Caribbean term, but *choko, shu-shu, chinchayote* and vegetable pear are among others. Unlike most gourds, it is native to Mexico but was widely grown throughout the tropics after the invasions of the Spanish.

Right: In China and Thailand, winter melon is often made into a soup and served in the shell.

Chayotes are pear-shaped fruits with a large central seed or stone, similar in appearance to the stone found inside a mango. The chayote seed, however, is edible. Chayotes have a smooth, pale green skin, which is often furrowed and may be covered in short spines. The fruit has a subtle aroma and the flavour is mild and delicate, similar to marrow (large zucchini), and the texture is fairly firm, not unlike that of a courgette (zucchini).

Buying and Storing

Chayote keeps quite well. Buy smooth, hard specimens and store in the salad compartment of the refrigerator. It will stay fresh for up to a week.

Preparing and Cooking

Chayotes are widely used in Mexican, Caribbean and Asian cooking, and may be eaten raw or cooked. Raw, they can be peeled and served in salads or salsas. To cook, they can be peeled and cooked in the same way as summer squash, or they can be baked in their skin. In Asian cooking, chayote is stir-fried or eaten in soups.

Above: Chayotes can be eaten raw, stir-fried or cooked in soups.

Baking Chayote

This is one of the simplest ways of cooking chayote.

1 Cut the chayote in half with a sharp knife. Brush the cut sides with a little vegetable or olive oil, then fill them with a vegetable stuffing or simply sprinkle them with a little salt and pepper.

2 Bake in a pre-heated oven at 190°C/375°F/Gas 5 for 25 minutes, or until tender all the way through when pierced with a skewer.

Preparing and Cooking

Luffa should always be cooked; it is never eaten raw. If the luffa is young, all you need to do is wash and slice it. As the luffa ripens, the ridges may become tough, in which case the ridges should be removed, leaving the skin in-between so that the luffa is striped green and white. If the skin is very tough, it is best to peel it off completely. Like cucumber, luffa should not be overcooked.

CHINESE BITTER MELONS

These are a common vegetable in all parts of Asia and go by many different names, including bitter gourd and bitter cucumber. Although grown in the West, they are only valued for their attractive foliage and unusual-shaped fruits.

Bitter melons are pale green and have distinctive warty, spiny skins. They have a rather sweet, fragrant smell, but the flesh itself is very bitter, especially when it is green and immature. The flavour mellows as the vegetable ripens and turns first pale green, then yellow-orange (when it is past its prime). In Asia, they are eaten very young.

Buying and Storing

A firm, green bitter melon will keep for 3–4 days, and should be allowed to ripen a little before use. Soft, yellowish melons should be used within a couple of days of purchase.

Preparing and Cooking

The bitter flavour can be an acquired taste, but it has a cooling effect in a hot climate. The flesh readily absorbs other flavours and its bitter tang can add a wonderful accent to dishes. Most Chinese recipes suggest halving the gourd, removing the pulp and then slicing before boiling for several minutes to remove the bitterness. The flesh can then be added to stir-fries or other Asian dishes.

Right: Chinese bitter melon has an unusual flavour, which can be an acquired taste.

Left: Young, fresh luffa can simply be washed and do not need to be peeled before cooking.

LUFFA

Also known as angled or ribbed luffa, silk gourd, silk squash or Chinese okra, this vegetable looks like a long, skinny courgette (zucchini) or a very large okra pod. The most common variety is ridged down its length and is dark green in colour. Although not so common, smooth luffa is larger and the shape is more cylindrical, with a slightly thicker base. It is much heavier than a ridged luffa, and is lighter in colour.

Luffa has a mild, delicate flavour, very similar to that of cucumber, and the two are interchangeable in most cooked dishes. Luffa is used mostly in stir-fries and soups. It goes particularly well with mild-tasting foods such as chicken, fish and shellfish, which do not overwhelm its delicate flavour.

Buying and Storing

Fresh luffa does not last long. It should be stored in the vegetable compartment of the refrigerator and used within two or three days of purchase before it begins to go limp.

WINTER MELON

This huge Asian vegetable can grow to 25cm/10in in diameter, and weigh more than 25kg/55lb. It has a subtle, delicate smell and tastes similar to courgettes.

Buying and Storing

Large melons are normally sliced and sold in sections. A whole winter melon will keep for weeks, but if it has been sliced open, it should be eaten as soon as possible as it will deteriorate rapidly.

Preparing and Cooking

Winter melon is always cooked before being eaten. The rind is removed, the seeds and fibres in the centre scooped out and the flesh cut into thin strips or wedges. It tastes good in stir-fries and soups. The juicy flesh readily absorbs other flavours, and is often cooked with strongly-flavoured ingredients such as dried shrimp and dried mushrooms.

VEGETABLE FRUITS

The fruits of the vegetable world are the most colourful, and probably most versatile of all vegetables. They are widely used to add colour, flavour and texture to numerous dishes.

TOMATOES

These vegetable fruits are related to potatoes, aubergines (eggplant) and sweet (bell) peppers and chillies, and all are members of the nightshade family. Some very poisonous members of this family may well have deterred our ancestors from taking to tomatoes. Indeed, the leaves of tomatoes are actually toxic and, if eaten, can result in very bad stomach-aches.

Tomatoes are native to western South America and a yellow variety was taken to Spain by the conquistadors in the 16th century. Spain was the first country to use them in cooking, stewing them with oil and seasoning. Italy soon followed suit, but elsewhere they were treated with suspicion. The first red tomatoes arrived in Europe in the 18th century, brought to Italy by two Jesuit priests. But it was not until the 19th century that they were accepted in northern Europe.

Today, along with onions, tomatoes are arguably the most important fresh ingredient used in the kitchen, and in Mediterranean cooking they are an essential ingredient. Along with garlic and the olive – whether in fruit or oil

Below: Brandywines are large beefsteak tomatoes with a rich flavour. They are good either used raw in salads or stuffed and baked.

Above: The purple beefsteak tomato is becoming increasingly popular, favoured for its attractive colour when sliced in salads.

Right: Flamme is a great all-round tomato with a wide variety of different culinary uses.

form – they create the basis of so many Italian, Spanish and Provençal recipes that it is hard to find any in which they are not included.

There are more than 7,000 different varieties of tomatoes, with new hybrids becoming available all the time. They come in a variety of shapes and sizes ranging from the huge, squat beefsteak tomatoes that measure about 10cm/4in across, to the common round salad tomato and the tiny cherry tomatoes that are not much bigger than a thumbnail.

BEEFSTEAK TOMATOES

These pumpkin-shaped tomatoes are large and often ridged. They are usually deep red or orange in colour. They have a good firm texture, plenty of flesh, and a sweet, mellow flavour due to their low acidity and often high water content. They are best eaten raw in salads and sandwiches or hollowed-out and stuffed and baked whole. The following are among the most popular beefsteak tomato varieties.

Brandywine These reddish pink fruits can weigh up to 900g/2lb and are noted for their succulent, rich flavour. Their balance of sweetness and acidity makes them a good choice for salads.

Dark Purple Beefsteak The classic beefsteak tomato, which can weigh between 350g/12oz and 450g/1lb is red. But specialities such as this dark purple variety are becoming popular.

Marmande These aromatic, fruity, ridged tomatoes are good for cooking and are frequently stuffed and baked.

ROUND OR SALAD TOMATOES

These are the most widely found tomatoes. They vary in size according to the variety and season. Sun-ripened tomatoes have the best flavour; however for year-round availability the fruit is often picked and ripened off the plant. Round tomatoes are good for everyday cooking. Add a pinch of sugar and take care to season the dish well to help overcome any weakness in flavour. Varieties include:

Flamme These spherical fruits are about the size of golf balls. They are excellent in salads, salsas and pasta sauces and can be dried successfully.

Gardener's Delight The flesh of these dark red tomatoes is meaty with a sweet yet tangy flavour.

Harbinger These are medium-sized tomatoes with a thin, smooth skin and a nice balanced flavour. They are good in salads.

Above: Harbingers are good for most culinary purposes.

Above: Supersweet 100 are a hybrid version of the popular salad tomato, Gardener's Delight.

CHERRY TOMATOES

These small, dainty tomatoes were once the prized treasures of gardeners but they are now widely available. They have a delightful sweet flavour and though more expensive than round tomatoes, are worth the extra for special occasions, whether in salads or cooking. Their skins can be a little tough, however. Varieties include:

Chadwick These bright red tomatoes measure about 2.5cm/1in across, and grow in clusters.

Phydra These pretty tomatoes have a sweet flavour and are popular with children. They make a good garnish.

Supersweet 100 These bright red hybrid tomatoes are about 2cm/¾in in diameter and have a sweet, rich, well-balanced flavour and firm texture.

PLUM TOMATOES

Richly flavoured with fewer seeds than regular tomatoes, this Italian-grown variety is usually recommended for cooking. It is the variety that is canned. Varieties of plum tomatoes include:

Roma These popular Italian plum tomatoes are scarlet in colour and each fruit weighs about 50g/2oz. If allowed to ripen on the bush, they have a good flavour with a firm, thick flesh and very few seeds. They are excellent for cooking and bottling.

San Marzano These tomatoes are very similar to Roma, but are larger and tastier. They are a good all-rounder, suitable for eating fresh in salads and sandwiches, but are also ideal for sun-drying or bottling.

YELLOW TOMATOES

These are exactly like red tomatoes – they may be round, plum or cherry-sized – except that they have bright yellow skins. Popular varieties of yellow tomatoes include:

Golden Sunrise These sunshine yellow tomatoes have a sweet and fruity flavour with a slight suggestion of citrus fruit.

Mirabelle These small yellow tomatoes have a sweet flavour. They are very versatile and may be used in salsas, salads and chutneys.

Pendulina This prolific, tumbling variety of cherry tomato bears bite-size fruits with a distinctive pointed tip. They have a sweet juicy flesh. They may also be red-orange in colour.

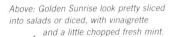

Above: Golden Sunrise look pretty sliced into salads or diced, with vinaigrette and a little chopped fresh mint.

Below: Orange Borgoin have a mild, sweet flavour.

ORANGE TOMATOES

These mild tomatoes have a sweet, delicate flavour and a low acidity. Like the red round tomatoes, they have quite a high seed ratio, although the seeds are often smaller than in red tomatoes. Orange tomatoes are particularly good in salads and soups and they make very pretty garnishes for all kinds of dishes. Popular varieties include:

Orange Borgoin These juicy tomatoes are similar in size and colour to apricots. They have a superb mild, fruity, sweet flavour.

Mini Orange These small round fruits, which are about 2.5–4cm/1–1¼in in diameter, are notable for their brilliant orange colour. They are an excellent addition to salads and they also make pretty garnishes.

Left: Roma tomatoes have a good flavour and few seeds, so are favoured for cooking.

GREEN TOMATOES

The term green tomato was originally used for the tangy, unripened tomatoes used for relishes and chutneys. However, ripe green tomatoes are now also available. They have a bright green skin and flesh, and a good flavour. They can be added to salads or used as a garnish. Varieties include:

Green Grape These green cherry tomatoes look decorative in salads.

Green Zebra These tomatoes have dark green stripes on a yellowish-green background and are about 7cm/3in in diameter. Their emerald-green flesh has a sweet/spicy flavour and a subtle tang.

VINE TOMATOES

These are just the same as ordinary tomatoes but are sold still attached to their stalk or vine. They have a good flavour and aromatic quality usually only found with home-grown tomatoes.

PEAR TOMATOES

This small category includes some of the most flavoursome tomatoes of all. They are pear-shaped and are generally quite small. Varieties include:

Red Pear These are full of flavour whether freshly picked or lightly cooked. The small fruits weigh around 25g/1oz and look like tiny light bulbs. The yellow variety does not have quite such a rich, sweet flavour.

Yellow Cocktail These bright yellow miniature tomatoes have a good flavour. They are good for salads and kebabs.

Buying and Storing

Ideally tomatoes should ripen on the plant so that their flavour develops naturally. Consequently, home-grown tomatoes are best, followed by organic ones, grown and sold locally. Vine-ripened tomatoes are noticeably sweeter with a more intense flavour.

Left: Green Zebra has an unusual stripy skin.

When buying tomatoes, look at the leafy tops; the fresher they look the better they will be. Buy locally grown beef-steak or cherry tomatoes for salads and plum tomatoes for rich sauces. Paler tomatoes or those tinged with green will redden if kept in a brown paper bag or the salad drawer of the refrigerator, but if you intend to use them straightaway, buy bright red specimens. Over-ripe tomatoes, where the skin has split and they seem to be bursting with juice, are excellent in soups. However, always check for any sign of mould or decay as this will spoil the flavour of the dish.

Cooking

When using tomatoes for salads and pizza toppings, slice them across rather than downwards. To make tomato wedges first cut them in half, then cut each half into two or three wedges, depending on the size of the tomato. When used in salads, the natural astringency of tomatoes means that they need nothing more than a sprinkling of fruity extra virgin olive oil and a little salt and freshly ground black pepper.

Above: Yellow Cocktails are tiny and pear-shaped.

Peeling Tomatoes

To loosen the skins of tomatoes and make them easier to remove, the tomatoes should be briefly submerged in boiling water.

1 Using a sharp knife, cut out the green stalk and core of the tomato, then make a shallow cross in the skin at the base of each tomato.

2 Place the tomatoes in a bowl and pour over enough boiling water to cover. Leave to stand for about 30 seconds, then drain and leave to cool slightly.

3 Pull away the loosened skin from the tomatoes. Discard the skins and chop the flesh as required.

PEPPERS AND CHILLIES

These are both members of the capsicum family. From a culinary point of view, the only difference between them is in their heat: chillies are hot and peppers much milder.

PEPPERS/BELL PEPPERS

These are known by various names, including sweet peppers, bell peppers and bullnose peppers. They come in a variety of colours and, to a large extent, this determines the flavour. However, sweet peppers are always mild, and never hot.

Green peppers are the least mature and have a fresh "raw" flavour. Red peppers are ripened green peppers and are distinctly sweeter. Yellow and orange peppers taste more or less like red peppers although perhaps slightly less sweet, and if you have a fine palate you may be able to detect a difference. Black peppers have a similar flavour to green peppers, and when they are cooked they turn green; so if you buy them for their dramatic colour, they are best used in salads. In Greece and other parts of southern Europe, longer, slimmer peppers are available, which have a more pronounced sweet and pungent flavour.

Left: Dark purple-black peppers lose their rather unusual and dramatic colour when cooked.

Buying and Storing

Peppers should look glossy, feel firm and have a crisp, juicy bite. Avoid any that look dull or whose skins wrinkle when pushed. Peppers can be stored for a few days in the salad drawer of the refrigerator.

Preparing and Cooking

To prepare stuffed peppers, cut off the top, and set it aside to replace when the pepper has been stuffed. Cut away the inner core and pith and shake out the seeds. The seeds and core are easily removed when halving, quartering or slicing the pepper.

There are countless ways of cooking peppers. Sliced peppers can be fried with onions and garlic in olive oil and then braised with tomatoes and herbs. Peppers are also wonderful roasted, or cooked with other vegetables such as onions, garlic, tomatoes and aubergines (eggplant).

Roasting Peppers

This gives a wonderful sweet, smoky flavour to the peppers.

1 Roast the peppers under a hot grill (broiler) for 10–15 minutes, turning regularly, until the skin is charred and blistered. Place in a polythene bag and leave until cool.

2 Carefully peel off the skin with your fingers. It will come away easily. Whole peppers, halves or quarters can be roasted and peeled in this way.

Left: Brightly coloured peppers are delicious either raw or cooked.

CHILLIES

The substance which makes the chilli hot is a volatile oil called capsaicin. This differs not only from one type to another, but also from plant to plant, depending on the growing conditions. The more the plant has to struggle to survive in terms of light, water and soil, the more capsaicin will be produced. It is not possible to give definitive values for heat, but the following is a guide.

Anaheim Chilli
This long thin chilli has a blunt end and is named after the Californian town. It can be red or green and has quite a mild, sweet taste.

Ancho Chilli/Pepper
These look like tiny sweet (bell) peppers. They are mild enough to taste their underlying sweetness.

Right: Cherry hot chillies are best peeled before use.

Below: Birds-eye chillies are exceedingly hot and fiery.

Left: The anaheim chilli can be red or green.

Right: Peppery Jalapeño chillies can be stuffed and roasted, then eaten whole.

Bird's-eye/Bird Chilli These small red chillies are fiery hot. They are also known in some places as piquin chillies.

Cherry Hot Chillies These pungent chillies have thick walls and look like rather large cherries. They have a sweetish flavour and make very good pickles. The skins can be tough so they are best peeled.

Early Jalapeño This popular American chilli starts off dark green and gradually turns to red.

Fresno These plump cylindrical chillies with tapered ends are most often sold red, though you will sometimes find green or yellow ones. They look similar to jalapeños and can be substituted for them if necessary.

Habanero These extremely fiery, lantern-shaped chillies have a wonderful, fruity flavour, and a surprisingly delicate aroma. When cooking with habaneros, a little goes a long way.

Hot Gold Spike This large pale yellow-green fruit is grown in the south-western United States. It is very hot so is principally for cooking.

Poblano This is a small, dark green chilli. They are mostly mild but you can get the rogue fiery one, so beware if eating whole.

Red Chilli These are long, rather wrinkled chillies which are green at first and then gradually ripen to red. They are of variable hotness and, because their shape is so long and thin, they are rather fiddly to prepare.

Below: Poblano chillies are eaten as they are in Spain, grilled or roasted and served whole.

Scotch Bonnets These pretty chillies are often confused with habaneros, which they resemble very closely. Scotch Bonnets are probably the hottest chillies of all and should be used with great caution. It is advisable to seed them and remove the pith where most of the capsaicin resides before use.

Below: Scotch bonnets are grown in Jamaica and are the principal ingredient in jerk seasoning.

Preparing Chillies

The capsaicin in chillies is most concentrated in the pith inside the pod and this, together with the seeds, should be cut away unless you want maximum heat. Capsaicin irritates the skin and especially the eyes, so take care when preparing chillies; either wear gloves or wash your hands thoroughly after handling chillies. If you rub your eyes, even if you have washed your hands, it will be painful.

2 Cut off the stalk from both halves of the chilli, removing a thin slice containing the stalk from the top of the chilli at the same time.

4 Cut out any white membrane from the centre of each chilli half, keeping the knife blade close to the flesh. Discard the membrane.

1 If the chilli is to be stuffed, and kept whole, merely slit it without separating the two halves. For all other purposes, hold the chilli at the stalk end, and, with a sharp knife, cut it in half lengthways.

3 Carefully scrape out all the seeds and discard them. Remove the core with a small sharp knife.

5 Slice each piece of chilli into strips. If diced chilli is needed, bunch the strips together and cut across them.

Serrano Chilli This extremely hot chilli is long and slender, and about 4cm/1½in long. Serranos are the classic Mexican green chilli, and are an important ingredient in guacamole. The flavour is clean and crisp, with a suggestion of citrus. They dry well.

Yellow Wax Pepper Pale yellow to green, these chillies can vary from mild to hot. They really do look waxy, rather like candles. It is not necessary to peel them and they are often used raw in salads.

Left: Serrano chillies are usually used while still bright green, but they ripen to red.

Buying and Storing

Some fresh chillies look wrinkled even in their prime and therefore this is not a good guide to their freshness. They should, however, be unblemished; always avoid any which are soft or bruised. To store chillies, wrap them in kitchen paper, place in a plastic bag and keep in the salad compartment of the refrigerator for a week or more. Chillies can also be frozen successfully: there is no need to blanch them if you plan to use them fairly soon. To dry chillies, thread them on a string, hang them in a warm place until dry, then crush or leave whole and store in a sealed jar in a cool, dark place.

Cooking

The pith and seeds should usually be removed before cooking, as this is where most of the heat resides. Depending on the type and heat of the chilli, they can be used, either raw or cooked, to add spice and flavour to dishes or be used whole, either grilled (broiled), roasted or deep-fried, or stuffed and roasted. In general, when using chillies, err on the side of caution and use sparingly as too much can render a dish inedible.

Chillies play a vital role in many cuisines around the world, including Mexican, Caribbean, Creole, Chinese, Asian, and Indian. Finely chopped raw chilli can be added to salsas and salads and, in Thailand, dried and pickled chillies are used as condiments. Sliced or chopped chillies, cooked in curries and spicy stews and casseroles, are an indispensable flavouring ingredient.

Left: Purple aubergines are the most common variety in the West.

AUBERGINES/EGGPLANT

These vegetable fruits are cultivated and cooked all over the world and feature in a multitude of different dishes. There are many different varieties of aubergines, differing in colour, size and shape, according to their country of origin. Small ivory-white and plump aubergines look rather like large eggs (hence their name in the United States – eggplant). Pretty striped aubergines may be either purple or pink and flecked with white irregular stripes. In Asia, the most common type of aubergine is tubular rather than ovoid and is usually straight or slightly curved. As a rule, Asian aubergines are much smaller and more slender than Western varieties and some are really tiny. In Thailand, there are aubergines that are not much bigger than peas. Colours range from black, to purple to orange, green and white. They have a tender, slightly sweet flesh.

The majority of aubergines found in stores and supermarkets are either a glossy purple or almost black and can be long and slim or fat like zeppelins. All have a similar bland yet smoky flavour and the flesh is spongy to touch when raw, but soft after cooking.

Buying and Storing

Aubergines should feel heavy and quite firm to the touch, and have glossy, unblemished skins. They will keep well in the salad drawer of the refrigerator for up to two weeks.

Cooking Aubergines

Aubergine slices can be fried in olive oil, as they are or coated in batter – both being popular in Italy and Greece as a starter. Alternatively, to make a purée first prick the aubergine all over with a fork and then roast in a moderately hot oven for about 30 minutes until tender.

Scoop out the flesh and mix with finely chopped spring onions, lemon juice and olive oil. For moussaka and other dishes where aubergines are layered with other ingredients, fry slices in olive oil.

Left: Aubergines come in a multitude of different shapes, sizes and colours.

Salting Aubergines

In the past, salting aubergines before cooking was advised to reduce their bitterness, but today's varieties are rarely bitter. However, aubergines tend to absorb large quantities of oil when frying and salting helps to reduce this.

To salt aubergines, cut into slices, about 1cm/½in thick, for fried slices, or into segments. Place in a strainer and sprinkle generously with salt. Leave to stand for about one hour, then rinse well and squeeze gently to remove excess moisture. Pat dry with kitchen paper before frying.

OLIVES

Olive trees have been grown in the Mediterranean since biblical times, when they were brought there from the East by the Romans. A wide variety of olives is cultivated all over the Mediterranean. The majority are destined to be pressed into oil (nearly 20 per cent of their weight is oil) but some are kept as table olives to be salted, pickled or marinated, and served as part of an *antipasto* or used in cooking. All olives have a high calorific content and are rich in iron, potassium and vitamins.

There are two main types of olive: green and black. The difference in colour in olives is not a matter of type, but simply when the olive is picked. Green olives are picked while immature in October or November. They have a sharper flavour and crunchier texture than black olives, which continue to ripen on the tree and are not harvested until December. Pale and dark brown olives are also grown in Italy, Sardinia, Morocco and Cyprus. From California there is a popular straw-coloured olive.

Spanish olives The most popular of the Spanish olives are called queens. These are normally sold whole. The Spanish olives most

Right: Black olives are more mature than the green ones.

Below: Wrinkled black olives from Liguria have a strong salty flavour.

Left: Green, unripe olives have a delicious, slightly sharp flavour.

frequently used for stuffing with pimiento, almonds or anchovies, are the manzanillas, which is a small and succulent green olive.

Italian olives Among the best Italian olives are the small shiny black Gaeta olives from Liguria and the wrinkled black olives from Lazio. Sardinian olives are semi-ripened and are brown or purplish in colour. The largest olives come from Apulia and Sicily, where giant, green specimens are grown. These are sometimes pitted and stuffed.

Greek olives The best Greek olives are black, including Kalamatas. They are enjoyed by themselves or added to tomato, cucumber and onion salads.

Buying and Storing

Cured olives vary enormously in flavour. The best olives are sold loose and you can therefore ask to sample them before buying. They can be kept in an airtight container in the refrigerator for up to a week. Alternatively, put olives in a jar of olive oil, or a mixture of olive oil, vinegar and water, and keep in the refrigerator or a cool place for up to 4 weeks. Always buy olives with pits as pitted olives tend to have a very poor flavour.

Culinary Uses

Olives can be served on their own, as a garnish or as a topping for pizza. There are numerous recipes where olives are an essential ingredient, such as *caponata*. Sicilian *caponata* is a dome-shaped salad of fried aubergines with celery, onions, capers, tomatoes and green olives, while the Ligurian dish of the same name consists of stale biscuits or bread soaked in olive oil and

Above: Kalamatas are considered among the best of Greek olives.

Below: Queens are the most popular Spanish olives.

topped with a mixture of chopped olives, garlic, anchovies and oregano. Olives combine well with Mediterranean ingredients such as tomatoes, aubergines, capers and anchovies. The Italian *pasta di olive* (olive paste) is made from pounded green, or more usually black, olives and can be bought in jars. It is very salty and rich, so a little goes a long way.

Below: Large green olives from Apulia and Sicily are often stuffed with pimiento.

Above: Avocados are a good source of protein, carbohydrate, vitamins and other valuable nutrients. They are also one of the few fruits or vegetables that contain fat.

AVOCADOS

The avocado has been known by several names, including alligator pear and butter pear. It earned the title butter pear because of its consistency, but alligator pear was the original Spanish name. It is a New World fruit, native to Mexico, but didn't become a popular food in Europe until the middle of the twentieth century, when modern transportation meant that growers in California, who started cultivating them in the middle of the nineteenth century, could market avocados worldwide.

There are four main varieties: Hass, the purple-black knobbly avocado, which is considered by many to have the superior flavour; Ettinger and Fuerte, which are pear-shaped and have smooth green skins; and the Nabal, which is rounder in shape. The Hass has golden-yellow flesh, while the others have pale green to yellow flesh.

Buying and Storing

A perfect avocado should have a clean, unblemished skin. If ripe it should "give" slightly if squeezed gently in the hand, but not so much that it actually feels soft. Avocados available in stores and supermarkets are often unripe but, if stored at room temperature, they will ripen in 4–7 days. Once ripe, they will keep well in the refrigerator for a few days. If you need to ripen an avocado quickly, place it in a brown paper bag with a banana.

Serving

Avocados are delicious served very simply. They can be halved, stoned and served with vinaigrette; or filled with prawns (shrimp), chopped tomatoes and cucumber, or sour cream potato salad. They may be thinly sliced and served with slices of tomato and mozzarella, sprinkled with olive oil and lemon juice to make the classic Italian tricolore salad. They are also very good chopped and added to salads or salsas, or puréed or mashed to make a rich dressing or dip. In Mexico, where avocados grow in abundance, the finely chopped vegetable fruit is used to garnish tacos and enchiladas and is an essential ingredient in guacamole – a mixture of avocados, tomatoes, garlic and hot, spicy chillies.

BREADFRUIT

This is actually the name for a tropical tree that grows on the islands of the South Pacific ocean. The fruit that grows on the tree is about the size of a small melon and has a rough rind and pale, mealy flesh.

Preparing and Cooking

The fruit should be peeled and the core removed. It can then be treated in the same way as a potato; the flesh may be boiled, baked or fried. Breadfruit is a staple food for the people of the Pacific Islands, who bake the flesh, or dry and grind it to make biscuits (cookies), bread and desserts. Breadfruit has a slightly sweet flavour and quite a soft texture when ripe.

Preparing Avocados

Avocado flesh discolours once exposed to air, so always sprinkle cut avocado with lemon juice.

1 Run a small, sharp knife all the way around the fruit, starting at the top and cutting right in until the knife touches the stone.

2 Gently prise the two halves apart using the flat part of the knife.

3 Push the knife blade into the stone, twist and lift it away. Remove any brown skin from the stone that remains on the avocado flesh.

4 To make slices, cut through the flesh, then strip off the peel.

Above: Outside the Caribbean, fresh ackee is rarely available and cooks have to make do with the canned vegetable.

ACKEE

This tropical fruit is used in a variety of savoury dishes, mainly of Caribbean origin, where the fruit is very popular. The fruit itself is bright red and, when ripe, bursts open to reveal three large black seeds and a soft, creamy flesh, resembling scrambled eggs. This flesh has a slightly lemony flavour and, in Jamaica is traditionally served with saltfish to make the national dish. It is also used to add flavour to a variety of vegetable and bean dishes.

Ackee should never be bought when underripe, because certain parts of the fruit are toxic. It is not widely available outside the Caribbean, however, although the fruit can be bought canned – and indeed most recipes call for canned ackee, which is an excellent substitute for the fresh fruit. The canned ackee needs very little cooking.

Preparing Plantain and Green Banana

Plantains and green bananas are inedible raw and must be cooked before eating them. If the fruit is unripe, the skin can be hard to peel.

1 Using a sharp knife, cut the fruit into short, manageable lengths.

2 Slit the skin along the natural ridge of each piece of fruit.

3 Gently ease the skin away from the flesh and pull the skin until it peels off completely. Once peeled, the fruit can be sliced horizontally or into lengths and then roasted or fried.

If cooking the fruit in their skins, slit the skin lengthways along the sides and place in a large pan of salted water. Bring to the boil and simmer for about 20 minutes. The peel can easily be removed once the fruit is cool.

Plantains and green bananas both have an excellent flavour. They can be either roasted or fried and then served simply with salt. If boiled, they can be sliced and served in a simple salad. If making crisps (US chips), use a mandolin or a potato peeler to produce the thinnest slices.

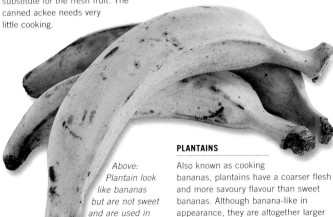

Above: Plantain look like bananas but are not sweet and are used in savoury dishes.

PLANTAINS

Also known as cooking bananas, plantains have a coarser flesh and more savoury flavour than sweet bananas. Although banana-like in appearance, they are altogether larger and heavier-looking, and must always be cooked before eating. They are normally eaten as a first or main course. Plantains can vary in colour from the unripe fruit, which is green, to yellow to a mottled black colour, which is when the fruit is completely ripe. They are delicious fried and are good combined with sweetcorn (corn) in soup.

GREEN BANANAS

These are widely used in African and Caribbean cooking – they should not be confused with the greenish bananas you normally find in supermarkets, which are eating bananas just waiting to ripen. If you need green bananas for a recipe, look out for them in Caribbean or African supermarkets and stores. They have a similar flavour to plantains.

SALAD VEGETABLES

The availability of salad leaves has grown enormously in recent years. Some are lettuces, while others belong to vegetable families. Their common feature is that they are eaten raw (although some can also be cooked).

LETTUCES

Lettuces have been cultivated for thousands of years. They were popular among the Romans, who are reputed to have introduced them to Britain. There are hundreds of different varieties, which can be divided into two main categories: the round lettuce and the cos lettuce. Lettuce contains vitamins A, C and E and the minerals potassium, iron and calcium.

ROUND LETTUCES

Sometimes called head or cabbage lettuces, round lettuces are spherical and have cabbage-like heads. Varieties include:

Butterheads These are the classic lettuces seen in kitchen gardens. They have a pale heart and floppy, loosely packed leaves. Butterheads have a pleasant flavour as long as they are really fresh.

Crispheads Crisp lettuces such as iceberg have an excellent crunchy texture and will keep their vitality long after butterheads have faded and died. Their flavour is not so pleasant, however.

Looseheads These are non-hearting lettuces with loose leaves and include lollo rosso and lollo biondo, oakleaf lettuce and red salad bowl. Although they do not have a remarkable flavour they look superb, especially when mixed with other salad leaves.

COS/ROMAINE LETTUCES

The name cos is derived from the Greek island where the lettuce was found by the Romans. Romaine is the name used by the French and also in the United States.

Above: Lamb's lettuce, despite its name, is not really a true lettuce.

Cos Considered the most delicious lettuce, this has a firm texture and a faintly nutty and sweet flavour. It is the correct lettuce to use when preparing a classic Caesar salad.

Little gems In appearance little gems are something like a baby cos crossed with a tightly furled butterhead. They have firm hearts and are enjoyed for their distinct soft flavour.

LAMB'S LETTUCE/CORN SALAD

This popular winter leaf does not actually belong to the lettuce family, although it is a lovely addition to the salad bowl. Called *mâche* in France, it has spoon-shaped leaves and an excellent nutty flavour that goes well with other milder-tasting leaves.

Buying and Storing

The best lettuces are those picked fresh from the garden. The next best thing is to buy from an organic farm shop or pick-your-own. If you buy lettuce – either pre-packed or from the shelf – it must be really fresh. Avoid any lettuce with limp, bruised or yellowing leaves and eat as soon as possible after purchasing.

*Above:
(Clockwise from top left) Cos, lollo rosso, curly endive, iceberg and butterhead lettuces are all delicately flavoured.*

OTHER SALAD LEAVES

As well as the lettuce family, there are a number of other delicious salad leaves.

ROCKET/ARUGULA

This wonderful salad leaf has become very fashionable in recent years. Rocket has dark green, elongated, indented leaves, rather like those of the dandelion, and has a hot, pungent, peppery flavour. It adds zest and flavour to any green salad and can also be enjoyed on its own with a simple olive oil and balsamic vinegar dressing and a few shavings of Parmesan cheese. As well as using as a salad leaf, rocket can be tossed with hot pasta or added to pasta sauces or risotto and cooked like spinach. However, cooking tends to diminish its wonderfully delicate, fresh and tantalizing flavour.

Buying and Storing

Home-grown rocket has a much better flavour but supermarket alternatives make a good substitute. Buy fresh green leaves that show no sign of wilting. Store in the refrigerator but use within a few days. Pre-packaged leaves tend to last longer than loose leaves.

Above: Rocket has a peppery flavour and is a good addition to a mixed green salad.

WATERCRESS

This is perhaps the most robustly flavoured of all the salad leaves and a few sprigs are ideal for perking up a salad of milder-tasting leaves. It is also delicious paired with fresh orange. It has a distinctive "raw" flavour, which is both peppery and slightly pungent, and this, together with its bright green leaves, makes it a popular garnish for cooked dishes. It is not widely available in the United States.

Buying and Storing

Choose fresh-looking leaves that show no signs of wilting. Store in the refrigerator and use within a few days of purchase.

Preparing and Cooking

Discard any yellow leaves and remove thick stalks that will be too coarse for salads or soups. Small sprigs can be added to salads. For soups and purées, either blend the cress raw, or cook very briefly in stock, milk or water. Cooking inevitably destroys some of the valuable nutrients, but cooked watercress has a less harsh flavour than raw, while still retaining its characteristic peppery taste.

Above: Watercress has a wonderful peppery flavour and is very nutritious.

WINTER CRESS

Also known as land cress, winter cress is often grown instead of watercress and it has a similar, possibly more assertive, flavour. Winter cress is a good source of vitamins and minerals.

Buying and Storing

Only buy very fresh-looking cress, with dark leaves. Avoid any with wilted or yellow leaves. It does not keep well. Stand the leaves in a jug (pitcher) of cold water and store in the refrigerator or a cool place, where it will keep for a few days.

MUSTARD AND CRESS

These delicate little sprouts are often grown together, to provide spicy greenery as a garnish for salads. They are available all year round. Mustard seedlings germinate 3–4 days sooner than the cress, so if you buy mustard and cress from the supermarket, or grow your own on the windowsill, initially only the mustard seedlings will show. They are always sold in tubs or punnets of earth. Mustard and cress are often enjoyed in sandwiches, either served on buttered bread, or with avocado or cucumber added. With its faint spicy flavour, cress can perk up a green salad, and it is also excellent in a tomato salad, dressed simply with olive oil and tarragon vinegar.

Below: Cress is widely used in sandwiches and is particularly good teamed with chopped egg and mayonnaise.

Below: Radicchio was developed from wild chicory.

CHICORY AND RADICCHIO

Chicory, radicchio, endive and escarole are all related to each other and when they are tasted together you can easily detect a similarity between them. Their names are occasionally interchanged: chicory is often referred to as Belgian or French endive and French and Belgian chicorée is the English curly endive.

CHICORY

Chicory was originally grown in Europe for its root, which was added to coffee, but during the 18th century, a Belgian discovered that the white leaves could be eaten. Chicory can be eaten raw, but is commonly baked, stir-fried or poached. To eat raw, separate the leaves and serve with fruit such as oranges or grapefruit which counteract a slight bitterness.

RADICCHIO

Looking rather like a small lettuce with deep wine-red leaves and striking cream ribs, radicchio owes its very striking foliage colours to careful shading. If it is grown completely in the dark, the leaves are marbled pink, and those that have been exposed to some light can be patched with a green or copper colour. Its flavour tends to be bitter but contrasts well with sweeter green salad leaves such as curly endive, chicory or rocket. Radicchio can also be eaten as a hot vegetable, either quartered and grilled (broiled) with olive oil, or stuffed with a mixture of breadcrumbs, anchovies, capers and olives and baked – although the leaves turn a disappointing dark green when cooked.

CURLY ENDIVE AND ESCAROLE

Although they look delicate, curly endive and escarole are robust salad ingredients both in terms of flavour and texture. The curly endive looks like a green frizzy mop and the escarole is broad-leafed; both have the same distinct bitter flavour. Serve mixed together with a well-flavoured dressing. This dampens down the bitter taste but gives the salad a pleasant bite. They are also good mixed with milder salad leaves.

Right: Curly endive has pretty leaves and makes an attractive addition to salads.

Baking Chicory

Chicory is delicious served hot, baked in a creamy sauce.

1 Using a sharp knife, remove the core at the base of the chicory. Discard any wilted or damaged leaves, then rinse and pat dry.

2 Blanch or sauté the chicory for 3–4 minutes. Wrap each head in a slice of Parma ham and place side by side, in a single layer in a greased ovenproof dish.

3 Pour over a white sauce or blend about 75g/3oz mascarpone cheese with 250ml/8fl oz/1 cup vegetable stock. Top with grated cheese and bake until golden and bubbling.

Above: English cucumber is the most popular variety for salads.

CUCUMBERS

These rightly belong with the squashes but they are so suited to salads that their culinary home is here. There are a number of varieties.

English cucumber These popular cucumbers have fewer seeds and a thinner skin than the ridged cucumber.

Gherkins These are tiny cucumbers with bumpy, almost warty skins and they are mostly pickled in vinegar and eaten with cold meats or chopped into mayonnaise to accompany oily fish, for example.

Kirbys These small cucumbers are available in the United States, and are used for pickling.

Ridged cucumbers These are smaller than most cucumbers with more seeds and a thick bumpy skin. You can buy them throughout France, but they are not widely available elsewhere.

Buying and Storing

Cucumbers should be firm from top to bottom. Remove the plastic packaging once you've started a cucumber. Discard once it begins to go soggy.

Preparing

Cucumbers are normally served raw. Wash cucumbers if you don't intend to peel them. Citrus peelers can remove strips of peel to give an attractive striped effect when sliced. Many cucumbers sold in Britain and the United States are waxed to give a glossy finish. These should always be peeled. Continental cucumbers are less likely to be waxed and the skin can be eaten.

RADISHES

These have a peppery flavour that, with the really strong varieties, can almost be felt in the nostrils as you bite into them. Their pungency depends not only on the variety, but also on the soil in which they are grown. Freshly harvested radishes have the most pronounced flavour and crisp texture. There are many different varieties worldwide.

Red radishes These small, turnip-shaped, red orbs are available all year round and have a pink skin, sometimes paler or white at the roots, and firm white flesh with a crisp, juicy bite. Their peppery flavour is milder in the spring and they are almost always eaten raw in salads or along with other raw vegetables as crudités.

French breakfast radishes These pretty radishes are red and white and slightly more elongated than the red radish. They also tend to be milder and are popular either eaten on their own or served with other raw vegetables as crudités.

Mooli or daikon radishes

Sometimes known as the Oriental radish, the mooli is a smooth-skinned, long, white radish that is much larger than Western radishes. Those bought in the shops have a mild flavour, less peppery than the red radish. They can be eaten raw, pickled, or stir-fried.

Buying and Storing

Buy red radishes that are firm with crisp leaves. If at all possible buy moolis which still have their leaves; this is a good indication of their freshness as the leaves wilt quickly. The leaves should be green and lively and the skins clear with no bruises or blemishes. They can be stored in the refrigerator for a few days.

Preparing and Serving

Red radishes need only be washed before being sliced or eaten whole by themselves or in salads. You can make a feature of them, but slicing into a salad of, for example, oranges and walnuts. To use moolis in a stir-fry, cut into slices and add to the dish for the last few minutes of cooking. They add a pleasant flavour and a wonderfully juicy, crunchy texture.

Above: Red radishes have a crisp, peppery bite.

Above: Mooli are good grated into salads.

MUSHROOMS AND FUNGI

These have always had a connection with the supernatural – circles of mushrooms appear inexplicably overnight in "fairy rings" and, in myth and folklore, pixies and elves have regularly been depicted sitting on or among mushrooms and toadstools.

Many types of mushrooms and fungi are either poisonous or hallucinogenic and their poisons have regularly been distilled for murderous reasons throughout history. The use of the terms mushroom, to mean edible species and toadstool, to mean those considered poisonous, has no scientific basis and there is no simple rule for distinguishing between the two.

WHITE MUSHROOMS

These are the most popular of the cultivated varieties of mushroom and are widely available in stores and supermarkets. When they are very young and tiny, they are sold as button mushrooms. The slightly larger ones are known as closed-cap mushrooms, while larger ones still are open capped or open cup mushrooms. They have ivory or white caps with pinky-beige gills which darken as they mature. All types have a pleasant, unassuming flavour.

Right: Button mushrooms are very young cultivated mushrooms.

Below: Chestnut mushrooms have a meatier texture than white mushrooms.

Below: Wide, flat field mushrooms are excellent for stuffing and baking.

Buying and Storing

It is easy to see whether or not button mushrooms are fresh – their caps should be clean and white, without bruises or blemishes. The longer they stay on the shelves, the darker and more discoloured the caps become, while the gills underneath turn from pale pink to darker brown.

If possible when buying mushrooms, use the paper bags provided by the supermarket. Polythene bags make mushrooms sweat in their own heat, and they eventually turn slippery and unappetizing. If you buy mushrooms in cellophane-wrapped cartons, transfer them to a paper bag and store in the refrigerator.

CHESTNUT MUSHROOMS

These have a thicker stem and a darker, pale brown cap. They have a more pronounced "mushroomy" flavour and a meatier texture than white mushrooms.

FIELD MUSHROOMS

These are actually the wild relative of the cultivated mushroom and when cooked have a wonderful aroma. Flat mushrooms, although indistinguishable from field mushrooms in appearance, have probably been cultivated but also have an excellent flavour.

Buying and Storing

During the autumn (fall), field mushrooms are sometimes available in farm shops. Since they are likely to have been picked recently, they should be fresh. Unless you intend to stuff them, don't worry if they are broken in places as you will be slicing them anyway. Use as soon as possible.

Preparing and Cooking

Mushrooms should not be washed but simply wiped with a damp cloth or a piece of kitchen paper if necessary. Unless the skins are very discoloured, it should not be necessary to peel them. Trim the stalk bases of field mushrooms and button mushrooms if necessary.

Mushrooms are largely composed of water and shrink noticeably during cooking. They also take up a lot of fat as they cook, so it is best to use butter or a good olive oil for frying. Fry them over a moderately high heat so that as they shrink the water evaporates and they don't stew in their own juice. For the same reason do not fry too many mushrooms at once in the same pan.

Field mushrooms can be used for stuffing, soups or any mushroom recipe. They will colour soups brown, but the flavour will be extremely good. When stuffing mushrooms, fry the caps on both sides for a few minutes. The stalks can be chopped and added to the stuffing, or used for soups or stocks.

OYSTER MUSHROOMS

These ear-shaped fungi grow on rotting wood. They grow in the same place in successive years, so if you are gathering them in the wild, remember where you picked them. However, they are now widely cultivated and available in most supermarkets. Cap, gills and stem are all the same colour, which can be greyish brown, pink or yellow. The cap is shaped rather like a fan, and larger specimens may have fluted edges. Delicious both in flavour and texture, they are softer than the button mushroom when cooked but seem more substantial.

Above: Shiitake mushrooms have a firm, meaty texture.

Buying and Storing

Fresh specimens should be erect and lively looking with clear gills and smooth caps. They are often sold packed in plastic boxes with cellophane wrapping and will go soft if left on the shelf for too long. Once purchased, remove them from the plastic packaging and use as soon as possible; or transfer to a paper bag and store in the refrigerator.

Below: Oyster mushrooms have a wonderful flavour and texture.

Preparing and Cooking

Oyster mushrooms rarely need trimming at all, but if they are large, tear rather than cut them into pieces. In very large specimens, the stems can be tough and should be discarded. Fry in butter until tender – they take less time to cook than white mushrooms. Do not overcook oyster mushrooms, or the flavour will be lost and the soft texture will become more rubbery.

SHIITAKE MUSHROOMS

These Japanese fungi are a variety of tree mushrooms (called *take* in Japan, the *shii* being the hardwood tree from which they are harvested). In appearance they resemble large, brown button mushrooms, and they have a meaty, rather acid flavour and a distinct slippery texture.

Dried Mushrooms

Many varieties of mushrooms are available dried. They have a rich, intense flavour and are a useful store-cupboard (pantry) standby. Once they have been soaked and reconstituted, they can be stir-fried, braised, steamed or added to soups, stews, sauces and risottos. Dried mushrooms often require longer cooking than fresh ones.

To reconstitute dried mushrooms, soak them in boiling water for 20–30 minutes, depending on the variety and size of the mushroom, until tender. Drain and rinse well to remove any grit or dirt.

Shiitake mushrooms, though once only found in Asian stores, are now widely available in most supermarkets.

Buying and Storing

Select firm specimens and store them in a paper bag in the refrigerator. Eat within three days of purchase.

Preparation and Cooking

Clean shiitake mushrooms as you would button mushrooms, but remove and discard the stalk, which is tough. Whole or sliced caps can be sautéed, used in stir-fries, cooked in braised dishes or added to soups. Because of their robust texture, shiitake need a slightly longer cooking time than button mushrooms, but they should not be cooked for too long otherwise they may begin to toughen. To serve shiitake mushrooms in a salad, boil them briefly in water or stock, then toss in a French dressing.

WILD MUSHROOMS AND FUNGI

Mushroom gathering, a seasonal event throughout Eastern Europe, Italy and France, is becoming a popular pastime in Britain, too. The French are particularly enthusiastic; in autumn (fall) whole families drive to secret locations to comb the ground for prizes like shaggy ink caps or ceps. Wild mushrooms are increasingly sold in supermarkets in autumn and this is the best way to obtain them, if you are reluctant to risk picking your own.

BAY BOLETUS

The bay boletus shares many qualities with the cep. Young specimens are particularly good. If picking your own, wipe the caps of any wet specimens and let them dry before cooking. They can be thinly sliced and eaten raw, or used in soups, stews and wild mushroom dishes.

CEP

Mushroom hunters regard this mushroom as a great prize; it has a wonderful nutty flavour and is extremely versatile. Small ceps are considered best, and good specimens are heavy for

Left: Chanterelles look pretty and have a wonderful flavour.

Below: Ceps are best when small and tight.

their size and have an almost leafy richness when eaten raw. Larger ceps are best cooked in butter with a few fresh chopped herbs. Clean the caps well and cut in half to check for maggots.

The cep dries extremely well. Do this by slicing the mushroom and placing on a tray in an airing cupboard or on a sunny windowsill. The mushrooms must be dried thoroughly, which may take several days. When the mushrooms are dry, pick over to remove any grit or other foreign bodies, then store in an airtight container.

CHANTERELLE

This mushroom is another favourite among enthusiasts, so much so that mushroom pickers will be intensely secretive about their chanterelle patches. The chanterelle is loved both for its looks and its flavour. The orange trumpet shape of the chanterelle is

most appealing and it has a scent of dried apricots with a hint of citrus. They are best tossed in nut-brown butter, although their colour and flavour remain true even after slow cooking. It is essential to avoid the false chanterelle *Hygrophoropsis aurantiaca* if you are picking your own, which can cause alarming hallucinations.

It is important to clean chanterelles well. Brush the caps and wipe with a damp cloth or kitchen paper if necessary. They can be successfully dried, or can be stored in extra virgin olive oil or vinegar.

HORN OF PLENTY

Although these mushrooms do not look inviting, they have a sweet earthy richness and are very versatile in cooking, going particularly well with fish. They are hollow and you will need to brush them out before using. With larger specimens, it is best to slice them in half and remove any debris that may have gone down the funnel-cap.

Below: The funnel-shaped horn of plenty has a very good flavour.

Above: Bay boletus can be eaten raw or cooked in soups and stews.

Right and below: Hedgehog fungus is very rare.

HEDGEHOG FUNGUS

This is one of the more unusual fungi and is rarely found for sale. The mushroom is quite difficult to find on the woodland floor, but it has great culinary value and so is much sought-after by collectors. After cleaning, smaller specimens can be cooked whole or sliced. It is a versatile mushroom, going well with both meat and fish. Young hedgehog fungus has a peppery watercress quality that is appreciated raw in salads. Mature specimens can be bitter and are best cooked with unsalted butter and herbs. With large specimens, remove the spines: although quite edible, the small hairs could spoil the appearance of the finished dish.

SAFFRON MILK-CAP

The saffron milk-cap is prized for its saffron-orange colour and firm texture. Mature specimens often harbour insect larvae in the stem and centre cap.

Below: Saffron milk-cap has a mild, unassuming flavour.

CHICKEN-OF-THE-WOODS

This is one of the most spectacular of all bracket fungi and is rarely available for sale so you will need to pick your own. It grows on deciduous trees, often in quite large quantities. This is the fungus you often see growing on old wood, commonly in the shape of a fan.

The colour is spectacular – lemon to orange-yellow, although it tends to darken with age. The flesh in young specimens is tender and exudes a yellow juice. The smell is quite pungent and a little acrid. The season is usually from late spring to early autumn (fall), but if the winter has been mild, it will often appear much earlier.

Pick young specimens that are still yellow. To remove the bitter taste, blanch for a few minutes in boiling salted water prior to cooking. The fungus can then be fried in olive oil or butter. The texture and flavour is similar to chicken, and it is much prized by chefs.

GIANT PUFFBALL

This huge fungus can be truly visually spectacular. It is also versatile, but only pick specimens that are fresh and young and sound hollow when tapped. It is pointless picking this mushroom once the flesh has become discoloured. When sliced open, the young giant puffball has a meaty rich aroma similar in some ways to the cep. Older specimens discolour to a yellow when cut and should never be eaten.

The giant puffball goes well in all wild mushroom dishes, soups and stews. It is also good for breakfast, sliced and fried with bacon or dipped in beaten egg and breadcrumbs and lightly fried.

Collecting Wild Mushrooms

Picking wild fungi and mushrooms is unsafe unless you are confident about identifying edible types. You may be able to arrange a mushroom-picking trip with a qualified mycologist. In autumn (fall) in France, people take the wild mushrooms they have gathered to the local pharmacy to have them identified. If you intend to pick your own mushrooms, it is essential that you can identify absolutely those that are poisonous. Many poisonous mushrooms grow next to or near some of the most prized edible ones. If you happen to add a poisonous specimen to a basket of edible fungi, you must discard all the items you have gathered because there is a possible risk of cross-contamination.

ORANGE BIRCH BOLETE

This is another favoured mushroom among collectors, and one that is rarely available in the stores. It is a lovely orange colour and can grow to a fairly large size. The young ones have a slightly fluffy appearance. It has a wonderful flavour, is very versatile, and is much sought after by chefs. It softens when cooked and provides a good texture for soups and casseroles.

Below: Giant puffballs should be picked while small and young.

WOOD AND FIELD BLEWIT

Wood blewits appear in woodland and hedgerows late in the season. The cap is blue when young but then turns an almost shiny tan, and the gills are lilac. This mushroom must be cooked before being eaten and some people are allergic to it, so take care if serving it to guests. The mushroom has an assertive pine-rich perfume and a strong flavour that goes well with other strongly flavoured vegetables such as onions and leeks.

Field blewits are paler than wood blewits, with whitish, rather than lilac, gills. The field blewit has a similar flavour to the wood blewit and is very good if chopped and added to stews. Like wood blewit, it can cause allergic reactions in some people, so take care.

MORELS

These are the most prized of the wild mushrooms, with a superb flavour that is much loved by connoisseurs and chefs. They are the first mushrooms of the year, appearing not in autumn but in the spring. The shape of morels is very distinctive: they are cone-shaped with a crinkled spongy cap that is hollow inside. They are pale brown in colour and darken to orange-yellow with age. The flesh is white to cream.

Because of all the nooks and crannies in their make-up, morels are often infested with small insects, so they need careful cleaning before either cooking or drying. The easiest way to clean them is to slice each one in half

Left: Morels have a superb flavour.

to make sure nothing is inside, rinse it in clear water and dry. Morels have an intense smell and flavour that goes well with eggs, beef and game. Take note that they must be cooked before eating; never eat them raw. They need longer cooking than most mushrooms: sauté them in butter, add a squeeze of lemon and then cover and simmer for up to an hour until tender. One of the tastiest ways of using fresh morels is to stuff them. They also make a deliciously rich sauce. Dried, the intensity of their flavour will enhance a wide range of dishes.

PIEDMONT OR WHITE TRUFFLE

Truffles are the elite of fungi and the white truffle is considered by all to be the best. It is the most sought-after of the truffles and is only found in very limited areas, mostly in northern Italy. Highly trained dogs or pigs are necessary to locate it. In order to develop their full aroma and flavour, the truffles must be left to mature, so truffle-hunters often cover up those which the animals have unearthed until they reach full maturity. The white truffle is irregular in shape and yellowish-brown in colour. The flesh is

Above: White truffles are considered by connoisseurs to be the best.

Below: Summer truffles have a less intense flavour than white truffles.

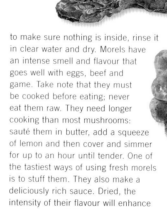

marbled and has a reddish-brown tinge. The smell is distinctive and very sweet. In cooking, they are normally finely sliced and cooked quickly. They can also be eaten raw.

SUMMER TRUFFLE

Less intensely flavoured than the white truffle, this warty black variety has a more delicate aroma associated with oak woodlands. All truffles have a very strong flavour and they are best used in small amounts; even a tiny quantity can transform a dish. They are delicious served with egg and pasta dishes.

Below: Blewits can cause allergic reactions in some people.

Above: Enokitake mushrooms need very little cooking, or can be eaten raw.

ENOKITAKE

This is a Japanese mushroom. The wild variety is orangey-brown with a shiny cap but outside Japan, you will only be able to find the cultivated variety. These are grown on the stumps of the enoki or Chinese hackberry tree and are similarly fine, with the same pin-size heads but are pale coloured with snowy-white caps. Enokitake mushrooms have a fine, sweet and almost fruity flavour reminiscent of white pepper and lemon. In Japanese cookery they are added to salads or used as a garnish for soups or hot dishes. They are also known as

Below: Shimeji is valued for its meaty texture more than its flavour.

enokidake or simply as enoki mushrooms. Since these mushrooms become tough if overcooked, add at the very last minute of cooking. If bought fresh, avoid any that have damp, slimy patches or that have discoloured. Enokitake mushrooms will keep for 4–5 days in the salad drawer of the refrigerator.

SHIMEJI

This is another popular Japanese mushroom. There are many varieties, but the most common has a light grey cap and grows to 2.5–10cm/1–4in in diameter. The shimeji has little aroma and an undistinguished flavour but it is valued for its fresh, meaty texture, which is similar to that of oyster mushrooms.

STRAW MUSHROOMS

These small, grey-brown mushrooms are grown on beds of rice straw, hence the name. They have a delicate, silky surface with a subtle, sweet flavour and a slippery texture. They are widely used in Chinese and Asian cooking, but fresh ones are not readily available in the West. Dried or canned ones can sometimes be found in Asian or Chinese food stores. Canned ones should be drained and rinsed before use. They can be combined with all sorts of ingredients in stir-fries, braised dishes and soups.

WOOD EARS

Also known as cloud ears, these dried black fungi are used widely in Chinese, Thai and Vietnamese cooking. The dried fungi are thin and brittle, and look like pieces of charred paper. They have a slightly smoky smell that disappears once they have been soaked. They have very little flavour but have an intriguing slippery, yet crisp, texture. They are generally used in stir-frying, braising and soups.

SILVER EARS

Also known as dried white fungus, this fungus is often used in Chinese cooking. They have a similar texture to wood ears but have a sweeter flavour. Silver ears are not regarded as an everyday ingredient and are usually reserved for special occasions.

Above: Straw mushrooms are an essential ingredient in Chinese dishes.

Below: Wood ears have little flavour but are valued for their crisp texture.

BEANS, LENTILS, PEAS AND GRAINS

Eaten for millennia, beans, lentils, peas and grains are still

the most important staple foods in many countries around the

world. They are delicious and nutritious and can be cooked

in hundreds of different ways to make satisfying, healthy

meals. In recent years, more and more interesting and

unusual varieties have become readily available and make

a wonderful addition to the kitchen repertoire.

BEANS

The edible seeds from plants belonging to the legume family are known as pulses, and include chickpeas and a vast range of beans. For the cook, their ability to absorb the flavours of other ingredients means that they can be used as the basis of an almost infinite number of dishes. The majority of beans require soaking overnight in cold water before use, so it is wise to plan ahead if using this ingredient.

Dried beans are a good source of protein, fibre, iron, potassium, phosphorous, manganese, magnesium, folate and most B vitamins. Soya beans are the most nutritious of all beans. Rich in high-quality protein, this "wonder pulse" contains all eight essential amino acids that cannot be synthesized by the body, but are vital for the renewal of cells and tissues.

HARICOT/NAVY BEANS

These pretty, small white beans are oval rather than kidney-shaped. When cooked, they are very tender, but still retain their shape. They are the beans most commonly used for canned baked beans and their versatility means they can be used for almost any dish where dried beans are called for. Haricot beans feature in many casseroles from Spain, Portugal and South America. Navy beans, as they are known in the United States, are a particularly small variety of haricot bean, and are commonly used for making the classic dish Boston baked beans.

FLAGEOLET BEANS

These young haricot beans are removed from the pod before they are fully ripe. They are a pretty mint-green colour and have a fresh delicate flavour. In France they are frequently sold semi-dried, when they are used in a number of classic dishes such as *gigot d'agneau* where the cooked beans are served in a fresh tomato sauce with roast lamb. They are also delicious treated simply; cooked until they are tender, then dressed with a little extra virgin olive oil and freshly squeezed lemon juice.

SOISSONS

These large white haricot beans are generally considered the prize of the bean family. They are particularly popular in France, where they are an essential ingredient in cassoulet, which is made with Toulouse sausage, lamb and preserved goose, topped with a layer of breadcrumbs.

PINTO BEANS

A smaller, paler version of the borlotti bean, the savoury-tasting pinto has an attractive orange-pink skin speckled with rust-coloured flecks – it is aptly called the painted bean. One of the many relatives of the kidney bean, pinto beans feature extensively in Mexican cooking, most familiarly in *frijoles refritos* – refried beans – where they are cooked until tender and then fried with garlic, chilli and tomatoes. The beans are then roughly mashed, resulting in a wonderful, spicy coarse purée that is traditionally served with warm corn tortillas. Sour cream and guacamole are good accompaniments. Pinto beans also feature in many Spanish dishes, including the Asturian bean stew.

Above: (Clockwise from left) Haricot, kidney, flageolet and pinto beans all originated in South America, but are now popular throughout the world.

Cooking Kidney Beans

Most types of beans, with the possible exception of aduki beans and mung beans, need to be soaked for 5–6 hours (or overnight). Some types need to be boiled rapidly for 15 minutes to remove toxins. This is particularly important with red kidney beans. Soya beans need to be boiled vigorously for 1 hour, as they contain a substance that prevents the body absorbing protein properly.

1 Wash the beans well, then place in a bowl that allows plenty of room for expansion. Cover with cold water and leave to soak for a minimum of 5 hours, or preferably overnight. Next day, drain and rinse well under cold running water.

2 Place the beans in a large pan and cover with fresh cold water. Bring to the boil and boil rapidly for 10–15 minutes, then reduce the heat and simmer gently for 1–1½ hours until tender. (Some types of beans may take longer.) Drain. The beans are now ready to be served or used in a recipe.

KIDNEY BEANS

Glossy, mahogany-red kidney beans retain their colour and shape when cooked. They have a soft, mealy texture and are much used in South American cooking. An essential ingredient in spicy *chilli con carne*, they can also be used instead of pinto beans to make refried beans. They are very popular, too, in the United States, Canada and the Caribbean, where they feature in vegetarian chillies, mixed bean dishes and as a filling supper cooked with bacon and onions. The popular Caribbean dish Peas and Rice, or Rice and Peas, depending on the island in question, is made with red kidney beans, not peas. Christopher Columbus introduced to them to Europe, where some countries, notably Spain, embraced them with enthusiasm. Cooked kidney beans can be included in a variety of salads, but they are especially good combined with red onion and chopped flat leaf parsley and mint, then tossed in an olive oil and vinegar dressing. When cooking a mixed bean dish, it is usually better to cook the red kidney beans separately because they

Right: Cannellini beans, which are widely used in Italian cooking, actually originate from Argentina.

have a tendency to colour any other ingredients. It is best to combine them with other ingredients towards the end of cooking time.

It is essential to cook red kidney beans thoroughly by boiling vigorously for the initial 10–15 minutes. This is because red kidney beans contain a substance that can cause severe food poisoning if the beans are not boiled sufficiently to eliminate it.

CANNELLINI BEANS

These creamy-white Italian beans are slightly larger and fatter than the white haricot beans and are more like a kidney in shape. They are related to the larger French soissons and, like them, have a fluffy texture when cooked. They are a popular addition to classic minestrone and a variety of other soups. Cannellini beans are an essential ingredient for *tonno e fagioli* – tuna and bean salad – and Florentine *fagioli all'uccelletto*, where the beans are stewed with sage, tomatoes and garlic. They are also good simply cooked with olive oil, onion rings, garlic and parsley.

Left: Dried chickpeas require long soaking and cooking to ensure a really delicious, tender result.

CHICKPEAS

Also known as garbanzo beans, robust and hearty chickpeas resemble shelled hazelnuts and have a delicious nutty flavour and creamy texture. They need lengthy cooking and are much used in Mediterranean and Middle Eastern cooking. They are the main ingredient in *falafel* and *hummus* and are essential also in the famous soup, harira. Chickpeas are hugely popular in Indian vegetarian cooking, and are also ground into a flour, called *gram*, which is used to make fritters and flat breads.

The skin on chickpeas can be quite tough and some recipes suggest removing it. Do this once the chickpeas are fully cooked and cooled. The skin comes away easily when the chickpea is pinched between the fingers and thumb. Although this is a fiddly job, it is worth the effort for making smooth pâtés and soups.

BLACK BEANS

These shiny black, kidney-shaped beans are often used in Caribbean and African cooking. They have a sweetish flavour and their distinctive colour adds a dramatic touch to soups, mixed bean salads and casseroles.

BLACK-EYED BEANS

Known as black-eye peas or cow peas in the United States, black-eyed beans are an essential ingredient in Creole and Cajun cooking and some spicy Indian curries. The small, creamy-coloured bean is characterized by the black spot on its side where it was once attached to the pod. Good in soups and salads, they can also be added to savoury bakes and

casseroles. In the southern United States, they are often cooked with ham hocks and spring (collard) greens, or with spiced rice, tomatoes and onions to make Hoppin' John. They can be used in place of haricot or cannellini beans in a wide variety of dishes.

BORLOTTI BEANS

These oval beans have red-streaked, pinkish-brown skin and a bitter-sweet flavour. When cooked, they have a tender, moist texture which is good in Italian bean and pasta soups, as well as hearty vegetable stews. In most recipes they are interchangeable with red kidney beans. They also require rapid boiling for 15 minutes to destroy any toxins.

FUL MEDAMES

These small Egyptian beans are a member of the broad bean family. They are eaten throughout the Middle East, often with eggs or bread, and are a traditional *mezze* dish. They have a strong, nutty flavour and tough, light brown outer skins. Ful medames need to be soaked overnight in cold water, then cooked slowly for at least 2½ hours and up to 4 hours until soft. In Egypt, they are traditionally cooked overnight in a pot buried in the ashes of a fire, so that they will be ready for breakfast.

Below: Ful medames form the base of Egypt's national dish. They are flavoured with ground cumin, then baked with olive oil, garlic and lemon.

Left: Black beans, black-eyed beans (peas) and borlotti beans are valuable sources of protein in many countries throughout the world.

MUNG BEANS

Also known as green gram in India, mung or moong beans are small, pretty, olive-coloured beans native to India. They are soft and slightly sweet when cooked, and are used in the spicy curry, *moong dhal*, which is flavoured with ground coriander, cumin, turmeric and cayenne pepper. Soaking the beans is not essential, but if they are soaked overnight, this will reduce the usual 40 minutes' cooking time by about half. Mung beans are one of the most popular beans for sprouting. They are also used to make the delicate transparent cellophane noodles that are very popular in Asian cooking.

ADUKI BEANS

Also known as adzuki beans, these tiny, deep-red beans have a sweet, nutty flavour and are popular in Asian dishes. They cook very quickly, and are more often used for sweet dishes than for savoury ones. In Eastern Asia they are cooked, puréed and mixed with sugar to make a sort of chocolate paste. They are also used in sweet soups and

desserts. In Chinese cooking, they form the basis of a sweet red bean paste used to fill *dim sum*.

Known as the king of beans in Japan, the aduki bean is reputed to be good for the liver and kidneys. In Japan, as in China, they are most frequently used to make a sweet paste, which is used to fill cakes. They are also ground into flour for use in cakes, breads and pastries, and are also sometimes used in casseroles and bakes. There are several festive dishes in Japan and Korea where aduki beans are combined with glutinous rice or rice flour to make savoury preparations. Aduki beans may be successfully sprouted for use in salads and stir-fries.

When making sweet bean paste, the beans need to be soaked in plenty of water for at least 24 hours before cooking, and any that remain floating should be discarded. If you are making a dish where you wish to retain the shape, colour and aroma of the beans – for example for a decoration for a dessert – the beans should not be soaked before cooking.

Left: (Top to bottom) Mung beans are the most popular type of bean for sprouting, but they are also good in soups, stews and casseroles, and curries. Red aduki beans are widely used in Asian cooking to make sweet dishes such as aduki bean paste.

Making Sweet Aduki Bean Paste

This classic Japanese paste, which is commonly used for filling cakes or pancakes, can be bought ready-made in jars, cans or in powdered form. However, making it fresh is very easy and it tastes far superior.

1 Put 200g/7oz/1 cup aduki beans in a large, heavy pan and pour over enough water to cover them. Bring to the boil, then drain.

2 Return the drained beans to the pan, add 750ml/1¼ pints/3 cups water and leave the beans to soak for about 24 hours. Discard any beans that remain floating.

3 Bring the beans and soaking water to a rolling boil, then reduce the heat and simmer for about 1 hour. Add water from time to time and stir frequently with a wooden spoon until the beans are very soft and the water is almost absorbed.

4 Add 200g/7oz/1 cup sugar and stir. Keep stirring until the beans are crushed. Add a pinch of salt, then mash to a smooth paste.

BUTTER BEANS AND LIMA BEANS

Similar in flavour and appearance, both butter beans and lima beans are characterized by their flattish kidney shape. Cream-coloured butter beans are well-known in Britain and popular in other parts of Europe, especially Greece. Lima beans are the favourite choice in the United States.

In Greek cooking, butter beans are baked with tomato, garlic and olive oil. The pale green lima bean is the main ingredient in *succotash*, an American dish that also includes corn kernels. Butter and lima beans are also good with creamy herb sauces. Care should be taken not to overcook them, as they become pulpy and mushy in texture.

Above: Butter beans have a soft floury texture and sweet flavour when cooked.

Below: Broad beans have a robust flavour and are often better skinned.

Below: White and black soya beans are rich in essential vitamins and minerals and are the most nutritious of all the beans.

Soya beans are extremely dense and need to be soaked for 12 hours before cooking, but once cooked they are very digestible. They are very bland, however, and need plenty of robust ingredients with distinctive flavours cooking alongside them, such as tomatoes, garlic, herbs and spices. They make a healthy addition to soups, casseroles and salads. Soya beans are also used to make tofu, tempeh, textured vegetable protein (TVP), soya flour and soy sauce.

BROAD/FAVA BEANS

These large beans were first cultivated by the ancient Egyptians. Usually eaten in their fresh form, broad beans change in colour from green to brown when dried, making them hard to recognize, although they retain their characteristic flat broad shape. The dried beans can be up to 2.5cm/1in long, and are rather floury in texture. The outer skin of the dried bean can be very tough and chewy and some people prefer to remove it after cooking. They can also be bought ready-skinned. Dried broad beans are good for adding to richly flavoured meat stews of lamb or beef, or to hearty vegetable soups.

BLACK AND WHITE SOYA BEANS

These small, oval beans vary in colour from creamy yellow through to brown and black. In China, they are known as meat of the earth and were once considered sacred. Soya beans contain all the nutritional properties of meat and dairy products, so they are a good choice for vegetarians and vegans.

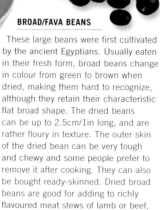

The Flatulence-free Bean

Many people are put off eating beans because of their unfortunate side effects. The propensity of beans to cause flatulence stems from the gases they produce in the gut. The United States' space programme NASA is involved in research into flatulence-free foods. One such food is the manteca bean, discovered by Dr Colin Leakey in Chile. This small, yellow bean is flatulence-free and easy to digest. It is now being grown in Cambridgeshire, England, and the Channel Islands and should become more widely available, called either manteca bean or Jersey yellow bean.

Buying and Storing Beans

Look for plump, shiny beans with unbroken skins. Beans toughen with age, so although they will keep for up to a year in a cool, dry place, it is best to buy them in small quantities from stores with a regular turnover of stock. Avoid beans that look dusty or dirty, and store them in an airtight container in a cool, dark, dry place.

Preparing and Cooking Beans

There is much debate as to whether soaking pulses before cooking is really necessary. It certainly reduces cooking times and can enhance flavour by starting the germination process. To prepare, first wash pulses thoroughly under cold running water, then place in a bowl of fresh cold water and leave to soak in a cool place for at least 6 hours, or overnight if you have time. Discard any pulses that float to the surface,

drain and rinse again. Put in a large pan and cover with plenty of fresh cold water. Boil rapidly for 10–15 minutes, then reduce the heat, cover and simmer gently until tender.

Do not add salt to beans while they are cooking, as this will cause them to toughen. Cook the beans first, then season with salt and pepper. Acidic foods and flavourings such as tomatoes, lemons and vinegar will also toughen the beans, so add these only once the beans are cooked and soft.

If you are short of time, the long soaking process can be speeded up by first cooking the beans in boiling water for 2 minutes, then removing the pan from the heat, covering and leaving to stand for about 2 hours. The beans can then be drained, rinsed and cooked as normal. Cooking beans in a pressure cooker will reduce the cooking time by around three-quarters.

Cooking Times for Beans

Depending on the age of the beans, cooking times can vary, so only use this table as a general guide.

Aduki beans	30–45 mins
Black beans	1 hour
Black-eyed beans (peas)	1–1½ hours
Borlotti beans	1–1½ hours
Broad beans	1½ hours
Butter/lima beans	1–1½ hours
Cannellini beans	1 hour
Chickpeas	1½–2½ hours
Flageolet beans	1½ hours
Ful medames	1 hour
Haricot (navy) beans	1–1½ hours
Kidney beans	1–1½ hours
Mung beans	25–40 mins
Pinto beans	1–1½ hours
Soya beans	2 hours

Canned Beans

These are a useful store-cupboard (pantry) standby because they require no soaking or lengthy cooking. Choose canned beans that do not have any added sugar or salt, drain and rinse well before use. The canning process reduces the levels of vitamins and minerals, but canned beans still contain a reasonable amount of nutrients.

Canned beans tend to be softer than cooked, dried beans so they are easy to mash, which makes them perfect for pâtés, stuffings, rissoles and croquettes, but they can also be used to make quick salads. They can be used for any dish that calls for cooked, dried beans: a drained 400g/14oz can is roughly equivalent to 150g/5oz/¾ cup dried beans. Firmer canned beans can be added to stews and re-cooked, but softer beans, such as cannellini beans, should just be heated through.

Right: Canned beans are excellent for making quick salads and for adding to soups and stews.

LENTILS AND PEAS

Above: Puy lentils are considered to have the best flavour and they also retain their shape well when cooked.

The humble lentil is one of our oldest foods and a staple in many countries around the world. It originated in Asia and North Africa, and continues to be cultivated in those regions, as well as in France and Italy. Lentils are hard even when fresh, so they are always sold dried. Unlike most other pulses, they do not need soaking.

Lentils are a good source of complex carbohydrates and plant protein. They also contain a range of vitamins and essential minerals, including iron, selenium, folate, manganese, zinc, phosphorus and some B vitamins.

GREEN AND BROWN LENTILS

Sometimes referred to as continental lentils, these disc-shaped pulses do not disintegrate when cooked. They take longer to cook than split lentils – about 40–45 minutes – and are ideal for adding to warm salads, casseroles and stuffings. Whole or puréed with cream or stock and/or butter, they are a traditional accompaniment to pork and gammon (smoked or cured ham) and also make a satisfying pilaff if combined with boiled brown or white rice or bulgur wheat.

Alternatively, green and brown lentils can be cooked and mashed or puréed with herbs or spices to make a tasty and nutritious pâté.

RED SPLIT LENTILS

Orange-coloured red split lentils, sometimes known as Egyptian lentils, are the most familiar variety. They cook in just 20–30 minutes, eventually disintegrating into a thick, rich purée. They are ideal for thickening soups and casseroles and, when cooked with spices, make a delicious dhal, a richly flavoured purée served as an accompaniment to meat or vegetable curries. In the Middle East, red or yellow lentils are cooked and mixed with spices and vegetables to form balls known as *kofte,* which are then fried.

Above: Red lentils cook relatively quickly and disintegrate to form a wonderfully thick, rich purée. They are delicious cooked with onions, garlic and spices to make hot and tasty Indian dhal.

PUY LENTILS

These tiny, dark blue-green, marbled lentils grow in the volcanic soil of the Auvergne region in central France and are named after the French town of Puy. They were originally called *lentilles à la reine* when the wife of Louis XV decided to dine on them.

Puy lentils may be more difficult to obtain than other types of lentils and they are usually more expensive. They are considered to be far superior in taste and texture to other varieties, and they retain their colour and bead-like shape after cooking, which takes about 25 minutes.

Puy lentils are a delicious addition to simple dishes such as warm salads, and are also good served with smoked fish, casseroled game and braised in wine and flavoured with fresh herbs. A traditional French country dish consists of Puy lentils braised with diced bacon, flavoured with herbs and enriched with double (heavy) cream.

Left: (Top to bottom) Hearty green and brown lentils have a firm texture and keep their shape during cooking.

Above:
Marrowfat peas
are a variety of
green pea that is dried whole.

YELLOW LENTILS

Lesser-known, yellow split lentils taste very similar to the red variety and are used in much the same way. They look a little like yellow split peas and, like red lentils, may be substituted for chana dhal and toovar dhal. They make a good accompaniment for winter dishes, being filling, nourishing and cheerfully bright.

YELLOW AND GREEN SPLIT PEAS

Dried peas come from the field pea not the garden pea, which is eaten fresh. Unlike lentils, peas are soft when young and require drying. They are available whole or split; the latter have a sweeter flavour and cook more quickly. Like split lentils, split peas do not hold their shape when cooked, making them perfect for dahls, purées, casseroles and soups. They are widely used in North European cooking, especially in Germany and Scandinavia, and are the main ingredient of the traditional English dish, pease pudding. They take about 45 minutes to cook.

MARROWFAT PEAS

The odd name of this variety of pea is derived from an unlikely comparison with the marrow found in bones, reflecting their high nutritional value. They are larger in size than split peas and are used to make the traditional British dish "mushy" peas, a kind of pea purée and another rather odd name that may simply be a corruption of mashed. Like other whole peas, they require soaking overnight before use. A large proportion of the marrowfat crop is used by the canning and food processing industry.

Buying and Storing Lentils and Peas

Although lentils and peas can be kept for up to a year, they will gradually become tougher with time, which means that they will have to be cooked longer. Buy from stores with a rapid turnover of stock and store in airtight containers in a cool, dark place. Look for bright, unwrinkled pulses that are not dusty. Rinse well before use.

Cooking Lentils

Lentils do not need to be soaked. Whole lentils hold their shape when cooked, while split ones cook down to a soft consistency. Whole lentils need a slightly longer cooking time than split lentils.

To cook whole green, brown and Puy lentils, put 250g/9oz/generous 1 cup whole lentils in a sieve and rinse well under cold running water. Tip into a pan. Add enough water to cover and bring to the boil. Lower the heat and simmer gently for 25–30 minutes until tender, replenishing the water if necessary. Drain well and season to taste with salt and ground black pepper.

Above: Yellow and green split peas
cook quickly and add substance to
soups, casseroles and stews.

To cook split red and yellow lentils, put 250g/9oz/generous 1 cup split lentils in a sieve and rinse under cold running water. Tip into a pan. Cover with 600ml/1 pint/2½ cups water and bring to the boil. Lower the heat and simmer for about 25 minutes, stirring occasionally, until the water is absorbed and the lentils are tender. Season to taste with salt and ground black pepper.

SPROUTED BEANS

Beansprouts have a lovely fresh flavour and a crisp texture, and they are an excellent addition to salads, stir-fries and other Asian dishes. All sorts of seeds can be sprouted, but beans are the most commonly sprouted ones. Beansprouts are also remarkably nutritious. There are almost 30 per cent more B vitamins and 60 per cent more vitamin C in the sprout than in the original seed, pulse or grain. Sprouted

Below: Lentil sprouts can be grown only from whole lentils, as split lentils cannot sprout.

Below: Mung beansprouts are the most commonly available type of beansprout.

Below: Chickpea sprouts are sturdy with a crunchy texture.

seeds, pulses and grains supply large quantities of protein, B vitamins and vitamins C and E, along with potassium, phosphorus and magnesium. Supermarkets and health food stores sell a variety of sprouts, but it is easy to grow them at home – all you need is a jar, a square of muslin (cheesecloth) and an elastic band. However, you can buy an inexpensive sprouter designed specifically for the purpose and if you want a constant supply of fresh sprouts, this will probably be worthwhile.

ALFALFA SPROUTS

Although alfalfa is more usually associated with animal fodder, the tiny, wispy, white sprouts have a mild, nutty flavour that is perfect in salads and sandwiches. They are tastiest eaten raw as this retains their lovely crunchy texture.

MUNG BEAN SPROUTS

These are the most widely available type of beansprouts. They have a fresh flavour and are very nutritious. They are popular in Chinese and Asian cooking, where they are used in soups, salads and stir-fries. They are fairly large, with a crunchy texture and a delicate flavour. Some people find them a little indigestible and may prefer to blanch them briefly in boiling water before using them. Canned mung beansprouts are also available.

Above: Alfalfa sprouts make a lovely, crisp addition to winter salads.

Using a Sprouter

Sprouters are usually made of clear plastic, resembling a square box with three tiers.

1 Rinse the pulses and put them in the two lower tiers. Fit the lid and place the sprouter in a warm place away from direct sunlight.

2 Rinse daily with fresh water poured through the perforated top tier. Tip the excess water out of the base.

3 Pale green shoots will appear within 3–6 days. Continue the daily rinsing until they are ready.

Tips on Sprouting
• Use whole pulses, as split ones will not germinate.
• Regular rinsing and draining is essential to prevent the beans from turning rancid.
• After 2–3 days, place the jar in sunlight to encourage the green pigment chlorophyll and increase the magnesium and fibre content.
• Other pulses, such as soya beans and snow beans, as well as many seeds, can be sprouted.
• Rinse soya bean and chickpea sprouts four times a day.

CHICKPEA SPROUTS

Sprouts grown from chickpeas have a nutty flavour and a crunchy texture. They add substance to baked dishes and casseroles.

LENTIL SPROUTS

These sprouts have a pleasant, slightly spicy, peppery flavour and thin, white shoots. Use only whole lentils for sprouting; split ones won't sprout.

ADUKI BEAN SPROUTS

These fine wispy sprouts have a sweet, nutty taste. Use in salads and stir-fries, on their own or in combination with another crunchier beansprout.

WHEAT BERRY SPROUTS

Sprouts grown from wheat berries have a crunchy texture and sweet flavour, and are an excellent addition to home-made breads. If they are left to grow, the sprouts will become wheatgrass, which can be made into a nutritious juice that is rich in essential vitamins and minerals.

Buying and Storing

If you can, choose fresh, crisp sprouts with the seed or bean still attached. Avoid any that are slimy or look musty. Sprouts are best eaten on the day they are bought but if fresh they will keep, wrapped in a plastic bag, in the salad compartment of the refrigerator for 2–3 days. Rinse well in cold water and pat dry before use.

Preparing and Cooking

Sprouted beans, lentils and peas tend to have a denser, more fibrous texture than sprouts grown from seeds, which tend to be much more delicate. Use a mixture of different types of sprouts for a variety of tastes and textures. Sprouted soya beans should always be cooked before use, but all other types of sprouts may be eaten raw.

Mung bean sprouts are often used in Asian dishes and require only very brief cooking. They are delicious stir-fried. Alfalfa sprouts are very good eaten raw in salads and as part of a sandwich filling. They are not suited to cooking because they are so delicate.

Sprouted grains make an excellent addition to breads, giving them a pleasant crunchy texture. Knead the grain sprouts into the dough after the first rising, before shaping the loaf or placing the dough in the loaf tin (pan). Chickpea and lentil sprouts are very good cooked in hearty casseroles and baked dishes.

Below: Aduki bean sprouts have a sweet taste and go well with other fresh beansprouts.

Left: Wheat berry sprouts are very nutritious and are very good served in wholesome salads.

Sprouting Beans, Peas and Lentils

Larger pulses such as chickpeas take longer to sprout than small beans, but they are all easy to grow and will be ready to eat in about 3 days. Store sprouts in a covered container or a plastic bag in the refrigerator for 2–3 days.

1 Wash 45ml/3 tbsp pulses or grains thoroughly in cold water, then place them in a large jar. Fill the jar with lukewarm water and cover the top with a piece of muslin (cheesecloth), secured with an elastic band. Leave in a warm place overnight.

2 Next day, pour off the water through the muslin and refill the jar. Shake gently, then turn the jar upside down and drain well. Leave the jar on its side in a warm place away from direct sunlight.

3 Rinse the pulses or grains in fresh water three times a day until the sprouts have grown to the desired size. Remove from the jar, rinse well and discard any ungerminated beans.

SOYA BEAN PRODUCTS

Nutritious soya beans are incredibly versatile and are used to make an array of foods that can be used in cooking – tofu, tempeh, textured vegetable protein (TVP), flour and miso, and also a variety of sauces. The soya bean is the most nutritious of all beans; rich in high-quality protein, it is one of the few vegetarian foods that contain all eight essential amino acids.

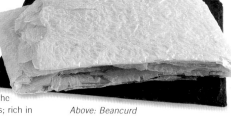

Above: Beancurd skins can be used to wrap around a wide variety of fillings.

TOFU

Also known as beancurd, tofu is made in a similar way to soft cheese. The beans are boiled, mashed and sieved to make soya milk, and the milk is then curdled using a coagulant. The resulting curds are drained and pressed to make different types of tofu.

FIRM TOFU

This type of tofu is sold in blocks and can be cubed or sliced and used in vegetable stir-fries, kebabs, salads, soups and casseroles. Alternatively, firm tofu can be mashed and used in baked dishes and burgers. When cutting firm tofu, always use a sharp knife; a blunt blade will cause it to break up. The bland flavour of firm tofu is improved by marinating, because its porous texture absorbs flavours and seasonings.

Right: Firm and silken tofu have different culinary uses.

SILKEN TOFU

This type of tofu has a silky, smooth texture and is ideal for use in sauces, dressings, dips and soups. It is a useful alternative to cream or soft cheese and can be used to make creamy desserts.

BEANCURD SKINS AND STICKS

Made from soya milk, dried beancurd skins and sticks have neither aroma nor flavour until they are cooked, when they will rapidly absorb the flavour of seasonings, sauces and other ingredients – just like fresh beancurd. They are used in Japanese and Chinese cooking and need to be soaked in water

Marinating Tofu

Tofu is relatively tasteless but readily takes on other flavours. It is used to best advantage when marinated in aromatic oils, soy sauce, spices and herbs.

1 Cut a block of tofu into 2cm/¾in cubes and marinate in a mixture of groundnut (peanut) oil, sesame oil, soy sauce, crushed garlic, grated fresh root ginger and clear honey for at least 1 hour.

2 Thread the cubes of tofu on to skewers with chunks of courgette (zucchini), onion and mushrooms. Brush with the marinade and grill (broil) or cook on the barbecue until golden, turning occasionally.

until pliable before use. Beancurd skins should be soaked for an hour or two; sticks need to be soaked for several hours or overnight. They can be chopped for soups, stir-fries and casseroles.

Above: Freeze-dried tofu is used to make a rich-tasting vegetable soup.

FREEZE-DRIED TOFU

Known as *koya-dofu* in Japan, freeze-dried tofu is thought to have been invented centuries ago by Buddhist monks living high on a mountain. It has a much stronger aroma and flavour than firm or silken tofu, even after it has been soaked in water, but its most striking feature is its unusual spongy texture. This enables it to absorb other

Below: Pressed beancurd is usually marinated in soy sauce, giving it a pale brown surface and white interior.

flavours extremely well. It is often sold in packets of five pieces, complete with powdered soup stock in which to cook it, but is available only from Japanese and some Chinese stores. An added advantage is that, however long it is cooked, it does not disintegrate.

FERMENTED TOFU

This is made by fermenting fresh tofu on beds of rice straw, then drying the curd in the sun before it is marinated with salt, alcohol and spices. Finally, it is stored in brine in sealed earthenware urns and left to mature for a minimum of six months before being packaged and sold. Fermented tofu is definitely an acquired taste. It is sometimes referred to as Chinese cheese because it smells very strong indeed and the flavour is pretty powerful, too. Two types of fermented tofu are available in the West, from specialist Asian stores: red fermented tofu is coloured on the surface only and white fermented tofu can be quite hot and spicy.

PRESSED TOFU

This is fresh tofu that has been compressed until almost all the liquid has been squeezed out, leaving a solid block with a smooth texture. It is usually marinated in soy sauce and seasoned with five-spice powder, so it is pale brown on the surface, but

Above: Fermented tofu, unlike many other kinds of tofu, has a distinctive and very powerful aroma and flavour.

remains white inside. It is available ready-pressed from Asian stores, but you can prepare it yourself. Wrap a tofu cake in a piece of kitchen paper and place a large plate on top of it, so that it is covered. Place a weight on top and leave it to press for up to 1 hour, until all the excess water has been absorbed by the kitchen paper.

Watchpoints

Although soya beans and products are nutritionally beneficial, they are also common allergens and in some people can provoke reactions such as headaches and digestive problems. Avoid eating excessive amounts of soya, and always cook sprouted soya beans before use.

DEEP-FRIED TOFU

There are various types of fried tofu. Deep-frying changes the texture and taste of somewhat plain non-crunchy tofu and not only provides extra protein and oil, but also gives the tofu some extra bite. It is easier to handle and cook than regular tofu and can be eaten heated up or cooked with vegetables and meat. It can be found, refrigerated, in Japanese and Chinese supermarkets. The tofu is fried in vegetable oil so is suitable for vegetarians.

Thick Deep-fried Tofu This is made of whole, coarse tofu and is available in blocks or cubes. The outside is golden brown, while the inside remains white. Before use, thick deep-fried tofu should be rinsed with boiling water, then lightly pressed dry with kitchen paper to reduce the oiliness. It can be eaten lightly grilled (broiled) with sauce, as tofu steak, and is also good added to soups and stews or simmered dishes.

Thin Deep-fried Tofu Sheets This is the most commonly used type of fried tofu in Japan. It is available fresh or frozen, usually in a standard size of 12 × 6cm/ 4½ × 2½in, and 1cm/½in thick, and is often used for cooking with other ingredients, mainly vegetables, and on its own as a source of vegetable protein. It can be added to soups and stews, or slit open like a pitta bread and stuffed with vegetables or sushi rice.

Deep-fried Tofu with Vegetables This variety of deep-fried tofu is very popular in Japanese cooking. It is made from chopped vegetables and seeds bound together with crumbled tofu and grated yam. The mixture is made into flat discs of about 8cm/3½in in diameter or small round balls, then deep-fried.

Buying and Storing

All types of fresh tofu can be kept in the refrigerator for up to a week. Firm tofu should be kept covered in water, which must be changed regularly. Freezing fresh tofu is not recommended because it alters the texture, although some deep-fried tofu can be frozen. Japanese thin deep-fried tofu is available both fresh and frozen. Silken tofu is often available in convenient, long-life vacuum packs, which do not have to be kept in the refrigerator and have a much longer shelf-life.

Below: (Clockwise from left) There are a number of different types of deep-fried tofu, including deep-fried tofu balls with vegetables, thin deep-fried tofu, and thick deep-fried tofu in blocks and cubes. They are very popular in Japan.

Preparing Deep-fried Tofu

Deep-fried tofu can either be heated up alone, or cooked with vegetables and/or meat. It should always be rinsed with boiling water before use, to reduce oiliness.

1 Put the tofu in a sieve and pour boiling water over it. Drain and pat dry with kitchen paper. If using fresh tofu, par-boil in boiling water for 1 minute, drain and squeeze out any excess water.

2 Cut each sheet in half and place on a chopping board. Pull each piece open by rubbing backwards and forwards across the outside with the palm of your hand to ease it apart. Use your fingers to open the bag fully, working your way carefully towards the bottom.

TEMPEH

This Indonesian speciality is made by fermenting cooked soya beans with a cultured starter. It is similar to tofu, but has a nuttier, more savoury flavour. It can be used in the same way as firm tofu and also benefits from marinating. The firmer texture of tempeh means that it can be used instead of meat in pies and casseroles.

Above: TVP chunks and mince can be used in place of meat in many dishes.

Buying and Storing

Tempeh is available chilled or frozen in health food stores and Asian supermarkets. It is sold in cakes about 2cm/³/₄in thick. Chilled tempeh can be stored in the refrigerator wrapped in a plastic bag for up to a week. Frozen tempeh can be left in the freezer for 1 month; thaw thoroughly before using.

TVP

Textured vegetable protein, better-known as TVP, is a useful alternative to meat and is usually bought in chunks or minced (ground). Made from processed soya beans, TVP is very versatile and readily

Below: Tempeh is a soya bean product from Indonesia that can be used in the same ways as tofu.

absorbs the strong flavours of ingredients such as tomatoes, herbs, spices and vegetable stock. It is very inexpensive and has a long shelf-life, making it a convenient store-cupboard (pantry) item. TVP needs to be rehydrated in boiling water or stock and can be used in stews and pies.

Gluten

Also known as mock meat, gluten is another source of vegetarian protein. In Asia it is commonly used by Buddhists and other vegetarians. There are several different varieties. Gluten used in most Chinese and Asian cooking is made from a mixture of wheat flour, salt and water, from which all the starch has been washed out. What remains is a sponge-like

Below: Gluten has a bland flavour so is best combined with strong flavours.

Right: Konnyaku has an interesting texture.

gluten, which has no particular aroma or flavour of its own. It can, however, be shaped, flavoured and coloured to resemble meat. Flavoured, coloured gluten is available in cans from Asian supermarkets and stores and needs only to be reheated before serving. Once opened, gluten can be stored in the refrigerator for up to a week. There are several other gluten products.

Seitan is a meat replacement made from gluten. It has a firm, chewy texture and can be found in health food stores. Seitan has a neutral flavour that benefits from marinating. It is good sliced or cut into chunks and stir-fried or added to soups or sauces during the last few minutes of cooking time.

Konnyaku is an unusual, dense gelatinous gluten product that comes from Japan. It is derived from the konnyaku plant, which is a type of yam. Konnyaku has no aroma or flavour and it has a slippery, hard jelly-like texture, for which it is most appreciated.

Fresh konnyaku is eaten raw or cooked with other vegetables and meat. In Japan it is also added to soups and hotpots. Konnyaku should be par-boiled before cooking. It does not easily absorb other flavours, so it needs to be simmered in a strongly flavoured sauce for several hours, or as long as possible.

CEREAL GRAINS

Grains have been cultivated throughout the world for centuries. The most popular types of grain such as wheat, rice, oats, barley and corn or maize come in various forms, from whole grains to flours. They are inexpensive and readily available, and form a hugely important part of our diet, whether eaten in bread, in pasta or noodles, baked into cakes or biscuits (cookies), or ingested in a less processed form, such as bulgur wheat, in salads or in breakfast cereals.

WHEAT

This is the largest and most important grain crop in the world and it has been cultivated since 7,000BC. The wheat kernel comprises three parts: the bran, the germ and the endosperm. Wheat bran is the outer husk, while wheat germ is the nutritious seed from which the plant grows.

Wheat is very important nutritionally, as it is an important source of complex carbohydrates, protein, vitamins and minerals. It is most nutritious when unprocessed and in its whole form. It is an excellent source of dietary fibre and is rich in B vitamins and vitamin E, as well as iron, zinc and selenium. The proteins in the wheat kernel form a mixture called gluten, to which some people are intolerant.

WHEAT BERRIES

These are the whole wheat grains with the husks removed and they can be bought in health food stores. Wheat berries may be used to add a sweet, nutty flavour and chewy texture to breads, soups and stews, or they can be combined with rice or other grains. Wheat berries should be soaked overnight, then cooked in plenty of boiling salted water until tender.

WHEAT FLAKES

Steamed and softened wheat berries that have been rolled and pressed are known as wheat flakes or rolled wheat. They are best used on their own or they can be mixed with other flaked grains in porridge or muesli (granola).

Above: Wheat berries can be allowed to germinate and sprout into highly nutritious wheatgrass.

CRACKED WHEAT

This is made from crushed wheat berries, and retains all the nutrients of whole wheat. Often confused with bulgur wheat, cracked wheat can be used in the same way as wheat berries (although it cooks in less time), or as an alternative to rice and other grains. When cooked it has a slightly sticky texture and pleasant crunchiness. Use cracked wheat in salads or serve as an accompaniment.

Right: Wheat flakes can be added to home-made cakes and breads to add extra nutrients, substance and flavour.

Right: Bulgur wheat is the main ingredient in the Middle Eastern salad tabbouleh, where it is combined with chopped parsley, mint, tomatoes and cucumber, and dressed with lemon juice and olive oil.

BULGUR WHEAT

This tasty grain is also made from wheat berries, but unlike cracked wheat, the berries are cooked, the bran is removed and they are then dried and crushed. Bulgur wheat has a wonderfully light and nutty flavour and is very easy to cook. It simply needs to be soaked in water for 20 minutes and drained before use. Some packet instructions specify cold water, but boiling water produces a much softer grain. It can also be cooked in boiling water until tender or used in place of rice to make wholesome pilaffs.

Below: Extremely nutritious wheat germ is found at the heart of the wheat grain and has numerous culinary uses.

*Above:
Semolina, made
from durum wheat,
has a wide variety of culinary uses and
is particularly good for baking.*

*Above:
Couscous
is a staple in
North African
cuisine, served with spicy stews.*

WHEAT GERM

This tiny wheat seed is extremely rich in B vitamins, vitamin E, salts, proteins and fatty acids. It is present in whole-meal (whole-wheat) flour, but has been partly removed from brown flour. Wheat germ can be bought separately in its natural state for adding to loaves or sprinkling over the sides of the loaf tin (pan) before cooking bread. It is also available ready-toasted for adding to breakfast cereals, porridge and yogurt. Wheat germ will keep for only a short period of time. Its natural oil gradually becomes rancid at room temperature, so it should always be stored in the refrigerator in an airtight container. Check the use-by date on the packet.

BRAN

This is the thin, papery skin covering the wheat grain. Some or all of it is removed when making brown and white flour respectively. Bran cannot be digested, but it does provide valuable fibre in the diet and can be bought separately for use in bran loaves and for other baking purposes. However, too high an intake of bran may have a negative effect on the body's absorption of minerals.

COUSCOUS

This is made by steaming and drying cracked durum wheat. It is popular in North Africa, where it forms the basis of a national dish of the same name in Morocco, Algeria and Tunisia. The traditional way to cook couscous is to set the grain in a *couscousière* over a stew of meat and vegetables. This couscous pot is a double boiler with a perforated upper container and lid. A colander or steamer set over a pan works just as well.

Couscous has a pleasant grainy texture. Although it is somewhat bland, it has the wonderful ability of absorbing accompanying flavours, whether a spicy stew or a dressing. Because of this ability, couscous is now a favourite ingredient in many modern restaurants, used for salads as well as stews.

SEMOLINA

This is made from the wheat kernel or endosperm of the wheat, once the bran and wheat germ have been removed in the process of milling. Like couscous, it is made from durum wheat, and can be ground either coarsely or finely. It is used in the West for making hot milk puddings and baby foods, or for adding to cakes, biscuits (cookies) and bread. In India, it is used for making certain kinds of breads.

Buying and Storing

Buy wheat-based foods from stores that have a high turnover of stock. Wheat berries can be kept for about 6 months, but most whole-wheat products, and particularly wheat germ, should be kept for no longer than 3 months because the oils present in them quickly turn rancid. Keep a note of the use-by dates of all wheat products – and don't forget to check them regularly. Always try to buy in small quantities.

Cooking Couscous

Lengthy steaming is not usually necessary as most couscous now available has been pre-cooked.

Place 275g/10oz/1⅔ cups couscous in a large bowl and pour over 550ml/18fl oz/2½ cups boiling water or stock. Stir well and leave to soak for 10 minutes. Fluff up the grains with a fork before serving.

Alternatively, moisten the grains with a little warm water and place in a steamer lined with muslin (cheesecloth). Steam for about 15 minutes, or until the grains are tender and fluffy.

CORN

The term corn has given rise to considerable confusion. In Britain, it was historically used to describe the predominant cereal crop of a region (for instance, wheat in England and oats in Scotland). An English field of corn, therefore, meant a field of wheat, rather than the tall annual grass with yellow edible grains, which was also known by its 16th-century Spanish name – maize (*maíz*).

Sailors from Spain and Portugal, who accompanied the early explorers to South and Central America were responsible for introducing corn into Europe, where it became a staple crop. Corn needs higher temperatures and more sunshine than wheat and, even with today's varieties, corn grows best in the more southerly parts of Europe. It is still widely grown in Mexico and the southern parts of the United States.

Corn is believed to be the only grain to contain vitamin A. It is also the source of some B vitamins, vitamin C and iron.

Corn is processed to produce many different products, including flour, meal and wholegrains.

WHITE AND YELLOW CORNMEAL

This meal is ground from white or yellow corn and is normally available in coarse, medium or fine grinds. Coarse-ground cornmeal is used for the Italian dish polenta; finer grinds are used for bread-making. Most cornbreads come from the United States. There are also some traditional cornbreads from Europe. *Broa de milo* is a Portuguese loaf and *pane di mais* comes from Italy. Corn contains no gluten, which is needed for bread to rise, so European breads all contain a proportion of wheat flour. On the other hand, breads from Central and North America such as Mexican tortilla are often made entirely from corn and are therefore flat.

Polenta This classic Italian cornmeal, which is cooked into a kind of porridge (oatmeal), comes in various grades, ranging from coarse to fine. You can buy polenta that takes 40–45 minutes to cook or a much quicker, part-cooked version that can be cooked in less than 5 minutes.

HOMINY

These are the husked whole grains of corn. If bought dried, the grains need to be soaked overnight and can then be cooked and served either by themselves or added to casseroles. Ground hominy is known as hominy grits.

POPCORN

This is a separate strain of corn that is grown specifically to make the popular snack food, known as popcorn. The kernel's hard outer casing explodes when heated in a little oil. Popcorn can easily be made at home by heating the corn in a large pan, and flavoured sweet or savoury according to taste.

GRITS

Very popular in the southern parts of the United States, grits are made from coarsely ground, dried yellow or white corn. They can be boiled to create a porridge- (oatmeal-) like dish or used to make pancakes or cakes, cookies and bakes (baked goods).

*Right:
(Clockwise
from top left)
Blue and yellow
cornmeal, cornflour,
popcorn, maize meal and
polenta are all derived from corn.*

OTHER CEREAL GRAINS

Wheat and corn may be the most commonly used grains in the West, but there are many other varieties that are enjoying a great revival or have been newly produced. These offer greater choice in every way – from flavour and texture to nutritional content.

BUCKWHEAT

In spite of its name, buckwheat is not a type of wheat, but is actually related to the rhubarb family. Available plain or toasted, it has a nutty, earthy flavour. It is a staple food in Eastern Europe, as well as in Russia, where the triangular grain is milled into a speckled grey flour and used to make blinis. The flour is also used in Japan for soba noodles and in Italy for some types of pasta. Buckwheat pancakes are popular in parts of the United States and France. The whole grain, which is also known as *kasha*, can be used to make a fine porridge or a creamy pudding.

Quite unusually, buckwheat is a complete protein, containing all eight essential amino acids. It is an excellent sustaining cereal, rich in iron and some of the B vitamins.

SPELT

This is one of the most ancient cultivated wheats and, because of its high nutritional value, it is becoming more widely available in the West. Spelt grains look very similar to wheat and the flour can be substituted for wheat flour in bread. Spelt is richer in vitamins and minerals than wheat, and are in a readily digestible form.

Right: (Clockwise from top) Buckwheat flour, toasted buckwheat and plain buckwheat are widely used in Eastern European cooking.

Making Polenta

Polenta makes an excellent alternative to bread or potatoes. If allowed to cool, it may be sliced, then grilled (broiled) or baked. It needs plenty of seasoning and is even better with a knob (pat) of butter and perhaps some grated cheese added.

1 Pour 1 litre/1¾ pints/4 cups water into a heavy pan and bring to the boil. Remove the pan from the heat.

2 In a steady stream, gradually add 185g/6½oz/1¼ cups instant polenta, whisking to prevent lumps forming.

3 Return the pan to the heat and cook, stirring constantly with a wooden spoon, until the polenta is thick and creamy and starts to come away from the sides of the pan – this will take only a few minutes.

4 Season to taste with salt and ground black pepper, then add a generous knob of butter and mix thoroughly. Remove from the heat and stir in some grated cheese, if liked.

5 Alternatively, pour the seasoned polenta into a greased tray and leave to set before further cooking.

TRITICALE

A hybrid of wheat and rye, triticale was created by Swedish researchers in 1875. It has a sweet, nutty taste and chewy texture. It can be used in the same way as rice and is also ground into flour. It contains more protein than wheat, but has less gluten so, for baking, the flour should be combined with a little wheat flour.

OATS

Available rolled, flaked, as oatmeal or oatbran, oats are warming and sustaining when cooked. Like rye, oats are a popular grain in northern Europe, particularly Scotland, where they are commonly used for porridge, oatcakes and pancakes. They are also used for coating herrings before frying and to add substance to stews and stuffings.

Whole oats are unprocessed with the nutritious bran and germ remaining intact. Oat groats are the hulled, whole kernel, while rolled oats are made from groats that are heated and pressed flat. Jumbo rolled oats, however, are made by rolling the whole oat grain. Rolled oats are used in breakfast cereals such as muesli (granola) and for making flapjacks and other biscuits (cookies). The largest and coarsest oatmeal, known as pinhead, is used for some porridge (oatmeal) and in haggis, while coarse oatmeal, the next size down, is good for oatcakes and biscuits (cookies). Medium oatmeal is best in cakes, especially parkin, and breads, while fine oatmeal is ideal for pancakes, and in fruit and milk drinks.

Oat flakes are made by steaming and rolling: pinhead oatmeal and a quick-cooking variety is widely available. Oat flour is gluten-free, which is useful for those who are intolerant to gluten. However, it has to be mixed with wheat flour if

Right: Barley is available both as whole grains and rolled flakes.

you want to use it to make leavened bread. Oat bran can be sprinkled over breakfast cereals and mixed into natural or fruit yogurt.

Oats are one of the most nutritious grains. They are high in soluble fibre and also contain vitamin E and some B vitamins, as well as iron and calcium.

BARLEY

Believed to be the oldest cultivated grain, barley is still a fundamental part of the everyday diet in Eastern Europe, the Middle East and Asia. Pearl barley, the most common form, is husked, steamed and then polished to give it its pretty ivory-coloured appearance. Pearl barley has a mild, sweet flavour and a rather chewy texture. It can be added to soups, stews and baked dishes and is also used to make old-fashioned barley water. Pot barley is the whole grain with just the inedible outer husk removed. It takes longer to cook than pearl barley. Barley flakes, which make a satisfying kind of porridge (oatmeal), and barley flour are also available.

Pot barley, which can be used like rice, is more nutritious than pearl barley, as it contains extra fibre, calcium, phosphorus, iron, magnesium and B vitamins.

RYE

This is the most popular grain for bread-making in many parts of northern and eastern Europe, Russia and Scandinavia. It produces a dark, dense and dry loaf that keeps well. It is a hardy grain that can grow where most others fail. Rye has a good gluten content, although the gluten is different from wheat gluten and rye doughs tend to be notoriously sticky and difficult to handle. For this reason, rye meal is often blended with other flours to create a dough that is more manageable.

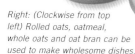

Right: (Clockwise from top left) Rolled oats, oatmeal, whole oats and oat bran can be used to make wholesome dishes.

Right: Rye grains and flour are widely used in northern and Eastern European cooking to make breads, crispbreads and vodka.

There are as many different rye meals as there are wheat flours, ranging in colour and in type of grind. Pumpernickel and other dense box-shaped rye breads use a coarsely ground wholemeal (whole-wheat) rye, while finer flour, containing neither the bran nor the germ, is used to make crusty black breads. Rye is a good source of vitamin E and some B vitamins, as well as protein, calcium, iron, phosphorus and potassium, and is high in fibre.

QUINOA

Hailed as the supergrain of the future, quinoa (pronounced keen-wa) is a grain of the past. It was known as the mother grain by the Incas, who grew it for hundreds of years, high up in the Andes. Today, quinoa is widely available. The tiny, bead-shaped grains have a mild, slightly bitter taste and firm texture. It is cooked in the same way as rice, but the grains quadruple in size, becoming almost translucent. Quinoa is useful for stuffings, pilaffs, baked dishes and breakfast cereals.

MILLET

Although millet is more commonly associated with bird food, it is a highly nutritious grain. It once rivalled barley as the main food of Europe and remains a staple ingredient in many parts of the world. Its mild flavour goes well with spicy stews and curries, and it can be used as a base for pilaffs or milk puddings. The tiny, firm grains can also be flaked or ground into flour. The flour can be used for baking, but needs to be combined with high-gluten flours. Millet contains more iron than other grains and is a good source of zinc, calcium, manganese and B vitamins.

Below: Quinoa is a complete protein, containing all eight of the essential amino acids.

Right: Wholesome millet is still a staple food in many parts of the world, including Africa, China and India.

AMARANTH

Native to Mexico, amaranth can be eaten as a vegetable or as a grain and is highly nutritious. It has a tiny pale seed or grain, and a strong and distinctive peppery flavour. It is best used in stews and soups, or it can be ground into flour to make bread and cookies. Flour made from the ground grains is gluten-free but should be mixed with wheat or other flours to make leavened bread. The leaves are similar to spinach.

SORGHUM

This grain is similar to millet and is an important staple in Africa and India. It can be used much like rice and, when ground into flour, can be used to make unleavened bread. Sorghum is often best-known for its thick, sweet syrup, which is used in cakes and desserts.

KAMUT

An ancient relative of wheat, this grain has long, slender, brown kernels. It is as versatile as wheat and, when ground into flour, can be used to make pasta, breads, cakes and pastry.

Below: Kamut has a deliciously creamy, nutty flavour when cooked.

RICE

This is the second most widely cultivated grain in the world and a staple in China, India, South-east Asia, Africa and Latin America. There are thousands of varieties of rice. In the world's major rice-growing areas, it is not unknown for each paddy field to yield its own particular strain. In the West, we classify rice by the length of its grain – a sensible classification since, as a rule, the grain length determines how it should be cooked and whether it is suitable for sweet or savoury dishes. It is always cooked before eating and is also made into other products such as flour and flakes.

There are a number of ways of cooking rice. Some types benefit from being rinsed in cold water, while others should be left to soak before cooking. Rinsing is suitable for most types of rice, unless using in a risotto. It helps to remove excess starch and any dust that may have accumulated in storage. If you rinse rice which is to be used in a paella or any other dish where it is fried at the beginning of the recipe, be sure to drain it thoroughly first. Soaking is suitable for basmati,

*Right:
American
long grain rice
is popular in
the West.*

brown basmati, glutinous rice and sometimes American long grain, brown long grain rice, short grain rice and Thai fragrant rice. It is seldom essential, but it does increase the moisture content of the grains, which means the rice will cook more quickly and will be less sticky. Soaking is particularly beneficial for basmati rice; less so for Thai fragrant rice, where a slight stickiness is an advantage. Risotto rice, of course, must not be soaked, as this would spoil the characteristic texture. Occasionally, rice that has been soaked will be fried; if this is the case, drain it well first.

LONG GRAIN RICES

This type of rice is three or four times as long as it is wide and, when cooked, the individual grains separate. Long grain rice is used for savoury dishes.

BROWN LONG GRAIN RICE

Sometimes called whole rice, this is the rice equivalent of wholemeal (wholewheat) bread – the whole of the grain complete with the bran, but without the husk. It has a pleasant texture and nutty flavour. Almost all brown rice is long or medium grain. Short grain rice, which is used for desserts, is almost always milled to remove the bran.

WHITE LONG GRAIN RICE

This is the most commonly available white rice and may come from any of a number of countries, although the United States is the most significant producer of the long grain rice bought in Britain.

Above: White and brown long grain rice form the basis of a massive range of both Western and Asian meals.

Boiling Rice

This method is suitable for most types of rice, but particularly for basmati, brown basmati, American long grain, red Camargue and brown rice. The method is not recommended for Thai fragrant rice. In Asia, cooks often add a few drops of vegetable oil as well as salt when cooking rice by this method.

1 Prepare the rice and put it in a large pan. Pour in about 1.2 litres/ 2 pints/5 cups for every 200g/7oz/ 1 cup rice and add a pinch of salt. Bring back to the boil, then lower the heat and simmer, uncovered, for the time indicated on the packet, or until the rice is tender.

2 Drain the cooked rice in a sieve or strainer and rinse thoroughly with plenty of hot water.

3 Either return the rice to the pan or set the sieve over the pan. Cover with the pan lid or a dishtowel and leave the rice to stand for about 5 minutes. Before serving, use a fork to full up the rice, adding a little butter or oil if you like.

Above: Basmati rice is enjoyed for its fragrance and for the slender grains, which provide such a unique texture.

Many countries, including China, India, Malaysia and Thailand produce a far greater amount of long grain rice than the United States, but their production is principally used for the home market and is not usually exported.

White long grain rice has been fully milled – in other words, all of the bran and outer coating have been removed. The grains are white and slightly shiny, a feature often described by the expression polished. While white rice doesn't have the flavour of basmati or Thai rice, it is still a firm favourite and is a good choice for a large number of Western-style and Asian meals.

Right: Thai fragrant rice, also known as perfumed and jasmine rice, is grown in Thailand and Vietnam. It is widely used in South-east Asian cooking, but most commonly used for feasts and celebrations, rather than for everyday meals.

BASMATI RICE

This type of rice comes from the Punjab region of India, from adjacent parts of Pakistan in the Punjab and from the foothills of the Himalayan mountains. The soil and climate of this region is thought to account for basmati's unique flavour and texture. The Hindi word *basmati* means "the fragrant one", and it is rightly considered by most rice lovers to be the prince of rice. "Old" basmati is especially highly prized, but it is rarely available. The grains of basmati rice are long and slender and, during cooking, become even longer, which partly accounts for its wonderful texture. Basmati is excellent in almost any savoury rice dish or served with curries. It is the essential rice for biriyani.

Brown basmati Like all types of brown rice, brown basmati comes with the bran but without the husk, has all the flavour of white basmati with the added texture of brown rice.

SURINAM RICE

This very thin, long grain rice from South America is highly prized by connoisseurs, but is difficult to obtain.

THAI FRAGRANT/JASMINE RICE

Cultivated in Thailand, this rice has a fragrant, almost milky aroma that goes well with the spicy dishes that are traditionally cooked in Indonesia, Malaysia and Thailand. It cooks quite quickly and salt is never added during cooking. Once cooked, the rice has a slightly sticky texture and is excellent for both savoury and sweet dishes.

Cooking Rice by the Absorption Method

This method is suitable for basmati, Thai fragrant rice, short grain rice and glutinous rice. It may also be used for brown basmati and for American long grain rice. The rice is cooked in a measured amount of water in a pan with a tightly fitting lid until the water has been fully absorbed. The proportion of rice to water, and the cooking time, will depend on the type of rice used.

1 Put the rice into a pan and pour in the measured cold liquid. Bring to the boil, then reduce the heat to the lowest possible setting.

2 Cover and cook gently until the liquid has been absorbed. This can take up to 25 minutes.

3 Remove the pan from the heat and leave to stand, covered with the lid, for 5 minutes. Steam holes will have appeared on the surface of the rice. If the grains are not completely tender, replace the cover and leave the rice to stand for a further 5 minutes.

Above: Patna rice goes well with spicy flavours and is excellent served with Indian food.

PATNA RICE

At one time, most of the long grain rice sold in Europe came from Patna in India, and the term was used loosely to mean any long grain rice. The custom persists in parts of the United States, but elsewhere the term Patna is used to describe a specific variety of long grain rice that comes from the Bihar region of India. It is a good, all-purpose rice, which cooks to light, fluffy, dry and separate, milky-white grains, with just a hint of firmness in the centre.

Patna rice takes flavourings very well – such as spices, saffron, butter, flaked almonds and herbs – which makes it very suitable for all kinds of Indian dishes. It is also suitable for rice salads and for stuffings.

SHORT GRAIN RICES

Also known as round grain rice, short grain rice is used almost exclusively for making desserts. However, some short grain rices should, perhaps, more properly be described as intermediate or medium grain, as their size is somewhere between pudding rice and long grain rice. These are usually used in savoury dishes requiring a creamy texture, notably Italian risotto rices such as Arborio and the short grain Valencia rice from Spain, best known for its use in paella.

PUDDING RICE

This is a catch-all name for any short grain rice. Virtually all pudding rice, with the exception of the very different glutinous rice, is white and the grains are short and plump. Short grain rice is particularly suitable for slow-cooked milky puddings, as the grains swell and absorb a lot of liquid. The rice becomes soft and sticky, giving a deliciously smooth and creamy texture.

CAROLINA RICE

This was the original name for a high-quality American short grain rice, named after the state where it was first grown. Now known simply as American rice, it is suitable for both sweet and savoury dishes and is widely used in the fillings for stuffed vegetables such as tomatoes and (bell) peppers.

JAVA RICE

This is a high-quality, all-purpose grain of intermediate size. It absorbs a large amount of liquid during cooking and is used for making desserts.

Left: Short grain pudding rice is popular for making milk puddings and traditional desserts.

Making Rice Pudding

Any of the short grain rices are suitable for making rice pudding.

1 Put 50g/2oz/¼ cup pudding rice and 45ml/3 tbsp caster (superfine) sugar in a non-stick pan and pour in 600ml/1 pint/2½ cups creamy milk. Stir well to mix. Bring the mixture to the boil, then lower the heat, cover the pan and simmer very gently for 1¼ hours, stirring frequently.

2 Remove the lid and simmer for 15–20 minutes until thick and creamy. Serve at once.

Flavouring Rice Pudding

• Flavour the milk by heating it with a vanilla pod until the milk is hot but not boiling. Remove from the heat and leave to infuse (steep) for about 1½ hours. Strain the flavoured milk over the rice and cook as above.
• Stir a little grated nutmeg into the rice and milk mixture and cook as described above.
• Add lemon grass, cardamom pods, or pared orange, lemon or lime rind to the rice as it is cooking.
• Nuts add both taste and texture to a rice pudding. Add chopped pistachio nuts or almonds at any time during cooking.

ITALIAN RICE

A large quantity and variety of rice is produced in Italy, more than in any other country in Europe. Most is grown in the Po Valley. The rice is classified by size, ranging from the shortest, *ordinario*, to *semi-fino* and *fino* to *superfino*. Most of the risotto rices come in *fino* and *superfino* varieties.

Arborio This is one of the best-known Italian risotto rices, taking its name from a town in the Vercelli region of north-west Italy. Unlike the finer risotto rices such as carnaroli, arborio has a comparatively large plump grain.

Vialone Nano A popular risotto rice, this has a plump grain and a firm inner starch, so that risottos made using this rice tend to have slightly more bite.

Carnaroli This premium risotto rice was developed by a Milanese rice grower who crossed Vialone with a Japanese rice. The outer part of the grain is made up of a soft starch that dissolves during cooking to leave the inner grain, which has a firm bite.

Instant Risottos

These are becoming increasingly popular. They are easy to make; all you need to do is add water, stir and heat. Most varieties need to be simmered for about 10 minutes.

Above: (Clockwise from top) Black cuttlefish, tomato, saffron and spinach risottos can make a quick, tasty meal in half the time that it takes to cook a classic risotto.

Above: Italian risotto rices produce a wonderful texture when cooked.

SPANISH RICE

Rice is grown extensively in Spain, particularly in the swampy regions outside Valencia. The most common is a medium short grain variety that has a slightly sticky consistency when cooked and is used for paellas. A longer grain rice is also grown and stirred into soups. Within Spain, rice is graded by the amount of whole grains included in the weight: *Categoria Extra* (red label) is the finest rice, with 95 per cent whole grains; *Categoria Uno* (green label) has 87 per cent whole grains; *Categoria Dos* (yellow label) has 80 per cent whole grains. Calasperra is a top quality short grain rice that can be found outside Spain.

Grano largo or Variedad Americanan This is a long grain white rice.

Bahia A medium grain rice for paella.

Bomba This plump paella rice, like Italian risotto rice, absorbs liquid.

Right: Valencia rice is traditionally used for making the Spanish dish paella.

Left: Black and white glutinous rices are normally used to make sweet desserts, rather than savoury dishes.

Right: Japanese sushi rice is not actually a glutinous rice, but it does become sticky when cooked.

SUSHI RICE

In the West, several varieties of suitable Japanese sushi rice are available. Although not actually a glutinous rice, it has sticky properties, a characteristic common to all Japanese rices. This is obviously important for sushi. Among the popular sushi rices available outside Japan, are Japanese rose, kokuho rose and calrose.

GLUTINOUS RICES

There are several types of glutinous rice that are very popular in Asian cooking. The name is misleading – the grain contains no gluten – but they are noted for the way they stick together after cooking. Often known as sticky or sweet rice, glutinous rice is sweetened and served with fruit as a dessert.

CHINESE GLUTINOUS RICE

In China, glutinous rice is sometimes known by the generic name for short grain rice, japonica or geng rice. There are white and black varieties, and also a pinkish-red rice that grows along the banks of the Yangtze River.

Above:
Chinese glutinous rice is often used for wrapping around other ingredients and for making the classic snack dim sum.

THAI GLUTINOUS RICE

Like Chinese glutinous rice, this rice is also available in white and black grains, and is very popular for making sweet puddings and desserts. The black rice is really a deep blue-purple.

JAPANESE GLUTINOUS RICE

This short grain rice becomes quite tender and moist when cooked, but retains a little crunchiness. It also becomes slightly sticky, a characteristic that makes it perfect for shaping as well as for picking up in mouthfuls with a pair of chopsticks. Even though it has a slightly sweet taste, it may be served for breakfast and eaten with meat, fish and other savoury dishes. There are over 300 varieties of short grain rice grown all over Japan in water-filled paddy fields, with brand names such as Mochigome and Koshihikari.

Right: Mochigome is a short, opaque Japanese rice that is often used for rice cakes and sweet cookies.

SHINMAI

This is a highly esteemed Japanese rice that is sold in Japan in late summer. It is the first rice of the season. Because of its high moisture content, it needs less water for cooking.

WILD RICES

These are not real rices at all, but aquatic grasses that grow in marshy areas around the North American Great Lakes. The rice was once a favourite food of the Native Americans, who would paddle out in small, two-man canoes to the grasses that grew around the lakes to collect the grain. Today much of the wild rice is still harvested by native people, who have treaty agreements to do so. Commercial production and mechanical harvesting are taking over from the labour-intensive methods of the past. Wild rice needs to be soaked for several hours and then cooked for about 35 minutes until the inner grain breaks through the husk, releasing its nutty aroma. It is quite expensive so is often served mixed with long grain rice.

GIANT CANADIAN WILD RICE

The Canadian version of wild rice is similar to the American one, but the dark, glossy grains are even longer and it is considered to have the superior flavour. As well as the northern lakes, wild rice is grown on lakes on

Making Sushi Rice
The rice used as the basis of sushi is lightly flavoured with vinegar.

1 Wash 350g/12oz/1¾ cups short grain sushi rice thoroughly in cold water. Drain the rice in a fine mesh strainer and set aside for 1 hour.

2 Put the rice in a deep pan and add 400ml/14fl oz/1⅔ cups cold water. (The water level should not be more than one third from the base of the pan.) Add a 5cm/2in square of konbu (dried kelp).

3 Cover the pan, and bring to the boil, removing the konbu just before it boils. Reduce the heat and simmer for about 10 minutes, or until the water has been absorbed.

4 In a small bowl, combine 45ml/3 tbsp Japanese rice vinegar, 37.5ml/7½ tsp sugar and 10ml/2 tsp sea salt. Stir until dissolved.

5 Transfer the rice to a bowl and sprinkle over the vinegar mixture. Fold into the rice and leave to cool.

Above: Red Camargue rice is grown in the Camargue region of France.

the west coast of Canada where native Canadians beat the overhanging stems of the grasses with canoe paddles. The grain that falls into their canoes is theirs – the remainder settling in the shallow water for next year's harvest.

RED CAMARGUE RICE

Also referred to simply as red rice, this delightful, nutty flavoured rice came about as a result of cross-pollination between the local white rice and an indigenous wild red rice. Uncooked, the grain is a reddish-brown, similar to many brown rices. However, as it cooks, the red intensifies and the water turns a distinct red colour. Wehani is a very popular variety of red rice that is grown in California.

Above: Giant Canadian wild rice is actually a marsh grass that was eaten as a grain by Native Americans.

RICE PRODUCTS

Being such a prominent and versatile grain, rice is processed into many other products, which are all equally popular and handy. Many of these originate from Asia. Lesser-known, cheaper rices are generally used for making products such as flakes and flour. Rice also forms the basis of mirin, sake and Chinese shaoxing rice wine.

Below: Flaked rice is widely used in Asian cooking to make savoury stuffings and sweet desserts.

Below: Ground rice has quite a coarse texture.

Below: Rice bran is used to flavour Japanese pickled vegetables.

FLAKED RICE

This is a commonly used rice product in many parts of Asia, including China, Thailand and Vietnam. Flaked rice is used to make a number of sweet and savoury dishes. The flakes are made from inexpensive rice, which has been husked, cleaned and par-boiled in hot water. The cooked rice is flattened with heavy rollers until wafer-thin and the resulting flakes are then dried mechanically. Depending on the weight of the rollers, flakes of varying thicknesses, from translucent to thick and opaque, are manufactured. In the West, flaked rice is used by the food trade for making snacks and breakfast cereals, but is seldom used in recipes. Flaked rice is widely available from Asian supermarkets.

Above: Rice cakes, or mochi, are traditionally eaten with soup at the Japanese New Year celebrations and can be bought ready-made from Japanese and Asian supermarkets.

GROUND RICE

This has a much more granular texture than rice flour, similar to semolina, and is creamy-white in colour. It is mainly used to make sweet dishes such as milk puddings and was once very popular in England. Ground rice is also widely used for biscuits (cookies) and baking, where it adds an agreeable sandy texture. It is a good substitute for wheat flour, especially for people who are unable to tolerate gluten.

RICE BRAN

This is removed from the rice grain during milling and processing and is often used as animal feed. However, in Japan, rice bran is traditionally used for pickling vegetables, known as *nuka-zuke*. The rice bran is first roasted to bring out its flavour, then mixed with water and salt to make a mash, which ferments and makes a unique pickling base for vegetables such as daikon, carrot and cucumber.

JAPANESE RICE CAKES

Known as *mochi* in Japan, these rice cakes are made from glutinous rice. They were traditionally made by hand, an arduous task involving pounding and steaming the rice to a very smooth, pliable consistency, then shaping the drying mass to make a rice cake block, which is usually circular in shape. Rice cakes can be fried, grilled (broiled) or very lightly boiled and served with other accompaniments.

SAKE

This Japanese rice wine is quite sweet with a mild flavour that belies its potency. It is served in small cups – about the size of eggcups – and can be chilled, but is more often served warm. Today, sake is commonly served with a meal, but traditionally sake was the central attraction, and the small portions of food that accompanied it were there to enhance the taste.

Right: Mirin is a delicate rice wine, which is widely used in Japanese cooking.

MIRIN

This is a sweet cooking sake with a light delicate flavour and a low alcohol content. Mirin is normally stirred into Japanese dishes during the final stages of cooking so that it does not lose its light flavour. It adds a mild sweetness to sauces or dips. Combined with soy sauce, it is the basis of teriyaki sauce, which is popular for basting grilled (broiled) foods. Mirin is available from any Japanese food store and from many of the larger supermarkets. If you cannot find mirin, dry sherry makes a good substitute, though the results will not be quite the same.

SHAOXING RICE WINE

This Chinese rice wine, which is made from glutinous rice, yeast and water, has a rich, mellow flavour. It is popular throughout China for cooking and drinking, and is available in Chinese stores and some wine stores. Although both are wines made from rice, do not confuse shaoxing with sake, which has a quite different flavour.

Far left: Shaoxing rice wine, which is named after the district in China where it is made, varies in colour from golden amber to dark brown.

Left: Japanese sake is most often served warm in cups.

RICE VINEGARS

White rice vinegar Made from glutinous rice, Japanese rice wine vinegar has a subtle, delicate flavour. It is excellent not only in Asian cooking, but for any dressing where you need a mild flavour.
Black rice vinegar Though dark in colour, this has a mild taste and can be used for soups and dipping sauces.
Red rice vinegar Much spicier than other vinegars, Chinese red rice vinegar is used in hot dipping sauces.

Processed and Easy-cook Rice

As well as specific rice products such as flour, rice grains are processed in a variety of ways, usually designed to make them easier to cook or to look attractive.
Polished rice After the grains have been milled to produce white rice, they are then passed through machines to remove any flour that still adheres. Camolino rice is a polished rice with the grains lightly coated in oil.
Steamed rice This is soaked and partially steam-cooked at low pressure before milling.
Easy-cook rice Also known as instant or pre-cooked rice, the grains are husked, soaked, briefly boiled and then heat-dried.
Boil-in-the-bag rice This is referred to as a convenience rice, although it takes just as long to cook as regular rice. The main convenience is that the pan does not need to be washed afterwards. Most boil-in-the-bag rices are prepared with easy-cook (par-boiled) rice.
Frozen rice This pre-cooked rice needs only to be thawed and then re-heated, which can often be done in the microwave; check the instructions on the packet.
Canned rice This type of rice couldn't be simpler to use: open the can, tip into a bowl and re-heat in the microwave or a conventional oven. However, it is a very expensive way to eat rice, and the flavour is severely diminished.

FLOURS

These are made by grinding grains or pulses until fine. The resulting type of flour – wholemeal (whole-wheat), white, brown, etc. – depends on the degree of processing, while the hardness or strength of the flour depends on the particular type of wheat used. Flour can be made from any grain, but wheat flour is far and away the most popular and the most versatile.

WHEAT FLOURS

The majority of flours are made from ground wheat and there are many different varieties.

White flour This flour contains about 75 per cent of the wheat grain, with most of the bran and wheat germ extracted. Plain (all-purpose) flour is used for pastry-making, sauces and biscuits (cookies), while self-raising (self-rising) flour, which contains baking powder, a raising agent, is used for cakes, scones (US biscuits) and desserts. American all-purpose flour is a medium-strength flour, somewhere between the British plain and strong white bread flour. Soft flour, sometimes known as American cake flour, has been milled very finely for making sponge cakes and similar baked goods.

Unbleached white flour is a creamier colour than other white flours, which have been whitened artificially. Bleaching flour, which involves treating it with chlorine, is becoming increasingly unpopular and rare and the majority of white flours are unbleached, but always be sure to check the packets to make absolutely certain.

Above: (Top to bottom) Malted brown and white flour

Below: (Clockwise from top right) Strong white flour, stoneground wholemeal, wholemeal, wheat germ, organic wholemeal, plain white flour, organic plain flour, semolina, organic stoneground wholemeal and Granary flour. (In the centre, clockwise from top) brown, spelt and self-raising flour.

Above: Spelt flour is ground from the small brown grains of an ancient variety of wheat, which is quite different from modern types of wheat.

Wholemeal/whole-wheat flour This flour is made using the whole of the wheat grain and is sometimes called 100 per cent extraction flour: nothing is added and nothing is taken away. If the flour is milled between rollers (as opposed to being stoneground), the bran and wheat germ are automatically separated from the white inner portion of the grain and are returned to the white flour at the end of the process.

Stoneground wholemeal/whole-wheat flour This wholemeal flour has been ground in the traditional way, literally between two stones. The bran and wheat germ are milled with the rest of the wheat grain, so there is no separation of the flour at any stage. Stoneground flour is considered to have a better flavour, owing to the slow grinding of the stones. However, because the oily wheat germ is squashed into the flour rather than churned in later, stoneground flour does not keep so well as most other flours.

Organic wholemeal/whole-wheat flour This flour has been milled from organic wheat, which is wheat produced without the routine use of artificial fertilizers or pesticides. There are organic versions of all varieties of wholemeal and white flours available from health food stores and many supermarkets.

Granary flour Granary is the proprietary name of a blend of brown and rye flours and malted wheat grain. The malted grain gives this bread its characteristic sweet and slightly sticky flavour and texture. It is available from most stores.

Graham flour This popular American flour is slightly coarser than ordinary wholemeal (whole-wheat). It is named after the Reverend Sylvester Graham, a 19th-century Connecticut cleric, who developed the flour and advocated using the whole grain for bread-making because of the health benefits of bran.

Brown flour This flour contains about 85 per cent of the original grain, with some of the bran and wheat germ extracted. It produces a lighter loaf than 100 per cent wholemeal (whole-wheat) flour, but retains a high percentage of the nutritious wheat germ.

Strong bread flour Strong bread flour – whether it is white or wholemeal – is the recommended type for bread-making. Strong flours are higher in a particular kind of protein which, when mixed with water, forms gluten. It is this that gives dough its elasticity, which in turn means that air can be trapped inside the dough, and this produces a wonderfully soft loaf when cooked.

Semolina This high-gluten flour is made from the endosperm of durum wheat before it is fully milled into fine flour. It can be ground to a coarse granular texture or a finer flour. The finer flour is traditionally used for making pasta, but also makes a delicious bread when combined with other flours.

Spelt flour Spelt is one of the oldest cultivated species of wheat. It is grown in only a few areas of Europe today, but some of the smaller flour mills produce a spelt flour that is available in some health food stores. It is popular in northern Europe, especially Germany, Switzerland and France, and is beginning to enjoy a revival in some other countries. This may be because the gluten it contains is fragile, so people with a gluten intolerance may be able to use it. It contains more B vitamins than other wheat grains.

OTHER FLOURS

Rice flour Polished rice, if ground very finely, becomes rice flour. It has a similar texture to cornflour and can be used as a thickening agent, mixed with a little water, milk or stock according to the recipe, and added while the dish is hot and still cooking. It is particularly useful to people with wheat allergies. In Asia, it is widely used for making rice papers and the dough for dumplings. It is often used to make sticky Asian cakes and sweets, but because rice flour does not contain gluten, bread and cakes are rather flat. Rice flour can be combined with wheat flour to make bread, but this produces a crumbly loaf.

Glutinous rice flour This is made from finely ground glutinous rice and is normally labelled rice powder.

Below: Glutinous rice flour is used in Asian cooking to make sweet desserts.

Maize meal Also known as *masa harina*, this is made from the cooked whole grain, which is ground into flour and commonly used to make the classic Mexican flat bread, tortilla.

Cornflour/cornstarch This fine white powder is made by grinding the white heart of the corn kernel. It is most commonly used as a thickening agent for sauces, soups and gravies.

Arrowroot This is not strictly a flour, but has very similar culinary properties to cornflour. It can be used as a thickener and, because it turns clear, is good for thickening desserts and fruit sauces.

Rye flour This is used extensively for Russian and Scandinavian breads, partly because the climates in these countries are cold and wet and not suitable for wheat cultivation. Light and medium rye flours are produced from the endosperm, while dark rye includes the whole grain, resulting in a coarser flour, which adds more texture to the bread. Rye contains gluten and, when used on its own, produces a heavy bread. Rye flour dough is very sticky and difficult to handle.

Millet flour This light yellow flour has a sweet flavour and a slightly gritty texture. It tends to give breads a dry, crumbly texture, so you may need to add extra fat when using. If using it to make bread, boost the gluten content by using at least 75 per cent white bread flour.

Barley flour This is made from pearl barley. Barley flour has a mild, slightly sweet, earthy flavour and gives breads a soft, almost cake-like texture due to its very low gluten content. To make bread, barley flour must be combined with white bread flour.

Buckwheat flour This greyish-brown flour has a distinctive, bitter, earthy flavour. It is traditionally used to make pancakes, Russian blinis and French galettes. To make bread, it is best used in combination with other flours.

Chickpea flour This very fine Indian flour is also called gram flour, or *besan*. It is used to make breads and for making onion and vegetable *bhajis*.

Above: (Clockwise from top right) Oatmeal, rye, barley, buckwheat and millet flours make a tasty alternative to the more common wheat flours.

Jowar flour Jowar grows over most of central and southern India. The flour ground from the pretty pale yellow grains is a creamy-white colour. It is mainly used for bread-making, and also for coating foods before frying.

Ata/Chapati flour This is a very fine wholemeal (whole-wheat) flour, which is normally found only in Indian stores, where it is sometimes labelled *ata*. It is used for making chapatis, parathas and other flat breads. If it is not available, well-sifted wholemeal flour may be used.

Soya flour This is a finely ground, high-protein flour made from the soya bean. It is used as a thickener in a wide range of sauces and soups. As it has a strong flavour, it is often mixed with other flours such as wheat flour to make bread and pastries, when it adds a pleasant nutty taste.

RAISING AGENTS

If you are baking cakes or bread, or making sponge puddings, some kind of raising agent is necessary to achieve a successful and light-textured result. There are a number of different, widely-used, leavening agents such as yeast and baking powder. Each one imparts its own unique character to the flavour and texture of the bread or cake.

FRESH YEAST

Yeast is the most popular leavening agent for bread-making, since it is considered to have the best flavour. It is the one preferred by almost all bakers. Fresh yeast is available from bakers, from health food stores and from most supermarkets that have an in-store bakery. It is pale beige, has a sweet, fruity smell and should crumble easily. It can be stored in the refrigerator, wrapped in clear film (plastic wrap), for up to 2 weeks, or can be frozen for up to 3 months. Yeast needs warmth to activate it, but must not be subjected to too high a temperature, or it will die.

DRIED YEAST

There are several different types of dried yeast, including easy-blend (rapid-rise) and fast-action yeasts. These are all produced for the convenience of people making bread at home. Although almost all bakers prefer fresh yeast, when this is not available or convenient, dried yeast is a handy substitute. Dried yeast is also the recommended yeast for breads made in a bread machine. Always check the use-by date on dried yeast. If the product is past its use-by date, it should be replaced as it may have lost its potency and will not give satisfactory results.

BAKING POWDER

This is made up of acid and alkaline chemicals. When these come into contact with moisture, as in a dough or batter, the reaction of the chemicals produces tiny bubbles of air so the cake, bread or pudding rises and becomes spongy. It is important to work fast when using baking powder, as the carbon dioxide will quickly escape and the cake or loaf won't rise as required, often causing it to collapse.

Using Yeast

Yeast needs warmth to activate, but must not be subjected to too high a temperature or it will die. Whether dissolving yeast in water or adding liquid to the yeast and flour, always make sure that the liquid isn't too warm. The optimum temperature is 38°C/100°F. If you do not have a thermometer, mix 300ml/½ pint/1¼ cups boiling water with 600ml/1 pint/2½ cups cold water, and measure the required quantity of water from the mixture.

BICARBONATE OF SODA/BAKING SODA

Also simply known as soda, bicarbonate of soda can often be used as a raising agent on its own in recipes where an acid ingredient is present. It is an alkaline chemical which, when mixed with an acid in a moisture-rich environment, reacts to produce carbon dioxide. Traditional Irish soda bread, that uses buttermilk, for instance, needs only the addition of bicarbonate of soda for the loaf to rise. If an acid ingredient is not used, then most recipes suggest cream of tartar to provide the necessary acid. Bicarbonate of soda used on its own as a raising agent can leave an unpleasant aftertaste.

CREAM OF TARTAR

This very fine white powder is most commonly used in conjunction with bicarbonate of soda to make soda breads. In fact, these two ingredients, when combined in the proportions of two parts cream of tartar to one part bicarbonate of soda, make baking powder. The acid is made by crystallizing grape acid. Buttermilk, soured milk or orange juice are naturally acidic and can be used instead.

Left: (Clockwise from top left) Fresh yeast, dried yeast, fast-action dried and easy-blend (rapid-rise) dried yeast can all be used to leaven bread.

BREAD

In almost every country around the world, bread is a staple food. Breads may be flat like Mexican tortillas or Indian chapatis or leavened like French baguettes or Italian ciabatta, they may have a crisp or soft crust or crumb, and are likely to come in all manner of shapes and sizes. The way the bread is made, the ingredients used and the way in which it is cooked all contribute to these many wonderful variations.

WHOLE LOAVES

There are numerous examples of leavened whole loaves – from those baked in tins (pans) such as farmhouse loaves, tins and split tins to traditional breads baked on baking sheets or straight on the sole of the oven. The traditional cottage loaf, the dumpy-looking cob and the slashed pain de campagne are among the many classic shapes of breads. Brown and wholemeal (whole-wheat) breads are now very popular although for a large part of the 20th century, it was mostly white bread that was produced commercially since it had the reputation of being more refined, and therefore a far superior product.

SHAPED BREADS

There are numerous breads that do not conform to the traditional loaf shape, such as the wheat-shaped epi from France and the plaited (braided) Jewish bread challah. Most of these are baked on the sole of the oven, although for home-bakers specially shaped tins for some loaves are available.

Baguette The baguette was developed in Paris in the 1930s and is now one of the most popular breads in the world. The bread owes its superb flavour and crust to the soft French flour, the small amounts of yeast used, the long kneading and rising period, and finally – but not least – to the skill of the baker. There are numerous variations using this same dough recipe, including *flutes*, *bâtards*, *ficelles* and *petits pains*.

Below: Pugliese is a popular Italian bread enriched with olive oil.

Above: Portuguese Rosquilha is usually eaten as a breakfast bread, or during mid-morning with a cup of coffee.

Breadsticks *Grissini* are probably the best-known breadsticks. These Italian breads are cooked until completely dry, so that they are basically all crust and no crumb. The better *grissini* are made using olive oil. Quite similar breadsticks are also available in Greece and Turkey. They are somewhat chunkier than the Italian variety, and are normally sprinkled with sesame or poppy seeds. The Greek *koulouria* are similar, but the bread has been formed into rings, like pretzels.

Sfilatino *Sfilatino* comes from Italy and is a popular addition to the dinner table. It is made with olive oil and goes very well with Italian food. It is similar in shape to the French baguette, but smaller and without slashes on the top. The crust is also crisper, darker and more floury than a baguette, and rather less flaky. It has a soft crumb.

Rosquilha This is an attractive ring-shaped white bread from Portugal. It has a pleasant crust, which forms as a result of its shape, and a slightly chewy texture and a salty flavour. It does not keep well so is best enjoyed really fresh.

Above: Sfilatino are crusty Italian loaves.

Olive Oil Breads

Throughout the Mediterranean region, breads are made with olive oil, which gives them a delicious flavour and wonderful texture.

Pan gallego This typical country-style bread from Spain, like many Spanish breads, has a soft flour crust, while the crumb is light with an open texture. Seed *gallego* is a similar loaf, studded with pumpkin and sesame seeds.

Pugliese This much-loved Italian bread was once the regional bread from Puglia, in the southern region of Apulia. Like many Italian breads, it is enriched with olive oil, and it is considered to be among the jewels of Italian breads. It is popular all over the country and beyond.

Below: Portuguese papo secos have a delicious soft crumb and a crust that is crisp without being too hard.

Below: Bagels are the classic Jewish roll to be enjoyed at any time of day.

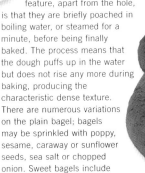

Left: Soft Scottish morning rolls are made with lard, which is rubbed into the flour.

SMALL BREADS

Rolls and small breads are extremely popular served for breakfast, for picnic lunches, at tea-time and served with dinner.

Papo secos These small white rolls are a popular breakfast bread all over Portugal. They have a soft white crumb and a delicious crust that is crisp without being hard. Like many breads from Portugal, *papo secos* are baked with lots of steam, which accounts for their crust, yet produces a crumb that is wonderfully light and airy.

Bagels Known as the roll with a hole, these are probably the most famous Jewish bread. They were traditionally made for *bar mitzvahs*, although today they can be bought almost anywhere and enjoyed at any time. Their unique feature, apart from the hole, is that they are briefly poached in boiling water, or steamed for a minute, before being finally baked. The process means that the dough puffs up in the water but does not rise any more during baking, producing the characteristic dense texture. There are numerous variations on the plain bagel; bagels may be sprinkled with poppy, sesame, caraway or sunflower seeds, sea salt or chopped onion. Sweet bagels include cinnamon or raisin varieties.

Morning rolls Also known as baps, morning rolls or just rolls, these soft, flattish, floury rolls are to be found in every bakery and supermarket in Scotland. The dimple in the centre of the roll is pressed into the dough just before baking to stop the tops blistering.

FLAVOURED BREADS

Bakers have been flavouring doughs with herbs, spices, cheese and seeds since time immemorial. As well as adding flavour, they add texture and interest to a loaf.

Focaccia Also known as *pizza rustica* or *pizza Genovese*, focaccia is a large flat bread, slightly puffy and dimpled all over the surface with indentations. The dough is often flavoured with sun-dried tomatoes or chopped black olives.

Below: Focaccia is popularly sprinkled with crushed rosemary before baking.

Left: German pumpernickel is probably the best-known of all the square-shaped, steamed rye breads.

Rossisky This bread is made from a sourdough starter, using 100 per cent rye flour. It has a distinctive, yet pleasant flavour and is one of the most delicious of all Russian breads.

Borodinsky Another classic Russian bread, borodinsky is flavoured with crushed coriander seeds. It can be made entirely with dark rye or with a blend of rye and wheat meal. Barley meal is also often used, giving an earthy flavour, while buttermilk or yogurt is occasionally added, both of which enhance the naturally tangy sourdough flavour.

Russian black bread Like many Russian breads, this is a substantial-looking loaf flavoured with molasses. It is usually made with an equal blend of rye and wheat flour and has a pleasant sweet/sour flavour that is characteristic of many rye breads. The combination of molasses and rye give it a wonderfully dark, moist crumb.

RYE BREADS

Along with wheat, rye is the other cereal that is widely used to make bread. It is extremely hardy and does well in climates that are too inhospitable to grow wheat. Because of this, rye is a hugely popular grain for bread-making in eastern and northern Europe and there are a countless number of different loaves. The use of rye flour gives them a characteristic, tangy flavour.

Kastenbrots These are the familiar box-shaped rye breads, and the name translates as box bread. The bread is steam-baked for some 20 hours in an enclosed tin (pan), which results in a dense and heavy loaf that is both moist and crumbly with a chewy texture. It has a sour flavour, but with a certain sweet and malty overtone. They are best eaten with strong tasting foods and malty types of drinks such as beer. Among the best-known varieties are pumpernickel, the darkest of the rye breads, vollkornbrot, another strongly flavoured rye bread, and roggenbrot.

Weisenkeimbrot This translates as wheat germ bread, and is made using the wheat germ along with rye grain.

Sonnenblumenbrot This bread is made using a small proportion of wheat flour along with the rye meal.

Krustenbrot This popular square rye bread from Germany is a crusty-style loaf. It is often just known as German rye but, unlike other rye breads, it has a pleasant, gentle flavour, owing partly to use of a blend of rye and wheat flours.

Right: (Left to right) Vollkornbrot and sonnenblumenbrot have the distinctive, sharp flavour of rye.

Above: Rossisky and borodinsky are both widely available outside Russia.

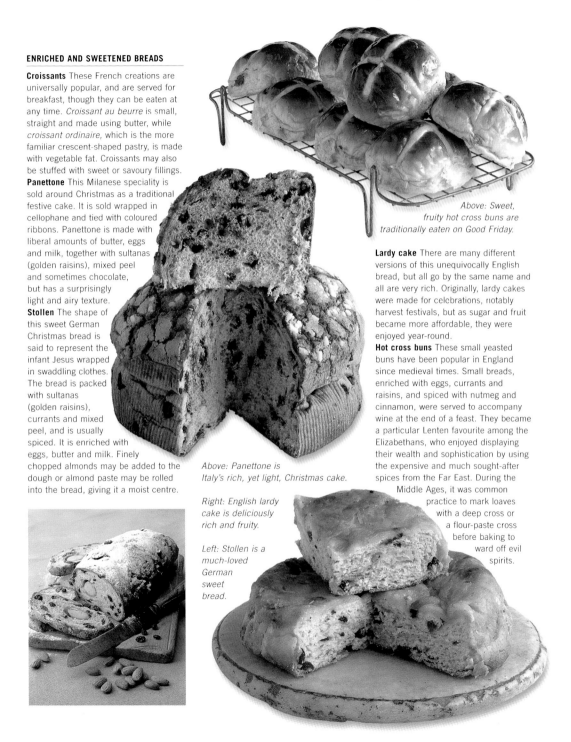

ENRICHED AND SWEETENED BREADS

Croissants These French creations are universally popular, and are served for breakfast, though they can be eaten at any time. *Croissant au beurre* is small, straight and made using butter, while *croissant ordinaire,* which is the more familiar crescent-shaped pastry, is made with vegetable fat. Croissants may also be stuffed with sweet or savoury fillings.

Panettone This Milanese speciality is sold around Christmas as a traditional festive cake. It is sold wrapped in cellophane and tied with coloured ribbons. Panettone is made with liberal amounts of butter, eggs and milk, together with sultanas (golden raisins), mixed peel and sometimes chocolate, but has a surprisingly light and airy texture.

Stollen The shape of this sweet German Christmas bread is said to represent the infant Jesus wrapped in swaddling clothes. The bread is packed with sultanas (golden raisins), currants and mixed peel, and is usually spiced. It is enriched with eggs, butter and milk. Finely chopped almonds may be added to the dough or almond paste may be rolled into the bread, giving it a moist centre.

Above: Sweet, fruity hot cross buns are traditionally eaten on Good Friday.

Lardy cake There are many different versions of this unequivocally English bread, but all go by the same name and all are very rich. Originally, lardy cakes were made for celebrations, notably harvest festivals, but as sugar and fruit became more affordable, they were enjoyed year-round.

Hot cross buns These small yeasted buns have been popular in England since medieval times. Small breads, enriched with eggs, currants and raisins, and spiced with nutmeg and cinnamon, were served to accompany wine at the end of a feast. They became a particular Lenten favourite among the Elizabethans, who enjoyed displaying their wealth and sophistication by using the expensive and much sought-after spices from the Far East. During the Middle Ages, it was common practice to mark loaves with a deep cross or a flour-paste cross before baking to ward off evil spirits.

Above: Panettone is Italy's rich, yet light, Christmas cake.

Right: English lardy cake is deliciously rich and fruity.

Left: Stollen is a much-loved German sweet bread.

FLAT BREADS

Contrary to popular belief, not all flat breads are unleavened – that is, made without yeast – although a significant few are. Pitta bread, naan and most Middle Eastern flat breads are made using a conventional yeasted dough but are cooked in a flat shape. They may be made with different types of flour, not just wheat.

MIDDLE EASTERN FLAT BREADS

Pitta bread Pitta breads, or *pide* to give them their Turkish name, are probably the best-known Greek and Turkish breads. This style of bread – flat and baked so that it contains a pocket – is popular throughout the Middle East, although often in different shapes and known by different names. It is made using wheat flour and is leavened with yeast, the flatness being the result of the method of baking – usually in an extremely hot clay oven. Pitta breads are popular almost everywhere, used as they are intended, for stuffing with meats and vegetables.

Khoubiz Similar to pitta bread, *khoubiz* means simply bread in Arabic. Like pitta, it is flat and slightly leavened, made in rounds, sometimes as large as 30cm/12in in diameter.

Barbari are sometimes called Persian flat breads. They have slightly more crumb than pitta and are sometimes flavoured with caraway or cumin seeds.

Lavash is the flattest of all the Middle Eastern breads and can be either leavened or unleavened.

Ragayig is very similar to lavash. It is an unleavened bread and is thought to be one of the world's most ancient breads.

Above: Pitta bread can be split open and stuffed with any type of filling.

Above: Khoubiz are one of the many flat breads from the Middle East.

Above: (Top to bottom) Indian chapatis and parathas are used to pick up food.

INDIAN FLAT BREADS

There are many Indian flat breads, many well known thanks to the popularity of Indian cuisine in the West. The majority of Indian breads are unleavened; they may be made using wheat flour, but frequently use the meal of other grains.

Right: Matzos are the classic unleavened bread eaten at Passover.

Chapatis These unleavened breads are popular in central and southern parts of India. They are served with most meals. Authentic chapatis are made with *ata* (chapati flour) which is a very fine wholemeal (whole-wheat) flour.

Parathas These are a richer and flakier version of chapatis. The chapati dough is spread with ghee, folded and then cooked over a *tava* (griddle) until puffy.

Naan Unlike the chapati, this is a leavened bread, which is made using yogurt. It is this that gives the bread its characteristic light and puffy texture and soft crust. The flavour comes partly from the yogurt and partly from the *tandoor*, in which the breads are cooked. Naan may be made plain or flavoured – a popular choice being garlic and coriander.

Matzo This crisp, brittle unleavened bread is served in Jewish households during Passover. Because any type of leavening is forbidden at Passover, matzos are made with great speed and under strict dietary regulations to make sure that the flour and water mixture does not start to ferment. Matzo is sometimes served at the table, but more commonly the bread is ground into meal and used for cakes, biscuits (cookies) and dumplings.

Above: Swedish krisprolls are commmonly eaten for breakfast.

Below: Wafer-thin flatbrød is one of the oldest of all the Norwegian breads.

OTHER FLAT BREADS

Tortillas There are basically two types: corn tortillas, made using *masa harina* – a type of cornmeal – and wheat tortillas. Both feature in Mexican cooking.

Flatbrød This was until fairly recently the bread most commonly eaten by the Norwegians. A long time ago, these wafer-thin crispbreads would have been made with any cereal that was to hand – mostly oats, rye, barley or pea-flour. The unleavened dough would have been rolled into very thin, large circles and baked on a griddle or on a stone over an open fire. The breads were known to last for months, even up to a year, and would be stored on the beams over the kitchen. Today they are factory-baked and sold cut into rectangles.

Polar flat breads Also known as polar rounds or polar thins, these very crisp cracker-like breads are widely available in our supermarkets. They contain a mixture of rye and wheat flours and have a pleasant, slightly nutty flavour.

Crispbreads

They are crisp throughout, with no soft crumb at all. There are a large number of different crispbreads and they are particularly popular in Scandinavia, although Dutch crispbreads are well known, too. Norwegian crispbreads are mainly made using whole rye or a blend of wheat and rye meal. Krisprolls, from Sweden, are eaten at almost any time of the day, but particularly at breakfast. They have a noticeably sweet flavour.

Left: Wheat tortillas are an essential part of many Mexican dishes.

PASTA, NOODLES AND WRAPPERS

Usually made from a simple flour and water dough, these

staples are enjoyed the world over. Italian pasta and Asian

noodles are strikingly similar and are normally cooked, then

combined with other ingredients — perhaps tossed with

stir-fried vegetables or a sauce, or added to a salad. Asian

pancakes and wrappers, on the other hand, are used to wrap

around ingredients, rather like a very thin flat bread.

PASTA

The many hundreds of different types of dried and fresh pasta are divided into categories. Long, short and flat shapes are the most common, but there are also stuffed shapes, shapes suitable for stuffing and tiny shapes for use in soup. Among these, you will find some lesser-known regional shapes and unusual and decorative designer shapes.

DRIED PASTA

Commercially produced dried pasta has always been highly regarded in Italy. It is in no way inferior to fresh home-made pasta, but is simply a different form of this fabulous food.

LONG PASTA

Dried long pasta in the form of spaghetti is probably the best-known pasta of all time, and was certainly one of the first types to be exported from Italy. Spaghetti is still very widely used, but today there are many other varieties of long pasta that look and taste just as good. There are no hard-and-fast rules when matching pasta to sauce, so experiment with alternative varieties to add interest to your cooking, always remembering that long pasta is best served with either a thin, clinging sauce or one that is smooth and thick. Clinging sauces made with olive oil, butter, cream, eggs, finely grated cheese and chopped fresh herbs are good with long pasta. When ingredients, such as vegetables, fish and meat, are added to a smooth thick sauce, they should be very finely chopped.

Long pasta comes in different lengths, but 30cm/12in is about the average. In specialist food stores, you may see dried pasta that is much longer than this, but think twice before buying it because extra-long pasta can be tricky to cook and eat, and is often not worth the bother. The width of long pasta differs according to the variety. The strands can be flat, hollow, round or square, and some long pastas have the strands coiled in nests.

Most long shapes are available in plain durum wheat only. The shapes made with egg (*all'uovo*) are very delicate, and are either packed in nests or compressed as waves. Fine long pasta, such as spaghetti, is far too delicate to be made with egg, but there is a short version from Emilia-Romagna.

Bavette This narrow, oval, flat pasta is known all over Italy, but is very common in the south. Bavettine is a narrower version of the same shape. Both types can be plain or made with egg.

Below: Bavette

Above: Bucatini

Below: Bucatini perciatellini

Bucatini This long, thin pasta looks like spaghetti but is slightly chunkier. The strands are hollow (*buco* means hole), rather like hard, inflexible drinking straws. This type of pasta is best known in the Roman dish called Bucatini all'Amatriciana, in which bucatini is served with a tomato, bacon and (bell) pepper sauce. In Sicily, bucatini is traditionally served with a sauce of fresh sardines. Bucatoni is a fatter version, while perciatelli is simply bucatini by another name.

Above: Capelli d'angelo a nidi

Below: Capelli d'angelo

Above: Capellini

Below: Capellini a nidi

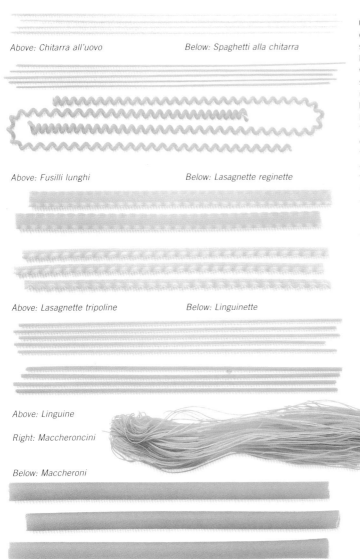

Above: Chitarra all'uovo

Below: Spaghetti alla chitarra

Above: Fusilli lunghi

Below: Lasagnette reginette

Above: Lasagnette tripoline

Below: Linguinette

Above: Linguine

Right: Maccheroncini

Below: Maccheroni

Chitarra Also known as spaghetti alla chitarra, this type of pasta is cut on a special wooden frame strung with wires like guitar strings (*chitarra* is the Italian word for guitar). It is therefore square-shaped, rather than round, but can be used as an alternative to spaghetti.

Fusilli These are spaghetti spirals that look like long opened-out corkscrews. You may see them labelled fusilli lunghi or fusilli col buco, to distinguish them from the more widely-known short fusilli and eliche. Fusilli is very good served with classic tomato sauces.

Lasagnette This flat, long pasta looks quite similar to tagliatelle, but the noodles are slightly wider. There are several types of lasagnette, most of which have frilly edges. Reginette is similar. You can use lasagnette in place of any type of ribbon pasta.

Linguine In Italian *linguine* means little tongues and describes the very thin spaghetti-like pasta that has flattened edges. You may also see linguinette and lingue di passera (sparrows' tongues), both of which are even narrower than linguine. There is also a whole-wheat variety of linguine available. All are good served with the olive oil-based sauces and smooth tomato sauces that are popular in southern Italy.

Maccheroni This is a very familiar form of pasta. We know a short version of it as macaroni, but in Italy, the long thick tubes are widely used for all kinds of sauces. In certain parts of Italy, the term maccheroni is even used as a generic term for pasta and maccheroncini is the name that is given to very thin, long pasta.

Maccheroni is available in many different lengths and thicknesses, with either straight or angled ends and in plain, egg and whole-wheat varieties. There is even a square-shaped chitarra version, which comes from Abruzzi. There, they call it maccheroni alla chitarra, but it is also commonly known as tonnarelli. Maccheroni is very popular and versatile because it goes with so many different sauces – from fresh tomato and vegetable sauces to rich, creamy, cheese sauces.

Capelli d'angelo In Italian, the name of this pasta means angel's hair, which is an evocative description for its shape of extremely fine, long strands. It is used in broths and soups, and is popular with children. Capelli d'angelo is most often found packed in nests, labelled capelli d'angelo a nidi. Packing them in this way helps to protect the delicate pasta from breaking, and the nests are simple to handle and cook – one nest per person is the usual serving, so it is easy to measure out portions. Other types of pasta that are very similar to capelli d'angelo include pretty capellini and capel Venere.

Spaghetti This familiar type of pasta takes its name from the word *spago*, which means string, so *spaghetti* means little strings. Spaghettini is a thinner variety, and spaghettoni is thicker. Spaghetti originally came from Naples, but today it is made in other parts of Italy too, and the length and width vary from one region to another. Numerous different brands, flavours and colours are available, including whole-wheat (*integrali*), spinach (*spinaci*) and chilli (*peperoncini*), so the choice is yours. Long Italian spaghetti is graded by number according to its thickness. Good-quality spaghetti made in Italy is still one of the best forms of pasta, despite the ever-increasing range of other shapes. It goes well with many different kinds of sauces.

Tagliatelle The most common form of ribbon noodle, tagliatelle are usually about 8–10mm/⅓–½in wide, but there are fine versions called tagliatellina, tagliarini and tagliolini. Traditional tagliatelle comes from Bologna. It is made both with and without egg and with spinach (*verdi*), as well as new flavours and colours, and is sold coiled in nests, which unravel during cooking. Paglia e fieno (which means straw and hay in Italian) is a mixture of half plain egg and half spinach egg pasta, packed together in separate bundles of each colour. Meat sauce is the classic sauce, as in tagliatelle alla Bolognese.

Below: (Top to bottom) Vermicelli, ziti and mezza ziti

Above: Spaghetti

Above: Spaghetti integrali

Above: Spaghetti con spinaci

Above: Spaghettoni

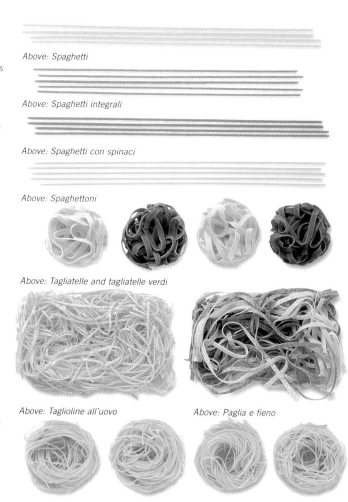

Above: Tagliatelle and tagliatelle verdi

Above: Taglioline all'uovo

Above: Paglia e fieno

Above: Taglierini all'uovo

Vermicelli The name of this very fine form of spaghetti means little worms. It comes in plain and egg varieties and is extremely versatile, going well with most light sauces, but especially the fresh tomato and shellfish sauces for which Naples is famous.

Ziti This pasta takes its name from the word *zita* (fiancée). It was traditional in southern Italy to serve ziti at wedding feasts. It is very long, thick and hollow and you break it into whatever length is required when you cook it. The tubes go well with robust, chunky sauces.

Types of Long Dried Pasta

Fettuccine These noodles come from Lazio and are used in classic Roman pasta dishes such as Fettuccine all'Alfredo. They are flat ribbons, like tagliatelle but narrower (about 5mm/¼in wide), and always sold coiled into loose nests. The three most common varieties are plain durum wheat, with egg (*all'uovo*), and with spinach (*verdi*), and you can use them in place of tagliatelle. Fettuccelle is similar, but is straight rather than coiled. Fettuccelle integrali is the whole-wheat variety.

Frappe This type of pasta from Emilia-Romagna. The 2.5–4cm/1–1½in wide noodles are flat, with wavy edges, about halfway in size between tagliatelle and lasagne. Made with egg and very delicate, the noodles are packed by a special machine that presses them into waves.

Pappardelle These broad ribbon noodles (2–2.5cm/¾–1in wide) with wavy edges come from Tuscany, where they are still made fresh with egg every day. Dried versions are now also becoming more widely available,

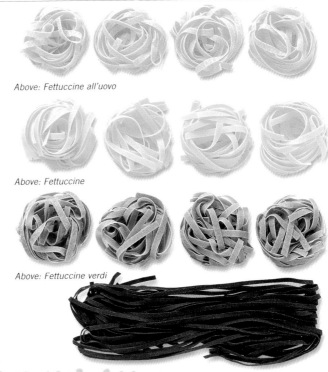

Above: Fettuccine all'uovo

Above: Fettuccine

Above: Fettuccine verdi

Above: Fettuccine all nero

Above: Frappe

Above: Pappardelle

many of them with only one wavy edge or straight edges. They are good with meat and game sauces. Nastroni are similar straight-sided noodles that are sold coiled into nests.

Trenette These noodles come from Liguria, where they are traditionally served with pesto sauce, a blend of olive oil, basil, pine nuts, garlic and Parmesan. The classic Genoese dish, Trenette alla Genovese, combines this long pasta with pesto, potatoes and beans. The noodles are about 3mm/⅛in wide, and are made with egg. They closely resemble bavette and linguine, which can be used as a substitute if you cannot find trenette in local stores or supermarkets.

Left: Trenette

SHORT PASTA

There are literally hundreds of different short pasta shapes, and new ones are constantly becoming available. Some people prefer short pasta simply because it is easier to cook and eat than long pasta. It also goes well with many different sauces and, in most cases, you can choose any shape you fancy, regardless of whether your sauce is a smooth tomato-, cream- or olive oil-based type, or is chunky with large pieces of fish, meat or vegetables. Exceptions are regional dishes that are traditionally cooked with a specific shape of pasta such as Penne all'Arrabbiata from Lazio.

Short pasta is divided into two main groups. Pasta secca is factory-made, using durum wheat flour and water. This is by far the largest group. *Pasta all'uovo* is made with the addition of eggs. It is naturally a brighter yellow than *pasta secca* and is more nutritious. Popular in the north of Italy, especially in Emilia-Romagna, *pasta all'uovo* has different properties from plain pasta and goes especially well with the rich, creamy and meaty sauces associated with that region. It has an advantage over plain durum wheat pasta in that it cooks slightly more quickly and is less likely to become overcooked and soggy. Although it tends to be slightly more expensive than plain pasta, egg pasta is becoming more popular and therefore more widely available, so keep an eye out for it in an increasing number of shapes and sizes.

New flavours and colours in short pasta shapes are on the increase too. For many years, tomato (*pomodoro*) and spinach (*verde*) were all that was

Below: Benfatti

available, but today there seems to be no end to the number of different colour and flavour combinations, ranging from garlic, chillies and herbs to beetroot (beet), salmon, mushroom and squid ink. Often red, white and green shapes are packed together, as pasta tricolore. Whole-wheat pasta is made from durum wheat and other cereals. It is higher in fibre than plain durum wheat pasta and takes longer to cook. It has a chewy texture and nutty flavour.

Benfatti Meaning well made, *benfatti* originally described the little offcuts or scraps of pasta left over from making other shapes. Traditionally, these were used in soups so they would not be wasted, but they proved so popular that they are now made and marketed as a shape in their own right. Benfatti are available plain and with egg, and are good in salads as well as soups.

Above: Chifferini rigatini

Chifferini Also called chifferi, chifferoni and chifferotti, these are small curved tubes like short, bent maccheroni. Some versions are ridged (*rigatini*). The holes in the middle fill with sauce, making them an excellent shape for all types of pasta sauces and soups.

Conchiglie These shapes resemble small conch shells. Sometimes they are ridged, in which case they are called conchiglie rigate. They are one of the most useful small shapes because they are concave and trap virtually any sauce. For this reason they are hugely popular and are widely available in many different colours and flavours. Sizes vary too, from tiny conchigliette for soups to conchiglione, which are jumbo shells for stuffing.

Above: Conchiglie rigate

Eliche The name comes from the Italian word for screws or propellers (as on a ship), which is exactly what these shapes look like. They are often mis-labelled as fusilli, which have a similar shape, but when you see the two side by side there is a marked difference. Eliche are short lengths of pasta, each twisted into a spiral, like the thread of a screw. They are available in different thicknesses, colours and flavours, including whole-wheat and tricolore, and are good with virtually all sauces, but especially those that are tomato-based. You may only be able to buy them labelled as fusilli – but the two are fairly interchangeable and their names often depend only on which region of Italy they come from.

Below: Eliche all'uovo

Below: Eliche tricolori

Above: Farfalle

Above: Farfalle verdi

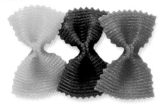

Above: Farfalle tricolore

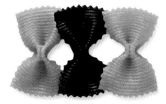

Above: Farfalle salmoseppia

Farfalle The name of this pasta means butterflies, but these shapes are also sometimes described as bow-ties – the Italian word for bow-tie being *cravatta a farfalla*. They are very pretty, with crinkled edges, and are sometimes ridged. Owing to their great popularity, they are available in a wide variety of colours and flavours, plain, with egg and tricolore. Farfalle can be served with almost any sauce, but they are particularly good with cream and tomato sauces. Children, in particular, love them. In Modena in Emilia-Romagna, farfalle are known as strichetti.

Fusilli These spirals of thin pasta look like tight coils or springs and are formed by winding fresh dough around a thin rod. The spiral opens out, rather than remaining solid as it does in the case of eliche, for which fusilli are often mistaken. Check when buying, because most packets of fusilli are in fact eliche. Genuine fusilli is likely to be plain, neither made with egg nor coloured. The shapes go well with thin sauces.

Lumache Snail shells were the inspiration for this attractively shaped pasta. Unlike conchiglie, they are not shaped like conch shells, but resemble a larger version of pipe, because they are fashioned out of hollow pasta. Lumache are excellent for trapping sauces. The most common type available is *lumache rigate* (ridged), and there is also a large version called lumachoni. Gomiti is a similar conch shell-shaped pasta.

Above: Fusilli

Above: Fusilli con spinaci

Below: Fusilli tricolore

Above: Lumache rigate

Above: Lumachoni rigati

Above: Maccheroni

Above: Maccaroncelli

Maccheroni In the south of Italy, the term is normally taken to mean the long variety, but in the north it is usually short. It is this short variety that is generally exported as macaroni (often labelled elbow macaroni, although some brands are straighter than others). This used to be the most common short pasta shape outside Italy, but other more interesting shapes now rival its popularity. Being hollow, it is a good shape for most sauces and baked dishes. Both plain and egg maccheroni are available, and there are also many different sizes, including a thin, quick-cooking variety. Tubetti is the name given to a miniature version for soups.

Above: Penne rigate

Above: Penne rigate con spinaci

Above: Penne lisce

Above: Mezze penne tricolori

Below: Penne mezzanine

Penne Like maccheroni, penne are hollow tubes, but their ends are cut diagonally so they are pointed like quills (*penne* means feather or quill pen). In the popularity stakes, they seem to have taken over from maccheroni, possibly because of their more interesting shape. They go well with virtually every sauce and are particularly good with chunky sauces as their sturdiness means that they hold the weight well. Penne lisce are smooth; penne rigate are ridged. Other less common varieties include the small and thin pennette and even thinner pennini and penne mezzanine, the short and stubby mezze penne or half penne, and the large pennoni. Penne made with egg and flavoured penne are very common.

Pipe These shapes look like a cross between conchiglie and lumache. They are curved and hollow (the name means pipes) and, more often than not, ridged (*rigate*). They are quite small. They are excellent for catching sauce and make an interesting change from other more common hollow varieties. Plain and wholewheat varieties are available, and there is also a smaller version known as pipette.

Rigatoni From the maccheroni family, these are ridged, hollow, chunky-looking shapes. They are very popular because they are sturdy enough to hold substantial sauces, and they come in many flavours. There is a short version called mezzi rigatoni and a straight, stubby version called millerighe. The texture of rigatoni always seems slightly chewier than that of other short pasta. Similar in shape but slightly narrower are elicoidali, which have curved ridges (their name means helixes). Elicoidali can be plain or flavoured.

Rotelle These are cartwheel shapes. There is a ridged variety, rotelle rigate, and sometimes this shape goes under other names such as ruote, ruote di carro and trulli. Although not a classic Italian shape, the spokes of the wheels

Above: Rigatoni

Above: Rigatoni con basilico

Above: Mezzi rigatoni

are very good for holding chunky sauces. Children like them, and most supermarkets sell them in different colours and flavours. The plain Italian brands taste very good.

Below: Rotelle

Below: Rotelle tricolore

Regional Types of Short Dried Pasta

Garganelli This tubular egg pasta shape comes from Emilia Romagna. Garganelli resemble a more intriguing version of penne, as they look more like scrolls than quills because you can clearly see how they have been rolled. This is done on a special tool, (*il pettine*) that looks like a comb.

Gnocchi sardi Also called malloreddus, this pasta comes from Sardinia. They are named after the gnocchi potato dumplings, but are smaller, and look like little razor shells. Gnocchetti sardi are smaller still, and are mostly used for soups. These shapes are often flavoured with saffron and take on a yellow colour. They are served with meat and vegetable sauces and are quite chewy in texture.

Orecchiette The name of this pasta means little ears in Italian. They come from Puglia in the south-east of Italy. Always made with durum wheat, they have a chewy texture and are served with the traditional sauces of the region, especially those made with broccoli and other vegetables.

Pizzoccheri are buckwheat noodles from Valtellina in Lombardy, not far from the border with Switzerland. They are thin and flat in shape, and usually sold in little nests (*a nidi*) like fettuccine, but the strands are about half the length. Pizzoccheri are also sometimes cut to make short noodles. Their flavour is quite nutty, and they go very well with the robust tastes of northern Italian cuisine, most famously with cabbage, potatoes and cheese in the baked dish of the same name.

Strozzapreti Literally translated, the name of this pasta means priest stranglers. They come from Modena and are said to derive their name from the story of a priest who liked them so much he ate too many, and nearly choked to death, but the name may have more sinister, political associations from the past. In fact, strozzapreti consist of two pieces of pasta twisted or "strangled" together. Other similar twisted shapes are caserecce, fileia and gemelli. The Genoese trofie, although not twisted, are similar in size and shape.

Above: Short-cut pizzoccheri

Above: Pizzoccheri a nidi

Above: Strozzapreti

Below: Trofie

Trofie are from the Ligurian port of Genoa, where it is traditional to serve them with pesto sauce. They are rolls of solid pasta with pointed ends, quite small and dainty. At one time you could get only home-made trofie, but now they are available from Italian delicatessens, in which case the shapes are sometimes open along one side. They are worth buying if you want to make an authentic Genoese Trofie al Pesto.

Above: Garganelli all'uovo   *Below: Garganelli paglia e fieno*

Above: Gnocchetti sardi   *Below: Orecchiette*

FLAT PASTA

Although there are many kinds of long flat ribbon pasta such as fettuccine and tagliatelle, there is really only one broad, flat pasta used for baking in the oven (*al forno*), and that is lasagne. Thin sheets of lasagne are designed to be baked between layers of sauce in the oven – the classic dish has layers of a meat sauce, béchamel and cheese. The sheets may also be cooked in boiling water until *al dente*, rolled around a filling to make cannelloni, then baked. All types of lasagne are designed to be used in this way, and are never served with a separate sauce.

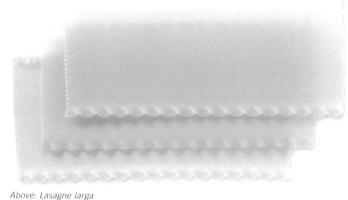

Below: Lasagne   *Above: Lasagne larga*

Below: Easy-cook lasagne all'uovo

Plain lasagne Made from durum wheat and water, this type of lasagne comes flat-packed in boxes. There are three different colours – yellow (plain), green (*verdi*), which is made with spinach, and brown or whole-wheat (*integrali*). The shape varies according to the manufacturer, ranging from narrow or broad rectangles to squares. Most sheets are completely flat, but some are wavy all over. Others have crimped or curly edges, which help to trap the sauce and look attractive, too. Get to know the different brands and their sizes and choose the ones that fit your ovenproof dish, to avoid having to cut them to fit. This will make the work of assembling the layers of ingredients before baking much quicker.

Always carefully check the cooking instructions on the packet because regular plain lasagne needs to be pre-cooked before being layered or rolled. The usual method is to plunge about four sheets at a time into a large pan of salted boiling water, boil for about 8 minutes until *al dente*, then carefully remove each sheet with a large slotted spoon and/or tongs and lay it flat on a clean damp dishtowel to drain. The sheets need to be drained in a single layer or they will stick to each other. This method is fairly time-consuming and messy, but once it has been completed and the lasagne has been assembled, the cooking time in the oven is usually only about 30 minutes.

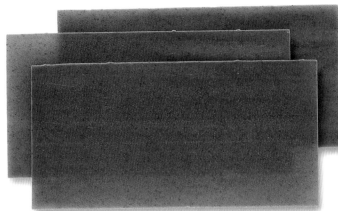

Above: Lasagne verdi

spinach, and brown or whole-wheat (*integrali*). It is available in different shapes and sizes and with a variety of different edgings. It is easiest to use if it is the right shape to fit neatly into your dish, although it can be broken to fit.

Baking time for easy-cook lasagne is slightly longer than for the preboiled varieties, so allow at least 40 minutes. Make sure that the sauce you use is runnier than usual because this type of lasagne absorbs quite a lot of liquid during baking and so needs extra sauce to keep it moist.

Below: Easy-cook lasagne verdi

Lasagnette These are long, narrow strips of flat pasta, which may be crimped on either one or two sides. They are used in the same way as lasagne, layered with sauces, then topped with grated cheese, usually Parmesan, and baked in the oven.

Festonelle are small squares of lasagnette, which are also used in baked dishes. Pantacce are tiny diagonal pieces cut from lasagnette. They can be used in baked dishes, but are more frequently added to soups.

Lasagne all'uovo This type of lasagne is made with durum wheat and water in the same way as plain lasagne, but with the addition of egg. This makes it a brighter yellow than the plain lasagne, and richer in flavour and nutrients. It is available as plain egg (*all'uovo*) and egg and spinach (*verdi all'uovo*). Like the plain lasagne, it comes in narrow or broad rectangles, or in squares of different sizes, and with a variety of different edgings – straight, crimped or curly.

Easy-cook lasagne Although a relatively recent innovation, easy-cook lasagne is fast becoming the number one favourite. Sometimes labelled as no pre-cooking required, it does not need to be boiled first, but is layered in the dish straight from the packet, thus saving lots of time and mess. As with the plain lasagne, it comes in yellow and green (*verdi*), which is made with

Above: Lasagne festonata   *Below: Lasagnette*

DRIED STUFFED PASTA

The most common type of dried stuffed pasta shapes are tortellini (little pies), a speciality of Bologna that is said to be modelled on the shape of Venus's navel. They are made from rounds or circles of pasta, so they look like little plump rings. Another name for them is anolini. Some Italian delicatessens also sell dried cappelletti (little hats), which resemble tortellini but are made from squares of pasta, so have little peaks. Cappelletti are more likely to be sold fresh than dried. The same goes for ravioli and agnolotti, although you may find them in larger supermarkets. Tortellini are popular dried because they are traditionally used *in brodo* (simmered in a clear beef or chicken stock until they swell and plump up to make a satisfying soup). Most Italian cooks keep a packet or two of tortellini in the store cupboard (pantry) for just

Below: Tortellini all'uovo stuffed with a meat filling

Above: Tortellini verdi stuffed with a pesto filling

Below: Tortellini verdi stuffed with a mushroom filling

this purpose, and Tortellini in Brodo is often served for an evening meal when the main meal of the day has been at lunchtime. It is also served as a pick-me-up if a member of the family is unwell. They are also traditionally served on New Year's Eve in Bologna, perhaps as an antidote to the excesses of Christmas celebrations.

Dried tortellini are generally available with a choice of fillings – with meat (*alla carne*) or cheese (*al formaggi*). The pasta is made with egg and may be plain and yellow in colour, green if flavoured with spinach, or pinkish-red if flavoured with tomato. All types of tortellini need to be cooked for at least 15 minutes to allow time for the pasta to swell and the filling to develop their flavour. Meat fillings are a mixture of ground pork sausage and beef with breadcrumbs, Parmesan cheese and spices. Cheese fillings usually consist of a minimum of 35 per cent cheese mixed with breadcrumbs and spices.

Dried tortellini are a useful store-cupboard (pantry) item as they will keep for up to 12 months (but always check the use-by date on the packet). For a soup, only a handful of the filled shapes are needed and the packet can be resealed. Tortellini are also good boiled, then drained and tossed in melted butter and herbs or a cream, tomato or meat sauce, and served with grated Parmesan. Children like their shape, and this is a good way of persuading them to eat meat and cheese. A 250g/9oz packet will serve four people.

DRIED PASTA FOR STUFFING

Large pasta shapes are commercially made for stuffing and baking in the oven. Fillings vary, from meat and poultry to spinach, mushrooms and cheese, and the pasta can be baked in either a béchamel or a tomato sauce. Keep the filling moist and the sauce runny to make sure that the finished dish will not be dry. Dried shapes make an interesting change from lasagne, especially for children's meals, and they are attractive as a first course for a dinner party. They do not need to be boiled before being stuffed.

Above: Agnolotti all'uovo

Below: Cannelloni

Above: Conchiglie giganti

Cannelloni These large pasta tubes (their name means large reeds) are about 10cm/4in long. Plain, spinach and whole-wheat versions are available. They are easy to stuff, using a teaspoon or a piping (pastry) bag and nozzle.
Conchiglie Sometimes also called conchiglioni, these jumbo conch shells are available in plain, spinach and tomato flavours, both smooth and ridged. There are often two sizes – medium and large – both of which are suitable for stuffing.
Lumachoni These are like conchiglie, but are elbow-shaped – like large snail shells – with an opening at either end. The ones most commonly available are plain and ridged, but you may find different colours in some delicatessens. You may also come across similar shapes called chioccioloni, gorzettoni, manicotti and tuffolini.

DRIED PASTA FOR SOUP

Tiny pasta shapes are called pastina, and there are literally hundreds of different varieties to choose from. They are mostly made from plain durum wheat, although you may find them made with egg and even flavoured with carrot or spinach. In Italy, they are always served in broths and clear soups, and they are regarded almost as nursery food because they are so often served for children's meals (many Italian babies are weaned on them), or as a pick-me-up for older people who are not feeling well. If you stay in an Italian hospital, you are likely to be served Pastina in Brodo.

Shapes of pastina vary enormously, and seem to get more and more fanciful as the market demands. The smallest and plainest *pasta per minestre* (pasta for soups) are like tiny grains. Some

Below: Tubettini

Above: Alfabet

Below: Anellini

Above: Conchigliette

Below: Ditalini rigati

Above: Farfalline

look like rice and are in fact called risi or risoni, while others are more like barley and are called orzi. Fregola, from Sardinia, look rather like couscous, and have a similar nutty texture and flavour. Semi di melone resemble melon seeds, as their name suggests, while acini de pepe or peperini are named after peppercorns, which they resemble in shape and size, if not in colour. Coralline, grattini and occhi are three more tiny shapes.

The next size up are the ones that are most popular with children. These include alfabeti and alfabetini (alphabet shapes), stelline and stellette (stars), rotellini (tiny wagon wheels) and anellini, which can be tiny rings, sometimes with ridges that make them look very pretty, or larger hoops. Ditali are similar to anellini but slightly thicker, while tubettini are thicker still.

Above: Occhi di lupo

Below: Peperini

Above: Rosini

Dried pasta is also appearing in all sorts of guises intended to appeal to children – animal shapes and space rocket shapes, for example.

Another category of *pasta per minestre* consists of slightly larger shapes, which are more like miniature versions of familiar types of short pasta. Their names end in "*ine*", "*ette*" or "*etti*", denoting that they are the diminutive forms. These include conchigliette (little shells), farfalline and farfallette (little bows), funghetti (little mushrooms), lumachine (little snails), renette (which are like baby penne), quadretti and quadrettini (little squares), orecchiettini (little ears) and tubetti (little tubes). The size of these varies: the smaller ones are for use in clear broths, while the larger ones are more often used in thicker soups such as minestrone.

DESIGNER PASTA

Relative newcomers to the market are the pasta shapes that bear very little, or no resemblance at all, to the traditional or regional Italian varieties. Many of these are made outside Italy in any case, while the ones made in Italy are often for export only. It seems that the majority of Italians are happy enough with the pasta they know and love.

Gourmet food shops, specialist delicatessens and even interior design shops are the best places to find these new shapes. Quality varies enormously, and some of them are nothing more than a gimmick, with very disappointing textures and flavours. Others are more successful, especially the ones made by long-established Italian firms. They make a change from the more usual shapes and are often an interesting talking point, especially when you are entertaining. As a general rule, flavoured pasta is best served with very simple sauces based on olive oil or butter, otherwise the flavours of the pasta and sauce tend to fight with one another.

Long shapes and noodles

Spaghetti and tagliatelle are often flavoured and coloured. These shapes are either long or coiled in nests (*a nidi*), and you can even buy a type of pasta called *spagliatelle*, which is like a cross between the two. You can choose from a single flavour in one packet, or up to five different flavours mixed together, and they can be either plain durum wheat pasta or made with the addition of egg (*all'uovo*).

Above: (Left to right) Three-colour tagliatelle and egg and smoked salmon-flavoured tagliatelle

Above: Coralli rigati

Above: Poppy seed tagliatelli

Below: Porcini-flavoured tagliatelli

Above: Garlic and chilli spaghetti

Below: Five-colour spaghettini

Spinach, tomato, mushroom, beetroot (beet), saffron and smoked salmon are all popular flavours, but there are also other stronger flavours such as chilli and garlic (singly and together) and black squid ink (*nero di seppia*).

One of the most fanciful combinations comes from Venice. Called arlecchino (harlequin), it is a mixture of black (squid ink), green (spinach and herbs), red (tomato and beetroot) and blue (blueberry and blue Curaçao liqueur). More common and perhaps most successful is tagliatelle speckled with herbs or seeds or, if it comes from Tuscany, flavoured with wild mushrooms (porcini).

A broad variety of tagliatelle called bavette from Puglia is also flavoured with porcini. Strangozzi is an unusual thin noodle from Umbria. It comes plain and flavoured with spinach, basil or tomato. It is sometimes sold twisted into a long, thick plait, which looks pretty in the packet, but is best broken into short lengths to cook.

Left: Basil-flavoured strangozzi

Above: Multi-coloured arlecchino

Below: Five-colour chioccioloni

Short shapes The most inventive and unusual designer shapes fall into this category. Manufacturers, ever on the lookout to make and sell more, quickly realised that new short shapes had the most appeal and so developed this sector of the market more than any other. Ever since the 19th century competition in the pasta industry has thrived on the design of different short shapes, with some more successful at holding sauces than others. Among these are the frilly ballerine, fiorelli, gigli del gargano, rocchetti rigati and spaccatella, all of which trap sauces quite well but somehow give a strange sensation in the mouth. Shapes such as banane, coralli rigati, creste di gallo, radiatori and riccioli are perhaps too gimmicky for their own good; so, too, are mixed bags of highly coloured pasta shapes such as the seven-colour orecchiette (little ears) and five-colour chioccioloni (snails), which includes chocolate-flavoured pasta along with the more run-of-the-mill plain, tomato, squid ink and wild mushroom (porcini) varieties.

Above: Seven-colour orecchiette

Below: Gigli del gargano

Above: Fiorelli tricolori

Below: Caserecce

Below: Handcrafted spinach, plain and tomato conchiglie for stuffing

Above: Spaccatella

Below: Rocchetti rigati

Above: Three-colour cappelletti

Below: Porcini-flavoured bavette

Below: Three-colour pennati rigati

FRESH PASTA

In Italy there has long been a tradition of buying fresh pasta, and now the custom has caught on in many other countries, too. Italians buy pasta from their local *pastificio* or baker, where the beautiful window displays are such a tempting feast for the eye, while outside Italy, we have to content ourselves with the delicatessens, supermarkets and food halls. Yet here, too, creative talent is running wild when it comes to making fresh pasta, and the choice of shapes, flavours and fillings is continually increasing due to popular demand. It seems that everybody loves fresh pasta, and we simply can't get enough of it. Quality is excellent, especially with the loose kinds sold in Italian delicatessens. Pre-packaged brands, although labelled fresh, are obviously not as "just-made" and silky-textured as the pasta made on a daily basis in an Italian delicatessen, but they are a very good substitute nevertheless. Flavours vary, but the most common ingredients include spinach, tomato, chestnut, beetroot (beet) juice, mushroom, saffron, herbs, garlic, chillies and squid ink.

Buy freshly made pasta on the day you need it or you defeat the object of buying it; otherwise keep it in its wrapping and use within 1–2 days of purchase (or according to the storage time given on the packet). If you buy fresh pasta loose from an Italian delicatessen, ask the storekeeper for advice on storage. Fresh pasta is made with egg, which shortens its storage time, but on the plus side, this increases its nutritional value and flavour, and gives the plain varieties a lovely sunshine yellow colour.

Fresh pasta takes far less time to cook than dried pasta, but the cooking technique is the same for each type. Most plain shapes will be *al dente* in 2–4 minutes, while stuffed shapes take about 6 minutes, but always ask advice in the delicatessen where it is made (or check the instructions on the packet).

The same rules apply for matching sauces to shapes as with dried pasta – long shapes are best with smooth sauces, while chunky sauces go better with short shapes.

LONG AND FLAT SHAPES

These were the first forms of fresh pasta to be available commercially, and were generally made in the local Italian delicatessen by the proprietor. The choice used to be between plain egg tagliatelle and fettuccine, possibly flavoured with spinach, but now there is a more extensive range of varieties.

Pre-packaged long fresh pasta comes in standard shapes and sizes, but some Italian delicatessens have weekend specials when they offer different flavours and colours according to the seasonal availability of the various ingredients. This is often the case when they supply a local restaurant with fresh pasta. If a special order is made for a restaurant, the delicatessen may make extra to sell to customers in the shop. These occasional treats are well worth looking out for, as are the regional specialities. If the owners of your local delicatessen are from Lazio, you may find fresh home-made fettuccine on sale. Ligurians are more likely to make trenette, whereas pappardelle indicates that the proprietors probably have family ties with Tuscany or Bologna.

Fettuccine These long, flat ribbon noodles are the narrow Roman version of tagliatelle, traditionally made about 5mm/¼in wide. Fettuccine are readily available, made with egg and flavoured with spinach. You may also see similar noodles called fettuccelle. The two are interchangeable, and are at their best simply tossed with butter and cream.

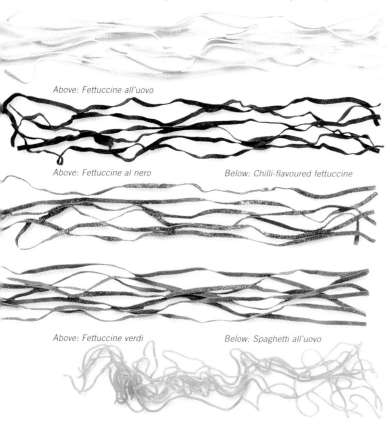

Above: Fettuccine all'uovo

Above: Fettuccine al nero   *Below: Chilli-flavoured fettuccine*

Above: Fettuccine verdi   *Below: Spaghetti all'uovo*

Below: Lasagne all'uovo

Spaghetti This pasta is widely available, in various widths. A narrow version, spaghettini, is popular, and can be found in some delicatessens. Serve fresh spaghetti or spaghettini Neapolitan-style with sauces based on olive oil and tomatoes. Both spaghetti and spaghettini are also good with fish and shellfish, as long as the pieces are cut small. Capelli d'angelo, plain or flavoured with spinach, is also available.

Lasagne Sheets of lasagne can be found plain, with egg, and flavoured with spinach or tomato. Depending on the manufacturer, they may be rectangles, squares or strips with plain or frilly edges. Lasagne al Forno (baked lasagne) made with fresh pasta tastes even more delicious and has a much better texture than Lasagne al Forno made with dried pasta, so the fresh sheets are well worth buying.

Linguine These look like strands of flattened spaghetti and are very narrow and thin. They are made with egg, and go very well with a simple dressing of olive oil and flavourings, such as finely chopped garlic, chillies or ground black pepper. Linguine is also excellent with fish and shellfish sauces.

Right: Pappardelle

Pappardelle These flat egg noodles vary in width from 2–2.5cm/¾–1in wide. Traditional pappardelle have wavy edges, but you may also see them with plain edges – the main thing is that they are wider than any of the other ribbon noodles. Pappardelle originated in Tuscany, but are also popular in the city of Bologna in Emilia-Romagna. In both these regions, pasta is often served with

Below: (Left to right) Spinach-flavoured tagliolini, tagliatelle all'uovo and spinach-flavoured tagliatelle

a rich meat or game sauce, and pappardelle are the perfect choice for these because the noodles are wide and strong enough to support the chunkiest of mixtures.

Pappardelle are available plain and flavoured, sometimes with sun-dried tomatoes or porcini.

Tagliatelle This is probably the best-known form of fresh pasta. The flat noodles are long and straight, and about 1cm/½in wide. They are available everywhere, in a wide variety of flavours and colours. After plain egg tagliatelle, spinach is the most popular, but it is also often flecked and flavoured with fresh herbs, garlic, porcini, sun-dried tomatoes, pepper, chillies and other spices, or beautifully coloured with saffron or tomato. When made with squid or cuttlefish ink, it is black and very dramatic in appearance.

Tagliatelle comes from Bologna, where it is traditionally served with Bolognese sauce, but it goes well with any meat sauce. Tagliarini and tagliolini are very thin versions of tagliatelle; they are about 3mm/⅛in wide, and sold either as plain egg (*all'uovo*) or half white and half green (*paglia e fieno*). Mixed packs are especially versatile and attractive because you can cook the different colours together or keep them separate, depending on the visual effect you are wanting to achieve when serving. They both go particularly well with tomato and cream sauces.

SHORT SHAPES

Supermarkets and other large outlets sell fresh short shapes, but the range is limited. Italian delicatessens sometimes sell a few simple home-made shapes, but because many short shapes need special machines for cutting and shaping there is seldom a wide range in small outlets, and making them by hand would be too time-consuming to be commercially viable. Short shapes tend to stick together, so in supermarkets they are kept in sealed bags in the

Below: Conchiglie

Below: Fusilli all'uovo

Below: Semi-dried garganelli

Below: Penne rigate

chilled cabinets; these packs are useful in that they can be stored in the freezer. Sometimes small stores remove excess moisture by briefly fan-drying the shapes straight after they are made. These are then described as semi-dried and must be sold within 24–48 hours. Shapes vary widely, depending on whether they have come from large manufacturers or individual shops. Conchiglie, fusilli and penne are easy to find, while other shapes such as garganelli and ballerine are much less widely available.

Conchiglie These shell shapes come in different sizes and colours, and conchiglie tricolore (red, white and green) are popular. They are one of the best shapes for trapping chunky sauces. If they are ridged, so much the better. Conchiglie are also good in cold pasta salads because they hold dressings very well.

Fusilli Resembling the threads of screws, these should correctly be called eliche, but they are almost always labelled fusilli. Plain, spinach and tomato flavours, either sold separately or mixed together, are easy to obtain. Squid ink fusilli are made in some stores. The versatile shape of this type of pasta means that it goes well with most sauces and is also good in salads.

Garganelli Sold in some specialist delicatessens, these are made from a very special type of egg pasta from Emilia-Romagna, and look like ridged scrolls. To make garganelli, squares of fresh dough are rolled around a rod and against a special tool called a *pettine*, which has teeth like a comb. The teeth produce the characteristic fine ridges on the outside of the pasta. Plain and spinach flavours are available, either sold separately or mixed together. In Emilia-Romagna, garganelli are traditionally served with a rich meat sauce, but you can use them in any recipe that calls for short maccheroni or penne. They are especially good with rich, creamy sauces.

Penne Sometimes called quills, these come in a variety of sizes and colours, both smooth and ribbed, just like their dried counterpart.

Above: (Top to bottom) Cappelletti all'uovo stuffed with mushroom filling and semi-dried tomato-flavoured cappelletti stuffed with sun-dried tomato filling

STUFFED SHAPES

Until recent years, the only stuffed fresh pasta shapes available were the classic ones traditionally associated with specific regions of Italy; ravioli was the best-known shape, followed by tortellini. These regional specialities are still popular, but today the traditional shapes and fillings are often varied, whether they are being made by a large-scale manufacturer or a single cook working for a local delicatessen. Individual interpretations on the basic shapes, a wide variety of seasonal ingredients for the fillings, plus eye-catching colour combinations for both the pasta and the fillings, make variations on the theme seemingly endless. New ideas are being developed all the time – some a little more successfully than others – so experiment with different kinds of stuffed shapes to find the ones you like the best. Listed here are the most popular and widely available shapes, following the regional tradition.

Agnolotti These filled pasta shapes come from northern Italy and are a speciality of Piedmont in particular. Traditionally, they were shaped like plump little half moons and stuffed with meat, but this is no longer the case: today you will see round and square shapes with vegetable fillings labelled as agnolotti. Square agnolotti with a

Above: Tomato-flavoured medaglioni all'uovo stuffed with prawn and trout

Below: Semi-dried cappelletti all'uovo

pleat in the centre are called dal plin (meaning with a pleat). One particular characteristic that all agnolotti should share is a crinkled edge, made by cutting the dough around the filling with a fluted pasta wheel.

Cappelletti These take their name from the Italian word meaning little hats. In Emilia-Romagna, small squares of dough are filled and folded to make triangular shapes, then two of the ends are wrapped around and the bottom edge turned up to make a party hat shape with a brim. In some central regions of Italy, however, cappelletti are made with either plain or fluted rounds of dough instead of squares. The dough for cappelletti can be plain or egg (*all'uovo*), or flavoured with tomato or spinach.

Cappelletti are traditionally filled with minced meat and cheese. They are eaten in northern and central regions of Italy at Christmas time and the New Year, especially served in clear broth – Cappelletti in Brodo. You can use them in this way or serve them as a pasta course with a little melted butter and freshly grated Parmesan cheese or, alternatively, toss the cappelletti in a tomato or cream sauce.

Ravioli These are usually square with fluted edges, but size and shape vary enormously. Along with tortellini, they are the most widely made of the fresh stuffed pasta shapes, and everyone seems to have their own favourite way of making them. Plain, spinach and tomato doughs are usually used for the pasta – although other flavours such as

Left: Large ravioli stuffed with minced (ground) chicken and asparagus.

Above: (Left to right) Hand-made plain and spinach-flavoured ravioli

Left: Ravioli all'uovo with a minced chicken filling

Below: Semi-dried raviolini all'uovo with a simple minced meat filling

Left: (Left to right) Plain ravioli with asparagus filling, squid ink-flavoured ravioli with a herb filling, and saffron ravioli stuffed with a smoked salmon and mascarpone cheese filling

Above: Sweet-shaped caramelle all'uovo stuffed with spinch and ricotta cheese

Below: Cappelli all'uovo stuffed with a minced salmon filling

Above: Sacchettini

squid ink and saffron are becoming increasingly available and there are even some ravioli that combine two different doughs such as egg and spinach or egg and tomato to give a striped effect. The fillings can be anything from vegetables such as spinach, artichoke and mushroom to fish and shellfish, and minced (ground) veal and chicken. Very tiny ravioli are called raviolini, and the smallest round ravioli are sometimes called medaglioni. The name for ravioli with a pumpkin filling is cappellacci. Large round, oval and rectangular ravioli, stuffed with cheese or vegetable fillings, are also

occasionally available from Italian delicatessens. Oval ravioli are sometimes called rotondi, while the large rectangular shapes may be called cannelloni rather than ravioli.

Pansotti Sometimes spelled pansoti, these stuffed pasta shapes are Ligurian. The word means chubby, and they are triangular in shape with little pot bellies of filling in the centre. It is traditional to fill pansotti with chopped cooked spinach, chopped hard-boiled eggs and grated Pecorino cheese, then serve them with a walnut sauce.

Tortellini Hugely popular, these look more or less the same as cappelletti, but are made from rounds or circles of dough rather than squares, so do not have peaks. They are usually slightly larger than cappelletti, while tortelloni and tortelli are larger still. Tortellini are a speciality from the city of Bologna in Emilia-Romagna, where the traditional filling is minced meats and prosciutto. At Christmas it is the local custom to eat Tortellini in Brodo as a first course soup before the main course of roast capon or turkey.

Today, tortellini are available everywhere and they are eaten all year round. There is a wide variety of colour combinations and all sorts of fanciful fillings. Black squid or cuttlefish ink, garlic, herbs, green olive, spinach and sun-dried tomatoes are among the many ingredients used to flavour the dough, while for the filling you can choose from such delicacies as white crab meat, pumpkin, ricotta, asparagus, cream cheese, caramelized onions, wild mushrooms, marinated tuna, aubergines (eggplant), sweet red (bell) peppers, artichokes and even white truffles. A mixture of four cheeses is a popular filling.

Other stuffed pasta shapes Creative cooks have started a trend for making shapes not based on regional traditions, so check out your local delicatessen or supermarket for the latest shapes – you will find new ones appearing all the time. Two very popular pasta shapes are caramelle and sacchetti. Caramelle means caramel, and this pasta shape takes its name from the familiar shape of caramels or toffees with wrappings twisted at both ends. The filling is encased in the centre and is often ricotta cheese-based, while the pasta itself is made with egg and may be plain, or spinach- or tomato-flavoured. Sacchetti look like little purses or money bags with scrunched tops. The pasta may be plain or flavoured and the fillings based on cheese or meat. Sacchettini are a tiny version, most often served in soups, but also good with smooth, creamy sauces.

Left: Sacchetti filled with spinach and ricotta

Below: Tortellini stuffed with an artichoke and truffle oil filling

Below: (Top to bottom) Plain tortelloni filled with five cheeses and spinach-flavoured tortelloni filled with spinach and ricotta cheese

Cooking Pasta

Before starting to cook either the pasta or the sauce to go with it, read through the recipe carefully. It is important to know which needs to be cooked for the longest time. Often, the sauce can be made ahead of time and reheated, and it is quite unusual for the timing of a sauce to be crucial, but pasta waits for no one. This is especially true if you are cooking fresh pasta, for which timing is often only a few minutes, so the sauce needs to be ready and waiting before the pasta goes into the pan of boiling water.

There needs to be plenty of room for the pasta to move around in the large amount of water it requires, so a big pan is essential. The best type of pan is a tall, lightweight, straight-sided, stainless steel pasta cooking pot with its own in-built draining pan. Both outer and inner pans have two handles each, which guarantee easy and safe lifting and draining. If you cook pasta a lot, it is well worth investing in one of these special pans; otherwise use the largest pan you have and a large stainless steel strainer, preferably one with feet.

Matching Sauces to Pastas

Some regional dishes are always made with the same pasta shape. Bucatini all'Amatriciana, Penne all'Arrabbiata and Fettuccine all'Alfredo are all classic Roman recipes, for example, and it is rare to see them served with anything other than the named pasta. The same applies to Tagliatelle alla Bolognese from Emilia-Romagna and Trenette con

Above, left and below: Classic regional dishes such as Fettuccine all'Alfredo, Bucatini all'Amatriciana and Penne all'Arrabbiata are almost always served with the named pasta.

Pesto from Genoa. These classics are few and far between, however, and with the ever-increasing number of different shapes on the market it may seem difficult to know which sauces and shapes go well together. Happily, there are no rigid rules, and common sense usually prevails. Heavy sauces with large chunks of meat are unlikely to go well with thin spaghettini or tagliolini, simply because the chunks will slide off, so these sauces and others like them are always served with wide noodles such as pappardelle, maccheroni and tagliatelle, or with short tubular shapes such as penne, fusilli, conchiglie and rigatoni.

In the south of Italy, olive oil is used for cooking rather than butter, so sauces tend to be made with olive oil and they are usually served with the dried plain durum wheat pasta such as spaghetti and vermicelli that is also popular in the south. These long, thin shapes are traditionally served with tomato and seafood sauces, most of

which are made with olive oil, and with light vegetable sauces. Spaghetti and vermicelli are also ideal vehicles for minimalist sauces such as Aglio e Olio (garlic and olive oil) from Rome. Grated cheese is not normally used in these sauces, nor is it sprinkled over them.

In the north, butter and cream are used in sauces, and not surprisingly these go well with the egg pasta that is made there, especially fresh egg pasta, which absorbs butter and cream and makes the sauce cling to it. Rich butter and cream also go well with tomato sauces when these are served with short shapes, especially farfalle and fusilli. Grated cheese is often tossed with pasta and sauce at the last moment, as well as being sprinkled over individual servings at the table.

Watchpoints

It is best not to cook more than 675g/1½lb pasta at a time, even if you have a very large pan, because of the danger in handling a large amount of boiling water. If you are using the microwave to cook pasta it is best not to cook more than 225g/8oz pasta at a time. Use a large heatproof bowl, don't overfill the bowl and carry it carefully.

How to Cook Pasta

It is very easy to cook pasta properly, but without care and attention, it is equally easy to cook it badly. There are a few simple guidelines to ensure pasta is cooked to perfection.

1 Use a large quantity of water: the recommended amount is 5 litres/ 8 pints/10½ US pints water for every 450g/1lb pasta. If you are cooking less than this, use at least 3 litres/ 5 pints/6 US pints water. If there is not enough water, the pasta shapes will stick together as they swell, giving an unpleasant, sticky result.

2 Before adding the pasta, bring the water to a fast rolling boil. The quickest way to do this is to boil water in a kettle, then pour it into the pasta pan, which should be set over a high heat. You may need as much as 3 kettlefuls, so keep the water in the pan simmering, covered by the lid, while you boil the kettle again.

3 When the water is boiling, add 30ml/2 tbsp salt for every 450g/ 1lb pasta. When the water bubbles furiously, add the pasta.

4 Tip in the pasta all at once so that it will cook evenly and be ready at the same time. The easiest way is to shake it out of the packet, covering the surface of the water as much as possible.

5 Make sure the pasta is completely submerged in the water. Cover the pan tightly with the lid to help bring the water back to the boil as quickly as possible. As soon as the water returns to the boil, remove the lid, reduce the heat slightly and let the water boil gently over a medium to high heat for the recommended cooking time.

6 Stir the pasta frequently while cooking to prevent the pasta strands or shapes from sticking together. Use a long-handled wooden fork or spoon.

7 Drain carefully and thoroughly. If you are using a pasta pot with an inner drainer, lift the draining pan up and out of the water. Shake the draining pan vigorously and stir the pasta well so that any water trapped in pasta shapes can drain out as quickly as possible.

8 Reserve a few ladlefuls of the pasta cooking water in case the pasta is too dry and needs a little extra moistening when it is tossed with the sauce just before serving.

Accurate Timing

This is essential for cooking pasta. Start timing the pasta from the moment the water returns to the boil after you have added the pasta. Always go by the time given on the packet or, in the case of fresh home-made pasta, by the time given in the recipe. For the greatest accuracy, use a kitchen timer with a bell or buzzer because even half a minute of over-cooking can ruin pasta, especially if it is freshly made. Dried egg pasta is more difficult to spoil, so if you are new to pasta cooking and nervous about getting it right, start with this type.

For fresh pasta As a general guide, thin fresh noodles will take only 2–3 minutes, thicker fresh noodles and pasta shapes 3–4 minutes, and stuffed fresh pasta 5–7 minutes.

For dried pasta The cooking time for dried pasta can vary greatly – from 8–20 minutes, depending on the type and the manufacturer. Always check the packet instructions.

GNOCCHI

These actually fall into a different category from pasta, being more like small dumplings – but they are cooked and eaten in very much the same way. They can be made with semolina (milled durum wheat), flour, potatoes, or ricotta and spinach, and may be shaped like elongated shells, ovals, cylinders or flat discs, or roughly shredded into strozzapreti (priest-stranglers). The best-known type of gnocchi are gnocchi di patate from northern Italy, made with potatoes and a little flour.

Buying and Storing

Gnocchi are usually sold loose on delicatessen counters. At their worst, they resemble large greyish maggots, but however they are made, they should be extremely light and almost melt in the mouth. They will keep in a plastic bag in the refrigerator for two or three days. Home-made gnocchi dough will also keep for a couple of days. Gnocchi are quite filling: allow 115g/4oz per serving for a first course.

Above: Spinach and Parmesan gnocchi

Right: Plain gnocchi

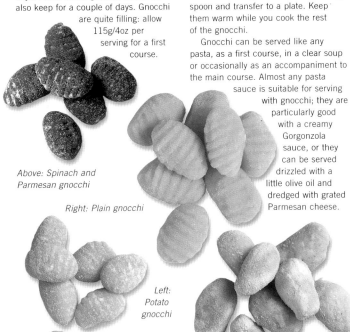

Left: Potato gnocchi

Right: Gnocchi made from semolina

Right: Spinach and ricotta gnocchi

Cooking

With the exception of oven-baked gnocchi alla romana, all gnocchi should be poached in a pan of lightly salted, barely simmering water. Drop the gnocchi into the water in batches and cook for 2–4 minutes. They will rise to the surface when they are done. Scoop out the cooked gnocchi with a draining spoon and transfer to a plate. Keep them warm while you cook the rest of the gnocchi.

Gnocchi can be served like any pasta, as a first course, in a clear soup or occasionally as an accompaniment to the main course. Almost any pasta sauce is suitable for serving with gnocchi; they are particularly good with a creamy Gorgonzola sauce, or they can be served drizzled with a little olive oil and dredged with grated Parmesan cheese.

Making Spinach and Ricotta Gnocchi

These green gnocchi originated in Tuscany where, rather confusingly, they were known as ravioli. To make gnocchi for 4 people, you will need: 350g/12oz cooked spinach, well drained and finely chopped; 225g/8oz ricotta, mashed until smooth; 2 eggs; 100g/3½oz/1 cup freshly grated Parmesan; 40g/1½oz/3 tbsp plain (all-purpose) flour; 65g/2½oz/5 tbsp melted butter; salt, ground black pepper and grated nutmeg.

1 Put the spinach, ricotta and seasoning in a large pan and cook gently, stirring, for 5 minutes.

2 Off the heat, beat in the eggs, 40g/1½oz/3 tbsp of the Parmesan and the flour. Chill the mixture for at least 4 hours.

3 Lightly shape the dough into small cylinders and roll them in a little flour. Drop them, in batches, into a large pan of lightly salted, barely simmering water and poach for 5 minutes, or until they rise to the surface. Scoop them out with a slotted spoon as soon as they rise.

4 Preheat the oven to 180°C/350°F/Gas 4. Pour a little melted butter into a serving dish and put in the cooked gnocchi. Sprinkle with some of the remaining Parmesan and place in the oven. Add the rest of the gnocchi as they are cooked and drizzle them with the melted butter and grated Parmesan cheese. Return the dish to the oven for another 5 minutes before serving.

NOODLES

These are a type of pasta made from flour, eggs and water, or just flour and water, and cut into flat strips of varying shapes and sizes. Asian noodles are made from a variety of flour pastes, including wheat, rice, mung bean, buckwheat, seaweed, corn, arrowroot and even devil's tongue, which is a plant related to the arum lily. There are hundreds of different types and, for the best selection, it is worth visiting a Chinese or Japanese supermarket or an Asian food store.

WHEAT NOODLES

The primary grain grown in northern China is wheat, and wheat noodles are widely sold, in bundles or compressed into packages. Dried wheat noodles, with or without eggs, are often called longevity noodles because of their association with long life.

Above: Japanese somen noodles are sold tied together in bundles.

Left: Plain wheat noodles are available in several different thicknesses.

EGG NOODLES

These are far more common than plain wheat noodles. In China, they come in various thicknesses and are sold either fresh or dried. They may be white or yellow in colour and either slightly wrinkled or plain. These are well-known in the West from dishes such as chow mein.

Yi noodles These very fine Chinese egg noodles, which resemble vermicelli, are named after the family that originally

Udon These are the most common type of Japanese noodle. Made from strong, plain wheat flour and water, they are long, narrow and ribbon-like. They are available fresh, pre-cooked or dried, but, in Japan, are usually sold fresh.

Somen These thin, delicate, white Japanese noodles are sold in bundles, held in place by a paper band.

Hiyamugi These Japanese dried wheat noodles are thicker than somen, but thinner than udon. They are most commonly served chilled.

Right: Bundles of dried Japanese udon noodles are commonly available in the West, although the fresh variety is often more difficult to find.

made them. They are also known as *yifu* or *efu* noodles. They are popular in Hakka-style cooking, especially in soup.

Ramen These are the Japanese equivalent of Chinese noodles and are usually sold in coils or blocks.

Shrimp noodles These seasoned egg noodles are flavoured with fresh shrimp and/or shrimp roe. They are usually sold dried, in coils of various widths.

Instant noodles Packets of pre-cooked egg noodles are a familiar sight in western supermarkets. They come in various flavourings such as chicken, prawn (shrimp) and beef.

Buying and Storing

Fresh and pre-cooked noodles will keep for up to 3 days in the refrigerator, well wrapped in clear film (plastic wrap).

Above: Fresh egg noodles are eaten throughout Asia.

Below: Ramen egg noodles

Right: Packets of instant noodles and sauces are perfect for a quick snack.

They can also be frozen and defrost quickly when dropped into boiling water. Dried noodles keep well for up to a year in the store cupboard (pantry).

Preparation and Cooking

Noodles are very easy to prepare. Some types benefit from being soaked before being cooked, so see individual recipes, read the instructions on the packet, or seek advice from someone in the store where you bought them. Both dried and fresh noodles have to be cooked in boiling water before use – the time depends on the variety of noodle, the thickness of the strips, and whether they will be cooked again in a sauce or soup. Dried noodles require about 3 minutes' cooking, while fresh ones will be done in less than 1 minute and may need to be rinsed under cold water to prevent them from over-cooking. After the initial boiling, noodles are then usually prepared and served in one of a variety of ways. They are usually served hot in soups, with sauces, or in stir-fries in China, Taiwan, Singapore, Malaysia, Indonesia, Vietnam and Thailand, whereas chilled noodle dishes are more common in Korea and Japan.

Noodles in soup This way of serving noodles is most popular in China, Korea, Japan, Vietnam, Burma and Singapore. It usually consists of noodles served in bowls of clear broth with pieces of cooked meat, poultry and shellfish, and sometimes including vegetables – or with vegetables on their own. The dish is often served with a sharp, tangy sauce on the side.

Braised noodles The difference between this and the noodles in soup described above is that braised noodles are first cooked in a broth, before serving with a thickened sauce.

Fried noodles This has to be one of the most popular Chinese dishes in the West (and in South-east Asia, but not so much in north China or Japan). The two basic types of fried noodles are dry-fried, which gives a crispy result, or soft-fried: the Chinese prefer them crisp on the outside and soft inside. Generally speaking, only the fine vermicelli-type of noodles are used for dry-frying; the thicker round or flat noodles are more suitable for soft-frying.

RICE NOODLES

These are more common than wheat noodles in southern China and in Cantonese restaurants, as this is the rice-growing area of the country. They are used as soup noodles and also in sauced dishes with meat and vegetables.

Unlike most other noodles, which are made from flour of one type or another, rice noodles are made from whole grains of rice, which are soaked and then ground with water into a paste. This paste is drained through a sieve to form a dough, which is divided into two. One half is cooked in boiling water for 15 minutes, before it is kneaded with the raw half to make a firm dough. The dough is then put through a press, which cuts it into various shapes and sizes. The finished strands are then blanched in water, drained and rinsed before being sold as fresh noodles, or dried in the sun before packaging.

Types of Rice Noodles

The rice noodles sold in southern China, Thailand and Vietnam are all very similar to each other. Like wheat noodles, they come in various widths, from the very thin strands known as rice vermicelli to rice sticks, which start at around 2mm/1⁄16in and can be as wide as 1cm/1⁄2in, as in the case of *ho fun*, a special variety from south China. Rice sticks are the main ingredient of the Singapore dish *kway teow*, when they are mixed with pork, prawns (shrimp) and (bell) peppers. In Thailand it is possible to buy a rice noodle enriched with egg, called *ba mee*, which is sold in nests. Malaysian rice noodles are known as *laksa* and are a central ingredient in the spicy fish broth of the same name. Very fine rice vermicelli can be deep-fried without pre-soaking and used as an attractive garnish. They also feature in a spectacular pyramid in the classic Thai dish *mee krob*, for which they are first deep-fried and then stir-fried with chicken, prawns (shrimp) and a chilli sauce. A wide range of dried rice noodles is available in Asian or Chinese stores, and fresh ones can occasionally be found in the chiller cabinets. Most supermarkets stock a limited range.

Preparing Rice Noodles

Because all rice noodles are pre-cooked, they need to be soaked in hot water for only a few minutes to soften them before use. If they are soaked for too long, they become soggy and lose the texture that is part of their special appeal. Add the noodles to a large bowl of water that has been recently boiled and leave for 5–10 minutes, or until just softened, stirring occasionally to separate the strands. You will need about 450g/1lb of noodles to serve four people.

Above: Very thin rice noodles, sometimes called lai fan or sen mee in China, are also known as rice vermicelli.

Left: Fine, delicate Japanese rice noodles need only to be soaked in hot water for a few minutes until softened.

Above: Flat Chinese rice noodles come in varying widths and are sold in square or rectangular bundles.

CELLOPHANE NOODLES

These noodles are known as *fensi* in China, *bun* in Vietnam and *harusame* (meaning "spring rain") in Japan. They are also known as transparent noodles, bean thread vermicelli or glass noodles. These very fine, rather brittle strands are made from green mung beans, which are the same beans as those used for sprouting. The Japanese version may be made from rice or potato flour. Although very thin, the strands are firm and resilient, and they stay that way when cooked, never becoming soggy, which doubtless contributes to their popularity.

Cellophane noodles are almost tasteless unless cooked with other strongly flavoured foods and seasonings, but they

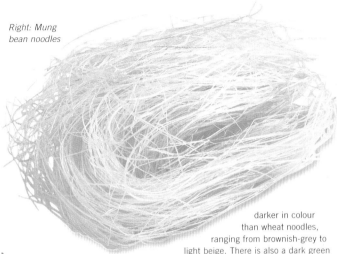

Right: Mung bean noodles

have a fantastic texture. For this reason, cellophane noodles are never served on their own. They are always used as an ingredient in a dish, notably in vegetarian cooking and in hot-pots. They are also often included in Vietnamese spring rolls. Cellophane noodles can be tied together and deep-fried. They are only available dried.

Preparing Cellophane Noodles

Soak cellophane noodles in hot or warm water for about 15 minutes to soften them. When they are soft, use a pair of scissors or a sharp knife to chop the noodles into shorter strands.

BUCKWHEAT/SOBA NOODLES

The best-known buckwheat noodles are the Japanese soba, which are usually sold in bundles of fine strands. They are made from a mixture of buckwheat and wheat flour, as buckwheat flour lacks elasticity and stickiness, and may also include yam flour. *Naeng myun* are very fine noodles made from a mixture of buckwheat, wheat flour and sweet potato starch. Soba are much

Left: Soba noodles from Shinshu, central Japan, are considered to be the finest of all soba noodles produced.

darker in colour than wheat noodles, ranging from brownish-grey to light beige. There is also a dark green variety called *chasoba* (tea soba), which is made of buckwheat and green tea. Fresh soba noodles are widely available in Japan, where they are a popular fast food. A *soba-ya* (noodle shop) is a common sight. Outside of Japan, prepacked dried soba noodles are sold in bundles in Asian stores and large supermarkets. Korean cooks also use a thin variety of buckwheat noodles.

Preparing Soba Noodles

Bring a large pan of water to the boil. Use at least 600ml/1 pint/ 2½ cups water. Add the noodles, allowing about 115g/4oz per person and bring back to the boil. Lower the heat and cook the noodles for 5–6 minutes, until they are half transparent and tender. Drain well, rinse in plenty of water to remove the outer starch and then drain thoroughly.

UNUSUAL NOODLES

Shirataki This is a popular Japanese noodle made from a starch derived from the tubers of the devil's tongue plant, which is related to the arum lily. The starch is formed into cakes, called *konnyaku*, from which the noodles are then cut. They are always sold wet and are available in cans or plastic tubes.
Bijon These South-east Asian noodles are made from corn.
Canton These Chinese wheat noodles are sometimes enriched with eggs.

ASIAN WRAPPERS

The pancakes and wrappers of Asia are quite different from either crêpes or pancakes in the West. For a start, they are almost always made from a plain dough of wheat flour and water, rather than a batter, which is then rolled out.

CHINESE PANCAKES

There are two types of pancakes in China – thin and thick. Thin pancakes (*bobing*) are also known as mandarin or duck pancakes, because they are used as wrappers for serving Peking duck. They are also served with other savoury dishes, most notably *mu-shu* or *moo-soo* pork, which consists of scrambled egg with pork and wood ears (dried black fungus). Making Chinese pancakes demands considerable dexterity, so many cooks prefer to buy

them frozen from Chinese food stores. They are usually cooked in pairs, then peeled apart before each one is cooked on the second side.

Thick pancakes are made with lard (shortening) and flavoured with savoury ingredients, such as spring onions (scallions). Both thin and thick pancakes are sometimes served as a dessert, with a filling of sweetened bean paste.

NONYA SPRING ROLL PANCAKES

These are the exception to the rule that most pancakes in the Far East are made from dough. Typical of the Singaporean style of cooking known as Nonya, they are made from a batter made of egg, flour and cornflour (cornstarch), and are traditionally served with a wide selection of fillings.

Above: Chinese thin pancakes are used as wrappers for savoury ingredients, or as part of a main meal.

Below: Chinese thick pancakes are eaten as a savoury snack, or filled with a sweet bean paste for dessert.

Reheating Chinese Pancakes
Cooked pancakes can be reheated just before serving.

1 Stack the pancakes on top of each other and interleave them with squares of greaseproof paper (baking parchment).

2 Carefully wrap the stacked pancakes in foil, folding over the sides of the foil so that the package is completely sealed.

3 Put the foil parcel in a bamboo steamer and cover. Place on a trivet in a wok of simmering water. Steam for about 4 minutes, or until the pancakes are hot, then use as required.

SPRING ROLL WRAPPERS

Also known as egg rolls in the United States, and pancake rolls in many other parts of the world, spring rolls must be one of the most popular Chinese snacks everywhere. While the fillings may vary from region to region, or even between different restaurants and fast food stalls, the wrappers are always more or less the same. They are made from a simple flour and water dough, except in Vietnam, where wrappers are made from rice flour, water and salt. In Vietnam, spring rolls are called *nem* and are traditionally filled with a mixture of chicken and crab meat seasoned with *nuoc mam* (fish sauce).

There are three different sizes of ready-made spring roll wrappers: small, medium and large. The smallest wrappers, which are about 12cm/4½in square, are used for making dainty, cocktail-style rolls, which are typical of

Thai cooking. The standard-size wrappers measure 21–23cm/8½–9in square, and usually come in packets of 20 sheets. The largest, 30cm/12in square, are too big for general use, so they are usually cut in half or into strips for making samosas and similar snacks.

Above: Wafer-thin small and medium-size spring roll wrappers are available frozen from Chinese and Asian food stores and supermarkets.

Preparing Spring Rolls

Use medium-size spring roll wrappers, which you will find in the freezer cabinet in Asian or Chinese stores. They should be thawed before use. For the filling, use ingredients such as beansprouts, bamboo shoots, water chestnuts and rehydrated dried mushrooms, with chopped prawns (shrimp) or finely minced (ground) pork. When you have prepared the rolls, deep-fry them, a few at a time, in hot groundnut (peanut) oil for 3 minutes, or until golden and crisp.

2 Divide the spring roll filling into the required number of portions. Spoon one portion diagonally across the wrapper.

4 Brush the edges of the wrapper with a little cornflour (cornstarch) and water paste.

1 Peel off the top spring roll wrapper. Cover the rest with a clean dishtowel to keep them moist.

3 Working quickly, carefully fold over the nearest corner of the wrapper to cover the filling.

5 Fold the edges towards the middle, then roll up into a neat parcel to enclose the filling.

Above: Wonton skins can be square or round and come in a variety of sizes.

WONTON SKINS

Wonton skins or wrappers are made from a flour and egg dough, which is rolled out to a smooth, flat, wafer-thin sheet. The sheet is usually cut into small squares, each measuring about 7.5cm/3in, although round wonton wrappers are also available. Ready-made wonton skins are stacked in piles of 25 or 50, wrapped and sold fresh or frozen. They can be found in Asian and Chinese food stores.

Fresh wonton skins are dusted with flour before being packed. This keeps each one separate from the others, making them very easy to use. Frozen wrappers must, however, be thawed thoroughly before use, or they will tend to stick together. Any unused skins can be refrozen, but should be carefully wrapped in foil so that they do not dry out when they are put in the freezer.

There are several ways of using wonton skins. They can be simply deep-fried and served with a dipping sauce, or used as a garnish, filled and boiled, steamed or deep-fried, or simply poached in a clear broth with a mixture of vegetables and flavourings. On most Chinese restaurant menus in the West, this last option is listed under soups, which is misleading, as in China and South-east Asia, wonton soup is always served solo as a snack – *dim sum* – and never as a separate soup course as part of a meal. Classic fillings for wontons include pork, crab meat, prawns (shrimp), water chestnuts, spring onions (scallions) and wood ears. Golden pouches, which are bite-sized, deep-fried wontons filled with minced (ground) pork and crab meat, flavoured with fish sauce, are a popular and delicious Thai snack.

You can also use wonton skins to wrap sweet fillings of fruit and nuts to make a tasty snack or dessert, and deep-fried, unfilled wontons, either plain or coated in egg white and sesame seeds and then dusted with icing (confectioners') sugar make an unusual substitute for ice cream wafers.

Preparing Wontons

Wontons are very simple to prepare and make a delicious snack.

Place the filling in the centre of the wonton skin. Dampen the edges of the skin with cold water. Press the edges of the wonton skin together to create a little purse shape, sealing the filling completely.

Below: Rice papers are dried on bamboo mats, which give them their familiar cross-hatch pattern.

RICE PAPERS

These are used in Vietnamese and Thai cooking and are quite different from the rice paper that is used for writing and painting in China and Japan; nor does it bear any resemblance to the sheets of rice paper British cooks use as pan liners when baking macaroons, which are not, in fact, made from rice at all. Made from rice flour, water and salt, it is a round, tissue-thin "crêpe", dried on bamboo mats in the sun, which results in the familiar crosshatch pattern being embedded on each sheet.

Rice paper is used for wrapping Vietnamese spring rolls and small pieces of meat and fish to be eaten in the hand. The sheets are rather dry and brittle, so must be softened by soaking in warm water for a few seconds before use. Alternatively, they can be placed on damp dishtowels and brushed with water until they are sufficiently pliable.

Spring rolls are usually deep-fried, but Vietnamese cooks also make an unfried version. Freshly cooked pork, prawns (shrimp), beansprouts and vermicelli are wrapped in rice paper, which has been dipped in cold water until it is pliable and transparent. The filling can clearly be seen through the wrappers, and the rolls look very pretty.

Storing

Rice papers are packaged and sold in 15cm/6in, 25cm/10in and 30cm/12in rounds. They will keep for months in a cool, dry place, provided the packets are tightly sealed. When buying, look for sheets that are of an even thickness, with a clear, whitish colour. Broken pieces are a sign of bad handling, so avoid any packages that look as if they have been knocked about, as broken rice paper is quite useless for wrapping any filling.

FRUIT, NUTS AND SEEDS

Fruits, nuts and seeds are some of nature's most bountiful

and versatile creations. No other foods offer such a variety

of colours, textures, scents and flavours. They are also

supremely healthy foods, bursting with natural energy-giving

sugars, minerals and vitamins. Most fruits, nuts and seeds

can be eaten raw, but they are also wonderful to cook with

and are enjoyed all over the world.

APPLES, PEARS, QUINCES AND MEDLARS

Ever since Adam bit into the fruit of knowledge, apples have been the stuff of myth and legend. The Greeks and Romans believed them to have aphrodisiac qualities, and for the Celts, crab apples were a symbol of fertility. There are thousands of varieties worldwide, although the choice of those available to buy is decreasing year by year. There are some 7,000 named varieties of apples but only about a dozen are readily available in stores and supermarkets. Nurseries often supply many more varieties for those who want to grow their own.

Pears are related to apples and there are almost as many varieties. Quinces and medlars are also related fruits.

DESSERT APPLES

The most popular of all fruits, apples are good eaten raw as a simple dessert, or as a healthy snack at any time of day.

Braeburn This crisp, juicy apple has a smooth pale green skin flushed with red and is an excellent eating apple. Braeburns are grown only in the southern hemisphere.

Right:
Egremont
Russet

Below: Beauty of Bath

Beauty of Bath A small, flattish green apple, flushed with red, and with sharp, sweet juicy flesh. Beauty of Bath apples should be eaten straight from the tree, as they rot very quickly after picking. Consequently, you are unlikely to find them in stores.

Cox's Orange Pippin A greenish-yellow apple of medium size, with some orange-red russeting. The firm, crisp juicy flesh of this sweet fruit, with its overtones of acidity, makes it one of the best and most popular of apples.

Above: Braeburn

Right: Empire

Egremont Russet These apples have rough, porous skins which allow the water to evaporate, giving a denser flesh and intensifying the nutty flavour. Egremont Russet is the most readily available of all russet apples. It is a golden russet colour, sometimes with an orange flush, and has a crisp texture and sweet taste. It can be used for both eating and cooking.

Left: Cox's Orange Pippin

Empire This dark red American apple has a shiny skin. It is best for eating raw, but is also suitable for cooking. It has crisp green, juicy flesh and a slightly tart flavour.

Gala This colourful eating apple from New Zealand has a yellow ground colour flushed with bright orange and red. The yellow flesh is very sweet, juicy and crisp. It is at its best when absolutely fresh. Royal Gala is similar, but red all over.

Above: Granny Smith

Granny Smiths are also good for cooking as they are only moderately sweet and retain their shape well once cooked.

Jonathon This smallish, round, orange-red North American apple has a white, juicy flesh and rather fragrant, slightly acidic flavour. Jonathon can be used for both eating and cooking.

Jonagold A hybrid of Jonathon and Golden Delicious, this large, round, green-tinged yellow apple has creamy white flesh and a superb flavour. It can be used for cooking or eating.

Crab Apples

These fruits have grown wild in hedgerows for thousands of years. They are smaller and often more colourful than cultivated apples. Today crab apples are often grown for ornamental purposes rather than their culinary qualities.

Crab apples are seldom worth eating raw (and may be totally inedible), but thanks to their high pectin content, they make truly wonderful jellies, either on their own or mixed with other wild fruits such as haw berries.

Golden Delicious Originally grown from a chance seedling in the United States, this conical, freckled golden apple has become ubiquitous. At its peak, the cream flesh is juicy and crisp with a mild flavour; unfortunately, most commercially grown Golden Delicious are sold when they are under- or over-ripe and are consequently tasteless and mealy in texture. Golden Delicious are suitable for cooking or eating.

Granny Smith First grown in Australia by the eponymous "Granny" Smith, this largish all-purpose apple is bright green, becoming yellow as it ripens. Usually sold underripe, it has a firm, crunchy flesh and a tart flavour.

Katy This is a highly coloured early apple bred in Sweden from the Worcester Pearmain. Its small size appeals to children, and its flesh is crisp, sweet and juicy.

Laxton's Fortune Similar to Cox's Orange Pippin, these apples have yellowish skin heavily tinged with red, and a sweet, juicy, lightly aromatic flesh that is sweet with some acidity. You are most likely to find them in farm stores rather than supermarkets.

Orleans Reinette One of the best apples of all, this large, orange-flecked russet has a rough skin, but juicy, sweet and aromatic flesh. Orleans Reinette is ideal for cooking and eating.

Above: Jonagold

Above: Katy are best eaten immediately after they have been picked.

Right: Golden Delicious are probably one of the most widely available varieties of apple found in stores.

Pink Lady A pretty Australian cross between Golden Delicious and Lady Williams, this large all-purpose apple has a mild flavour and is becoming increasingly available in supermarkets and greengrocers.

Spartan A Canadian apple raised in . 1926 from McIntosh and Newton's Pippin, the Spartan inherits a tough skin from McIntosh, but tastes highly aromatic with a floral perfume.

Below: Pink Lady

Left: Spartan apples have a rather aromatic, sweet flesh.

Below: Worcester Pearmain

COOKING APPLES

Bramley's Seedling The nonpareil of cookers, this large, flattish green apple (sometimes faintly flushed with red) has coarse, white, juicy acid flesh that cooks into a frothy purée. Bramleys are perfect for stuffing and baking whole.

Grenadier An irregularly shaped conical apple with yellow skin, the Grenadier has acid flesh and is faintly green, firm and juicy. It breaks down during cooking. Grenadiers do not keep.

Howgate Wonder This apple can grow to an enormous size. The juicy white flesh breaks up during cooking and has a dull flavour, so this variety is grown mainly for exhibition.

Reverend W. Wilkes This large conical apple with pale greenish-white skin has fine, very white flesh that is crisp, juicy and acidic. The apple can be eaten raw, but it is best used as a cooker.

Ida Red By far the favourite North American apple for making apple sauce, this apple can also be used as an eating apple. Like many American-grown fruits, it has a good acid flavour.

Blenheim Orange This apple has a pleasantly nutty flavour and is suitable for dishes such as apple Charlotte and apple crumble, and for serving raw as a dessert fruit.

Worcester Pearmain A conical fruit, pale yellow-green flushed with bright red or scarlet, the juicy, sweet white flesh of this apple has a hint of strawberry and is strongly perfumed. Worcester Pearmain apples are crisp and best eaten picked straight from the tree, but they can also be used for cooking, as they keep their shape very well.

Above: Bramley's Seedling are extremely good for cooking in sauces and pies.

Buying and Storing

Choose unblemished apples with no bruising and undamaged skins. Check there are no signs of insect damage. If possible, smell the fruits to determine their fragrance and squeeze gently to make sure they are firm (not easy when they are pre-bagged). Do not let yourself be seduced by the colour of an apple's skin; those gorgeous-looking specimens with thick, brilliant red, waxy skins often have woolly, tasteless flesh.

Apples continue to ripen after they have been picked, so their colour and texture may change during storage. For short-term storage, they can be kept in a ventilated plastic bag in the refrigerator. To store home-grown or pick-your-own apples, first make sure that they are in perfect condition, then wrap each one in newspaper and place, folded-side down, in a single layer in wooden or fibre trays or baskets. Keep in a cool, dry, dark place and check occasionally to make sure none has gone rotten. A bad fruit will taint all the others, so remove it immediately.

Preparing

Most apples can be eaten with the skin on, but they should be thoroughly washed first in case there are any residual pesticides. To peel, use a vegetable peeler or small, sharp knife, either in a spiral around the apple, or peeling downwards in strips from stem to calyx. The flesh of peeled apples goes brown very quickly; brush them with lemon juice or drop them into a bowl of water acidulated with lemon juice or cider vinegar immediately after peeling. You could also use one or two unflavoured, effervescent vitamin C tablets to acidulate the water without affecting the flavour of the apples.

Cooking

Some apples are only suitable for eating raw, but most can be cooked in such classic sweet dishes as apple pies, cobblers, crumbles, crêpes, tarts, strudels and baked apples. When a soft, fluffy texture is required, it is best to use a cooking variety, but firmer eating apples are ideal for decorative dessert toppings and the classic French upside-down tart, *tarte tatin*. Sweet apples combine well with other fresh fruits such as blackberries and quinces, and with dried fruits such as raisins and sultanas (golden raisins). Aromatic spices such as cinnamon, nutmeg and cloves, highlight their flavour.

A useful tip when making apple pie is to toss the sliced fruit in a little flour, which may be seasoned with spice, before adding it to the pie dish. This helps to soak up the juices and thicken them so that they don't leak out of the pie during cooking and spoil its appearance. Use apples with other fruit for jams and jellies, as they have a high level of pectin, but will not overpower the other flavours.

Sharply flavoured apples make excellent accompaniments for game birds, particularly pheasant, black and white pudding (blood sausage) and sausages, and rich meats such as pork – traditionally served in Britain and the United States with apple sauce – duck and goose. They also make a good substitute for gooseberries in a compôte to serve with oily fish such as herring and mackerel, and complement delicately flavoured fish, such as sole and skate. They go particularly well with red cabbage and are often included in salads, partnering celery, beetroot (beet) and nuts. They are an essential ingredient in Waldorf salad. Not very surprisingly, they are often used in dishes cooked in cider or Calvados, apple brandy from Normandy.

Raw apple and cheese is a favourite combination, but cheese also features in some traditional cooked apple dishes such as Austrian apple and raisin strudel and British top-crust apple pie.

Apples combine well with other fruit and vegetables to make delicious cooked chutneys and relishes. Classic combinations are apple and mango, apple and red onion and apple, pineapple, (bell) pepper and ginger. Apple cheese is an English speciality, while apple butter comes from the United States. They are a popular fruit for juicing on their own, with other fruits and with vegetables.

Making Apple Purée

The secret to a traditional apple sauce is to add a knob (pat) of butter to the pan with the apples.

1 Peel, core and thickly slice the apples, immediately dropping the pieces into a bowl of cold water acidulated with lemon juice.

2 Barely cover the base of a pan with cold water. Add the apple and cook over a low heat for about 10 minutes until pulpy. Add sugar to taste towards the end of cooking.

3 If you are using firmer dessert apples that do not disintegrate when cooked, simmer until tender, then rub through a coarse sieve.

Left: Comice pears

Left: Conference

Anjou

These large pears have greenish yellow skin with small brown spots. The flesh is juicy and sweet. Suitable for eating and cooking.

Beurré Superfin Large, with a tough, golden green, russeted skin, this is the perfect eating pear. Its flesh is sweet and juicy and it is less grainy than other pears.

Conference

First cultivated in the English county of Berkshire in 1770, these long, conical pears have remained a favourite in Britain because they keep so well. The yellowish-green skin with extensive russetting turns yellower when the pears are mature. The granular flesh is tender, sweet and juicy. Conference pears are excellent for eating and cooking.

PEARS

There are almost as many varieties of pears as there are apples but, again, only a dozen or so are readily available in stores. Pears are related to apples, but are much more fragile and are more often eaten raw than cooked. They have fine white granular flesh and a core containing the pips (seeds). Most pears are wider at the bottom than the top, but some are apple-shaped, while calabash pears have an elongated neck, like a gourd. Pears tend to be less vividly coloured than apples, usually varying from bronze to gold, green or yellow, although there are also some red-blushed varieties such as Red Williams and Forelle.

Right: Forelle

Comice/Doyenné du Comice

This large, roundish pear is one of the finest of all pears, with creamy white, melting, very juicy flesh and a sweet, aromatic flavour. The thick, yellowish-green skin is covered with speckles and patches of russetting. Comice are best eaten raw and they are delicious served with Camembert or Brie cheese.

Forelle This beautiful golden pear has a dark red flush on one side. The grainy flesh is crisp, with a fresh flavour. Eaten raw, it goes particularly well with cheese, but is at its best when cooked.

Laxton's Foremost Yellow-skinned and lightly russeted, this is one of the largest pears. Its creamy coloured flesh is very juicy and granular. It does not keep well and, as it turns brown from the inside out, there may be no external signs that the fruit is past its best.

Above: Anjou

Left: Packham's Triumph

Above: Williams Bon Chrétien

Below: Asian pears

Left: Red Williams

Packham's Triumph The first successful Australian pear was produced by Charles Packham in 1896 and remains a favourite. Slow-ripening, it is a largish dessert pear, with a smooth green, lightly russeted skin that changes to yellow as it ripens. The soft white flesh is succulent and sweet, with a touch of acidity.

Red Williams These pears have shiny, speckled skins, at first green with a red blush, turning to yellow flushed with red. The flesh is sweet and juicy.

Williams Bon Chrétien Known as Bartlett in the United States, these irregularly shaped pears are generally swollen on one side of the stalk. The speckled skin is golden yellow with russet patches and sometimes a red tinge. The delicious tender flesh is creamy-white and very juicy, and the flavour is sweet and slightly musky. Williams Bon Chrétien are suitable for cooking and eating, but unfortunately these superb pears do not keep very well.

Winter Nelis This roundish medium-size pear has thick but tender greenish yellow skin with cinnamon-brown russeting and sometimes a pink flush. The creamy-white flesh is soft and very juicy, and the flavour is sweet. These pears can be cooked or eaten raw.

Perry pears With the demise of the most famous of the sparkling alcoholic pear drinks, perry pears have largely fallen into disfavour. A few small producers still press perry pears into juice, wine or "champagne" perry, but although there are still about 300 known varieties, you will never find these in the stores. Perry pears are smaller than their dessert counterparts. Although they look delicious, they contain large quantities of tannin and taste bitter and astringent, whether raw or cooked.

Asian/Nashi pears There are many varieties of Asian pear, but their characteristics are very similar. They are round rather than a pear shape, the fruits have a golden brown russet skin and they have very crisp, white juicy flesh. The crunchy texture resembles that of an apple, but is more granular. It would be a shame to spoil the crisp texture by cooking. Asian pears are best eaten straight from the refrigerator, to be enjoyed as a "drink on a stalk". They also make an excellent addition to fruit salads or savoury winter salads.

Tientsin These Asian pears from China and Korea are very similar to Asian Nashi pears in taste and texture. They are available when Asian pears are out of season. They look rather like elongated apples, tapering gently at both ends. The skin is pale yellow, slightly speckled with patches of light brown. The pure white flesh is exceptionally juicy and crunchy.
Hosui These pears have much the same crunch and juiciness of the Tientsin pears, but look more like apples, with greeny-brown mottled flesh that tastes like a cross between an apple and an unripe pear.

Buying and Storing

Always buy pears when in perfect condition, as they deteriorate quickly. Once past their best, they become woolly or squashy and unpleasant. Test for ripeness by pressing gently; the fruit should give a little, but still be quite firm. Once ripe, eat within a couple of days. They can be kept at the bottom of the refrigerator for a few days. Store unripened pears at room temperature, where they will ripen in two or three days.

Preparing and Cooking

The majority of pears are eaten raw, by themselves or with a robust cheese such as Stilton or Roquefort. Pears Savarin, halved fruit filled with Roquefort mashed with a little butter and served chilled with double (heavy) cream and paprika, is a popular appetizer. Pears also make a good addition to winter salads. Whether or not to peel pears before eating raw is a matter of preference, but they should always be peeled before cooking. Pears discolour quickly once they are peeled, so rub the cut surface with lemon juice or place in a bowl of water acidulated with lemon juice. If the recipe involves cooking the pears in wine or sugar syrup, the fruit can be put directly into these to prevent them turning brown.

Most varieties of pears are suitable for cooking, but some are specifically designated cooking pears, although commercial production of these is now decreasing. If appearance is important, choose even-size, classic, pear-shaped pears such as Comice, Conference or Williams (Bartlett). For whole poached pears, simply peel with a stainless steel vegetable peeler, leaving the stalk on. Use an apple corer to core the pears if you want to stuff them with nuts or

Below: Tientsin pears are best eaten chilled.

dried fruit. Poach in port or red wine spiced with cinnamon, cloves and thinly pared lemon rind, or in a vanilla-flavoured syrup. For sautéed or grilled (broiled) pears, peel and quarter the fruit and scoop out the cores with a melon baller. Sauté over a low heat in unsalted (sweet) butter or grill (broil), turning once, watching very closely to avoid the fruit scorching.

Pears can be used in a wide variety of desserts, including tarts, mousses, soufflés, sorbets (sherbets) and ice creams. Classic dishes include *poires belle Hélène, à l'Impératrice* and *Condé*. They are also delicious grated into tea breads. Pears go particularly well with nuts, especially walnuts and almonds, in both sweet tarts and savoury winter salads.

Like apples, pears complement game, particularly duck and hare, while venison garnished with pears is a German speciality. For additional luxury, the pears may be cooked in pear brandy, also known as Williamine, or pear liqueur. Pears can also be roasted with small game birds and then rubbed through a sieve and served as a sauce. A slightly more unusual, but delicious combination is lamb and pears, slow-cooked in a casserole. Pears also feature in soups, most famously with watercress and also with garden peas.

Fruit vinegars are coming back into fashion and steeping pears in vinegar to flavour it has a long history in country and farmhouse cooking. The vinegar is a rich golden colour. It can be used in salad dressings, as part of a basting mixture when roasting rich meats, especially duck, or for deglazing the cooking juices after pan-frying liver or duck to make a sauce. Pear chutney is also a traditional rural favourite, not least because you can use hard, windfall pears that would otherwise have to be thrown away. Pears can also be steeped in brandy for several weeks to make a liqueur for drinking after dinner. A more modern variation of this is to steep the fruit in vodka.

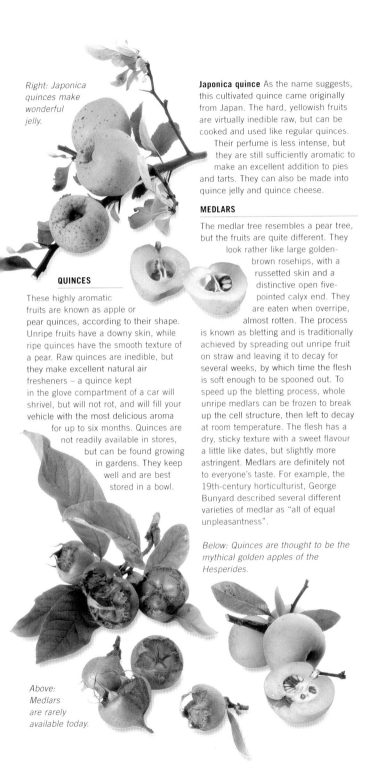

Right: Japonica quinces make wonderful jelly.

Japonica quince As the name suggests, this cultivated quince came originally from Japan. The hard, yellowish fruits are virtually inedible raw, but can be cooked and used like regular quinces.

Their perfume is less intense, but they are still sufficiently aromatic to make an excellent addition to pies and tarts. They can also be made into quince jelly and quince cheese.

MEDLARS

The medlar tree resembles a pear tree, but the fruits are quite different. They look rather like large golden-brown rosehips, with a russetted skin and a distinctive open five-pointed calyx end. They are eaten when overripe, almost rotten. The process is known as bletting and is traditionally achieved by spreading out unripe fruit on straw and leaving it to decay for several weeks, by which time the flesh is soft enough to be spooned out. To speed up the bletting process, whole unripe medlars can be frozen to break up the cell structure, then left to decay at room temperature. The flesh has a dry, sticky texture with a sweet flavour a little like dates, but slightly more astringent. Medlars are definitely not to everyone's taste. For example, the 19th-century horticulturist, George Bunyard described several different varieties of medlar as "all of equal unpleasantness".

Below: Quinces are thought to be the mythical golden apples of the Hesperides.

QUINCES

These highly aromatic fruits are known as apple or pear quinces, according to their shape. Unripe fruits have a downy skin, while ripe quinces have the smooth texture of a pear. Raw quinces are inedible, but they make excellent natural air fresheners – a quince kept in the glove compartment of a car will shrivel, but will not rot, and will fill your vehicle with the most delicious aroma for up to six months. Quinces are not readily available in stores, but can be found growing in gardens. They keep well and are best stored in a bowl.

Above: Medlars are rarely available today.

Making Quince Jelly

Quince jelly is time-consuming to make but well worth the effort.

1 Coarsely chop 1kg/2¼lb quinces. Put in a large heavy pan with 2 litres/3¼ pints/8 cups water.

2 Bring to the boil, then lower the heat and simmer until the quinces are very tender.

3 Pour the fruit into a jelly bag set over a bowl. Let the juice run through. Do not squeeze the bag or the finished jelly will be cloudy.

4 Measure the strained juice and pour into a large heavy pan. Add 500g/1¼lb/2½ cups preserving sugar for each 600ml/1 pint/ 2½ cups of the juice. Bring to the boil, stirring until the sugar has dissolved completely. Boil rapidly until 105ºC/220ºF in temperature.

5 Skim the foam from the top of the jelly and pour or ladle into warm, sterilized jars. Cover the jars while the jelly is still hot. When the jars are cool enough to handle, label.

STONE FRUITS

These delicious fruits all belong to the *prunus* family and share the same characteristics of soft, juicy flesh and a single stone (pit) in the centre.

Above:
Elegant Lady is a
very popular variety of
yellow peach.

Above:
Mireille is a commonly available variety of white-fleshed peach.

PEACHES

Sometimes known as the queen of fruits, the peach is certainly among the most beautiful. Their downy, velvety skin is yellow, flushed with red, and they are voluptuously curvaceous – the French call one variety *tétons de Venus*, meaning Venus's breasts.

The most familiar peaches are round or beaked (with a pointed end) but they can also be flat and disc-shaped. The delicate fine-textured flesh, which can be yellow, white or tinged with red, encloses a heavily ridged stone (pit). They may be cling peaches – when the flesh clings tightly to the stone – or freestone varieties.

Peaches are seldom sold by variety but by the colour of their flesh – yellow or white. Which you choose is a matter of preference. Yellow varieties include Elegant Lady, Royal George and Bellegarde, and Mireille is a popular

white peach. The finest peaches of all are the *pêches de vigne*, red-fleshed fruits that are grown in vineyards. They do not look attractive, being covered in a greyish down, but the flavour is superb. You are unlikely to find them outside markets in France, however.

NECTARINES

These are a smooth-skinned variant of peaches and are native to China. They taste similar to peaches, with a touch more acidity. The flesh can be yellow, white or pinkish, and is delicate and sweet. Unlike peaches, they do not need to be peeled, so some people prefer to eat them as a dessert fruit.

Slightly underripe fruit can be poached, but otherwise nectarines are best eaten raw, as cooking them spoils their delicate flavour and texture.

Both peaches and nectarines are a good source of vitamins A, B and C. Nectarines have a lower calorie count than peaches. Neither fruit ripens successfully after picking, so always make sure it is ripe when you buy. Press gently to make sure that the fruit is firm, with some give. Never buy greenish peaches and avoid fruit with bruised or damaged skin. Peaches do not keep well, but firm fruit can be kept at room temperature for a day or so to soften; ripe peaches can be kept in the refrigerator in a plastic bag for a couple of days.

Right: Ripe apricots are deliciously fragrant.

APRICOTS

These round, yellow-orange fruits have velvety skins flushed with pink. The flesh is firm, sweet and fragrant, and contains little juice. The kernel of the stone is edible and is used to flavour jams, biscuits (cookies) and Amaretto.

Apricots do not continue to ripen after picking, so choose ripe fruit with a rich colour and smooth skin. Avoid very pale or greenish fruit, or wrinkled specimens, which will have begun to soften. Store at room temperature for a few days, or store in the refrigerator in a plastic bag for up to five days.

Below: White nectarines

Below: Smooth-skinned yellow nectarines

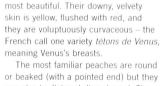

PLUMS

There are thousands of varieties of plum, differing in size, shape, colour and flavour. There are three main types: European, Japanese and Western Asian, their skins varying from blue-black to purple, red, green and yellow. They have a long season and one variety or another is available almost all year round. All plums have smooth skins, with a bloom, and juicy flesh with plenty of acidity.

Dessert Plums

These can be eaten on their own, although most of them can be cooked as well as eaten raw. They are usually larger than true cooking plums and are sweet, fragrant and juicy. Buy unblemished fruit, which should be plump and firm. The flesh should have a little give without being squashy. Plums should have a pleasant aroma; avoid any with blemishes or bruising. They ripen quickly, so store them in the refrigerator for no more than a day or two.

Victoria These were originally cultivated in England in 1840 from a stray seedling. Since then, these large oval fruits with yellow skins flushed with scarlet, and sweet, juicy flesh, have become ubiquitous. They are also widely used for cooking.

Santa Rosa and Burbank Large and round, with bright red skins, these two North American varieties of plum are mainly grown in California. They have juicy, deep yellow flesh and a pleasantly tart flavour, which makes them good for both cooking and eating.

Denniston's Superb This early variety of plum is a medium-sized green fruit flushed with red, with an excellent sweet flavour.

Above:
Victoria plums are the most prolific dessert plums.

Below: Greengages have a firm flesh.

Below: Damsons

Cooking Plums

These are drier, with tart flesh that is ideal for pies, flans and cakes. They can be poached, baked or stewed. Cook plums until just tender; do not let them disintegrate. Plums are also good for preserves.

Mirabelles/Cherry plums These very small wild plums are round and grow on long stalks like cherries. They have black, red or yellow skins, which can taste rather bitter, but all have sweet juicy flesh. They are best stewed or baked or made into jams or jellies.

Other varieties include Beach Plums, Czar, Quetsch, Angelino and Autumn Rose.

GREENGAGES

A small member of the plum family, greengages are known for their green skins and loved for their wonderful, honeyed flavour. This deliciously sweet flavour of greengages makes them ideal for eating raw. They can also be poached gently in syrup, puréed for mousses and fools, or made into compôtes and jam.

DAMSONS

These plum-like fruits have deep blue-black skins with an attractive bloom and a strong, tart flavour which makes them more suitable for cooking than for eating raw. In addition, they have proportionately larger stones (pits) than other members of the plum family. Damsons can be stewed for pies, tarts, ice creams and fools, but are most commonly used for bottling, or for jams and jellies. The robust flavour of damsons makes them particularly suitable for savoury dishes, and they make an excellent addition to pork or lamb casseroles.

CHERRIES

One of the great delights of spring is cherry trees in blossom, followed in summer by clusters of bright shiny fruit hanging in pairs from long elegant stalks. The skin of these small round stone fruits can vary in colour from pale creamy-yellow to deepest red or almost black. The firm juicy flesh can be sweet or sour, depending on the variety, of which there are hundreds. Cherries contain vitamins A and C as well as some dietary fibre.

Cherries are categorized into three main groups: sweet (for eating), sour (for cooking) and hybrids such as the nobly named Dukes and Royals, which are suitable for eating raw or cooking. The original wild sweet cherries, known as *mazzards*, were found in Asia Minor and were cultivated by the Chinese 3,000 years ago. Mazzards were known to the Ancient Egyptians, Greeks and Romans, and still exist today. Sour cherries were brought to Rome from Greece and all the modern varieties are derived from these early wild specimens.

Sweet Cherries

These fall into two main groups: bigarreaus, which have firm crisp flesh, and geans or guines, which have a softer texture. Nowadays, there is also a large number of hybrids.

Below: Bing cherries are widely grown in the United States.

Above: Bright red Colney cherries have a lovely sweet flavour.

Below: Napoleons are a variety of sweet cherry, with slightly crisp, tart, fragrant flesh.

Bigarreaus The best known of these are Napoleons, large pale yellow cherries tinged with light red. They have a crisp fragrant flesh, which is slightly tart. Napoleons are also known as Royal Annes and for a time in 19th-century England, became known as Wellingtons, a name chosen because of the loathing at the time of anything to do with Napoleon. Bing cherries are a large, heart-shaped, deep-red fruit with a truly superb flavour.

Geans/Guines These delicious cherries have soft, juicy flesh and come in many colours. Black Tartarian are a deep purplish-black colour, from the skin right through to the stone (pit). Early Rivers have dark purple skins and flesh and very small stones. They are fragrant, sweet and juicy. Ranier has golden skin with a pink blush. The famous Swiss black cherry jam is made from intensely dark guines. Sweet, juicy black guines are also used for making *clafoutis*, the classic French batter pudding from the Dordogne region of France. The English version of this wonderful dessert is known rather more prosaically as battered cherries.

Sour Cherries

These range
from almost
sweet to bitter;
they are full of
flavour and are mainly used
for preserving or in the
manufacture of liqueurs. Most are
too tart to eat, but are ideal for cooking.
The two main types are morello, with
dark juice, and amarelle, with light,
almost colourless juice.

Montmorency These are bright red
cherries with a sweet-sour flavour.

English cherries These small, orange-
red fruit with soft translucent flesh are
mainly used for preserving in brandy.

Maraschino cherries These small wild
fruit from Dalmatia are damasca or
amaresca cherries. They are distilled
into the Italian liqueur, Maraschino.
The bottled Maraschino cherries were
originally damasca cherries preserved
in Maraschino liqueur; today, the
vibrant red fruits sold as Maraschino
tend to be ordinary cherries tinted with
artificial colouring and steeped in syrup
flavoured with bitter almonds.

*Above: Maraschino
cherries are often
bottled with their stalks.*

*Above: Morello cherries, which are often
preserved in brandy.*

Buying and Storing

Choose plump cherries with shiny,
unblemished skins. It is best to buy
them still on the stalk, and indeed the
stalks are a good indication of their
freshness. The stalks should be green
and flexible: dry, brown, brittle stems
tell you that the cheries were picked
some time ago. As a rule of thumb, pale
cherries are very sweet, while dark
cherries tend to be more acidic; if
possible, taste before you buy.

Unwashed cherries will keep for a
few days in the refrigerator; wash them
just before serving. They can also be
removed from their stalks and frozen.

Preparing and Cooking

Sweet cherries need no preparation
other than washing and are best eaten
on their own or in a fruit salad. They
make unusual sweets (candies) when
left on the stalk and
dipped into melted
dark chocolate.

Removing Cherry Stones

If you wish to stone a large number
of cherries, a cherry stoner will
make light work of the task.

Put the cherry in the cup of a
cherry stoner and squeeze the
handles together to push the bar
into the fruit. The stone will be
ejected, leaving the fruit whole.

Pitted cherries make a delicious filling
for sponge (pound) cakes and pavlovas,
or an attractive decoration for cakes
and desserts. There is no reason why
you shouldn't cook sweet cherries, but
they may not have much flavour owing
to their low acidity. Although fresh
cherries can be served as they are, for
cooking they should always be pitted.

Dual-purpose and sour cherries can
be cooked in tarts, pies, compôtes and
sauces. They go well with sweet spices,
citrus flavours and chocolate. In Eastern
Europe and Alsace, cherries are made
into sweet-sour soup and are used to fill
the dumplings served with these soups,
as in the Russian *vareniki*. They are
also pickled in spiced vinegar and
served as an accompaniment for rich
meats. Cherries go well with all game
and are classically served with duck.

Any dish described on a
menu as Montmorency will
be accompanied by cherries,
originally of the Montmorency variety.

Amarelle and morello cherries are
good used for making jam (jelly) and
preserves as well as for crystallizing in
sugar to make glacé (candied) cherries,
which are a very popular, used with
dried fruit, in baking.

CITRUS FRUITS

All citrus fruits have a tough, bitter peel that is highly scented and contains aromatic oils. Inside, the fruit is segmented and encloses juicy flesh.

ORANGES

Despite their name, oranges are not always orange; they can also be yellow or mottled with red. The size can vary too – an orange can be as large as a football or as small as a cherry – and the flavour can range from sweet to intensely sour. The beautiful, waxy white, star-

Above: Pretty blood oranges make a good addition to fruit salads.

shaped flowers also have an intense aroma, which is captured in orange flower water. Like other citrus peel, orange rind contains essential oils, which are used both in cooking and perfumery. Oranges fall into two distinctive groups. Bitter oranges have to be cooked before they can be eaten. Sweet oranges can be eaten raw and are divided into four main categories, which are available at different times of the year.

Navel and Navelina These seedless oranges take their name from the navel-like protuberance at the end, which contains a tiny embryonic fruit. They have thick, pebbly skins and very sweet juicy flesh. The skin is particularly good for making candied peel.

Above: Navel

Right: Valencia

Peeling and Segmenting Oranges
When using oranges for cooking, peel them with a serrated knife.

1 Cut a thin slice from each end of the orange to expose the flesh. Cut off the peel in a circular motion, removing the white pith.

2 Holding the fruit over a bowl to catch the juice, cut out each segment by slicing between the membranes, then squeeze the juice from the membranes into the bowl.

Right: The flesh of bitter Seville oranges is best used for cooking.

Blonde These pale-skinned winter oranges include Jaffa and Shamouti. The large fruit have thick skins that are easy to peel. The flesh is crisp and juicy. If you are lucky you may find Salustianas oranges, which are full of juice and contain no pips (seeds).

Blood oranges These small oranges have red-flushed skins and jewel-like flesh, which can range from golden to deep ruby-red. These are the best oranges to use for sorbets (sherbets) and desserts where colour is important. They are an essential ingredient of *sauce Maltaise*, an orange-flavoured mayonnaise which takes its name from the sour but juicy Maltese blood orange.

Valencia These are among the late oranges. They have smooth, thin skins and contain few or no pips (seeds). Valencia is the world's most popular variety. Their pale flesh is very juicy with a sharp flavour and they are the best oranges for juicing.

Bitter Seville As well as the sweet oranges, there are bitter oranges. Seville (Temple) or Bigarade cannot be eaten raw, but are used for making marmalade, jams and jellies. Vast numbers are grown in Seville but, surprisingly, the Spaniards never make marmalade; almost all their oranges are exported to Britain. Seville oranges are used in the classic *sauce bigarade*, which is traditionally served with roast duck. In the south of France, these

oranges are crystallized, while the blossoms on the trees are distilled to make aromatic orange flower water. The aromatic oils from the peel are used to flavour such liqueurs as Grand Marnier and Cointreau. Bitter oranges have a very short season and are only available in January in the northern hemisphere.

Buying and Storing

Choose firm oranges that feel heavy for their size – this indicates that they will be juicy. Oranges keep well; they can be stored at room temperature or in the refrigerator for up to two weeks. The juice and grated rind of fresh oranges can be frozen.

Preparing and Serving

Oranges are best eaten in their natural state, but can be used in an almost infinite variety of desserts and sweet dishes. Use the juice and rind for mousses, soufflés, ice creams and *crêpes suzette* and segments for fruit salads. They also go well in vegetable dishes. Combine with watercress, beetroot (beet) or chicory (Belgian endive) and thinly sliced raw red onion for a refreshing salad, or glaze carrots in orange juice and butter. They also have a natural affinity with tomatoes. Oranges feature in a wide range of savoury dishes with game, chicken, duck, fish, particularly trout, veal and liver. Many recipes that traditionally use bitter oranges are prepared these days with sweet varieties.

Making Candied Peel

Choose thick-skinned oranges and wash and dry them well.

1 Thinly peel the oranges and cut the peel into thin julienne strips.

2 For each orange, combine 250ml/ 8fl oz/1 cup water with 115g/4oz/ generous ½ cup sugar and bring to the boil. Add the strips of orange peel, half-cover the pan and simmer until the syrup has reduced by about three-quarters. Leave to cool.

3 Sift icing (confectioners') sugar in a thick layer over a baking sheet. Roll the peel in the sugar. Dry in a cool oven. Store the candied peel in a jar for up to 3 months.

Above: Tangerines are easy to peel and have sweet, juicy flesh.

TANGERINES AND MANDARINS

There is a huge range of "easy peelers" that come under this general heading. Although each fruit has a discernibly different flavour, what they have in common are their aromatic skins, which can be easily detached from the fruit, and segments that separate easily. The flesh is sweet and perfumed, but often contains a large number of pips (seeds). The names of many types of tangerines are commonly interchanged, so you may find a bewildering variety of fruits that are essentially the same.

Clementines These are the smallest of all the tangerines, with bright skins and no pips (seeds). This, and their sweet, aromatic flesh, makes them the most popular variety.

Mandarins Commonly sold canned, tiny peeled tangerine segments are sold as "mandarin oranges". The deliciously sweet, vibrantly coloured segments make an attractive decoration for a dessert and are popular with children, set in orange jelly.

Satsumas These large tangerines from Japan have loose skin and a refreshing, rather tart flavour. Satsumas contain very few pips (seeds).

Ortaniques Also known as honey tangerines because of their delicious sweetness, ortaniques are a hybrid that can be found growing on the same trees as tangerines or oranges.

Tangelos These are a cross between a tangerine and a grapefruit and are easy to peel. They are irregularly shaped and have a tart, refreshing flavour.

Minneolas Another tangerine-grapefruit hybrid, minneolas have a distinctive bulge at their stalk end. They have bright orange skin and are easy to peel. The sweet, juicy flesh has no pips (seeds).

Buying and Storing

Many varieties of tangerine have loose, puffy skins, which are no indication of quality. Choose fruits that feel heavy for their size; they will contain more juice. Avoid fruits with damaged skins and, if you are buying pre-packed fruits, check that none are mouldy as they will quickly taint the others. Tangerines do not keep as well as other citrus fruits, but can be stored in the refrigerator for up to a week. Canned mandarin oranges are a useful store-cupboard (pantry) standby. It is also possible to buy canned whole mandarins in syrup, which makes a very simple but sensational dessert.

Preparing and Serving

All varieties of tangerine can be used in the same way as oranges. The peel is as useful as the flesh, and the zest can be candied or used to flavour sweet liqueurs. Strips of peel can be dried and used in savoury stews or included with herbs to make a bouquet garni. Tangerine segments can be eaten on their own. Dipped in melted chocolate or crystallized, they make a delicious after-dinner sweet (candy) served with coffee. Tangerine juice can add flavour to marinades for pork and poultry.

Above: Clementines are the smallest variety of tangerine.

LEMONS

Arguably the lemon is the most useful of all fruit. The skin contains aromatic essential oils, and a good lemon will perfume the air with its fragrance.

The juicy, pale yellow, acid flesh enhances almost any food and never fails to awaken and refresh the taste buds. The lemon is rich in vitamin C.

Buying, Storing and Cooking

Choose lemons that are firm and heavy. Smooth-skinned lemons are best for juicing and cooking, while the knobbly skinned varieties are easier to grate. Lemons become paler as they ripen and lose some juiciness and acidity, so avoid light yellow fruit. Every part of the lemon can be used in sweet and savoury cooking, from the juice to the zest.

Kaffir Limes

These pale green, gnarled fruits have a scented citrus bouquet but are not actually true limes. They belong to a sub-species of the citrus family. The flesh is inedible but the finely grated rind and torn leaves are widely used in South-east Asian cooking.

Above:
Knobbly-
skinned lemons
are easy to grate.

LIMES

These have thin, fairly smooth green skins and a highly aromatic, acid flavour. Unlike lemons, limes will grow in tropical regions and are an essential ingredient in South-east Asian, Mexican, Indian, Caribbean, Brazilian and Latin American cooking. Limes are high in vitamin C and other nutrients. There are basically three types of lime available.

Tahitian These are large limes, with pale, fine-grained pulp and a very acidic, extremely sour flavour.

Mexican Smaller than the Tahitian, this variety has bright green skin and a very aromatic flavour.

Key lime These are a pale yellowish-green fruit, and are very juicy with a strong, sharp flavour. They are the main ingredient of Florida key lime pie.

Buying, Storing and Cooking

Choose unblemished limes that feel heavy for their size and avoid those with yellowish skins, as they may have lost some of their flavour. They can be stored for up to a week in the refrigerator. Limes can be used in the same way as lemons, but will add a sharper flavour, so use fewer of them. In Caribbean and Latin American cooking, limes are cooked with fish, poultry and meat.

Above:
Bright green
limes have a
sharper, rather
more astringent
flavour than
lemons.

Zesting and Grating a Lemon

Choose an unwaxed lemon that has not been treated with diphenyl.

1 Hold the lemon firmly in one hand and scrape a zester down its length to pare off slivers of rind.

2 Chop the pared zest finely with a sharp knife if you like.

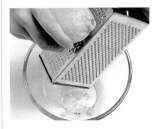

3 For grating, choose a knobbly-skinned lemon, if possible. Grate the lemon rind on the fine side of a grater, taking care to remove only the yellow zest and avoiding the bitter white pith. Work over a bowl – this makes it easy to transfer the grated rind to a bowl or pan with the aid of a pastry brush.

GRAPEFRUIT

This is one of the largest citrus fruits and can vary in diameter from 10–18cm/4–7in. Most grapefruits have deep yellow skins but the flesh can range from very pale yellow (confusingly called white), through rosy pink to deep pink (known as ruby). Generally speaking, the pinker the flesh, the sweeter the grapefruit will be.

Grapefruits are an excellent source of dietary fibre and vitamin C. When buying, choose a fruit that feels heavy for its size, as it will be juicy. The skin can be thick or thin depending on the variety, but it should be plump and firm; if it is puffy and coarse, the flesh will be dry. Avoid grapefruit with bruised or damaged skin. You cannot ripen grapefruits once they have been picked, but they can be kept in a cool place or in the refrigerator for a week.

Grapefruits can be squeezed for their juice, or eaten for breakfast. Segmenting a grapefruit is simple – all you need is a curved, serrated grapefruit knife. Run the knife between the skin and flesh, then use a small sharp paring knife to cut carefully between the membrane that separates the segments.

Above: Pomelos can be used in the same way as grapefruit, but may need more sugar.

The main varieties of grapefruit are white, pink or ruby, but you may also find the green-skinned Sweetie, whose flesh, as the name implies, is so sweet that it needs no added sugar.

Pomelos Although they resemble grapefruit, true pomelos are actually a species in their own right. They are also known as shaddocks. Much larger than grapefruit and not quite so juicy, they are pear-shaped and have thick yellow dimpled skin, coarse, pinkish flesh and a sharp flavour.

Above: White grapefruit have a pale yellow flesh.

Kumquats

These are not true citrus fruits, but belong to a similar species, *fortunella*. Their name comes from the Cantonese *kam kwat*, which means golden orange. The small elongated fruit is about the size and shape of a large olive, with a thin orange rind that is edible. The rind is sweeter than the sour pulp and the two parts eaten together provide a delicious sour-sweet sensation.

Kumquats can be eaten whole or sliced into rings and used in fruit salads. They can be kept in the refrigerator for up to a week.

Ugli Fruit Despite its large size, baggy shape and mottled green skin, the ugli fruit is a hybrid of the grapefruit, orange and tangerine. It may not be the beauty of the citrus world, but the flavour is sweet and delicious – a cross between grapefruit and tangerine – and it is extremely juicy. The peel can be candied in the same way as grapefruit peel and served as a sweet.

BERRIES

Whether wild or cultivated, these delicate soft fruits have a wonderful flavour and are always a treat.

STRAWBERRIES

For centuries, strawberries have been the most highly prized soft fruit. They were valued for their therapeutic properties in Ancient Rome and have been cultivated in Europe since the Middle Ages. The cultivated strawberries we enjoy today were developed in the 19th century from

Above: Cultivated strawberries are widely available in most supermarkets and stores.

small, scarlet, wild strawberries from Virginia. The enthusiasm engendered for cultivated strawberries blossomed and they remain one of the world's favourite fruits. They are rich in vitamin C and B vitamins and contain potassium, iron and fibre.

The best-flavoured varieties are summer strawberries, but perpetual strawberries go on to fruit continuously throughout the autumn (fall). Although not so sweet as the summer varieties, they can be used for jams (jellies), sauces and compôtes.

Cambridge Favourite These medium-sized berries have an attractive colour and flavour and are a favourite with all strawberry-growers.

Elsanta Largish and firm, these berries have attractive glossy flesh and an excellent sweet flavour.

Elvira This Dutch variety was developed in the 1970s. The oval berries are a deep glossy red.

Gorella This is a deep red conical berry with paler red flesh. It is a very consistent variety.

Fraises des bois The smallest wild strawberries are the Hautbois varieties, whose tiny red fruits taste wonderfully fragrant. Alpine strawberries are generally a little larger and less juicy, with a highly perfumed flavour. Yellow and white varieties look less appealing, but have a delicious flavour of vanilla.

Buying and Storing

Always try to buy locally grown fruits and check those at the bottom of the bag or container, making sure they are damaged. Ideally, strawberries should be eaten the day they are bought. If this is not possible, keep the berries in the refrigerator, loosely covered with clear film (plastic wrap) for no longer than two days. Remove at least an hour before serving.

Preparing and Serving

It is best not to wash strawberries, as they easily become waterlogged. If they are dirty, wipe them gently. Strawberries can be served with cream and perhaps a little sugar. They may be steeped in wine or Champagne or sprinkled with pepper or balsamic vinegar. They feature in a huge variety of desserts. They are rarely used in savoury dishes, but may be served with sliced avocado as an appetizer.

Below: Tiny wild fraises des bois have a lovely perfumed flavour.

Preparing Strawberries

Although these fruits are easy to prepare, hulling a large quantity may take a little time.

1 Wipe the strawberries with a piece of damp kitchen paper.

2 Hold the strawberry between your thumb and forefinger and twist off the stalk and frill, removing the central hull in the same movement.

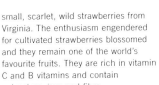

RASPBERRIES

These are a member of the rose family. Native to the hilly areas of Europe and Asia, they grow best in a cool, damp climate and can be found even in Alaska. The deep red (or sometimes yellow) jewel-like fruits have a sweet, intense flavour. They are a valuable source of vitamin C, potassium, niacin and riboflavin, and dietary fibre. Raspberry juice is said to be good for the heart and the fruit is also thought to enhance brain function.

There are many different varieties of raspberry with new ones constantly being developed. Stores and markets do not tend to identify varieties but gardeners have their own favourites.

Heritage This is a late-fruiting variety with outstanding flavour.

Malling Jewel Fruiting in mid-season, this raspberry is a heavy cropper.

Yellow and Golden These clear golden berries are not widely available, but are worth seeking out for their fine flavour.

Wild raspberries You will often find these fragrant fruits growing in cool, damp areas of woodland. They are full of pips (seeds), but have an exquisite flavour. The salmonberry is a wild raspberry from the United States.

Buying and Storing

Raspberries are ripe when they are bright and evenly coloured. If buying in a carton, check the base to make sure it is not stained red or leaking, a sure sign that the fruit has become soft and is past its best.

Above: Raspberries have a wonderfully intense flavour.

If possible, always eat raspberries on the day they are bought or picked; if necessary, they can be stored for up to two days in the bottom of the refrigerator, but bring them out at least an hour before serving. Raspberries freeze very well: open-freeze the fruit in a single layer on a baking sheet, then pack into rigid containers. Raspberry purée may also be frozen.

Preparing and Serving

Do not wash raspberries unless this is unavoidable; they are seldom very dirty and washing will ruin the texture and flavour. All you need to do is gently pick off any bits of leaf or stalk. The less you handle them, the better.

Good raspberries have such a wonderful flavour that they are best eaten on their own, with a little sugar or cream. They can also be used for pavlovas, meringues, mousses, jellies, flans and tartlets. They are an essential ingredient in the traditional English summer pudding and combine very well with other berries such as strawberries and blueberries in fruit desserts and sweet soups. Raspberry coulis, an integral part of the classic peach melba, is an easy-to-make sauce that tastes delicious with ice cream.

Raspberry jam – with or without seeds (pips) – is delicious and very popular. Raspberries also feature

in savoury dishes. Their slightly tart, acidic flavour complements the rich meat of duck and game birds such as guinea fowl and quail and they also go well with lamb. Use them whole or crushed in a marinade. Raspberry vinegar is a traditional country recipe, made by steeping the crushed berries in white wine vinegar and then straining it. It is useful in salad dressings and makes a refreshing drink diluted with still or sparkling water. It may also be used in deglazed sauces and basting mixtures for roasting ham or duck.

Making a Raspberry Coulis

This simple sauce is classically spooned over a lightly poached peach in peach melba, but it is good served with any number of other desserts such as chocolate cake or ice cream.

1 Put the raspberries in a bowl and crush to a purée with a fork. Tip the purée into a sieve set over a bowl. Rub through, using the back of a large spoon.

2 Sweeten to taste with icing (confectioners') sugar and stir.

CLOUDBERRIES

These relatives of raspberries grow on boggy land in the northern climates of Scandinavia, Siberia and Canada, where they are known as baked apple berries, and even within the Arctic Circle. They ripen slowly, allowing the flavour to develop to an extraordinary intensity and sweetness. They are very highly prized in Scandinavia for making jams (jellies), desserts and fruit soups. They are a good source of vitamin C and are rich in dietary fibre. They also contain calcium, phosphorus and potassium.

BLACKBERRIES AND DEWBERRIES

These two relations of the rose and the raspberry are virtually indistinguishable, the main difference between them being that blackberries are larger and grow on thorny bushes or brambles, while dewberries trail. Blackberries grow wild in temperate zones everywhere in the world, but are also cultivated to give a larger, juicier and slightly sweeter berry with better keeping properties.

Buying and Storing

Whether you pick or buy blackberries, they should be plump and tender, not wet or mushy. Look for large, shiny fruit, with no green patches or signs of mould, and if you are buying them in a carton, check that the underside is not stained. Blackberries do not keep well. If you are not going to eat them at once, store them for no more than one day in the bottom of the refrigerator. They do freeze well; place in a single layer on a baking sheet then, once frozen, pack into rigid containers.

Preparing and Cooking

If you must wash blackberries, do so just before serving and drain well. They are best eaten as they are, with sugar and cream, but can also be puréed and sieved for a coulis or used for fools, ice creams and sorbets (sherbets). Blackberries are also popular used for making jam (jelly).

BLUEBERRIES AND BILBERRIES

These small, round blue-black berries grow on small shrubs on peaty moors and uplands. American blueberries are generally larger and sweeter than bilberries. Today they are often cultivated, resulting in large, perfect berries that sometimes lack the distinctive flavour of the wild fruit. Blueberries and bilberries are a source of vitamin C, iron and dietary fibre. They also have antibacterial properties and are thought to improve sight.

Above: Blueberries have a mild, sweet flavour.

Above: Blackberries are delicious baked with apples in a crumble.

Buying and Storing

The best blueberries and bilberries are those you pick yourself. If you buy them, look for plump berries of uniform size with the characteristic bloom. Reject shrivelled specimens. Unwashed blueberries will keep for a week in the bottom of the refrigerator, but bilberries do not keep so well.

Preparing and Cooking

Blueberries and bilberries have soft seeds, so they can be eaten raw. Simply rinse and drain them first. However, they are more commonly used for making pies and tarts, or added to muffins, breads and pancakes. They may also be lightly cooked and flavoured with lemon or orange and spices and used as a jam-like topping for cheesecake. They make simply fabulous ice cream. Blueberries can also be made into a sauce to serve with game.

Above: Bilberries are smaller and less sweet than blueberries.

GOOSEBERRIES

These are a peculiarly British favourite of the fruit world. A botanical cousin of the blackcurrant, they have been popular in Britain for centuries, growing wild in many kitchen gardens. The Tudors served them in savoury sauces and in all manner of sweet dishes. Their popularity never extended across the English Channel though: even today the French use them only in a sauce to cut the richness of oily fish and there is no specific French word for gooseberry. They are known there as *groseilles à maquereau* – mackerel currants.

Gooseberries have a long season. Early fruit are usually bright green and rather hard. These are followed by the softer, mid-season fruits, which are not generally identified by variety when sold in supermarkets, but that you may find in gardens and farm stores.

Gooseberries are high in vitamin C and also contain vitamins A and D, potassium, calcium, phosphorus and niacin, as well as fibre.

Early Sulphur This very early variety has golden, almost transparent berries and a lovely, sweet flavour.
Goldendrop This small, round yellow gooseberry has a fine, rich flavour, which makes it ideal for eating raw as a dessert fruit. It ripens in mid-summer.
Langley's Industry A large, red, hairy berry, this has a lovely sweet flavour.
Leveller This mid-season, yellowish-green berry has a sweet flavour.

Above: Early season green gooseberries cannot be eaten raw but are delicious cooked.

London These huge, deep red or purple dessert gooseberries can be eaten fresh, just as they are.
Worcestershire berries These are a species of gooseberry from North America. The small purplish-red berries are the size of large blackberries, but they have the distinctive veining of gooseberry and a gooseberry flavour. They can be eaten raw or cooked.

Buying and Storing

Choose slightly underripe gooseberries for cooking, but check that they are not rock-hard. Dessert varieties should be yielding and juicy (if possible, taste before you buy). Gooseberries will keep in the refrigerator for up to a week. To freeze whole gooseberries, top and tail them with a sharp knife or kitchen scissors and open-freeze on baking sheets. Pack the frozen berries into plastic bags. Alternatively, purée and sieve them, sweeten and freeze in containers.

Above: Fully ripe red gooseberries are quite sweet enough to be eaten just as they are.

Preparing and Cooking

Unless making jam (jelly) or if you are going to sieve the cooked fruit, it is not necessary to top and tail gooseberries before use. Gooseberries are rich in pectin, which makes them ideal for making firm jams. They can also be used in pies, tarts or crumbles, or can be cooked with a little water and sugar and puréed, sieved and mixed with whipped cream for a gooseberry fool.

Gooseberries have a tart flavour, and a sauce made with the fruit is an excellent foil for mackerel and other oily fish, and also goes well with duck and rich meats such as pork.

Making Gooseberry Fool
Gooseberries have a great affinity with elderflowers, which may be included to give a subtle fragrance.

1 Top and tail 450g/1lb gooseberries and put into a pan with 30ml/2 tbsp water. Cover and cook for 5–6 minutes, until the berries pop open.

2 Add 50g/2oz/¼ cup sugar and 30ml/2 tbsp elderflower cordial and stir or mash until the fruit forms a pulp. Remove from the heat, spoon into a bowl and set aside to cool.

3 Stir a 400g/14oz carton of ready-made custard sauce into the fruit. Whip 300ml/½ pint/1¼ cups double (heavy) cream and fold into the mixture. Spoon into dessert glasses and chill before serving.

CRANBERRIES

These tart, bright ruby-red berries grow wild on evergreen shrubs in peaty marshland all over northern Europe and North America. They are closely related to blueberries and bilberries, but are much more sour and are always served cooked. They are closely related to cowberries and lingonberries.

Cranberry and Chestnut Stuffing

The traditional Christmas accompaniments of cranberries and chestnuts can be combined to make a stuffing for turkey or other poultry. To make about 450g/1lb stuffing, soften 115g/4oz chopped onion in 25g/1oz butter in a pan. Stir in 175g/6oz unsweetened chestnut purée and 30ml/2 tbsp cooked cranberries or chunky cranberry sauce. Season with salt and pepper and mix thoroughly. Take the pan off the heat and stir in 225g/8oz fresh white breadcrumbs. Coarsely chop 115g/4oz cooked chestnuts and fold into the stuffing mixture. Leave to cool before using.

*Above:
Bright red cranberries can be used in both sweet and savoury dishes, or can be juiced and served as a drink.*

Cranberries are sometimes known as bounceberries since they were traditionally tested for firmness by being bounced seven times. Any which failed the bounce test were too squashy and were, therefore, discarded. Because of their waxy skins, cranberries keep for much longer than other berries, which helps to explain their popularity.

Cranberries contain useful amounts of vitamins C and D, potassium and iron. They used to be considered to be a good protection against scurvy, and they are known to contain a natural antibiotic. Cranberry juice has long been recommended as a natural remedy for cystitis, kidney, bladder and urinary tract infections.

Buying and Storing

Look for plump, firm, bright red berries and check the base of the carton in case of squashed or shrivelled berries. Fresh cranberries will keep in the refrigerator for four weeks, or freeze them in plastic bags.

Preparing and Cooking

Cranberries can be used in sweet or savoury dishes. Their most famous incarnation is as cranberry sauce. The berries are high in pectin, so they make excellent jams (jellies). They also combine well with orange and apple, and can be mixed with blackberries and raspberries for an autumn (fall) version of summer pudding. Cranberry sorbet (sherbet) is a delicious treat. When cooking them for a sweet dish, do not add the sugar until the skins have popped or they will become tough.

Making Cranberry Sauce

Cranberry sauce and roast turkey have featured as part of the American Thanksgiving feast since 1620. The sauce also goes well with goose, red meat and game.

1 Using a sharp knife or vegetable peeler, thinly pare the rind of an orange. Put the rind and the juice of the orange into a pan.

2 Add 350g/12oz/3 cups of cranberries. Cook over a low heat for about 3 minutes.

3 Stir in caster (superfine) sugar to taste and simmer for 5 minutes. Add a splash of port if liked. Pour into a bowl, then cool and chill.

HYBRID BERRIES

There is a variety of raspberry/blackberry crossbreeds. Some, like the loganberry, have occurred naturally; others have been cultivated to produce a more robust or better-flavoured fruit. All these hybrids can be cooked and frozen in the same way as raspberries or blackberries.

Loganberries The loganberry first appeared in 1881 at Santa Cruz in California in the garden of Judge J.H. Logan. It was a natural hybrid, probably derived from a cross between a native dewberry and a raspberry. Since then, loganberries have been cultivated to produce very large, juicy, dark wine-red berries, with the consistency of a blackberry but with an intense raspberry flavour. Loganberries are very tart, so need plenty of sugar.

Youngberries These dewberry/loganberry hybrids resemble a dark red, elongated blackberry, but taste rather like a sweeter loganberry.

Boysenberries This cross between a youngberry and a raspberry resembles a large red-purple blackberry. Boysen-berries are sweeter than loganberries and can be eaten raw, although they are more often used to make jam (jelly).

Tayberries These wonderful berries are a cross between the American blackberry and a raspberry. They grow on long, spiny canes. The elongated berries have a slightly tart, aromatic flavour and are usually cooked.

Right: Tayberries were first bred in Scotland.

Tummelberries
These are similar to tayberries, but fruit later in the season. Similar crossbreeds include sunberries and wineberries.

MULBERRIES

These grow on dome-headed trees that can often be very ancient and grow up to about 10m/30ft across. They are more likely to grow on village greens or, in France, in the town square or in a large farmhouse courtyard.

Black mulberries are native to western Asia. They were known to the Ancient Greeks, but it was the Roman Emperor Justinian who deliberately encouraged their propagation as part of an enterprise in silk production. In the sixteenth century, it was discovered that silkworms preferred to feed on the leaves of the white mulberry, and many of these trees were planted in Europe in the vain hope of stimulating a silk trade. Some of these white mulberry trees still survive today. Mulberries have a slightly musky flavour.

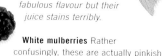

Above: Mulberries have a fabulous flavour but their juice stains terribly.

White mulberries Rather confusingly, these are actually pinkish or pale red. There is also an American red mulberry, whose leaves turn beautifully yellow in autumn (fall).

Black mulberries These are considered finer than the white variety. The dark wine-red, elongated berries resemble loganberries in appearance and the luscious black juice stains everything with which it comes into contact.

Preparing and Serving

Ripe mulberries can be eaten just as they are, with or without cream, and are usually sweet enough not to need sugar. They are a good addition to summer pudding and make excellent ice creams, fools and sorbets (sherbets). They can also be steeped in white wine vinegar to flavour it for salad dressings or in vodka for a fruity drink. Overripe fruit is best used for jams (jellies) and sauces. Mulberry sauce goes well with richly flavoured roast meats such as game, duck and lamb.

HUCKLEBERRIES

These berries, which gave their name to Mark Twain's character Huckleberry Finn, are similar to blueberries, but have a tougher skin and hard internal seeds. They have a sharper flavour than blueberries, but can be eaten and cooked in the same way.

Tangleberries, which grow on the coast of North America, are another variety. These purplish berries are sweeter than huckleberries.

Below: Elderberries are good cooked with other fruits to make pies.

Below: Rosehips are very rich in vitamin C.

ELDERBERRIES

Although you can seldom buy them, you will find elderberries growing all over the countryside throughout the late summer. The pretty flowers can be used to make cordials and the dark, tiny berries used for fabric dye and for making wine.

If picking elderberries for wine-making, choose those growing well away from a road so that they will not be contaminated with dust and pollution. Good elderberries should be shiny and black. If making elderflower cordial, choose cream coloured flowerheads that are fully open, but whose petals have not yet begun to drop. Use both flowers and berries soon after picking.

Like most hedgerow berries, elderberries are an excellent source of vitamin C. Strip off the berries using a fork and cook them in the same way as redcurrants or other berries. They can be made into jellies, included in savoury sauces for pork and game, or used to bulk out other berries, especially blackberries, in pies, tarts, fools and ice creams. They are used to make flavoured vinegar and are a popular choice for country wines. Sprigs of elderflowers can be dipped in batter for fritters, or made into a flavoured syrup. The flowers have a particular affinity with gooseberries.

ROWANBERRIES

These bright orangey-red berries, the fruit of the mountain ash, grow in large clusters. They can be used for making jelly, a gloriously deep orange, jewel-like preserve with a bittersweet flavour. The jelly goes well with rich meats.

Below: Rowanberries

ROSEHIPS

These are the seed pods of roses and appear after the plants have finished flowering. Rosehips are an excellent source of vitamin C, a single rosehip typically containing twenty times more vitamin C than an orange. Rosehips are used for country-style wines, and for making a bittersweet jelly, which is delicious with poultry or game. Rosehip syrup, sweetened with honey or sugar, makes a popular dessert sauce for children. Since each seed contains numerous prickly hairs that will irritate the stomach, the seeds and hairs must be scooped out of the halved hips before cooking. Any rosehip liquid should always be strained twice through a double layer of muslin (cheesecloth).

HAWS

The fruit of the hawthorn or may tree, these small, wine-red berries have a bitter, pungent taste. They are not eaten raw, but can be combined with crab apples or elderberries for a delicious hedgerow jelly. They can also be made into a good sauce to serve with rich meats, poultry and game.

Below: Haws have a rather bitter taste.

CURRANTS

These native European berries, with their glowing colours, make a beautiful sight in summer, hanging like miniature bunches of grapes on the bush. Each berry contains a mass of small seeds. Currants can be eaten whole, but because they are highly acidic, this is seldom the preferred option.

Currants grow wild all over Europe and even as far north as Siberia. They became popular only in the sixteenth century when they were prized for their health-giving properties. All currants, particularly blackcurrants, are very rich in vitamin C. Blackcurrants are used in cordials, throat lozenges and other remedies designed to ward off colds; in the past, they were used as a cure for quinsy. The Russians add blackcurrant jam (jelly) to tea for colds. Tisanes, made from blackcurrant leaves, are also often taken as a health-giving drink.

Buying and Storing

Choose plump, firm currants with shiny skins. They will keep in the refrigerator for several days. They can be frozen very successfully. Strip the currants from the stalks, then rinse and drain them and freeze in rigid containers. Blackcurrant purée also freezes well.

Preparing

Strip the currants from the stalks if this hasn't already been done. If you wish, pick off the calyx tops before cooking the currants by pinching them between the nails of your forefinger and thumb. However, this is a tedious process and is seldom worth the effort.

BLACKCURRANTS

Although they are often combined with other currants in cooking, as in summer pudding, blackcurrants are different from other types. They have tougher skins and, unlike other currants, which grow on old wood, they fruit on new wood. Both the bushes and the currants themselves are highly aromatic and the fruits have a luscious tart flavour.

Cooking

Blackcurrants can be added raw to fruit salads if they are not too tart, but are usually cooked in a little water, with sugar to taste. Simmer until they are just tender – do not overcook them or they will lose their lovely fresh flavour. Blackcurrants make wonderful jams (jellies) and combine well with soft cheeses, rich meats and game.

Stripping Currants off the Stalk
The simplest way to strip currants from the stalk is with a fork.

Hold the bunch of currants by the stem and strip off the berries with the tines of a fork.

To serve blackcurrants with meat, sauté them lightly in butter, adding a pinch of sugar. They also adapt well to other flavourings such as mint and lemon.

Above:
Buffalo currants
are a type of
blackcurrant with
larger
berries.

Left: Blackcurrants have a tart flavour and are usually cooked before eating.

Blackcurrant Whip
For a light and refreshing summer dessert, heat 15g/½oz gelatine gently in 450ml/¾ pint/scant 2 cups of blackcurrant juice. Add sugar to taste. Cool, then whisk until a thick foam is produced. When the whisk leaves a trail in the foam, spoon into a glass dish.

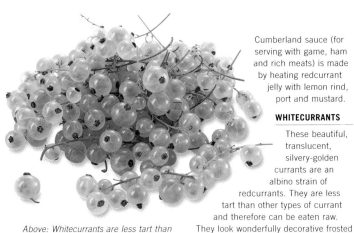

Above: Whitecurrants are less tart than other currants and can be eaten raw.

REDCURRANTS

Redcurrants can be eaten raw, and small bunches look decorative if frosted with egg white and caster (superfine) sugar. They are an essential ingredient for summer pudding and make a good addition to creamy desserts, such as *crème brûlée*. The most familiar use of redcurrants, however, is in the jewel-like jelly that is so often served with lamb and venison.

Cumberland sauce (for serving with game, ham and rich meats) is made by heating redcurrant jelly with lemon rind, port and mustard.

WHITECURRANTS

These beautiful, translucent, silvery-golden currants are an albino strain of redcurrants. They are less tart than other types of currant and therefore can be eaten raw. They look wonderfully decorative frosted with egg white and sugar.

PINK CURRANTS

These are an even more attractive variety than the whitecurrant, with a beautiful pink flush.

Redcurrant Cooler

To make a refreshing summer drink, purée 450g/1lb/4 cups redcurrants with 550ml/18fl oz/ 2 cups water and sugar to taste, then press the purée gently through a sieve placed over a jug (pitcher). Dilute the puréed fruit with sparkling water or soda water (club soda), add a few ice cubes – and a dash of vodka or gin, if you like.

Left: Redcurrants are one of the essential ingredients in the classic dessert, summer pudding.

Making Redcurrant Jelly

This brightly-coloured jelly goes well with lamb or venison.

1 Put the redcurrants in a pan with enough water to cover. Bring to the boil and simmer for 8–10 minutes.

2 Strain the mixture through a jelly bag. Measure the liquid, then pour back into the pan. Add 350g/12oz/ 1¾ cups sugar for every 600ml/ 1 pint/2½ cups liquid and stir over a medium heat until dissolved.

3 Boil for 10 minutes until setting point is reached, skimming off any scum. Pour the jelly into warm sterilized jars. Seal and, when cool enough to handle, label.

EXOTIC FRUITS

Thanks to modern transportation methods, tropical fruits are now widely available all over the world.

BANANAS

These are surely the best-known tropical fruit. Neatly packaged in their attractive, easy-peel skins, hygienically enclosing the sweet, creamy white flesh, bananas are the perfect convenience food and are very versatile. Bananas originated in South-east Asia and have grown in the tropics since ancient times.

Bananas are extremely nutritious, being rich in potassium, riboflavin, niacin and dietary fibre. They also contain vitamins A and C, and some calcium and iron. They have a high level of natural sugar, which provides a rapid energy boost and this, together with the high level of potassium, which is essential for muscle and nerve function, makes them a powerhouse snack for children and for athletes.

Hundreds of different varieties of banana flourish in the Tropics, from sweet yellow pygmy fruit to large fibrous plantains and green bananas, which can be used only for cooking. The most common varieties of sweet banana are the long, curved yellow dessert fruit, which develop a speckled brown skin as they ripen. The most widely available of these is the Cavendish, but unless you are a banana expert, it is virtually impossible to differentiate between the individual varieties.

Lady Finger/Sugar bananas These are tiny finger bananas, often no more than 7.5cm/3in long – hence their name. They have a lovely creamy flesh and a very sweet flavour.

Left: Bananas come in a variety of shapes, sizes and colours and are very easy to peel.

Below: Red bananas have a yellowish-pink flesh.

exact degree of ripeness, so they can sometimes prove rather disappointing. It is best to allow a few blackish patches to develop on the skin before eating.

Buying and Storing

Bananas are harvested unripe and stored in a humid atmosphere to ripen slowly. Unripe bananas are green all over; these are inedible. Fruit with green-tinged ends are slightly under-ripe, with a crisp texture and refreshing taste. Perfectly ripe bananas are uniformly yellow. As the fruit continues to ripen, brown speckles appear on the skin, until it is covered with brown mottling. At this stage they are best for mashing, but once the banana has turned brown all over, it is too ripe to eat, but can still be used for cooking. Do not buy bananas with damaged skins, or those that are too ripe. Never store bananas in the refrigerator, as the skins will blacken and everything else stored there will smell of banana.

Apple These yellow bananas are also very small. They have golden flesh and, when very ripe, have a faint taste and aroma of apples.
Red bananas These bananas from Ecuador have brownish-red skins and smooth, yellowish-pink, sweet flesh with a creamy texture. Their colour makes it hard to assess the

Left: Apple bananas

BABACOS

This five-sided fruit is a hybrid of the papaya, pointed at the stem end and blunt at the other. The waxy skin is pale green but gradually matures to yellow. When ripe, the pale orangey-pink flesh is succulent and juicy, with a faint aroma of fresh strawberries, although the flavour resembles that of a rather bland, tasteless papaya.

Babacos can be stored in the refrigerator or, if still pale green, kept at room temperature for a few days until ripe. They are normally eaten raw, sliced and served with a sprinkling of sugar, lemon juice and spices. They can also be used unsweetened in salads and other savoury dishes in the same way as cucumber.

Right: Babacos are ripe when they are yellow all over.

Below: Custard apples have soft flesh with a mellow flavour.

Below: Carambolas

CARAMBOLAS

Native to Indonesia and the Moluccas, carambolas or star fruit are now widely available in supermarkets. The uncut yellow or pale amber fruit has a waxy skin and is cylindrical in shape, with concave sides and five ridged edges, so that when the fruit is sliced crossways, it resembles a star. The flesh is refreshing and juicy to eat and makes a pretty decoration for fruit salads, although it has little flavour. The degree of sweetness can vary and there is no way of knowing in advance how sweet individual fruits are. It can also be eaten with vinaigrette as a salad. Carambolas are a good source of vitamin C. When buying, choose firm, undamaged fruits. They will keep in the refrigerator for up to a week.

CHERIMOYAS, CUSTARD APPLES AND SOURSOPS

Cherimoyas are a fruit belonging to the annona family, of which custard apples are the most widely available. Native to South America and the Caribbean, they are a heart-shaped or oval fruit, made up of many concave sections rather like the appearance of a pine cone. Inside the fruit are inedible, large, black seeds surrounded with creamy-white flesh which has a sweet-sour flavour reminiscent of pineapples and bananas.

Custard apples have a light tan or greenish quilted skin that develops brown patches as the fruit ripens. The custard-like flesh has a more mellow flavour than that of cherimoyas.

Soursops, also called prickly custard apples and guanabanas, have prickly dark green skins. They are pear-shaped and larger than cherimoyas. The white juicy flesh has a tangy, acidic flavour.

When buying cherimoyas, choose fruit with unblemished skin and tightly packed carpels. They should be eaten as soon as possible after buying, but can be kept in the bottom of the refrigerator for a day or two. They can be eaten simply with a spoon, added to fruit salads or used to make sorbets (sherbets) and drinks.

CURUBAS

Also known as the banana passion fruit, the curuba looks like an elongated passion fruit with soft yellowish skin and a sharp, but rich flavour. It is delicious in sorbets (sherbets).

DATES

These are one of the world's oldest cultivated fruits. It is likely that the Babylonians grew them as long as 8,000 years ago and, in early times, the date palm was regarded as the tree of life. Every part was used: the buds and fruit were eaten or dried, the sap was drunk, the fibres were woven, and the date stones (pits) were used as fuel or fodder for donkeys and camels.

Of the many varieties of date, only a few are exported, and even these are seldom known by name. The most popular is the golden brown *deglet noor* (date of the light) from North Africa and Israel. Dates are extremely nutritious, and contain more natural sugar than any other fruit. They also contain substantial quantities of dietary fibre and potassium.

Ripe fresh dates, which are available in cartons, should be plump and moist with a slightly crunchy texture. They are ripe when burnished brown. Unripe dates are more golden and the flesh will taste less honeyed than ripe dates. They can be stuffed with cheese or nuts, combined with nuts in tarts, teabreads and other baked goods, and are widely used in savoury stews in North Africa.

DRAGON FRUIT

Dragon fruit come in both yellow and pink versions. The pink fruit is large, covered with green-tipped scales. The flesh is sweet and refreshing, with a slightly acidic, melon-like flavour. The edible black seeds give it a similar texture to kiwi fruit. Yellow dragon fruit look more like prickly pears, but taste exactly like the pink variety. Buy fruit

that is slightly yielding. It is best eaten as soon as it is ripe, but can be kept in the refrigerator for up to three days.

FEIJOAS

A distant member of the guava family, feijoas come from South America. The thin, tough skin protects a soft jelly-like flesh containing tiny hard seeds, with an aromatic strawberry-like flavour. Treat it as you would a guava.

Left: Dried deglet noor is a popular variety.

Above: Halawi dates have a lovely chewy texture and a sweet flavour.

Below: Dragon fruit is good served chilled with a sprinkling of lime juice.

DURIANS

The disgusting, all-pervading, sewage-like smell of the durian is legendary, and only the most adventurous – or those lacking any sense of smell – go on to sample the flesh, which is paradoxically rich and delicious. It is used to make jams, jellies and sweets (candies) and in Indonesia, unripe fruit is cooked like a vegetable. The edible seeds are often roasted or boiled.

Below: Feijoas taste a little like fresh strawberries.

*Above:
Granadillas can
be eaten in the
same way as passion fruit.*

GINUPS

These small round tropical fruits grow on trees in bunches like grapes. Not unlike a lime with its bright green dimpled skin, the fruit sometimes goes by the name Spanish lime. The pink, jelly-like pulp is juicy and sweet, with a slightly acidic note. The juice stains.

GRANADILLAS

These are the largest members of the passion fruit family. They can weigh several kilos and, in their unripe state, are often used as vegetables. Ripe granadillas are round, smooth and orange-skinned, with greyish pulp that contains small hard seeds. They taste less fragrant than passion fruit.

Preparing Guavas
To eat guavas raw, they need very little preparation.

Cut the guava in half and squeeze over a little lime juice. Scoop out the flesh using a teaspoon.

GUAVAS

This versatile fruit is used for all sorts of confections and desserts such as ice creams, sorbets (sherbets) and sweet drinks. They are also delicious eaten raw. Similar in shape to pears or plums, guavas can be as small as 2.5cm/1in or as large as 10cm/4in in diameter. They have thin, pale green skins that turn light yellow as they ripen. The flesh varies from white through to deep pink or salmon red and contains a number of flattish, hard but edible seeds.

Guavas are highly scented, with an aromatic sweet-acid flavour, not unlike that of quinces. They are exceptionally rich in vitamin C and are a good source of niacin, potassium and dietary fibre. As well as being used for sweet dishes, guavas can also be incorporated into sauces to serve with duck or game. They make an interesting addition to salads and can be stuffed with cream cheese and served as an appetizer. They can also be poached but should be cooked gently as the flesh tends to disintegrate.

JACKFRUIT

Related to breadfruit, these large, irregularly shaped oval fruits originated in the rainforests of India and Malaysia, and are now grown in Asia, Africa, America and Australia. They can weigh 20kg/44lb, but you will find only smaller specimens in the stores. They have a rough spiny skin that ripens from green to brown and each fruit contains large, white, edible seeds. Ripe jackfruit have a musty odour and a sweet, but rather bland flavour. They may be peeled and eaten raw, but are better boiled, roasted or fried and used as a vegetable or in a curry. The seeds may be roasted or boiled and eaten like chestnuts.

JAMAICAN PLUMS

Also known as hoy or hog plums, golden apple, *limbu* and *mombin*, this fruit belongs to the same family as the mango and is grown in Central and South America, the Caribbean, South-east Asia and India. Although much smaller than mangoes, they have a similar soft skin and a large central stone (pit). The firm yellow flesh is juicy, fragrant and sweet. It is more akin to pineapple or apple than mango, and the distinctive flavour has an acidic tang. The fruit can be eaten raw, sweetened with brown sugar, or sprinkled with rum or liqueur and served with cream.

Above: Guavas are delicious eaten raw with a squeeze of lemon juice.

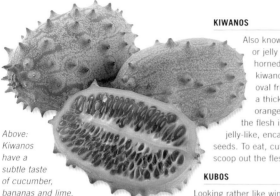

Above: Kiwanos have a subtle taste of cucumber, bananas and lime.

JUJUBES

Also known as Chinese dates, these small greeny-brown fruits have been cultivated in northern China for more than 4,000 years and are now grown extensively in India and other parts of the world. The fruit can be oblong, egg-shaped or round and has crisp pearly-white flesh enclosing a single stone (pit). The sweet flavour and texture is reminiscent of an unripe pear. Most fruits are deep brown when ripe, but can be bought while still firm. Leave at room temperature for a few days to ripen. They can be eaten raw or stewed with orange juice, or made into jams (jellies). They can also be dried.

KIWI FRUIT

The dull exterior of this fruit belies its pretty flesh. Also known as Chinese gooseberries, kiwi fruit originated in the Yangtze Valley. They are now grown extensively in New Zealand, Australia, South America and parts of Europe.

Kiwi fruit can be eaten as a fruit in its own right, or added to fruit salads, open fruit tarts and pavlovas. Kiwi fruit contains enzymes that make an excellent meat tenderizer. Rub the peeled skin or slices of kiwi into both sides of the cheaper cuts of meat and leave for 20 minutes. A marinade of lightly crushed kiwi can also be used for tenderizing squid. The same enzymes, however, will prevent gelatine and aspic from setting and will curdle milk, so do not try to make ice cream with kiwi fruit.

KIWANOS

Also known as horned or jelly melon or horned cucumber, kiwanos are an oval fruit with a thick, spiky, orange skin. Inside, the flesh is green and jelly-like, encasing edible seeds. To eat, cut in half and scoop out the flesh.

KUBOS

Looking rather like wine-red guavas, kubos are pear-shaped fruit with thick bitter skins. They have refreshingly sweet, tangy, creamy-white flesh, spattered with tiny edible black seeds. To eat, cut in half and scoop out the flesh with a spoon.

LYCHEES

The knobbly, reddish skin of this fruit encloses translucent, pearly flesh that encases a shiny, inedible stone (pit). The flesh is juicy, sweet and fragrant, reminiscent of grapes and pineapple.

When buying lychees, choose fruit whose shells are as pink or red as possible. Greenish fruits are underripe, while brown-tinged fruit are past their prime. They can be stoned (pitted) and added to fruit salads, or poached in lemon-scented syrup and served chilled. In some Chinese recipes, they are combined with fish or meat.

Below: Kiwi fruit are very rich in vitamin C.

Above: Lychees are best eaten raw.

LONGANS

Related to the lychee, longans are small, round fruit with a brittle, light brown skin enclosing translucent flesh around a single large stone. They taste similar to lychees.

RAMBUTANS

These are closely related to the lychee, with a similar, although sharper flavour. The dark reddish-brown skin is covered in soft, hairy spines and the flesh is white and translucent.

MANGOES

Regarded by many as among the most delicious and luxurious of all tropical fruits, mangoes are grown throughout the Tropics. Within their green, pinkish-gold or red skin, the meltingly soft flesh is always juicy and sweet. Some mangoes have fibrous flesh, others are succulent and buttery. Certain varieties are said to have a flavour of mint, lemon, banana, peach or pineapple, but, in reality, mangoes have their own distinctive taste, quite unlike that of any other fruit.

There are over 2,500 varieties of mango. They can be round, oval, heart- or kidney-shaped, and can weigh as much as 675g/1½lb. All mangoes are green when unripe, some remaining green even when they ripen, others turning golden or bright red. There is a number of popular varieties. Alphonso, from India, has supple buttery flesh and a heady, sweet flavour. The small Julie and the round, juicy Bombay are Caribbean varieties. Cultivated mangoes include Parvin, Kent and Tommy Atkins, which all have thinner skins than wild mangoes.

Ripe mangoes are rich in vitamins, especially A and C, and are a good source of betacarotene.

Buying and Storing

Colour is not necessarily an indication of a mango's ripeness. The best test is its aroma, which should be highly perfumed. The fruit should be just yielding when pressed. They will ripen at home if left in a warm place. Eat the mangoes as soon as they are ripe.

Left: Kent mangoes are just one of the 2,500 varieties that are grown around the world.

Left: Ripe mangoes have meltingly soft flesh that is juicy and sweet with the perfumed fragrance that is unique to the mango.

Above: Tommy Atkins mangoes have a thinner skin than wild varieties and a rather fibrous flesh.

Left: Parvin mangoes are a popular cultivated variety.

MANGOSTEENS

Despite their name, mangosteens have nothing to do with mangoes. Nor are they related to lychees, although their pearly white flesh looks very similar.

About the size of an orange, mangosteens are an apple-shaped fruit with rather leathery, reddish-brown skin, which is deep purple when ripe. The flesh is divided into five segments, each containing a large seed. The segments are enclosed in dark pink pith, which should be removed before eating. Do this carefully, as it stains everything it touches. Mangosteens have a sweet, refreshing flavour, rather like a plum, but are more highly perfumed and are best eaten raw, the flesh scooped out with a teaspoon. They can also be used for making jams and sorbets (sherbets) and, in Indonesia, they are used to flavour vinegar.

MARACOYAS

Also known as yellow passion fruit, the South American maracoya is a largish fruit with vibrant green, thick shiny skin which turns yellow as it ripens. Inside is a mass of translucent orange pulp enclosing hard grey seeds, just like a passion fruit, but sharper and less aromatic. Use for jellies and desserts.

Below: Maracoyas can be used in the same way as passion fruit.

PASSION FRUIT

Native to the Americas, but now widely cultivated elsewhere, these round or oval fruits have a leathery, purplish-brown skin that wrinkles when the fruits are fully ripe. Inside, the crunchy edible seeds are surrounded by an intensely fragrant, translucent, greenish-orange pulp with a distinctive sour-sweet flavour and a wonderful scent. Passion fruit contains vitamins A and C, and is a good source of dietary fibre.

Above: Mangosteens have a sharp, highly perfumed flavour.

Left: Passion fruit takes its name from its flower, which is said to symbolize the Passion of Christ.

Buying, Storing and Preparing

When buying passion fruit, choose ones that feel heavy for their size, with firm, slightly wrinkled skins. They can be ripened at room temperature. Do not store them in the refrigerator.

The simplest way to eat passion fruit is on its own: cut the fruit in half and scoop out the pulp and seeds with a teaspoon. Both are edible, but the pulp can be sieved to make a smooth coulis or a topping for pavlova or cheesecake. Passion fruit combines well with other tropical fruits. The sieved pulp is also popular in ice creams and sorbets, added to yogurt or as a dressing for tropical fruit salads. If you process the fruit in a blender or food processor, sieve it first to remove the seeds, as they taste bitter when crushed.

Passion fruit jelly goes well with roast meats, or it can be spread on toast. Passion fruit curd can be made in the same way as lemon curd. The juice makes an excellent marinade for rich meats. Passion fruit syrup has taken up residence in cocktail bars, where it features in a number of mixed drinks.

PAPAYAS

Also known as paw-paws, papayas are native to tropical America, but are now grown in most tropical or sub-tropical regions. Some varieties remain green when ripe, but most turn deep yellow or orange. They have a beautiful deep salmon-pink flesh, with an abundance of grey-black seeds in the central cavity, which are edible although they are usually scooped out and discarded. The soft, juicy, sweet flesh tastes like a cross between melons and peaches.

Papayas contain large quantities of the enzyme papain, which breaks down protein and can be used to tenderize meat. When buying, choose uniformly yellow fruit with a delicate scent. Avoid any with damaged or shrivelled skins. Fruit that is not quite ripe should be left at room temperature until soft and yellow.

Papayas are excellent fresh, in fruit salads, on pavlovas, or served with ice cream. Papaya is also wonderful finely chopped and served with chopped fresh chillies in a salsa.

Below: Ripe persimmons are plump and very soft.

Left: Papayas are a good source of valuable vitamin A.

Below: Physalis are native to South America.

PERSIMMONS

These fruit resemble large orange tomatoes, but they have a wide, pale brown calyx. At their best, persimmons are delicious, having a sweet honeyed flesh. However, unripe persimmons are almost inedible, being horribly sour. Persimmons, rich in vitamin A, are a source of potassium, calcium and iron. Care should be taken when buying this fruit, as an underripe specimen will only disappoint. The fruit should look as though it is about to burst. Handle with care and eat immediately. To eat raw, simply slice off the top, spoon out the flesh and serve with cream or yogurt.

Sharon Fruit Developed in the Sharon Valley in Israel, this is a non-astringent variety of persimmon. They are not so highly flavoured as persimmons and benefit from a squeeze of lemon juice before serving.

PHYSALIS

Early settlers in South Africa cultivated physalis in the Cape of Good Hope, which gave rise to their common name, Cape gooseberries. Physalis are related to tomatoes, (bell) peppers, aubergines (eggplant) and potatoes. The small, orange-gold berries are encased in a papery, beige husk, similar to a Chinese lantern. They have a tart, mildly scented flavour, reminiscent of a ripe gooseberry with a slight hint of strawberry.

Physalis are best eaten raw, with the papery husk simply peeled back and used as a handle. They can be eaten as they are, or dipped in fondant icing or melted chocolate to make *petits fours*, or decorations for gâteaux. They can also be cooked, and they make delicious-tasting jams (jellies).

Drying Persimmons

Peel the fruit, leaving the calyxes and stems intact. Arrange on a rack over a baking sheet and dry in a very low oven. The sugar that is naturally present in persimmons will crystallize on the outside. Dried persimmons taste like a mixture of dried figs, prunes and dates. They can be used in place of these fruits and added to cakes and puddings.

PINEAPPLES

These are probably one of the most recognizable of all fruit. In fact, they are multiple fruits, consisting of dozens of lozenge-shaped protuberances, each one being the fruit of a single flower. Native to South and Central America, pineapples have been cultivated for centuries. It was Christopher Columbus who brought them back to Europe, where they were regarded with wonder.

Pineapples are rich in vitamin C and dietary fibre. They contain bromelain, an enzyme that aids digestion, so are the perfect fruit to finish a rich meal. The enzyme breaks down protein so can be used to tenderize meat, but it will prevent gelatine from setting.

There are hundreds of varieties, ranging from very large to miniature fruits. They are seldom sold by name, although Sweet Gold is becoming familiar in some stores. The colour of the skin varies from orange to greenish-yellow, while the degree of juiciness and sweetness depends upon the season.

Peeling a Pineapple

1 Cut the pineapple across into round slices of the desired width.

3 Hold each slice upright and carefully cut out the dark "eyes".

2 Using a small, sharp knife carefully cut off the tough rind from each slice.

4 Using an apple corer, remove the central core of each slice.

Buying and Storing

Choose a plump pineapple that feels heavy for its size, with a fresh stiff plume. To test for ripeness, gently pull out one of the bottom leaves; it should come out easily. Avoid bruised or withered fruit with browning leaves. Use as soon as possible after purchase. Do not store the whole pineapple in the refrigerator. Once cut and peeled, it can be chilled for up to three days.

Preparing and Cooking

Served in wedges or rings, pineapples are delicious on their own. They go well with other fruits, and can be made into a variety of desserts. They can also be used in savoury dishes. Traditionally, pineapple is cooked with gammon, but it also goes just as well with lamb, poultry, and fish.

Above: Pineapples come in a variety of different sizes.

Pomegranate seeds are rich in vitamin C and are a good source of fibre. Buy fruit that feels heavy for its size, as it is likely to be full of juice. The fruit will keep in the refrigerator for up to a week. Dried pomegranate seeds are used in Middle Eastern cooking.

Above: Pomegranates are filled with seeds, giving it its French name, which means grain apple.

POMEGRANATES

This attractive, apple-shaped fruit has leathery, reddish-gold skin. Inside is a mass of creamy-white edible seeds, each encased in a translucent sac of crimson pulp. Pomegranates have been a symbol of fertility since ancient times. Venus, the goddess of love, was said to have given pomegranates as gifts to her favourites.

PRICKLY PEARS

These are the fruit of a cactus and certainly live up to their name, the skin being covered in tiny prickles. The greenish-orange skin protects the orangey-pink flesh, which has a melon-like texture and a sweet aromatic flavour. Prickly pears are usually peeled and eaten raw with a squeeze of lime or lemon. Wear rubber gloves when handling them. They go well with other fruit and are also good in fruit salads. They can be made into jams (jellies) or mixed with oranges to make an unusual and delicious marmalade.

SAPODILLAS

The oval fruit has a delicious flavour that is reminiscent of vanilla-flavoured banana custard. Inside the rough, light brown skin of the ripe fruit, the honey-coloured flesh is sweet and luscious, with a core containing inedible, black seeds. Ripe sapodillas should have wrinkled brown skins and give slightly when pressed. Unripe fruit has smooth skin with a greenish tinge: avoid this as unripe fruit is full of tannin

Left: Sapodillas come from Central America.

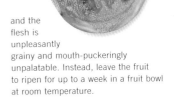

Below: Prickly pears

and the flesh is unpleasantly grainy and mouth-puckeringly unpalatable. Instead, leave the fruit to ripen for up to a week in a fruit bowl at room temperature.

SNAKE FRUIT

Also known as salak, this member of the lychee family acquired its nickname because of the beautifully patterned, scaly brown skin. The creamy flesh is divided into four segments, each enclosing a large inedible brown stone (pit). The flesh is denser and less juicy than a lychee and has a distinctive apple flavour. The flesh dries out quickly so snake fruit should be eaten soon after purchase.

Below: Snake fruit obtain their name from their skin, which is patterned and scaly like that of a snake.

MELONS, GRAPES, FIGS AND RHUBARB

Some fruits do not fall into a specific group. Melons, grapes and figs have little in common, except that they are all fruits; rhubarb is really a vegetable.

MELONS

Sweet melons are members of a large family of fruits and vegetables that grow on trailing vines, which includes cucumbers and squashes. They come in a huge number of varieties and range in size from a melon that provides only a single portion to those that could serve 12 or more. They have a hard, often beautifully patterned rind and very juicy, refreshing flesh enclosing a central cavity filled with a large number of pale, pointed, edible seeds.

Melons have a very high water content. The more orange the flesh, the more beneficial carotenes it contains. All melons are very low in calories.

SUMMER MELONS

These include all those varieties with cross-hatched skin, like brown netting.

Cantaloupe This summer melon takes its name from the town of Cantaloupe near Rome, where the fruits were grown in profusion on the papal estate. Most cantaloupes are elongated,

Below: Galia melons have fragrant, sweet-tasting flesh.

with craggy pale green or golden rinds, marked into segments, and have aromatic orangey-yellow or delicate pale green flesh.

Charentais These have smooth grey-green rinds and very fragrant orange flesh. A ripe charentais gives off a heady aroma. Most charentais melons are grown around Cavaillon in France, and may be sold under this name.

Galia A relative of the ogen, the galia is round with a raised pattern of fine netting on the skin. The skin turns from green to golden as it ripens; the flesh is green and juicy.

Musk These summer melons, which are also known as nutmeg melons, and as cantaloupe melons in the United States, are round or oval, with a raised pattern of lacy netting on the rind. The skins can be green or orange and the sweet, highly aromatic flesh ranges from orangey-pink to pale green. They take their name from the Romans' habit of sprinkling the fruit with powdered musk to accentuate the flavour. They are often hothouse-grown.

Ogen A hybrid developed in Israel, this cantaloupe melon has a smooth pale green skin, marked with green or orange lines, which turns golden when the fruit is ripe. The juicy flesh is sweet and aromatic.

Pineapple/Khoob melons These large oval melons have orangey-yellow netted skin and juicy orange flesh, which has the aroma and flavour of pineapple. The larger khoob melons come from Iran.

WINTER MELONS

These have smooth or finely ridged pale or bright yellow rinds and delicately flavoured, pale flesh.

Casaba This is a walnut-shaped melon with ridged, deep yellow skin and pale creamy flesh.

Crenshaws Pointed at the stem end, these melons have smooth golden skins. They have the best flavour of all winter melons, with sweet, juicy salmon-pink flesh and a scented aroma.

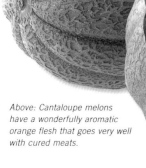

Above: Cantaloupe melons have a wonderfully aromatic orange flesh that goes very well with cured meats.

Above: Honeydew melons are the most commonly available of the different types of winter melon.

Honeydew A honeydew melon can be disappointingly bland, but if eaten when perfectly ripe, it has a pleasant refreshing sweetness.

Watermelons

These are believed to have originated in India, but may have come from tropical Africa. They can weigh up to 12kg/26lb – much larger than sweet melons. There are several varieties of watermelon now available, including those of a more manageable weight – 3–5kg/6½–11lb. Sugar Baby is a particularly sweet, round variety with very dark green skin and red flesh. Tiger has a paler

Above: Piel de Sapo meaning toad's skin, is a type of honeydew melon.

green skin striped with yellow or green. Golden watermelons have bright yellow flesh and a more delicate (or dull) flavour than the red-fleshed varieties. However, they look very pretty combined with red ones.

Buying and Storing

Melons should feel heavy for their size and give off a pleasant, sweet aroma; they should not smell too musky, as this is a sign that they are overripe. Gently press the stalk end with your thumb; it should give a little. To ripen a melon, keep it at room temperature. Ripe melons are best kept in a cool airy place. If keeping in the refrigerator, wrap in clear film (plastic wrap).

Preparing and Serving

Aromatic melons are best eaten raw, on their own sprinkled with ginger, in a fruit salad or as an hors d'oeuvre with prosciutto or salami. They should always be chilled.

GRAPES

These vine fruits grow in pendulous bunches on a stalk. The skins can be green, pale yellow, purple, bluish or red; green grapes are known as white and purple grapes are known as black. Some grapes have a bloom; others have almost waxy skins. Inside, the pulp is translucent and usually contains a few seeds, although there are several varieties of seedless grapes. Grapes are very nutritious, containing natural sugars, potassium, iron and dietary fibre. Some varieties are grown as dessert or table grapes, others are cultivated exclusively for wine-making, while others are grown for drying.

A wide variety of table grapes is available, both seedless and seeded. The finest by far are Muscat. Seedless grapes contain less tannin than the seeded fruit and are easier to eat.

WHITE GRAPES

Italia These are very large, roundish, seeded fruit with greenish-yellow skins and a luscious musky flavour. They are the nearest inexpensive alternative to Muscat grapes.

Perlette These are small, seedless, fairly thin-skinned grapes with a tart flavour.

Sultana These are small, elongated grapes with thin, greenish-gold bloomy skins and a sweet, juicy pulp. The varieties Perlette and Thompson are both hybrids of Sultana.

Thompson seedless These attractive, medium-size grapes have a slightly elongated shape and a thin, bloomy skin. The flesh inside is very sweet, succulent and juicy.

Left: The deliciously sweet flesh of Thompson seedless makes it a popular dessert grape.

Below: Flame seedless are grown mainly in Chile.

BLACK GRAPES

Alphonse Lavalle These large, round seeded grapes have thick, purplish-black skin.

Cardinal These large, oval fruit have reddish-purple skin and firm, fleshy pulp that can sometimes lack flavour.

Flame seedless
This small grape has thin, wine-red skin and sweet, juicy pulp.

Napoleon The thick, dark purple skin on these large grapes has a heavy white bloom. The flesh is particularly sweet, although not very juicy.

Muscat Without doubt, these are the king of grapes, with a wonderful perfumed flavour, almost like nectar. The best are hothouse-grown and are displayed in shops cocooned in padded paper to preserve their beautiful bloom. All Muscats are large; the white varieties are pale green or golden, while black Muscats can be red or black.

Buying, Storing and Serving

The best way to make sure grapes are ripe and sweet is to taste a stray fruit. White grapes should have a golden or amber tinge; avoid any that are uniformly vivid green. Black varieties should not be tinged with green. Overripe grapes normally show traces of browning or mould. Store grapes in a bowl in a cool dry place; they will keep for up to a week depending on room temperature, and even longer if kept in a plastic bag in the refrigerator.

Grapes are best eaten on their own as a snack or dessert, or at the end of a meal with cheese or nuts. For an unusual sandwich, try Brie with halved grapes. They are also widely used in tarts and pâtisserie.

Left: Black Muscat grapes can be dark purplish-black (as here) or red.

Below: Alphonse Lavalle grapes have a lovely firm and crisp texture.

Left: Turkish purple figs look stunning when cut open.

FIGS

These oval or pear-shaped fruits are one of the most luscious of all fruit, and can be eaten fresh or dried. They are not juicy, nor do they have a particularly strong flavour, but they are succulent and sweet.

Figs come in three main varieties – white, black and red – and range in colour from palest green to dark gold. The entire fig is edible (although some people prefer to peel them), from the soft thin skin to the sweet, succulent red or purplish flesh and the tiny seeds.

Figs contain vitamins A, B and C. They are also a good source of calcium and are high in natural sugars and in fibre. Since they are very delicate, they do not travel well, so it is often difficult to find imported fruit at a perfect stage of maturity. Look for unblemished fruit that is soft and yielding when gently squeezed, but still holds its shape. If overripe, they will smell sour. They are best eaten on the day they are bought, but can be stored in the refrigerator for up to three days. Remove well before serving.

Figs are delicious served fresh, either whole or cut into four and opened out to resemble a flower. Cream cheese mixed with honey and chopped nuts is delicious either served alongside fresh figs or stuffed in the centre.

Making Fig Flowers
With a sharp knife, cut each fig downwards into quarters, without cutting right through to the base. Gently pull the sections apart to open them out like the petals of a flower. Serve plain or stuffed with a creamy filling.

RHUBARB

Strictly speaking, rhubarb is not a fruit, but a vegetable; it is the fleshy leaf stalk of the rhubarb plant, a relative of sorrel and dock. The stalks are succulent, but too sour to eat raw, and the leaves contain oxalic acid, which make them highly poisonous.

Rhubarb has significant amounts of calcium, potassium and thiamine (vitamin B_1) and has laxative properties. When buying rhubarb, choose crisp, firm stalks that look bright and release sap when you snap them. Rhubarb can be stored for a few days in the bottom of the refrigerator, but wilts quite quickly.

Unlike most fruit, rhubarb has to be cooked before it is palatable. It also needs to be sweetened, normally with sugar. This can be added at the outset, or when it has been cooked and is tender. Use a stainless steel pan and only a spoonful or two of water. Poach gently until the fruit is tender. Rhubarb makes a wonderful pie or tart filling, and a delicious crumble. Puréed rhubarb can be made into ice cream, sorbets (sherbets), mousses and fools. It goes well with preserved stem ginger.

Above: Early forced rhubarb, grown under pots, is pink and tender.

Right: Maincrop rhubarb is grown outdoors. It is delicious poached until soft, and sweetened to taste with sugar.

DRIED, BOTTLED AND CRYSTALLIZED FRUITS

Many fruits are available dried. The fruit's natural sweetness becomes more intense when the fruit is dried, so they are good for adding sweetness to many dishes. The best dried fruits are those that have been sun-dried, without undergoing any chemical processes.

DRIED GRAPES

Raisins The best raisins are made from Muscat grapes and come from Spain or California. These large, deep amber fruit are tender and sweet, and can be eaten on their own, with cheese or nuts, or used in rice and couscous dishes. Smaller black raisins are useful for making cakes and puddings, muesli (granola) and mincemeat. All raisins benefit from being plumped up in brandy, or other liquid such as orange juice, before cooking.

Currants These small dried fruits are made from Turkish and Greek seedless black grapes.

Sultanas/Golden raisins More golden-coloured than raisins, sultanas are made from seedless white grapes. They are deliciously moist, with a tender texture and delicate flavour.

Right: (Clockwise from left) Sultanas, currants and raisins

PRUNES

These are dried purple or red plums. The plums can be left to dry naturally on the tree, but are more often sun-dried. The finest variety of pruning plum is the Agen, which is grown in France and California. These prunes are sold complete with stones (pits) and must be soaked overnight before being cooked.

Today, stoned (pitted) ready-to-eat prunes are widely available, but they tend to be flabbier than the traditional variety. Apart from their famed laxative qualities, prunes have other healthful properties. They are said to be a cure for hangovers, they give a great energy boost and are purported to be an aphrodisiac.

Prunes are delicious served with hot custard, but they are equally good with thick cream. They make excellent ice cream, especially with an additional splash of French Armagnac. Prunes are often used in savoury dishes, particularly in Middle Eastern cooking, and they go well with pork and chicken.

Below: French Agen prunes are the finest variety of prune.

Left: Californian prunes are succulent and go well in sweet and savoury dishes.

Soaking Prunes

Prunes must be soaked for at least 4 hours before using. Place in a bowl and cover with cold water or tepid weak tea for added flavour. Leave overnight if possible to plump up. For compôtes and purées, it is not necessary to soak the prunes: cook them directly in wine, water or fruit juice until they are very tender.

DRIED FIGS

These are made from the very ripe autumn (fall) fruits, usually golden Smyrna figs or deep purple Mission figs from Turkey. They are spread out on hurdles to dry in the sun and must be turned several times before they are dried completely. This process flattens the figs into a cushion shape. Dried figs contain large quantities of sugar and other nutrients. The best have a soft texture. Less high-quality dried figs are commonly

sold in blocks or strung together like a necklace. Store them in a cool dry place. Eat dried figs as they are or stuff them with marzipan, nuts or a cream cheese filling. They can be used in compôtes, poached in wine or served with creamy custard puddings. They can be baked in cakes, steamed puddings and teabreads. They can be used for savoury dishes: figs are extensively used in Middle Eastern cooking and go especially well with poultry or game. They can also be substituted for prunes in chicken, pork and rabbit recipes such as in terrines, stews and casseroles. Soak them – preferably in red wine – for several hours to rehydrate before cooking.

Below: Crinkly-skinned Medjool dates have intensely sweet flesh and a lovely moist texture.

DRIED DATES

Sticky, sweet dried dates may be packaged whole in a long, narrow box or pressed into blocks. Since the advent of widely available fresh dates, the popularity of dried dates has declined. Some Chinese and Asian supermarkets stock tiny, wrinkled red dates and smoky black dates with the flavour of a bonfire, which are only suitable for cooking. Semi-dried dates are sold in clusters on the

Above: Dried dates

Stuffed Dates

These can make good canapés or after dinner sweets (candies).

1 Cut the dates in half, then remove and discard the stones (pits). Fill with cream cheese and sandwich the halves together.

2 Alternatively, mould a little marzipan to fill the cavities, roll the date halves in granulated sugar and top with a walnut half.

stem. They have wrinkled skins and a chewy texture, but a wonderful flavour with a balanced sweetness.

Dried dates will keep for months, but do not store them near strong-smelling foods such as onions as they readily absorb odours. Sorbic acid or potassium sorbate are sometimes added to both dried dates and figs as a preservative to help stop them from going mouldy.

Dried dates make an excellent addition to moist fruit cakes, hot sticky puddings and fresh fruit salads, and combine very well with nuts, particularly walnuts and almonds. When cooking with dates, they should be stoned (pitted) and chopped.

DRIED CHERRIES

These can be made from sweet or sour cherries. Sour dried cherries, popular in the United States, are a rich browny-red and have a sweet-sour flavour. As well as using in muffins and desserts, they can also be used in sauces for meat.

DRIED APRICOTS

The best dried apricots come from Turkey; they are burnished orange and have a rich flavour. All dried apricots are wonderfully tart, which makes them an excellent addition to sweet desserts and compôtes, and to a range of savoury dishes where a sweet-sour flavour is required. Use them just as they are in slow-cooked dishes that contain plenty of liquid. Semi-dried apricots don't need soaking, but fully dried apricots should be soaked in warm water for a couple of hours before using them in sweet dishes.

Above: Moist semi-dried apricots can be eaten just as they are.

Below: Turkish sun-dried apricots have a very good, rich, sweet flavour.

Above: Dried peaches have a lovely delicate flavour.

DRIED PEACHES

Like dried apricots, dried peaches (and nectarines) have a delicious sweet-sour flavour. They are best eaten as they are, as cooking tends to destroy their intense flavour, but they are also very good in winter compôtes served with dried apricots, dates, and fresh and dried pears. Just be careful not to cook them for too long.

DRIED APPLES

These have a sweet, concentrated flavour. Eat them straight from the packet as a snack, add them to muesli (granola), or soak them in water, then cook them in sweet and savoury dishes such as fruit compôtes, apple sauce or casseroles. Dried apples are available commercially, but it is easy to dry your own, and you can choose your favourite varieties. Russet apples are particularly delicious when dried.

DRIED PEARS

Although dried pears are most often used in winter fruit compôtes and savoury casseroles – they complement venison and wild duck superbly – they have a delicate flavour and are delicious eaten as they are. They are readily available in stores and supermarkets, but it is also very easy to prepare your own.

Above: Dried apple rings are a very useful store-cupboard ingredient.

Below: Dried pears have quite a subtle flavour that goes well with game.

DRIED BLUEBERRIES

These are surprisingly sweet and tasty and make a pleasant addition to home-made fruit cakes and muesli (granola). They are good sprinkled into fresh fruit salads or over breakfast cereal. They are available in specialist food stores.

DRIED CRANBERRIES

These are much sweeter than the fresh fruit, with a distinct flavour. They can be eaten as they are or after soaking in water or orange juice. They can be added to muesli (granola) or stirred into fresh or dried fruit salads. They are also good in steamed puddings, cakes and muffins, and in savoury stuffings for poultry and rich meat such as pork.

Below: Dried pineapple makes a good addition to cakes and desserts.

Below: Crystallized pineapple makes a healthy alternative to sugary snacks.

DRIED EXOTIC FRUITS

A number of exotic fruits lend themselves to drying. They do not require soaking and are normally eaten simply as snacks.

Dried mango This can be bought in small pieces, long strips or in large half-fruit size. The dried fruit is intensely sweet and chewy. Add to chutneys and relishes, mix with other dried fruits in cake and teabread recipes or enjoy as a snack.

Dried papaya This is usually available cut into small cubes, which have been sugared. Dried papaya is mostly enjoyed as a confection, rather than a cooking ingredient.

Dried pineapple This has an intense, almost fragrant, sweet flavour. Eat as it is or use for making cakes and puddings.

CANDIED, GLACÉ AND CRYSTALLIZED FRUIT

The peel from oranges, lemons and citron are the most commonly candied fruit. The peel is simmered in a syrup until tender. The best candied peel is that available in large slices, which has more flavour than the "cut" peel, since the essential oils are more likely to be retained.

Crystallized and glacé fruit is usually candied fruit with a granular coating of sugar or glazed with a sticky coating of sugar syrup. Crystallized pineapple, cherries, kumquats, clementines and figs are among the many glacé and crystallized fruits available in supermarkets and stores, especially at Christmas, when they are used as decoration or simply eaten as sweets (candies).

Above: Bottled figs are good served with yogurt or cream.

BOTTLED FRUITS

Throughout history, fruit has been bottled to preserve it over the winter months. The fruit is preserved in sugar syrup, an alcoholic liqueur, or a mixture of both. Some varieties of bottled fruits have become particularly popular. Maraschino cherries are often bottled with their stalks intact, and are used for decoration, in cooking or as a sweet. Figs, apricots, peaches and small clementines are all popular bottled fruits. If bottling your own, pack the fruit into pretty glass jars as gifts.

Below: Glacé cherries are sometimes available in bright colours.

NUTS

With the exception of peanuts, nuts are the fruits of trees. The quality and availability of fresh nuts varies with the seasons, although most types are sold dried, either whole or prepared ready for use. Shelled nuts come in many forms: they may be whole, blanched, halved, sliced, shredded, chopped, ground or toasted.

All nuts are rich in B complex vitamins and vitamin E, as well as the minerals potassium, magnesium, calcium, phosphorus and iron. They are an excellent source of protein, but do contain a hefty number of calories and should be used in moderation and balanced with other foods for a healthy diet. Most are rich in monounsaturated and polyunsaturated fats, with the exception of Brazil nuts and coconuts, which are high in saturated fat, but do not contain cholesterol. Polyunsaturated fats provide essential fatty acids, which help protect against heart disease. The highest concentration is found in almonds, hazelnuts and walnuts. Nuts are one of the richest vegetable sources of the antioxidant vitamin E, which has been associated with a lower risk of heart disease, stroke and certain cancers, and Brazil nuts contain high levels of the cancer-fighting nutrient selenium.

ALMONDS

There are two types of almonds – sweet and bitter. The best sweet variety is the flat and slender Jordan almond from Spain. Heart-shaped Valencia almonds from Portugal and Spain, and the flatter Californian almonds are also available.

For the best flavour, buy shelled almonds in their skins and blanch them yourself. Cover with boiling water, leave for a few minutes, then drain; the skins will peel off easily. Almonds are available ready-blanched, flaked (sliced) and ground. The latter adds a richness to cakes, tarts, pastry and sauces. Sweet almonds feature in a wide variety of desserts and pâtisserie and form the basis of both marzipan and frangipane.

Almonds also feature in a wide variety of savoury dishes, especially couscous, rice and other Middle Eastern recipes. Trout and almonds is a classic French combination and the nuts also go well with chicken and some game birds. Almonds are also cultivated for their aromatic oil, used in baking. Bitter almonds, which are smaller than sweet almonds, are used in almond oil and essence. They should not be eaten raw, as they contain traces of the lethal prussic acid (cyanide). Bitter almonds are not available in the United States.

Nut Allergies

Any food has the potential to cause an allergic reaction, but peanuts, as well as walnuts, Brazil nuts, hazelnuts and almonds, are known to be common allergens and nut allergies appear to be becoming more common. In cases of extreme allergy, nuts can trigger a life-threatening reaction known as anaphylaxis. Typical symptoms include facial swelling, shortness of breath, dizziness and loss of consciousness. Should this happen, immediate medical attention is essential. Sufferers need to take every precaution to avoid nuts, including nut oils. Modern research suggests that children may even develop an allergy to nuts before birth and pregnant women, especially if they or their partners suffer from a food allergy, asthma, eczema or hayfever, are advised to avoid eating nuts.

BETEL NUTS

These small nuts are seeds from the areca palm. This is not the plant from which betel leaves come, an evergreen that is related to pepper. Betel nuts are particularly popular in India and probably originated there.

BRAZIL NUTS

These are, in fact, seeds, and they are grown mainly in the Amazon region of Brazil and other neighbouring countries. Between 12 and 20 Brazil nuts grow, packed snugly together in a large brown husk, hence their three-cornered wedge shape. Brazil nuts have a sweet, milky taste and are used mainly as dessert nuts, and also in confectionery. Because of their size, they are easy to grate and can be added to cakes and biscuits (cookies). Brazil nuts have a high fat content, so will turn rancid very quickly.

Above: Almonds, cashews and Brazil nuts taste delicious and can be eaten as snacks or as a dessert after a meal, or used for cooking.

CANDLE NUTS

These cream-coloured, round, oily nuts come from Indonesia and Malaysia, where they are roasted and then crushed before being added to curries and stews to give a wonderful texture and richness. They are never eaten raw, as they contain a toxic substance that is only destroyed by cooking. They are not widely available outside their native countries, but macadamia nuts have a similar flavour and can be used as a very satisfactory substitute.

CASHEW NUTS

These are the seeds of the "cashew apple" – a Brazilian evergreen tree with bright orange fruit. Cashew nuts are now widely cultivated in India and other tropical countries. They have a sweet flavour and crumbly texture. They

Roasting and Skinning Nuts

The flavour of most types of nut, particularly hazelnuts and peanuts, is improved by roasting them. It also enables the thin outer skin of the nuts to be removed more easily.

1 Place the nuts in a single layer on a baking sheet. Bake in a preheated oven at 180°C/350°F/Gas 4 for 10–20 minutes, or until the skins begin to split and the nuts are golden.

2 Tip the nuts on to a clean dishtowel and rub to loosen and remove the skins. The nuts may be eaten as they are, or lightly salted, if preferred.

Above: Macadamia nuts are native to Australia but are now also grown in California and South America.

make delicious nut butters, or can be sprinkled into stir-fries – Chinese chicken with cashew nuts is a hugely popular dish – or over salads. They also feature in a variety of Indian dishes, including lamb curries and rice with prawns (shrimp), as well as in cakes and biscuits (cookies).

Cashew nuts are never sold in the shell because they have to undergo an extensive heating process to remove the seed from its outer casing. The cashew apple is eaten on its own with a little sugar, as it is rather tart, or made into jams and jellies.

HAZELNUTS

Grown in the United States and Europe, hazelnuts are usually sold dried, and can be bought whole, shelled and ground. In England they are often called cobs and in the United States filberts. They can be eaten raw but are also very good toasted. Coarsely grate or chop them for use in and on cakes, and in crumble toppings for sweet and savoury dishes. Grind them finely and mix with flour to make biscuits (cookies) or meringues.

MACADAMIA NUTS

This round nut is about the size of a large hazelnut. They are sold shelled (the shell is extremely hard to crack). Macadamias have a crisp, yet almost soft, texture, a rich buttery flavour and quite a high fat content.

PEANUTS

Actually a member of the pulse family, peanuts bury themselves just below the earth after the plant has flowered. They are a staple food in many countries and are widely used in South-east Asia, notably in satay sauce, and in African cuisines, where they are used as an ingredient in stews. They are one of the ingredients of the Indian *paans*, a mixture of chopped betel nuts and other nuts, spices and shreds of coconut that is wrapped in betel leaves and offered to guests after a meal.

In the West, peanuts are a popular snack food, mostly eaten roasted and salted. They are also used to make peanut butter, which, in turn, can be used as an ingredient – for example in peanut butter cookies. Peanuts are highly nutritious, but they are also particularly high in fat so should be eaten in moderation.

Below: Peanuts are also known as groundnuts and may be used in both sweet and savoury dishes.

Below: When shelled, hazelnuts have a husky brown skin, which is best removed before chopping.

CHESTNUTS

Raw chestnuts are not recommended, as they are not only unpleasant to eat, but also contain tannic acid, which inhibits the absorption of iron. Most chestnuts are imported from France and Spain, and they are excellent after roasting, which complements their soft, floury texture. Out of season, chestnuts can be bought dried, canned or frozen, whole or puréed. Add whole or chopped chestnuts to winter stews, soups, stuffings or pies, or serve unsweetened purée with game. The sweetened purée is delicious in creamy desserts.

Peeling Chestnuts

This method makes quick work of the fiddly job of peeling chestnuts.

1 Place the chestnuts in a pan of boiling water, turn off the heat and leave to stand for 5 minutes.

2 Remove the chestnuts with a slotted spoon, then leave until cool enough to handle. Peel with a sharp knife, making sure you peel away the inner, as well as the outer shell.

Above: Unlike any other nut, chestnuts have a very low fat content.

PECAN NUTS

A glossy, reddish-brown, oval shell encloses the kernel, which looks like an elongated walnut but has a sweeter, milder flavour. The native American nut is a favourite in sweet pies, especially the classic pecan pie, but it is also good eaten on its own, or added to salads. Pecans have the highest fat content of any nut so should be eaten in moderation and enjoyed only as an occasional treat.

PISTACHIO NUTS

These have pale-green flesh and thin, reddish-purple skin. Sold shelled or in a split shell, these mild nuts are often used chopped as a colourful garnish, sprinkled over both sweet and savoury foods. They have a wonderful flavour and are good in all manner of desserts, and can be made into a delicious ice cream. They are widely used in Turkish and Arabic sweets (candies). Always check the label before buying pistachio nuts for cooking, as they are often sold salted.

Right: Walnuts are an essential ingredient in the classic Waldorf salad, combined with apple, celery and mayonnaise.

WALNUTS

When picked young, walnuts are referred to as wet and have fresh, milky-white kernels, which can be eaten raw, but they are often pickled. Dried walnuts have a bittersweet flavour and can be bought shelled, chopped or ground. They are one of the most versatile of all nuts. They taste good raw, and can be used to make excellent cakes, breads and biscuits (cookies), as well as rich pie fillings, but are also good added to savoury dishes.

Above: Pistachios have a mild yet distinctive flavour.

Above: Pecan nuts are popular in their native America.

Above: Tiny pine nuts are the fruit of the Mediterranean stone pine and are widely used in Mediterranean and Middle Eastern cooking.

Making Nut Butter

Nut butters are easy to make at home, and there is the added advantage of knowing that they do not contain additives or excessive amounts of sugar.

1 Place 75g/3oz/¾ cup shelled nuts in a food processor or blender and process until they are finely and evenly ground.

2 Pour 15–30ml/1–2 tbsp sunflower oil into the processor or blender and process to a coarse paste. Store in an airtight jar.

PINE NUTS

These very small, cream-coloured nuts have a rich, aromatic flavour that lends itself well to toasting. Pine nuts are a key ingredient in Italian pesto sauce, where they are pounded with Parmesan cheese, garlic, olive oil and basil. They are traditionally used, too, in the Middle Eastern sauce, *tarator*, in which toasted pine nuts are combined with bread, garlic, milk and olive oil to make a delicious creamy paste.

COCONUT

This versatile nut grows all over the tropics. The white dense flesh is made into desiccated (dry unsweetened shredded) coconut, blocks of creamed coconut, and thick and creamy coconut milk. It is a popular ingredient in Asian, African and South American cooking, and lends a sweet, creamy flavour to desserts, as well as being used extensively in savoury dishes. When buying, the nut should be full of liquid.

Buying and Storing

Always buy nuts in small quantities, from a store with a high turnover of stock as they do not keep well. Nuts in their shells should feel heavy for their size. Never buy nuts with damp or mouldy patches on their shells. Nuts should be stored in airtight containers in a cool, dark place or in the refrigerator. They should keep fresh for at least 3 months.

Cooking

There are many traditional recipes in which nuts feature, from sweet walnut cakes and teabreads to savoury pesto sauce. Nuts can also be used to make attractive garnishes and decorations. Simply sprinkle finely chopped nuts or shredded coconut over a finished dish or, for a more elaborate decoration on desserts, arrange halved nut kernels in an attractive pattern. Toasted nuts are always good sprinkled over salads.

Making Coconut Milk

Coconut milk or cream can be bought in cans or cartons, but it is easy to make at home. Put 225g/8oz/2⅔ cups desiccated coconut and 450ml/¾ pint/scant 2 cups near-boiling water into a food processor and process for about 30 seconds. Leave to cool slightly, then tip into a sieve, lined with muslin (cheesecloth), placed over a bowl and gather the ends of the cloth. Twist to extract the milk.

Below: (Clockwise from top left) Coconut milk, thick coconut cream and dessicated coconut can be used in both sweet and savoury dishes.

SEEDS

They may look small and unassuming, but seeds are nutritional powerhouses, packed with vitamins and minerals, as well as beneficial oils and protein. They can be used in a huge array of sweet and savoury dishes, and will add flavour and texture to rice and pasta, salads, stir-fries, soups and yogurt.

Seeds contain protein, dietary fibre and valuable vitamin E, which enhances the immune system and helps to protect cells from oxidation. Vitamin E also improves the circulation of the blood and promotes healing and normal clotting, as well as reducing infections associated with the ageing process, and improving the memory.

Seeds, particularly sunflower seeds, may help to reduce blood cholesterol levels in the body because they contain plentiful amounts of linoleic acid.

Above: Black and white sesame seeds can add a nutty flavour and lovely texture to dishes.

Above: Sunflower seeds are often recommended for their restorative qualities.

For their size, seeds contain a huge amount of iron. Sesame seeds are particularly rich – just 25g/1oz/2 tbsp provides nearly half the daily requirement of iron, and 50g/2oz/scant 1 cup pumpkin seeds provide almost three-quarters of the iron we need each day. Pumpkin seeds are also a very useful source of zinc, especially for vegetarians because many other sources of this valuable mineral are animal-based.

Quick Ideas for Seeds
• Sprinkle over breads, cakes and biscuits (cookies) before baking.
• Combine with dried or fresh fruit, chopped nuts and natural (plain) yogurt to make a nutritious and energizing breakfast.
• Add to flapjacks, scones and pastry to give them a nutty flavour.
• Add a spoonful of seeds to rissoles and casseroles.
• Mix with rolled oats, flour, butter or margarine, and sugar to make a sweet crumble topping. Omit the sugar to make a savoury topping and combine with chopped fresh and dried herbs.
• Use sunflower or pumpkin seeds in place of pine nuts to make a variation of pesto.
• Sprinkle over a salad of mixed green leaves.
• Add an instant nutritional boost to stir-fries or noodle dishes by sprinkling a handful of seeds over the top before serving.

SESAME SEEDS

These tiny white or black seeds are a feature of Middle Eastern and Asian cooking. In the Middle East, they are ground into tahini, a thick paste that is a key component of hummus. Sesame seeds are also ground to make halva, a sweet confection from Greece, Israel and Turkey. *Gomassio*, or *gomashio*, is the name of a crushed sesame seed condiment used in Japan. It can easily be made at home; toast the seeds, then crush with a little sea salt in a mortar using a pestle. Try a ratio of one part salt to five parts sesame seeds.

The flavour of sesame seeds is improved by roasting: this gives them a distinctive nuttiness. The toasted seeds make a good addition to salads and noodle dishes. Unroasted seeds can be used as a topping for breads, buns, cakes, sweet biscuits (cookies) and crackers, and they can also be added to pastry.

When buying, try to find sesame seeds that have been rolled mechanically – the tell-tale sign is a matt appearance. Seeds processed in other ways such as salt-brining or a chemical bath are usually glossy and the techniques can affect the flavour and nutritional value of the seeds.

Above: Black and white poppy seeds contain useful amounts of calcium.

Above: A handful of pumpkin seeds can make a convenient, healthy snack.

SUNFLOWER SEEDS

These are the seeds of the sunflower – a symbol of summer and an important crop throughout the world. The impressive golden-yellow flowers are grown for their seeds and oil; the leaves are used to treat malaria and the stalks are made into fertilizer. Rich in vitamin E, the pale green teardrop-shaped seeds have a semi-crunchy texture and an oily taste that is much improved by dry-roasting. Sprinkle sunflower seeds over salads, rice pilaffs and couscous, or use in bread doughs, muffins, casseroles and baked dishes.

POPPY SEEDS

These are the seeds of the opium poppy but without any of the habit-forming alkaloids. Poppy seeds can be blue (they are usually described as black) or white. The black variety looks good sprinkled over cakes and breads, and they add a pleasant crunchiness.

Black poppy seeds can be used to make delicious seed cakes and teabreads, and they are used in German and Eastern European pastries, strudels and tarts. They combine well with creamy cheeses. In India, the ground white seeds are used to thicken sauces and curries, adding a nutty flavour. In Jewish cookery, they are pounded to a paste, sweetened with honey and used to coat dumplings and bagels. Poppy seeds – on their own or combined with breadcrumbs – are also useful for adding a colour contrast to pale dishes such as noodles.

PUMPKIN SEEDS

Richer in iron than any other seed and an excellent source of zinc, dark green pumpkin seeds are delicious lightly toasted, tossed in a little sesame seed oil or soy sauce, and stirred into a mixed leaf or rice salad to give additional texture and flavour. Pumpkin seeds are widely used in South American cooking, where they are roasted and ground, to make into sauces.

HEMP SEEDS

The cultivation of hemp has a long history, but, for various reasons, it fell out of fashion. Today, hemp is making a comeback as a food. Hemp seeds are best roasted, as this enhances their nutty flavour, and they can be used in a variety of sweet and savoury dishes.

LINSEEDS

The oil obtained from linseeds has long been used to improve the look of wooden furniture. However, the golden seed, which is also known as flaxseed, is a particularly rich source of poly-unsaturated fat, including the essential fatty acid, linoleic acid. Linseeds can be added to muesli (granola) and other breakfast cereals, mixed into bread dough or tossed into savoury salads.

Buying and Storing

Seeds are best bought in small quantities from stores with a high turnover of stock. Purchase whole seeds, rather than ground. Store them in an airtight container in a cool, dark place or the refrigerator as they do not keep well and are prone to turning rancid due to their high fat content.

Roasting Seeds

The flavour of seeds is much improved by roasting them in a dry frying pan. Black seeds obviously won't turn golden brown, so watch them carefully to make sure that they don't scorch.

1 Spread out a spoonful or two of seeds in a thin layer on the base of a large, non-stick frying pan and place over a low heat.

2 Cook over a low to medium heat for 2–3 minutes, gently tossing the seeds frequently until they are golden brown.

Other edible seeds such as mustard, caraway and fennel are classed as spices, although it is sometimes difficult to understand the distinction. Seeds that are used to impart their flavour to other ingredients are usually referred to as spices, while those that retain their own distinctive character are thought of as simply as seeds.

Above: Linseeds and hemp seeds are good sprinkled over salads.

HERBS AND SPICES

Both herbs and spices enhance the flavour of foods, and

many have medicinal or nutritional properties. Spices are the

aromatic parts of plants that thrive in tropical regions —

usually the dried buds, fruits, berries, roots or bark. Herbs

are the leaves of fresh or dried plants. Today, an ever-

widening range of fresh and dried herbs, and packaged spices,

is available in the supermarkets.

HERBS

These have been highly prized for centuries, both for their aroma and flavour, and for their healing and medicinal properties. In cooking, herbs can make a significant difference to a dish, enlivening the simplest meals. Fresh herbs can be grown easily at home in the garden, or in a pot or window box, and are also widely available from supermarkets, as sprigs, leaves and growing in pots. Dried and frozen herbs are also available.

BASIL

This delicate aromatic herb is widely used in Italian and Thai cooking. The herb has a sweet, slightly pungent perfume, which you will notice just by brushing the leaves. The flavour is elusive but distinct, adding its own particular stamp to a wide range of dishes. Basil has a great affinity with tomatoes and other Mediterranean vegetables such as aubergines (eggplant) and fennel and is the herb you are most likely to associate with Italian and Provençal cooking. Basil, garlic, pine nuts, Parmesan and olive oil make up Italian

Left: Thai sweet basil is used in stir-fries, curries and salads.

pesto and its Provençal equivalent, pistou. Besides the familiar sweet basil, there are numerous other varieties, many now available in our stores. Purple basil has beautiful dark wine-red leaves, while handkerchief basil has particularly large leaves and Neapolitan basil has crinkly leaves. All varieties have a similar aroma and flavour.

When using basil, add it to dishes at the last minute or use raw, as cooking will destroy the flavour. The leaves bruise easily, so are best used whole or torn, rather than cut with a knife.

THAI BASIL

Also known as Asian basil, sweet Thai basil has a more aniseed flavour than the basil that comes from around the Mediterranean, with a more pungent aroma. There are a number of varieties, and *horapa* (sweet basil) comes closest to the basil with which we are familiar, with glossy pointed leaves. *Krapow*, commonly known as holy basil, is another sweet basil but with narrower leaves that tend to be dull rather than shiny. The leaves have serrated red or purple edges. Holy basil is the more pungent of the two, with a lemon scent and a peppery flavour.

Left: Basil derives its name from the Greek word basilikos, *which means royal, because it was regarded as such a special herb that only the king was allowed to cut it.*

Chopping Herbs

Most herbs can be either coarsely or finely chopped with an ordinary kitchen knife. There are, however, a few exceptions: basil leaves are better torn or shredded by hand, and both dill and chives can be snipped with kitchen scissors.

A mezzaluna is a tool specifically designed for chopping herbs. It has a sharp, crescent-shaped blade with a handle at either end and is used in a rocking motion. Its design makes sure that the downward pressure is even. Some types have two or even three blades to speed up the process. An hachoir also has a crescent-shaped blade, but only a single handle. It is used with an identically curved wooden bowl for chopping small quantities of herbs, as well as garlic and ginger.

1 Remove the leaves from the stalk and place on a clean, dry board.

2 Using a large, sharp cook's knife, chop the herbs as finely or coarsely as required, by holding the tip of the blade on the board and rocking the handle up and down.

CORIANDER/CILANTRO

Fresh coriander looks similar to flat leaf parsley, but the flavour is completely different, with an unmistakable piquant taste and an intense aroma.

Coriander is used extensively throughout the world, wherever a distinctive fresh pungency is required – in curries, dhals and chutneys in India; in kebabs, meatballs and stir-fries in the Middle and Far East; and in salsas in South America. It is often sold with its root intact. The root has a more intense flavour than the leaves and can be used in curry pastes. The leaves make a good garnish.

Below: Flat leaf parsley has a good flavour.

Above: Fresh coriander has a great affinity with spicy foods such as curry.

PARSLEY

There are two types of parsley: curly and flat leaf. Curly parsley is more commonly available. Once used indiscriminately when any herb was called for, it still has a role to play in the kitchen, adding a pleasant fresh flavour to sauces and stuffings. It has a particular affinity with white fish and potatoes, and goes well with garlic and capers in Italian and French dishes.

Flat leaf parsley has a more robust flavour and some people argue that it has the better flavour. The two types can be used interchangeably.

Use parsley stalks for stocks, whole stalks of flat leaf parsley in salads, and the finely chopped herb as a garnish whenever a touch of green is required.

BURNET

The tender, pale green leaves of the burnet plant have a faint cucumber flavour and can be added to salads.

Freezing Herbs

Freezing is an excellent way of preserving fresh delicate herbs that cannot be successfully dried. They will lose their fresh appearance and texture but are still suitable for use in cooking. They will keep for 3 months.

1 To freeze chopped herbs, half-fill ice-cube trays with chopped herbs and top up with water. Freeze, then remove the cubes from the tray and place in freezer bags.

2 To use, add the appropriate number of frozen cubes to soups, stews and stocks, and heat until melted. A standard-sized ice cube tray will hold about 15ml/1 tbsp chopped herbs.

3 Alternatively, pack chopped herbs in plastic pots and freeze. Sprinkle them directly into soups and stews.

4 To freeze whole sprigs or leaves, place in freezer bags, expel any air, tightly seal and freeze.

5 Alternatively, open-freeze whole sprigs or leaves on trays. When the herbs are frozen, transfer them carefully to freezer bags, expel any air, seal tightly and return to the freezer until ready to use.

COOK'S TIP

Delicate herbs that cannot be dried successfully but that are suitable for freezing, include: basil, chives, tarragon, chervil, coriander (cilantro), dill and parsley.

Below: Dill has a sweet, aromatic bouquet.

CHERVIL

Chervil looks similar to flat leaf parsley, but it is more delicate with a fine stem and soft, almost wilting leaves. Chervil has a faintly aniseed flavour and can be used in salads, or added to egg dishes. It is an essential part of *fines herbes*.

DILL

Native to southern Europe and western Asia, dill grows wild in Spain, Portugal and Italy. It thrives in the warmer regions of the northern hemisphere and is widely used in Scandinavian cooking.

Dill goes well in potato salads, and with courgettes (zucchini) and cucumber. It makes a good addition to creamy sauces and can be added to a wide variety of egg dishes. It has a great affinity with fish, especially oily fish such as mackerel, herring and salmon, and is an essential ingredient for making gravadlax (Scandinavian marinated salmon). It can also be used as a flavouring for dressings and marinades, and is a good partner for mustard. Add to dishes just before serving, as its mild, delicate flavour diminishes with cooking.

FENNEL

The herb fennel is noted for its fine wispy leaves, which are used as a herb, and for its seeds, which are a popular spice. The plant is a member of the same family as parsley and dill and is native to southern Europe and the Mediterranean, where it grows abundantly near the sea and in damp places, and has been used in cooking for thousands of years.

Fennel leaves have a mild, sweet, slightly aniseed flavour, reminiscent of dill and, like dill, fennel has a great affinity with fish. Chopped fresh fennel leaves may be added to mayonnaise and other dressings, creamy sauces, stuffings and soups.

TARRAGON

Fresh tarragon is deservedly one of our most popular herbs. The slender-leafed French variety has a uniquely intense, sweet aniseed/vanilla flavour and is considered superior to the coarser tasting Russian tarragon. This herb has an affinity with egg and cheese dishes, tastes good with poultry, particularly chicken, and can be added to green salads. It is used to enliven dressings and mayonnaise, and is excellent finely chopped and stirred into cream and egg-based sauces to serve with salmon or trout. Tarragon is essential for béarnaise sauce and is used both commercially and in the home for flavouring vinegar.

Above: Tarragon is one of the classic fines herbes.

SWEET CICELY

This pretty, fern-like herb is rarely available today, although is often grown in old-fashioned gardens and by gardening enthusiasts. The herb has a sweet, faintly aniseed or liquorice flavour and can be used in salads and fruit pies and desserts. It also makes a very attractive decoration.

LOVAGE

This strongly flavoured herb was once a popular addition to stocks and soups, but is not so widely available today. The plant has large, rather tough-looking leaves that have a distinctive smell. Use sparingly in casseroles and soups. It goes especially well with potato dishes and omelettes.

LEMON BALM

With its distinctive lemon fragrance and flavour, this herb complements all ingredients that go well with citrus fruit or juice – fish, veal, poultry and beans. Whole or finely chopped leaves are excellent in salads and stuffings and add a delicious flavour to cream, syrup and custard for desserts. Lemon balm also makes a refreshing herbal tea.

ANGELICA

Although best known in its candied form, angelica is actually a herb. The stem of this pretty plant is soft and fibrous and, once candied, has an unassuming flavour. The leaves of the angelica plant are delicate and can be used for flavouring desserts. It has a particular affinity with sharply flavoured rhubarb.

Above: Mint is one of the oldest and most popular herbs, grown around the world and used in almost every cuisine.

MINT

There are many different varieties of mint, each with subtle differences in flavour and aroma. Spearmint is the most popular mint. It has pointed, serrated leaves with the fresh familiar flavour we mostly associate with mint. This is the preferred type for mint sauce or mint jelly to accompany lamb. It is also used for the tea that is such a favourite in North Africa and the Middle East, and for Kentucky mint julep.

Peppermint, with its longer, darker leaves, has a stronger flavour. The pretty, soft green leaves of apple mint have a more subtle, fruitier flavour. There is also lemon and pineapple mint, which may come your way via a friendly gardener since they are not readily available in the shops. These, like apple mint, have a nice fruity flavour and make a refreshing summer drink.

Mint is used as a flavouring in a wide variety of dishes, from stuffings to fruit salads. It is an essential ingredient in the Middle Eastern salad, tabbouleh, and is also mixed with natural (plain) yogurt to make raita, a soothing accompaniment to curries. In Thai cooking, mint is added to soups and to some highly spiced curries. Asian mint is much more strongly flavoured than most European types, with a sweet, cool aftertaste.

BORAGE

The borage plant can be found almost everywhere, growing wild on wasteland. The plant grows quite tall and has soft green leaves and a bristly stem that renders a mild sting. The plant is quite unremarkable apart from the exquisite tiny blue flowers that appear from early summer onwards. The flowers can be used for garnishing salads, but more famously are used, sometimes along with the smaller of the plant's furry leaves, for decorating the celebrated summer drink, Pimms.

MARJORAM

Closely related to oregano, marjoram has a slightly sweeter flavour and a sweet, almost perfumed aroma. There are two types, sweet marjoram and the more strongly flavoured pot marjoram. Marjoram goes particularly well in Mediterranean-style vegetable dishes such as ratatouille or in casseroles and tomato sauces, but should be added at the last minute as its flavour diminishes when heated. It also makes a good addition to a marinade and is the classic herb for pizza toppings. In Greece, it is widely used as a flavouring for lamb.

Left: Marjoram has a deliciously sweet aroma and goes well with Mediterranean-style flavours.

OREGANO

This herb is a wild variety of marjoram, with a more robust flavour. It has a heady, warm aroma and a pleasant, slightly musty flavour that brings out the flavour of tomatoes and aubergines (eggplant).

Right: Oregano is often used on pizzas.

Using Dried Herbs

Although fresh herbs have the best flavour and appearance, dried herbs can be a convenient and useful alternative, especially in the winter months when some fresh herbs are not readily available.

• Although available commercially, a few herbs, such as basil, dill, mint, tarragon and parsley, do not dry well, losing most of their flavour.

• Oregano, marjoram, rosemary, thyme, summer savory and bay retain their flavour when dried and are useful substitutes for fresh.

• Dried herbs have a more concentrated flavour than fresh, so a much smaller quantity is required – usually a third to a half as much as fresh herbs.

• When using dried herbs in cooking, always make sure you allow sufficient time for them to rehydrate and soften.

• Dried herbs do very little for uncooked dishes, but they are useful for flavouring marinades for meat or fish, and are good in slow-cooked stews and soups.

• When you are buying dried herbs, they should look bright, not faded. Store them in sealed, airtight jars in a cool, dark place because light spoils their flavour and shortens their shelf-life.

*Below: (Left to right) Rosemary
and sage are both robust
in flavour.*

ROSEMARY

Rosemary has a
wonderfully fragrant aroma
and flavour, and an intensity that
means it is particularly suited to meat
dishes. It goes beautifully with lamb,
chicken and game. Its slightly pungent
taste can also enliven hearty bean and
vegetable dishes.

Use this herb sparingly, as its flavour
can be overpowering. Rosemary is
normally added in whole sprigs, either
tucked inside pieces of meat, or under
vegetables, so that it can be removed
before serving.

SAGE

The leaves of this herb have a potent
aroma and a little goes a long way. The
flavour is musky. It is commonly used
for flavouring sausages, and in stuffings
for meats, particularly fatty meats such
as pork and goose, because it aids
digestion. It is a favourite herb in Italy,
often used for flavouring oil before
cooking calf's liver, or cut into tiny thin
slivers and used for stuffings for veal.

*Below: Thyme has a delicious aroma
and flavour and is one of the standard
ingredients used in a classic
bouquet garni.*

THYME

This Mediterranean herb has a
wonderfully aromatic and heady scent.
It has small, grey-green leaves and
purple flowers and is valued for the
antiseptic properties of its essential oil
as well as for its culinary usefulness.
There are a number of varieties besides
common thyme. Lemon thyme, which
has a spicy, lemon flavour, has an
affinity with fish.

One of the most frequently used
kitchen herbs, thyme goes particularly
well in slow-cooked dishes, adding an
earthy, sweetly pungent flavour. It
harmonizes well with Mediterranean
vegetables – tomatoes, (bell) peppers,
courgettes (zucchini) and aubergines
(eggplant) – and is also wonderful in
stuffings, pâtés and terrines. It is widely
used in marinades for beef, pork, lamb
and game and goes well with baked
fish. It also makes a tasty addition to
plain lentils and scrambled eggs.

SAVORY

Used in the same way as thyme, savory
has an earthy, aromatic flavour.
Looking a little like thyme, but
with slightly more straggly
stems, savory can be used in
whole sprigs with chicken and
rabbit, or finely chopped for
stuffings. It goes exceptionally well
with beans of all types, both fresh
and dried. There are summer and
winter varieties, with similar
flavours. Savory is one of the
few herbs that does not lose its
flavour when it is dried.

Making a Bouquet Garni

This bunch of herbs is useful when
you want the flavour of herbs but
do not want them to show in the
finished dish. A classic bouquet
garni is made up of parsley stalks, a
sprig of thyme and a bay leaf, but
you can tailor the contents to suit
the dish you are cooking. You may
like to include a stick of celery for
poultry dishes, a rosemary sprig
for beef or lamb, or a piece of
fennel to flavour fish dishes.

1 Bundle the herbs together and tie
with a short piece of string. Add to
the soup, stew or casserole and
cook. When it has added sufficient
flavour, remove the bundle.

2 Alternatively, the herbs can be
wrapped in a square of muslin
(cheesecloth). This is ideal if the
herbs are dried and may crumble
easily. Break or tear the herbs into
small pieces and place in the
centre of a 10–13cm/4–5in square
of clean muslin. Bring the edges of
the muslin together and tie firmly
into a bag with a length of string
and use as above.

Below: (Left to right) Chives are often used raw, while bay leaves are added to cooked dishes.

BAY LEAVES

This herb, from a Mediterranean evergreen, has a heady aroma and adds a distinct pungency to food. For this reason bay leaves go best with strongly flavoured dishes – beef, lamb or game casseroles and broths, as well as pâtés and terrines. They are also used to line the grill (broiler) pan when cooking fish and may be threaded on to kebab skewers. They are traditionally included in a bouquet garni, along with parsley and thyme, and used in making stocks, marinades and court-bouillons for fish. Bay leaves may also be used to flavour sweet dishes such as apple pie. Place a bay leaf in a jar of caster (superfine) sugar to flavour it in the same way as a vanilla pod (bean) and use the sugar for desserts.

Bay leaves are best left to dry for a few days, and if you do have your own bay tree, the leaves are easy to dry and can be used for up to a year. To dry bay leaves, place them in a single layer on a large sheet of plain paper and leave in a dry, dark place for several days.

CHIVES

These tufts of aromatic spikes with edible pale lilac flowers are the mildest members of the onion family. Chives can be snipped with scissors and added to egg dishes, or used as a garnish for salads and soups, adding a pleasant but faint onion flavour. They are an essential flavouring in potato salad. Along with parsley, tarragon and chervil, they are a component of *fines herbes*. Chives also make a delicious addition to soft cheeses: if you combine the herb and cheese yourself it will give a much tastier result than commercially bought cheeses. Snipped chives mixed into soft butter also makes a good alternative to garlic butter. Spread chive butter on to French bread and bake as for garlic bread. If adding chives to cooked dishes, heat for only a very brief time, otherwise their flavour will be lost.

CHINESE CHIVES

Chinese chives, sometimes called garlic chives, have a delicate garlic flavour, and if you see them for sale in your local Chinese supermarket, they are worth buying as they add a delicate onion flavour to stir-fries and other Asian dishes. Use them as you would chives – both green and white parts are edible.

Cutting Chives

It is much easier to prepare chives by snipping them with kitchen scissors, rather than by chopping them with a knife.

1 Holding a bunch of chives in your hand, snip the bunch level at one end with kitchen scissors, then snip off the amount you require.

2 Cut straight across, or obliquely to form slanting chives.

Below: Chinese chives are delicious served as a vegetable in their own right and are good in stir-fries.

Left: Fresh lemon grass is widely available in the West.

LEMON GRASS

Few ingredients have seized the Western imagination in recent years quite so dramatically as lemon grass. At one time, this scented grass was little known outside the tropics of South-east Asia, but today it is widely grown in many parts of the world. Lemon grass is a perennial tufted plant with a bulbous base that grows in dense clumps. The cut stems are about 20cm/8in long, and resemble fat spring onions (scallions). It is only when the stems are cut that the citrus aroma can be fully appreciated. This is matched by a clean, intense lemon flavour which has the citrus tang but none of the acidity associated with lemon or grapefruit. Only the bottom 7.5cm/3in of the stem is edible and this part can be finely chopped or thinly sliced. Alternatively, the entire stem can be bruised, added to a dish to flavour it and then discarded before serving. Lemon grass can be added to curries, soups and casseroles, particularly those made with chicken and seafood.

Lemon rind may be suggested as a substitute, but it lacks the intensity and liveliness of fresh lemon grass.

Above: Ground lemon grass does not have the same quality of flavour as fresh lemon grass stalks.

CURRY LEAVES

These come from a tropical tree of the citrus-rue family, which is native to southern India and Sri Lanka. The long slender leaflets are shiny, dark green on top with paler undersides. Curry leaves have a strong, warm, spicy aroma when they are bruised or rubbed. They impart a curry flavour that cannot be replicated by any other ingredient.

A classic way of using curry leaves is by frying mustard seeds in hot ghee, then adding a little asafoetida and several curry leaves and cooking them for just a few seconds before stirring them into a plain dhal or dhal-based Indian soup. Curry leaves may be added whole to curries, in which case they should be removed before the dish is served. Alternatively, the leaves can be very finely chopped or minced (ground).

Left: Curry leaves have a very distinctive aromatic, curry-like flavour.

Preparing Lemon Grass

The fleshy, bulbous end of lemon grass can be sliced and added to stews or stir-fries, while the stalk can be bruised and used to flavour dishes, although it should be removed before serving.

1 Trim and discard the root end of the stem, then cut 7.5cm/3in from the bulbous end. Slice it finely and use as directed in the recipe.

2 To use the tough top end of the stalk, bruise it with a pestle to help release its flavour.

3 To make a brush for basting meat or fish with oil or marinades, bruise one end of the stalk.

Above:
Kaffir lime
leaves are
widely used in
South-east Asian cooking.

KAFFIR LIME LEAVES

Also known as makrut, kaffir limes are not true limes, but belong to a subspecies of the citrus family. The tree is native to South-east Asia and, while the rind of the dark green knobbly fruit is sometimes used in Thai cooking, it is the leaves that are the most highly prized part of the tree. The flesh of the fruit is inedible.

Kaffir lime leaves have an unmistakable citrus smell that is released when the leaves are torn or shredded. They are used extensively in Thai cooking and are also a popular flavouring in the cuisines of Indonesia, Malaysia, Burma and Vietnam. The leaves are torn or finely shredded and used in soups, especially hot-and-sour soups, and curries.

WASABI

This is the Japanese answer to horseradish, although the flavour is not so harsh. It comes from a plant related to watercress and also grows with its roots in running water. The peeled root reveals delicate, apple-green flesh which is either finely grated, or dried and powdered. The dried powder is made into a cream with a little soy sauce or water. Wasabi is always served as an accompaniment to sashimi, a dish of raw fish. It is fairly expensive, so beware of bargain-price "wasabi", which may be made from horseradish.

HORSERADISH

This is a member of the same family as mustard, cabbage and, curiously, wallflowers. The plant has large, long leaves with pronounced pale veins. The long, tapering root is not unlike a parsnip, with rings and rootlets sprouting from the main root.

Below: Fresh horseradish has a powerful smell and fiery taste and should be handled with great care.

Below: Bright green wasabi paste is made from wasabi powder mixed with water or soy sauce.

Horseradish is a good accompaniment for rich or rather fatty foods. It is richer in vitamin C than lemons or oranges. To prepare fresh horseradish, peel only the amount needed and grate, or shred in a food processor. Once grated, it quickly loses its pungency, so prepare in small quantities. Horseradish sauce, with a creamy consistency, varies in strength according to the brand. Creamed horseradish is milder and slightly sweeter. Both can be used as an accompaniment to beef, steaks and venison, served with strong-flavoured, oily fish such as mackerel, tuna or smoked trout, or spread on toast with meat pâtés.

Making Wasabi Paste

Put 5ml/1 tsp powdered wasabi in an egg cup and add the same volume of tepid water. Stir to make a firm, clay-like paste. Place the cup upside down on a board to stand for at least 10 minutes before use. This helps to develop the flavour without the paste drying out.

SPICES

DRIED CHILLIES

These are simply the dried version of fresh chillies and are, as such, treated as a vegetable. However, some dried chillies are so hot that, for most people's palates, they are only used in tiny quantities and are therefore thought of as a spice.

The characteristic pungency of chillies is caused by the presence of capsaicin. The heat is said not to come from the seeds themselves, which contain no capsaicin, but rather the placenta – the pithy white part of the fruit surrounding the seeds and to which they are attached. The heat of chillies is measured in Scoville units, ranging from 0 (for sweet peppers) to 300,000 (for the habañero). To provide a simple guide here, the heat scale has been reduced to 0–10, with habañeros, the hottest chillies, having a scorching rating of 10. There are numerous varieties of dried chillies, the majority coming from Mexico.

Nyora Heat scale 1–2. A dried Spanish chilli with a sweet fruity flavour. It is great for mild salsas, soups and stews.

Above and below: Whole and ground ancho chillies have a sweet, fruity, mild flavour.

Left: Mulato

Ancho/Dried Poblano
Heat scale 3. These mild chillies can be stuffed, cut into strips or added to Mexican mole sauces (sauces that are enriched with bitter chocolate or cocoa).
Mulato Heat scale 3. Similar to ancho, mulatos have a more smoked taste, and a hint of liquorice flavour. They can be stuffed, cut into strips or used in Mexican mole sauces.
New Mexico Red Heat scale 2–4. This is a large red chilli with a clean heat and earthy, fruity flavour. It is excellent for flavouring red sauces.
Guajillo Heat scale 3. These dried chillies are about 15cm/6in long, with rough skin. The mature fresh pods are a deep reddish-brown and have a smooth texture. They have a mild, slightly bitter flavour, suggestive of green tea. They are used in many classic salsas.
Pasado Heat scale 3–4. Very dark brown and skinny, pasados are about 10cm/4in long and have a toasted flavour combined with apple, celery and citrus accents. They have an affinity with black beans, and make a fine salsa.

Above and below: Ground and whole pasilla chillies can be used in soups and stews.

Grinding Chillies
Soaking and dry-frying dried chillies before grinding them gives a distinctive smoky taste to home-made chilli powder.

1 Place the chillies in a small bowl and pour over hot water. Leave to soak for 30 minutes, then pat dry with kitchen paper.

2 Heat a heavy frying pan without adding any oil. Add the chillies and dry-fry until crisp.

3 Leave to cool slightly, then transfer to a mortar and grind to a fine powder with a pestle. Store in an airtight container.

Pasilla/Little Raisin Heat scale 4. Open a packet of these deep-purple dried chillies and the first thing you notice is their rich liquorice aroma. They are good with shellfish, mushrooms and in Mexican mole sauces.
Cascabel/Little Rattle Heat scale 4. These small, pretty chillies have a medium "rounded" heat. They are thick-fleshed and are great in sauces, soups, stews and salsas.

Above: Dried cascabel chillies have a nutty, woody flavour and add body to spicy sauces and salsas.

Chipotle/Smoked Jalapeño Heat scale 6. These smoke-dried jalapeños have wrinkled, dark red skin and thick flesh. Chipotles need long, slow cooking to soften them and bring out their full flavour, which is hot, tasty and smoky.
De Arbol Heat scale 8. Usually sold dried rather than fresh, these chillies combine blistering heat with a clean, grassy flavour. They can be added to soups or used to enliven vinegar or oil.
Tepin/Flea chilli Heat scale 8. This small chilli has a searing heat and tastes of corn and nuts. Crush the chilli over food or use it to flavour vinegar or oils.

Right: Hot and fiery habañero chillies are good used in salsas and to make bottled hot chilli sauces.

Below: Dark chipotles have a hot, smoky flavour.

Habañero Heat scale 10. This is a chilli so hot that when it is puréed, even the fumes from the blender can scorch the skin. Lantern-shaped, it is about 4.5cm/1³⁄₄in long and 3cm/1¹⁄₄in wide. It has a wonderful, fruity flavour and a delicate aroma.

Buying and Storing

Good quality dried chillies should be flexible, not brittle. Store them in an airtight jar in a cool, dry place. For short-term storage, the refrigerator is ideal, although they can also be frozen. Do not keep dried chillies for more than a year, or the flavour may depreciate.

Culinary Uses

Dried chillies are used extensively in almost all parts of the world. Central and South America, West and East Africa, the whole of the Asian continent and most parts of the Middle East use chillies in a significant proportion of meat, vegetable and rice dishes. Even in those countries where chillies are less apparent, they still have a walk-on role, in the pasta sauces of Italy, for instance, and in pickles, relishes and chutneys of northern Europe.

CHILLI POWDER

Prepared from a variety of mild to hot chillies, different types and brands vary in their degree of heat. Check the ingredients list before buying, as some chilli powders may contain other flavourings such as garlic, onion, cumin and oregano. Some even contain cocoa, intended as a spice mix for Mexican mole sauces. For best results, make your own pure chilli powder by seeding, dry-frying and grinding dried chillies. If the dish requires other herbs and spices, you can add these individually to taste.

Right: Most brands of chilli powder are milder than cayenne pepper.

Soaking Dried Chillies

In order to appreciate their full flavour, dried chillies are best soaked before being used.

1 Wipe the chillies to remove any dirt, and brush away any seeds that are accessible. Place in a bowl.

2 Pour over hot water to cover and leave to soak for 30 minutes. Drain, reserving the soaking water if it can usefully be added to the dish.

3 Use the pieces of chilli as they are, chop them or purée with a little soaking water in a blender or food processor, depending on the recipe.

CRUSHED CHILLIES

These dried chilli flakes contain both the flesh and seeds from red chillies and can be used in place of some or all of the chilli powder in a dish.

PAPRIKA

This fine powder is made from very mild varieties of (bell) pepper, including *Capsicum annum*. The mild-flavoured peppers had been introduced to Hungary by the Turks only in the 19th century, although, by that time, they had been known in Europe for some 300 years. The Hungarians dried and powdered the peppers and used the rich red spice in many of their traditional dishes – goulash being the most famous. Paprika is also widely used in Austrian cooking, hardly surprisingly, given the close political association between the two countries at that time.

Paprika can be anything from mild to pungent, but it is never as hot as chilli powder or cayenne pepper. As a rule, it is faintly sweet with a slight hint of bitterness. When buying, always check the label, which will give a guide to its pungency, usually describing it as either sweet or hot. If you find paprika labelled "noble sweet", it will almost certainly have been produced in Hungary, and should be the best quality with no bitter aftertaste. Spain is also a major producer of paprika but, for the Spanish spice, the peppers are smoked first.

Below: Cayenne pepper includes the fiery seeds and white pith of the chilli.

Right: In Thailand, crushed chillies are used as a condiment for sprinkling on food.

Paprika should be stored in a cool, dark place in an airtight container, as it loses its flavour and aroma very quickly, becoming brown and stale if kept too long.

In addition to flavouring Hungarian and Austrian meat and chicken stews, sauces, soups and stuffings, paprika goes well in many Spanish and Portuguese dishes. It is used to flavour fresh cheeses and may be rubbed on the rind of some hard cheeses such as Spanish Queso Ibores, during their manufacture. Paprika makes a good garnish for light-coloured, creamy dishes such as egg mayonnaise. If you find the true fresh paprika peppers, which look very like ordinary or sweet red peppers, but are more pointed, try stuffing them with minced (ground) lamb, seasoned with oregano or thyme, cooked in a tomato sauce – they are excellent. They are also known as Hungarian peppers.

When adding paprika to other ingredients, either add it with liquid or remove the pan from the heat first. Otherwise, the natural sugar it contains may caramelize and spoil both the flavour and colour of the dish.

CAYENNE PEPPER

This is the very fine ground powder made from the fiery hot and very pungent *Capsicum frutescens* variety of chilli. It is named after the Cayenne region of French Guyana, although the chillies it is made from now come from other parts of the world including India, Japan and East Africa. Cayenne is widely used as a seasoning – in tiny amounts – for example, in savoury biscuits (crackers) and in cheese and egg dishes. It is also added to some curries. A tiny pinch of cayenne added to a basic white sauce can give a wonderful lift to rather bland dishes such as fish pie and macaroni cheese.

Above right: Paprika has been adopted as the national spice of Hungary and is used extensively.

OTHER CHILLI PRODUCTS

A wide range of flavouring ingredients is produced from chillies. Many of these such as chilli paste, chilli vinegar, chilli oil and chilli sauce are invaluable store-cupboard (pantry) items. They are all commercially available and can be made at home. They provide instant, trouble-free seasoning and have a relatively long shelf-life.

CORIANDER

Just as fresh coriander (cilantro) is one of the most important herbs of Indian cuisine, so the seeds of the coriander plant are also up there with the other great Indian spices – cumin and cardamom. The seeds look like tiny, pale, creamy-brown peppercorns. When they are dry-fried, the seeds have a heady, slightly burnt orange aroma which is very appealing. The ground seeds give a pleasing, mild and sweet

Mixed Spice

This traditional English blend of spices, also called pudding spice, is used to flavour steamed puddings. Like all mixtures, the proportions and the ingredients vary according to personal taste. Grind together 15ml/1 tbsp coriander seeds, a 5cm/2in cinnamon stick, 5ml/1 tsp allspice berries and 5ml/1 tsp cloves. Stir in 15ml/1 tbsp grated nutmeg and 10ml/2 tsp ground ginger.

Above: Coriander seeds impart a warm, aromatic flavour to dishes.

Above: Ground coriander is widely used in many classic Indian dishes.

taste that is not overwhelming. Every Indian household uses huge quantities of ground coriander in curry powders, garam masala and a variety of other spice mixes. Coriander seeds are frequently combined with cumin seeds, the two spices being dry-fried together before being ground. This combination is common in Middle Eastern dishes, too, and coriander seeds also feature as a flavouring in many South-east Asian recipes. They are not so widely used in European cuisines – hardly at all in France – although they are becoming increasingly popular. In Germany, they are added to marinades for game and used for seasoning cabbage. Whole coriander seeds may be added to chicken and pork casseroles and they are one of the ingredients in basic pickling spice. Whole or ground seeds may be used in chutneys, particularly with green tomatoes. Whole or coarsely ground coriander must be used in

dishes cooked *à la grecque* (prepared with herbs, spices, olive oil and lemon).

CUMIN

Native to eastern Mediterranean countries and Upper Egypt, cumin is now grown almost anywhere where the climate is dry and warm. The spice comes from the seed of this plant, which grows to about 30cm/1ft high and has flowers that range in colour from mauve or rose-pink to white. Black cumin, which grows in Iran, has a smaller seed, and is occasionally confused with nigella.

Above: White cumin is the most commonly available variety.

Below: Black cumin seeds have a slightly sweeter aroma and a more delicate flavour than the white seeds.

Left: Ground cumin loses its aroma quickly so should be bought in small quantities.

Cumin has a strong, spicy, sweet aroma with a warm, slightly bitter and pungent taste. These last two qualities are particularly noticeable in the ground spice, although this is counterbalanced when it is used with ground coriander.

Dry-frying before grinding brings out a toasted, nutty flavour, making the spice less harsh. Buy the whole seeds and grind them as required for superb flavour. Cumin, with its distinct and strong flavour, is a hugely popular spice in India, the Middle East, North Africa, Mexico, and practically any country where highly spiced food is enjoyed. It is used in almost all Indian curry mixtures and in garam masala. The spice is added to soups and stews, especially Moroccan lamb dishes and Mexican meat dishes.

Dry-frying Cumin Seeds

The flavour of cumin and many other seeds is greatly enhanced by dry-frying before use.

Heat a heavy frying pan without adding any oil. Add the cumin seeds and toss them over a low heat until they begin to give off a rich aroma. Leave to cool slightly before grinding them.

GINGER

Native to India and China, ginger is one of the most enduringly popular spices around the world. It is now grown in many tropical and subtropical areas including the Caribbean and Africa.

Ginger has a wonderful aroma. When cut, it has a refreshing sharpness, with a hint of lemon. Jamaican ginger is said to have the finest aroma, with the Kenyan spice being of good quality, too. African and Indian gingers have a darker skin and a less pleasant flavour.

Fresh root/Green ginger This is the fresh spice. Look for plump, silvery-skinned pieces. Avoid ginger that is wrinkled, softening or very light in weight. Similarly, reject pieces where the cut ends look dehydrated. Asian stores sometimes sell "young" ginger with a thinner skin. Buy it when you find it to sample the smooth, juicy and tender texture, and the light, hot, refreshing, almost citrus flavour.

Dried whole ginger root This is used traditionally as a pickling spice, the whole root being placed in a muslin (cheesecloth) bag of spices for flavouring vinegar or pickle mixtures.

Ground ginger This spice is widely used in baking and desserts.

Pickled ginger This condiment is used in Asian cooking. The most familiar type is Japanese pickled ginger, which is traditionally served with sushi.

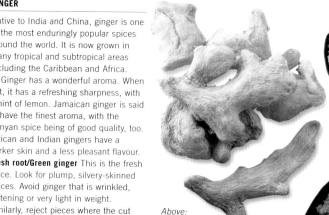

Above: Dried ginger root is rarely used when fresh is available.

Above: Ground ginger has a particular affinity with stewed apple.

Right: Crystallized ginger makes a delicious sweet.

Preserved/Stem ginger

Traditionally packed into decorative Chinese ginger jars, this plump, tender young ginger is peeled and preserved in syrup.

Chopped candied ginger The ginger is preserved in a strong syrup and chopped, then packed in a small quantity of heavy syrup.

Crystallized ginger This is preserved by cooking in syrup, then drying and rolling in sugar.

Culinary Uses

Fresh root ginger is extremely popular in a huge variety of stir-fry and curry dishes. It can be used in all sorts of different ways: large slices may be added to curries or vegetable dishes, the pieces discarded on the side of the plate or bowl as the food is eaten; grated, chopped or crushed ginger is used in marinades, pastes and braised dishes; finely shredded ginger is added

Above: Fresh ginger root has a fresh and zesty aroma and flavour.

Left: Pickled ginger takes on a very pretty pale pink colour.

to fried and stir-fried dishes or may be used raw in salads. Pickled and preserved types are served as appetizers or used in savoury cooking. Fresh root ginger is used to flavour fish and shellfish, poultry, meat, vegetable and noodle dishes.

Ginger is also widely appreciated in new cooking styles, for example with chicken and game in casseroles. Fresh or ground ginger is widely used in Western baking, for gingerbreads, cakes and biscuits (cookies). It is worth noting that ground ginger cannot be used as a substitute for the fresh root, especially in dishes such as stir-fries because it cannot withstand the high cooking temperature. However, grated fresh root ginger can replace the dried spice in baked goods. The spice is also used in chutneys, pickles and sweet preserves, as well as in drinks such as ginger beer or wine.

Below: Preserved or stem ginger is sweet with a wonderfully fiery bite.

Preparing Fresh Root Ginger

Fresh ginger is usually peeled, then sliced, chopped, bruised, pounded or grated and used in stir-fries, braised dishes or spice pastes.

1 Using a sharp knife, thinly peel a piece of fresh root ginger.

2 Grate the peeled root ginger, taking care not to graze your fingers.

3 Alternatively, cut thin, peeled slices into thin batons. The strips can be cut across to provide coarsely chopped ginger or pounded in a mortar with a pestle.

4 To bruise the root, place it on a board and press down using the flat blade of a knife.

GALANGAL

This is a member of the ginger family. There are several different varieties – greater and lesser galangal, and a variety known as kaempferia galangal, which is quite different in appearance, looking like a clutch of fingers.

Greater galangal is, as you would expect, the larger plant, and the root or rhizome is creamy-white with brown rings at intervals

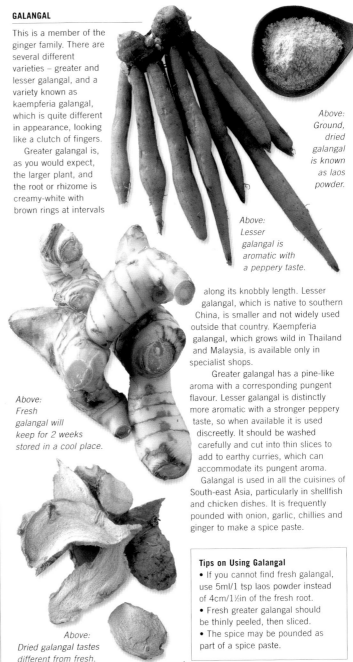

Above: Ground, dried galangal is known as laos powder.

Above: Lesser galangal is aromatic with a peppery taste.

Above: Fresh galangal will keep for 2 weeks stored in a cool place.

Above: Dried galangal tastes different from fresh.

along its knobbly length. Lesser galangal, which is native to southern China, is smaller and not widely used outside that country. Kaempferia galangal, which grows wild in Thailand and Malaysia, is available only in specialist shops.

Greater galangal has a pine-like aroma with a corresponding pungent flavour. Lesser galangal is distinctly more aromatic with a stronger peppery taste, so when available it is used discreetly. It should be washed carefully and cut into thin slices to add to earthy curries, which can accommodate its pungent aroma.

Galangal is used in all the cuisines of South-east Asia, particularly in shellfish and chicken dishes. It is frequently pounded with onion, garlic, chillies and ginger to make a spice paste.

Tips on Using Galangal

• If you cannot find fresh galangal, use 5ml/1 tsp laos powder instead of 4cm/1½in of the fresh root.
• Fresh greater galangal should be thinly peeled, then sliced.
• The spice may be pounded as part of a spice paste.

Left: Green cardamoms have an aromatic flavour.

Below: Cardamom seeds can be found inside the coarse pod.

Above: Ground cardamom is made from the seeds only and is best made fresh – as and when it is needed.

Left: Black cardamoms come from India and Vietnam.

Culinary Uses

Cardamom plays an essential role in both sweet and savoury dishes worldwide. It is an essential flavour in Indian curries, pilaus, garam masala and other spice mixtures, and is also essential to the flavour of many Indian sweetmeats, desserts, ice creams and drinks such as the classic *chai*. The spice is also used widely in Scandinavian and German cooking – in pickles, with herrings and in cakes and pastries. It is one of the spices that flavour Aquavit, along with caraway. It is also said that chewing cardamom seeds helps to freshen the breath. The Ancient Egyptians used the spice for this purpose, simultaneously whitening their teeth. The eucalyptus and camphor of cardamom does seem to be an antidote to the smell of garlic or alcohol on the breath. Cardamom is also widely used in Arab and North African cooking in spicy stews.

Right: Saffron imparts a wonderfully rich yellow colour to dishes such as risotto, paella and pilaus.

Right: White cardamoms are bleached green pods.

CARDAMOM

Along with cumin and coriander seeds, cardamom is an essential Indian spice. The pungent and warm bouquet of cardamom seeds with their distinct aroma is unforgettable, and the spice adds a pleasing, warm, slightly lemon-like flavour, with an element of eucalyptus and camphor.

The plant grows in tropical and subtropical areas and comes mainly from India, which produces 80 per cent of the world's crop. It is a tall shrub with short stems that, after flowering, carry small green seed capsules. Green cardamoms are the most common and useful; white cardamoms are the same type of pods that have been bleached (they are used in Indian desserts). Black cardamoms are quite different; the black spice is used in long-cooked, highly flavoured savoury Indian dishes. The flavour is coarse and too over-powering for light dishes.

SAFFRON

Highly prized as a dye, medication and culinary spice since Greek and Roman times, saffron is the stigma of a type of crocus, *Crocus sativus,* which was once grown all over Europe, including in England. It has a distinctive and lasting aroma, and a pleasant pungency if used sparingly. Because of its striking colour, as well as its distinctive flavour, saffron is frequently added to celebration dishes; for example, pilaus from India, Spanish paella and Italian risotto Milanese. *Bouillabaisse,* the famous French fish and shellfish soup-stew, is flavoured with saffron. The spice is also widely used in sweet recipes, including milky rice and sweet custard-like desserts. Baked goods flavoured with saffron include breads and cakes.

Infusing Saffron

Saffron threads can be infused (steeped) in a little warm water or milk until the colour of the liquid is even. Add the liquid and the threads to the dish, usually towards the end of the cooking process. Saffron powder can be added to food without soaking, but not to hot oil.

Above: White mustard seeds are not actually white and have an initial sweetness with a mild taste.

Above: Black mustard seeds have a pungent flavour and are not as widely used as the popular brown seeds.

MUSTARD SEEDS

The word mustard comes from the Latin *mustum* or *must*, the name for the grape juice used to mix the ground seeds to a paste, known in turn as *mustum ardens*, the burning paste. There are three different types of mustard seed: white (*alba*), brown (*juncea*) and black (*nigra*). These are all part of the family of *Cruciferae* (cross bearer) plants, which produce flowers in the shape of a cross.

Mustard seeds have little or no smell. The hot taste that gives mustard its bite is released only when the seeds are crushed and mixed with water. Crushing and moistening the mustard, or mixing powdered mustard with water, activates an enzyme present in the seeds, and it reacts with other natural constituents to develop the essential oil, which gives

mustard its characteristic taste. Black seeds have the sharpest, most pungent flavour; white seeds are much milder, while the brown seeds come somewhere between the two.

White mustard seeds These, in fact, are sand- or honey-coloured and are slightly larger than the other two varieties. The pale outer husk is removed before the seeds are used. This is the type of mustard grown in mixed cartons of mustard and cress, although rapeseed is sometimes substituted for the mustard seed. The plant is native to the Mediterranean, but is now grown throughout Europe and North America. The yellow flowers form seed pods, which grow horizontally, each holding about six seeds.

Black mustard seeds Black mustard seeds have been superseded in popularity by the brown seed for a very good reason: the black mustard seed plant grows tall and drops its seed very easily when ripe. This makes harvesting by machine almost impossible, so the plant is now grown only in places where harvesting by hand is the norm. Black mustard seeds have an initial bitter taste and a sharp, biting pungency.

Brown mustard seeds These have largely replaced the black seeds, although they are not so intensely pungent as the black seeds. Their colour varies from light to darker brown. Native to, and grown throughout India, the plant produces pale yellow flowers, and seed pods that are larger than those of the other mustard plants.

Below: Brown mustard seeds are milder than the pungent black seeds.

Above: Yellow mustard seeds are a type of white mustard and have a mild taste.

Below: Crushed yellow mustard seeds are widely used to make the delicious, peppery condiment.

Culinary Uses

Mustard is an indispensable ingredient in cooking: the different whole seeds, ground or powdered seeds, prepared pastes and oil are all used. The white seeds are used in pickling, and the brown seeds are used throughout India in curry powders and in spiced ghee. The seeds are cooked in hot oil until they pop and turn grey and are then stirred into a variety of vegetable or dhal dishes. Mustard oil, available in Asian stores, is used in many Indian recipes. Mustard is used in salad dressings and in mayonnaise, where it helps to emulsify the egg yolk and oil. It is also added to cheese sauce, Welsh rarebit and sauces for cabbage or cauliflower, Jerusalem artichokes or leeks.

The seeds can also be sprouted in a glass jar, in a similar way to beansprouts. The delicate sprouts can be used in salads and sandwiches.

TURMERIC

This is hugely popular in India, and not only as a cheap alternative to saffron. It is – and should be – appreciated for its own virtues. It has a peppery aroma and adds a warm, musky flavour to food.

Fresh turmeric looks a little like small pieces of ginger, and is becoming increasingly available, mostly from Asian stores. Most turmeric comes in its ground form (almost all India's crop is ground and sold as powder). If you do find fresh turmeric, peel it in the same way as ginger, then slice, grate, chop or grind to a paste with other ingredients. Turmeric stains heavily, so make sure you wear protective gloves.

Turmeric is best appreciated as an ingredient in curries (especially fish curries) and curry powders, contributing flavour as well as colour. It is also used in chutneys and pickles.

Left: Under its dull skin, fresh turmeric is a vibrant yellow-orange colour.

Below: Ground turmeric is easy to use.

Right: Ground ajowan is used to flavour the Indian snack Bombay mix and parathas.

AJOWAN

Pronounced aj'owen, this Indian spice is particularly popular in Indian recipes such as savoury pastries, snacks and breads.

It also goes well with bean and pulse recipes, all of which illustrates the affinity ajowan has with starchy foods. Ajowan can be crushed in the hand, when it releases a powerful thyme-like aroma and flavour.

ASAFOETIDA

This is the dried resin obtained from the thick stems and root of *Ferula asafoetida*, a plant that is indigenous to Iran, Afghanistan and northern India. In its raw state, the resin has an unpleasant smell, but this completely disappears when the spice is used in cooking, when it adds a strong onion/garlic flavour. Asafoetida is used widely in Indian vegetarian cooking, especially that of the Brahmin and Jain castes, where the use of onions and garlic is prohibited.

Although those keen on Indian

Below: Asafoetida is used widely in pickles from west and south India.

cooking are used to working with lumps of asafoetida resin, from which they will break off tiny bits as required, for most, the powdered version is easier to handle. It is often sold, usually mixed with flour to provide bulk, in a bright yellow tub.

NIGELLA

These seeds have little aroma, but when rubbed in the fingers, they give off a peppery smell – they are sometimes used as a substitute for pepper. Additionally, they have a herb-like taste, similar to oregano or carrots. Nigella is one of the five spices in Bengali five spices. It is widely used in Indian

Above: Crushed nigella seeds have a peppery aroma and flavour.

Below: Nigella is the seed of the pretty garden flower love-in-the-mist.

cooking – where it is known as *kalonji* – in dhal and vegetable dishes, pickles and chutneys. The seeds are often sprinkled on naan bread, to which they give a distinctive, peppery flavour. In Middle Eastern kitchens, the seeds are often sprinkled over breads and cakes, and are sometimes mixed with sesame seeds for the same purpose. The seeds are sometimes called black cumin, although they are a different spice.

FENUGREEK

Fenugreek is a highly aromatic spice, smelling of curry. The whole plant has this mild curry-powder aroma. The spice itself has a tangy flavour, rather like burnt sugar, and anyone who has tried old-fashioned or inexpensive curry powder will instantly recognize the distinctive smell of fenugreek.

Fenugreek seeds are used in a wide range of home-made or commercial curry powders. The small seeds, which resemble tiny, irregular, beige stones, are extremely hard and difficult to grind at home. Add to spiced fish dishes and vegetable curries, but use judiciously because fenugreek has a strong penetrating flavour. Fenugreek leaves can also be used. They are rich in protein, minerals and vitamins, which makes it an important ingredient in vegetable and dhal dishes eaten in the poorer areas of India, where the plant is also grown as fodder for animals.

Fenugreek seeds can be sprouted very easily in a jar covered with muslin (cheesecloth). They should be rinsed with cold water once or twice a day until the seeds sprout. The delicate sprouts add an intriguing flavour to salads, or can be used as a sandwich filling, with avocado, tomato or cheese.

SUMAC

This spice grows wild and is also cultivated around southern Italy, Sicily and throughout the Middle East. It is widely used in Lebanese, Syrian, Turkish and Iranian cuisines. The red berries of the sumac bush have little aroma, but have a definite astringent quality, with a pleasing sour-fruit flavour. They are used whole or can be ground

and can also be cracked, then soaked for about 15–20 minutes in water and squeezed to release their astringent juice. Ground sumac is available from specialist Middle Eastern stores; it may be rubbed on to fish, chicken, steaks or kebabs to flavour them before cooking. The juice can be used to add flavour to marinades and salad dressings.

TAMARIND

This is a popular Indian and Asian spice that adds a distinctly sour, yet fruity flavour to Asian dishes, a flavour that lemon juice – often suggested as an alternative to tamarind – sadly cannot quite equal. Tamarind comes in several versions, most commonly as a compressed block, looking a little like a block of dates. Although the word translates in India as date of India, tamarind is not actually a member of the palm family, but is a type of legume. The sticky pulp that surrounds the seeds of the tropical tree has a high tartaric acid content, which accounts for its wide use as a souring agent. Tamarind is used throughout India and South-east Asia in curries, chutneys and bean dishes.

Below: Ground sumac is widely used in Middle Eastern cooking.

Below: Tamarind pods contain the sticky pulp used in cooking.

Compressed block tamarind Tear off the equivalent of 15ml/1 tbsp and soak it in 150ml/¼ pint/⅔ cup warm water for 10 minutes. Swirl with your fingers, then strain the juice through a nylon sieve. Discard the pulp and seeds and use the liquid as required.

Tamarind slices Soak in 150ml/¼ pint/⅔ cup warm water for about 30 minutes. Squeeze, then strain the juice.

Tamarind concentrate Simply mix 15ml/ 1 tbsp with 60–90ml/ 4–6 tbsp warm water and use as required.

Left: Dried tamarind slices should be soaked before use.

Below: Tamarind concentrate is very simple to use.

CARAWAY

The caraway plant is grown widely in Europe, particularly in Holland, where it thrives in the heavy clay soils. Caraway seeds have a warm, sweet and slightly peppery aroma. Their distinct flavour has a hint of fennel or aniseed, and a slight eucalyptus-like tang. For this reason, they are often chewed to sweeten the breath.

Caraway seeds are used extensively in Eastern European, German and Austrian cooking. They feature in savoury as well as sweet dishes, including sauerkraut, cabbage soups, coleslaw, goulash, and potato- and cheese-based dishes. Many breads from these countries are flavoured with caraway, and it is also used to flavour cheese, with medieval recipes for caraway-flavoured Dutch cheese still popular today. Caraway is also an

Above and below: Whole caraway seeds and the ground spice are a popular flavouring for traditional rye breads.

Right: Fennel flower-heads

Right: Fennel seeds have a distinctive aroma and flavour.

essential ingredient in the liqueur Kümmel, in Aquavit – a Scandinavian liqueur – and as an ingredient in gin and schnapps. To round off a meal, the seeds can be infused (steeped) in boiling water and served as a tisane.

FENNEL

Known to herbalists and doctors since time immemorial, fennel was believed to be a cure-all and to make people young, strong and healthy.

Fennel seeds, like the herb, have a delightfully sweet and warm aroma, with a flavour of mild anise. Fennel is best bought in seed form and dry-fried or ground as required. It complements pork, lamb and veal, but is most enjoyed with fish, particularly oily fish, with which it has a great affinity. The crushed seeds can be used for flavouring sauces to serve with fish. Ground fennel is used in many curry powders and in Chinese five-spice powder. Crushed or ground seeds are used in savoury and sweet baking – in breads, cakes and biscuits (cookies). Drinking hot water infused with fennel seeds is said to restore a jaded palate.

CELERY SEED

Celery seeds are the seeds of the vegetable celery. They are small and grey-brown in colour. They should be used with discretion, as they have a fairly strong and sometimes rather bitter flavour. There is no mistaking their distinctive aroma. Celery salt and celery pepper are both made by grinding the seeds with either salt or whole peppercorns. Celery salt is a key flavouring in the classic tomato and vodka drink, Bloody Mary. Whole celery seeds can be added to bread dough or when making cheese crackers. A few seeds can also be sprinkled over lightly boiled carrots, grilled tomatoes or salads, and they are especially complementary to egg and fish dishes.

Grinding Seeds

You can use a spice mill or even a coffee grinder kept especially for the purpose, but the traditional way to grind seeds is in a mortar with a pestle. Dry-frying and crushing fennel seeds before using them heightens their flavour.

1 Dry-fry the seeds first in a heavy pan for 1–2 minutes, until they release their aroma, then leave them to cool slightly.

2 Tip the cooled seeds into a mortar, but do not fill it more than one-third full. Roll the rounded head of the pestle over the seeds to crush them.

Above: Dill seeds have a delightfully aromatic flavour and are good for flavouring vinegars and oils.

Above: Japanese and Indian dill seeds are thinner and paler than their Western counterparts.

DILL SEED

Dill seed, like the fresh herb, has a sweet and aromatic bouquet with a hint of caraway in flavour. There are two main varieties of dill seed: one is grown in North and South America, and the other comes from Japan and India.

Dill seeds are invariably found in jars of pickled cucumbers. Crushed dill seeds marry well with almost all fish dishes: add a little to a creamy sauce for a fish pie, or stir some into thick yogurt with a teaspoon of chopped chives and serve as a sauce with grilled (broiled) fresh salmon or cod fillet. You can also use them to flavour gravadlax if fresh dill is unavailable. Dill seeds are also good with egg and potato dishes. Use dill vinegar or crushed seeds to make a dressing for a shellfish salad.

ANISE

A member of the parsley and carrot family, this feathery plant grows in countries as far apart as Russia and South America. The seeds have a delicately sweet and aromatic bouquet and a distinctive liquorice flavour. The spiciness of the seeds is similar to fennel – a flavour heightened by dry-frying the seeds. Anise is used in savoury and sweet cooking, in spicy dishes from India as well as lightly flavoured cuisines. This spice flavours fish soups, sauces, breads (particularly rye bread), cakes, biscuits and confectionery. Popular aniseed-flavoured drinks include French *pastis*, such as Ricard, a liqueur called *anisette*, Spanish *ojen*, Turkish *raki*, Greek *ouzo* and Arab *arak*.

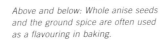

Above and below: Whole anise seeds and the ground spice are often used as a flavouring in baking.

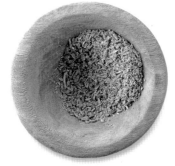

STAR ANISE

This is one of the most important spices in Chinese cuisine and is the dominant flavour in Chinese five-spice powder. The whole spice is a dried eight-pointed star, the fruit of an evergreen tree native to south-west China. Inside the husk are tiny, amber-coloured seeds. Star anise tastes and smells like anise, with a liquorice-like aroma and flavour. In China, the whole star, or part of it, is used. Star anise is used as a flavouring in drinks, such as *pastis* and *anisette*. The ground spice goes well with duck or partridge, while the whole spice can be used in slow-cooked dishes.

Left: Star anise seeds are found in each point of the star-shaped husk.

Below: Whole star anise makes a pretty addition to fruit dishes.

Below: Ground star anise is made from the seeds and the husk.

Right: Cassia can be used whole or ground.

CINNAMON AND CASSIA

These two spices have much in common. Both spices grow on small, evergreen, laurel-like trees and in both cases it is the delicate inner bark that is harvested to make the spice. Cassia bark is dried into woody strips, while cinnamon bark is curled up into neat quills or sticks. Cassia is native to Burma, while cinnamon originates from Sri Lanka. Most of the cassia produced today is grown in China, Indochina, Indonesia and Central America.

Although both spices share similar characteristics, cassia is coarser, more pungent and less fragrant than cinnamon. Cinnamon has a delightfully exotic bouquet, sweet and fragrant, and is very much the nobler cousin.

Making Mulled Wine

This warming drink is great served on cold winter nights. It is also a good drink for Christmas parties.

1 Gently heat 1 bottle of dry red wine with the juice and thinly pared rind of 1 lemon, 45ml/3 tbsp sugar, 2.5ml/½ tsp freshly grated nutmeg, 1–2 cloves and 1–2 cinnamon sticks for about 10 minutes; do not allow the mixture to boil.

2 Remove the pan from the heat, then pick out and discard the lemon rind, cinnamon and cloves. Serve the wine piping hot in glasses or cups with handles.

Culinary Uses

Chinese cooks make much use of cassia. It is one of the constituents of five-spice powder and is also an important ingredient in the elaborate spiced stock know as *lu*, which is used throughout China for simmering foods. When this stock is first made, it is very strongly flavoured, and is generally used for cooking beef; it is then used again, perhaps with poultry. Cassia is also commonly used in mixed (apple pie) spice and

Right: Cinnamon sticks are an essential ingredient in the classic mulled wine that is popular in northern Europe.

Below: Ground cinnamon can be used in both sweet and savoury dishes.

Using Cinnamon

• Sprinkle prepared fruit such as peaches, nectarines, pears and apples with cinnamon-flavoured sugar, and grill (broil) until the sugar is golden. Serve hot with chilled crème fraîche.

• To make cinnamon toast, toast bread on one side, then butter the uncooked side, sprinkle with cinnamon sugar and toast until golden brown.

• To make cinnamon French toast, dip slices of white bread in beaten egg and fry in butter on both sides until golden brown. Sprinkle with cinnamon sugar.

• Add cinnamon to bread dough to make savoury buns to serve with tomato or pumpkin soup.

• Stir a cup of hot, sweet, fresh coffee with a cinnamon stick or sprinkle ground cinnamon over cappuccino coffee.

pickling spice. Though generally used in savoury dishes, in Germany cassia is used to flavour chocolate.

Cinnamon has a flavour that is dulcet and warm, and it has universal appeal as a flavouring in both sweet and savoury dishes. It is appreciated in a multitude of dishes from around the world. Ground cinnamon is used in cakes, pastries and biscuits (cookies). The quills or cinnamon sticks are added whole to casseroles, rice dishes, mulled wines and punches, and to syrups for poaching fruit. In Mexico, they are used to stir mugs of steaming hot chocolate. In Asia, they are used in spicy meat dishes, often with star anise, with which cinnamon has an affinity. Indonesian cooks use cinnamon in their famous spiced beef and coconut milk stew, *rendang*.

NUTMEG AND MACE

These spices are different parts of the same fruit of the nutmeg tree. This is a large evergreen tree native to the Banda Islands in the Moluccas. The fruit of the tree splits when ripe to reveal brilliant red arils encasing the brown nut. The red arils are the mace, which turn to an orange colour as they dry. The mace is removed from the nut and dried. The nut is also dried until the kernel inside rattles and this is removed by tapping the end of the nutmeg shell. Mace and nutmeg smell gloriously aromatic, sweet and warm. Both spices have a similar flavour, with the nutmeg being slightly sweeter.

Culinary Uses

Mace is sold either as whole blades or as the ground spice, and it can be used in both forms. Mace is used in savoury dishes, and nutmeg, although used in savoury dishes too, is especially good in desserts, cakes and drinks. In Malaysia, the fleshy outer husk of the nutmeg is crystallized or pickled, then halved or sliced and sold in packs as a snack.

Right: Ground mace adds a delicious flavour when used in baking.

Below: Mace is the web-like covering that encases the whole nutmeg nut.

Above: Whole nutmeg can be grated as and when it is required.

Above: Ground nutmeg is a useful standby, but freshly grated nutmeg has a much better flavour.

Both spices have well-established roles in classic cuisines. Mace is used to flavour milk-based sauces such as béchamel, and it is widely used in processed meats, such as sausages and charcuterie. It is also superb when added sparingly to delicate soups and sauces with fish, shellfish and eggs. Pickles and chutneys may be seasoned with mace.

Nutmeg is delicious added to fillings for pasta, especially those using spinach and cheese. It may also be added to risotto, tomato sauce or sauces for fish or chicken pies. It is excellent in cheese or onion sauces, as well as in creamy mashed potatoes. Nutmeg is a traditional flavouring for cakes, gingerbreads, biscuits (cookies) and fruit or milk puddings, and will add an extra dimension to fruit desserts. For a refreshing end to a meal, try sprinkling a little grated nutmeg and sugar on to slices of well-chilled fresh orange. The spice can also be added to hot milky drinks at the end of the day. Nutmeg is a well-known narcotic, not dangerous in small quantities, but even a little is said to aid sleep.

Grating Nutmeg

Nutmeg graters have very fine perforations and a curved surface, so they produce a fine powder. Nutmeg grinders are also available.

To grate nutmeg, firmly rub the whole nutmeg up and down the grater, being very careful not to grate your fingers.

Alternatively, place the whole nutmeg in a nutmeg grinder and twist in the same way as you would a pepper grinder.

CLOVES

The name cloves comes from the Latin word *clavus* (a nail), because of the appearance of the dried, unopened flower buds. Cloves belong to the myrtle family, a tree that is native to the Moluccas in South-east Asia, but they are now widely grown in the tropical maritime climates of the Caribbean, Indonesia, Malaysia, Madagascar, Tanzania and Sri Lanka. They are picked when the pink buds are small – about 1cm/½in long and 2mm/1⁄16in in diameter – before the purple or crimson flowers develop. The buds change from a pale russet colour to a darker brown as they slowly dry in the sun. Cloves have a sweet, pungent flavour and aroma. They can be quite bitter on their own, making them an uncommon spice in everyday cooking, but the heat of cooking tempers their flavour.

Buying and Storing

Whole cloves have a long shelf-life if kept in a cool place away from strong light. Powdered cloves are available, but buy the powder in small quantities as required, as the flavour and colour soon dissipates. You can make your own powder by grinding the central bud at the top of the clove.

Above and below: Ground and whole cloves have a strong, pungent flavour.

Studding with Cloves

As whole cloves must be removed from the cooked dish before it is served – biting into a clove is an unpleasant sensation – sticking them into a larger ingredient, such as a whole onion or orange, is a way to keep them under control.

Peel an onion and cut off the roots. Stick 4–6 whole cloves around the centre so that the tiny bud heads just protrude. Place the onion in the body of a duck before roasting or in the pan with gammon or other meat to be boiled. This is an essential ingredient in the French dish *blanquette de veau* and can equally well be used in other stews.

Culinary Uses

Cloves are included in many classic spice mixtures, including Chinese five-spice powder and in numerous Indian and Asian curry powders. They are also used in European whole pickling spices, spice mixtures for mulling wine and mixed (apple pie) spice for baking. The whole clove is frequently used to flavour cooking liquids for simmering fish, poultry, game or meat. They are traditionally arranged in a diamond pattern on baked and glazed ham. Cloves have an affinity with apples and are added whole or ground to apple puddings, pies, tarts and sauces, and they also go well with dried fruit. Ground cloves are used to spice rich cakes, biscuits (cookies), gingerbreads and satisfying desserts from all over the world.

ALLSPICE

Although allspice is a native of the New World, unknown elsewhere until it was introduced into Europe in the 16th century by the Spaniards, it is now used in cuisines the world over. The best berries come from Jamaica, which produces most of the world's supply. Like cloves, allspice belongs to the myrtle family: the tree grows to a considerable height and the berries are the size of large peppercorns. The berries are green when unripe, at which time they are harvested and sun-dried. They turn brown when dry and are then ready for use. Allspice is suitably named for its bouquet and flavour: the spice smells of cloves, nutmeg and cinnamon and some even detect a hint of mace and peppercorns in its aroma.

Buying and Storing

Ideally, buy the whole spice and grind it when required, as the ground spice soon loses its punch.

Culinary Uses

The best-quality allspice berries come from Jamaica: a local drink, known as Jamaica dram, is made from rum and allspice. In European cooking, allspice is used for Christmas puddings, cakes and biscuits (cookies). The ground or whole spice may be used in preserves and chutneys, as well as the Christmas mincemeat. Many Scandinavian herring dishes are enhanced by the distinctive flavour of allspice. It is also one of the ingredients in the liqueurs Bénédictine and Chartreuse. The whole berries are a popular ingredient for mulled wine.

Left: Whole and ground allspice go well with sweet flavoured dishes.

LIQUORICE

This is the root of a plant that is native to the Middle East and south-east Europe and cultivated in many parts of the world, including Russia, where it is particularly popular.

When cut, the root is bright yellow with a sweet smell. It tastes strongly of anise, with a rather bitter-sweet flavour. Liquorice is best known as an ingredient in confectionery. It is also used in the making of the famous Irish stout Guinness, as well as other beers and soft drinks (sodas).

Below: Liquorice powder is made from the ground root.

Below: Dried whole and sliced liquorice root can be used to impart flavour to sugar.

Above: Juniper berries give gin its distinctive flavour and aroma.

JUNIPER

This is a member of the cypress family and the berries of the tree have long been popular in Hungary and southern Europe where the trees grow. The berries have a very distinctive aroma.

Juniper is a valued seasoning for game birds, venison, duck, rabbit, pork, ham and lamb. It is also widely valued as an excellent flavouring in meat pâtés and terrines. The berries can be ground in a peppermill for use in marinades or as a barbecue seasoning. Otherwise, crush the berries using a mortar and pestle or by pressing them with the back of a teaspoon in a small cup. The spice is used in the production of gin, liqueurs, bitters and Swedish beer.

VANILLA

This is the seed pod of a tropical climbing orchid. The drying process is lengthy and this contributes to the high price, but its highly fragrant aroma and fine, soft flavour are well worth it. Vanilla is used almost exclusively in sweet cooking, added to cakes, biscuits (cookies) and desserts. It is used to flavour confectionery and has a special affinity with chocolate. Flavouring, extract and essence are all sold as a more convenient way of using vanilla. Some are made using the genuine article, and the result is light years away from the artificial vanilla flavourings.

If you buy whole vanilla pods (beans), they can be used more than once. After splitting a whole bean to scrape out the seeds for use in a recipe, leave the bean to dry for several days. Place the dried bean in a sealed jar of sugar, which will take on the delicate vanilla aroma. Add more beans to maintain a steady supply of flavour. Alternatively, split the beans, extract the seeds, place them in a bowl and pour over some boiling milk. Sweeten to taste and allow to stand for 15 minutes. Use the flavoured milk in rice puddings.

Right: Vanilla extract has quite a strong flavour so only a little is needed to impart flavour.

Above: Vanilla essence is a convenient flavouring.

Left: Whole vanilla pods can be used several times if rinsed in cold water after use, then dried and stored in an airtight container.

CONDIMENTS, FLAVOURINGS AND OILS

Simple ingredients such as salt can help to bring out the flavour of ingredients while more complex condiments and sauces such as mustard, soy sauce or curry paste can complement and enhance the flavours of the other ingredients. A myriad different sauces, pastes, pickles, vinegars and oils are indispensable in the kitchen, each contributing their own unique character to the overall flavour of a finished dish.

SALT

This simple ingredient is one of the most widely used throughout the world, both as a flavouring during cooking and as a condiment to be added at the table. Salt consists of two elements, sodium and chlorine, sodium being an essential trace element for maintaining animal and human life. The human body requires about 5g/⅙oz salt each day, but Western diets tend to include more than four times as much. Some research has suggested that a high salt intake may be linked to coronary disease, although the most recent research is questioning this theory. Many commercially produced foods often have a high salt content.

Salt is a universal seasoning in every cuisine, used to bring out the flavour in both sweet and savoury dishes. It is odourless, but strongly flavoured – and without it our meals would be fairly dull and insipid. Throughout history, salt has been used for preserving food. The ancient Romans salted fish, meat and cheese, and this method of storing fresh ingredients is the origin of salted butter. It remains an important preserving commodity in today's food industries, including canning and the manufacture of sausages and cured meats.

Right: Table salt

Below: Fine and coarse sea salt

Salt should be stored in an airtight container in a cool dry place and must never be kept in silver salt cellars or left sitting with a silver spoon in it. The chlorine in the salt will react with the silver, causing it to turn green.

Culinary Use

Salt is widely used in preserving meat, fish and vegetables. Chicken or fish can be baked in a thick crust of salt, producing sweet, tender, juicy chicken or fish. The salt can be used again after baking.

Rock salt This salt comes from underground deposits, formed over the millennia by the drying up of inland lakes and seas. Water is pumped into the salt caves and the brine is pumped to the surface. The brine is then boiled

Right: Maldon salt comes from Essex, England.

and allowed to crystallize. The term rock salt is usually used to describe the larger crystals produced by the process. Some believe it to be superior in flavour. The salt is either ground in a salt mill or pounded in a mortar with a pestle.

Cooking salt This type of salt is obtained from rock salt. In the past, it was sold as block salt, but is now sold as a fairly coarse, refined salt kept free-flowing by the addition of magnesium carbonate to prevent it taking in moisture from the air.

Table salt Finer in texture than kitchen salt, this is the salt of choice to be presented at table. A few grains of rice used to be added to salt cellars; the rice absorbed any moisture from the salt,

Left: Black salt

keeping it dry. This is still practised in some countries where salt tends to become damp and lumpy.

Sea salt Also known as bay salt and, in England, Maldon salt, sea salt is produced by the evaporation of sea water, either naturally or by artificial means. It is believed that there is enough salt in the sea to cover the world's landmass to a depth of over 30m/100ft. Some people find that the flavour of sea salt is better for both cooking and table use. The characteristic flakes have an excellent flavour and can be sprinkled on to bread rolls and savoury biscuits (crackers) before baking.

Black salt This is actually dark grey and it has a pinkish tinge when ground. It is used both as a seasoning and a spice in Indian cooking. It has a definite tang and hint of smokiness.

Low-sodium salt Produced in response to health fears about sodium intake, this is available both as table salt and as sea salt.

Iodized salt This is table salt with the addition of sodium iodide. Iodine is an essential mineral, but it is better to use sea salt which contains less sodium.

Celery salt A mixture of fine table salt and dried ground celeriac, rather than celery sticks, this is used in stocks and in fresh vegetable juices, notably tomato, and a number of cocktails such as the classic Bloody Mary.

Spiced salt Widely used in Germany and some other northern European countries, this consists of salt, white pepper and mixed spices.

Hickory salt This is an American condiment consisting of a combination of sea salt and finely powdered smoked hickory. It is used for flavouring meat for cooking on the barbecue, but is gradually becoming less popular than in the past because of health fears.

PEPPER

Above and right: Ground white pepper and whole white peppercorns are milder than their black counterparts.

This spice is one of the oldest and most popular flavourings in the world, used both in cooking and as a condiment. It was the search for the source of pepper more than any other spice that led early sailors eastward.

At one time, peppercorns were more valuable than gold. By the Middle Ages, pepper was considered as a desirable currency: dowries, taxes, rents and even ransoms were frequently paid in

peppercorns. This gave rise to the rather quaint term peppercorn rent, which indicated payment in full. Today the term means a nominal sum.

The name pepper comes from the Sanskrit word *pippali*, meaning berry. There are many different varieties of pepper. The plant, *Piper nigrum*, is native to Java and India, but grows in any tropical or subtropical area, and is cultivated throughout the Far East, Africa, the South Sea Islands and Brazil. The term pepper is also used loosely to describe a number of unrelated spices, including cayenne.

Black peppercorns The green pepper berries are dried on mats in the sun and raked several times a day for a week until they are wrinkled and black. Sometimes, the berries are scalded with boiling water before drying. Black peppercorns have a special earthy, rich scent and they taste highly pungent with a richness and strength reflected in the aroma.

White peppercorns The red and orange berries are packed in sacks and soaked for a week under slowly running water. This rots the outer husks of the berries so that they can then be removed by rubbing them between the hands over sieves. The husked berries are white peppercorns. White peppercorns are less earthy and not as pungent or rich as the black spice. The flavour of white pepper is cleaner and not so complex.

Culinary Uses

Pepper is one of the most versatile spices, used in virtually all savoury cooking. Black and white pepper are used in cuisines worldwide, at all stages of the cooking process and as a table condiment. Not only does pepper contribute its own special seasoning, it has the capacity to enhance other flavours as well.

This spice is also used in sweet cookery: black pepper is added to fruit cakes and gingerbreads, sometimes in quite considerable quantities, and it can

Crushing Peppercorns
Peppercorns can be crushed by placing them in a plastic bag and pressing them with a rolling pin. The resulting coarsely crushed peppercorns are ideal for steaks, or they can be pressed on to a duck breast before cooking. Peppercorns can also be crushed using a mortar and pestle, or in a coffee grinder reserved for spice grinding. For everyday use, it is best to keep a pepper mill full of the whole spice to be ground as required.

be served as a light seasoning on fresh fruit. Try grinding pepper on slices of fresh pineapple, sauté them in unsalted (sweet) butter and flambé them with rum. Fresh strawberries taste good when topped with a light grinding of black pepper, as do sweet juicy figs.

Above and below: Crushed peppercorns and ground black pepper are widely used in cooking.

Above: Green peppercorns are often sold stored in brine.

Above: Coarse ground pepper

Right: Long peppercorns

Right: Green peppercorns are sometimes available fresh, still attached to their long, woody stems.

Left: Pretty pink peppercorns are often available bottled in brine.

Fresh green peppercorns Used particularly in Thai cooking, green peppercorns also complement game and duck dishes, terrines and creamy sauces. *Colvert au poivre vert* is a classic Parisian dish and green peppercorns are also traditionally used to season avocado salad. Green peppercorns are available either pickled in brine or vinegar in jars or cans, or freeze-dried. Occasionally, they are available fresh. Green peppercorns are lighter and more delicate in flavour than the black spice, but just as hot. They do not smell or taste as complex as the other peppers.

Pink peppercorns These attractive rose-coloured berries are not actually true peppercorns as they are not from the *Piper nigrum* family. They are native to South America and are available freeze-dried or pickled in brine. Pink peppercorns do not have a strong aroma until they are crushed, when they give off a faintly sweet-peppery smell. Their flavour is sweet and slightly scented, with only a peppery aftertaste.

Valued for their appearance and once the subject of a food fashion trend, dried pink peppercorns are frequently mixed with green, black and white peppercorns to make an attractive-looking table spice. Although pink peppercorns are an interesting seasoning ingredient, they do not have the same effect as the hot, pungent black, green and white peppercorns and should not be used instead of ordinary pepper. They are popular for seasoning fish, and used widely in Mediterranean cooking.

When pink peppercorns were in vogue and added generously to all sorts of dishes, there were reports of ill effects when consumed in large quantities or on a frequent and regular basis. Therefore, it is recommended that pink peppercorns be used only in small quantities (for example, limit the use to 12 to 15 peppercorns in any one dish) to avoid any likelihood of adverse health reactions to them.

Above: Dried pink peppercorns have a mild, sweet, aromatic flavour that goes very well with delicate fish dishes.

Above: Peppercorn mix looks very pretty served as a table condiment, in a clear plastic pepper mill.

Sichuan Pepper
Sometimes spelt as Szechuan and also known as anise pepper and *farchiew*, this spice is often wrongly assumed to be part of the pepper family, when, in fact, it is the berry of the prickly ash tree. The spice, which is the ground husks of the berries, is common in the Sichuan region of China. The ripe seed pods of the tree open out in a similar way to star anise, which is probably why they were named anise pepper.

Sichuan pepper has a pungent aroma with a hint of citrus. Dry-frying brings out the flavour, which is pleasantly peppery. It can be bought whole or ground. It is one of the spices in Chinese five-spice powder together with star anise, fennel, cloves and cinnamon, and it is used in Japanese seven-flavour seasoning mix.

Sichuan pepper is also used to make spicy salt and pepper. Heat a wok. Add 5ml/1tsp Sichuan peppercorns and 30ml/2 tbsp coarse sea salt and dry-fry, stirring constantly, for about 3 minutes, until lightly coloured. Remove from the heat and stir in 2.5ml/½ tsp Chinese five-spice powder, then set aside to cool. Grind the cooled mixture to a fine powder in a mortar with a pestle.

Below: Sichuan peppercorns are much used in Chinese cookery to flavour chicken and duck.

SAUCES AND PASTES

There are many different sauces and pastes that are indispensable in the kitchen. They are used to add flavour and colour to a wide variety of dishes.

TOMATO PURÉE/PASTE

This thick paste is the most intensely flavoured of all the many tomato products, and is extremely useful for adding flavour and colour to dishes. It is made from tomatoes, salt and citric acid and can vary in strength depending on the manufacturer.

It is worth finding a brand of tomato purée that you like and sticking to it, because some brands are quite bitter and sharp, and others can be quite overpowering. Tomato purée should be used in small quantities as it can make a dish too acidic. To counteract acidity, add a pinch or two of sugar.

Tomato purée is normally available in tubes or in small cans. Both should be kept in the refrigerator once opened. Canned purée will last only 2–3 days once opened; tomato purée in a tube can be kept for 3–4 weeks.

SUN-DRIED TOMATO PASTE

This is similar to standard tomato purée (paste), but is made from intensely flavoured sun-dried tomatoes and olive oil. Although thick in texture, the flavour of sun-dried tomato paste is sweet and mild compared with regular tomato purée. It can be used to add an intense flavour and colour to tomato-based pasta sauces, stews and casseroles.

Below: Tomato purée is an invaluable ingredient in every kitchen.

Passata, Sugocasa and Polpa

These crushed tomato products from Italy are not strictly sauces but they are an invaluable cooking ingredient. Passata (bottled strained tomatoes) is simply made from sieved ripe tomatoes and can be smooth or slightly chunky, depending on the degree of sieving. Sugocasa and polpa are also made from crushed tomatoes but they have a slightly chunkier texture than passata.

Passata, sugocasa and polpa are a wonderfully convenient short cut wherever tomato pulp is required. They are available in cartons and from most supermarkets. They

Right: (Clockwise from top right) Sugocasa, passata and polpa are all made from crushed tomatoes.

can be used as a basis for soups and sauces, and as a substitute for fresh tomatoes in all recipes where they require long cooking.

To make a very quick pasta sauce, sweat some finely chopped onion and garlic in olive oil, add a jar of passata and simmer the sauce while the pasta is cooking. Add chopped fresh herbs or some chopped olives, capers and/or anchovies for added flavour.

TOMATO KETCHUP

This sweet, vinegary, slightly spicy sauce is the classic condiment served with sausages, burgers and chips (fries). It is also extremely useful as a flavouring ingredient and can be added to soups, barbecue sauces and dressings. When added as a flavouring, tomato ketchup should be used in moderation as its pungent flavour can be quite over-powering and will drown more delicate flavours.

Making Tomato Ketchup

This tastes much better than the commercial kind and uses up tomatoes if you grow your own and have a glut. Chop 2.75kg/6lb tomatoes into quarters and put in a preserving pan with 25g/1oz salt and 600ml/1 pint/2^1/$_2$ cups vinegar. Simmer until the tomatoes are soft, then strain through coarse muslin (cheesecloth). Return the purée to the pan, add 225g/8oz sugar and simmer until the ketchup starts to thicken. Add 2.5ml/^{1}/$_2$ tsp each of allspice, ground cloves, cinnamon and cayenne. Pour into bottles.

Above: Red pesto obtains its colour from the addition of sweet red peppers.

PESTO

This classic basil sauce originated in the Italian port of Genoa. It is made with fresh basil, pine nuts, Parmesan or pecorino cheese and olive oil and is sometimes also flavoured with red (bell) peppers or sun-dried tomatoes. It is available fresh or bottled.

Pesto can be used as a dressing for pasta or potato gnocchi, or as a stuffing for grilled (broiled) fresh sardines. It gives a lift to risottos and tomato sauces, and is delicious stirred into minestrone or tomato-based soups. A spoonful of pesto adds a new dimension to bottled mayonnaise, creating a rich, pungent *maionese verde,* and it is also excellent tossed with little mozzarella *bocconcini* cheeses. As basil loses its flavour when dried, a spoonful of pesto is a good substitute for fresh basil in the winter.

Making Pesto

Nothing tastes as good as home-made pesto. Crush 115g/4oz/ 4 cups fresh basil leaves with 25g/ 1oz/¼ cup pine nuts, 2 peeled garlic cloves and a pinch of salt in a mortar with a pestle. Work in 50g/ 2oz/⅔ cup freshly grated Parmesan cheese. Slowly add about 120ml/ 4fl oz/½ cup olive oil, working it in well with a wooden spoon to make a thick, creamy sauce. Store for up to 1 month in a sealed jar in the refrigerator. This quantity is enough to dress pasta for 4–6 servings.

Above: Green pesto is traditionally served with the Ligurian pasta, trofie.

PISTOU

This basil sauce from the south of France is very similar to pesto, although it does not include grated cheese or pine nuts. It can be stirred into vegetable soups and used to dress boiled potatoes, steamed broccoli and grilled vegetables such as courgettes (zucchini) and aubergines (eggplant).

OLIVE PASTE

At its simplest, olive paste consists of olives pounded to a paste with olive oil and salt and packed in small jars. Also known as *pasta di olive* in Italy, it tends to be very salty and rich, so a little will go a long way. Olive paste can be spread very thinly over pizza bases, or scraped on to toasted croûtons and topped with tomatoes or mushrooms to make crostini. It is delicious spread thinly on veal or pork escalopes (scallops) or lamb chops before coating them in egg and breadcrumbs and frying them. A little olive paste adds a rich flavour to a tomato sauce, while a spoonful stirred into a vinaigrette makes a good dressing for a robust salad.

Making Italian Olive Paste

Process 115g/4oz/1 cup chopped, pitted black olives, 2 chopped garlic cloves, 60ml/4 tbsp chopped fresh parsley, 15ml/1 tbsp chopped fresh thyme and 75ml/5 tbsp olive oil in a food processor. Season to taste with ground black pepper.

TAPENADE

This olive paste from Provence in the south of France is often served as a dip for crudités. The name tapenade is derived from the Provençal word for caper – *tapeno*. The paste is a delicious blend of pitted black olives, capers, anchovies, olive oil, lemon juice and, sometimes, a splash of brandy. Additional ingredients may include garlic, mustard, thyme, bay leaves, other aromatic herbs and even small pieces of tuna. It is popular spread thinly on bread, served with grilled (broiled) meat or fish and used as a garnish for hard-boiled eggs. Hard-boiled quail's eggs served with a small dish of tapenade for dipping are very good served with drinks.

Below: Green olive paste is good used as a simple dressing, stirred into pasta.

Below: Black olive paste is more commonly found than the green version.

Above: Good quality garlic paste is a useful substitute for fresh garlic.

Making Roasted Garlic Purée
This delicious purée can be added to sauces, pasta and dressings.

1 Cut a slice off the top of 5 heads of garlic. Wrap the garlic and 2–3 sprigs thyme in foil and pour over 45ml/3 tbsp olive oil. Bake at 190°C/375°F/Gas 5 for 60 minutes.

2 When cool, squeeze the garlic out of its skin into a bowl, then mash, beat in more olive oil and season with salt and pepper to taste.

GARLIC PURÉE/PASTE

There is now a variety of convenient, easy-to-use garlic products, including garlic purée in a tube, garlic paste that comes in small jars, and bottled whole garlic cloves, which have been skinned. Garlic purée and paste can be added to sauces, stir-fries, soufflés, omelettes and tarts, or to any recipe where garlic is called for. It can also be simply spread on bread. Use sparingly at first until you can gauge the strength of the purée, but as a general rule, 5ml/1tsp is equivalent to 1 medium-size clove.

To make a simple sauce for pasta, stir 2–3 tbsp of garlic purée into 150ml/¼ pint/⅔ cup of heated double (heavy) cream, season with salt and pepper, and add a little lemon juice and some chopped thyme or basil.

Bottled garlic is normally served as an apéritif, or with canapés, in a similar way to cocktail onions.

ANCHOVY ESSENCE AND PASTE

Anchovy essence comes in familiar glass bottles and is useful for adding to fish dishes and sauces that are served with fish, adding a distinct, salty/fishy flavour. It can be mixed with soy sauce and used as a substitute for fish sauce such as the Thai *nam pla*, which is widely used in Asian cooking. Anchovy paste comes in pots and is normally spread thinly on toast.

WALNUT AND MUSHROOM KETCHUP

These were once popular condiments, used for flavouring casseroles or for perking up soups and sauces. Both are a dark colour and have a fairly robust flavour, so use judiciously with meat dishes or in well-flavoured sauces.

WORCESTERSHIRE SAUCE

Despite its name, Worcestershire sauce was developed in India by the English. It was brought to Britain by Lord Marcus Sandys, an ex-Governor of Bengal. In 1835, he approached a chemist's shop in Worcester belonging to John Lea and William Perrins, and suggested they made a sauce from his recipe. The result was impossibly fiery, and the mixture was left in a barrel and

Left and below: Anchovy, essence and Worcestershire sauce

forgotten.
Then one day the chemists came across the barrel again. On trying the mixture a second time, they discovered that it had matured to a superb mellow-tasting liquid, and the sauce was born.

Worcestershire sauce is still often referred to as Lea and Perrins. It is used to flavour meats, soups and vegetable dishes. Among the many ingredients used in its making are tamarind, garlic, soy sauces, molasses, onions, lime, anchovies and vinegar. A vegetarian version, which omits the anchovies, is also available. As well as being used as a flavouring and condiment, Worcestershire sauce is an essential ingredient in a Bloody Mary.

Above: West Indian hot
pepper sauce has a peppery bite.

Above: Chilli sauce can be very fiery
so should be used sparingly.

CHILLI SAUCE/WEST INDIAN HOT PEPPER SAUCE/TABASCO SAUCE

There are numerous varieties of chilli sauces, since each country that grows and uses the chilli produces its own version. Tabasco sauce is a favourite North American seasoning made from extremely hot tabasco or cone chillies. It has been made by the same family business in Louisiana since the nineteenth century. The original red version, made from red chillies, is still the most popular, but green Tabasco sauce is also now widely available. The chillies, whatever their colour, are mixed with salt and vinegar, then matured in white oak casks for several years.

In the Caribbean there are also many styles of chilli sauce. Most, like Tabasco, are made from steeping the chillies in vinegar and all are very hot. Chilli sauces are widely used in small quantities as a general seasoning. Tabasco is served with tomato juice, and is commonly served with couscous to pep it up a little. It also goes well with bean and egg dishes. Besides its

use in the kitchen and as a condiment, Tabasco sauce is also used in a number of cocktails and may be substituted for Worcestershire sauce in a Bloody Mary to produce a spicier flavour.

Most chilli sauces are thick and bright red. They can range from sweet and mild to fiery hot. Many contain other ingredients, depending on where they come from; you will need to check the label to discover what these might include, and also to find out the heat index. Thai chilli sauces, mainly used for dipping, are often quite sweet, but may also be very hot, while Chinese sauces, served with a wide variety of dishes, are usually fairly salty. Chilli sauce can be added to stews, casseroles and curries, or simply used as a condiment at the table.

CHILLI PASTE

Ready-made chilli paste is sold in small jars and can be used, like chilli sauce, for spicing up stews, bean dishes and curries.

To make your own chilli paste, halve and seed 10 hot chillies, then pound the flesh to a paste in a mortar with a pestle or process to a purée in a blender or food processor. Scrape the purée into a bowl and stir in 1 finely chopped onion, 10ml/2 tsp finely grated fresh root ginger and salt to taste. Transfer to a clean jar and add groundnut (peanut) or sunflower oil to cover. Seal and store in a cool, dark place or the refrigerator for at least 2 months before using. The paste will keep for a long time, especially if you change the oil from time to time to prevent it from becoming rancid.

HARISSA

This hot chilli purée comes from the Middle East and North Africa, where it is widely used as a condiment and, diluted with stock, water or fresh tomato sauce, to flavour couscous, soups and meat stews. In Tunisia, small dishes of harissa topped with olive oil are placed

on the table at most meals. Pieces of flat bread are torn off and dipped into the mixture. Harissa is available from supermarkets and Middle Eastern stores, or you can make your own.

A classic harissa paste is made from a blend of fresh red chillies, garlic, salt, ground coriander, ground cumin, dried mint, fresh coriander (cilantro) and sufficient olive oil to make a fairly stiff consistency. It should be left to stand for at least 12 hours before using.

Below: Hot chilli paste is a handy
substitute for fresh chillies as it
requires no preparation.

Below: Red Tabasco
sauce is the most
common variety.

Left: Green
jalapeño
sauce has a
vibrant hue and
a spicy flavour.

CURRY PASTES

A wide range of commercial curry pastes is available from supermarkets and Asian stores and many of them are of excellent quality. Fresh spice pastes can be time-consuming to prepare so these ready-made products are great for making delicious, authentic curries when you're in a hurry.

INDIAN CURRY PASTES

Spice pastes tend to have a more authentic flavour than curry powders, which often include a dry-tasting imbalance of spices that produces a slightly stale flavour. A typical recipe for a paste might include coriander and cumin seeds, tamarind, peppercorns, cardamom, ginger, chilli powder, cloves and nutmeg, all finely ground and mixed with oil. Other spices that might be added are mustard and fennel seeds, ajowan and cinnamon. Like curry powders, pastes are available as mild, medium and hot.

If you are using commercial curry pastes, you can give them an extra lift and a personal touch by adding fresh herbs such as chopped coriander (cilantro) and a squeeze of lime or lemon juice.

Right: Green and red Thai curry pastes are based on fresh green and red chillies respectively.

THAI CURRY PASTE

There are a number of different types of Thai curry pastes, but the most common ones are red and green. Thai spice pastes tend to be very hot and aromatic, as they are based on fresh chillies and contain a variety of other spices and fresh herbs. They can be used to make all kinds of curries with meat, poultry, fish, shellfish and vegetables.

Traditional Thai spice pastes require lengthy pounding and grinding. However, there are several good commercial brands available, which take the effort out of cooking Thai food. Recipes vary, but green curry paste usually contains coriander and cumin seeds, lemon grass, galangal or fresh root ginger, garlic, onion, shrimp paste, fresh coriander (cilantro), salt, sugar and oil as well as green chillies. It may also include other herbs and spices, such as mint, caraway and nutmeg. Red chilli paste often consists of onions, garlic, galangal or fresh root ginger, lemon grass, kaffir lime leaves, coriander (cilantro) roots, peppercorns, ground turmeric, cinnamon, coriander and cumin seeds, shrimp paste, salt and oil, as well as plenty of fresh red chillies. The degree of heat depends on the variety of chilli used – Thai birds-eye chillies are extremely hot and fiery but, if you prefer a slightly milder taste, you can use a less intense variety.

Above: Japanese curry roux tends to be quite sweet, even the very hot varieties.

JAPANESE CURRY ROUX

Japan was first introduced to curry in the middle of the nineteenth century, not directly from India but via England, where curry powder was concocted and exported. Since then, curry has become one of the most popular daily foods in Japan. The Japanese further developed the powder into an instant curry sauce roux, mixing together all the necessary ingredients such as herbs and spices, fruits, soup stock, sauces and seasonings. It comes in the form of a soft slab, resembling a chocolate bar, in a sectioned plastic tray. All you need to do is boil the fresh ingredients such as meat or shellfish, potato, onion and carrot, and add some of this sauce mix. There are degrees of hotness: mild, medium, hot and very hot. There are also separate roux for meat and fish. An average packet normally serves 12, but remember that a Japanese portion is very small and it really makes enough for only six to eight adult appetites, particularly if eaten on its own.

ASIAN SAUCES AND PASTES

There is a great deal of overlap with many store-cupboard (pantry) ingredients, and many foods that are distinctly Western in character are just as likely to turn up in Indian and Asian kitchens as in our own. Similarly, many Asian-style sauces and flavourings have become familiar in the West, but nevertheless they still belong to the Eastern-style of cooking.

SOY SAUCE

This is one of Asia's most important contributions to the global pantry. It is used all over the world, not merely as a condiment, but as an ingredient in a host of home-made and manufactured foods. Making soy sauce is a lengthy process. The soya beans are cleaned, soaked until soft, then steamed before being mixed with a yeast culture and wheat flour and fermented for up to two years before being filtered and bottled.

Above: Japanese soy sauces range from dark and thick to lighter, less rich types.

Right and below: Dark and light Chinese soy sauce are widely used both in cooking and as a condiment to be added to food at the table.

Chinese Soy Sauce

There are basically three types of Chinese soy sauce on the market, which differ in aroma and flavour.

Light soy sauce This sauce comes from the initial extraction and has a delicate, but quite salty flavour. It is light brown, with a lovely "beany" fragrance.

Dark soy sauce This type of soy sauce is left to mature for longer and has caramel added to it. The final result is slightly sweeter and darker with a very powerful aroma.

Regular soy sauce This is simply a blend of light and dark soy sauce and has many uses.

Japanese Soy Sauces

There are several different types of Japanese soy sauce, all of them rather different in character from Chinese soy sauces, so it is best to use these when cooking Japanese dishes. Usukuchi soy sauce is light in colour and tastes less salty than Chinese light soy sauce. Tamari is dark and thick with a strong flavour, and is even less salty than the light type. Shoyu is a full-flavoured sauce that is aged for up to two years. In between there is the very popular Kikkoman,

which is a brand name for the equivalent of the Chinese regular soy sauce. It is ideal as a dipping sauce to be used at the table rather than for cooking. Japanese soy sauces are mainly used for seasoning tofu, grilled (broiled) dishes, cold fish salads and the classic sashimi.

Indonesian Soy Sauce

Indonesia produces *kecap manis*, which is a thick, black soy sauce with a powerful aroma and a very sweet syrupy taste, and *kecap asin* which is much thinner and weaker and is sometimes described as white soy. *Kecap sedang* comes somewhere in between but is less popular than *kecap manis*. They are all mainly used as condiments rather than in cooking.

Below: (Top to bottom) Kecap manis and kecap asin are the most popular varieties of Indonesian soy sauce.

Above:
Sweet chilli
sauce is widely used in Thai cooking.

Below: Lemon sauce goes well with
chicken and fish
dishes.

PLUM SAUCE

Made from plum juice with
sugar, salt, vinegar and
a thickening agent,
plum sauce is a sort
of sweet-and-sour
accompaniment.
There is a variety of
sauces from China,
Thailand and Vietnam.
They all have slightly different
aromas and flavours, according
to the seasonings added. Plum sauce
is most commonly used for seasoning
Peking duck or served as a dip for
spring rolls or dim sum.

LEMON SAUCE

Lemon sauce is not actually
an Asian sauce, but a
condiment that was
especially created for
the Western market.
It is thick, smooth
and velvety and has a
delicious piquant
citrus aroma and spicy,
tangy, sweet flavour.

HOISIN SAUCE

This is another Cantonese speciality.
Its Chinese name literally means
sea flavour, which is a
reflection on how delicious it
is rather than an indication
of its ingredients. In fact
it is made from fermented
soya beans, sugar, vinegar,
salt, chilli, garlic and sesame
oil and may also include a
variety of other spices, but there
is no standard formula so the aroma
and flavour of different brands can
vary quite considerably.

Hoisin sauce is a fairly versatile
sauce and makes a valuable
contribution to the kitchen.
Mainly intended to be used
as an accent in marinades, it
can also be used at the table
as a dipping sauce, but
should not accompany Peking
duck, as is the practice in some
restaurants in the West. Peking
duck has traditionally always been

CHILLI SAUCE

The best known Asian chilli sauce
comes from China, although the
Vietnamese have a very hot version and
there is also a thick, spicy chilli sauce
made in Thailand.

Chinese bottled chilli sauce made
from fresh red chillies, salt, vinegar and
apples or plums is hot and spicy, with
a touch of fruitiness. The Thai version
includes both hot and sweet chillies,
along with ginger, spices and vinegar.
There is also a thick Chinese sauce
which is made exclusively from chillies
and salt. This is usually sold in jars and
is much hotter than the bottled sauce.
Chilli sauce can also include other
ingredients such as tomatoes.

The bottled sauce is used both for
cooking and as a dip, but the thicker
sauce is mainly used for cooking as
an alternative to chilli bean paste. Use
sparingly, as it can be quite fiery. It goes
especially well with shellfish.

> **Making Chilli Dipping Sauce**
> This is good served with spring rolls
> and other appetizers. Gently heat
> 50ml/2fl oz/¼ cup rice vinegar,
> 30ml/2 tbsp water and 50g/2oz/
> ¼ cup caster (superfine) sugar in
> a small pan, stirring constantly until
> the sugar has dissolved. Bring to
> the boil and boil rapidly, without
> stirring, until the mixture forms a
> light syrup. Remove the pan from
> the heat and stir in 2 seeded and
> finely chopped fresh red chillies.
> Allow to cool before serving.

partnered by plum sauce. However,
hoisin is a very good accompaniment
to all kinds of roast meats. It is also
an excellent sauce to use in stir-fries
with chicken, prawns (shrimp) or
vegetables. Hoisin sauce is widely
available from Chinese stores and from
most large supermarkets.

Below: (Top to bottom) Light and dark
hoisin sauce should have a rich, warm,
sweet, yet salty taste.

MISO

This is one of the best-known Japanese ingredients. Miso is the collective name for several different types of soya bean paste. The various pastes are made from steamed soya beans, fermented with the aid of different natural yeasts. Some of these starter moulds are based upon rice, while others are based on wheat or barley, and yet more on soya beans themselves. The pastes come in a range of different colours, textures and flavours, depending on the type of yeast used and the length of the fermentation process.

Red miso, known as *mugi miso* in Japan, is the most popular paste. It is more strongly flavoured than the sweeter white miso. Miso is the key ingredient in a soup served at almost every Japanese meal, *miso ramen*. The paste is also stirred into sauces, used as a marinade for meat and fish, and is an ingredient in dressings. When miso is mixed with mayonnaise it makes the increasingly popular *miso-may*.

If miso is overcooked it loses its subtle aroma, so add the paste towards the end of the cooking time. In soups, use sparingly. Dilute a little with some of the liquid and mix it into the soup. Check the taste and add more if needed.

Right: Black bean sauce goes well with strongly flavoured ingredients such as beef and pork – beef with green (bell) peppers and black bean sauce is a very popular Chinese dish.

Above: (Left to right) Red mugi miso is the most popular type of miso, while the much darker hacho miso is the most strongly flavoured type.

BLACK BEAN SAUCE

This sauce made from a mixture of puréed salted black beans with soy sauce, sugar and spice is manufactured for the convenience of Western cooks, since Chinese and Asian cooks generally make their own version at home by crushing whole fermented black beans in the wok while cooking.

Fermented black beans have a powerful aroma and flavour. The sauce should not be used cold straight from the jar or bottle, but should always be heated first. It is usually blended with other strongly flavoured seasonings, such as spring onions (scallions), garlic, ginger and chillies, before being added to stir-fries, and braised and steamed dishes. Ready-made black bean sauces, seasoned either with garlic or chillies, are available, too. These should also be heated before being used, to bring out the aroma and flavour.

1 Spread a thin layer of shiro-miso on a large plate. Cover with kitchen paper and press down lightly so that the paper absorbs the miso.

2 Place fish fillets, flesh-side down, on the paper and cover with another piece of kitchen paper.

3 Using a knife, press a thin layer of miso on top of the paper so that it covers the fish. Leave to marinate for about 3 hours.

4 Remove the fish from the paper and marinade and grill (broil).

YELLOW BEAN SAUCE

Also known as brown bean sauce and ground bean sauce, this Chinese favourite is the basis of many more elaborate sauces, including hoisin sauce, Sichuan sauce, chu hou sauce and Peking duck sauce. It is made from crushed fermented soya beans mixed with salt, wheat flour and sugar. It is not as salty as black bean sauce, and cooks in every region of China add their own choice of spices and seasonings to make their individual blends.

Yellow bean sauce is very versatile in the kitchen, adding an extra dimension to most meat, poultry, fish and even some vegetable dishes, whether in stir-fries, braised dishes or roasts. It is also the ideal basis for a marinade, usually with additional ingredients, such as garlic, spring onions (scallions), ginger and rice wine.

Below: (Top to bottom) Crushed yellow beans and yellow bean sauce have a wonderful "beany" aroma and flavour.

CHILLI BEAN PASTE

This is a Sichuan speciality made from a type of broad (fava) bean. There are several varieties of chilli bean paste available, ranging from mild to hot, but all have a lovely "beany" aroma with a rich flavour. While similar, chilli bean paste and chilli sauce are not interchangeable: each has its own distinct flavour and consistency. Chilli bean paste is slightly thicker than chilli sauce and is an indispensable seasoning in Sichuan cooking, the style from the West of China where hot, spicy foods predominate. It is used to add flavour to stir-fries and braised dishes. Chilli bean paste must be heated before use and should not be served cold as a dipping sauce.

Above: Chilli bean paste is also known as chilli bean sauce, hot bean sauce and Sichuan sauce.

RED BEAN PASTE

Also known as red bean pâté, this thick, smooth paste is made from either red kidney beans or aduki beans, and is sweetened with rock sugar. It is very easy to make, and Asian cooks usually make their own. However, it is also available in small cans, which are available from Asian food stores and most large supermarkets. The paste has a pleasant, mild fragrance with a subtle flavour. Although it is sweetened, the sauce is never cloying, and Asian cooks often add extra sugar to intensify the flavour. Occasionally, other flavourings such as essence of sesame seeds or ground cassia are blended in.

Above: Sweet red bean paste is very popular served spread on pancakes, which are then deep-fried.

Red bean paste is most commonly used in sweet dishes served for dessert, and it is also very popular used as a filling for cakes, pastries, steamed buns and glutinous rice balls.

Storing Asian-style Sauces

Bottled sauces and pastes should be kept in the refrigerator once they have been opened. Most will keep almost indefinitely, but check the use-by dates for safety. Canned beans or paste should be transferred to a plastic tub with a secure, airtight lid. They, too, will keep very well but, again, check the use-by dates.

JAPANESE SAUCES

A number of ready-to-use sauces have been developed in recent years making Japanese cooking much easier.

MEN-TSUYU

This is a dashi-based condensed sauce for serving with soba and udon noodles. It is made of dashi stock, shoyu, salt, sugar and other ingredients, and is used as a dipping sauce or as a soup. The instructions on the packet will state how much water should be added to make a dip for soba and somen, or soup in which to cook udon and soba. It is usual to dilute 1:1 for a dip and 1:8 for soup. Once opened, store the sauce in the refrigerator.

TONKATSU SAUCE

Tonkatsu (pork cutlet) is one of the most popular dishes in Japan, and this thick brown sauce is the ideal

Right: (From left to right) Ready-made sauces include tonkatsu sauce, sukiyaki sauce, men-tsuyu sauce, ponzu, men-tsuyu sauce for somen and yakiniku no tare.

accompaniment, together with shredded cabbage and mustard. It is made of fruits, spices and seasonings. You can easily make your own *tonkatsu* sauce by mixing a fruit sauce such as ketchup and Worcestershire sauce.

TEN-TSUYU

This tasty dipping sauce for tempura is made of dashi stock, shoyu, mirin and a number of seasonings. Ten-tsuyu is normally used undiluted together with a little grated daikon and finely shredded fresh root ginger.

YAKINIKU NO TARE

This Japanese version of barbecue sauce is made of shoyu, spices and various seasonings. It is slightly sweeter than the Western barbecue sauces and is also used for griddled food.

Making Simple Sauces

Most Japanese have a number of sauces in their repertoire that can be easily made on the day of use.
Yuan sauce This sauce gives a subtle flavour to bland white fish, and enhances the flavours of stronger-flavoured fish, such as salmon. Mix together 5 parts mirin, 3 parts shoyu to 2 parts sake and 2 parts lime juice. Marinate the fish in the sauce for at least 15 minutes before frying or cooking over a barbecue.
Tonkatsu sauce This sauce is delicious with fried pork. Mix 1 part Worcestershire sauce with 5 parts tomato ketchup. Coat pork slices in flour and beaten egg and deep-fry. Dip into the sauce to eat.

SUKIYAKI SAUCE

This is a sweet shoyu sauce for cooking *sukiyaki*, made of dashi stock, sugar, sake and seasonings. First thinly sliced beef is pan-fried, then this sauce is added, with vegetables.

Above: Fish sauce is an essential flavouring used in all Asian cuisines, and each country has its own version.

Above: Thick, dark, sweet-tasting oyster sauce is used extensively in Chinese cooking and as a garnish.

OYSTER SAUCE

This is a Cantonese speciality. The thick brown soy-based sauce is flavoured with oyster juice, salt and caramel, then thickened with cornflour (cornstarch). It is thicker than both soy sauce and fish sauce, but is lighter in colour.

Oyster sauce has a pleasant, fragrant aroma and a delicious and quite delicate flavour that surprisingly doesn't taste of fish at all. Nevertheless, it is widely used in many fish dishes, soups and sauces. It is a highly versatile flavouring and can be used in a wide variety of dishes. It is especially good with fairly bland foods such as chicken and tofu but also works very well with more strongly flavoured ingredients, such as beef and shellfish. Beef in oyster sauce is one of the most popular Chinese dishes in the West. Oyster sauce can be used as a garnish and 15–30ml/2–3 tbsp are often sprinkled over the top of cooked dishes such as rice and noodles. It may also be used as a substitute for fish sauce, if the latter is unavailable. The bottled sauce is only used as a cooking ingredient and is never served as a dip or sauce at the table. To enjoy it at its best, oyster sauce is best added to dishes towards the end of cooking time. There are a number of different brands available, and the more expensive versions are usually far superior, and have a much richer flavour than the cheaper versions. Once opened, the bottle should be stored in the refrigerator where the sauce will keep for a very long time, although it is best used before the expiry date on the label.

FISH SAUCE

This seasoning is widely used in Vietnamese and Thai cooking in much the same way that soy sauce is invaluable in the Chinese and Japanese cuisines. In Vietnam, it is usually made using shrimp, but in Thailand the sauce is more often made using salted fermented fish.

All types of fish sauce have a very pungent flavour and aroma, although not excessively fishy, and they are extremely salty. The colour of fish sauce can vary considerably; as a general rule, lighter-coloured sauces are usually considered to be of a better quality than darker versions.

Fish sauce is used extensively in all South-east Asian cooking as a seasoning in many different savoury dishes, including those made with meat. It is also used to make a popular dipping sauce, when it is blended with extra flavourings such as finely chopped garlic and fresh chillies, and sugar and lime juice. As a general rule, about

Right: Thai nam pla sauce has a slightly stronger aroma and flavour than the Chinese and Vietnamese fish sauces.

30ml/2 tbsp fish sauce is sufficient to season a curry or stew for 4–6 people. Thai fish sauce is widely available in supermarkets and Asian food stores, but the Vietnamese variety may be more difficult to find. If it is not available, soy sauce is an adequate substitute. Asian fish sauce is generally sold in either glass or plastic bottles. Once opened, it should be kept in a cool, dark place where it will keep for up to a year. Use before the expiry date.

SHRIMP PASTE

Also known as *blachan, terasi, kapi* and *ngapi*, according to its country of origin, shrimp paste is an essential ingredient in scores of savoury dishes from South-east Asia. It is made from tiny shrimp that have been salted, dried, pounded and then left to ferment in the hot, humid equatorial conditions until the aroma is very pungent. The colour of the paste can be anything from pale oyster pink to purplish brown, depending upon the type of shrimp and the precise process used to produce it.

There's no disguising the main constituent of this paste. The moment you unwrap it or lift the lid, the smell of rotten fish is quite overwhelming. Do not let this put you off, however. The odour vanishes when the paste is cooked, and this is one of those ingredients that really does make a difference to the food, adding depth, pungency and a recognizable South-east Asian signature. It should be used sparingly – a piece about 1–2 cm/½–¾ in long is sufficient for most dishes.

Above: Shrimp paste is compressed and sold in blocks or packed into tiny tubs.

Dried shrimp Strongly flavoured, tiny salted and dried shrimp are used as a condiment throughout South-east Asia in much the same way as shrimp paste. They can be used to flavour stir-fries or garnish salads and are used in the classic "eight-treasure stuffing". Rehydrate by soaking in warm water until soft, then pound to a paste in a mortar with a pestle or process in a food processor or a blender.

Right: Dried shrimp are pale pink in colour, having been boiled before being spread out in the sun to dry.

Preparing Shrimp Paste

Shrimp paste can be used straight from the packet if it is to be fried with other ingredients, but it needs to be heated to temper its raw taste before using in sambals and salads.

1 Cut off a piece of paste and shape it into a 1cm/½in cube. Mould it on to a metal skewer.

2 Holding the skewer in a cloth, rotate the paste over a low gas flame, or under an electric grill (broiler) until the outside begins to look dry, but not burnt.

3 Alternatively, wrap the cube of paste in a piece of foil and dry-fry in a frying pan for 5 minutes.

SAMBALS

In the West, sambals have come to mean the side dishes served with a curry, but this is several steps away from the original South-east Asian term, which was, and still is, applied to a number of hot, spicy relishes, sauces and similar accompaniments that are based on chillies. Sambals are most notably associated with Indonesia, where they are particularly popular, and feature strongly in the famous *rijstafel*, a veritable banquet that includes dozens of different dishes and that was developed in the days when Indonesia was still a colony and known as the Dutch East Indies. Thanks to this European connection, *rijstafel* is also well-known and highly popular in The Netherlands, and bottled sambals are widely available in that country.

In Indonesia, a sambal can also be a main dish. *Sambal goreng*, for instance, is a spicy chilli sauce, which may include a variety of foods such as tiny meatballs, cubes of fish, wedges of hard-boiled eggs or vegetables.

In Malaysia, Singapore and Indonesia *sambal blachan* (chilli and shrimp paste sambal) is a favourite. Fresh red chillies are coarsely chopped, then pounded with a little salt and prepared shrimp paste. This sambal is extremely hot – especially when the seeds have been left in the chillies. *Sambal oelek* is similar, but a little brown sugar is added to bring out the flavour of the chillies. Sometimes labelled chopped chilli, this product is now sold in jars in many shops and supermarkets. One teaspoonful (5ml) is approximately equivalent to one small chilli. Although sambals usually feature red chillies, a typical Malaysian sambal might include tomatoes and onion, as well as green chillies, mixed with lime juice and garnished with a sprinkling of grated coconut.

At a typical Thai meal, there may be one or two sambals in addition to the much-loved *nam prik*, a combination of dried prawns, shrimp paste, garlic, chillies, fish sauce, lemon juice and brown sugar. *Nam prik* complements raw, steamed, fried or boiled vegetables and is often simply stirred into a bowl of plain boiled or steamed Thai rice. Another popular sambal is made from fish sauce, lemon juice, shallots and chillies – a blend that enhances all kinds of fish and shellfish dishes.

In Vietnam, the salt and pepper of the Western table is replaced by *nuoc cham*. This is a piquant sambal made from chillies, garlic, sugar, lime juice or rice vinegar, and fish sauce. It demonstrates beautifully the classic combination of hot, sweet, sour and salt flavours that is so typical of Vietnamese cooking.

Sambals and sauces are usually served in small bowls or saucers, with pieces of cooked meat, fish or vegetables for dipping, or a tiny spoonful may be put on to each plate.

Above: Nuoc cham is a classic table condiment served in Vietnam.

Sambal Blachan

Deseed 2–4 fresh red chillies and put them in a mortar with a little salt. Pound to a paste using a pestle. Cut off a small piece of shrimp paste, shape it into a 1cm/ 1/2in cube and heat, pressed on to a metal skewer, over a low gas flame until the outside begins to look dry, but not burnt. Add the shrimp paste and pound to mix well. Add lemon juice to taste.

Left: (Clockwise from top right) Nam prik sauce, sambal blachan and sambal oelek are very hot relish-like sauces based on fiery fresh chillies, which are served at the table with other savoury dishes.

MUSTARDS

Above: English mustard

*Above:
English
mustard powder*

ENGLISH MUSTARD

Made from yellow mustard or blended seeds, English mustard is very hot. It is sometimes mixed with wheat flour for bulk and turmeric for colour.

English mustard powder should be mixed 10 minutes before it is required to allow the clean pungent flavours to develop. It will lose its pungency in a few hours, so fresh mustard should be made daily or as required. For fiery results, mix mustard powder with cold

Below: Fench's American mustard

liquids – water, milk or beer – never with boiling water or vinegar, as both kill the enzyme that gives the condiment its temperature, resulting in a mild, but bitter, mustard. Similarly, when mustard powder is to be added to hot dishes, such as sauces and stews, stir it in at the end of the cooking and heat gently on the lowest heat to retain its bite.

AMERICAN MUSTARD

The obligatory accompaniment to the all-American hot dog, this is made from mild white mustard seeds, vinegar, sugar, spices and turmeric. It is mild with a slight hint of sweetness.

Above: German mustard

GERMAN MUSTARD

This is a smooth, dark mustard made from black seeds and vinegar to give a sweet-sour flavour with just a hint of sharpness. There are also several types of extra-strong German mustard.

Below: Dijon mustard

Above: French mustard

DIJON MUSTARD

Traditionally prepared from only black seeds, Dijon mustard is now made from brown seeds. The seed husks are removed, resulting in a mustard with a pale blond colour. The mustard is blended with wine or verjuice (the sour juice from unripe grapes or wild apples), salt and spices. This is the classic French mustard that is eaten with steaks and grills (broils). It is smooth, salty and sharp, with a good mustardy flavour.

BORDEAUX MUSTARD

Often referred to as French mustard, this is darker in colour than Dijon mustard. It is also made from a blend of black and brown seeds and the husks are retained, which results in the darker colour. Bordeaux mustard is mixed with vinegar and sugar, plenty of tarragon, plus other herbs and spices, which produces a mustard with a mild sweet-sour taste that goes best with cold meats and sausages.

MEAUX MUSTARD

For this classic mustard, the black seeds are partly crushed and partly ground to give it its distinctive crunchy texture. The seeds are then mixed with vinegar and spices, producing a mustard with a medium to hot flavour and an interesting spiciness. It goes particularly well with cold meats, meat pies and sausages. Meaux mustard is frequently sold in attractive stoneware jars with a sealed cork stopper.

Above: *Provençal mustard*

Below: *Honeycup mustard*

Above: *Red grape mustard*

Below: *Moutarde verte a l'estragon*

Above: *Old style grey mustard*

Below: *House neri karashi*

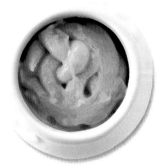

Below: *Wholegrain mustard*

ORLÉANS MUSTARD

This is the fourth in the group of great French mustards. It is prepared with wine vinegar.

ALSACE MUSTARD

This is the exception to the French rule that only mustards with black and/or brown seeds merit the word mustard or *moutarde*. Those made from white or yellow mustard seeds are simply called condiments. This particular type, however, does contain white seeds.

CREMONA MUSTARD

Also known as *mostarda di frutta*, this Italian mustard is more like a crystallized fruit chutney than a conventional mustard. It is made from a mixture of crystallized fruit such as apricots, clementines, melons, figs and cherries infused in mustard seed oil.

It is traditionally served with Italian sausages, roast beef and *bollito misto*, a mixture of boiled chicken, beef and veal. It can also be served with sweet dishes such as ice cream, creating a wonderful contrast between the peppery bite and the creamy sweetness.

OTHER MUSTARDS

There are dozens of other mustards, such as French Maille mustard; Verona mustard, which is mixed with apple purée; and Provençal mustard, which is flavoured with garlic and red (bell) peppers. Tarragon, tomato, basil, paprika and honey are all popular flavourings. Mustards flavoured with citrus fruits became popular in the last quarter of the twentieth century. Mustards are mixed with a variety of ingredients, including red and white wine, wine vinegar and grape juice.

Storing Mustard
Always store mustard in a glass or stone pot or jar and make sure it is securely covered. Mustard is best kept in the refrigerator.

PRESERVED INGREDIENTS

There are a number of ingredients that have been dried or preserved in salt, vinegar or oil that are invaluable as flavouring ingredients. They often have an intense taste and aroma that can impart a richness to the dishes to which they are added.

SUN-DRIED VEGETABLES

Vegetables can be dried in the sun, which intensifies their natural flavour. They can be added to sauces, stews, casseroles and simmered dishes to impart a wonderfully rich flavour.
Sun-dried tomatoes These are perhaps the best-known of all the dried vegetables and can be found in most stores and supermarkets. The process of sun-drying tomatoes intensifies their flavour to an astonishing sweetness and pungency and allows you to enjoy the full savour of tomatoes, even in winter. If you are extremely lucky, you may still find in markets in southern Italy locally grown tomatoes that have been spread out to dry in the sun. The commercially produced "sun-dried" varieties are air-dried by machine and don't actually see the sun.

Dry tomatoes are brick-red in colour and have a chewy texture. They can be eaten on their own as a snack, but for cooking they should be soaked in hot water until soft. The tomato-flavoured soaking

Right: Sun-dried tomatoes are available dry in packets or preserved in oil.

Above: Sun-dried aubergines have a meaty texture.

Above: Sun-dried peppers have a more peppery, piquant flavour than sun-dried tomatoes.

water can be used as an ingredient for a soup or sauce. Bottled sun-dried tomatoes are sold in chunky pieces. The tomato-flavoured oil can be used in salad dressings and in cooking instead of all or part of the quantity of unflavoured oil specified in the recipe. Sun-dried tomatoes add piquancy to vegetable dishes, soups and sauces. They make an excellent appetizer or antipasto combined with fresh tomatoes, mozzarella and basil, or with other preserved vegetables, and they add extra flavour to egg dishes.

Sun-dried char-grilled aubergines/ eggplant These thin slices of aubergine are not used as a substitute for fresh, but are added to fresh vegetable sauces and stews for their characteristic earthy flavour. They need to be rehydrated in boiling water with a splash of wine vinegar for 2 minutes before use, then drained and patted dry with kitchen paper. Once rehydrated, they can be snipped into strips with kitchen scissors and either added immediately to sauces or first fried in olive oil.
Sun-dried peppers These resemble wrinkled, dark red sun-dried tomatoes and are used in the same way, to add a meaty bite to soups and stews, especially vegetable dishes. Before use, they should be rinsed under the cold tap, then dried and cut into narrow strips or finely chopped.
Dried porcini These are invaluable for the intense, musky aroma and flavour they impart to sauces, soups, stews and risottos. When buying, look for packets with large pieces. Although they may seem expensive, a little goes a long way, and 15–25g/$^{1}/_{2}$–1oz is the most you will need for a recipe that serves 4–6.

Below: A few dried porcini make a delicious addition to ordinary fresh mushrooms, giving them a flavour of wild mushrooms.

Before use, dried porcini must be reconstituted in warm water for about 20 minutes. Drain, rinse and squeeze dry, then slice or chop as required. The soaking water can be strained and added to soups or stocks.

VEGETABLES PRESERVED IN OIL

Italians produce a wide variety of vegetables preserved in virgin olive or sunflower oil, or a mixture of both. The choicest are often cooked *alla brace*, that is, lightly grilled (broiled) before being packed in the best extra virgin olive oil – tiny, baby artichokes, porcini and other wild mushrooms, red and yellow (bell) peppers and aubergines (eggplant), which look as beautiful as they taste. Perhaps the most luxurious and certainly the most expensive preserved vegetables are truffles. You will also sometimes find large bulbous jars containing colourful layers of different vegetables in oil; these are packed by hand and are extremely expensive, but incomparably delicious.

Not only is a mixture of preserved vegetables great served with cured meats as part of an antipasto, but they can also be chopped or sliced and used to dress hot or cold pasta. Stirred into

Below: Artichoke hearts bottled in olive oil make a delicious, simple antipasti.

cold rice they make a wonderful salad and they also make a delicious topping for crostini or pizza. Preserved small artichokes or artichoke hearts are one of the traditional toppings for the classic Four Seasons pizza.

PICKLED VEGETABLES

Pickling is a very old method of preserving foods, either by immersing in salt or brine, or in vinegar. There is an almost countless number of different types of pickles, chutneys and relishes, but whether from Britain, Europe, India or Asia, they are all made by similar traditional methods. Among the vegetables popular in pickling for the West are cabbage (sauerkraut), cucumbers (dill pickles) and onions (pickled onions), but almost any vegetable or fruit can be pickled, either by themselves or mixed with others. Most are flavoured with herbs and spices.

Mixed pickled vegetables are sold packed in vinegar and oil. Single varieties, such as peeled or unpeeled aubergines (eggplant) and courgettes (zucchini) are available, but a mixture of these vegetables along with artichokes, baby (pearl) onions, carrots, celery and (bell) peppers is more colourful. These vegetables are called *giardiniera* or sometimes *all contadina*, meaning peasant-style.

CAPERS

These grow in profusion in the warm dry climate of the Mediterranean. They have to be picked by hand, which is labour intensive and makes them expensive. The bushes are checked each morning for small hard buds that are at just the right stage for harvesting. The capers are washed and allowed to wilt for a day before being put into jars and covered with salted wine vinegar, brine or olive oil. Alternatively, they can be preserved in

Above: Capers stored in brine should always be well-rinsed before use.

Above: Salted capers tend to be more versatile than the pickled variety.

Left: Whole caper berries can make a very pretty garnish.

salt alone. Capers have a distinctive sour, salty flavour. They are used in a huge range of classic sauces, such as tartare, *rémoulade* and *ravigote* sauces, and Italian *tonnato* sauce, which is used in the classic cold braised veal dish, *vitello tonnato*. In Britain, hot caper sauce is traditionally served with boiled mutton, but try it with salmon or pan-fried or grilled (broiled) fish with the addition of a little grated lemon rind. They are also used for flavouring meatballs and as a garnish for pizza.

Capers should always be stored submerged in their pickling medium, otherwise they will develop an unpleasant flavour.

PICKLED ALLIUMS

In many countries, onions, shallots and garlic are pickled in vinegar, spices and herbs. These preserved alliums make a delicious addition to mixed salads, egg and rice dishes. Bottled green shoots of sprouting garlic are a popular spring flavouring in Spain, Italy and China. Pungent pickled onions go very well with cold roast meats or cheeses.

PICKLED GHERKINS

These are very small cucumbers with bumpy skins and are normally found pickled in vinegar. They can be eaten with cold meat, pâtés or terrines, or can be finely chopped and then added to mayonnaise with chopped capers to make tartare sauce. In Russia and some parts of northern Europe, gherkins are treated as a vegetable, rather than as an accompaniment.

Pickled gherkins are available in three different sizes. The smallest ones with a rough skin are called cornichons; a little larger are

the prickly skinned gherkins that are normally eaten with herrings, while sweet or dill pickles are made from large, smooth-skinned gherkins.

BREAD AND BUTTER PICKLES

Quick and easy to make, these pickles are very popular in the United States. They can be made with small, pickling cucumbers or courgettes (zucchini), combined with onions, white wine vinegar, sugar, yellow mustard seeds, ground turmeric and salt. Bread and butter pickles are usually served in sandwiches, often made with rye bread, with roast beef, cured or smoked ham, salt beef or pastrami.

Right: Large dill pickles go particularly well with cold meats such as pastrami and salt beef.

Below: (From left) Garlic, small onions and shallots are popular pickled and served as an accompaniment.

Making Pickled Gherkins

Large dill pickles are very easy to make at home. Scrub 20 small, ridged pickling cucumbers and leave to dry. Add 175g/6oz/³/4 cup coarse sea salt to 2 litres/ 4 pints/2 quarts water and bring to the boil. Turn off the heat and leave to cool. Lightly crush 20 garlic cloves. Pack the cucumbers tightly into four 1.2 litre/ 2 pint wide-necked, sterilized jars, layering them with the garlic, fresh dill, 15ml/1 tbsp dill seeds and 30ml/ 2 tbsp mixed pickling spice. Add a small piece of hot chilli to each jar, if desired. Pour over the cooled brine. Cover and leave to pickle for about 6 days before serving.

Chutneys and Relishes

Around the world, there are many different chutneys and relishes that are served as condiments. Most have a sweet-and-sour, piquant flavour that goes particularly well with cold meats and cheeses, in sandwiches and with hot, spicy dishes such as curries.

Sweet mango chutney Mango chutney is hugely popular in Britain served not only with curries, but with cold meats, salads and in cheese sandwiches. It is made using ripe but firm mangoes.

Mango pickle Of varying degrees of hotness, this is popular in India. It is hot, spicy and sour and is quite different from mango chutney.

Piccalilli Popular in the United Kingdom, piccalilli is part mustard and part pickle. It is basically a medium-strong mustard to which cauliflower, pickling onions, chillies and ginger have been added, giving the pickle a crunchy texture, with turmeric providing the distinctive yellow colour. Although it is not everybody's preferred condiment, piccalilli is good with cold meats, especially pork and cured or smoked ham. Like most pickles, piccalilli should be stored in the refrigerator once opened, where it will keep for several months.

PICKLED TURNIPS

Also known as *torshi*, this is a classic Middle Eastern speciality and a traditional food enjoyed by the Jews of Persia, Israel and the Arab lands. The turnips, rich red in their beetroot-spiked brine, not only look gorgeous in their jars but also make a delicious pickle to add to falafel, or to be served as part of an assortment of appetizers.

PICKLED CHILLIES

Jars of whole chillies stored in white wine vinegar are an extremely useful storecupboard (pantry) standby. Once opened, the jar should be tightly closed and stored in the refrigerator.

MUSTARD FRUIT PICKLE

This sweet crystallized fruit pickle has a piquant undertone of mustard. It is a classic Italian pickle, created over one hundred years ago in Cremona and Venice. Its vibrant multicolour comes from the assortment of candied fruits from which it is made – cherries, pears, melons, figs, apricots and clementines, infused in mustard seed oil. Mustard fruit pickle is traditionally served with boiled pork sausages like *zampone* and *cotechino*, or roast and boiled beef, veal or port. For an unusual dessert, it can be served with creamy mascarpone.

PRESERVED LEMONS

These are used extensively in Middle Eastern and North African cooking. Whole lemons, or sometimes lemon slices, are packed in jars with salt. The interesting thing with preserved lemons is that you eat only the peel, which contains the essential flavour of the lemon, rather than the flesh. They have an intense flavour and go very well with chicken. They are often added to savoury dishes such as tagines and spicy stews and are sometimes used to enliven salads.

Below: Pickled chillies can be used as an ingredient or chopped finely and served as a condiment.

Making Preserved Lemons

Wash 10 unwaxed lemons and cut each into 6–8 wedges. Press a generous amount of salt into the cut surfaces. Pack the wedges into two 1.2 litre/2 pint sterilized jars. To each jar, add 30ml/2 tbsp salt and 90ml/6 tbsp lemon juice, then top up with boiling water. Cover and leave for 2–4 weeks before using.

Below: Italian mustard fruit pickle is traditionally enjoyed at Christmas.

ASIAN-STYLE PICKLES

Preserved and pickled food plays an important part in the Asian diet. In the days before refrigeration and rapid transportation, fresh food had to be preserved for the lean months, and also so that it could be conveyed to regions that were often a long way from the source of supply.

Preserved and pickled vegetables – and to a lesser extent fruit – are used as an accompaniment to meals all over Asia. Some of the more famous examples include *chow chow*, the Chinese sweet mixed pickles that are now an American favourite, and *kimchee*, the tart, garlicky pickle that is served at almost every Korean meal.

Sichuan preserved vegetables This pickle, made from the stems of mustard cabbage, originated in Sichuan province, but is now made in other parts of China. The stems are dried in the sun, then pickled in brine. After being trimmed and cleaned, they are pressed to extract excess liquid before being blended with chillies and spices and stored in sealed urns to mature.

Below: There is a wide range of Chinese pickles available in the West.

Above: Pickled mustard greens can be served raw as a powerful relish.

They have a pungent, salty, peppery flavour and smooth and crunchy texture. They can be added to stir-fries, soups and steamed dishes during cooking. Rinse in water to remove some of the excess salt and chillies before using, finely sliced or shredded. Once open, store the pickle in an airtight container in the refrigerator, where it will keep for several months.

Chinese pickles These are available in packets, bottled in jars, or preserved in cans. A pickle may consist of a single ingredient, such as ginger, garlic, spring onion (scallion) bulbs, cucumber or chillies, or a mixture of some or all of these. Individual items are generally pickled in dark soy solution, while mixed vegetables tend to be pickled in clear brine to which sugar, Sichuan peppercorns, distilled spirit and fresh root ginger have been added.

Japanese pickles There are many different varieties of the Japanese pickles known as *tsukemono*. The vegetables that are used are more or less the same as those used in China, but the method of pickling is somewhat different. To start with, instead of earthenware urns, only wooden barrels are used in Japan and, instead of being pickled in a brine solution, the vegetables are layered with salt. When the barrel is full, a lid is put on top, and this is weighted down with a large stone or a similar heavy object. The combined effect of the compression and salt forces the liquid out of the vegetables and they are pickled in their own juices to delicious result.

Japanese pickles form an essential part of a meal. They are served as a relish to accompany the cooked food, as well as a dessert or as a means of cleansing the palate at the end of a meal. They are either served singly or in groups of two or three, and they are always beautifully arranged in small individual dishes.

PICKLED BAMBOO SHOOTS

These tasty pickles are a great delicacy in Vietnam. The fresh bamboo shoots are sliced and then pickled in a spiced vinegar. Before using, the pickled bamboo shoots should be soaked in water to remove some of the bitterness. They are mainly used in soups and stocks, and are often served with duck.

PICKLED GARLIC

This is a great favourite in Thailand. Small bulbs of garlic are pickled whole in a sweet and sour brine.

Above: Umeboshi are often chopped and used as a filling for rice balls.

UMEBOSHI

These small pickled plums are a particular Japanese delicacy. The plums are picked before they are ripe and are then pickled in salt with red *shiso* leaves, which gives them their distinctive colour. They have a sharp and salty taste.

PICKLED LIMES

Whole limes preserved in brine or a mixture of soy sauce, sugar, salt and vinegar are a Thai speciality.

JAPANESE SALT-PICKLED VEGETABLES

Salt-pickled vegetables are widely eaten in Japan. Popular vegetables include daikon, cucumber, aubergine (eggplant) and mustard leaves. Japanese cucumber and aubergine are smaller than Western varieties, so it is worth looking out for those in particular.

PICKLED GINGER

Pieces of fresh root ginger are sprinkled with salt, then pickled in a mixture of rice vinegar, sugar and water. Pickled ginger is served with sushi and sashimi in Japan and with preserved duck eggs in Hong Kong. Once opened, store the jar in the refrigerator, where the pickle will keep for up to six months.

MIRIN PULP PICKLES

These traditional Japanese pickles are available in Japanese stores, either loose or in packets. Vegetables such as aubergine (eggplant), carrot, cucumber, daikon and turnips are pickled in a mash made of rice bran mixed with warm brine.

PICKLED KUMQUATS

These little, orange-like fruits are first soaked in brine and then pickled in a vinegar syrup flavoured with cinnamon and cloves. They are delicious with chicken or duck and the vinegar can be used to flavour sauces and gravies.

Below: (From left) There are a great many Japanese salt-pickled vegetables, including aubergines, radishes and tiny sliced cucumbers.

Above: Pickled ginger is known as gari *in Japan.*

Below: Mirin pulp pickles have a mildly sweet enriched flavour.

VINEGARS

One of our oldest condiments, vinegar is made by acetic fermentation, a process that in effect converts alcohol into acid. Many home wine-makers discover that if their fermenting wine is exposed to the air, they are left with vinegar. Most countries produce their own type of vinegar, usually based on their most popular alcoholic drink – wine in France and Italy; sherry in Spain; rice wine in Asia; and beer and cider in Great Britain. Apple cider vinegar is the standard vinegar in the United States. Any fruit can be used as a base, but grape (i.e. wine) produces the most versatile vinegar and is normally the one used when creating herb- and fruit-flavoured vinegars.

Vinegar is used as a preservative in pickles and chutneys; it is also an ingredient in marinades and salad dressings. A spoonful or two of a good-quality vinegar can lift many cooked dishes, giving an intensity particularly suited to meat and poultry.

Above: Cider vinegar is a clear, pale brown colour and has a distinct, yet subtle flavour of apples.

MALT VINEGAR

Made from soured beer, malt vinegar is used in Britain and other northern European countries for pickling onions and other vegetables, or for sprinkling over potato chips (French fries). It can be clear, but is more often sold coloured with caramel, making it dark brown in colour. Malt vinegar has a robust, harsh flavour and is not suitable for salad dressings.

DISTILLED VINEGAR

This is a colourless vinegar that is mostly used for pickling onions and other vegetables when you wish to preserve the colour of the vegetable.

SPIRIT VINEGAR

This is a strong vinegar with a faintly lemon flavour. Use it very sparingly, added to dressings.

CIDER VINEGAR

Made from cider and praised for its health-giving properties, cider vinegar is made in the same way as wine vinegar. However, it is too strong and sharp to use in the same ways as wine vinegar. It can be used for salad dressings, but it is perhaps best kept for pickling fruits, such as pears.

RED AND WHITE WINE VINEGAR

These can be made from white, red or rosé wine. The quality of the vinegar will depend on the quality of the original ingredient. The finest wine vinegars are made by the slow and costly Orléans method. Cheaper, faster methods of fermentation involve heating, producing a harsher vinegar that lacks the complexities of the original wine. Use in dressings, mayonnaise and some classic sauces, or to add flavour to savoury stews and soups.

Left and above: Red and white wine vinegars are used in many dishes.

BALSAMIC VINEGAR

This is a rich dark, mellow vinegar which has become hugely popular. Balsamic vinegar is made from grape juice (predominantly from Trebbiano grapes), which is fermented in vast wooden barrels for a minimum of four or five years and up to 40 or even more years, resulting in an intensely rich vinegar with a concentrated flavour. Its production is strictly controlled by law. Vinegars aged for 20 or more years are called *stravecchio*. Balsamic vinegar is delicious in dressings or sprinkled over roasted vegetables. It is even good with fresh strawberries.

SHERRY VINEGAR

This vinegar can be just as costly as balsamic vinegar and, if left to mature in wooden barrels, equally good. Sweet and mellow, sherry vinegar is caramel in colour and can be used in the same way as balsamic vinegar – in dressings, sprinkled over roasted vegetables or added to sauces and stews.

Above: Rice vinegars are fermented or distilled from rice and are used extensively in Asian cooking.

Left: Balsamic vinegar is produced in Modena in the north of Italy.

Left: Sherry vinegar can be used in dressings, sprinkled over roasted vegetables or added to stews or sauces.

RICE VINEGARS

The vinegar fermented from rice is dark amber in colour and is referred to in China as red or black vinegar. Vinegar distilled from rice grains is clear, so it is called white vinegar. The raw ingredients used for making rice vinegar consist of glutinous rice, long grain rice, wheat, barley and rice husks. It is fermented twice and is matured for up to 6–7 months. Japan has a brown rice vinegar which is dark and heady. This vinegar, which has been likened to balsamic vinegar, has a robust flavour, yet is wonderfully smooth.

Rice vinegar is an important ingredient in Chinese sweet-and-sour and hot-and-sour sauce and is added to many other dishes to impart flavour. It is used in Thai cucumber and dipping sauces such as Vietnamese vinegar and garlic fish sauce. It is also widely used for pickling and preserving. Thai cooks add rice vinegar to several dishes, including their hot-and-sour soup. In Japan, rice vinegar is used for sushi rice. If rice vinegar is heated for too long, its fragrance will be lost and the food will taste tart and unpleasant. In Asian cooking, therefore, it is usually added at the last minute before serving.

Most Japanese vinegars, unless they are labelled *yonezu* (pure rice vinegar), contain other grains besides rice. If less than 40g/1¹/₂oz rice was used to make 1 litre/1³/₄ pint/4 cups of vinegar, it is labelled as *kokumot-su* (grain vinegar).

FLAVOURED VINEGAR

Wine vinegar is the most popular choice as the base for making flavoured vinegars, although cider vinegar can also be used. Herbs such as tarragon, basil, thyme and mint can be added, as can garlic, chillies, anchovies and capers. Soft fruit can be used to enhance the flavour of white wine vinegar, with raspberries being the most popular choice.

Flavoured vinegars can be bought ready-made but are also very easy to make at home, simply using red or white wine vinegar and very fresh unblemished fruit or herbs. Flavoured vinegars should always be stored in a cool dark place.

When using flavoured vinegars, pair them with appropriate ingredients. For example, robust meats will go well with more pungently flavoured vinegars such as rosemary, whereas a delicately flavoured fish will be better suited to a milder vinegar such as a fruit vinegar.

COCONUT VINEGAR

This amber coloured vinegar is highly regarded in the Philippines. It is made from coconut nectar tapped from the flower sheaves of mature coconut palms. The tip of the flower stem is cut off to release the sap, which then ferments naturally. The "toddy" is either drunk as it is, or it is allowed to ferment further to become flavoursome coconut vinegar.

PON VINEGAR

This Japanese vinegar is made from the juice of a citrus fruit similar to limes. Pon vinegar is used to make the classic Japanese table condiment and dipping sauce, *ponzu*, which is served with poached meats, fried foods and fish and shellfish. Pon has a delicate, limey flavour.

Right: (From left to right) Pon vinegar and coconut vinegar are popular and widely used flavourings in Asian cooking.

Above: Raspberry vinegar is one of the most popular types of vinegar flavoured with soft fruit; it is particularly good used in salad dressings.

Dressings

Although dressings are quick and simple to make at home, there is a wide range of very good ready-made varieties available in supermarkets and stores. As with most things, you get what you pay for, so the better flavoured dressings that contain natural ingredients and fewer additives are more expensive. Many supermarkets sell "fresh" dressings, normally found in the chilled counters, either with other delicatessen ingredients or with the food with which they are most frequently served. Most fresh dressings should be kept in the refrigerator, and should be eaten within a fairly short period of time (check the use-by date on the label). Other dressings should also be kept in the refrigerator once opened. They tend to keep a little longer, but again, check use-by dates to make sure.

French/Vinaigrette This dressing is normally a blend of oil, vinegar, mustard and salt. Most commercial dressings also include sugar. Lower-quality dressings are made using sunflower or a similar oil, whereas the better ones are made with olive oil.
Mayonnaise Made with egg yolks, vinegar and oil, there are numerous brands available. Fresh mayonnaise usually has a good flavour.
Thousand Island This variation on mayonnaise includes tomato purée (paste) and chopped stuffed olives, onion, green (bell) pepper and herbs.
Tartare sauce This combination of mayonnaise, chopped capers and gherkins is a classic accompaniment to goujons of fish and fried scampi (extra large shrimp).
Aioli Garlic cloves are pounded to a pulp with salt and then form the basis of mayonnaise. The flavour of this dressing is quite powerful.

Making Flavoured Vinegars

It is simple to make flavoured vinegars at home. Make sure the bottle or jar is sterilized before making the vinegar.

Raspberry vinegar Macerate 450g/1lb fresh raspberries in 1.2 litres/2 pints/5 cups good quality wine vinegar for 2–3 weeks. Once the mixture is strained, use to flavour salad dressings or sauces.

Tarragon vinegar Put 3–4 sprigs of fresh tarragon into a clean jar and cover with white wine vinegar. Keep in a warm place for about 2 weeks, shaking the jar occasionally. Strain the vinegar, then pour into a bottle with another sprig of fresh tarragon. Use other herbs such as basil or rosemary in the same way.

Fennel seed vinegar Place about 30ml/2 tbsp fennel seeds in a preserving jar and pour over about 600ml/1 pint/2½ cups white wine vinegar. Cover and leave to infuse in a cool, dark place, shaking the jar occasionally, for 2–3 weeks, or until the flavour is sufficiently pronounced. Use to make dressings or to sharpen herb sauces.

Garlic vinegar Crush 3–4 garlic cloves in a mortar with a pestle, then place in a stainless steel or glass mixing bowl. Heat about 250ml/8fl oz/1 cup white wine or cider vinegar until just boiling and pour it over the garlic. Leave to cool, then add a further 250ml/8fl oz/1 cup cold white wine or cider vinegar. Pour into a clean jar, cover tightly and leave for 2 weeks, or less for a milder flavour. Shake the jar occasionally. Strain the vinegar into a clean bottle.

Ginger vinegar Finely chop a 5cm/2in piece of fresh root ginger and pound to a paste in a mortar, then place in a stainless steel or glass mixing bowl. Meanwhile, heat 250ml/8fl oz/1 cup rice vinegar until just boiling and pour it over the ginger. Leave to cool, then add a further 250ml/8 fl oz/1 cup cold rice vinegar. Pour the mixture into a clean jar, cover tightly and leave for 2 weeks, or less if you prefer a milder flavour, shaking occasionally. Strain the vinegar into a clean bottle, cover and store in a cool, dark place.

Chilli vinegar This spicy vinegar is perfect for pepping up soups and sauces or to deglaze a pan after cooking venison or beef steaks. Place 25g/1oz (about 8) dried chillies in a preserving jar. Heat 600ml/1 pint/2½ cups red wine or sherry vinegar until just boiling, then pour over the dried chillies. Leave the mixture to cool, then cover tightly and leave to infuse for 2 weeks, shaking the jar occasionally. Taste for flavour and strain the flavoured vinegar into a clean bottle when sufficiently strong. (If necessary, leave the mixture to infuse for a further week or so until the desired flavour is achieved.) Make sure that the bottle is full to the top. Cover and store in a cool, dark place.

Chilli Ho Ho Use this colonial-style vinegar to liven up dull stews. Fill a clean bottle with small red chillies and top up with sherry vinegar. Cover the bottle and leave to infuse for about 2 weeks, shaking occasionally. This vinegar can be very spicy so use only a few drops at a time. As you use the vinegar, top up with more sherry vinegar to keep the ho ho going.

Left: (From left to right) Garlic-, chilli- and ginger-flavoured vinegars can add extra flavour to dressings and sauces.

OILS

There is a wide variety of cooking oils and they are produced from a number of different sources: from cereals such as corn; from fruits such as olives; from nuts such as walnuts, almonds and hazelnuts; and from seeds, including rape seed, safflower and sunflower. They can be extracted by simple mechanical means, such as pressing or crushing, or by further processing, usually involving heat. Virgin oils, which are obtained from the first cold pressing of olives, nuts and seeds, are sold unrefined, and have a characteristic flavour. They are the most expensive.

OLIVE OIL

Indisputably the king of oils, olive oil varies in flavour and colour, depending on how it is made and where it comes from. Climate, soil, harvesting and pressing all influence the end result – generally the hotter the climate, the more robust the oil. Thus oils from southern Italy, Greece and Spain have a stronger flavour and a darker colour than those from the rest of Italy and France. Olive oil is rich in monounsaturated fat, which has been found to reduce blood cholesterol levels, thereby reducing the risk of heart disease. There are several different grades of olive oil to choose from.

Extra virgin olive oil
This premium olive oil has a superior flavour. It comes from the first cold pressing of the olives and has a very low acidity – less than one per cent. Extra virgin olive oil is not usually used for cooking by itself, as heat impairs its wonderful flavour. However, it can be used with equal quantities of sunflower or another bland-flavoured oil to give the cheaper oil a better flavour. Extra virgin olive oil comes into its own when used in salad dressings, either by itself or combined with lighter oils. It can also be drizzled over bread as a tasty and healthy alternative to butter.

Virgin olive oil Also a pure first-pressed oil, this has a slightly higher level of acidity than extra virgin olive oil and can be used in much the same way. With the exception of deep-frying, it is an ideal all-purpose oil and, although it is quite expensive, it is worth using on its own if you are cooking Mediterranean dishes, as it gives them their authentic flavour.

Pure olive oil Refined and blended to remove impurities, this type of olive oil has a much lighter flavour than virgin or extra virgin olive oil and is suitable for all types of cooking. However, the flavour does not really justify the expense.

CORN OIL

One of the most economical and widely used vegetable oils, corn or maize oil has a deep golden colour and a fairly strong taste. It is suitable for cooking and frying, but should not be used for salad dressings owing to its rather overwhelming and powerful flavour.

SUNFLOWER OIL

This is perhaps the best all-purpose oil. Sunflower oil is very light and almost tasteless. It is very versatile and can be used for frying and in other types of cooking, or to make salad dressings, when it can be

Left: Extra virgin olive oil can be used as a sauce on its own, stirred into pasta with chopped garlic and black pepper, or drizzled over steamed vegetables.

Below: (Left) Sunflower oil has a very mild flavour.

Above: (Right) Safflower oil is best used for cooking strongly flavoured ingredients and is ideal for cooking spicy foods.

combined with a stronger flavoured oil such as olive oil or walnut oil. It is a good choice – on its own or combined with virgin olive oil – for making mayonnaise, when a stronger flavoured oil might be overpowering. Sunflower oil is extracted from the seeds of the sunflower. It is high in polyunsaturated fat and low in unhealthy saturated fats.

SAFFLOWER OIL

This is a light, all-purpose oil, which comes from the seeds of the safflower. It can be used in place of sunflower and groundnut (peanut) oils, but is a little thicker and has a slightly stronger flavour so is best used with more strongly flavoured ingredients. It is suitable for deep-frying. Safflower oil contains more polyunsaturated fat than any other oil and is low in saturated fat.

GROUNDNUT/PEANUT OIL

This relatively tasteless oil is useful for frying, cooking and dressing salads. Because it is very stable it can be heated to the high temperatures required for deep- and stir-frying and also the same batch of oil can be safely used more than once. Chinese peanut oil is darker in colour than groundnut oil and has a more distinctive nutty flavour. It is good in Asian salads and stir-fries.

Groundnut oil is also widely used in the canning industry and in the manufacture of various types of margarine. Anyone with an allergy to peanuts should avoid using the oil.

SOYA OIL

This neutral-flavoured, all-purpose oil is extracted from soya beans. It is useful for frying because it has a high smoking point, and remains stable at high temperatures. It is also widely used in

Below: Soya oil is probably one of the most widely used oils in the world and is thought to be healthier than some other oils.

the manufacture of margarines. Soya oil is rich in both polyunsaturated and monounsaturated fats and low in saturates, so it is thought to be useful in the prevention of heart disease. Try to find a brand that is not made from genetically modified soya beans.

RAPE SEED/CANOLA OIL

This bland-tasting, all-purpose oil can be used for frying, cooking and for salad dressings. It contains a higher percentage of monounsaturated fat than any other oil, apart from olive oil.

GRAPESEED OIL

This is a delicate, mild-flavoured oil, which does not impose on other ingredients. Grapeseed oil is pressed from the grape seeds left over from the wine-making process. It is good in cooking and for frying, and can be used to make salad dressings, especially when combined with a stronger flavoured oil such as walnut oil or extra virgin olive oil. Grapeseed oil is particularly good for marinating meat.

Right: Rape seed oil is good for most cooking purposes.

Above: Palm oil is very high in saturated fats so should be used sparingly.

VEGETABLE OIL

This blend of various oils, including coconut oil, rape seed, cottonseed and palm oil is usually very cheap. It is highly refined and commonly a deep golden colour. It is a good choice for frying, as it has a high smoke point, but is not a good choice for dressings, as it lacks any discernible character or flavour and has a rather greasy texture.

PALM OIL

A bright orange waxy oil from the oil palm, this is one of the main cooking fats in Central and South America, the Caribbean and West Africa. Elsewhere, it is usually heavily refined, losing its colour, and is used in the manufacture of vegetable fats and oils. If you find unrefined palm oil, use it in highly coloured and spiced dishes, as it has a nutty flavour. It is high in saturated fats.

COCONUT OIL

Solid at room temperature, coconut oil is white and buttery in texture. It has a distinctive coconut flavour and is widely used in South-east Asia and India. It is high in saturated fats.

Making Flavoured Oils

Flavoured oil can be used both for cooking or drizzling over finished dishes. They can be bought ready-made but are easy to make yourself. There are no hard-and-fast rules about the type of oil or the spices to use, but it is best if you choose flavours that complement each other such as olive oil and garlic.

Ginger, garlic and shallot oil This is ideal for fish, shellfish and chicken. To flavour 475ml/16fl oz/2 cups oil, peel and bruise a 6cm/2½in piece of fresh root ginger and place it in a clean bottle with the oil, 2 peeled garlic cloves and 3 small, peeled shallots. Cover tightly and leave to stand in a cool place for 2 weeks. Strain into a clean bottle.

Below: (From left to right) Ginger oil, garlic and spice oil, lemon grass oil, and spiced nut oil are all good for adding extra flavour to dishes.

Garlic and spice aromatic oil To flavour 600ml/1 pint/2½ cups extra virgin olive oil, peel and halve a large garlic clove, then place in a clean bottle with the oil, 3 fresh red chillies, 5ml/1 tsp coriander seeds, 3 allspice berries, 6 black peppercorns, 4 juniper berries and 2 bay leaves. Cover tightly and leave to stand in a cool place for 2 weeks.

Cinnamon and coriander spiced nut oil To flavour 600ml/1 pint/2½ cups walnut or hazelnut oil, place 1 cinnamon stick in a clean bottle with the oil and 10ml/2 tsp coriander seeds. Cover tightly and leave in a cool place for about 2 weeks. Strain into a clean bottle.

Cinnamon and citrus oil Use to make dressings and mayonnaise. To flavour 600ml/1 pint/2½ cups walnut or hazelnut oil, place 1 cinnamon stick in a clean bottle with the oil and a piece of orange or lemon rind. Cover tightly and leave in a cool place for 2 weeks. Strain into a clean bottle.

Chilli oil Use as a dipping sauce or drizzle over South-east Asian soups. Do not use for cooking. Place about 20 seeded and chopped dried chillies in a heatproof container. Heat 250ml/8fl oz/1 cup groundnut (peanut) or corn oil in a small pan until the oil just reaches smoking point. Remove the pan from the heat and set aside for 5 minutes to cool. Pour the oil into the container and leave for 1–2 hours. Strain into a clean bottle, and store in a cool, dark place or in the refrigerator.

Lemon grass and lime leaf oil Almost fill a clean bottle with groundnut oil. Trim and discard the root end from a lemon grass stalk. Lightly bruise the bulbous end and cut the stem into lengths to fit the bottle. Tear 3–4 lime leaves into pieces, and put the lemon grass and lime leaves into the bottle. Cover tightly and leave in a cool, dark place for 2 weeks, or longer if the flavour is not sufficiently pronounced.

SPECIALITY OILS

These are the expensive oils with very distinctive flavours. They should always be used sparingly.

ALMOND OIL

This pale, delicate oil is mainly used in confectionery and desserts. It has the subtle sweet flavour of almonds, but not enough to give an almond flavour to cakes and biscuits (cookies). Almond oil is rich in monounsaturated fat as well as vitamins A and E. It is reputed to be very good for the skin and is often used as a massage oil.

WALNUT OIL

This is an intensely flavoured oil that is delicious in salad dressings and marinades, but shouldn't be used for frying, as heat diminishes its rich taste. Instead, drizzle a little over roasted or steamed vegetables, or use to make a simple sauce for pasta. Walnut oil plays a significant role in the regional cooking of some parts of France such as the Périgord. It can be used in small quantities in place of some of the fat or oil in a recipe, to add flavour to cakes and biscuits (cookies), especially those that contain walnuts. Walnut oil does not keep for long; after opening, store in a cool dark place to prevent it from becoming rancid. It can be stored in the refrigerator, although this may cause the oil to solidify. If this happens, remove from the refrigerator and leave at room temperature for a few hours until ready to use.

SESAME OIL

There are two types of sesame oil – the pale and light version that is pressed from untoasted seeds, and the rich, dark toasted oil that is used in Asian cuisines. The lighter oil, popular in India and the Middle East, has a mild flavour and a high

Right: (From left to right) Walnut, sesame and hazelnut oils are good for dressings.

smoking point and is useful for cooking. Dark sesame oil, which has a wonderfully nutty aroma and taste, is useful for flavouring marinades and stir-fries. It has a much stronger taste than either walnut oil or olive oil and is too overpowering to use in large quantities. However, it can be mixed with milder oils such as soya or groundnut (peanut). Heating helps to intensify the aroma, but it should never be heated for too long or it will burn.

HAZELNUT OIL

This fine, fragrant oil is rich brown in colour and has a delicious roasted hazelnut flavour. It is quite expensive to buy but because it has such a strong flavour, only a little is needed. It is good combined with less strongly flavoured oils, for salad dressings and sauces, and can also be used to add a nutty flavour to teabreads, cakes, biscuits (cookies) and pastry.

MUSTARD SEED OIL

This delicious oil is widely used in Indian cooking, where it is often used instead of ghee. Mustard seed oil has a distinctive aroma and flavour when cold but this is driven off when it is heated.

WHEAT GERM OIL

Often used as a health supplement owing to the significant amounts of vitamin E present in wheat germ, this oil adds a pleasant nuttiness to salad dressings and is particularly delicious stirred into pasta.

AVOCADO OIL

Rich in vitamin E and monounsaturated fat and containing no cholesterol, this is fast becoming the most fashionable oil. Its delicate, yet distinctive flavour makes it ideal for salad dressings and for crostini or bruschetta. Some producers combine avocado oil with extra virgin olive oil.

POPPY SEED OIL

Also known as *huile blanche*, this is a subtle and flavoursome oil that is good in salad dressings and for serving with crudités. Always buy an unrefined version, as it has the finest flavour.

PUMPKIN SEED OIL

The delicate, yet distinctive flavour of this oil is perfect for salad dressings and for dishes made with squash and courgettes (zucchini). However, it may be too strong for some tastes.

TEA, COFFEE, CHOCOLATE AND SWEETENERS

Tea, coffee and chocolate can be enjoyed as hot or cold

beverages or as flavourings in sweet, and sometimes savoury,

dishes. There are many different varieties, all with their own

unique character and flavour. Sweeteners too come in many

different forms from dry sugar to sticky syrups. Some simply

add sweetness or bring out the flavour of other ingredients,

while others such as honey can be used to add flavour too.

TEA

Native to south-west China, tea has been drunk by the Chinese for many centuries. It was introduced to Europe in the early seventeenth century, brought from China by Dutch merchants. By the middle of the seventeenth century tea was well established in both France and Britain, firstly as a medicinal brew, but later ceremonies for the drinking of tea became a popular pastime amongst the well-to-do, with fine cups and saucers, teapots and tea caddies adding to the ritual.

Teas are named after their leaf size, their type and the place of origin, and many are blended, a practice that began centuries ago, when people realized that blending gave a more balanced brew, the characteristics of different teas complementing and enhancing each other.

BLACK TEAS

These are fully fermented teas, and all English teas are made using various blends of black teas. Black teas come mostly from India, Sri Lanka and Africa. Unlike green teas, where the leaves are dried immediately after picking, the plucked leaves for black teas are first allowed to wilt on drying racks, then bruised by rolling, and lastly fermented in the open air. This fermentation/oxidation process causes the leaves to turn red-brown and acquire the flavour, strength and body characteristic of black teas. The teas are then graded by the size of their leaf: whole and large leaf tea is lighter and more fragrant, while broken leaf tea is made up of smaller and broken leaves and produces a darker, stronger brew.

Darjeeling These teas are grown on the foothills of the Himalayas in northern India and are considered the finest of teas, enjoyed for their superior flavour. They are also the most expensive.

Ceylon These Sri Lankan teas are another superior product, especially those teas that grow above 1,800m/6,000ft. Many of the planters forced out of Sri Lanka for political reasons went to Africa and similar high-quality teas are beginning to be produced in this area of the world as well.

Keemum This is a China tea from the Huangshan Mountains in southern Anhwei province. Regarded as one of the best black teas, it is full-bodied and very aromatic.

Assam In the north-east of India, between Darjeeling and Kohima, lies Assam – an extremely important tea-producing area. The teas are full-bodied, providing strength to many blends.

Orange Pekoe The word *pekoe* once meant white haired in Chinese, indicating that the leaves of this tea were sometimes tipped with white. Orange blossoms were once added for extra fragrance; however, this practice was discontinued centuries ago. Orange Pekoe tea has long leaves, which are occasionally tipped with yellow or white, and it has small leaf buds mixed in with the leaves.

Souchong This large-leafed tea from China includes lapsang souchong, which is smoke-cured and has a distinctive, almost tarry flavour.

Blended Teas

Most of the popular teas sold in Britain and the United States are made not of just one leaf, but are a blend of several different teas. This is done with a view to reducing deficiencies in a single tea and producing a balanced brew with good body, aroma and flavour. Cost, of course, is inevitably a factor as well. Expert blenders, while aiming to achieve the best possible brew, need to be constantly aware of the fluctuating price of individual teas, an exact science in these days of ever-changing political regimes, not to mention floods and droughts, and so on.

There are more than 3,000 different blends of tea and if you visit a specialist store, you should have the opportunity to sample some of the better known or more highly prized ones. Failing that, sample some of the teas available in the supermarket, bearing in mind whether you prefer a full-bodied cup of tea, or a lighter, more fragrant kind.

Earl Grey This is a blend of Indian and Chinese tea, scented with oil of bergamot, which gives the tea its characteristic citrus flavour. It takes its name from the second Earl Grey, who asked his grocer to make up the blend according to his own formula. The name for the tea was never registered, however, and consequently the blend was copied by other tea companies. It is one of the earliest types of blended teas.

English Breakfast This is one of the most popular of all teas, producing a full-bodied, well-flavoured brew. It is normally made up of a blend of Indian and Ceylon teas.

Irish Breakfast This is a blend of good quality Ceylon and Assam teas.

Uva Uva is a blended Ceylon tea.

Above: Darjeeling is considered to be one of the finest teas available.

Left: Lapsang souchong tea has a wonderful smoky flavour.

Brewing Black Tea

The quality of the water that is used will affect the flavour of the tea. Most people use ordinary tap (faucet) water, but chlorination or the presence of lime or iron may spoil the brew. In that case, use purified water or a light mineral water. Do not use water that has previously been boiled.

As the water comes to the boil, rinse the teapot with it to warm, then add the tea. The quantity required will depend on the type of tea – the better it is, the less will be required. The rule of thumb is 5ml/1 tsp per person, plus 5ml/1 tsp for the pot. Take the teapot to the kettle, not the other way round, and pour the freshly boiled water over the leaves. Leave the tea to steep for 3–5 minutes, then stir before pouring into cups, through a strainer.

The flavour of tea does not improve or strengthen if the leaves are left to steep for any longer than the time recommended. In fact, it becomes darker and tastes bitter as the tannins begin to spread. A good way of avoiding this is to use tea bags or an infusion ball, which can be removed once the tea has brewed.

The tea can be drunk on its own or with the addition of a slice of lemon or a little cold milk. Never use hot milk. It is a matter of personal taste whether you add the milk to the cup before or after the tea. If liked, tea may be sweetened with a little sugar or honey.

GREEN TEAS

Unlike black teas, where the leaves are fermented, green teas are dried immediately after picking, preventing the oxidation that causes the leaves to blacken and the flavour to develop. The brew has a fresher, more astringent taste, with none of the body or depth of flavour of black teas. Green teas should never be served with milk, being a refreshing beverage by themselves, or brewed with mint or other herbs.

Green teas are mostly produced in China and Japan where they are very popular. They are also widely drunk in Muslim countries, where fermented tea is forbidden. They are available in Britain and the United States, but are nowhere near so popular as black teas, and most people have become familiar with them from drinking tea in Chinese and Japanese restaurants.

Gunpowder Also known as Chao Chen, this is one of the best known Chinese green teas. The leaves are tightly rolled into balls and the tea, once brewed, is pale with a sharp but pleasant flavour.

Young Hyson This, together with Hyson, is another Chinese green tea, with an exceptionally good flavour.

Moyunes A highly popular green tea in China, Moyunes is liked for its rich flavour and clarity.

Gyokuro Meaning jewel dew, this Japanese tea is made from fresh young leaves. It is extremely fragrant and mellow and is brewed with warm, rather than boiling water.

Bancha Yellowish green in colour, this Japanese tea is a coarse everyday brew, often served with meals. There are many grades of bancha and the lower the grade, the more stems and twigs are included.

Left: Gyokuro is considered to be the best quality green tea.

Making Gyokuro Tea

This method will provide enough tea for four people.

1 Fill a small teapot with freshly boiled water, then use this water to fill four small teacups or bowls and leave to cool for about 5 minutes, or until it is 50–60°C/122–140°F.

2 Empty the teapot and add 20ml/ 4 tsp gyokuro. Pour the warm water in the cups back into the pot and let it brew for 2 minutes.

3 Shake the pot gently, half-fill the cups, then top them up in turn so that the infusion of the tea is evenly distributed. For second cups, pour slightly hotter water into the pot.

Matcha This powdered tea is used mainly for the Japanese tea ceremony. It is made from steamed leaves that are dried flat before being made into a powder that retains the vivid light green colour and fragrant aroma. The tea is made by whisking the powder in hot water in individual cups or tea bowls with a whisk, rather than by brewing in a pot. Only a tiny amount, 5–10ml/1–2 tsp per 120ml/4fl oz/½ cup water per person, is used. To fully appreciate its flavour, eat something sweet before drinking the tea.

Making Matcha Tea

If you don't have a bamboo whisk, use a small fork instead.

1 Warm a large cup (a rice bowl is ideal) with hot water. Soak the tip of a bamboo whisk in the hot water. Empty the cup.

2 Put 5–10ml/1–2 tsp matcha, to taste, in the cup and add about 120ml/4fl oz/½ cup hot water.

3 Using the bamboo whisk, first stir, then whisk vigorously until frothy and the powder dissolves.

Above:
Oolong teas have a delicate, fragrant flavour.

OOLONG TEAS

This type of tea consists of partially fermented leaves, and they are thus halfway between green and black teas in character. The large leafed oolong teas are mostly produced in China and Taiwan. Among the best-known oolongs are the Formosa oolongs from Taiwan, with their deep amber colour and delicious fruity flavour, and Pouchong, which is an oolong mixed with jasmine, gardenia and other scented flowers, producing a highly fragrant, aromatic tea with a lovely flavour.

Above:
Organic teas are grown without the use of potentially harmful chemicals.

ORGANIC TEAS

These are becoming increasingly popular. Organic teas are grown with respect for the land and the people who tend it. The teas are generally fairly traded, with communities far away from the end beverage gaining real benefits whenever a packet is sold. Pesticide residues are at issue here. Although these are not high in agrochemically grown teas, the crop is generally sprayed intensively throughout its growth. This pollutes the land and poses a serious health threat to the workers. Organic teas are full of flavour, and are readily available in lots of different varieties, including loose leaves and tea bags containing either single estate varieties or blends. Flavoured or spiced teas are also on sale. All these products contain vitamins and minerals as well as powerful antioxidants that protect the heart and help to prevent cancer. When you buy organic, even the tea bags are better for the environment, because unlike non-organic tea bags, they have to be chlorine-free.

Above: Herbal tisanes are made from the leaves, seeds and flowers of herbs.

TISANES AND AROMATIC TEAS

There are numerous tisanes and spiced or aromatic teas. As well as producing a fragrant and/or fruity beverage, they have the virtue of being free of caffeine or tannin. Many also are said to have medicinal properties. Once of rather limited popularity, contemporary interest in healthy eating means that these teas are much more mainstream, and are now available in almost all supermarkets, although the more specialist teas are likely to be found only in health-food stores.

FRUIT TEAS

These are made from a blend of fruit flavours such as rosehip, strawberry, orange, raspberry and lemon along with fruit pieces and sometimes herbs or real tea. It is a good idea to check the packaging to make sure the tea is naturally, rather than artificially, flavoured. Fruit teas, providing they don't contain real tea, make refreshing caffeine-free drinks.

HERBAL TISANES

Although herbal tisanes are of little nutritional value, herbalists have prescribed them for centuries for a multitude of ailments and diseases. These teas are a simple way of taking medicinal herbs. They do, however, vary in strength and effectiveness. Store-bought teas are generally mild in their medicinal properties, but are good, healthy, caffeine-free drinks. Even so, some varieties are not recommended for young children and pregnant women, so check the instructions on the packaging.

Peppermint tea This tea has a distinctly minty flavour and is highly recommended as a digestive to be drunk after a meal. It is effective in settling other stomach problems and for treating colds. It is also said to act as a tonic and stimulant.

Below: Naturally flavoured fruit teas are caffeine-free and contain few calories.

Camomile tea This tea is thought to soothe and calm the nerves, relieve stress and induce sleep. It is also said to relieve the symptoms of migraine.

Raspberry leaf tea With its pleasant fruity flavour, raspberry leaf tea is said to reduce labour pains and to relieve the symptoms of premenstrual syndrome and menstrual cramps.

Rosehip tea This is a sweet tea and is high in vitamin C. It may help to ward off colds and other infections.

Lemon balm This pleasantly flavoured tea is said to be good for giddiness.

Lemon verbena tea This tea has a pleasant citrus flavour and is believed to have a calming effect.

Dandelion tea Like lemon verbena tea, dandelion tea has a diuretic effect.

COFFEE

The coffee plant is thought to be native to Ethiopia, where it is still possible to find it growing wild. It was first cultivated on a large scale in the fifteenth and sixteenth centuries in Yemen. Shortly after that, the coffee beans were brought to Europe, where coffee houses were opened in London, Paris and Venice. As consumption increased, so various imperial powers were prompted to cultivate the bean in their colonies such as the Dutch colonists in Indonesia. In the early eighteenth century, the French succeeded in establishing coffee plants in their colony of Martinique in the Caribbean, from which the great plantations of Latin America sprung.

There are two main types of coffee bean: arabica is the original coffee, and is considered the superior bean. Robusta coffee is more prolific, cheaper and is used for blending.

AFRICA

As the birthplace of coffee, it is fitting that the continent of Africa produces some of the world's finest coffees. In many countries, however, social, political and economic problems make the production of coffee a difficult task.

Ethiopia The earliest accounts of coffee all refer to its being a native of this region of old Abyssinia: indeed the coffee processed today by many Ethiopian villagers is simply picked off untended wild bushes. In spite of its poverty, Ethiopia is a significant producer of coffee, both in quantity and quality, and still manages to export some of the world's finest and most individual beans. Some of the best-known Ethiopian coffees are Djimmah, Ghimbi and Limu.

Ivory Coast This is usually Africa's second-largest coffee producer, thanks to its stable political regime and the fact that it receives aid from its former ruler, France. The coffee, although only of average quality, is consistent, and the reliable supply makes Ivory Coast robusta attractive to many coffee blenders throughout the world.

Congo This country of nine provinces includes a small section of Atlantic coastline, and was once the middle part of French Equatorial Africa. The equator runs across the top third of the country, and its climate is basically the non-varying heat and humidity of equatorial regions. The all-robusta crop produced

Above: Kenyan peaberry green beans

in the republic seems to be increasing. Unusually, the coffee is not graded by size, as the beans are generally uniform, but rather by number of defective beans, of which the top grade, Extra Prima, has none. The cup quality is that of an average-to-good robusta, neutral and clean.

Kenya The Kenyan peaberry, one of the world's great coffees, produces single round beans and is famed for its sharp, fruity and sometimes almost citrus flavour. It is considered so fine that it is rarely blended and should be drunk black.

Tanzania Coffee is Tanzania's number one crop, and both robusta and arabica coffee are produced. The coffee is excellent, similar to Kenyan coffee, but the acidity is less intense and the overall feel is milder and lighter.

Above: Ivory Coast robusta

Above: Congo Kivu arabica

Left: Ethiopian Sidamo

Right: Tanzanian Chagga

Left: Costa Rican Finca de Tres Rios

Below: Cuban Extra Turquino

Above: Costa Rican Tuj san Marcos de Tarrazu

CENTRAL AMERICA AND THE CARIBBEAN

Costa Rica This little Central American republic enjoys the best possible conditions for growing superb coffee: a high-altitude central plateau basking in a mild temperate climate with good moisture and cool nights. The coffee is all arabica – it is socially unacceptable even to mention the word robusta. Once considered inferior to Brazil's beans, the best of the Costa Rican coffees are now rated as exceptional, with a mild flavour and sharp acidity, and a clean and pure aftertaste. Tarrazu is considered among the best of Costa Rican coffees.

Cuba Coffee has been grown in Cuba since the mid-1700s. It is clean and flavoursome and is lower in acidity than most other Caribbean coffees due to Cuba's lack of high altitudes. Cuban coffee is, however, pleasant in the cup and is best dark-roasted.

Guatemala This coffee is considered by the experts to be one of the best coffees in the world. Unlike the Costa Rican coffees, Guatemalan coffees vary considerably from region to region. Those from the higher regions of Guatemala produce a delicious, full-flavoured coffee bean that is known for its high acidity. Others are described as medium-to-full-bodied and have a rather pleasant spiciness.

Jamaica Most famous is Jamaica's Blue Mountain coffee – an arabica coffee of outstanding quality that is thought by many to be the best coffee in the world. The coffee has an exquisite balance of nutty aroma and delicate sweet flavour, which results from the natural sugars in the bean caramelizing during roasting. Take note that producers in other countries sometimes label their coffee "Blue Mountain". You can be certain that it will be inferior to Jamaican Blue Mountain. Check the packaging to make sure, or buy from a reputable source.

Mexico Most Mexican coffees are arabica, some of which are extremely good, characterized by a light body, but with a slightly sharp, dry acidity, which sometimes has nutty or chocolate hints. These coffees tend to come from the more mountainous regions such as Veracruz and the alturas of Huatusco and Orizaba.

Nicaragua The world's largest coffee bean comes from Nicaragua, but apart from this distinction, the country is not noted for its coffee. Nevertheless, the arabica coffee has a medium-to-full body and a good aroma. Nicaraguan coffees are often sold in stores helping to promote the economies of developing countries. Nicaragua is one of the poorest countries of Central America. Coffee is the country's main export, the best coming from Matagalpa and Jinotega.

Above: Jamaican Blue Mountain green beans

Right: Jamaican Blue Mountain roasted beans

Below: Nicaraguan SHG medium roast

Above: Guatemalan Huehuetenango green beans

SOUTH AMERICA AND REST OF WORLD

Brazil Brazil is the world's largest coffee grower, producing about one-third of all the world's coffee. It grows many different grades of coffee – both arabica and robusta – some excellent, others less so. Much of Brazil's coffee is used

Above: Brazilian Santos medium

Above: Colombian Popayán Excelso

Below: Colombian Supremo medium

Below: Peruvian washed arabica

Above: Hawaiian Kona medium

Below: Venezuelan Maracaibo

Below: Indian plantation medium

Below: Australian Skybury

for the manufacture of instant coffee. Tastiest and best known of the Brazilian beans is Santos, particularly Bourbon Santos. Named after the port through which it is exported, the bean is usually medium-roasted and has a smooth, mild and mellow flavour.

Colombia A good proportion of coffees grown in Colombia are arabica, some of which are very highly regarded. Beans are medium- or dark-roasted and have a heady aroma with a good balance of flavour and acidity. The acidity of Colombian coffees seldom match that of certain Kenyans and Costa Ricans but, in general, Colombia produces a balanced cup of coffee, with good body. Best known is Medellin Excelso, which has a mildly acid, slightly nutty flavour. Coffee is also produced in the Andean foothills.

Peru Coffee is one of Peru's main crops. The coffees are mostly good quality, and some are certified as organically grown. In general, Peruvian coffees are excellent for blending, as they are mild, pleasant and sweet.

Venezuela These coffees, unlike other South American beans, tend to be delicately light, if not actually thin. They have only moderate acidity, with a rather appealing individual aroma and flavour, popular for breakfast blends.

Hawaii The most famous Hawaiian coffee is Kona, which is the name of the only variety of coffee grown in the United States. Hawaiian Kona is sometimes compared to Jamaican Blue Mountain. Both have a mild acidity, medium body and fine aroma. Some experts also detect a spicy, cinnamon-like flavour, a quality not found in Jamaican coffee at all.

Australia Some of Australia's coffee is very highly regarded, particularly Skybury, which is grown from a Blue Mountain variety of coffee.

India This country produces several well thought of coffees, including Mysore, which is considered to have good body, low acidity and a mellow sweetness. Another, Monsooned Malabar, has a unique flavour that is brought about by exposing the coffee to the humid south-west monsoon winds for six weeks in May and June. Its characterful flavour makes it an excellent choice for using in blends.

Above: Indonesian Lintong grade 2 medium roasted beans

Indonesia Indonesia produces a rich, full-bodied, low acidity coffee with a prolonged aftertaste. Sumatra, the largest island of Indonesia, produces a number of highly thought-of coffees. Blue Sumatran is strong and assertive; Gaya Mountain is sweetly spicy and exotically herbal, and Mandheling is rich and smooth and merits the title "world's heaviest coffee".

Below: Indonesian Old Brown Java

*Above:
Indonesian Java Jampit green beans*

Below: Indonesian Mandheling grade 2 green beans

The Coffee Roasts

The colour and flavour of coffee depends partly on the length of time the beans are roasted.

Unroasted Before roasting the seeds of the coffee plant are normally pale, varying from very pale, through yellow to green. They can be round or oval in shape. Some pods contain only one seed, which is known as a peaberry bean owing to its shape, which is similar to a pea.

Light roasted This type of roast is suitable for mild coffees with a delicate aroma and flavour. The coffee beans are pale to medium brown in colour. It is best for breakfast coffee.

Medium roast This is best for coffees with a well-defined character. The flavour and aroma are stronger, yet the coffee is still suitable for drinking black or with milk for breakfast, as well as for a mid-morning pick-me-up and after meals.

Dark roast A dark roast or full roast gives a full-bodied coffee with a fairly strong aroma and a slightly bitter flavour. The beans are dark and glossy and are excellent for after-dinner coffee.

High roast This is sometimes called a Continental roast, giving a strong, bitter coffee. The beans are almost black and glossy, looking almost as if they are coated with oil.

Espresso Intensely black glossy beans produce a dark roasted coffee, with a full-bodied, bitter flavour. The beans are used for Italian espresso and Austrian moka coffee.

Below: Light roasted beans have a mild flavour and provide a good, all-purpose, "daytime" coffee that can be drunk from breakfast onwards.

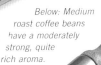

Below: Medium roast coffee beans have a moderately strong, quite rich aroma.

Left: Dark roast beans make perfect after-dinner coffee – full bodied, strongly flavoured and slightly bitter.

The Coffee Grinds

Different coffee-makers require different grinds of coffee – from coarse to very fine. A truly successful cup of coffee depends on the correct grind being used.

Medium grind This is suitable for fairly light coffees made in a cafetière (press pot) or using the Neapolitan flip machines.

Omni grind This comes between fine or filter grind and medium grind. It is supposed to work equally well for both, but, in reality, is more medium than fine, and provided that you know the requirements of your particular coffee maker, it is better to go with the precise grind. Omni grind works quite well with Neapolitan flip machines and other equipment that calls for a medium-fine grind.

Fine (filter) Use this grind for the glass balloon/vacuum method, and for filter or drip methods of making coffee. It produces a stronger coffee with a good, full-bodied flavour.

Espresso (very fine grind) This is a very fine grind of coffee. Use for espresso machines.

Turkish This is sometimes called pulverized or powdered coffee (not to be confused with instant coffee), and makes an exceptionally strong cup of coffee. The flavour of the beans is intensified by the grinding process.

Below: Omni grind is not quite as all-purpose as its name suggests. However, it can be used for any coffee maker that requires a medium-fine grind.

Left: Medium grind is ideal for cafetières (press pots), Neapolitan flip machines and the similar, but smaller, French drip pots.

Left: Fine (filter) grind is designed for filter methods of coffee making and for the balloon/vacuum method, producing a richly flavoured, clear coffee with a full body.

Left: Espresso grind is designed for making coffee with the appropriate Italian machine to produce a potent, strong-tasting brew that is always drunk in very small quantities.

Right: Turkish grind is very fine and used for making coffee in an ibrik – a small, long-handled copper pan that narrows towards the top. It is popular in Turkey and Greece.

Making Coffee

Correct coffee brewing depends on a balance of several factors, and each coffee will react differently to exactly the same balance of factors.

Degree of grind of the ground coffee The finer the grind, the greater the surface area exposed to the water and the faster the extraction of soluble solids. Finely ground coffee therefore needs faster brewing than coarser grinds.

Ratio of coffee to water No matter how good the quality of the coffee grounds, the amount of water used is also very important. Most experts agree that a cup of coffee tastes best when the liquid consists of 98.4–98.7 per cent water and 1.3–1.6 per cent soluble solids. For European tastes the ideal proportion of coffee to water is 50–75g/2–3oz per 1 litre/33fl oz/4 cups of water. Much of North America drinks a weaker cup.

Condition of the water The condition and taste of water affects the final brew. For the best results, experts recommend slightly hard water.

Water temperature Water of any temperature will extract coffee, but hot water extracts faster than cold. Never pour boiling water over coffee as it brings out a harsh flavour. The optimum temperature for coffee preparation is between 92°C/197°F and 96°C/205°F. When coffee is intentionally boiled, as with Turkish brewing, sweetening offsets any bitterness.

Contact time between the coffee and the water When ground coffee and water are combined, a certain amount of time is needed for the water to saturate the coffee grounds and extract the various soluble solids, some of which take longer than others to pass into the water. For the first few minutes of the brewing cycle, the blend of the flavour compounds in the liquid is changing continuously. Finer grinds require a shorter brewing time.

OTHER COFFEE PRODUCTS

Instant coffee Sold in a jar, instant coffee is made by brewing coffee beans into a concentrate. For coffee granules, the concentrate is then freeze-dried and processed to make dry, crisp particles, and the best of this type uses arabica coffee. Coffee powder is generally cheaper than granules and is mostly made from robusta beans. The concentrate is dried to a fine powder. Better powders are heated further to make a granular type of powder.

Decaffeinated coffee Although coffee lovers and experts alike are still convinced that decaffeination destroys the taste of coffee, many would find it difficult to differentiate between a regular coffee and a decaffeinated one. There are some fabulous decaffeinated coffees available, particularly from specialist shops. Try to choose brands that have removed the caffeine without the use of chemical solvents.

Left and right: Kahlua and Tia Maria are two of the most popular coffee liqueurs.

Below: Chilled canned coffee is a Japanese creation.

Coffee bags Popular in the late 1980s, these were intended to provide convenience with flavour. However, they tended to take a long time to brew, and the resulting coffee was weak, pale and lacked body.

Coffee essence This is convenient for flavouring cakes, desserts and ice creams. Make sure you buy pure coffee essence and not chicory and coffee essence.

Coffee liqueurs Tia Maria is the most famous coffee liqueur, made using Jamaican rum liqueur with coffee extracts and spices. Kahlúa is a Mexican coffee liqueur with an altogether different flavour, suitable for many Italian-style desserts.

Canned coffee Ready-to-drink canned coffee was launched by the Japanese in 1969. This was partly owing to the popularity of vending machines in Japan. Uptake in Europe and the United States has been slow, but it is popular throughout Asia, where cold drinks are perhaps more welcome.

CHOCOLATE

Chocolate is one of our most luxurious and indulgent foods. The cacao or cocoa bean is native to South America and the plant was cultivated by the Aztecs for hundreds, perhaps even thousands, of years before being discovered by European explorers. By the seventeenth century, drinking chocolate had spread across Europe and was particularly popular among royal and aristocratic families.

Only in the nineteenth century was the cocoa bean put to use to make confectionery. Chocolate is made by pulverizing and then mixing the cocoa bean with sugar and cocoa butter, to make a paste. This is then further treated by conching, a process that agitates the liquid chocolate over a period that may be as long as seven days. It is this process that allows the flavour of chocolate to develop and mellow. As a rule, the longer the conching, the better and smoother the chocolate. Once this stage has been completed, the chocolate is tempered before being moulded into the bars we know and love. The tempering process, which involves gently heating and cooling the chocolate, helps to distribute the cocoa fat evenly and produces a glossy finish.

COCOA PRODUCTS

There are a great number of cocoa products available, which can vary dramatically in appearance, flavour, texture and quality.

Unsweetened cocoa This fine, dark brown powder is made from the pure cocoa mass after most of the cocoa butter has been extracted. The mass is roasted, then ground to make a powder. It is probably the most economical way of giving steamed desserts and baked goods a rich chocolate flavour.

Above: Plain, dark chocolate has an intense flavour, making it ideal for flavouring desserts and cakes.

Plain dark/Bittersweet chocolate
Often called luxury, bitter or Continental chocolate, this has a high percentage of cocoa solids – around 75 per cent – with little added sugar. In unsweetened chocolate, which is found only in specialist shops, cocoa solids are as high as 98 per cent.

Above: Organic chocolate is a little more expensive than other types, but is a quality product, as well as being produced without the use of pesticides.

Left: Couverture, with its high percentage of cocoa butter and glossy finish, is the best choice for decorative use and handmade chocolates.

Below: Plain chocolate is the most popular choice for cooking, as it gives a good flavour and is easy to handle.

Left: Cocoa powder is widely used for flavouring cakes, cookies and hot, chocolatey drinks. Because it is unsweetened, it usually requires the addition of sugar.

Right: Mild-tasting white chocolate contains cocoa butter, but does not contain any cocoa solids.

Right: Milk chocolate is popular for sweet snacks, but is not so suitable for melting and cooking.

Below: Mexican Ibarra chocolate comes in a distinctive yellow hexagonal box.

Couverture This fine quality, pure chocolate with a high percentage of cocoa butter, which gives it a high gloss, is the professional's choice. It is suitable for decorative use and for making hand-made chocolates. It must generally be tempered before using in a recipe.

Plain/semisweet chocolate This is the most widely available chocolate for use in cooking. It contains between 30 and 70 per cent cocoa solids, so check the label before you buy. The higher the cocoa solids, the better the flavour.

Milk chocolate To some *aficionados*, this is not really considered chocolate, but increasingly there are good brands around, even though they may be difficult to find. A good brand will have a cocoa solid content of 40 per cent, but most mass-produced milk chocolate contains only 20 per cent. Mass-produced milk chocolate usually has a very high sugar content, often up to 50 per cent. It can also contain up to 5 per cent vegetable fat, used as a substitute for expensive cocoa butter, and artificial flavouring. Although this is the most popular eating chocolate, it is not so suitable for melting and cooking.

White chocolate

This type of chocolate is basically cocoa butter without any cocoa solids, but with the addition of sugar, flavouring and milk. White chocolate does not have the same depth of flavour as plain (semisweet) chocolate. It is mainly sold for its novelty value or to provide an attractive colour contrast in chocolates and chocolate desserts. The best quality brands tend to be French and Swiss. British brands usually contain vegetable oil instead of cocoa butter, as well as some synthetic flavourings. White chocolate must be melted with care – preferably over boiling water – as it does not withstand heat so well as plain chocolate.

Making Mexican Chocolate
If you cannot buy Mexican chocolate, you can still make an acceptable substitute using dark bitter chocolate with a minimum of 70 per cent cocoa solids.

1 Break about 115g/4oz dark chocolate into small pieces and put into a food processor. Add 25g/1oz/ ¼ cup ground almonds and 10ml/ 2 tsp ground cinnamon.

2 Process the ingredients to a fine powder, then tip into an airtight container and store in the refrigerator for up to 2 weeks.

Above: Drinking chocolate powder has a mild, sweet taste, popular with children and useful for baking.

Right: Chocolate-flavoured cake covering is easy to use and convenient, but the flavour tends to be rather poor.

Mexican chocolate This is made using dark and bitter chocolate mixed with sugar, ground nuts and cinnamon, and pressed into discs. The chocolate has a grainy quality and is crumbly when broken. It comes in packs, each containing five or six discs that are individually wrapped in waxed paper. Its main use is in beverages. Mexicans are very partial to *champurrada*, a chocolate corn drink, and classic Mexican hot chocolate, which is served with churros for dunking.

Below: Popular for baking, chocolate chips are available in plain (semisweet), milk and white flavours.

Chocolate powder This sweetened powder is mainly used for making drinks but can also be used for baking. Chocolate powder has a lower percentage of cocoa solids than pure (unsweetened) cocoa and has a much milder, sweeter taste. It dissolves easily in liquids.

Chocolate-flavoured cake covering This is a blend of sugar, vegetable oil, cocoa and flavourings. The flavour is poor, but the high fat content makes it suitable for making chocolate curls – to improve the flavour, add some plain chocolate to the cake covering.

Chocolate chips These are small pieces of chocolate of uniform size. They contain fewer cocoa solids than ordinary chocolate and are available in plain dark, milk and white flavours. They melt readily and are widely used in baking, for example in chocolate chip cookies.

Storing Chocolate

Chocolate can be stored successfully for up to a year if the conditions are favourable. This means a dry place with a temperature of around 20°C/68°F. At higher temperatures, the chocolate may develop white streaks as the fat comes to the surface. Although this will not spoil the flavour, it will mar the appearance of the chocolate, making it unsuitable for use as a decoration. When storing chocolate, place inside an airtight container, away from strong smelling foods. Check the best before dates on the wrapper.

Carob and Carob Powder

This is a caffeine-free alternative to chocolate which is made from the aromatic, fleshy bean pod of a Mediterranean tree. Carob powder looks and tastes fairly similar to (unsweetened) cocoa powder and can be used to replace it in hot drinks, confectionery and baked goods. It is naturally sweeter and lower in fat than cocoa, as well as being more nutritious, providing iron, calcium, vitamin B6, riboflavin and potassium.

Right: Carob and carob powder are a popular chocolate alternative.

Melting Chocolate

If chocolate is being melted on its own, all the equipment must be completely dry. Water may cause the chocolate to thicken and become a stiff paste. For this reason, do not cover chocolate either during or after melting it, as condensation could form. If chocolate does thicken, add a little pure white vegetable fat (not butter or margarine) and mix well. If this does not work, then start again. Do not discard the thickened chocolate; melt it with cream to make a sauce for ice cream or desserts.

With or without liquid, chocolate should be melted very slowly. It is easily burned or scorched, which will cause the chocolate to develop a bad flavour. Dark chocolate should not be heated above 50°C/120°F. Milk and white chocolate should not be heated above 45°C/110°F. Take care when melting white chocolate, which clogs easily when subjected to heat.

Melting Chocolate in the Microwave

When melting chocolate in the microwave, check it at frequent intervals during the cooking time. These times are for a 650–700W oven and are approximate, as microwave ovens vary from model to model.

1 Place about 115g/4oz chopped or broken dark (bittersweet) or plain (semisweet) chocolate in a bowl suitable for microwaving and cook on medium power for about 2 minutes. The same quantity of milk or white chocolate should be melted on low power for about 2 minutes.

2 Check the chocolate frequently. It will not change shape, but will start to look shiny. It should then be removed from the microwave and stirred until completely melted and smooth.

Melting Chocolate Using Direct Heat

If you need to melt chocolate with a liquid such as milk, cream or butter, it can be done in a pan over direct heat.

1 Heat the chocolate and liquid in a heavy pan over a low heat, stirring frequently, until the mixture is smooth.

2 To melt chocolate in the oven, put it in an ovenproof bowl and place in the oven for a few minutes at 110°C/225°F/Gas ¼. Remove before it is completely melted and stir until smooth.

Melting Chocolate Over Water

If you are using a bowl set over a pan of boiling water rather than a double boiler, make sure that the base of the bowl sits just above the surface of the water, and does not touch it.

1 Break or chop the chocolate into small pieces to enable it to melt quickly and evenly.

2 Put the chocolate pieces in the top of a double boiler or in a heatproof bowl set over (not in) a pan of barely simmering water.

3 Heat gently until completely melted and smooth, stirring occasionally. Remove the chocolate from the heat and stir again.

SWEETENERS

Although it is generally acknowledged that, in the West, most people eat too much sugar and sweeteners, sugar is nevertheless necessary for a whole host of cooking techniques and recipes, without which we would be very much the poorer. Sugar, like salt with vegetables, acts as a preservative for fruit, inhibiting the growth of bacteria, yeasts and moulds. This is how jams and marmalades came to be made by our ancestors – the only way fruits such as strawberries, raspberries and plums could be eaten outside their short season. Equally, many foods are too bitter to be eaten without some sweetener, whether it is sugar, syrup or honey. Finally, all our desserts, cakes, biscuits (cookies) and puddings rely on sugar in their preparation or serving.

SUGAR

There are many different sorts of sugar providing a range of flavours, textures and possibilities. Most of the sugar that we consume today comes from two sources: the sugar-cane grown in the Tropics, and the sugar beet grown mainly in temperate climates.

Right: Demerara sugar has a very granular texture, which can give a delicious crunch to cookies and crumbles.

Below: Muscovado sugar has a rich flavour and lovely texture.

*Above:
Light and dark soft brown sugar have a distinctive flavour.*

BROWN SUGAR

Natural brown sugars are produced from raw sugar-cane. The difference in colour and flavour of the various brown sugars depends on the quantity of molasses present. The greater the amount of molasses, the stickier the crystals, the darker the colour and the stronger the flavour. Unrefined sugar, because of its high molasses content, contains a minute proportion of minerals, vitamins and proteins but the amounts are so small that their nutritional value is negligible.

Providing they are unrefined, as opposed to being flavoured and coloured white sugar, brown sugars are naturally slightly moist and sticky and, as such, will go hard over time. When this happens, cover the sugar with a damp cloth for a few hours and it will soften.

Muscovado/ Molasses sugar

This is a dark brown, strong-flavoured sugar that is moist and fine-grained. It is useful for baking rich fruit cakes and other dark rich desserts.

Demerara/Raw sugar Demerara is a partly refined sugar, but still contains a small amount of molasses, which gives it its pale golden colour. It is gritty in texture and can add a lovely texture to biscuits (cookies) and desserts. Cubed demerara sugar, either smoothly cut or rough cut, looks attractive and is most usually served with coffee.

Light soft brown sugar This is the most popular sugar for making fruit cakes and puddings where a slightly fuller flavour is required. It has a mellow syrupy flavour and colour, and creams extremely well with butter.

Dark soft brown sugar This is a dark sugar with a strong flavour and colour, making it ideal for rich fruit cakes, gingerbread, puddings and chutneys.

Artificial Sweeteners

There are a number of artificial sweeteners on the market that can add a sweetness to foods, without offering the calories of sugar. Many processed foods and drinks, particularly those labelled as "diet" contain artificial sweeteners. For use at home, there are sweeteners for tea and coffee, which usually come in the form of a tiny tablet. There are also some granular varieties, which can be used for sprinkling. The best-known and most widely-used sweeteners are saccharin and aspartame.

WHITE SUGAR

This is simply refined brown sugar, the molasses having been removed. White sugars are equally sweet, but the finer the powder, the sweeter they seem. Refined sugar is 99.9 per cent sucrose.

Preserving/Jam sugar There are various jam sugars available that have added pectin, which makes sure of a good set when making jams and preserves. Preserving sugar has larger crystals and requires less stirring when making marmalades and jams. It does not form a dense mass at the base of the pan, which helps prevent burning.

Granulated sugar Used for sweetening tea and coffee, and in cooking, this is a basic all-purpose sugar.

Above: Lump sugar and sugar crystals look very pretty served with coffee or tea for special occasions.

Caster/Superfine sugar This has finer crystals that dissolve easily, making it the better sugar for creaming with fats. It is used for custards, mousses and meringues, and for sprinkling over fruit.

Vanilla sugar This is caster sugar to which at least 10 per cent pure vanilla extract or essence has been added. It is used in pastries and sweet dishes.

Icing/Confectioners' sugar This is very fine white sugar, made by grinding granulated sugar into a powder, with an anti-caking agent such as calcium phosphate. It dissolves instantly on contact with a liquid. It is mostly used for making icings and frostings for cakes and desserts, confectionery and syrups for fruits.

Lump sugar Even-size and uniform sugar lumps are simply granulated sugar stuck together into lumps. They are used for sweetening tea and coffee. Unrefined sugar lumps are available.

Sugar crystals/Rock candy This is simply white sugar produced as large crystals. It may be coloured golden or multi-coloured. Rainbow crystals are usually slightly smaller than golden ones. Sugar crystals are used for sweetening coffee and for decorating cakes and biscuits (cookies). Make your own by putting a few crystals in a saturated sugar solution; as the water evaporates, the sugar joins with seed crystals to form larger ones.

Left: Jars of granulated (far left) and caster sugar can be found in almost any kitchen.

Making Flavoured Sugar

To make vanilla sugar, fill a jar with caster (superfine) sugar and press a whole vanilla pod into the centre. Seal and leave for 2–3 weeks.

Alternatively, make spiced sugar in the same way, using whole spices such as cloves, cinnamon sticks or cardamom pods.

SYRUP

Some syrups may be used as toppings or to accompany ice creams and desserts. Others are used as an ingredient in recipes.

Maple syrup This is made from the sap of the maple tree. Look for pure varieties rather than maple-flavoured syrup, which contains additives and is usually blended with corn or cane syrup. Maple syrup has a rich distinctive flavour and is sweeter than sugar, so less is required in cooking. It is popular poured on to pancakes and waffles and is also used to glaze ham.

Grain syrups Barley, wheat and rice can be transformed into syrups that are used in place of sugar in cakes, biscuits (cookies) and sauces. Grain syrups tend to be easier to digest and enter the bloodstream more slowly than other forms of refined sugar, which causes swings in blood sugar levels. Grain syrups are not as sweet as sugar and have a mild subtle flavour. Malt extract, a by-product of barley, has a more intense flavour and is good in breads, cakes and biscuits (cookies).

Cane syrup This intermediate syrup, produced during the sugar refining process, is very popular in the United States.

Corn syrup Made from corn starch, this useful, all-purpose syrup may be light or dark. The dark variety has a stronger flavour.

Palm/Date syrup This syrup is obtained from date and other palms. It is dark and sweet, and is produced in India, the Middle East and Latin America, where it is used in local recipes.

Golden syrup This traditional British light golden treacle has a distinctive taste and is something you either love or loathe. The famous Lyle's golden syrup was launched over 100 years ago and is still packaged in the same classic green and gold can. Although it can be eaten neat (it is delicious on warm drop scones, if you are one of the people who love it), the syrup is mostly used in baking, for making cakes, flapjacks, biscuits (cookies), fudge and toffee sauces to pour over ice cream. It is also used, like maple syrup, as a topping for pancakes.

Above: Black molasses are a good source of valuable nutrients, including iron, calcium, copper, magnesium, phosphorus, potassium and zinc.

Black treacle Black treacle is made by refining molasses. It is thick, black and extremely sticky, less sweet than honey, and with a strong flavour. It is used in recipes that call for its colour and distinctive flavour, notably gingerbread, some fruit cakes, and Christmas puddings and toffee. It also adds sweetness and its distinctive flavour to some traditional American dishes such as Boston baked beans.

Dark syrup This is a blend of golden syrup and black treacle. It is used in a similar way to golden syrup, but is not as sweet and has a darker colour.

Molasses This rich, syrupy liquid is a by-product of sugar refining and ranges in quality and colour. The most nutritionally valuable type is thick and very dark blackstrap molasses, which contains less sugar than lighter alternatives. However, it may be better to choose organically produced molasses, which doesn't contain the chemicals and additives that are used in the sugar-refining process.

Fruit syrup This is a blend of fruit juice and concentrated sugar syrup and is often used to flavour cakes, desserts and sauces for fish. It may also be diluted with water for a refreshing drink and poured over ice cream. It is usually made from sweet, soft fruits such as raspberries, strawberries, blackberries and blackcurrants.

Above: (Clockwise from left) Date syrup, barley malt syrup and brown rice syrup are used in baking in place of refined sugar.

HONEY

This is one of the oldest sweeteners used by man and was highly valued by the Ancient Egyptians for its medicinal and healing properties. The colour, flavour, consistency and quality of honey depend on the source of the nectar, as well as the production method used. In general, the darker the colour, the stronger the flavour. Many commercial brands of honey are pasteurized and blended to give a uniform taste and texture, but from the point of view of both flavour and health, it is best to buy raw unfiltered honey from a single flower source.

Honey contains several of the B vitamins, including thiamine, riboflavin and niacin. Trace elements include iron, copper, calcium, potassium and magnesium.

Honey is widely produced in the United States, Canada, South America, Mexico, China, Greece, Hungary, Australia and New Zealand.

Honeycomb This is honey that is still sealed within the cells. You can buy (or be given it) whole, halved or chunks of honeycombs,

normally sealed in wax so the honey doesn't run out. More commonly available commercially is cell honey, which comes bottled in jars.

Clear clover This honey has been heat-treated, a process that prevents it from crystallizing, which will happen naturally after a few weeks. Many people prefer clear or runny honey as it is easier to use in cooking. Clover honey is pale straw in colour and has a delightful sweet, mild flavour. It is good for cooking and eating and is popular in both the United States and Britain. At one time, clover honey was the most commonly produced honey in Britain. It has declined in recent years owing to the loss of pastureland.

Acacia This fragrant, pale-coloured honey is produced in China, Canada, France, Hungary, Romania and Italy. Unlike most other honeys, it does not crystallize with time.

Lavender This thick, dark, fragrant honey is mainly produced in the Provençal region of France.

Orange blossom This reddish-gold honey from China, California and Florida has a lovely aroma and delicate flavour.

Lemon blossom Delicately flavoured and a pretty golden colour, this delicious honey comes from Mexico.

Hymettus This is the most famous Greek honey. It is dark in colour, heavily scented, and tastes strongly of thyme. It is named after Mount Hymettus, not after a flower. It is one of the most expensive honeys in the world.

Scottish Heather This is light in flavour and reddish-brown in colour, with a pleasant aromatic tang. Honey made from ling has a bitter edge to it.

Alfalfa Thick and creamy yellow, this honey is often used in blends. It is very popular in the United States.

Leatherwood The flowers of the Tasmanian leatherwood tree are the source of this delicate honey.

Eucalyptus Produced by both Australia and some Mediterranean countries, this highly aromatic honey has a powerfully pungent flavour.

Manuka This is the best-known New Zealand honey. It is made from the flowers of the manuka or tea tree, which is also known for its aromatherapy oil. It has a rich flavour and deep, rich golden colour.

Blended honey Much of the honey available commercially is blended from differing sources.

Above: Honey comes in many forms, including crystallized honey, clear, runny honey and chunks of honeycomb.

KITCHEN
EQUIPMENT

There are hundreds of different pieces of cooking equipment

that can be found in today's kitchens. Some items such as

knives and cooking vessels are essential, while others

such as electric bread machines and ice cream makers are

luxury items. The following chapter looks at a few of the basic

items of kitchen equipment that will prove invaluable and

make light work of most preparation and cooking techniques.

COOKING PANS

A set of pans, a large ovenproof casserole and a good frying pan are essentials in every kitchen. Other useful items include a fish kettle, a large preserving pan, and a wok.

PANS

It is useful to have three sizes of pan, typically 16cm/6¼in, 19cm/7½in and 23cm/9in. Look for heavy, durable pans that distribute heat quickly and evenly. The best are heavy stainless steel, with a core of copper and silver alloy in the base. Look for strong handles that do not conduct heat well and reinforced rims designed to pour cleanly. Look for a long guarantee from a reputable manufacturer and remember that high-quality, expensive pans will give a lifetime's service.

Non-stick coatings do not last as long as stainless steel. All-metal pans, which can be used in the oven as well as on the stove, are useful if you have a large oven. It is worth taking plenty of time over the choice. Ask friends, read consumer reports and try out one pan before investing in the whole set.

Right: A set of three different-sized, good quality pans is ideal.

Above: A fish kettle is invaluable for cooking whole fish.

Above: Round and oval stock casseroles are very useful for slow-cooked dishes such as stews.

PRESERVING PANS

These traditional large, deep pans can be useful for boiling ham or making jams.

CASSEROLES

These ovenproof cooking dishes with lids can be used on the stove, for browning ingredients, as well as braising and stewing in the oven. Choose a casserole that is big enough to serve six, even if you usually cook for four as this gives plenty of room for stirring.

STOCK POTS

These large, deep pans are intended for making stock and cooking large cuts of meat. Heavy-duty stainless steel will last a lifetime. Look for a pan with metal handles on both sides, then it can double as a huge ovenproof casserole, ideal for baking ham.

FISH KETTLES

These long, deep pans have a handle at either end and a tight-fitting lid. Inside is a perforated rack or grid on which to lay the fish. This, too, has handles that allow the cook to lift out the fish without breaking it. Fish kettles are used on the stove and are invaluable for cooking whole, large fish such as salmon. Fish kettles can also be used for steaming other foods that are difficult to fit into a conventional round pan.

GRIDDLES

These cast-iron cooking pans may be flat or, more commonly, ridged, and they are used for cooking on the stove. Grilling, especially on a ridged pan, provides a healthy and attractive alternative to frying.

WOKS

These can be the most useful items in the kitchen. The Asian wok need not be reserved solely for stir-frying. It is the ideal pan for quick-cooked creamy dishes or risottos, or for deep-frying. Many woks come with an attachment upon which to drain fried foods. Woks with a flat base can be used on all types of hob, while those with a round base can only be used over a flame.

FRYING PANS

A good-quality, heavy frying pan is invaluable for frying, sautéeing and browning meat. A pan with a handle that can withstand heat is useful when cooking dishes that are placed under the grill (broiler) or in the oven such as frittata or tarte Tatin. Oval frying pans suitable for cooking fish are also available. A non-stick frying pan can be used for dry-frying meat and vegetables.

Above: There are many different types of wok available – they may have a flat or round base and may have either one or two handles. Steal woks must be seasoned before use.

Right: Heavy omelette pans with metal handles are ideal for making Spanish tortilla, which needs to be finished under the grill (broiler).

Below: Flat and ridged griddles are good for cooking fish, meat and vegetables.

OMELETTE PANS

If you are a keen omelette maker, a pan used exclusively for making omelettes can be a good investment. An omelette pan should be made of aluminium, steel or cast iron and have gently curving sides and a thick base that spreads the heat evenly across the base of the pan.

PANCAKE PANS

These should be light with low sides that allow the pancake to be tossed easily. Pancake pans may be non-stick or made of steel, which will need to be seasoned before use to prevent sticking. To season a pan, heat it with oil, then allow to cool and wipe clean with kitchen paper rather than washing it with soap and water.

DISHES AND OVENWARE

Every kitchen needs a few basic oven-proof baking dishes and a roasting pan, as well as baking tins (pans) and sheets for cakes and cookies.

BAKING DISHES

These large, shallow ceramic dishes come in different sizes and shapes – the most popular being round, oval and rectangular. They are good for making dishes such as roasted vegetables, layered vegetable bakes and oven-baked pasta dishes such as lasagne and cannelloni.

GRATIN DISHES

These shallow ovenproof dishes are available in various sizes and are ideal for baking eggs or holding gratinéed fruits or vegetables that are topped with a sauce and browned under the grill (broiler) or in the oven.

SOUFFLÉ DISHES

These are characterized by straight sides that help a hot soufflé mixture rise high and straight. They can also be used to make chilled soufflés – a paper collar can be tied around the dish to support the mixture while it sets, then removed. Classic soufflé dishes are made of white porcelain.

Below: A roasting pan with a rack is good for cooking poultry and joints of meat.

Below: Gratin dishes come in a wide variety of different sizes.

Above: Baking dishes can be used for cooking and serving food.

RAMEKINS

These deep, straight-sided dishes look a little like small soufflé dishes. They are used for individual dishes such as moussés and may be used as both a cooking and serving dish. Their undersides are unglazed, allowing heat to penetrate quickly and evenly. Th' ' iekins will retain heat so food will continue cooking even when removed from the oven.

ROASTING PANS

Used for roasting meat, poultry and vegetables, a roasting pan should be tough enough to withstand high heat and stove-top cooking as well as long, slow cooking in the oven without buckling. High-quality, heavy stainless steel or enamel pans are a good choice. Handles are a bonus and make lifting pans with heavy roasts much easier. A rack fits inside on which to support the meat.

Bowls

A number of different-sized bowls are invaluable for any cook. Large and medium sized bowls are useful for mixing, beating or whisking ingredients, while small bowls are good for holding measured and prepared ingredients such as chopped herbs or ground spices.

Below: Tins come in a range of sizes and shapes. They may have loose bases or clipped sides for easy removal of a pie or tart.

MUFFIN PANS AND PATTY TINS

These metal sheets contain several cups. Muffin tins are deeper and are useful for making muffins and rolls, while the larger, flatter patty tins are good for making Yorkshire puddings.

PIE DISHES

There are a wide variety of dishes specifically designed for making pies. The traditional pie dish is oval with a rim and sloping sides and is often made of glazed earthenware. The rim is wide and flat, so that the pastry crust can be attached easily. Pie dishes, however, can also be round, square or rectangular, and may also be made of glass or metal. Springform tins (pans) may also be used for making pies. They have a loose base and clip on the side to make releasing the pie easier.

BAKING SHEETS AND TRAYS

Heavy baking sheets and trays can be used as a base on which to cook, for example, cookies, pizzas and free-form breads. They are also handy for using as trays to help lift other dishes out of the oven, or to catch ingredients that have bubbled over the top of the cooking dish. Choose a heavy, good-quality baking tray that will not buckle at high temperatures and that are large but will fit easily in your oven.

TARTLET TINS/PANS

These little tins come in a huge variety of shapes and sizes. Single portion round ones are popular, but boat-shaped moulds known as *bateau* and *baquette* moulds are also available. They are particularly good for making small pastry cases and tartlets. Tiny fluted tins are usually reserved for petit fours.

Above: Glass, metal and earthenware pie dishes can also be used for pasta and other baked foods.

FLAN TINS/QUICHE PANS

These metal tins (pans) come in all shapes and sizes including square, round and heart-shaped. The best flan tins have loose bases, which makes turning out delicate tarts, flans and quiches easier. Tins with fluted edges add strength to pastry cases, while those with a dull finish rather than a shiny one will produce a crisper pastry crust. Porcelain flan dishes are also available but they absorb heat slowly so are less good for baking pastry.

Below: Muffin pans and baking sheets are very useful kitchen items.

UTENSILS

All kinds of utensils are available to make work in the kitchen quicker and easier. Good quality knives are essential; the use of other utensils depends on the individual cook.

KNIVES

Select knives that are comfortable to hold and well balanced. Blades of high-grade stainless steel, fully forged and with the tang running through the handle, are strong and durable.

Cook's/Chopping knife With a 20 cm/8 in long blade, this is invaluable for most kitchen chopping such as cutting up meat or fish steaks.

Paring knife This good basic knife has a 10 cm/4 in blade.

Boning knife This has a narrow, flexible blade, which bends easily for cutting around curved bones.

Carving/Slicing knife This knife with a 20–25 cm/ 8–10 inch blade is useful for carving roasts. A ham knife has a 25 cm/10 in serrated blade, which is good for carving thicker slices of meats.

Meat cleaver This heavy, wide-bladed knife is used for chopping meat bones and finely chopping meat.

Palette knife This wide, round-bladed spatula is useful for a variety of tasks including mixing doughs, smoothing tart fillings and icing (frosting) and lifting small delicate items such as tarts or cookies from baking sheets.

VEGETABLE PEELERS

These are good for removing layers of peel or skin from vegetables or fruits. Swivel-blade peelers are good for paring thin layers, while fixed-blade peelers can be used to remove a thicker layer.

SCISSORS

Kitchen scissors are well suited to certain preparation techniques such as snipping herbs, trimming skin from poultry or the rim of fat on bacon, or cutting the fins off fish. They are also useful for opening packets of ingredients and tasks such as cutting string for trussing meat.

EGG SLICERS

These are great for slicing hard-boiled eggs into neat slices for sandwiches or garnishes. The egg is placed in the hollow and then the frame of wires can be gently pulled through the egg, cutting it neatly and evenly.

Above: Draining spoons can be used to lift cooked ingredients from cooking liquids such as hot fat or water.

GRATERS

There is a huge range of graters that are suitable for different purposes. Simple stainless steel box graters have a range of teeth suitable for coarse, fine and very fine grating. There are also rotary graters with a handle that are good for grating Parmesan cheese.

METAL TONGS

These are very useful for lifting and turning small cuts of meat during cooking.

BASTING SPOONS

These are large metal spoons for basting roasts and baked dishes while cooking.

DRAINING SPOONS

These large, perforated or slotted spoons are useful for removing ingredients from a pan, leaving the water or fat behind for the next batch.

PASTRY BRUSHES

This is an essential item for brushing a thin layer of egg or milk glaze or melted butter on pastry or jam glazes over fruit tarts.

*Above:
A selection of knives, suitable for different tasks, are an essential part of every kitchen.*

Below: Wooden spoons and spatulas are useful for mixing and stirring.

WOODEN SPOONS AND SPATULAS

These come in a variety of shapes and sizes and are suitable for different tasks: a large round spoon is for mixing cake and bread mixtures, while a flat-ended wooden spatula is for making chunky scrambled eggs or tossing stir-frying ingredients in a wok. It is useful to have a selection of different sized and shaped spoons suited to the various kitchen tasks.

FISH SLICES/METAL SPATULAS

These can be bought in various sizes, with varying widths of blade. They are useful for turning large pieces of meat, delicate fish, omelettes and other foods that need support as they are turned or lifted from the pan.

LADLES

These are useful for serving soups, sauces and gravies as well as moist casseroles and stews, fruit salads and punches. Sizes can vary from small and pointed with a lip to very large and round without a lip.

MASHERS

These are useful for mashing cooked vegetables such as potatoes or other ingredients that are too large to mash with a fork – such as chickpeas when making hummus.

MEASURING SPOONS

These are essential for accurate measuring, as they are calibrated in sizes from ¼ teaspoon to 1 tablespoon.

MEASURING CUPS

Widely used in the United States for measuring dry and wet ingredients, these vary in size from ¼ cup to 1 cup.

MEASURING JUGS/PITCHERS

Heatproof glass jugs are the most convenient, and measurements should be clearly marked; buy jugs with both imperial and metric measurements.

WHISKS

There is a wide choice of whisks, suitable for different culinary tasks.
Wooden and straw whisks These can be used to lightly mix ingredients such as eggs and sauces.
Balloon whisks These are for whisking sauces, and smoothing out lumps.
Small round whisks These are for mixing small quantities such as cornflour (cornstarch) and water.
Flat whisks These give an airy result when whisking egg whites but it can take a long time to achieve a stiff result.
Conical, floppy whisks These are good when making sauces and custards.
Long-handled swirled whisks These can be used in tall glasses or jugs (pitchers) where there is limited space. They are used in the same way as balloon whisks.
Rotary beaters The best alternative to a hand-held electric beater, these are useful for whisking small quantities.

WOODEN HAMMERS OR MALLETS

This can be used to break open crab claws or tenderize meat. The flat side is for beating; the dimpled side is for tenderizing.

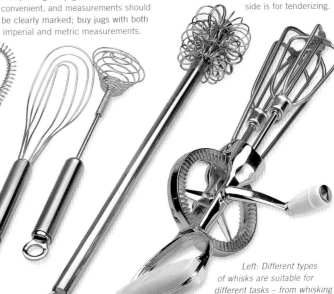

Left: Different types of whisks are suitable for different tasks – from whisking egg whites and whipping cream to removing lumps from sauces.

OTHER USEFUL EQUIPMENT

As well as pans, dishes and utensils, there are a number of other pieces of useful kitchen equipment.

MORTAR AND PESTLE

This is used for crushing spices and aromatics. Smooth china mortars and pestles vary in size and are good for grinding small amounts of dry spices. Asian stone mortars and pestles are usually large and have a pitted surface that is ideal for pounding fresh spices such as ginger and garlic – the rough surface grips the pieces and prevents them flying out of the bowl.

ROLLING PIN

A thick, heavy, wooden rolling pin is invaluable for rolling out doughs and crushing ingredients such as ice.

KITCHEN SCALES

There is a wide range of kitchen scales available, from spring scales that are not particularly accurate to balance scales with weights (these can be precise) and digital scales, which vary in quality, but can be excellent, particularly for small amounts.

CUTTING BOARD

Sturdy plastic composite boards are more hygienic than the traditional wooden ones because they are not absorbent. However, they still need thorough scrubbing, as the surface becomes scored with use. Sturdy plastic cutting boards can be put in the dishwasher.

TIMERS

These are useful for accurately timing cooking. A large timer with a rotating dial is good for longer cooking times but not so accurate for shorter ones, such as boiling eggs.

THERMOMETERS

Sugar thermometer This can be very useful for checking the temperature of a syrup or to determine whether the setting point of a jam has been reached.
Meat thermometer This can be used to check the cooking progress when roasting a cut of meat. Some thermometers are inserted into the raw meat, then placed in the oven with it. Others are inserted at the end of cooking, once the meat is removed from the oven. The point of the thermometer should be inserted into the middle of the thickest part of the meat.

Left: A kitchen timer is very useful when accurate timing is required.

Below: A sugar thermometer ensures success when making toffee, fudge or jam.

Oven thermometer Temperature gauges on ovens, particularly older ones, can sometimes be inaccurate, so it is a good idea to invest in a small, neat thermometer that will hang on the oven shelf and give an accurate reading.

STEAMERS

Cooking food such as fish and vegetables in steam is delicious and very healthy. There are a number of different types of steamer on the market. The most common are stainless steel ones that fit inside a lidded, deep outer pan; collapsible, perforated stainless steel steamers that also fit inside a larger, lidded pan; and Asian bamboo steaming baskets that sit on top of the pan, and can be stacked several layers high.

SIEVES/STRAINERS

It is handy to have several different sizes of sieve with different-sized mesh. They can be used for draining boiled vegetables, sifting flour and sprinkling sugar or cocoa powder over cakes and biscuits (cookies).

WIRE RACKS

Breads, cakes and bakes (baked goods) are best cooled on a wire rack. This allows air to circulate freely under them and helps to prevent trapped warmth turning into moisture and producing a soggy base.

Left: Balance scales can be used to accurately weigh dry and solid ingredients.

ELECTRICAL EQUIPMENT

There are a great number of electrical gadgets designed for kitchen use. Some such as food processors and blenders can speed up everyday kitchen tasks, while others such as ice cream makers, bread machines, rice cookers, omelette makers and centrifugal juicers for fruits and vegetables are definitely luxury, rather than essential, items.

FOOD PROCESSORS

These are incredibly useful for quick chopping, grating, blending, slicing, beating, grinding and many more culinary tasks. Select a processor with a bowl to suit your requirements, big enough to prepare the amount with which you normally cook and not so large that it is too big to be of use for everyday amounts.

Keen cooks can easily use their food processor every day, so try to buy one that will sit on your kitchen work surface, rather than one that has to be stored in a cupboard and taken out every time you use it. Some large food processors have smaller bowls that fit inside the main container when processing small amounts – for example, when chopping herbs or making a small amount of mayonnaise. Look for a model with a powerful motor.

Left: A food processor can be used for chopping, grating, slicing, grinding and beating.

Left: An electric mixer is useful for making cakes and batters.

BLENDERS

These are great for blending and puréeing and can be useful for making blended drinks, batters, sauces, soups and mayonnaise.

Single unit blender These have a single jug (pitcher) on top and are quick and easy to use. The jug can be immersed in water or taken apart for washing.

Hand blenders These are very useful and versatile and can be used either with a purpose-built jug (pitcher) or, for example, directly in the pan when blending vegetable soup.

FREE-STANDING ELECTRIC MIXERS

With a balloon whisk, beater and extra large bowl, these are good for mixing up batters and cake mixtures, whipping cream and whisking eggs. These mixers are slower than food processors so can be left to whisk, beat or mix while you work on another part of the recipe.

INDEX